LOCAL GOVERNMENT G

Financial and Legal Aspects of Implementing the Local Government Act 2000

LOCAL GOVERNMENT GOVERNANCE

Financial and Legal Aspects of
Implementing the Local Government Act 2000

General Editors

Richard Lester, formerly First Vice-President, ACSeS and currently
Consultant, Eversheds
Sandra Moss, Barrister, Manager of the CIPFA Better Governance and
Counter-Fraud Forum

Contributors

Division 1 – Modernising Democracy
Claer Lloyd-Jones (with a team from Brighton & Hove City Council),
Vice-President ACSeS and City Solicitor and Head of Corporate
Governance at Brighton & Hove City Council

Division II – Ethical Standards
Mark Heath, Head of Legal Services, Southampton City Council

Division III – Community Focus
Graeme Creer, City Solicitor, Liverpool City Council

Division IV – Financial Property
Michael Crich, Consultant

Division V – Employment Implications
Tim Rothwell, Managing Director, GWT Rothwell

Butterworths
London, Dublin and Edinburgh

United Kingdom	Butterworths, a Division of Reed Elsevier (UK) Ltd, Halsbury House, 35 Chancery Lane, LONDON WC2A 1EL and 4 Hill Street, EDINBURGH EH2 3JZ
Australia	Butterworths, a Division of Reed International Books Australia Pty Ltd, CHATSWOOD, New South Wales
Canada	Butterworths Canada Ltd, MARKHAM, Ontario
Hong Kong	Butterworths Asia (Hong Kong), HONG KONG
India	Butterworths India, NEW DELHI
Ireland	Butterworths (Ireland) Ltd, DUBLIN
Malaysia	Malayan Law Journal Sdn Bhd, KUALA LUMPUR
New Zealand	Butterworths of New Zealand Ltd, WELLINGTON
Singapore	Butterworths Asia, SINGAPORE
South Africa	Butterworths Publishers (Pty) Ltd, DURBAN
USA	Lexis Law Publishing, CHARLOTTESVILLE, Virginia

© Reed Elsevier (UK) Ltd 2001

A CIP Catalogue record for this book is available from the British Library.

ISBN 0-406-94153-X

9 780406 941534

Typeset by Kerrypress Ltd, Luton, Beds
Printed and bound by Bookcraft (Bath) Ltd, Midsomer Norton, Avon

Visit Butterworths LexisNexis *direct* at: http://www.butterworths.com

FOREWORD

Up and down the country local authorities are grappling with the great challenge of our time, 'modernisation'.

It is not by any means an easy challenge. There are so many different (though interconnected) elements to a modernisation programme that advocates such high standards. Alongside the restructuring of local authorities, the Local Government Act 2000 has promoted the importance of scrutiny, accountability and ethics.

In view of this, local authority lawyers, accountants and managers generally are helping authorities to make significant progress, to be more innovative, flexible, responsible and accountable. They are working towards the implementation of codes of conduct, new powers and monitoring whilst ensuring that governance sits comfortably with Best Value, finance and employment issues.

'Change' and 'risk' are opposite sides of the same coin. Authoritative guidance, both internally from management teams and externally from the sharing of experience and advice, is crucial to achieve the balance between change and risk. Through ambitious and skillful management the ideals of modernising democracy, ethical standards, community focus and financial property can be achieved.

Local Government Governance is designed to assist those managing the implementation of such changes with practical advice and guidance in order to transform ideals into reality.

Chris Hurford
President – CIPFA

PREFACE

The term 'governance' is one which has gained increasing prominence in the language of local government in recent times. It is defined in the dictionary as 'the act or manner of governing'.

The Local Government Act 2000 and its implementation bring governance to the fore. For those of us working at the corporate centre of local government the concept of good governance has risen very much up our agendas as we advise our councils of all the implications of the 2000 Act.

In drafting new constitutions and putting into place all the arrangements necessary to implement those constitutions, in whatever form, we are to a significant extent re-inventing the governing of our local authorities. The Act has provided us with both an unprecedented opportunity and a challenge to help shape the way our councils are going to be governed in the twenty-first century. These are exciting as well as demanding times for lawyers and administrators in local government.

Given that background, the publication of *Local Government Governance* could not be better timed. The approach adopted is an extremely practical one that covers all aspects of the governance agenda. Included are sections on the new constitutional arrangements including the overview and scrutiny function, the new ethical framework, the community leadership role (including well being power and community strategy) and financial propriety as well as the major implications for local authorities as employers which flow from these changes.

Contributions by leading and experienced practitioners in the field of local government governance make this work necessary reading for all those who either have an interest in or are involved in whatever was in preparing or implementing new governance arrangements for their authorities.

As president of the Association of Council Secretaries and Solicitors I am delighted to have the opportunity of endorsing the work on behalf of the Association.

COLIN G LANGLEY
President – ACSeS
August 2001

PUBLISHERS NOTE

With relation to references to the DETR/DTLR in the text of this work, please refer to the summary of changes to former DETR responsibilities at the following internet address:

http://www.dtlr.gov.uk/changes/index.htm

CONTENTS

page

Foreword v
Preface vii
Table of Cases xv
Table of Statutes xix
Table of Statutory Instruments xxv

DIVISION I
Modernising Democracy

1. New Political and Administrative Structures An introduction 1
    Claer Lloyd-Jones

2. Power to promote or Improve Economic, Social and
    Environment Well-Being 6
    Dianne Bates

3. Community Leadership Roles and Local Strategic
    Partnerships 31
    Dianne Bates

4. Cabinet Government 47
    Elizabeth Culbert

5. The Oview and Scrutiny Function 68
    John Chard

6. Alternative Arrangements 78
    Sean Morris/Elizabeth Culbert

7. Referendums, Mayoral Elections and Constitutions 88
    Elizabeth Culbert

8. Modernising Elections 96
    Paula Slinn

DIVISION II
Ethical Standards
Mark Heath

9. What is meant by Ethics and Ethical Standards? 115

Contents

10. The Monitoring Officer 120

11. Standards Committee 140

12. Procedures and Documentation 151

13. Setting the Standards – Legislation, Codes and Protocols 160

14. Promoting and Monitoring Standards.............................171

15. National Standards Board, the Adjudication Panel and Case
    Tribunals 179

16. Conducting an Investigation 184

17. Best Value, Oview and Scrutiny and Ethics and Probity.............185

Division III

Community Focus
Graeme Creer

18. Community planning and Corporate Strategy..............................191

19. Partnership With Others 202

20. Consultation...218

21. Openness and Freedom of Information 229

Division IV

Financial Propriety
Michael Crich

22. Introduction...247

23. Risk Management of Strategic and Operational Risks 254

24. Monitoring and Reviewing Performance 262

25. Internal and External Audit – Reporting and Controls 273

26 Involvement of Staff and Partners.....................................285

27 Regulation of Investigatory Powers Act 2000..............................289

28. Countering Fraud and Corruption...294

Division V
Employment Implications
Tim Rothwell

29 Cultural Issues 301

30. Codes of Conduct..320

31. Changing Roles of Statutory Officers............................328

32. Employee Relations Implications..................................335

33. Whistle-Blowing..342

34. Human Rights 347

35. Training and Information..357

Division VI
Appendices

1. Examples of Local Strategic Partnerships in Development
    and Contact Details 365
    Chapter 3

2. Regulations and Directions under the Local Government
    Act 2000 369
    Chapter 4

3. Main Similarities and Differences Between the Mayor and
    Cabinet, Leader and Cabinet and Mayor and Council
    Manager Models 371
    Chapter 4

4. Local Government Act 2000 (Constitutions) (England)
    Direction 2000 375
    Chapters 7 and 10

5. Local Government and Housing Act 1989, ss 5, 5A, 19,
    21 and 31..379
    Chapters 10 and 13

6. Local Government Act 2000, ss 51, 53, 54, 57, 59, 60,
    64–66, 78–83 387
    Chapters 10, 11 and 12

7. The New Role of the Monitoring Officer (ACSES)......................401
    Chapter 10

8. Terms of Reference of Standards and Governance
    Committee...411
    Chapter 11

Contents

9. Local Authorities (Executive Arrangements) (Modification of Enactments and Further Provisions) (England) Order 2001, SI 2001/1517, reg 8...413
    Chapter 12

10. Notes to Scheme of Delegation 415
    Chapter 12

11. Safeguards for Authorisation of Subordinate Officer to Discharge Particular Function in Scheme of Delegation..............419
    Chapter 12

12. Local Government Act 1972, ss 94–98, 105 and 106.................421
    Chapter 13

13. National Code of Local Government Conduct (DoE Circular 8/90)...425
    Chapter 13

14. The General Principles of Conduct...431
    Chapter 13

15. Officer/Member Protocol 433
    Chapter 13

16. Draft Model Code of Conduct for Members 443
    Chapter 13

17. Ethical Governance Audit – Methodology....................................453
    Chapter 14

18. Ethical Governance Audit – Questionnaire 457
    Chapter 14

19. Special Procedure and Protocol Standards Committee...............463
    Chapter 15

20. Local Government and Finance Act 1988, ss 113 and 114.........469
    Chapter 22

21. LGMB Code of Conduct for Local Government Employees (1994) 473
    Chapter 30

22. Code of Conduct for Qualifying Employees of Relevant Authorities in Wales 477
    Chapter 30

Index 481

TABLE OF CASES

A

Ahmed v United Kingdom (Application 22954/93) (1998) 29 EHRR 1, [1999] IRLR 188,
5 BHRC 111, [1998] HRCD 823, (1998) Times, 2 October, 1 LGLR 94, ECtHR................34.2
Allsop v North Tyneside Metropolitan Borough Council (1992) 90 LGR 462, [1992] ICR
639, [1992] RVR 104, CA..2.3

H

HSBC Bank plc (formerly Midland Bank plc) v Madden [2001] 1 All ER 550, [2000] ICR
1283, [2000] IRLR 827, 652 IRLB 7, CA...34.4
Hazell v Hammersmith and Fulham London Borough Council [1990] 2 QB 697, [1990]
3 All ER 33, [1990] 2 WLR 17, 88 LGR 433, 134 Sol Jo 21, [1990] 2 LS Gaz R 36,
[1989] RVR 188; on appeal [1990] 2 QB 697, [1990] 3 All ER 33, [1990] 2 WLR
1038, 88 LGR 433, 134 Sol Jo 637, [1990] 20 LS Gaz R 36, [1990] RVR 140, CA;
affd [1992] 2 AC 1, [1991] 1 All ER 545, [1991] 2 WLR 372, 89 LGR 271, [1991]
RVR 28, HL...2.3

L

Lawrence v Regent Office Care [2000] IRLR 608, 645 IRLB 7, CA..29.2
Link v Secretary of State for Trade and Industry [2001] IRLR 416, EAT.....................................34.4

M

Merton London Borough Council v Gardiner [1981] QB 269, [1981] 2 WLR 232, 79
LGR 374, [1981] ICR 186, sub nom Gardiner v London Borough of Merton [1980]
IRLR 472, 125 Sol Jo 97, CA...29.2

R

R v Barnet London Borough Council, ex p B [1994] 2 FCR 781, [1994] 1 FLR 592, [1994]
ELR 357 ....20.6
R v Bexley London Borough, ex p Barnehurst Golf Club [1992] NPC 43, [1992] COD
382 ....20.3
R v Birmingham City Council, ex p Dredger (1993) 91 LGR 532, [1993] COD 276 ....20.3
R v Birmingham City Council, ex p Ferrero Ltd (1990) 154 JP 661; revsd [1993] 1 All ER
530, 89 LGR 977, 155 JP 721, [1991] 26 LS Gaz R 32, CA 20.4
R v Brent London Borough Council, ex p Gunning (1985) 84 LGR 168 ....20.3
R v Brent London Borough Council, ex p Morris (1996) 28 HLR 852; affd (1997) 30 HLR
324, CA 20.3
R v Broadland District Council, ex p Lashley [2000] LGR 708, 2 LGLR 933; affd sub nom
R v Broadland District Council, ex p Lashley [2001] EWCA Civ 179 [2001] All ER
(D) 71, Times, 20 March, CA 11.3
R v Camden London Borough Council, ex p Bodimead unreported 20.5
R v Chief Constable of North Wales Police, ex p AB [1997] 4 All ER 691, [1997] 3 WLR
724, [1997] NLJR 1061; affd sub nom R v Chief Constable of North Wales Police,
ex p Thorpe [1999] QB 396, [1998] 2 FLR 571, [1998] Fam Law 529, sub nom R
v Chief Constable of North Wales Police, ex p AB [1998] 3 All ER 310, [1998] 3
WLR 57, [1998] 3 FCR 371, [1998] 17 LS Gaz R 29, CA...21.5

R v Devon County Council, ex p Baker (1992) Times, 20 October; on appeal [1995] 1 All
ER 73, 91 LGR 479, 11 BMLR 141, 6 Admin LR 113, CA...20.4
R v Falmouth and Truro Port Health Authority, ex p South West Water Services [2001]
QB 445, [2000] 3 All ER 306, [2000] 3 WLR 1464, [2000] EGCS 50, [2000] Env LR
658, CA 20.4
R v Governors of Small Heath School, ex p Birmingham City Council (1989) Times, 31
May; affd [1990] COD 23, CA 20.3
R v Gravesham Borough Council, ex p Gravesham Association of Licensed Hackney
Carriage Owners (1987) Independent, 14 January..20.4
R v Greater Manchester Police Authority, ex p Century Motors (Farnworth) Ltd (1996)
Times, 31 May, (1998) unreported, CA..19.11
R v Gwent County Council and Secretary of State for Wales, ex p Bryant [1988] COD 19 ....20.4
R v Hounslow London Borough Council, ex p Dooley (1999) 80 P & CR 405 ....20.4
R v Islington London Borough Council, ex p Rixon [1997] ELR 66, 32 BMLR 136, 1 CCL
Rep 119 ....20.5
R v Lambeth London Borough, ex p N [1996] ELR 299 ....20.6
R v Leeds City Council, ex p N [1999] Ed CR 735; affd [1999] ELR 324, [1999] Ed CR
949, CA 20.6
R v Liverpool Corpn, ex p Liverpool Taxi Fleet Operators' Association [1972] 2 QB 299,
[1972] 2 WLR 1262, 71 LGR 387, 116 Sol Jo 201, sub nom Re Liverpool Taxi
Owners' Association [1972] 2 All ER 589, CA..20.3
R v Local Comr for Administration for the North and East Area of England, ex p Bradford
Metropolitan City Council [1979] QB 287, [1979] 2 All ER 881, [1979] 2 WLR 1,
77 LGR 305, 122 Sol Jo 573, [1978] JPL 767, CA 13.3
R v Local Comr for Administration in North and North East England, ex p Liverpool City
Council [2001] 1 All ER 462, [2000] LGR 571, 2 LGLR 603, [2000] NPC 18, CA..........13.3
R v London Borough of Wandsworth, ex p P (1988) 87 LGR 370, [1989] 1 FLR 387,
[1989] Fam Law 185 ....20.4
R v Norfolk County Council Social Services Department, ex p M [1989] QB 619, [1989]
2 All ER 359, [1989] 3 WLR 502, 87 LGR 598, [1989] FCR 667, [1989] Fam Law
310, [1989] NLJR 293, sub nom R v Norfolk County Council, ex p X [1989] 2 FLR
120 ....20.4
R v North and East Devon Health Authority, ex p Coughlan (Secretary of State for Health
intervening) (1998) 47 BMLR 27, [1999] COD 174, 2 CCL Rep 27; affd [2001] QB
213, [2000] 3 All ER 850, [2000] 2 WLR 622, 97 LGR 703, 51 BMLR 1, [1999] 31
LS Gaz R 39, 143 Sol Jo LB 213, [1999] Lloyd's Rep Med 306, [1999] 2 CCL Rep
285, CA 20.5
R v North and East Devon Health Authority, ex p Pow (1997) 39 BMLR 77, [1998] 1 CCL
Rep 280 ....20.6
R v Powys County Council, ex p Hambridge [1998] 1 FLR 643, [1998] Fam Law 136, 40
BMLR 73, 1 CCL Rep 182; affd (1998) 96 LGR 627, [1998] 3 FCR 190, 45 BMLR
203, [1998] 32 LS Gaz R 30, 142 Sol Jo LB 232, 1 CCL Rep 458, CA...............................20.3
R v Richmond upon Thames London Borough Council, ex p McCarthy & Stone
(Developments) Ltd [1992] 2 AC 48, [1990] 2 All ER 852, [1990] 2 WLR 1294, 60
P & CR 174, [1990] 27 LS Gaz R 41, [1990] NLJR 362, CA; revsd sub nom
McCarthy & Stone (Developments) Ltd v Richmond upon Thames London
Borough Council [1992] 2 AC 48, [1991] 4 All ER 897, [1991] 3 WLR 941, 90 LGR
1, 63 P & CR 234, [1992] 3 LS Gaz R 33, [1992] JPL 467, 135 Sol Jo LB 206, HL..............2.3
R (on the application of Wainwright) v Richmond upon Thames London Borough
Council [2001] 18 EG 174 (CS) 20.6
R v Secretary of State for Social Services, ex p Association of Metropolitan Authorities
[1986] 1 All ER 164, [1986] 1 WLR 1, 83 LGR 796, 130 Sol Jo 35 ....20.6
R v Secretary of State for the Environment, ex p Hillingdon London Borough Council
[1986] 1 All ER 810, [1986] 1 WLR 192, 84 LGR 628, 52 P & CR 409, 130 Sol Jo
89, [1986] LS Gaz R 525, [1986] NLJ Rep 16, [1987] RVR 6, [1986] JPL 363; affd
[1986] 2 All ER 273n, [1986] 1 WLR 807n, 84 LGR 628, 55 P & CR 241n, 130 Sol
Jo 481, [1986] LS Gaz R 2331, [1987] RVR 6, [1987] JPL 717, CA...................................21.1
R v Secretary of State for the Environment, ex p Kent (1988) 57 P & CR 431, [1988] 3 PLR
17, [1988] JPL 706; affd [1990] COD 78, [1990] JPL 124, CA 20.3
R v Secretary of State for the Home Department and London Fire and Civil Defence
Authority, ex p London Borough of Greenwich unreported..20.4
R v Shropshire Health Authority, ex p Duffus (1989) Times, 16 August, [1990] COD 131 ....20.6

R v Waltham Forest London Borough Council, ex p Baxter [1988] QB 419, [1987] 3 All
ER 671, [1988] 2 WLR 257, 86 LGR 254, 132 Sol Jo 227, [1988] LS Gaz R 36,
[1987] NLJ Rep 947, [1988] RVR 6, CA 13.3
R v Wandsworth London Borough Council, ex p Beckwith (1995) 159 LG Rev 929; revsd
[1996] 1 FCR 304, 25 BMLR 144, [1995] 31 LS Gaz R 34, CA; affd [1996] 1 All ER
129, [1996] 1 WLR 60, [1996] 1 FCR 504, 30 BMLR 105, [1996] 02 LS Gaz R 28,
140 Sol Jo LB 27, HL 20.4
R v Worcestershire Health Authority, ex p Kidderminster and District Community Health
Council (1989) unreported 20.3
R v Yorkshire Purchasing Organisation, ex p British Educational Suppliers Ltd (1997) 95
LGR 727, [1998] ELR 195, [1997] COD 473, CA 19.12

S

Scanfuture UK Ltd v Secretary of State for Trade and Industry [2001] IRLR 416, EAT................34.4
South Ayrshire Council v Morton [2001] IRLR 28, EAT 29.2

T

Tehrani v United Kingdom Central Council for Nursing, Midwifery and Health Visiting
[2001] IRLR 208, 2001 SLT 879, OH..34.4
Tenby Corpn v Mason [1908] 1 Ch 457, 6 LGR 233, 72 JP 89, 77 LJ Ch 230, 98 LT 349,
24 TLR 254, CA 21.1

V

Venables v News Group Newspapers Ltd [2001] 1 All ER 908, [2001] 2 WLR 1038,
[2001] 1 FLR 791, [2001] Fam Law 258, [2001] 12 LS Gaz R 41, [2001] NLJR 57,
145 Sol Jo LB 43 ....21.5

W

Wilson v Secretary of State for the Environment [1988] JPL 540 ....20.3

TABLE OF STATUTES

References in this Table to *Statutes* are to Halsbury's Statutes of England (Fourth Edition) showing the volume and page at which the annotated text of the Act may be found.
References in the right-hand column are to paragraph numbers.
Paragraph numbers in **bold** indicate where the material is reproduced in the text.

PARA

A

Access to Personal Files Act 1987 (7
Statutes 245) 21.3
Audit Commission Act 1998
s 14, 15 ....21.1 C
Children Act 1989 (6 Statutes 370)
Sch 2
para 1A 18.2
Civic Restaurants Act 1947 (25 Statutes
80) 2.30
Companies Act 1985 (8 Statutes 88)
....19.4
Consumer Protection Act 1987 (39
Statutes 150) 20.4
Credit Unions Act 1979 (21 Statutes
1151) 19.3
Crime and Disorder Act 1998 ....19.1–19.3
s 5, 6, 40 ....18.2
115 ....21.5

D

Data Protection Act 1984 (7 Statutes
192) 21.3
Data Protection Act 1998 (7 Statutes
389) 13.2, 21.4
s 13 ....21.3
Sch 1 ....21.3
2, 3 ....21.3, 21.5
Deregulation and Contracting Out Act
1994 (25 Statutes 1438)
s 70 ....18.6, 19.11
71 ....19.11

E

Education (Scotland) Act 1996 ....29.2
Employment Rights Act 1996 (16
Statutes 557) 33.3
s 1 ....30.5
Pt IVA (ss 43A–43L) 33.1
s 108(1) 29.2
146 ....29.2

PARA

Employment Rights Act 1996—*contd*
s 230(4), (5) 29.2
231 ....29.2
Environment Act 1995 (35 Statutes
1019)
s 63 ....30.3
84(2)(b) 2.35
Environmental Protection Act 1990 (35
Statutes 712) 20.4
s 49(1)(c) 2.35
Equal Pay Act 1970 (16 Statutes 34)
s 1(3) 29.2

F

Factories Act 1961 (19 Statutes 646)
....34.6
Fatal Accidents Act 1976 (31 Statutes
251) 21.4
Fire Services Act 1947 (18 Statutes 6)
....30.3
Food Safety Act 1990 (18 Statutes 478)
....18.2
Food Standards Act 1999 ....18.2
Freedom of Information Act 2000 ...21.3, 21.4

G

Greater London Authority Act 1999
s 30(1), (2) 2.23
32 ....2.23

H

Health Act 1999 ....2.18, 19.1, 19.3,
19.8, 19.11
Health and Safety at Work, etc Act 1974
(19 Statutes 796)
s 2 ....**34.6**
(3) 34.6
28 ....21.5
Health and Social Care Act 2001 .5.2, 5.7, 5.10
Home Energy Conservation Act 1995
(21 Statutes 786)
s 2 ....2.35

PARA

Housing Act 1988 (21 *Statutes* 608) 21.1
s 105 ....20.3
Human Rights Act 1998 (7 *Statutes* 497)....20.5,
21.1, 34.1
Sch 1
art 2 ....21.5
6(1) **34.4**
8 ....21.5
10 ....21.5, **34.3**
11(1) **34.5**

I

Industrial and Provident Societies Act
1965 (21 *Statutes* 1064) 19.5
Industrial and Provident Societies Act
1967 (21 *Statutes* 1119) 19.5
Industrial and Provident Societies Act
1975 (21 *Statutes* 1147) 19.5
Industrial and Provident Societies Act
1978 (21 *Statutes* 1149) 19.5
Interception of Communications Act
1985 (45 *Statutes* 304) 27.3
Interpretation Act 1978 (41 *Statutes* 985)
Sch 1 ....2.13

J

Jobseekers Act 1995 (40 *Statutes* 813)
....19.3

L

Learning and Skills Act 2000 ....19.3
Leasehold Reform, Housing and Urban
Development Act 1993 (23 *Statutes* 495)
....19.3
Limited Liability Partnerships Act 2000 ....19.1
Local Authorities (Admission of the
Press to Meetings) Act 1908 ....21.1
Local Authorities (Goods and Services)
Act 1970 (25 *Statutes* 139) 2.30, 18.6,
19.12
Local Government (Access to Information) Act 1985 (25 *Statutes* 712) ...21.1
Local Government Act 1972 (25 *Statutes*
166) 2.1, 4.1, 11.1, 11.3, 11.6, 12.11
s 7(2), (8) 7.9
12A 4.21
26(1) **13.3**
30(3A) **13.3**
83 ....13.3
87 ....10.23
94–97 ....13.2, 13.3
98 ....13.2
Pt VA (ss 100A–100K) 502, 6.2, 21.1
101 ....6.2, 12.10, 19.9–19.11
102 ....6.2, 19.8
105, 106 ....13.2
111 ....1.1, 2.3, 19.4, 19.12, 21.5

PARA

Local Government Act 1972 (25 *Statutes* 166)
—*contd*
Pt 112 ....32.2
(2) 22.2, 32.11
117(2) 30.1
135 ....12.5
(2) 19.11
137 ....2.6, 2.16, 2.27, 2.36
(1)(b) 2.4
(3) 2.5
141, 142 ....19.12
143 ....19.8
151 ....10.6, 22.2–22.4, 25.5,
31.1, 31.2, 31.4, 32.2
157(a), (b) 22.2
161, 166 ....22.2
Pt IX (ss 179–215) 2.3
Sch 12A 5.2, 21.1
Local Government Act 1974 (25 *Statutes*
495) 21.1
Local Government Act 1985 (25 *Statutes*
714)
Pt IV (ss 23–42) 30.3
Local Government Act 1988 (25 *Statutes*
870)
Pt II (ss 17–23) 19.12
s 17 ....29.11
Local Government Act 1992 (25 *Statutes*
1248) 19.11
Local Government Act 1999 ...2.19, 2.43, 3.3,
8.1, 17.4, 18.3, 18.5, 19.12, 21.1
s 1 ....27.4
3 ....20.2, 29.5
(1) 2.43
(2)(d) 29.5
5 ....5.2
6(1) 18.2
16 .1.1, 1.2, 2.20, 2.24, 2.33, 18.6, 19.1
Local Government Act 2000 ...2.4, 2.40, 2.43,
4.4, 4.15, 4.23, 4.25, 6.5,
6.8, 7.1, 7.6, 8.1, 8.2,
8.4, 8.41, 9.1, 10.1, 10.2, 10.4,
11.1, 11.6, 18.5, 19.3, 19.11,
21.2, 25.6, 29.1–29.3, 29.5,
29.11, 30.1, 31.1, 31.5, 32.1,
32.3, 32.6, 32.10, 32.11,
34.1, 35.1, 35.3
Pt I (ss 1–9) 1.1, 1.2, 2.2, 2.3,
2.7–2.11, 2.25, 2.30,
3.1–3.3, 10.27, 17.2,
18.3, 18.6
s 1 ....**2.9**, 4.2
2 ....2.29, 19.1, 19.4, 19.10,
19.11, 21.1, 21.5
(1) 2.7, 2.12, 2.15, 2.19,
2.27, 2.33, 2.37
(2) 2.13
(3) 2.14
(4) 2.15, 2.19, 19.12
(a), (b) 2.16

PARA

Local Government Act 2000 —contd
s 2(4)(c), (d) 2.17
    (e), (f) 2.18
    (5) 2.13, 2.15, **2.19**, 2.22
    (6) 2.15
3 ....2.33, 19.1, 19.12
    (1) 2.26
    (2) 2.24, **2.27**, 2.28–2.30
    (3)–(6) 2.31
4 ....2.14, 2.32, 18.2, 20.2, 20.8
    (3) 18.3
    (a), (b) 3.2
5 ....2.33, 2.38, 2.44, 18.6
    (5) 2.35
6 ....2.34, 2.35, 2.38, 18.6
7(2)(d) 2.35
8 ....2.5, 2.36
9 ....2.33
    (1)–(4), (6) 2.38
Pt II (ss 10–48) 1.1, 1.2, 2.11, 3.3,
                3.30, 4.2, 4.3, 5.1, 6.7,
                7.5, 10.25, 11.2, 11.7, 12.5,
                18.2, 29.4
s 11(2) 4.3
    (3) 4.3
    (b) 4.6
    (4) 4.3
    (5) 6.7
    (6)(a), (b) 4.9
    (8), (9) 4.5
12(3) 4.9
13 ....4.10
    (3) 10.25
    (4), (5) 4.12
14 ....12.9, 12.10
    (2)–(5) 4.5
15 ....12.9, 12.10
16 .....4.7, 12.9, 12.10, 31.6, 31.7, 32.7
17 ....12.9
21 ....6.2
    (1) 5.2
    (2) 5.2
    (a) 5.9
    (3) 5.2, 5.9
    (b) 5.9
    (4)–(11) 5.2
    (13)(a), (b) 5.2
    (14), (15) 5.2
25 ....**4.2**, 6.6
    (4) 4.1
26 ....4.5
27(1)(b) 6.7
    (2) **6.7**
    (b) 6.1
    (4) 6.7
    (6) 7.3
    (7) 7.8
    (8) 6.7, 7.8
    (12) 6.7
    (13) 6.7

PARA

Local Government Act 2000 —contd
s 29(2) 6.2
31 ....4.24, 6.6
    (2) 6.1
32 ....4.24
    (1), (3) 6.2
33(2), (3) 6.2
    (4), (7), (9) 6.10
34(5), (6), (9) 6.10
35, 36 ....6.10
37 ....**10.26**
    (1)–(3) 7.10
39 ....8.5
    (6) 4.5, 7.9
40(1), (2) 8.5
41 ....8.5
42 ....8.6
44 ....8.8
Pt III (ss 49–83) 1.1, 1.2, 4.22, 6.2,
                6.4, 9.2, 10.3, 10.5, 10.20,
                10.25, 10.28, 31.3, 31.7
s 49 ....30.2
    (6) 30.3
51 ....10.21, 30.2
53 ....11.2–11.4, 14.10
    (10) 11.8
54 ....11.2, 14.10
55(12) 11.7
Pt III, Ch II (ss 57–67) 15.3
s 57(5) 15.4
    (c) 10.6
59 ....10.22
    (4)(c) 10.7
60(1) 10.22
    (2) 10.15, 10.22
    (b) 10.8
    (3) 10.9
64(1) 10.10
    (2) 10.15
    (b), (c) 10.11
    (3)(c) 10.12
    (4) 10.10, 10.13
65(5)(b) 10.14
66 ....10.15, 10.22, 16.2
Pt III, Ch III (ss 68–74) 15.3
s 78(7)(b) 10.16
79 ....10.16
    (9), (15) 10.23
80(4), (5) 10.24
81(1), (2) 10.17
    (6) 10.18
    (7) 10.19
82 ....30.6
    (1), (2) 30.3
    (3)(a) 30.3
    (7) 30.3, 30.6
    (8) 12.6, 30.3
83(12), (13) 10.20
Pt IV (ss 84–89) 1.1, 1.2, 8.3, 31.7
s 85–88 ....8.3

PARA

Local Government Act 2000 —*contd*
Pt V (ss 90–104) 1.2
s 101 ....2.16
 151 ....10.25
Sch 1
  para 1 ....4.5
    2(2)(a), (b) 4.6
    3(13) 4.7
    7 ....5.2, 6.2
    8 ....6.2
    9 ....5.2, 6.2
    10, 11 ....6.2
    13 ....31.2
  Sch 2 ....8.6, 8.7
  Sch 3 ....4.7
  Sch 5 ....10.23
    para 24 ....31.2
  Sch 6 ....2.7, 2.37, 13.2
Local Government and Housing Act
  1989 (25 *Statutes* 987) 2.4, 10.20,
                         20.2, 21.2, 32.8, 34.3
  s 1 ....34.2
  1A 10.3
  s 2 ....10.3, 21.1
    (6)–(8) 32.2
  2A 10.3
  4(1) 31.2
  5 ....10.1, 10.3, 10.5, 10.6, 10.27,
                         10.29, 30.2, 31.3
    (1) 10.2, 31.2
    (2), (2A) 10.4
  5A 10.3
  8 ....32.2, 32.5, 32.7
  8A 10.3
  9 ....32.2, 34.2
  15 ....5.2, 6.2, 11.8
  16 ....5.2, 6.2
  17 ....6.2
    (1)(b) 5.2
  19(1) 13.2
    (4)(a) 13.2
  21(1) 10.2, 31.2
  31, 32 ....13.3
  Pt III (ss 33–38) 2.6
  s 33, 34 ....2.7, 2.37
  35 ....2.7, 2.37, 18.3
  33(1) 2.6
  35(3) 2.6, 2.7
  Pt V (ss 67–73) 2.24, 19.4
  s 97, 98 ....5.2
  150 ....2.29, 18.6
  Sch 1 ....5.2
Local Government Finance Act 1988
  (36 *Statutes* 1109) 22.2
  s 113 ....10.6, 22.3, 22.4
  114 ....30.2
    (1) 22.3
    (7) 22.4
Local Government Finance Act 1992
  (25 *Statutes* 1130) 6.3

PARA

Local Government Finance Act 1992 (25
  Statutes 1130) —*contd*
  s 19 ....13.2
  65 ....20.2
  106 ....13.2
Local Government Finance Act 1998
  ....21.1
Local Government (Miscellaneous
  Provisions) Act 1976 (20 *Statutes* 60)
  s 38 ....2.30, 19.12
Local Government (Scotland) Act 1973
  (25 *Statutes* 489)
  s 33A 13.3

N

National Assistance Act 1948 (40
  Statutes 18) 20.5
National Health Service and
  Community Care Act 1990 (40 *Statutes*
  242)
  s 46 ....18.2

O

Offices, Shops and Railway Premises
  Act 1963 (19 *Statutes* 744) 34.6

P

Parliamentary Commissioner Act 1967
  (10 *Statutes* 323) 13.3
Partnership Act 1890 (32 *Statutes* 782)
  s 1 ....19.1
Police Act 1997
  Pt III (ss 91–108) 27.7
Political Parties, Elections and
  Referendums Act 2000 ....7.7, 8.2, 8.31
  Pt VII (ss 101–129) 7.1
Prevention of Corruption Act 1906 (12
  Statutes 155) 30.1
Prevention of Corruption Act 1916 (12
  Statutes 179) 30.1
Public Bodies (Admission to Meetings)
  Act 1960 (25 *Statutes* 111) 21.1
Public Interest Disclosure Act 1998
  ....12.16, 33.2–33.9, 34.3
  s 1 ....33.1
  9 ....33.5
Public Libraries and Museums Act 1964
  (24 *Statutes* 206)
  s 1(2) 18.2

R

Race Relations (Amendment) Act 2000
  ....18.3
Rates Act 1984 (36 *Statutes* 1076)
  s 13 ....20.2
Recreational Charities Act 1958 (5
  Statutes 893) 19.7

PARA

Regional Development Agencies Act
1998 ....19.3
Regulation of Investigatory Powers Act
2000 ....27.1–27.9, 28.3
s 26 ....27.10
Regulatory Reform Act 2001 ....2.33
Representation of the People Act 1983
(15 *Statutes* 1312) 8.2, 8.8
s 1, 2, 3A, 4 ....8.12
5 ....8.13, 8.15
6 ....8.15
7 ....8.13, 8.15
7A, 7B 8.13
8, 9 ....8.15
Sch 1, 2 ....8.14
Representation of the People Act 2000 ......8.2,
8.8–8.11, 8.14,
8.16, 8.34, 8.35, 8.41
s 1(1), (2) 8.12
2 ....8.12
3(2) 8.13
4–6 ....8.13
10 ....8.17
11 ....8.31
12 ....8.15, 8.20
Sch 4 ....8.15

PARA

S

School Standards and Framework Act
1998 ....19.3, 19.8, 21.1
s 6, 26, 120 ....18.2
Social Security and Housing Benefits
Act 1982 (40 *Statutes* 127) 13.2

T

Town and Country Planning Act 1990
(46 *Statutes* 500)
s 13, 16 ....20.2
27, 54 ....18.2
Trade Union and Labour Relations
(Consolidation) Act 1992 (16 *Statutes* 180)
s 152(1)(a), (b) 34.5
(2) **34.5**
154 ....34.5
Transport Act 2000 ....19.8
s 108 ....18.2

W

Welfare Reform and Pensions Act 1999 ...19.3
Wireless Telegraphy Act 1949 (45
Statutes 30) 27.7

TABLE OF STATUTORY INSTRUMENTS

References in the right-hand column are to paragraph numbers.
Paragraph numbers in **bold** indicate where the material is reproduced in the text.

PARA

C

Community Health Councils Regulations 1996, SI 1996/640
reg 18(1) 20.3
Contracting Out (Functions in Relation to the Provision of Guardian ad Litem and Reporting Officers Panels) Order 1997, SI 1997/1652 ....19.11
Contracting Out (Management Functions in Relation to Certain Community Homes) Order 1996, SI 1996/586 ....19.11

D

Data Protection (Subject Access Modification) (Education) Order 2000, SI 2000/414 ....21.3
Data Protection (Subject Access Modification) (Health) Order 2000, SI 2000/413 ....21.3
Data Protection (Subject Access Modification) (Social Work) Order 2000, SI 2000/415 ....21.3

E

Education (School Organisation Plans) (England) Regulations 1999, SI 1999/701 ....18.2
Education (School Organisation Plans) (Wales) Regulations 1999, SI 1999/499 ....18.2
Education Standards (Fund) (England) Regulations 2000, SI 2000/703 ....18.2

L

Local Authorities (Alternative Arrangements) (England) Regulations 2001, SI 2001/1299 ....6.1, 6.6
reg 3 ....6.3
5 ....6.2
6, 8–16 ....6.5
Sch 1 ....6.3

PARA

Local Authorities (Alternative Arrangements) (Wales) Regulations 2001, SI 2001/2284
reg 5(2) 6.11
8–10 ....6.11
13(b) 6.11
Sch 1–4 ....6.11
Local Authorities (Changing Executive Arrangements and Alternative Arrangements) (England) Regulations 2001, SI 2001/1003
reg 2(2), (3) 4.24
3(1) 4.24
10 ....4.24
Local Authorities (Companies) Order 1995, SI 1995/849 ....2.24, 19.4
Local Authorities (Conduct of Referendums) (England) Regulations 2001, SI 2001/1298 ....7.1
reg 3 ....7.2
4 ....7.4
5 ....7.5
6(3) 7.7
9 ....7.2
Sch 1 ....7.2
Sch 2 ....7.7
Local Authorities (Contracting Out of Allocation of Housing and Homelessness Functions) Order 1996, SI 1996/3205 ....19.11
Local Authorities (Contracting Out of Highway Functions) Order 1999, SI 1999/2106 ....19.11
Local Authorities (Contracting Out of Investment Functions) Order 1996, SI 1996/1883 ....19.11
Local Authorities (Contracting Out of Tax Billing, Collection and Enforcement Functions) Order 1996, SI 1996/1880 ....19.11
Local Authorities (Executive Arrangements) (Access to Information) (England) Regulations 2000, SI 2000/3272 ....4.16, 4.18, 4.21, 21.2

PARA

Local Authorities (Executive Arrangements) (Modification of Enactments and Further Provisions) (England) Order 2001, SI 2001/1517
art 8(4) 12.5
Local Authorities (Functions and Responsibilities) (England) (Amendment) Regulations 2001, SI 2001/2212 ....4.12, 4.13
Local Authorities (Functions and Responsibilities) (England) Regulations 2000, SI 2000/2853 ....4.10
reg 2(1) 4.11
3 ....4.12
4 ....18.5
5 ....4.12
Sch 1 ....4.11, 32.2, 32.4, 32.11
Sch 2 ....4.12
Sch 3 ....4.13
Sch 4 ....18.5
Local Authorities (Members' Interests) Regulations 1992, SI 1992/618 ....13.2
Local Authorities (Standing Orders) Regulations 1993, SI 1993/202 ....4.7, 10.25, 31.7
reg 3(1) 31.6, 32.6
Local Elections (Principal Areas) Rules 1986, SI 1986/2214 ....7.4
Local Government Act 2000 (Commencement No 3) Order 2000, SI 2000/2836 ....2.2, 2.7, 2.8
Local Government Act 2000 (Constitutions) (England) Direction 2000 ....7.10, 10.26, 13.5
para 3 ....12.9
Local Government Best Value (Exclusion of Non-commercial Considerations) Order 2001, SI 2001/909 ....29.11, 30.4
Local Government (Best Value) (Performance Plans and Reviews) Order 1999, SI 1999/3251 ....18.2
Local Government (Best Value) (Review and Performance Plans) (Wales) Order 2000, SI 2000/1271 ....18.2
Local Government (Committees and Political Groups) Regulations 1990, SI 1990/1553 ....6.2
Local Government (Elected Mayors) (Elections, Terms of Office and Casual Vacancies) (England) Regulations 2001, SI 2001/2544 ....4.5
reg 2 ....7.9
Local Government (Inspection of Documents) (Summary of Rights)

Order 1986, SI 1986/854 ....21.1
Local Government Officers (Political Restrictions) Regulations 1990, SI 1990/851 ....34.2
Local Government Pension Scheme (Amendment, etc) Regulations 1999, SI 1999/3438 ....29.10
Local Government Pension Scheme (Amendment) Regulations 2000, SI 2000/1005 ....29.10
Local Government Pension Scheme Regulations 1997, SI 1997/1612 ......29.2, 29.10
Local Government (Promotion of Economic Development) (Amendment) Regulations 1990, SI 1990/789 ....2.6
Local Government (Promotion of Economic Development) (Amendment) Regulations 1992, SI 1992/2242 ....2.6
Local Government (Promotion of Economic Development) (Amendment) Regulations 1995, SI 1995/556 ....2.6
Local Government (Promotion of Economic Development) Regulations 1990, SI 1990/763 ....2.6
Local Government Redundancy (Continuity of Employment in Local Government, etc) (Modification) Order 1999, SI 1999/2277 ....29.2
NHS Bodies and Local Authorities Partnership Arrangements Regulations 2000, SI 2000/617 ....19.3
Parent Governor Representatives (England) Regulations 2001, SI 2001/478 ....5.2
Public Interest Disclosure (Compensation) Order 1999, SI 1999/1548 ....33.5
Relevant Authorities (General Principles) Order 2001, SI 2001/1401 ....30.2
Representation of the People (England and Wales) Regulations 2001, SI 2001/341 ....8.14
Telecommunications (Lawful Business Practice) (Interception of Communications) Regulations 2000, SI 2000/2699 ....27.3, 27.9
Town and Country Planning (Development Plan) Regulations 1991, SI 1991/2794 ....20.2
Transfer of Undertakings (Protection of Employment) Regulations 1981, SI 1981/1794 ....29.2, 29.5, 29.8–29.11

DIVISION I
Modernising Democracy

CHAPTER 1
New Political and Administrative Structures –
An Introduction

The Modernising Agenda

[1.1]
Local government matters. Not least because it accounted for some £71 billion spending in the first year of the new Labour Governments' first term in 1997/1998 (some 25% of all general government spending) when the modernising agenda was being developed.

The vision for local government in the run up to the 1997 General Election was to be found in the pledge to modernise the country and bring government back to the people. This is echoed in the introduction to the subsequent Green Paper:

> 'Local government has a key role to play in our country if people are to have the quality of life they deserve. So modernising local government is at the heart of this pledge'[1].

The modernisation agenda for local government aimed to address the following weaknesses:

- low turn out at elections;
- a culture of apathy about democracy;
- councillors over-burdened by committee meetings;
- corruption and misbehaviour amongst councillors; and
- mixed picture of service delivery.

Radical change was proposed in the form of democratic renewal, best value in service delivery, a new ethical framework and changes to the local government finance system. Green Papers and consultation documents addressing each of these areas were issued during early 1998.

Councils were told they would need to develop a vision for their locality, provide a focus for partnership and guarantee quality services for all.

Prior to the issue of the local democracy Green Paper, the Local Government (Experimental Arrangements) Bill had already been introduced in the Lords, not as a government Bill, (although with government backing) but by Lord Hunt. The Bill received its first reading in December 1997.

The purpose of the Bill was to enable local authorities in England and Wales to operate, for temporary periods, experimental arrangements with respect to decision-taking. It would have allowed the creation of an elected mayor and political executives.

Its philosophy reflected the Labour Party manifesto[2] commitment to 'encourage democratic innovation in local government including pilots of the idea of elected mayors with executive powers in cities'. Its existence also seemed to reflect the fact that powerful pressure groups such as the new Local Government Network could bring real influence to bear on government policy.

The Bill was overtaken (and subsequently ran out of time) by the publication of the Green Paper *Local democracy and community leadership* and subsequently by the Local government White Paper *Modern Local Government: In Touch with the People*[3].

The White Paper was heralded as 'outlining the greatest reform agenda for local government in 20 years'[4].

The White Paper's key proposals were:

- a new duty to promote the economic, social and environmental well being of their areas[5];
- the beacon council scheme[6];
- authorities to review their decision-making processes – the options of mayor and cabinet, leader and cabinet and mayor and council manager emerge[7];
- referendum for Mayors – to be proposed by authorities, or triggered by 10% of the local electorate[8];
- electoral processes to be reformed[9];
- crude and universal capping to be scrapped[10];
- CCT to be abolished and the creation of a new duty of Best value[11]; and
- a new ethical framework – all councils to have standards committees, and end to surcharge and the creation of a new independent standards board[12].

The tone of the modernisation suggested in the White Paper seemed to be much more that local government could chose to be either part of the problem or be seen to be part of the solution delivered by central government[13]. This somewhat harsher tone is reflected in the words of the Prime Minister, Tony Blair MP.

He wrote:

> '... I want the message to Local Government to be loud and clear. A changing role is part of your heritage. The people's needs require you to change again so that you can play your part in helping to modernise Britain and in partnership with others, deliver the policies for which this Government was elected. If you accept this challenge you will not find us wanting. You can look forward to an enhanced role and new powers. Your contribution will be recognised. Your status enhanced. If you are unwilling or unable to work to the modern agenda then the government will have to look to other partners to take on your role'[14].

The next stage of implementing the modernisation agenda came with what was to become the Local Government Act 1999. This Act removed Best Value from the cohort of policies in the White Paper and implemented it first. Lack of parliamentary time was the ostensible reason. Whatever the real reason, there are now some perceived advantages in being able to marginalise a cumbersome and expensive regime. The disadvantages are the lack of joined-upness of the modernising agenda, for example how best value is divorced from the community planning process.

The draft Bill on *Organisation and Standards* published in March 1999, along with a consultation document *Local Leadership, Local choice*, was subject to a unique scrutiny by a committee of both houses of parliament. It was the precursor to the Local Government Act 2000, but had the effect of lengthening the process between policy development and legislation.

For lawyers, the real test emerged on publication of the final version of the legislation. Between February 1998 and July 2000, the ideas that were to become the Local Government Act 2000 went through the several different versions of Green Paper, White Paper, draft Bill and Bill. Late compromises such as the '4th option' emerged during the bill's final passage through parliament in order to soothe the House of Lords and gain royal assent.

For the local government lawyer these ideas painted a bright future studded with discretion to innovate on modernisation and an end to committees. Vires issues seemed a million miles away.

Yet what might have been a long awaited general power of competence emerged into a much blunted power of well being with no overhaul of s 111 of the Local Government Act 1972. This is disappointing. Promised freedoms within Best Value as part of implementing s 16 of the 1999 Act have also yet to emerge[15]. Our main job was to read all these consultation papers and draft Bills and suggest intelligent responses that our councillors might like to make.

1   John Prescott MP Deputy-Prime Minister: Green Paper – *Introduction to Local Democracy and community leadership*. Green paper (February 1998).
2   New Labour – *Because Britain Deserves Better*.
3   Published 30 July 1998.
4   Local Government Association briefing on the White Paper – August 1998.
5   Subsequently forming Pt I of the LGA 2000.
6   Not supported by a statutory framework.
7   Subsequently becomes Pt II of the LGA 2000.
8   Forms part of Pt II of the LGA 2000 and 10% reduced to 5% of the electorate for a petition to trigger a referendum.
9   Subsequently forming part of Pt IV of the LGA 2000.
10   Subsequently enacted as Pt II of the LGA 2000.
11   Subsequently Pt I of the LGA 2000.
12   Pt III of the LGA 2000, drawing on the work of the Nolan Report – *Third Report of the Committee on Standards in Public Life: Standards of conduct in Local government in England, Scotland and Wales* (July 1997, Cm 3702).
13   See Chap 1 of the White Paper – *The Need for Change*.
14   *Leading the Way: A New Vision for Local Government* (Institute for Public Policy Research, 1998).
15   See consultation document: *Working with Others to Achieve Best Value* (DETR, March 2001).

A Brief Introduction to the Local Government Act 2000

[1.2]
Part I of the Act deals with the promotion of economic, social or environmental well-being etc. It covers the power of well-being, limits on the power and strategies to promote it, better known as community strategies. Powers to modify other legislation are set out in ss 6 and 7 but are so far unimplemented. Details of Part I of the Act are set out fully in Chapters 2 and 3 of this Division.

Part II of the Act covers arrangements with respect to executives and covers the move to executive arrangements, referenda, alternative arrangements, scrutiny and new constitutions. Chapters 4, 5, 6 and 7 of this Division cover these areas in full.

Part III of the Act introduces the new ethical framework.

Part IV of the Act covers election schemes and is yet to be implemented.

Part V of the Act, entitled 'Miscellaneous' covers a mixed bag of measures, perhaps the most significant among which is the repeal of surcharge. The introduction of pensions for councillors and amendments to the allowances scheme are to be found at s 99 and the long-awaited indemnification of members and officers of authorities is at s 101.

With many parts of the legislation either yet to be implemented in their infancy can any lessons be drawn from the modernisation of local government so far?

Could it be said that the modernisation agenda confuses an interest in politics with democracy? Democracy seems to be measured by turnout at elections when it is well documented that turnout is affected by activity generated by political parties. The electorate is interested in good basic services but has little interest in structures. Why did we expect larger turnouts in consultation on democratic structures and Mayoral referendums?

Scrutiny, although allegedly well modelled by central government, has not caught local councillors' imaginations yet. This may be linked to a perceived weakness in failing to address the calibre of local councillors.

Can central prescription ever deliver change? Doesn't detailed prescription prevent innovation?

Would it not be better in achieving effective change to work with councils and not against them? For example the stick of inspection in the best value regime far outweighs the carrots of the yet to be defined freedoms introduced by s 16 of the 1999 Act.

Finally, there is no parallel modernisation agenda for central government so the opportunity to motivate local government by leading by example is lost.

The agenda for local government for the second term of this government will be set out in a White Paper in Autumn 2001. It promises to look at more deregulation and further democratic renewal measures. There has also been much speculation about how the Prime Minister's references to finding other partners might be translated into an imperative to allow more private sector partners to deliver council services.

The modernising agenda in local government, whatever it looks like in future, is here to stay because local government does matter and therefore we need to understand the implications of what is already on the statute book.

CHAPTER 2
Power to Promote or Improve Economic, Social and Environmental Well-Being

The Power of Economic, Social and Environmental Well-Being

Background – local authorities' powers to act

[2.1]

Local authorities are creatures of statute. As statutory corporations they have no powers to act unless there is express authority in law for them to do so. The legal framework in which local authorities operate bestows on them a wide range of duties which they are required to undertake, an even wider range of discretionary powers which enable them to undertake specific activities should they choose to and a small number of more general powers. Taken together, these duties and powers are the statutory functions of local authorities.

To act without the necessary express or implied powers will open an authority to the risk of challenge. Subsequent judicial interpretation of the legality of that activity will render the authority's action ultra vires and void.

It is in relation to the use of the small number of general powers available to local authorities that judicial interpretation has on occasion taken a restrictive view of the activities that authorities can legitimately pursue. This has created uncertainty amongst local authorities as to the extent to which they can rely on their general powers to undertake certain activities. Increasingly, the doctrine of ultra vires has been criticised as imposing a negative control over authorities to the detriment of innovation, enterprise and the development of a positive and proactive role for local authorities, in leading and developing their communities[1].

---

1   The Maud Report concluded that: 'Our view is that ultra vires as it operates has a deleterious effect on local government because of the narrowness of the legislation governing local authorities' activities. The specific nature of legislation discourages enterprise, handicaps development, robs the community of services which the local authority might render and encourages too rigorous oversight by central government. It contributes to the excessive concern over legalities'. See also eg M Loughlin, *Ultra Vires: Hail and Farewell* in 'A Framework for the Future' (LGIU, 1997) for an analysis that even if the legislative framework up to and including the LGA 1972 was conducive to innovation and flexible responses by local authorities, subsequent developments have resulted in a less facilitative and more restrictive climate than existed previously.

What the Law Used to Say

[2.2]
Prior to Pt I of the Local Government Act 2000 coming into force (on 18 October 2000[1]) local authorities already had a small number of 'general' powers.

1 Sections 1 to 9 of the Local Government Act came into force 18 October 2000 in relation to England via SI 2000/2836 (c 82) 'The Local Government Act 2000 (Commencement No 3) Order 2000'.

The general power under s 111 of the Local Government Act 1972

[2.3]
The most obvious general power is s 111 of the Local Government Act 1972 – the power for local authorities to undertake activity which is 'calculated to facilitate, or is conducive or incidental to the discharge of their functions'. The drawback to s 111 as a general power is that the power conferred by it must be ancillary to an intra vires function of a local authority. There are those who argue that s 111 merely restates the implied general powers which all corporations have anyway.

The courts in recent years have done harm to the use of s 111 and it has now become unclear whether the function must be expressly conferred by statute or can be impliedly conferred. The broader view that s 111 can extend to support activity which a local authority is impliedly authorised to perform is supported by some case law[1] but so too is the narrower view that the function must be expressly conferred before section III can be relied on[2]. Further complications to the use of s 111 resulted from the decision in *R v Richmond Upon Thames London Borough Council, ex p McCarthy & Stone (Developments) Ltd*[3] where the point was not argued in the House of Lords that the giving of pre-planning application advice was an implied function of the local authority. The point therefore remains open as to whether there can be such functions[4].

Consequently, although s 111 has not been repealed under Pt I of the Local Government Act 2000, reliance on its use may well shift in favour of reliance on the broad well-being power contained in s 2 of the 2000 Act.

1 Eg *Hazel v Hammersmith and Fulham London Borough Council* [1990] 2 QB 697, 722–723, Woolf LJ in his definition of 'functions' said: 'What is a function for the purposes of the sub-section (III(I)) is not expressly defined but in our view there can be little doubt that in this context 'function' refers to the multiplicity of specific statutory activities the council is expressly or impliedly under a duty to perform or has' power to perform under the provision of the act of 1972 or other relevant legislation'.
2 Eg *Allsop v North Tyneside Metropolitan Borough Council* (1992) 90 LGR 462 where in the Court of Appeal, Parker LJ suggested a preference for a narrow view and that the term 'function' is 'plainly referring to the functions set out in Pt IX of the Act.'
3 [1992] 2 AC 48.
4 In *R v Richmond Upon Thames London Borough Council, ex p McCarthy & Stone (Developments) Ltd* [1992] 2 AC 48, the House of Lords held that the giving of pre-planning application advice was incidental to the function of determining planning applications and

that to charge for such advice by reliance on s 111 was unlawful since this was 'incidental to the incidental'.

The general power under s 137 of the Local Government Act 1972

[2.4]
The other significant general power was s 137 of the Local Government Act 1972. Section 137 permitted authorities to incur expenditure which in their opinion was in the interests of their area. However the use of s 137 powers was constrained:

- s 137 could not be used for any purpose for which there was authority in other legislation, or to overcome any limitations, prohibitions or conditions in other legislation (s 137(1));
- by an expenditure limit currently ranging from £2.50 to £5.00 per head of population depending on the class of authority.

The scope for expenditure under s 137 was further restricted by the Local Government and Housing Act 1989. As a result of the 1989 Act authorities had to be able to demonstrate that any expenditure incurred under s 137 was of 'direct' benefit to their area and was proportionate to the benefits the expenditure was intended to bring (see s 137(1)(*b*)).

Where the judiciary has been called upon to interpret the vires of activities pursued under s 137, it has, on occasion, taken a narrow and restrictive view. In some cases the judiciary has inferred from the absence of specific powers in other legislation that certain activities were prohibited and that an authority was therefore unable to rely on s 137 powers to circumvent that prohibition. Consequently, despite the original aim of s 137, it is no longer thought of as a vehicle for undertaking new or innovative activities[1]. Authorities saw s 137 'as very much a fallback or safety net to provide the vires for an activity if no other powers were available'. This 'power of last resort' is the antithesis of the 'power of general competence' that local government has been calling for over the last 20 years[2].

1 *Local Authority Activity under s 137, Local Government Act 1972* (York Consulting, DETR – February 1999).
2 See *Get in on the act: Local Government Act 2000 explained* (Local Government Association, published September 2000).

Modification of s 137

[2.5]
Section 8 of the Local Government Act 2000 has removed most of the s 137 powers from all the principal councils to which the 2000 Act applies. All that is retained for principal councils is s 137(3) which permits them to make contributions to the funds of charities operating in the UK, to not for profit bodies providing public services in the UK and for mayoral appeals.

Section 137 will continue in force as a general power for parish and town councils.

Sections 33 to 35 of the Local Government and Housing Act 1989

[2.6]
The Widdicombe Committee was set up in 1984 to consider 'the conduct of local authority business'. It reported in 1986[1] and took a special interest in local authority involvement in economic development and in discretionary expenditure under existing s 137 powers[2].

It was not until 1989 that the Local Government and Housing Act was passed. Part III of this Act was concerned with economic development. For the first time, economic development was recognised as a discretionary function of local authorities. Authorities were given the power to take such steps as they may from time to time consider appropriate for promoting the economic development of their area (s 33(1)).

However, the powers to promote economic development were heavily constrained by the restrictions placed on their use by the four sets of regulations made under s 34[3].

Flexibility in the use of economic development powers was further constrained by the provisions of s 35(3). Under this section, authorities who chose to exercise their discretionary economic development powers were required to 'prepare a document'[4] each financial year setting out what money they intended to spend and what outcomes they expected to achieve from this expenditure. Authorities were then required to consult with the private sector locally on the contents of the annual document. If expenditure proposals on specific items were not included in the annual document there was no flexibility allowed to authorities to make provision during the course of that financial year either to take advantage of an unforeseen opportunity or to adapt to accommodate a change of circumstance such as the closure of a local enterprise.

1   Report of the Committee of Enquiry into the Conduct of Local Authority Business (1986, Cm 9797).
2   Phillip Ransdale and Stuart Capon, *An analysis of Local Authority Discretionary Expenditure in 1984–85, Research Volume IV* (Committee of Enquiry into the Conduct of Local Authority Business, 1986, Cm 9801, pp 11–35).
3   These regulations are: (a) the Local Government (Promotion of Economic Development) Regulations 1990, SI 1990/763); (b) the Local Government (Promotion of Economic Development) (Amendment) Regulations 1990, SI 1990/789); (c) the Local Government (Promotion of Economic Development) (Amendment) Regulations 1992, SI 1992/2242); and (d) the Local Government (Promotion of Economic Development) (Amendment) Regulations 1990, SI 1995/556.
4   NB a document, not a strategy or a plan. These documents could vary substantially from being a few paragraphs to lengthy policy statements.

Repeal of ss 33 to 35 of the Local Government and Housing Act 1989

[2.7]
Schedule 6 to the Local Government Act 2000 has repealed the economic development powers in ss 33 to 35 of the 1989 Act because they have been rendered obsolete by the new well-being powers[1].

Economic development is now subsumed within the new power of well-being contained in s 2(1) of the Local Government Act 2000. In addition, the requirement to produce an annual document on the use of the economic development power (s 35(3) of the 1989 Act) is also repealed (see Sch 6 to the LGA 2000) freeing authorities to be more flexible in providing for economic well-being under Pt I of the Local Government Act 2000.

1   Sections 34 to 35 were repealed on 18 October 2000 in relation to England by SI 2000/2836 (c 82) Local Government, England, The Local Government Act 2000 (Commencement No 3) Order 2000. Section 33 currently remains on the statute books simply as a 'reassurance' to authorities. Section 33 is to be repealed on 28 July 2001 though it is a redundant provision now that the new well-being power of s 2 of the Local Government Act 2000 is in force.

What the Law Now Says Following the Implementation of Pt I of the Local Government Act 2000

Promotion of economic, social or environmental well-being

[2.8]
Introduction

The Local Government Act 2000 received Royal Assent on 28 July 2000. Part I, 'Promotion of Economic, Social or Environmental Well-being', came into force on 18 October 2000[1] in respect of principal authorities in England. It consists of nine sections.

1   See the Local Government (Commencement No 3) Order 2000, SI 2000/2836.

[2.9]
The new power of well-being

Part I of the Act introduces a major change to the legal framework that local authorities operate within. The key provision of this new framework is the broad power contained in s 2 which gives all principal authorities[1], though not parish or town councils, the discretionary power 'to do anything which they consider is likely' to promote or improve the economic, social or environmental well-being of their communities, subject to certain constraints.

This represents a significant change to the legal framework since in the past local authorities needed to locate a specific power in legislation, authorising them to undertake an activity before they were able to do so. This broad well-being power now shifts the previous balance of presumption away from the need for certainty and reliance on a specific power. Instead local authorities can now assume they have the power to act in pursuit of promoting well-being without the need to sift through the statute books to find a specific power. The statutory guidance on promoting well-being advises authorities to regard this 'can do' power as being 'the power of first resort'[2].

Will this prove to be the case? Will it obviate the need for local authorities to search for legal powers to act? Will it give them reassurance where there had been uncertainty over their powers? These points are covered in this chapter and summarised in the conclusion.

1 The definition of the local authorities which are subject to the provisions in Pt I of the Act is given at s 1. Section 1 states:
'In this Part 'local authority' means–
(a) In relation to England–
    (i) a county council;
    (ii) a district council;
    (iii) a London borough council;
    (iv) the Common Council of the City of London in its capacity as a local authority;
    (v) the Council of the Isles of Scilly
(b) In relation to Wales, a county council or a county borough council.
2 DETR Guidance, *The Power of Economic, Social or Environmental Well-being*, para 10 (28 March 2001). The Guidance can be obtained from the DTLR's web-site at http://www.local-regions.detr.gov.uk/wellbeing/index.htm.

[2.10]
Community Leadership: The duty to prepare a Community Strategy and Partnership Working

Part I of the Act introduces further changes to the legal framework in respect of the community leadership role of local authorities and specifically includes a new duty to prepare a comprehensive community strategy developed with local people, businesses, public and voluntary organisations.

The government's policies for the radical reform of local government were spelt out in the White Paper *Modern Local Government: In Touch with the People*[1]. This clarified that community leadership should be at the heart of the role of modern local authorities.

Community leadership take into account that many issues facing communities today are cross-cutting issues which require partnership working at a local level between the public, private, community and voluntary sectors to achieve integrated and more coherent delivery of local services. Such cross-cutting issues include health, transport, social inclusion and equalities, community safety, unemployment, sustainable development, the environment, economic growth, educational improvement, regeneration etc. No one organisation on its own can provide the solution to these issues. Instead an integrated approach is needed. All sectors need to work together each contributing its part to delivering the local objectives of the community strategy. With proper co-ordination duplication of effort can be avoided and resources can be used to better effect. Part I of the Act carries into effect the community leadership role for local authorities.

Local authorities are now enabled as part of the new legal framework to be the engine driver, to be the community leader in facilitating the building of effective local partnerships for the delivery of integrated and coherent services serving the interests of and enhancing the quality of life of their communities.

To enable local authorities to develop their community leadership role and respond to the needs of local communities, s 4 of the Act places a duty on local authorities to prepare a comprehensive community strategy to enhance the quality of life of local communities and contribute to the achievement of sustainable development in the UK[2] through actions to improve well-being. The community strategy will set out how the authority and its partners will work together to promote the well-being of their local community.

The community strategy will allow authorities and other bodies who provide local services to establish common priorities and identify the steps each will take to deliver these priorities. 'The involvement of local people is central to the development and implementation of the community strategy and is key to change in the longer term'[3]. The community strategy puts local people at the heart of partnership working and needs to respond to the needs and concerns of local communities.

The discretionary well-being power, the duty to prepare a community strategy and the remaining provisions of Pt I are central to the modernisation of local government. Together, they provide authorities with a modernised legal framework enabling them to develop their community leadership role and deliver the longer term community vision over the next decade and more (see Chapter 3 of this Division for further details on community leadership and the new partnership arrangements for local strategic partnerships. Further detail on the duty to prepare community strategies is given in Division III – Chapter 18).

1   (July 1998, Cm 4014).
2   See DETR, *A Better Quality of Life: a strategy for sustainable development for the UK* (May 1999, Cm 4345).
3   See government Guidance to local authorities, *Preparing Community Strategies*, para 50 (December 2000).

The Nine Provisions of Pt I of the Local Government Act 2000 and the DETR Guidance on the Power to Promote or Improve Economic, Social or Environmental Well-Being[1]

Section 1 – meaning of 'local authority' in Pt I

[2.11]
The following local authorities are subject to the provisions of Pt I:

* In England–
    - county councils;
    - district councils;
    - London borough councils;
    - the Common Council of the City of London; and
    - the Council of the Isles of Scilly.
* In Wales[2]–
    - county councils; and
    - county borough councils.

Part I does not apply to[3]:

- parish or community (town) councils;
- police authorities; or
- fire and civil defence authorities.

The responsibility for exercising the use of the well-being power is the responsibility of the executive under executive arrangements set out in Pt II of the Act. (See Chapter 4 below for full details on executive arrangements).

All principal councils to which executive arrangements apply will need to adopt a new constitution involving the creation and operation of an executive. The executive will be the accountable, corporate leadership for the council and will lead the search for Best Value and be the focus for partnership working with other local public, private and voluntary sector bodies. The full council will set the policy and budgetary framework and approve the community strategy based on proposals from the executive. So unless the executive intended to use the well-being power in a manner contrary to the council's policy or budgetary framework then only the executive can determine how the power is to be exercised. Decisions which are contrary to the policy and budgetary framework must under executive arrangements be taken by full council[4].

Where councils are operating under 'alternative arrangements' set out in Pt II of the Act, such councils can also opt for a streamlined committee system where the relevant policy committee undertakes the same role as that outlined above for the executive. (See Chapter 6 below for details on Alternative Arrangements).

1   This Guidance can be downloaded from the DTLR website at http://www.local-regions.detr.gov.uk/wellbeing/index.htm.
2   The National Assembly for Wales has power to bring Pt I into force in Wales and to issue guidance to Welsh authorities.
3   For reasons as to why the provisions of Pt I do not apply to these authorities: see p 17 of *Powerpack – using the new power to promote well-being* (LGA, December 2000).
4   See the Annex to the DETR Guidance on the well-being power.

Section 2 – the promotion of well-being

[2.12]
Section 2(1) provides that every local authority is to have power to do anything it considers is likely to achieve any one or more of the following objects:

(a)   the promotion or improvement of the economic well-being of their area;
(b)   the promotion or improvement of the social well-being of their area; and
(c)   the promotion or improvement of the environmental well-being of their area.

Each of these three components can be used separately or in combination.

Section 2(2) – who benefits?

[2.13]
Section 2(2) provides that the well-being power may be exercised in relation to or for the benefit of:

(*a*)   the whole or any part of a local authority's area; or
(*b*)   all or any persons resident or present in a local authority's area.

This is further broadened by s 2(5) which allows authorities to apply the well-being power for the benefit of any person or area outside the authority's boundary if that action contributes to well-being in the authority's own area. Schedule 1 to the Interpretation Act 1978 clarifies that the term 'person' includes 'a body of persons corporate or incorporate'. It therefore includes local authorities, police, fire, civil defence, health and park authorities, businesses and other organisations that constitute legal entities as well as any individual or particular groups of people within the community. The definition of 'persons present' in an area includes groups such as tourists, commuters and travellers[1].

The DETR Guidance issued on the use of the well-being power (published 27 March 2000) outlines the scope for collaborative working, eg to address issues which do not recognise administrative boundaries. The emphasis in the Guidance centres on the need for consultation, consensus and co-operative working between authorities when exercising the power for the benefit of people or areas outside their own boundary[2].

1   See para 30 of the DETR Guidance.
2   See paras 50 to 56 of the DETR Guidance. Any further reference in this chapter to paragraph numbers refers to paragraphs in the DETR Guidance on the power to promote or improve economic, social or environmental well-being – the DETR's website address is http://www.local-regions.detr.gov.uk/wellbeing/index.htm.

Section 2(3) – must have regard to the Community Strategy

[2.14]
Section 2(3) states that a local authority when exercising the power must have regard to its community strategy prepared under s 4. 'The requirement in section 2(3) is intended to ensure that local authorities consider the impact that using the well-being power will have on the achievement of the aims and objectives of the community strategy (including the contribution to sustainable development). However, this does not mean that a council has to wait until its community strategy is in place before using the well-being power'[1]. Importantly, each and every use of the new power does not need to be referenced in the community strategy[2]. Although this is what the DETR Guidance says there is some need for caution. Incurring any significant expenditure under the new power without any demonstrable regard to the community strategy might risk a successful judicial review challenge. A point for lawyers to feed into any draft community strategy may be the need for it to include flexible general principles which are adaptable enough to cover a wide variety of uses of the power not necessarily foreseeable when the plan is adopted.

1   DETR Guidance, paras 11 and 25.
2   DETR Guidance, para 26.

Section 2(4) – possible uses of the well-being power

[2.15]
Section 2(4) provides six examples of actions that local authorities can undertake using the well-being power. Authorities can:

*   incur expenditure;
*   give financial assistance to any person;
*   enter into arrangements or agreements with any person;
*   co-operate with, or facilitate or co-ordinate the activities of, any person;
*   exercise on behalf of any person any functions of that person; and
*   provide staff, goods, services or accommodation to any person.

This is not an exhaustive list of the sorts of activities that can be undertaken under the well-being power. Section 2(6) states explicitly that: 'Nothing in subsection (4) or (5) affects the generality of the power under sub-section (1)' (ie the well-being power)[1].

1   DETR Guidance, para 32.

Section 2(4)(a) and (b) – the power to incur expenditure and the power to give financial assistance

[2.16]
Section 2(4)(a) and (b) make it clear that local authorities now have a broad spending power to use in the pursuit of promoting well-being. No longer is there the limitation on spending which was contained in s 137 of the Local Government Act 1972. Financial assistance may now be given by any means authorities consider appropriate including by way of grants, loans, investment in well-being activities or by the provision of guarantees[1].

The position on authorities ability to grant indemnities against personal financial loss to their members or officers in all the circumstances in which indemnities would be appropriate is to be put beyond doubt. The Guidance at para 35 sets out the government's intention to make an order later in 2001 under s 101 of the 2000 Act conferring power on local authorities to provide such indemnities. Such an order should enable local authorities to take out insurance and indemnity for members and officers in connection with council business which should also cover them where they undertake appointments by their council to outside bodies provided the action to be indemnified is taken in good faith.

1   See DETR Guidance, paras 33 and 34.

Section 2(4)(c) and (d) – the power to enter into arrangements or agreements with any person and the power to co-operate with, or facilitate or co-ordinate the activities of any person

[2.17]
Section 2(4)(*c*) and (*d*) confer wide discretion for authorities to engage in partnership working so that authorities can act effectively in their community leadership role to drive forward the addressing of cross-cutting issues through multi-disciplinary working with partners from the public, private, voluntary and community sectors.

The government's view is that only through the strategic co-ordination of partnership working and through active community involvement will this lead to effective action to improve the well-being of an area. Partnership working involves all the statutory, non-statutory and voluntary organisation that provide services or whose actions affect local quality of life.

Non-statutory Guidance on *Local Strategic Partnerships*[1] stresses the importance of establishing successful overarching partnerships which bring together the public, private, community and voluntary sectors building on existing good practice wherever possible. These local strategic partnerships will provide an opportunity to bring together new and existing partnership working arrangements, to help authorities reduce local 'partnership fatigue'. See Chapter 3 of this Division for further details on local strategic partnerships.

1   The Guidance on LSP's published 27 March 2001 is available at http://www.local-regions.detr.gov.uk/lsp/guidance/index.htm.

Section 2(4)(e) and (f) – the power to exercise on behalf of any person any functions of that person and the power to provide staff, goods, services or accommodation to any person

[2.18]
Section 2(4)(*e*) clarifies that the well-being power enables local authorities to take on the functions of other service providers. The Health Act 1999 already provides local authorities and health authorities with the power to carry out functions on behalf of one another, by agreement. This provision allows authorities to extend this partnership approach to other bodies in addition to the NHS[1]. However, where a local authority does undertake a function on behalf of another body this does not transfer any statutory responsibility or accountability for the carrying out of that function from that other body. It simply provides local authorities and their partners with the ability to decide how best to discharge their functions[2].

Section 2(4)(*f*) is self-explanatory. It effectively clarifies that as well as providing financial assistance, local authorities can provide assistance in the form of contributions 'in kind'.

1   DETR Guidance, para 39.
2   DETR Guidance, para 40.

Section 2(5) – action outside an authority's area and in multi-tier areas

[2.19]
Section 2(5) states:

> 'The power under sub-section (1) includes a power for a local authority to do anything in relation to, or for the benefit of, any person or area situated outside their area, if they consider that it is likely to achieve one or more of the objects in that sub-section'.

This sub-section enables local authorities to exercise the well-being power outside their own area providing that such use contributes to well-being within their own area. It facilitates partnership working between a local authority and other bodies that provide local services and with other tiers of local government, enabling such partnerships to act in the interests of communities.

The Guidance states that s 2(5) opens up the scope for:

*   more collaborative working within local authorities and local strategic partnerships[1];
*   co-operation between neighbouring local authorities and local strategic partnerships; and
*   initiatives at the regional, cross-regional and sub-regional level (such as the provision of sub-regional leisure facilities, or to address issues which do not recognise administrative boundaries, such as the prevention of pollution and the conservation of biodiversity).

Taken together, s 2(4) and (5) powers provide local authorities with broad powers for collaborative working and with opportunities for innovation in the way that services, which improve well-being, can be delivered.

Collaborative working is a key power in relation to local authorities' partnership working with other public service providers. It provides a range of opportunities for collaborative action between neighbouring local authorities and local strategic partnerships.

A local authority and its local strategic partnership will need to consider, in drawing up the community strategy, whether they could be more effective, economic and efficient in promoting well-being by working across more than one local authority area. In doing so the objectives of Best Value could be furthered.

The Guidance makes it clear (at para 54) that a single community strategy can cover several authorities' areas of responsibility. There may be circumstances where co-operation and working together between neighbouring authorities with similar priorities could be carried out within a single local strategic partnership framework.

The following paragraphs identify a number of ways in which collaborative working to take action outside an authority's area can be undertaken using the key power provided by s 2(5). Such actions can also fulfil the authority's duty to secure Best Value under the Local Government Act 1999.

1   See Chapter 3 for further details on local strategic partnerships. The Guidance on local strategic partnerships, published by DETR on 27 March 2001, can be obtained from DETR, PO Box 236, Wetherby, West Yorkshire, LS23 7NB or downloaded from the DETR website at http://www.detr.gov.uk.

Collaborative Working – Lead Commissioning[1]

[2.20]
Lead commissioning allows for one Best Value authority, or one of its partners, to take a lead commissioning role on behalf of others involved in the partnership.

It provides the facility to commission on a collaborative basis a range of commodities, goods, services, works or other assets for a client group. One partner takes on the role of commissioner on behalf of the others to arrange contracts with a range of providers in the public, private and voluntary sectors.

An example of lead commissioning would allow two or more neighbouring authorities to appoint one of their number as a lead commissioner to undertake a function on their behalf to exploit economies of scale for the participating authorities. A unified service could provide a range of services either collectively or individually, such as refuse collection, grounds maintenance, leisure services and/or revenues and benefits services.

Where a Best Value authority transfers responsibility for the delivery of a function, under a lead commissioning agreement, the originating authority still retains accountability for that function. The originating authority must therefore make arrangements to monitor the effectiveness of the commissioned contract/s.

1   For details of lead commissioning and other ways of collaborative working see *Working with Others to Achieve Best Value* consultation paper, available from the DTLR website at http://www.local-regions.dtlr.gov.uk/consult/bestvalue/index.htm. This consultation paper was issued under s 16 of the LGA 1999. Section 16 provides the Secretary of State with the power to make an order to modify enactments which prevent or obstruct Best Value authorities from achieving Best Value and to confer new powers on local authorities to facilitate the achievement of Best Value objectives. At the time of writing it is expected that the order will be made at some point in 2002.

Collaborative Working – Joint Commissioning[1]

[2.21]
Under a joint commissioning agreement the partners share the responsibility for commissioning without giving the lead role to a particular partner. Joint commissioning of integrated services can therefore be provided across organisational or administrative boundaries to provide, for example, joined

up contracts for schemes, where increased volume will lead to more interest and/or more competitive tenders from the private sector than would otherwise have been the case had one local authority acted alone. The consultation paper[2] gives the example of joined up PFI schemes between neighbouring authorities, to jointly commission the renewal or upgrading of street lighting. However, joint commissioning can be used in the interests of well-being, wherever two or more authorities acting together can deliver economies of scale to serve the interests of community groups.

The consultation paper referred to[3] also details other ways of collaborative working, including secondments of staff, pooled budgets and integrated provision. See Chapter 3 for details of partnership working.

1   See n 1 at para **[2.20]** above.
2   See n 1 above.
3   See n 1 above.

Non-collaborative action by one authority outside its area

[2.22]
The scope of s 2(5) clearly enables a local authority to use the well-being power outside its area, without necessarily working in collaboration with neighbouring authorities, providing that such action benefits the originating authority's area. Under these circumstances there is the possibility that a local authority may use the power in ways that are perceived by other local authority tiers or neighbouring areas as being detrimental to them. The Guidance makes it clear (at para 56) that local authorities will be expected to consult and take the views of the other authority into account prior to exercising the power outside their own boundaries. Additionally where a local authority plans to use the well-being power in a way that will have a major impact beyond its boundaries, it should assess these impacts in consultation with the relevant neighbouring authorities. Having assessed these impacts in consultation, can a local authority still proceed with its proposed actions without the expressed support of the relevant neighbouring authority? Clearly authorities should strive to seek consensus but such agreement does not appear to be a statutory requirement.

London and Greater London Authority – para 57

[2.23]
Section 30(1) of the Greater London Authority Act 1999[1] provides that the Greater London Authority (GLA) has power to do anything which it considers will further any one or more of its principal purposes. The principal purposes are set out in s 30(2). These cover in respect of Greater London:

• the promotion of economic development and wealth creation;
• the promotion of social development; and
• the promotion of the improvement of the environment.

Section 32 requires the GLA to consult with the London boroughs and other bodies appropriate to a particular case (although their consent is not required before the power in s 30(1) can be exercised). Similarly, London boroughs will wish to consider how any action taken by the GLA will affect their own proposals and ensure that any action taken to promote well-being is co-ordinated to avoid unnecessary duplication.

1   Available at http://www.legislation.hmso.gov.uk/acts/acts1999/19990029.htm.

The power to form companies and other corporate bodies

[2.24]
As part of partnership working the well-being power will also enable local authorities to form or participate in companies, trusts or charities, including joint venture companies. This is provided that they are satisfied that the primary purpose behind the formation of, or participation in, a particular company is likely to achieve well-being objectives. Authorities will also be able to receive dividend payments in their capacity as a shareholder from its investment activity in such companies, since the receipt of dividends will not amount to raising money for the purposes of s 3(2)[1].

However, formation of and participation in companies using the well-being power will currently still be subject to the capital control mechanisms set out in Pt V of the Local Government and Housing Act 1989 and the accompanying Local Authorities (Companies) Order 1995[2].

These capital control mechanisms are to be reconsidered following any new system of capital controls which may result from the current review of local government finance[3].

Additionally, in the consultation paper, *Working with Others to Achieve Best Value*[4], it is proposed to provide Best Value authorities with a new power to form and participate in a range of corporate (company) structures to facilitate the achievement of Best Value. The provisions of this new general power are intended to help overcome the risk of challenge some authorities claim they may face in forming and participating in companies as a result of the ultra vires doctrine.

Statutory guidance, to be issued under s 16 of the Local Government Act 1999 will set out how companies can be used to assist authorities achieve Best Value in service delivery.

1   DETR Guidance, para 42.
2   SI 1995/849.
3   For details of the current review of local government finance see *Modernising Local Government Finance* – a Green Paper published by DETR (September 2000); available at http://www.local.dtlr.gov.uk/greenpap/index.htm.
4   Available at http://www.local-regions.detr.gov.uk/consult/bestvalue/index.htm – published 29 March 2001 by the DETR.

Section 3 – limits and restrictions on the power to promote well-being

[2.25]
Although Pt I of the 2000 Act provides significant new powers for local

government 'to do anything which it considers is likely to achieve' the promotion or improvement of the economic, social or environmental well-being of its area it is subject to certain constraints on its use.

Section 3(1) – local authorities must observe express statutory restrictions

[2.26]
Section 3(1) 'does not enable a local authority to do anything which they are unable to do by virtue of any prohibition, restriction or limitation on their powers which is contained in any enactment (whenever passed or made)' including constraints contained in subordinate legislation. A knowledge of these statutory restrictions will still, therefore be essential to anyone advising on the use of the well-being power.

Section 3(2) – local authorities cannot raise money

[2.27]
Section 3(2) states:

> 'The power under section 2(1) does not enable a local authority to raise money (whether by precepts, borrowing or otherwise)'.

Although local authorities are no longer subject to the spending limits in s 137 of the Local Government Act 1972, they can only use existing sources of income to promote or improve well-being. Specifically, local authorities are prevented from levying a new tax, though they are not prevented from setting annual council tax levels, having regard to the ways they intend to use the well-being power. Nor does the well-being power broaden local authorities' existing powers to borrow money.

Section 3(2) – incidental charging for well-being

[2.28]
The government's view is that the effect of the provision in s 3(2) is to prevent local authorities from using the well-being power *primarily* to raise money. Paragraph 67 introduces the principle of *incidental* charging. For example, where a local authority uses the well-being power for a different purpose and only *incidentally* receives income as a result, this does not amount to raising money and is not, therefore, prohibited. A local authority can, therefore, receive dividends from a formerly struggling local enterprise which it has invested in by purchasing shares to provide it with capital. Where that investment leads to the subsequent success of the enterprise, and as a result the authority receives income from its shares, that is *incidental* income and does not amount to raising money within the meaning of s 3(2). An authority may also receive, where the receipt of income by the authority is incidental and not the primary purpose of its use of the well-being power, income from for example:

- lending money and charging interest;
- jointly obtaining sponsorship for a partnership project;
- receiving an indemnity from an organisation for costs which may be incurred; and
- receiving revenue income from a trust.

Local authorities may also receive contributions on a voluntary basis from partner organisations, since such contributions or cost recovery is not considered to be raising money within the meaning of s 3(2)[1].

1   DETR Guidance, para 68.

Section 3(2) – charging for well-being services

[2.29]
Importantly, local authorities are prevented from using the well-being power to charge for the services they provide in pursuit of well-being objectives, unless such charges can be seen as incidental charges – see the above paragraph. Therefore, unless there is a power in previous legislation that allows for charging for a specific function, which could be regarded as promoting well-being, local authorities are currently prevented from charging for well-being services:

> 'The government did not consider that a general power to charge was appropriate in the context of the well-being legislation, in the light of the broader review currently being carried out into the local government finance system. But it did appreciate that there was a case that local authorities should have greater ability to charge for discretionary services than they currently enjoy' (para 69).

Instead of a general power to charge, the government proposes that charging for certain discretionary services provided under the well-being power should be authorised by means of charging orders under s 150 of the Local Government and Housing Act 1989. Section 150 of the 1989 Act allows charges to be authorised by regulations. It applies to all discretionary and mandatory services, if there is no other statutory power or duty to make a charge. Work is to begin on these regulations in 2001.

There is no indication from government as yet as to whether regulations under s 150[1] will leave the charges for prescribed activities to a local authority's discretion or may impose a maximum charge or stipulate a method of calculating the amount. Nor is there any indication as to the extent the prescribed activities may cover or any underlying principles on which these may be based. The major drawback in respect of the use of s 150 is that it provides no power to issue statutory guidance on the power to charge. DETR has recognised that if this was considered necessary a new general power to charge for discretionary services would need to be sought.

The Guidance clarifies, at para 70, that where an authority chooses to use its powers under s 2 to set up a company, that company as a separate entity is not subject to the restrictions provided by s 3(2) and such a company can charge for any service it provides to others.

1   Work will begin on these regulations in 2001 now that the consultation on *Modernising Local Government Finance* has been completed.

The power to trade

[2.30]
The pre-2000 Act powers to trade have not been altered by Pt I. Where local authorities do not have specific powers[1], they may rely on the provisions of the Local Authorities (Goods and Services) Act 1970 ('the 1970 Act') to enable them to supply goods and materials and various administrative and technical services, to other local authorities or to designated 'public bodies'. The 1970 Act defines a 'public body' to include a local authority, a police authority, a Housing Action Trust or such bodies specified in orders made by the Secretary of State.

The 1970 Act restricts the type of services provided and the bodies with whom an authority can trade. The range of goods and services which authorities are permitted to supply under the 1970 Act is narrower than that permitted under the well-being power. The well-being power enables local authorities to provide staff, goods, services and accommodation to any person where to do so will achieve well-being of their area, but s 3(2) prevents authorities from charging for them. This unhelpfully constrains the use of the well-being power in the supply of goods and services to others in return for a fee or charge.

It is proposed that as part of the current Local Government Finance review local authorities should be given powers to charge for discretionary services, including those provided under the well-being power.

The 1970 Act also limits those bodies to whom authorities can supply goods and services. This is inconsistent with the requirement in the Local Government Act 2000 for partnership working between authorities and other public bodies and with the private and voluntary sector. To extend the power to trade the government proposes to bring into effect a new legislative framework[2] to allow all Best Value authorities to enter into agreements with any other person to provide staff, goods and services or accommodation so long as it is directed towards the achievement of Best Value in the related function.

The government will also take steps to create a single unified statutory framework for local authority trading. The government proposals on the new legislative framework are detailed in the consultation paper – *Working with Others to Achieve Best Value*.

It is to be regretted that at a point where the government is expecting local authorities to seize the new opportunities provided by the broad well-being power that clarification on further powers to charge and trade have not as yet accompanied the well-being legislation.

1   Such as the Civic Restaurants Act 1947 (enables district councils and London Boroughs to establish restaurants and other similar facilities for the public); and s 38 of the Local Government (Miscellaneous Provisions) Act 1976 (spare computer and IT capacity).

2   Paragraphs 4.1 to 4.6 of the consultation paper on *Working with Others to Achieve Best Value.*

Sections 3(3) to (6) – other restrictions

[2.31]
Before exercising the well-being power an authority needs to check whether the Secretary of State has used his power in s 3(3) to make an order preventing the particular action under consideration. There are no plans at present to make such orders[1]. An authority must also have regard to any guidance issued under s 3(5) about the exercise of the well-being power. The Guidance (paras 71 to 72) indicates that local authorities may not use the well-being power to make regulations or byelaws but should instead continue to rely on the existing powers to create byelaws.

1   DETR Guidance, para 73.

Section 4 – the duty to prepare a Community Strategy

[2.32]
See Division III – Chapter 18 below.

Section 5 – amending or repealing enactments

[2.33]
If the Secretary of State thinks that an enactment prevents or obstructs local authorities from exercising the power of well-being in s 2(1), he may by order, amend, repeal, revoke or disapply that enactment in relation to:

(a)   all local authorities;
(b)   particular local authorities; or
(c)   particular descriptions of local authorities.

Section 3 does not permit local authorities to circumvent statutory restrictions contained in legislation. However, s 5 provides the power for the Secretary of State to amend or remove legislative barriers to the promotion of well-being, subject to an affirmative resolution of both Houses of Parliament.

This power adds to the Secretary of State's existing power under s 16 of the 1999 Act to modify or repeal enactment's that prevent authorities from achieving Best Value or to confer new powers on Best Value authorities for this purpose.

In addition, the provisions in the Regulatory Reform Act 2001 provide a further power by which unnecessary burdens to the promotion of well-being can be removed.

The procedure for making such orders is set out in s 9 and in the DETR Guidance on the well-being power at paras 83 to 85.

It is not intended that there should be a formal application process for authorities to make application to the Secretary of State for such orders. However, para 78 of the Guidance states the hope that local authorities will themselves come forward with examples where they believe that they are being impeded by existing legislation from using the new power effectively. Local authorities who wish to put forward suggestions for orders under s 5 can do so by writing directly to the Secretary of State[1]. In doing so, authorities need to provide the Secretary of State with the information as set out in para 81. Paragraph 80 states that the government has also been discussing with the 20 local authorities who are piloting local Public Service Agreements, legislative barriers which inhibit effective performance, with a view to making deregulatory orders. There is no indicative timetable set out in the Guidance as to how long the process will take to make an order but what is clear is that the procedure for the Secretary of State to make such orders will not be a quick fix but will be a lengthy process (see paras 83 to 85).

1   Write to the Secretary of State, Department of the Environment Transport and the Regions, Eland House, Bressenden Place, London SW1E 5DU – e-mail: lgr@detr.gov.uk.

Section 6 – power to modify enactments concerning plans

[2.34]
Section 6 allows the Secretary of State to suspend, disapply or repeal any enactment which requires local authorities to prepare a plan or strategy. The duty to prepare an overarching community strategy should make some statutory plans unnecessary. The power to modify enactments concerning plans may be exercised in relation to:

(*a*)   all local authorities;
(*b*)   particular local authorities; or
(*c*)   particular descriptions of local authorities.

It is clear that the sheer number of plans that local authorities must produce is time consuming and can reinforce service silo mentalities at the cost of effective partnership work in responding to the cross-cutting priorities that emerge from the community planning process.

The s 6 power can therefore be used to streamline the plethora of plans that local authorities currently produce. Surprisingly, the Guidance contains no detail at all in relation to s 6 powers or the procedure and/or the application process for modifying such enactments. However the Local Government Association's publication *Powerpack* does contain commentary on s 6. The Local Government Association is encouraging all local authorities to provide potential examples of redundant planning requirements that could be abolished using the power in this section. Local Authorities are asked to write direct to DETR[1] in the first instance but to copy their correspondence to the Local Government Association[2].

1   Write to the Secretary of State, Department of the Environment Transport and the Regions, Eland House, Bressenden Place, London SW1E 5DU – e-mail: lgr@detr.gov.uk.
2   Send copy correspondence to the Local Government Association, Local Government House, Smith Square, London SW1P 3HZ.

Sections 7 and 5 in relation to Wales – the power to modify enactments concerning plans etc in Wales

[2.35]
Section 7 allows the National Assembly for Wales (NAW) to exercise the powers in s 6 to amend, repeal, revoke or disapply the need to produce the plans specified in the enactments listed in s 7(2). The list of plans in s 7(2) is not yet comprehensive because not all the statutory plans where the NAW has a relevant role have yet been identified. The enactments and plans currently listed in s 7(2) include:

(a)   s 49(1)(c) of the Environmental Protection Act 1990 concerns the plan for air quality;

(b)   s 2 of the Home Energy Conservation Act 1995 concerns the plan for energy conservation;

(c)   s 84(2)(b) of the Environment Act 1995 concerns the plan for waste disposal.

As the list of plans is currently incomplete s 7(2)(d) therefore provides the Secretary of State with the powers to add further plans to the list, by order.

The power can be exercised in relation to:

(a)   all local authorities in Wales;

(b)   particular local authorities in Wales;

(c)   particular descriptions of local authorities in Wales.

In relation to the Secretary of State's power under s 5 to amend, repeal, revoke or disapply enactments by order which prevent or obstruct local authorities from exercising the well-being power, the Secretary of State must not make any provision which has effect in relation to Wales unless he has consulted the NAW and gained its consent to make that order.

The NAW does not have powers similar to those in s 5 to amend, repeal, revoke or disapply enactments which may prevent or obstruct the pursuit of well-being. However the NAW may under s 5(5) submit proposals to the Secretary of State to make an order in relation to Wales to remove any legislative barriers which obstruct or prevent the achievement of well-being objectives by some or all relevant local authorities in Wales.

Section 8 – modification / repeal of s 137 of the Local Government Act 1972

[2.36]
Section 8 of the 2000 Act, with effect from 18 October 2000, repealed most of the power for principal local authorities to incur expenditure under s 137 of the Local Government Act 1972.

Repeal of ss 33 to 35 of the Local Government and Housing Act 1989

[2.37]
The economic development powers in ss 33 to 35 of the 1989 Act in respect of principal authorities to whom the power of well-being applies, have been repealed by Sch 6 to the Local Government Act 2000. These economic development powers have been subsumed within the new power of well-being contained in s 2(1) of the Local Government Act 2000.

Section 9 – procedure for orders under ss 5 or 6 of the 2000 Act

[2.38]
Section 9 states the procedure to be followed by the Secretary of State before making an order under ss 5 or 6 to amend, repeal, revoke or disapply enactments. Section 5 in particular has the potential to confer broad powers on local authorities. The process for making proposed orders under s 9 therefore incorporates the opportunity for parliament to scrutinise the Secretary of State's proposals.

The procedure under s 9 requires the Secretary of State:

- before preparing an order under ss 5 or 6 to consult such local authorities, representatives of local government and such other persons as appear to him to be likely to be affected by his proposals (s 9(1));
- where those proposals affect any local authorities in Wales, the Secretary of State must also consult the National Assembly of Wales (s 9(2));
- to lay before each House of Parliament a document which explains his proposals, sets them out in a draft order and gives details of the consultation carried out including where consultation has taken place under s 9(2) the views of the National Assembly of Wales (s 9(3));
- to allow 60 days for parliament to scrutinise the document before a draft order is laid before parliament (s 9(4)); and
- to consider any representations made during the scrutiny period (s 9(6)).

The draft order will then be subject to affirmative resolution by both Houses of Parliament.

The timing and frequency with which this process is undertaken and orders are laid is not clarified in the Guidance. However, it is stated that this will need to be considered by the government in consultation with the Local Government Association[1].

1   Paragraphs 85 and 86 of the Guidance on the Power of Well-Being.

What some councils are already thinking of doing with the new power

[2.39]

The Local Government Association's publication *Powerpack*[1] on using the new power to promote well-being provides some ideas from councils outlining initial thoughts on how they may use the power. The following are a few examples from that publication.

1 Published in December 2000 – http://www.lga.gov.uk/lga/blg/compact/powerpack.pdf.

[2.40]
Being able to pool budgets – Salisbury District Council

Salisbury DC aims to create pooled budgets with its partners to support joint community initiatives. Up until the 2000 Act, it had been necessary to identify the action required and then the budget holder responsible. This did not facilitate partnership working. When, for example, the county council responded to a rural transport issue and provided a community bus for a local group, this was seen as a county project rather than a joint initiative of the local partnership because budgets were unable to be pooled.

[2.41]
Combating anti-social behaviour – Dover District Council

Dover DC may use the power to assist residents who are not council tenants to combat anti-social behaviour. This may for example include the provision of security patrols either directly by the council or by contracting out the service to security firms.

[2.42]
CCTV – Kerrier District Council

Kerrier DC had experienced problems in partnership working across boundaries. They are, for example, the lead authority in a six-town CCTV scheme and a number of regeneration initiatives. In these situations it had been a legal worry about the ability to lead on initiatives that involve a wider geographical area than its own district.

The power now enables councils to benefit people outside their area as long as it also benefits people insider the council's area.

The Power of Well-Being and the Links to Best Value

[2.43]

The Local Government Act 1999 places a duty on all Best Value authorities including police, fire and passenger transport authorities as well as principal councils to make arrangements to secure continuous improvement in the way in which they exercise their functions, having regard to a combination of economy, efficiency and effectiveness[1].

Where a principal authority exercises the power to promote well-being under the provisions of the 2000 Act, it must also discharge that function in accordance with the duty to achieve Best Value under the 1999 Act.

The statutory guidance on Best Value[2] states at para 7 that:

> 'The [community] leadership role will entail the development of a community strategy, which sets out the broad objectives and visions for the community in the area. Such strategies need to reflect the contribution which the authority and its partners expect to make to improve the economic, social and environmental well-being of their areas. It should provide the starting point for the first step under best value – the setting of strategic objectives and corporate priorities'.

The Guidance on the well-being power notes that the well-being provisions have been drafted in such a way as to provide councils with considerable scope over the means they use in pursuit of well-being, including working in partnership with other service providers in the public, private and voluntary sectors. To that end, councils are able to establish companies and other forms of corporate body, to create pooled budgets, to undertake lead or joint commissioning and to integrate the provision of their services with those of other service providers.

However, it is not only in pursuit of well-being objectives that authorities will need the widest possible range of means of service delivery. The government's view is that this range should equally be available to the discharge of all authority functions and to all Best Value authorities not just to principal councils.

The government has therefore published the consultation paper, *Working with Others to Achieve Best Value*[3], to provide new and amended powers for ensuring that all Best Value authorities have available to them a variety of new structures or vehicles designed to promote and facilitate the achievement of Best Value through partnership working. The consultation paper contains guidance on innovative means of service delivery such as pooled budgets, lead and joint commissioning, integrated service provision and extended trading powers. It also includes proposals for Best Value authorities to provide a wider range of goods and services to partners in the public and private sector.

Further links between Best Value and the power of well-being are outlined in the Local Government Association's publication *Powerpack* published December 2000. *Powerpack* can be downloaded from the LGA website at *http://lga.gov.uk/lga/blg/compact/powerpack.pdf*.

How authorities set about meeting the requirements of Best Value is a matter for them. However, the Guidance states that authorities will in particular wish to reassess their Best Value review programme to ensure that it is cast in sufficiently strategic terms to support the delivery of improved well-being in the area, in particular concentrating on cross-cutting issues such as community safety, promoting neighbourhood renewal and tackling social exclusion[4].

1   The duty of Best Value is set out in s 3(1) of the LGA 1999. More information on Best Value can be obtained on the DETR website at http://www.local-regions.detr.gov.uk/bestvalue/bvindex.htm.

2   See DETR Circular 10/99 – published December 1999.
3   Available at http://www.local-regions.detr.gov.uk/consult/bestvalue/index.htm – published
    29 March 2001 by the DETR.
4   Paragraph 13 of the Guidance on the Power of Well-Being.

Conclusion

[2.44]
Is it true that local authorities can regard the 'can do' power of well-being as
the power of first resort? Yes, but only to some extent. Although the
well-being power constitutes an important step towards the power of general
competence long sought by local government, it remains heavily constrained
by restrictions in existing legislation. Until, and to the extent that, the
Secretary of State exercises the power in s 5 of the 2000 Act to disapply
barriers in existing legislation which either prevent or obstruct local
authorities from exercising the well-being power, they will still have to resort
to searching the statute books to check for any statutory restrictions on its use.

So while the 'power of first resort' may obviate the need to search for legal
powers to act, it certainly does not obviate the need to search for restrictions
contained in existing legislation.

Does the new power give them re-assurance where there had previously
been uncertainty over their powers? Yes, but again only to some extent. This
is unlikely. Uncertainty may well arise, for example when local authorities
interpret what constitutes incidental charges for well-being services as
opposed to what constitutes primary purpose charges.

The prohibitions on charging are also disappointing. Moreover to still be
waiting for charging orders to be made to clarify what services provided
under well-being can be charged for and to what extent, is unsatisfactory.

On the whole the broad well-being power is to be welcomed but it is to be
hoped that the defects in the tool-kit for exercising the use of it will be swiftly
corrected.

CHAPTER 3

Community Leadership Roles and Local Strategic Partnerships

Community Leadership – What Is It?

[3.1]
The new well-being power in Pt I of the Local Government Act 2000, enshrines in law a concept of local government as the community leader. The new legal framework embodied in Pt I recognises that local authorities have wide-ranging concerns to improve the social, economic and environmental well-being of their areas and s 2 now provides councils with the new broad-ranging power to do anything to promote and improve the well-being of their communities (subject to certain constraints).

However, there are many issues of concern to local communities – environmental improvement, crime reduction, unemployment, regeneration, reducing discrimination to build a fairer and more equitable society, improving health etc – that cannot adequately be resolved by local authorities or by any single organisation working alone.

The new community leadership role for local authorities seeks to change the current fragmented structure at a local level where a multiplicity of different statutory agencies, the voluntary and business sectors all deliver services to the community in a non co-ordinated way.

Local authorities, for the first time, have now been given the power to achieve this community leadership role. The role is to build effective local partnerships between the wide-range of public, private, voluntary and community sectors involved at a local level and to develop effective processes for doing this.

Community leadership is about making joined-up action happen at a local and sub-regional level to confront and address the cross-cutting issues that can only be tackled effectively through partnership working.

Partnership

[3.2]
Part I of the LGA 2000 not only gives local authorities new powers to improve well-being but it also places a duty on them to prepare community strategies[1] to promote and improve the social, economic and environmental well-being of their areas with local people and partner organisations. The Act requires

local authorities, in preparing community strategies, to consult and seek the participation of such organisations and people as they consider appropriate[2] and to have regard to government guidance[3].

In its role as community leader, a local authority can kick start this consultation role and secure the participation of other organisations by facilitating and driving forward the building of a 'local strategic partnership' (LSP) whose task it will be to prepare and implement the community strategy. The detail on LSPs is set out in the Guidance on *Preparing Community Strategies* issued in December 2000 by the former Department for the Environment, Transport and the Regions (now the Department for Transport, Local Government and the Regions) and in the non-statutory Guidance *Local Strategic Partnerships* issued in March 2001[4].

1   LGA 2000, s 4.
2   LGA 2000, s 4(3)(*a*).
3   LGA 2000, s 4(3)(*b*).
4   The statutory Guidance *Preparing Community Strategies* is available at www.local-regions.dtlr.gov.uk/pcs/guidance/index.htm and the non-statutory Guidance *Local Strategic Partnerships* is available at www.local-regions.dtlr.gov.uk/lsp/guidance/index.htm.

Setting the Local Strategic Partnership (LSP) in the Wider Context of the Modernisation of Local Government

[3.3]
Although it is not a statutory duty to have a LSP the following diagram places the LSP in the wider context of the modernisation of local government and shows the relationship between the LSP, the local authority and:

Within the wider context of modernising local government, LSPs have the potential to give substance to local authorities' community leadership role. They also represent one of the mechanisms to reconnect the authority with their communities to achieve the required culture change of service provision being centred on the priorities identified by service users and taxpayers. They provide the means through which meaningful consultation and genuine involvement of the community can happen in the preparation and implementation of the community strategy. In particular, LSPs provide the avenue not only to prepare but to implement the community strategy and to tackle cross-cutting issues that no one organisation on its own can resolve. Through the LSP, local authorities have the opportunity to demonstrate new and innovative ways of working that will improve the local quality of life and deliver Best Value:

> 'Best Value is beginning to be seen by many councils as also the mechanism for aligning the council behind the priorities identified in the community strategy and ensuring delivery of the council's contribution to local joint action plans. Therefore the strategic framework set in place by the LSP should enhance this process'[1].

32

● the new power of well-being	**LGA 2000, Pt I**
● the new duty to prepare community strategies	
● the new democratic arrangements	**LGA 2000, Pt II**
● the duty of Best Value	**LGA 1999**

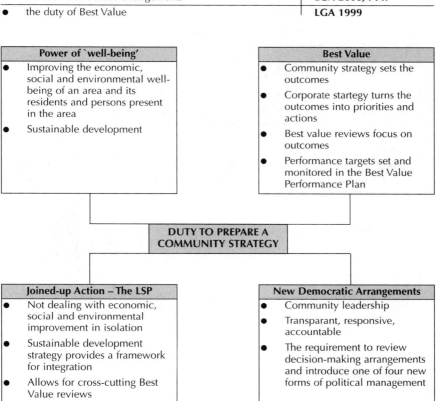

Power of `well-being'
- Improving the economic, social and environmental well-being of an area and its residents and persons present in the area
- Sustainable development

Best Value
- Community strategy sets the outcomes
- Corporate startegy turns the outcomes into priorities and actions
- Best value reviews focus on outcomes
- Performance targets set and monitored in the Best Value Performance Plan

DUTY TO PREPARE A COMMUNITY STRATEGY

Joined-up Action – The LSP
- Not dealing with economic, social and environmental improvement in isolation
- Sustainable development strategy provides a framework for integration
- Allows for cross-cutting Best Value reviews

New Democratic Arrangements
- Community leadership
- Transparant, responsive, accountable
- The requirement to review decision-making arrangements and introduce one of four new forms of political management

Note
This diagram is reproduced with the consent of Miffa Salter from the Office for Public Management

For all these reasons it is appropriate that all local authorities are active in developing and being involved in an LSP.

1   See LGA paper issued 17 July 2001 – *Facts about LSPs: Useful lessons from the New Commitment to Regeneration*; available at http://www.lga.gov.uk.

LSPs and Links to Sources of Government Funding

[3.4]

Some local authorities will need to be involved in an LSP should they wish to secure the following sources of government funding.

Local public service agreements

[3.5]
LSPs will have a role in contributing to the development of local public service agreements (PSAs).

Local PSAs offer local authorities the opportunity to enter into an agreement with central government to deliver the most important national and local priorities for their areas in return for receiving agreed operational flexibilities, pump-priming funding and financial rewards if they meet their targets.

There are 20 authorities piloting local PSAs in 2001/2002[1] and proposals for the national roll out of local PSAs are to be published in a prospectus for the national scheme in Summer 2001[2]. The national scheme will offer the opportunity to conclude a local PSA to a further 130 'top-tier' authorities including all shire counties, unitaries, metropolitan districts and London boroughs from 2002/2003. Arrangements are being developed for district councils to enter into local PSAs but it is already open to districts to get involved in county-led agreements.

To successfully conclude a local PSA, local authorities will need to show their proposals are supported by local people and other local partners. Many of the agreed local PSA targets can only be achieved by joint working between the authority and other local organisations. LSPs provide a mechanism for securing joint working.

1   Re the prospectus for the 2000 Pilot Scheme see: *Local Public Service Agreements: A Prospectus for Local Authorities* issued by DTLR (July 2000).
2   See DTLR *The National Roll-Out of Local PSAs: Update – May 2001*; available at http://www.local-regions.dtlr.gov.uk/lpsa/rollout/index.htm.

Neighbourhood Renewal Fund

[3.6]
The Neighbourhood Renewal Fund provides new money for local authorities in the 88 most deprived areas, amounting to £200 million in 2001/2002, £300 million in 2002/2003 and £400 million in 2003/2004. It is intended as a way to help local authorities and their partners to begin improving services in the most deprived neighbourhoods, including contributing to the achievement of PSA targets to narrow the gap between deprived neighbourhoods and the rest of the country[1].

The 88 authorities eligible for Neighbourhood Renewal Fund money must produce a local neighbourhood renewal strategy, agreed by the LSP, by April 2002 so they must have committed to developing an LSP in 2001. Government Offices for the Regions will act as accreditors to assess whether Neighbourhood Renewal Fund grant conditions have been met and that the LSPs in these areas are effective and actively involve all the key players including the public, private, community and voluntary sectors[2].

1   Paragraph 4.8 of the non-statutory Guidance on LSPs. The statutory Guidance *Preparing Community Strategies* is available at www.local-regions.dtlr.gov.uk/pcs/guidance/index.htm; and the non-statutory Guidance *Local Strategic Partnerships* is available at www.local-regions.dtlr.gov.uk/lsp/guidance/index.htm.

2   See Annex B of the Guidance on LSPs for further details on the Neighbourhood Renewal
    Fund. The national strategy to renew the 88 most deprived neighbourhoods was published
    by the Social Exclusion Unit of the Cabinet Office – January 2001 *A New Commitment to
    Neighbourhood Renewal: National Strategy Action Plan*; available at www.cabinet–
    office.gov.uk/seu/2001/Action%20Plan.htm.

The Beacon Council Scheme

[3.7]
The Beacon Council Scheme does not as yet present councils with the
opportunity to tap into new sources of funding. However, it may in the future
provide those councils who have regularly been successful in achieving
beacon status with additional financial freedoms and flexibilities. For this
reason it is worth covering the aims of the scheme and how councils and
their partners may, amongst other benefits, reap potential financial ones from
regular participation in the scheme.

The scheme was introduced as a result of the Government's 1998 White
Paper *Modernising Local Government: In Touch with the People.* There are
two phases by which the White Paper proposes that the scheme becomes
operational.

[3.8]
Phase One

Phase One, now in its third year of operation, aims to identify the best
performing councils who can act as centres of excellence from which other
councils can learn. Those councils who are successful in their application for
beacon status, enter an agreement with the Secretary of State to share their
experiences, their practices and the lessons they have learned with other
local authorities. This is done through a national programme of activities
co-ordinated and supported by the IDeA.

Beacon status is granted by the DTLR. Each year the government chooses
themes for the beacon scheme. These cover service delivery and include
service specific or cross-cutting themes. The scheme is open to all English
county and district councils including unitary and metropolitan district
councils, and London Boroughs. Applications may be submitted by a single
authority or by two or more councils who are working in partnership to
deliver their services. Councils can apply for beacon status in up to a
maximum of three themes but normally the status is awarded for just one
service area. To achieve the award councils must demonstrate: exceptional
best practice in a beacon theme, that additionally they have good overall
council performance and have plans for effective dissemination. Any
partnership arrangements that make a positive impact on service delivery
need to be clearly outlined.

In the first two rounds of the scheme 76 beacon awards have already been
made in 18 service themes. Round Three applications for beacon awards, for
2002 to 2003, are currently being assessed by the DTLR and IDeA and it is
expected that between 40 to 50 awards will be made. Round Three themes,
comprise eleven in all, including, adoption, crime reduction in rural areas,

promoting racial equality and better access and mobility. Clearly partnership working is critical to be able to demonstrate best practice in cross-cutting themes.

There is no financial reward attached to beacon status in phase one other than a Special Grant to support beacon councils in their dissemination of best practice. However there are promises of financial benefits to come under Phase Two.

[3.9]
Phase Two

The White Paper proposes that the key role of beacon councils in spreading best practice will continue in phase two. In addition it is proposed that certain councils, who through regular participation in the scheme have proved themselves to be excellent across the board in service delivery, will be allowed to test bed new local freedoms and flexibilities. These new freedoms and flexibilities may eventually be applied to local government more widely.

Under Phase Two proposals, these overall beacon councils will have power to raise additional business rates in consultation with the local business community, will be given greater freedom when levying council tax. They would have wider freedom on capital investment to decide the amount of capital expenditure they can afford and would have additional regulatory freedoms and flexibilities including the power to take initiatives where currently councils have no power to do so.

Freedoms and flexibilities granted under phase two would be in relation to exercising the new well-being powers and will be for the particular service or cross-cutting area for which beacon status is awarded. Whereas in phase one beacon status is awarded normally for one year, in Phase Two beacon councils may be designated for a set period perhaps for as long as three to five years.

Legislation will be required to give these overall beacon councils this new role and new powers. Unfortunately, at the time of writing, there is no proposed parliamentary timetable to make this legislation or any indication of when phase two will be brought into operation. Further information on the beacon council scheme is available from the DTLR web-site at: http://www.local-regions.dtlr.gov.uk/beacon/index.htm.

Background to the Concept and the Proposals to Develop LSPs

[3.10]
The concept of LSPs has emerged from the DLTR's work on community strategies, from the Social Exclusion Unit's *New Commitment to Neighbourhood Renewal: National Strategy Action Plan* and from what is seen as being the precursor to the LSP – the partnerships resulting from the testing of *New Commitment to Regeneration* in 22 pathfinder areas.

New Commitment to Regeneration was an LGA initiative for which the LGA succeeded in securing government backing for testing in 22 pathfinder areas. Research into the ideas and lessons learned by the pathfinders has been jointly commissioned by the LGA, DLTR and the Joseph Rowntree Foundation from Liverpool John Moores University. The final evaluation report on this research will be published in September 2001. The interim report was published by the LGA on 17th July 2001[1].

As the thinking behind LSPs draws heavily on the ideas and lessons from the new commitment pathfinders, local authorities and their partners could benefit in developing LSPs by familiarising themselves with this research and the different examples of partnership working which it cites.

Relevant lessons for LSPs, learned from *New Commitment to Regeneration Pathfinders* include:

- the importance of mainstream services in affecting the quality of life;
- the greater potential of harnessing mainstream resources through partnership working;
- government must learn to be a proactive partner and positively facilitate the development of partnerships;
- the need for a long-term approach;
- partnership building cannot be rushed – trust and understanding will develop at its own pace;
- build on the experience and commitment of existing partnerships;
- leadership by an organisation is needed to provide momentum and continuity but no one organisation should dominate;
- all those involved in the partnership need to change the way they work and understand what drives the others and how they operate;
- partnership structures must be sensitive to agencies statutory and territorial roles;
- capacity building of each partner is key to success;
- feedback mechanisms need to be firmly established so that decisions made by the partnership are fed back into the individual organisations and influence their operation;
- representatives on the partnership need to be of sufficient seniority to make partnership decisions happen within their own organisations;
- prioritise what is going to be achievable and have short-term deliverable goals; and
- resource partnerships by jointly paying the costs of an individual or small team to make progress more quickly. Benefits include a separate identity for the partnership independent of any one organisation, administrative support in setting up meetings, providing papers, co-ordinating and monitoring activity and keeping up the momentum.

1   See LGA paper issued 17 July 2001 – *Facts about LSPs: Useful lessons from the New Commitment to Regeneration*; available at http://www.lga.gov.uk.

Resourcing partnerships

[3.11]
The experience of the NCR pathfinders show that it is usually the local

authority who provides the resources to pay the costs of an independent individual or small team.

However, for those of the 88 authorities entitled to receive Neighbourhood Renewal Funding (NRF)[1] the Guidance states that formal approval by the Secretary of State will be given to spend some of the funding on the administration of the partnership.

For these 88 authorities the Community Empowerment Fund[2] is available specifically for the purpose of assisting the voluntary and community sectors and the wider community to participate in the LSP. This funding will be given directly to these sectors through the Government Office for the Region.

Given that the research findings from the NCR pathfinders recommends that government must learn to be a proactive partner and positively facilitate the development of partnerships, it is to be hoped that government funding will be made available on a wider basis than just to the 88 qualifying authorities for NRF funding, to assist the successful development of LSPs in all local authorities' areas. To date, however, there is no indication that this will be the case.

1   See para **[3.6]** above.
2   See para **[3.25]** below on the Community Empowerment Fund.

The Local Strategic Partnership (LSP)

What is a LSP?

[3.12]
A Local Strategic Partnership is a single body comprising all the key public, private, community and voluntary sectors that provide local services or whose actions affect the local quality of life. The common purpose of all LSP partners is to act as a strategic body to identify the top priorities and needs of the communities they serve and to tackle the issues that matter to local people such as crime, health, housing, employment, regeneration, the environment, education etc.

The LSP should bring together all existing local partnership activity to provide one umbrella organisation to co-ordinate and monitor overall partnership activity and ensure the delivery of the communities' priorities. The LSP sets out the partnership's central aims, keeps track of progress made, and reviews and updates issues to be addressed.

Below the LSP, different coalitions of organisations can be brought together to tackle and deliver theme specific issues. The issues that the sub-groups deal with will reflect those priorities identified in the community strategy.

Annexe F of the Guidance on LSPs[1] sets out examples of partnership structures that different types of local authorities have followed. These range from unitary authorities, those involving both district and county councils through to those involving broader groups of authorities and provide insight for authorities who are in the process of developing LSPs. Further information is available from the LGA in a paper issued in July 2001 Examples of Local

Strategic Partnerships in Development. This latter paper provides details about the LSPs developed in 13 different local authorities, who the members of the partnership are and the involvement of the different sectors. Moreover it shows the wide variation in the size of the membership that these LSPs have adopted. These 13 partnerships, together with their contact details, are listed at Division VI – Appendix 1 below.

1   The statutory Guidance *Preparing Community Strategies* is available at www.local-regions.dtlr.gov.uk/pcs/guidance/index.htm and the non-statutory Guidance *Local Strategic Partnerships* is available at www.local-regions.dtlr.gov.uk/lsp/guidance/index.htm.

Core tasks

[3.13]
The non-statutory Guidance on LSPs states that its core tasks are to:

*   prepare and implement the community strategy – the long-term vision – for the area and bring about improvements to the well-being of the area;
*   prepare the action plan identifying shorter term priorities and set outcome based targets, develop common arrangements for monitoring progress made on achieving the targets and review and update the contents of the community strategy and action plan;
*   bring together local plans, partnerships and initiatives to streamline existing partnerships, avoid duplication and 'partnership fatigue';
*   work with local authorities that are developing a local public service agreement (PSA); and
*   develop and deliver a local neighbourhood renewal strategy to secure more jobs, better education, improved health, reduced crime and better housing to close the gap between the most deprived neighbourhoods and the rest of the country.

Structure of the LSP

[3.14]
The Guidance on *Preparing Community Strategies* states that there is no definitive approach to the way in which LSPs should be structured, the bodies that should be represented or the way in which the partnership should operate. This is a matter for the partnership itself to determined[1].

While this provides flexibility, what happens when there is conflict about who should or should not be a member of the LSP? There are few mechanisms within the Guidance to resolve this. Instead Government Offices for the Region have been given the role of acting as mediators to resolve difficulties which may arise. It is yet to be seen whether this will prove to be sufficient.

1   See para 25 of the Guidance.

Process – building and developing the Partnership

[3.15]

'The process by which community strategies are produced is as important as the strategy itself'[1].

It is important to note that the single most important lesson learned from the experience of the New Commitment to Regeneration pathfinders – the precursors to LSPs (see para **[3.10]** above) is that building partnership and the trust and understanding that is essential in joint working across the public, private, voluntary and community sectors cannot be rushed. It takes time to develop an effective LSP.

There is no prescriptive process for preparing and producing the community strategy and it should not be under-estimated the degree of challenge, potential difficulties and frustrations that this may pose to LSP partners.

1   See para 16 of the Guidance on *Preparing Community Strategies.*

Community involvement and the LSP

[3.16]

The Guidance states that the preparation process (of the community strategy) is the means by which local people and organisations can be drawn into democratic decision-making, to give their voice to identifying what they see as their priorities to shape the community strategy. Widespread consultation with and the engagement of local communities is key to the preparation and implementation of the community strategy and will require LSPs to develop a variety of means to work with and consult local people, including faith, black and minority ethnic communities, geographic communities and communities of interest.

At the outset of the partnership, putting consultation into practice so that the whole process of community planning becomes an inclusive one will be one of the initial challenges for the LSP. Details on involving local people in community strategies is provided in the Community Development Foundation's publication *The New Community Strategy – How to involve local people*[1].

1   Published December 2000; available from The Publications Unit, Community Development Foundation, 60 Highbury Grove, London N5 2AG; Tel: 020-7226-5375.

Timing

[3.17]

There is no prescribed date by which the preparation of the community strategy is to be completed. However authorities and their partners are expected to set realistic targets for putting their first community strategy into place.

Starting the LSP

[3.18]
Since the statutory duty to prepare a community strategy falls on local authorities, this provides the impetus for local authorities to take on the initial responsibility of bringing together key partners to establish the LSP.

Membership and size of the LSP

[3.19]
Membership of the LSP should be determined locally and will vary dependent on the issues and community priorities with which it is dealing. The core membership needs to include key partners operating in the area that the community strategy is to cover including partners from the public, private, voluntary and community sectors. Annex C of the non-statutory Guidance on LSPs sets out information on engaging and involving these sectors.

The degree to which organisations need to be involved in the LSP will vary depending on the nature of their work, their potential contribution to establishing the long-term vision or their contribution to delivering the action plan by providing key services.

Key partners

[3.20]
Ways to draw in key partners include:

- Build on existing partnerships, plans and initiatives that involve working with other organisations and agencies. Existing partners will have experienced the benefits of joint working and will be committed to the process. It is not necessary to start from scratch.
- Involve other local providers of public services. Where the engagement of public service providers in the LSP proves a problem, raise this in the first instance with the Government Office for the Region. In the Government Offices new role as facilitators and mediators, Government Offices can offer advice to LSPs on building the LSP and provide information on networks and partnership working arrangements already in place and emerging good practice in joint working.
- Involve representatives of umbrella voluntary and community sector forums and organisations. Voluntary organisations are a key element in the social fabric of communities and are well placed to involve local people who might otherwise prove hard to reach. Similarly use the knowledge of officers working on community issues and neighbourhood projects to identify community groups who might not be tied into the voluntary or community sector infrastructure.
- Involve local councils of faith or inter-faith networks. If none exist locally approach the main faith group.

LSPs in multi-tier authorities

[3.21]
In multi-tier authorities, unless the county and the districts work out suitable arrangements for joint working in the process of preparing community strategies, before they involve other partners, it is likely to lead to considerable duplication, conflicting priorities and consultation/partnership fatigue.

Membership attributes and skills

[3.22]
Representatives of the member organisations on the LSP must be of sufficient seniority to speak for their organisation, to sign it up to the long term vision and to commit resources – where they have them – to implement the action plan. They should recognise the operational autonomy of the other partners and develop an understanding of how the organisations of other partners operate and be sensitive to the statutory roles of relevant partners.

Each partner will need to develop mechanisms so that decisions made by the partnership are fed back into their own organisations and influence their operation. Without this the LSP will not be in a position to deliver all the priorities identified in the community strategy or achieve all the short-term goals set out in the action plan. There needs to be shared commitment to implement the community strategy and action plan. To ensure that this happens and that each partner plays its part it is essential that representatives are at the top of their organisation and can exert influence within their organisation to give effect to the decisions of the LSP, commit resources and adjust corporate priorities and deliver the necessary changes to front line services directly.

For local authorities, in order for them to be effective, it is important that the leader of the council and chief executive are actively involved in the LSP.

Leadership / chairing the LSP

[3.23]
The Guidance sets out that the organisations that leads a LSP needs to command the confidence of the other partners. In many cases the local authority will be in the lead but where another partner can command a greater level of confidence and support, the chairing arrangement should reflect this. The members of the LSP should decide who should take the lead. One organisation needs to take the lead to provide the necessary momentum but it is important that one organisation is not seen to be dominating.

Capacity building of LSP partners

[3.24]
The idea behind LSPs is a simple one – co-ordinating services for local

people can make good services get even better. However working in partnership with other organisations to co-ordinate service delivery requires all those involved to change the way they work. This part of the process will not be simple nor will it be achieved quickly.

Training of all those partners involved in the LSP is an essential starting point to drive forward this organisational change. Each partner needs to understand the benefits that joint working will bring and what steps they will need to take to effect change within their own organisation. This will equip their representative to participate fully in the work of the LSP and deliver the decisions of the LSP through their own organisation.

The Community Empowerment Fund – capacity building of the voluntary and community sectors

[3.25]
The Community Empowerment Fund is available in the 88 most deprived authorities eligible for the Neighbourhood Renewal Fund. A core principle is that one use of this government funding is to build the capacity of the community and voluntary sectors to enable their representative to play a full part in the LSP. Government Offices will oversee the distribution of this funding as well as Community Chest money for the more general activities of community groups. This funding will be distributed directly to these sectors in these 88 local authority areas. The new Neighbourhood Renewal Unit, operational from April 2001, will provide advice and guidance on the use of this fund[1].

Many community and voluntary sector bodies operate on a short-string. Clearly the participation of these groups to the work of the LSP is vital to assist identifying and delivering community needs. The Guidance emphasises that both these sectors are at the heart of the partnership process. However government funding to assist building capacity of groups outside of the 88 deprived areas has not been addressed.

1   The Neighbourhood Renewal Unit is at the DTLR, Eland House, Bressenden Place, London SW1E 5DU (tel: 020-7944-3000).

The principles guiding the relationship between members of the LSP

[3.26]
There are three guiding principles firmly embedded within the Guidance to govern the relationship between members of the LSP.

[3.27]
Equality

Each member is an equal partner. Better resourced partners should support the involvement of the less well resourced so that they can play an equal part and it is important that no one organisation or a small number of partners should be seen to be dominating. Experience on the other hand often suggests that this is not what happens in practice and that partnerships are notorious for being exclusive.

[3.28]
Accountability

Individual partners will remain autonomous and be responsible and accountable for the decisions on their services and resources to their customers and in the case of public sector partners to the wider community. The accountability arrangements to the LSP will need to build on these, to see that common monitoring, evaluation and reporting mechanisms are put in place within the partnership action plan to keep partners informed of progress and performance. Such accountability arrangements will provide grounds for challenging a partner if their performance is poor. Some examples of the kind of partnership accountability systems that have been put in place are given in research carried out for DTLR on regional and sub-regional partnerships[1].

1   G Fordham et al (DETR, October 1998).

[3.29]
Transparency

LSPs need to operate within a transparent and robust framework of local accountability. Publicising common aims and priorities, setting common performance monitoring and evaluation systems is at the heart of the work of the LSP. Keeping partners and the wider community fully informed is a fundamental element of the community strategy.

The Role of Elected Members in Relation to LSPs and the Community Strategy

[3.30]
All councils to which Pt II of the Local Government Act applies are expected to have introduced a new constitution by June 2002 at the latest. The roles that councillors will have in relation to the LSP and the community strategy will include the following.

1   See Chaps 4 and 6 below for the details on these new democratic arrangements.

Full council

[3.31]
Full council must approve the community strategy following proposals from the executive in councils operating executive arrangements or from the relevant policy committee in councils operating alternative arrangements.

Local authorities do not have sole responsibility for the preparation of the community strategy. Increasingly this is now prepared by the LSP. It would therefore be counter-productive and destructive of the trust and confidence developing between partners on the LSP, if the full council were, at the final approved stage, to overturn or change elements of the strategy.

To avoid this, effective and regular consultation and communication between the executive, the relevant overview and scrutiny committees and other members of the local authority needs to take place during the development of the strategy. Local authorities should adopt protocols to ensure that any councillor who is neither a member of the executive nor a member of the LSP has opportunities to feed their views into the development of the community strategy.

Where a dispute arises between the executive and the full council in setting either the budget or the policy framework, including the adoption and implementation of the community strategy, mechanisms for conflict resolution are triggered. See Chapter 4 for details of conflict resolution mechanisms and the new democratic arrangements.

Overview and Scrutiny Committee

[3.32]
Following the adoption of the community strategy non-executive members of scrutiny committees will be able to monitor the achievements of the local authority and other accountable partners such as health authorities, in delivering the goals and targets set out in the action plan. They may also wish to play a role in monitoring and evaluating the strategy as it develops against sustainable development criteria and initiating audits of resources to meet expressed priorities.

The Executive for councils operating executive arrangements or Chairs of Committees for councils operating alternative arrangements

[3.33]
In order for the LSP to be effective, representatives of the partner bodies need to be of sufficient seniority to speak for their organisation, to commit resources and to take action to deliver the priorities agreed as part of the action plan. It is therefore important that the leader of the council, as well as other executive members (in those councils operating executive arrange- ments) or the chairs of relevant committees (in those councils operating alternative arrangements) and the chief executive are actively involved in the LSP

Non-executive councillors – the local champion role

[3.34]
As elected representatives, councillors have an important leadership and

representational role in their communities. The changes to the political management arrangements within local authorities reinforce the role of councillors within their communities. Councillors gain valuable grass roots information about the concerns of local residents and the services provided to neighbourhoods. They may also lead and listen to formal and informal discussion and consultation and feedback these community views to the executive or to the members serving on the LSP, to influence the content of the community strategy. As 'local champions' non-executive councillors can take a lead in developing a network of local organisations and individuals, providing local interpretations of the community strategy and promoting local democratic engagement.

Many authorities have or are establishing neighbourhood forums or area committees in which councillors participate. By feeding back community views from these bodies, councillors will provide useful contributions to assist the work of the LSP. Such structures provide a framework for the local champion role of non-executive councillors.

CHAPTER 4
Cabinet Government

Introduction

[4.1]
The Local Government Act 2000 ('the Act') has signalled the modernisation of local authority decision-making structures. Of all the elements of the new arrangements, the creation of a 'split' between executive and non-executive members has caused the greatest debate. The executive, whether headed by a leader or mayor, is a group of councillors who will lead on and implement policy and whose role will be scrutinised by non-executive members. These arrangements are referred to as 'cabinet government' or 'executive arrangements'.

The impetus for a change in political management structures first came from the White Paper, *Modern Local Government: In Touch with the People*[1]. The White Paper argues that 'traditional committee structures, still used by almost all councils, lead to inefficient and opaque decision-making'[2]. The basis for this argument is that key decisions under the committee system are taken by political groups – behind closed doors. The White Paper concludes there is too much time spent by councillors in unproductive committee meetings and not enough time spent in direct contact with those they represent[3].

The idea behind cabinet government is that a small number of people can act quickly to take decisions and that the public are clear who is responsible for taking those decisions.

The new legislation promised in the White Paper was first seen in the draft Local Government (Organisation and Standards) Bill in January 1999, published as the consultation document *Local Leadership: Local Choice*[4]. The consultation paper again emphasised that the real action was 'off stage'[5] under the committee system and provided research findings about the number of hours councillors spent in committee[6] and the mismatch between what they did and what they aspired to do[7]. The Act itself received Royal Assent on 28 July 2000 and has had the effect of removing many of the restrictions on decision-making formerly imposed by the Local Government Act 1972.

The proposed benefits of the separation of the roles of executive and non-executive members advocated by the Government Consultation papers can be summarised as providing greater efficiency, transparency and accountability for local governance. These aims were translated in the Act into s 25(4) which requires authorities to consider the extent to which the proposals are likely to assist in securing continuous improvement in the way

47

in which their functions are exercised, having regard to a combination of economy, efficiency and effectiveness.

We are provided with a definition of some of these terms[8] against which the new structures must be tested.

- **Efficiency** – where decisions can be taken quickly, responsively and accurately to meet the needs and aspirations of the community;
- **Transparency** – where it is clear to people who is responsible for decisions;
- **Accountability** – where people can measure the actions taken against policies and plans on which those responsible were elected to office.

The challenge for authorities is to be rigorous in evaluating new proposals against these principles and to revisit the principles as the new structures develop. This will be particularly challenging in view of the fact that local authorities have not been offered any new resources to help support this significant change agenda and also because the options available for local government are strictly prescribed.

1   *Modern Local Government: In Touch with the People* (30 July 1998) available at http://www.local-regions.dtlr.gov.uk/lgwp. All references in the text to 'White Paper' are to this document.
2   *Modern Local Government: In Touch with the People*, Pt 2, Chap 3 – New Political Structures.
3   The White Paper states at para 3.7: 'People often do not know who is really taking decisions. They do not know who to praise, who to blame or who to contact with their problems. People identify most readily with an individual, yet there is rarely any identifiable figure leading the community.'
4   Published by the Stationery Office (March 1999, Cm 4298).
5   *Local Leadership: Local Choice*, para 1.14.
6   *Local Leadership: Local Choice*, para 1.16: 'A sample of councillors showed them spending an average of over 60 hours per month on preparing for, travelling to and attending council meetings.' This research came from *Managing Change: Councillors and the New Local Government*, Nirmala Rao (Joseph Rowntree Foundation, 1992).
7   *Local Leadership: Local Choice*, para 1.15: 'A councillor's representational work directly with the community should be central to his or her role as an elected member. There is evidence of a '*radical mismatch between what councillors aspire to do and what the pressures of council business require them to do*'. This research came from K Young and N Rao, *The Local Government Councillor in 1993* (Joseph Rowntree Foundation/LGC Publications, 1994).
8   *Local Leadership: Local Choice*, para 1.21.

Cabinet Government under the Local Government Act 2000

Part II of the LGA 2000

[4.2]
The relevant provisions of the Act which relate to new decision-making arrangements for authorities are contained in Pt II of the Act (ss 10 to 48). These provisions came into force in stages between 7 August 2000 and 15 February 2001. The key requirement in Pt II is that it places principal councils in England and Wales[1] under a duty to consult local people on and draw up

proposals for executive arrangements[2]. Consultation requirements are dealt with separately in Chapter 7 below.

There are a considerable number of sets of Regulations and Directions in force which have been issued giving full effect to the provisions of Pt II. A list of the Regulations and Directions made under the Act is set out in Division VI – Appendix 2 below.

At the time of writing, further Regulations and Directions are still awaited in relation to the conduct of Mayoral Elections.

In addition to the legislation, the government has issued Guidance on the detail of the proposed new arrangements. The Guidance, entitled *New Council Constitutions: Volume One*, is regularly updated as new Regulations come into force and so it is worth using the DTLR website to check that you are referring to the most up to date version. The Guidance contains statutory guidance to which authorities must have regard (marked with a maroon tick) and also descriptive examples of good practice. The Guidance deals in detail with the requirements of Pt II of the Act and is an essential handbook when looking to understand the complex process of moving to new arrangements under the Act. The Guidance applies to English authorities.

1   In relation to England, this means county councils, district councils, London Borough Councils, the Common Council of the City of London in its capacity as a local authority, the Council of the Isles of Scilly. In relation to Wales, it means a county council or county borough council: LGA 2000, s 1.
2   LGA 2000, s 25. Executive arrangements are defined in s 10 as arrangements:
     '(a) for and in connection with the creation and operation of an executive of the authority, and
     (b) under which certain functions of the authority are the responsibility of the executive.'

Options for executive arrangements

[4.3]
As set out above, Pt II of the LGA 2000 places principal councils in England and Wales under a duty to consult on and draw up proposals for executive arrangements. Where the model chosen by the authority includes a directly elected mayor, councils are further required to consult on and choose a fall-back proposal and to hold a binding referendum. If the referendum does not support a mayor, the council implements its fall-back arrangements. Referendums are considered in Chapter 7 below.

District councils in the area of a county council with a population of less than 85,000, as estimated by the Registrar General on 30 June 1999, can choose to draw up proposals based on **either** executive arrangements **or** alternative arrangements[1].

Alternative arrangements are considered at Chapter 6 below. It should be noted that alternative arrangements are not only available to authorities with a population of less than 85,000 but are also available as a fall-back option for **all** authorities whatever their size whose primary proposals involve a mayoral option and will therefore require a referendum.

The options for executive arrangements on the face of the Act are:

- An elected mayor with a cabinet[2];
- A leader with a cabinet[3]; and
- An elected mayor with a council manager[4].

1   LGA 2000, s 31.
2   LGA 2000, s 11(2).
3   LGA 2000, s 11(3).
4   LGA 2000, s 11(4).

The key features of executive arrangements

[4.4]
The table in Division VI – Appendix 3 below sets out the main similarities and differences between the mayor and cabinet, leader and cabinet and mayor and council manager models.

In this chapter we consider the main elements of the executive models that appear on the face of the Act and the features common to all the executive models, namely:

- The role of the executive;
- The role of full council;
- Conflict resolution;
- The role of all councillors;
- Accountable decision-making;
- The Standards committee;
- Officer support for cabinet government; and
- Monitoring, review and change.

Mayor and Cabinet

[4.5]
An authority must hold a referendum to approve their proposals before this model can be adopted[1].

The mayor will be elected in accordance with the Local Government (Elected Mayors) (Elections, Terms of Office and Casual Vacancies) (England) Regulations 2001[2]. The usual term of office for the mayor will be four years[3], although the term of the first mayor can be between two to five-and-a-half years to bring the mayoral election within the normal electoral cycle.

The mayor appoints his or her executive. The size of the executive must be between two and nine members of the authority[4], plus the mayor. The LGA 2000 does give power to the Secretary of State to amend this figure by Regulations but only to **decrease** the maximum size of the executive not increase it[5]. The membership of the executive under this and the other models for cabinet government is not required to be politically balanced. It is quite possible, therefore, to have an executive made up of one political party. If that is the case, the means of holding the executive to account will need to be especially carefully organised and supported in order to ensure that allegations of 'behind closed doors' decision-making are to be avoided.

The DTLR Guidance requires the elected mayor to have regard to any relevant responses to the consultation undertaken by the local authority when deciding the size and membership of the executive. However, authorities were not specifically required or advised to consult on the size of the executive and so it is not clear whether the composition of many of the first round of executives will be based on consultation results. Perhaps of more significance is the fact that the mayor is required to consider whether further consultation is necessary if s/he is considering changing the size of the executive[6].

The mayor appoints the members of the executive and determines the scheme of delegations in respect of executive functions[7]. For example, the mayor will decide whether to discharge an executive function him or herself or whether to delegate that function to the executive as a whole, an individual member of the executive, a committee of the executive or to an officer. Specific delegations are permitted as follows:

- from the executive to a committee of the executive or to an officer;
- from an individual member of the executive to an officer;
- from a committee of the executive to an officer[8].

In addition, the mayor or the body to whom the mayor has delegated a function, can arrange for area committees, other local authorities or a joint committee with other local authorities to undertake an executive function. In deciding the scheme of delegations the mayor can limit the delegations, for example, by directing that the function cannot be delegated onwards. Once a function is delegated, the person or body who delegated it continues to be able to exercise that power.

Executive members are not permitted to have formal substitutes or deputies who are not themselves members of the executive. There is also no power to co-opt other councillors or others on to the executive.

As the mayor will decide the membership and the roles of the executive, it is clearly a powerful role. The mayor can make decisions on his or her own in relation to executive functions. Add to those powers the mandate of an election on a manifesto and some commentators see a potential for abuse of power. The checks and balances to executive powers (such as overview and scrutiny, the forward plan and call-in arrangements) are the response to such concerns and, depending on how effective the checks and balances are, may or may not address them.

The mayor is required to appoint a deputy who holds office for the same term as the elected mayor[9]. The elected mayor can remove and replace the deputy 'if he thinks fit'. If neither can act the executive must act in the mayor's place or arrange for a member of the executive to do so.

1   LGA 2000, s 26; see further Chapter 7 below.
2   SI 2001/2544.
3   LGA 2000, s 39(6).
4   LGA 2000, s 11(8).
5   LGA 2000, s 11(9).
6   See 'Monitoring, review and change' at para **[4.24]** below.
7   LGA 2000, s 14(2).

8   LGA 2000, s 14(3) to (5).
9   LGA 2000, Sch 1, para 1.

Leader and Cabinet

[4.6]

This model does not require a referendum and many councils moved straight to a leader and cabinet form of government following their consultation. Alternatively, the leader and cabinet is available as the fall-back option for an authority moving to a referendum on a mayoral model and, in that case, may be implemented if the referendum does not support a mayor. The leader is an elected councillor appointed as leader by full council. The council can make provisions for the election and term of office of the leader (but there is no requirement to do so)[1]. Any arrangements for removing the leader from office need to be clearly explained in the constitution.

The executive must again be limited in size to between two and nine councillors plus the leader.

There are two broad options available – either the leader can appoint the executive or the full council can do so[2]. The two options have been labelled the 'strong' and 'weak' leader models but this is somewhat misleading as the two alternatives are not mutually exclusive. The council can decide to divide up the jobs of choosing the executive and deciding the scheme of delegations between the council and the leader in any way that it wishes. For example, the council might choose the executive with the leader then deciding on the delegations or vice versa. Examples of such 'hybrid' arrangements are given in the DTLR Guidance (fig 4.4).

Where the arrangements are for the council to choose the members of the executive, the council can choose to make provision for the terms of office for the executive members as well as for the leader[3]. Where the leader appoints the executive members the authority does not control their term of office.

Unlike the mayor and cabinet model, there is no requirement for the leader to appoint a deputy.

Other aspects of the leader and cabinet model reflect the principles of the mayor and cabinet model. The leader is required to consider further consultation, for example, if s/he is considering altering the size of the executive. Delegations can be made to the same individuals or bodies, including area committees and joint committees with other councils. The arrangements for the framework of checks and balances to the system are the same for all cabinet government models and are considered under common features below.

The significant differences between the mayor and cabinet and leader and cabinet models then are the need for a referendum for the mayoral model and the fact that the leader is not directly elected but chosen by the council from one of the elected councillors. The model potentially looses some of its visibility in terms of the identifiable figurehead but runs less risks for those concerned about the abuse of power because the leader can be removed by the council, whereas the elected mayor will only be replaced at the end of his or her term.

1   LGA 2000, Sch 1, para 2(2)(*a*).
2   LGA 2000, s 11(3)(*b*).
3   LGA 2000, Sch 1, para 2(2)(*b*).

Mayor and Council Manager

[4.7]
The third form of cabinet government available on the face of the Act is the directly elected mayor and council manager. The model requires a referendum before it can be adopted by an authority. If a referendum supports the model, the mayor would be elected in the same way as in the mayor and cabinet form of government with the same provisions regarding term of office applying.

The difference is that, instead of an executive of a further two to nine councillors, the mayor in this model has an executive of two comprised of him or herself and the council manager[1].

The council manager is appointed by full council and can be dismissed by the full council. Dismissal would, of course, be subject to employment legislation but the statutory protections afforded to the head of paid service[2] will not apply where the council manager is also the head of paid service.

The council manager is entitled to attend and speak but not vote at all committee and sub-committee meetings of the authority including overview and scrutiny committees, if invited to do so. The council manager is a politically restricted post and cannot be held by the monitoring officer or chief finance officer. In addition the Secretary of State recommends in the DTLR Guidance that the council manager should not be the proper officer for verifying petitions, or publishing records of decisions nor the returning officer[3].

As the cabinet in this model is only made up of two people, there is provision in the Act for the elected mayor to appoint one or more committees to advise the executive. Advisory committees are not required to be politically balanced.

The mayor must appoint a deputy mayor[4], who will need to be kept fully informed as s/he will not be a member of the executive but may have to take on the mayor's role at short notice.

The council manager in this model will be responsible for appointing all staff (the Secretary of State intends to make Regulations requiring the delegation of all staff appointments to the council manager). It is clearly envisaged that the council manager would also be the head of paid service and chief executive[5].

The executive/ non-executive split which is the key feature of cabinet government is reflected in this model by the roles of the mayor and the council manager. The role of policy development is undertaken by the mayor and the council (with the support of advisory committees). The responsibility for implementing the policy framework that is developed and making the day to day decisions for delivery will lie with the council manager.

The council manager can discharge executive functions him or herself or delegate them to either the executive (ie him or herself and the mayor together) or to an officer of the authority[6]. The DTLR Guidance, however, does state that the council manager should not generally delegate matters to the executive, which indicates the model envisages virtually all decisions being taken by officers or other devolved structures where these are in place. As with all of the cabinet government models, the council manager can make arrangements for functions to be delegated to area committees, another local authority or a joint committee of more than one authority. The Act specifically requires the council manager to have regard to the advice of the mayor when deciding delegations.

One feature of this model that may cause a potential for conflict is that as a member of the executive, the council manager must be held to account by the overview and scrutiny committee(s) of the authority. However, the council manager as head of paid service will also be responsible for resourcing scrutiny and there may be a conflict between these two roles. The DTLR Guidance therefore suggests a separate officer support structure for scrutiny with a different chief officer being responsible for scrutiny, with staff who report to him or her rather than to the council manager.

At the time of writing, it does not appear that any authorities have chosen the mayor and council manager to put forward as their proposals to the electorate. It may be that this is because the model has not appeared attractive to councillors who see it as reducing the level of involvement by councillors in decision-making. Those who do think the model is attractive see it as modern and professional and mirroring commercial practice.

This model has featured in the consultation exercises. When consulting, authorities are required to put all of the options to the electorate and this can lead to the possibility of some interesting interpretation of consultation results. For example, if an authority is keen to move to a referendum, it is possible to add up the responses in favour of the mayor and cabinet and mayor and council manager and interpret this as an expression of interest in a mayoral model which would justify a move to a referendum. Similarly, for those councils who do not wish to move to a referendum, it is possible for them to treat the two mayoral models quite separately. This does provide some support for criticism of the real influence of the consultation process.

1   LGA 2000, Sch 1, para 3(13).
2   Under the Local Authorities (Standing Orders) Regulations 1993, SI 1993/202.
3   At para 4.81 of the DTLR Guidance *New Council Constitutions: Volume One*.
4   LGA 2000, Sch 3.
5   Paragraph 4.92 of the Guidance.
6   LGA 2000, s 16.

Leader and Council Manager

[4.8]
No provisions have been made for a leader and council manager model.

However, it is possible for the leader to have a small executive (of only two other members) and to delegate heavily to the chief executive. This would effectively make the chief executive a council manager. This is an option envisaged in the DTLR Guidance[1].

1   See paras 4.76 to 4.79 of the Guidance.

Other Executive Arrangements

[4.9]
The Act includes at s 11(6) the possibility for other models of executive arrangements to be prescribed in regulations made by the Secretary of State. Examples of the kind of additional executive arrangements that may be provided for are given in the Act. They include members of the executive being directly elected to specific posts, and members of the executive being directly elected but not to specific posts[1].

Regulations under s 11(6) extending the models for executive arrangements have not been made. However, Local Authorities can at any time make proposals for different forms of executive arrangements to the Secretary of State.

When making proposals for a different form of executive arrangement, authorities must show[2]:

- that the proposed arrangements would be an improvement on the arrangements the authority currently has in place;
- that the proposals would ensure efficient, transparent and accountable decision-making;
- that the proposals would be suitable for all local authorities or a particular description of authority to consider.

The DTLR Guidance on *New Council Constitutions* at Chapter 4 sets out the reason for the above requirements as being that there is already 'considerable scope' to tailor the three models on the face of the Act to suit the needs of individual authorities and explains that 'the Secretary of State would be unlikely to make available a form of executive which was very similar to an existing form or one which was only applicable to a single authority'[3].

Although most authorities are moving to new arrangements with one of the 'off-the-shelf' forms of executive arrangements, proposing alternative executive arrangements may be an option that authorities wish to consider as the new arrangements develop and authorities see opportunities to build on and improve them.

1   LGA 2000, s 11(6)(*a*) and (*b*).
2   Contained in s 12(3) of the LGA 2000.
3   DTLR Guidance *New Council Constitutions: Vol 1*, chap 4, para 4.6.

The Role of the Executive

[4.10]

The majority of local authority functions (for example, housing and social services) are required to be the responsibility of the executive. The position is that, unless specified otherwise, a function is presumed to be an executive function[1]. The potential delegations within and outside the executive have been considered separately under each model above.

The Local Authorities (Functions and Responsibilities) (England) Regulations 2000[2] divide the functions of an authority into the following categories:

- functions which **cannot** be the responsibility of an executive;
- functions which **may** be the responsibility of an executive ('local choice functions'); and
- functions **not** to be the **sole** responsibility of an executive.

The broad approach to the division of functions is that deciding the policy framework and budget as well as constitutional and quasi-legislative functions are to the responsibility of the full council. All other functions are executive functions.

1   LGA 2000, s 13.
2   SI 2000/2853.

Functions which cannot be the responsibility of the Executive[1]

[4.11]

Functions which cannot be the responsibility of the executive include functions relating to town and country planning and development control, licensing and registration functions, health and safety functions and electoral functions.

The question that is left in respect of these functions is who or what body will exercise them, having determined that the executive cannot? This will be for individual councils to decide but there is some further guidance from the Secretary of State, who recommends that these functions should be the responsibility of full council. The Guidance further recommends that where these decisions are currently delegated to officers or committees, those delegations should continue.

The number of committees the council establishes and the membership of those committees should be kept to a minimum and be proportionate to the size of the authority[2].

1   Listed in reg 2(1) and Sch 1 to the Local Authorities (Functions and Responsibilities) (England) Regulations 2000, SI 2000/2853.
2   DTLR Guidance, para 5.12.

Local choice functions

[4.12]
There are certain functions which authorities can decide whether they are to be the responsibility of the executive or not[1]. These functions include conducting Best Value reviews, arrangements for education appeals, functions under local Acts and the appointment of individuals to an office outside the council.

In relation to these functions, authorities must make a decision where they will lie, and make the arrangements clear in their constitution. It is possible for the functions to be shared between the executive and the council (or its committees)[2]. This may be appropriate where the function incorporates several roles, such as policy delivery, strategy development and direct regulation of persons.

The Guidance given on how to decide where Local Act functions should lie refers back to the broad distinction set out above – ie licensing, consent, permission, registration decisions should not be executive functions but policy decisions and implementation of policy should be.

The executive has responsibility for drafting the budget and the plans and strategies which make up the policy framework[3] but certain functions in relation to the policy framework are retained by the authority. These are:

• giving instructions requiring the executive to reconsider a draft plan or strategy;
• amending a draft plan or strategy;
• the approval of plans or strategies which are required to be submitted to the Secretary of State or other Minister;
• the adoption of a plan or strategy.

Amendments to plans and strategies can only be made by the executive where they are either giving effect to a requirement by a Minister or where the council authorises in year modifications by the executive at the point of approving the plan or strategy.

Where the executive goes beyond its functions and makes a decision which is not in accordance with the budget or a plan or strategy approved by full council, overview and scrutiny committees will have the power to call-in such decisions and refer the matter to the full council. If the matter was in fact a matter for the council to decide (for example, where the executive amended a plan which the council had not authorised it to), full council could take a decision themselves. If the matter was found not to be contrary to the budget or policy framework and therefore appropriate for the executive to decide, the council can request the executive to reconsider the decision, but ultimately it is for the executive to decide the issue.

There are urgency procedures where a decision which is contrary to the budget or policy framework can be taken if it is agreed as urgent by the chair of the relevant overview and scrutiny committee or the chair of the authority if the overview and scrutiny chair is not available[4]. After making such a decision, the decision-maker is required to report to the council the decision, the reasons for it and the reasons for the urgency.

For the urgency provisions to work well, it will be important for the council's constitution to set out which chair should be consulted for each category of executive function and to provide some guidance to the overview and scrutiny chairs as to the sort of issues which may be considered urgent.

In order for the workload of the executive to be manageable, it is likely to mean that there will need to be an increase in delegation to officers or other bodies, for example, area committees, to enable the executive to concentrate on strategic matters. Even with increased delegation, there is a question as to whether it is realistic to assume that the role of an executive councillor can be anything other than a full-time one. The LGA 2000 does require authorities to set up Independent Panels to assess the level of members allowances and consider whether they should be pensionable but Government Consultation is still awaited which may impede the progress towards a fully functioning executive.

As we have seen under each of the models, it will be possible and expected for executive functions to be delegated to individual executive members. There will be no hiding behind the group, a committee or the whole council in these instances. The confidence of individual members to make decisions will have a significant impact upon how cabinet government will work and authorities will need to think carefully about support and training for members, including media training, to enable them to embrace their new role.

1   Set out at reg 3 and Sch 2 of the Local Authorities (Functions and Responsibilities) (England) Regulations 2000, SI 2000/2853; and also in the Local Authorities (Functions and Responsibilities) (England) (Amendment) Regulations 2001, SI 2001/2212.
2   LGA 2000, s 13(4) and (5).
3   The plans and strategies which are subject to full council approval or adoption are referred to collectively as the policy framework. They are listed at para **[4.13]** below.
4   Set out in reg 5 of the Local Authorities (Functions and Responsibilities) (England) Regulations 2000, SI 2000/2853.

The Role of Full Council

[4.13]
There are certain functions reserved to the full council in cabinet government arrangements. The consultation paper *Local Leadership: Local Choice* summarised the role of full council under new arrangements as being required to:

- 'Agree the council's overall community strategies, including such key plans as its education development plans, local transport plans, and its local performance plans;
- Determine each year its revenue and capital budget;
- Take those decisions which would represent a departure from the strategies and budgets which the council has previously agreed as well as making certain appointments and settling the form of governance'.

The plans and strategies that the full council is required to approve are listed in Sch 3 of the Local Authorities (Functions and Responsibilities) (England) Regulations 2000[1] (as amended[2]). They are:

- Annual Library Plan;
- Best Value Performance Plan;
- Children's Services Plan;
- Community Care Plan;
- Community Strategy;
- Crime and Disorder Reduction Strategy;
- Plans and alterations which together comprise the Development Plan;
- Early Year Development Plan;
- Education Development Plan;
- Local Transport Plan;
- Youth Justice Plan.

In addition, local authorities can choose other plans or strategies that it wishes to be adopted by full council. The Secretary of State recommends the following[3]:

- Food Law Enforcement Service Plan;
- The strategy and Plan which comprise the Housing Investment Programme;
- Local Agenda 21 Strategy;
- Adult Learning Plan;
- Quality Protects Management Action Plan;
- The Local Authorities Corporate Plan (if any).

This means that many plans which were formerly dealt with in committees will go to full council. The arrangements for council meetings will need to be reviewed to accommodate this. There is likely to be a need for more meetings and councils will need to think about how the full council is best able to determine policy. When a draft plan or strategy is submitted to full council for consideration, the full council will need to give time and thought to how to deal with it. There may be a need to have a form of 'first reading' (like the American model) to allow the council to consider and debate the issues and make recommendations followed by a 'second reading' where the plan or strategy, with any amendments that flowed from the first debate, is formally adopted. Without such a mechanism it is difficult to see how the council could give proper consideration to the issues raised and avoid the 'rubber stamping' of polices, which is clearly not the role of the council anticipated by the government under executive arrangements.

The council may want to build in consultation with members outside the executive before a plan comes to it. For example, overview and scrutiny committees are expected to have role in policy development. Before a plan goes to full council for approval, the executive would be wise to consult non-executive councillors and this could be achieved by going to the relevant overview and scrutiny committee with draft proposals for plans or strategies.

In addition to policy determination, the full council will be an important arena for holding the executive to account. This is a role that will clearly need to work alongside overview and scrutiny who will lead the process of monitoring the performance of the executive. Authorities will need to decide where questions from members and the public to the executive should be put – at overview and scrutiny meetings, at full council or at both? The full council will receive overview and scrutiny reports and a process for dealing with recommendations will need to be incorporated into the arrangements.

An example of problems that can arise if the process is not clear is that the reports of an overview and scrutiny committee get delayed whilst awaiting an executive response so that by the time the report gets to full council it is no longer the live issue that it was. Alternatively, the report could go swiftly to full council but without clear expectations about what would then happen to it – will the executive respond, will the council itself be asked to make any decisions?

The council will have the power to require the executive to reconsider decisions which have been called-in and could pass a notice of no confidence in the executive or individual members. Where the council appoints the executive it will also have the power to dismiss them.

Academics and commentators on local government have taken the opportunity of the requirements of these new roles for council meetings to highlight concerns about the council meeting being a sterile place which does not engage local people. It has been suggested that when moving to new arrangements authorities should take the opportunity to reinvigorate the public debate at council meetings and realise the potential of community leadership that the council meeting has.

In his paper on the role of the council meeting, Professor Stewart suggests:

> 'One possibility is that every year the council should hold a state of the city (county town or district) debate to focus on the key issues faced not by the authority, but by the area and the communities within. Such a debate would symbolise the outward looking council and could involve as part of the meeting the representatives of other stakeholders and the public generally. Such a meeting could be part of the community planning process'.

Of course, local government did not require the introduction of cabinet government to put life into its council meetings, make them outward looking or take innovative approaches to engaging the public. This has always been possible. However, it would seem that the trend has been for councils to discourage rather than encourage public participation and to be firmly inward rather than outward looking. The modernisation process may be what is required to push councils into rethinking their council meetings.

1   SI 2000/2853.
2   Local Authorities (Functions and Responsibilities) (England) (Amendment) Regulations 2001, SI 2001/2212.
3   Para 2.22 of the Guidance.

Conflict Resolution

[4.14]
All executive models will require thought to be given to resolving conflict

between the executive and the council. This is well illustrated when looking in particular at models with an elected mayor. The mayor will be directly elected on a manifesto and will be likely to consider him or herself as having a mandate to represent the community. The manifesto commitments may not be the same as the priorities of the council.

The DTLR Guidance indicates that the Secretary of State intends to introduce Regulations requiring a conflict resolution mechanism to be adopted between the executive and the full council in respect of setting the budget and policy framework. At the time of writing these Regulations are not in place. However, the Guidance informs us of three of the intended mandatory features, as follows[1]:

- the leader or mayor to have at least five days to object to a full council decision contrary to executive proposals;
- the council to meet to reconsider in the light of the objection;
- provision for the council to insist on its decision by either a simple or greater majority. (The Guidance suggests that a two-thirds majority should be required in a mayoral model for the council to insist on its decision because of the direct mandate that the mayor will have.)

1 Para 2.35 of the Guidance.

The Role of All Councillors

[4.15]
A common feature of all cabinet models is that the majority of councillors will not be on the executive and will therefore have some form of 'back bench' role. It makes sense, then, for councils to pay as much, if not more, attention to the roles of non-executive members. Authorities need to ensure that the community is getting the full value of the representation of all its democratically elected councillors and that councillors themselves are engaged in their new roles and do not feel left out.

The LGA established a task group to look at the range of roles available to non-executive members and the practices of local councils in piloting such arrangements. Their report *Real Roles for Members* describes a range of roles that non-executive members will need to play under executive arrangements.

There should be plenty for non-executive councillors to do. They will be on overview and scrutiny committees, area committees, have direct contact with and represent electors, become involved in partnerships and joint ventures, and support and advise the executive. The idea of non-executive councillors being 'redundant' as some councillors have felt is really not an option if cabinet government is to work. Members who are not on the executive need to take the lead in holding the executive to account and representing community views.

However, some councillors have felt that the new arrangements will shut them out and that all of the important decisions will be made by the executive. It is understandable why some councillors should feel this because of the tendency for authorities to concentrate on executive arrangements when moving to a new cabinet government system. The view has also not been helped by many of the pilots run by authorities where a kind of cabinet government was put in place but without the non-executive side properly supported. For example, under the Act there will be a requirement for a forward plan of key decisions (see para **[4.20]** below) and this will be a crucial source of information for the public and non-executive councillors. Many authorities have been working with an executive but without the information flow properly developed, leading to accusations that the executive is making its decisions without any input from other councillors.

Therefore, the checks and balances of the cabinet system must be put in place. Call-in, the forward plan, mechanisms for member briefings are all essential elements of the cabinet government system. Going back to the aims of the new system – efficiency, transparency and accountability – the executive is supposed to provide the first but the onus is on non-executive councillors to provide the second two.

By ensuring adequate focus on non-executive members the accusation of a less democratic system may be addressed but there will to some degree still be the need for a culture shift among councillors, especially those who have been used to the committee system for many years. They will need to learn to receive information in different ways and be willing to do this. They will also have to embrace the fact that non-executive roles are different but not second class to executive positions. Again, the responsibility is on authorities to approach member training in a proactive and innovative way to reflect the new roles for councillors.

Accountable Decision-Making

[4.16]
The Local Authorities (Executive Arrangements) (Access to Information) (England) Regulations 2000[1] set out requirements for access to information and meetings under executive arrangements.

1   SI 2000/3272.

Recording decisions

[4.17]
Where an executive decision is taken by:

- the executive or a committee of the executive meeting in public or private;
- an individual member; or
- an officer;

a **record** of that decision must be made and must include:

- the decision;
- reasons for the decision;
- the alternative options considered;
- any conflicts of interests declared; and
- any dispensation granted by the standards committee relating to a conflict of interest.

The record, supporting reports and the background papers, must be made available for public inspection as soon as practicable.

Meetings of the executive or their committees must be held **in public** (and papers available three days on advance) where:

- a key decision (see below) is to be made; or
- a matter is to be discussed, with an officer present, relating to a key decision and the decision is going to be made within 28 days of the meeting.

This includes key decisions discussed or taken which are not contained in the forward plan due to timing (see below).

Briefings and political debate are not covered by the requirement to meet in public as long as a key decision is not taken.

Key decisions

[4.18]

Key decisions are defined in the Regulations as decisions which either:

- result in significant expenditure or savings having regard to the budget for the service; or
- result in a significant effect on communities in the area covering two or more wards.

When considering what is 'significant' the DTLR Guidance suggests that authorities should agree financial thresholds and check that there is consistency between neighbouring authorities at the same tier. The government is currently consulting on whether financial thresholds should be prescribed.

When considering the significance of a decision in terms of its effect on the area, the Guidance requires the decision-maker to consider whether the outcome will have an impact on a significant number of people living or working locally.

Individual executive decisions

[4.19]

Where an individual officer or member receives a report upon which s/he intends to make a key decision, the decision cannot be made unless the report has been available for at least three clear days. The report author must also make a copy of the report available as soon as reasonably practicable to each relevant overview and scrutiny chair.

The forward plan

[4.20]
The Regulations require councils to publish a forward plan. The forward plan must contain details of the matters likely to be subject to key decisions for a period of **four months** – starting with the first working day of the month. The plan must be updated monthly and produced at least 14 days before the first day of the month.

The forward plan must contain the following details:

- the matter;
- the decision-maker;
- the date the decision is to be made;
- the groups/organisations to be consulted;
- the means of consultation;
- how individuals can make representations; and
- a list of the relevant documents.

Where it is impracticable to include a key decision in the forward plan, the decision can only be made if the relevant chairs of overview and scrutiny have been informed of the matter and that notification has been made public for at least three clear days.

Where it is not possible to comply with the above requirements for publicity, the decision can only be made with the agreement of the relevant chair of overview and scrutiny that the decision is urgent and cannot reasonably be deferred.

Access to information for members

[4.21]
Rights of access to information for members are set out in the Regulations, in particular relating to documents held by the executive.

Extended rights are given to members of overview and scrutiny committees, who are entitled to exempt or confidential information contained in documents held by the executive where it is relevant to a scrutiny review.

Where a decision is made and is not treated as a key decision, an overview and scrutiny body can require the executive to report to the council if it thinks the decision should have been treated as a key decision.

The full council must receive quarterly reports of each decision taken which was agreed as urgent and did not therefore comply with the publication timescales.

The provisions of s 12A of the Local Government Act 1972 (access to information: exempt information) are not affected by these Regulations. In addition, the advice of a political advisor or assistant is not required to be disclosed.

A criminal offence is committed if a person refuses to supply a document or intentionally obstructs the inspection of a document in breach of the regulations.

In order to produce a forward plan, authorities will need to have excellent communications between departments and central services to be clear about what decisions are coming up over the next four months. Internal protocols will be required to explain what will be a key decision. The plan should help to determine the scrutiny work programme and, if it used effectively, should limit the need for call-in of executive decisions.

Standards Committee

[4.22]
Another feature common to all of the cabinet arrangements is the require-ment for authorities to establish a Standards Committee under Pt III of the Act. The roles and responsibilities of standards committees are considered in Division II. It is mentioned here only to emphasise that cabinet arrangements require other structures to work alongside the cabinet for it to work effectively whilst still achieving openness and accountability.

Officer Support for Cabinet Government

[4.23]
Officers and members need to work differently together under a system of cabinet government. There are specific provisions in the Act to address the role of the monitoring officer, the head of paid service and the finance officer – these are dealt with in Division V – Chapter 33 and further, in relation to the monitoring officer, in Chapter 30.

An issue which councils are already dealing with under new arrangements is the role of officers in relation to supporting both the executive and overview and scrutiny. It is a difficult issue because, as has already been identified, there are no new resources to support the new arrangements. Officers will spend much of their time liasing with the executive in respect of the implementation of policy and are also expected to give support to scrutiny reviews of the executive's performance. There is a risk that overview and scrutiny will not get adequate support unless there are dedicated staff who report to it. At the same time it will not be feasible or desirable for authorities to set up a parallel officer structure to support scrutiny, so officers need to work across the executive/scrutiny split.

Guidance on arrangements for officer support is contained in Chapter 8 of the DTLR Guidance. The Guidance correctly identifies the potential for conflict in some areas in respect of officer support for different aspects of the new arrangements and helpfully suggests that that potential for conflict should be 'taken into account' and that authorities 'draw up procedures for resolving such conflicts of interest'!

The main difficulties for councils is likely to be wrestling enough support for the overview and scrutiny function out of the budget and it is easy to underestimate how much support in depth reviews of council services or performance requires. It is also a difficult balancing act to justify those resources when there will be a direct impact on the resources available to provide the services in question. Overview and scrutiny is likely to win more support (politically and financially) if it is seen to produce recommendations that improve service delivery and, possibly, save the council money. Some 'quick wins' in this respect are essential to get the function moving in the right direction. For example, in Haringey the scrutiny review of parking enforcement resulted in recommendations which saw as a direct result substantial financial savings.

Monitoring, Review and Change

[4.24]
As authorities develop their new structures there will be minor changes to the structure to be made and there will also be authorities that wish to change the arrangements in their entirety – ie move from one model to another.

The Local Authorities (Changing Executive Arrangements and Alternative Arrangements)(England) Regulations 2001[1] and the accompanying Direction set out the procedure for both minor and major changes.

Where an authority wishes to review and amend its existing executive or alternative arrangements, reg 2(2) and (3) require authorities to draw up proposals for the different arrangements. The council must pass a resolution before the changes can be implemented[2].

In addition, the DTLR Guidance requires authorities to consult local electors for, and other interested parties in, their area when changing their executive arrangements in any respect which has previously been the subject of consultation. The Guidance states that such consultation 'should be proportionate in scale, scope and extent to the scale of the proposed changes to the executive arrangements'.

Councils will therefore find that they must have regard to the questions asked in the initial consultation to see whether they need to consult again when making changes. It would appear that authorities that have conducted less thorough consultation will not be required to consult again if they didn't consult on the issue the first time. For example, some authorities will have conducted in depth consultation on the structure of overview and scrutiny in the authority. If so, any changes to overview and scrutiny will need further consultation.

Where an authority wishes to move from one set of arrangements to an entirely different one, the Regulations prescribe the process to be followed, which mirrors the process of the initial move to new arrangements from the committee structure.

When proposing to move from one form of executive to another, local authorities must take reasonable steps to consult local electors[3]. The Direction sets out what the consultation must involve. Following the consultation, the proposals must be sent to the Secretary of State with the usual consultation statement.

Where either the existing or the proposed arrangements involve a mayoral model, the council must also draw up fall-back proposals – which must be the existing arrangements – and hold a referendum (not before two months after sending the proposals to the Secretary of State.) On the basis of the three models that are on the face of the Act this means that any change of executive arrangements will involve a referendum.

If the referendum does not support the new proposal, then the existing arrangements continue. If the referendum does support the new proposals, they can be implemented. However, if there is an elected mayor in office, the new arrangements cannot be implemented until the end of the term or s/he resigns or dies. The Regulations specify the content of statutory notices that must be published following a referendum, whatever the outcome.

Similarly, there are provisions for small shire district councils who are operating alternative arrangements under s 31 of the Act to change from executive to alternative arrangements and vice versa. The same consultation requirements apply as does the requirement for a referendum if either the existing or the proposed new arrangements include an elected mayor.

There is no option for larger councils who are operating executive arrangements to move to alternative arrangements. However, reg 2(4) does give power to local authorities operating alternative arrangements to move to executive arrangements.

1   SI 2001/1003.
2   SI 2001/1003, reg 10.
3   SI 2001/1003, reg 3(1).

Conclusion

[4.25]
There is scope within the Act for councils to develop their arrangements very differently. Power could be centralised with the executive or the role of full council strengthened. Ideally there will be a balance between a strong leadership role for the cabinet and effective checks and balances and real roles for non-executive members.

The structure of cabinet government alone will not result in the provision of better services. It should, however, provide councils with the opportunity to re-evaluate their community leadership role and to re-design their structures in a way which reflects this focus.

CHAPTER 5
The Overview and Scrutiny Function

The Legal Basis for Scrutiny

[5.1]
The legal basis for overview and scrutiny is provided in Pt II of the Local Government Act 2000 and in particular s 21. The provision in the LGA 2000 was anticipated in the government Green Paper published in 1998 – *Modernising Local Government: Local Democracy and Community Leadership* – that proposed a radical change to the way that local authorities discharged their responsibilities.

The Green Paper proposed to abandon the traditional committee system and separate the decision-making and accountability processes. Formerly the same committee often carried out these two processes. The decision-making process, the executive function, was comparatively easy to understand but the accountability function, scrutiny, has been a much more difficult concept to develop.

In introducing the Local Government Act 2000 the government has provided the main framework for local authorities to develop the new processes but has left the detailed implementation to local discretion.

What are local authorities required to provide?

[5.2]
Section 21(1) of the LGA 2000 requires all local authorities' executive arrangements to include provision for the appointment of overview and scrutiny committees.

Section 21(2) requires that a local authority's executive arrangements provides an overview and scrutiny committee(s) that has power to:

- review or scrutinise decisions or action taken in respect of any functions that are the responsibility of the executive;
- make reports or recommendations to the local authority or the executive in respect of any functions that are the responsibility of the executive;
- review or scrutinise decisions or actions in respect of any functions that are not the responsibility of the executive;
- make reports or recommendations to the local authority or the executive in respect of any functions that are not the responsibility of the executive; and

- make reports or recommendations to the local authority or the executive in respect of matters that affect the local authority's area or its inhabitants.

Section 21(3) makes provision for an overview or scrutiny committee to recommend that a decision that has been made but not implemented in respect of a function that is the responsibility of the executive be reconsidered by the person or body that made the decision. In addition the overview or scrutiny committee may also arrange for the full council to review or scrutinise such a decision and to decide whether or not to recommend that the decision be reconsidered.

Section 21(4) and (5) provide that an overview and scrutiny committee may not discharge any functions other than the functions conferred on it by s 21 of the LGA 2000 and the function of conducting Best Value reviews under s 5 of the Local Government Act 1999.

Section 21(6) and (7) enable an overview and scrutiny committee to delegate any of its functions to a sub-committee of itself.

Section 21(8) provides that any member of an overview and scrutiny committee (or sub-committee) may ensure that any matter relevant to the remit of the committee (or sub-committee) be placed on the agenda and discussed at a meeting of the committee (or sub-committee).

Section 21(9) provides that a member of the executive may not be a member of overview and scrutiny committees (or sub-committees).

Section 21(10) provides that an overview and scrutiny committee may include anyone who is not a member of the local authority but (with the exception of church and parent governor representatives in respect of education matters) such members are not entitled to vote.

Section 21 (11) provides that:

- where party groups have been declared in the local authority, overview and scrutiny committees (and sub-committees) must reflect the political balance of the local authority, in accordance with ss 15 to 17 of, and Sch 1 to, the Local Government and Housing Act 1989. Section 17(1)(b) of that Act provides that a local authority may adopt different arrangements for the allocation of seats if the local authority so approves without any member present voting against[1]; and
- overview and scrutiny committees (and sub-committees) must meet in public in accordance with the access to information provisions in ss 100A to 100K of, and Sch 12A to, the Local Government Act 1972, as amended by ss 97 and 98 of the Local Government Act 2000, except where those provisions allow the public to be excluded.

Section 21(13)(a) enables an overview and scrutiny committee (or sub-committee) to require members of the executive and officers of the local authority to appear before it and answer questions. Section 21(13)(b) enables an overview and scrutiny committee (or sub-committee) to invite any other persons to attend its meetings but it cannot require them to do so. However, provisions in the Health and Social Care Act 2001 require the Chief Executives of National Health Bodies to attend at least two meetings a year.

Section 21(14) and (15) make it a duty of the persons mentioned above to comply with requirements to attend meetings but that are not obliged to answer any question that they would be entitled to refuse to answer in a court of law.

Paragraph 7 of Sch 1 to the LGA 2000 makes provision for providing rights for Church of England and Roman Catholic representatives to be members of any overview and scrutiny committee of a local education authority whose functions relate to education. Those members will also have full voting rights on those committees in respect of education matters. Paragraph 7 also provides for similar rights to be granted by direction to representatives of other denominations and faiths. Paragraph 9 of that Schedule also makes provision for regulations to grant parent governor representatives the right to be full voting members of the same committees. Such regulations have now been made and are the Parent Governor Representatives (England) Regulations 2001[2].

1   See also relevant Regulations.
2   SI 2001/478. The Regulations require local education authorities operating executive arrangements to appoint parent governor representatives to overview and scrutiny committees and sub-committees dealing wholly or partly with education functions. They also cover the number of parent governor representatives to be elected, their speaking and voting rights and the procedure for their election.

Comparison Between Local Authority Overview and Scrutiny Committees and Parliamentary Standing and Select Committees

[5.3]
The term 'standing committee' survives from earlier years when such committees were appointed to consider a series of bills on related subjects, as distinct from select committees which were then mostly appointed to consider a single bill or inquire into a particular matter. Nowadays, the memberships of the majority of standing committees are appointed for a whole Parliament or session. The two types of committee are fundamentally different in character. Select committees are committees of inquiry that mostly proceed by the taking of evidence and the making of reports on their findings. Procedure in standing committees follows that of the Committee of the whole House: the committees proceed by debate.

As mentioned above, the powers of overview and scrutiny committees enable them to require members of the executive and officers of the local authority to appear before it and answer questions. They can invite other persons to attend its meetings but it cannot require them to do so.

However, Parliamentary Select Committees can require any person to appear before it with the exception of members of either the House of Commons or the House of Lords. Failure to appear would be contempt of Parliament and subject to penalty. The only exception to this is the Committee on Standards and Privileges with regard to Members of the Commons. By Notice of Motion, Parliament can require any member of either House to appear before a Select Committee. The government has frequently confirmed that ministers and civil servants will attend committees when requested and provide committees with the information necessary to their inquiries.

Models for Scrutiny

[5.4]

According to statutory guidance[1] the Secretary of State has advised that all but the smallest local authorities should have more than one overview and scrutiny committee and that they should meet frequently, for example on a monthly or six-weekly cycle. In addition overview and scrutiny committees should take a cross-cutting rather than a narrow service-based view of the conduct of the local authority's business and therefore the aim should be for local authorities to have, at any given point in time, a relatively small number of such committees. Apart from this the arrangements for overview and scrutiny (including the membership and remits of the committees) are a matter for local choice.

1   *New Council Constitutions: Guidance Pack*, Vol 1, chap 3, para 3.20.

So what different models are there?

[5.5]

In advance of the legislation a number of authorities have experimented with different approaches. A number of different authorities have appointed a single 'Scrutiny Management Committee'. Such a committee does not generally carry out specific reviews but considers, consults on and in some cases recommend to the council a programme of overview and scrutiny activity. In one authority[1] the committee establishes time limited ad hoc panels to examine specific issues, sets their broad terms of reference, and requires each panel to report regularly but briefly on its progress against its objectives and timetables. The aim of this approach is to ensure flexibility and experimentation and to ensure that a balanced programme of overview and scrutiny is set and achieved each year.

In another authority[2], the overview and scrutiny co-ordinating group includes in its remit:

- co-ordination and action on all requests for the call-in of an executive decision;
- liaison with its individual standing committees – each with a cross cutting theme and each chaired by a member of the co-ordinating group;
- overall management of the work programme; and
- regular liaison and joint discussion of future policy issues and the Best Value review programme with the executive.

Another local authority[3] sets its overview and scrutiny programme by considering the whole range of performance data available to it. It uses sources such as opinion surveys, Best Value performance data, external audit and inspection reports, surveys of its own members, and so on, to determine its programme. It ensures that overview and scrutiny complements rather than competes with the programme of Best Value reviews and feeds into community planning and other statutory timetables. It also takes into account the capacity of the organisation to undertake overview and scrutiny work.

Another example[4] is where a local authority has drawn up arrangements for overview and scrutiny where a Scrutiny Management Board co-ordinates and plans the work of three overview and scrutiny committees for the environment and the economy; cultural and social issues; and finance and resources. The arrangements also include a 12-month scrutiny plan that is approved by the full council.

Statutory guidance suggests that overview and scrutiny committees are encouraged to consider different approaches and formats for their meetings for their different roles; scrutinising decisions and decisions making; reviewing policy; and investigating other matters of local concern.

There are also good examples of good practice and innovation in overview and scrutiny. These include:

- holding time limited inquiries;
- holding new style meetings outside the town hall involving informal dialogue with local residents, linked to the community planning process;
- co-optees from a wide range of community and voluntary groups who in turn are helping to change the character and style of meetings; and
- annual reports of individual reviews in a new style, drafted by members of the committee.

1   *New Council Constitutions: Guidance Pack*, Vol 1, chap 3, fig 3.1.
2   See n 1 above.
3   See n 1 above.
4   See n 1 above.

Types of Scrutiny

What is scrutiny?

[5.6]
There is no one definition of scrutiny and this is where the problem starts. Historically, best practice evolves as word spreads about the best way local authorities can provide better and more efficient services. And so it is with scrutiny. The government has provided the basic framework to provide scrutiny and left local authorities to develop their own processes to meet the legislation. But what is scrutiny? The answer is no one actually knows. There are a number of specific areas that have thus far been identified but undoubtedly these will change and evolve as experience demonstrates otherwise. So what is there so far?

- Developing and Reviewing Policy; and
- Holding the Executive to Account.

The new arrangements enable the non-executive member to fulfil a specific function and to contribute to the development of the authority. The perception so far is that non-executive members are being sidelined and are in many ways second tier members because they have not yet appreciated the part that they can play in moving the authority forward.

Developing and Reviewing Policy

[5.7]
In relation to developing and reviewing policy potentially the overview and scrutiny committees have a very important role to perform. In reviewing policy decisions overview and scrutiny committees will help to develop future policy. These reviews could be specific and look at a particular policy to decide:

* if it has been implemented in accordance with previously determined criteria;
* if it has been implemented successfully;
* whether the desired outcomes have been achieved; and
* if not, what changes could be introduced to ensure that the desired outcomes would be achieved.

In addition, overview and scrutiny committees could carry out wide ranging reviews of policy, for example, education and life-long learning. In this way the overview and scrutiny committees will be able to influence future policy because it would be a brave executive that ignored recommendations of a properly constituted review, providing that the overview and scrutiny committee could demonstrate that the recommendations were soundly based.

As part of this review comes Best Value. Whilst the executive must have a role in developing Best Value the overview and scrutiny committees can also play an important role. In fact some local authorities are seeking to merge the two roles within the scrutiny function.

The government has also seen a role for overview and scrutiny committees in examining and investigating the work and impact of outside bodies on the communities that the local authorities serve. However whilst there are recognised benefits to this there are also dangers. Such reviews will help the local authority to understand the benefits of partnership working but they will need to be carried out carefully to ensure that relationships are not compromised. This will be very important with health scrutiny that the government has identified in the NHS Plan and the Health and Social Care Act 2001.

Holding the Executive to Account

[5.8]
Holding the executive to account can be done in one of two ways. The first is

scrutinising decisions either before they are made or before they are implemented and the second is scrutinising decisions after they have been implemented.

Scrutinising decisions before they are made raises a difficult issue that overview and scrutiny committees will have to resolve and it will be a matter for individual local authorities to overcome. If on the one hand the overview and scrutiny committees are too aggressive and apparently unreasonable it is likely to result in the executive being uncooperative and being increasingly inventive in looking for other routes to implement policy without involving scrutiny. This would be dangerous and potentially divisive and a waste of limited resources. On the other hand, if overview and scrutiny committees are always supportive of the executive and do not challenge decisions or fail to investigate issues of concern that have been identified then they would rightly be accused of failing to carry out their duties properly.

Call-in and Conflict Resolution Procedures

[5.9]
As mentioned earlier, s 21(2)(*a*) and (3) of the LGA 2000 provide that a local authority's executive arrangements must ensure that overview and scrutiny committees have specific powers, in respect of functions that are the responsibility of the executive, to recommend that a decision made but not yet implemented be reconsidered by the person or body that made the decision or to recommend that the full council consider whether that person or body should reconsider the decision.

Guidance issued to local authorities confirms that they should make provision in their executive arrangements as to how these procedures are to operate. Such provisions may include a standard of delay before those decisions are implemented. In addition these provisions should also ensure that there is an appropriate balance between effectively holding the executive to account, being able to question decisions before they are implemented and allowing effective and efficient decision-making by the executive within the policy framework and budget agreed by the full council. The provisions should ensure that the decision-maker could only be asked to reconsider a decision once. The provisions also preclude the day to day management and operational decisions taken by officers being subject to any call-in procedure.

If the executive wishes to make a key decision after consulting the chair of an overview and scrutiny committee (or where there is no chair of the overview and scrutiny committee with the chairman or vice-chairman of the authority) on the basis that the decision is urgent, the local authority's call-in procedure should allow such decisions to be exempt from the call-in procedure or in any other way being delayed.

Local authorities should also determine how to respond to called in decisions. If, after considering a decision, the overview and scrutiny committee decides to recommend an alternative course of action, the call-in procedure should establish how the executive should respond to the alternative course of action recommended and what the timescale should be.

For example, one method for call-in could be as follows:

- the executive publishes decisions made either at an executive meeting or which an individual member has taken;
- the executive arrangements provide that decisions that can be subject to call-in procedures will be implemented within a given period unless an overview and scrutiny committee calls it in;
- during that period at least two members of the appropriate overview and scrutiny committee can request a meeting of the committee to review the decision by the submission of a requisite notice;
- any action to implement the decision is suspended for a period of up to 10 working days from the date of receipt of the notice to enable the overview and scrutiny committee to meet and to decide whether to decide to invoke the powers in s 21(3) of the LGA 2000;
- if the committee decides to disagree with the decision it may exercise the powers in s 21(3) having regard to statutory guidance;
- the decision-maker reconsiders the decision and decides whether to change it explaining her or his reasons to the next ordinary meeting of overview and scrutiny or full council as appropriate. One way of dealing with this would be for the decision to be re-examined at the next meeting of the executive with one or more of the representatives of the overview and scrutiny committee being present to put forward the views of the committee.

Local authorities should ensure that any call-in procedure is not abused or used unduly to delay decisions or slow down the process of decision-making. In particular the executive will from time to time be required to take decisions that need to be implemented quickly. Therefore local authorities will need to develop protocols and conventions to prevent abuse of an overview and scrutiny committee's power to recommend that a decision that has been made but not yet implemented, be reconsidered. In addition local authorities should keep the operation of any call-in arrangements under review to assess their effectiveness.

Some local authorities have experimented with this type of process. For example one authority with six review and scrutiny committees requires that the call-in of any executive decision must be within three days of the decision. It requires five members of any review and scrutiny committee to request a decision to be called in. In addition the five members must represent at least two political groups.

Another authority publishes a fortnightly members' information sheet that includes all decisions made by the executive or executive members. At least three members need to request the call-in of a decision and a call-in committee of members that are not members of the executive consider the request for the call-in.

Statutory advice[1] suggests local authorities will need to consider, when designing such mechanisms that under normal circumstances where a decision relates to a function that is the responsibility of the executive, ultimately only the executive can decide the matter.

In addition, statutory guidance also suggests that to avoid the possibility of calling numerous emergency council meetings the Secretary of State recommends that overview and scrutiny committees should only consider the use of power in s 21(3)(*b*) to refer matters to the full council if it is considered that the decision is contrary to the policy framework or contrary to or not in accordance with the budget. In the circumstances where an overview and scrutiny committee refers a decision to the full council there should be a clear timescale set out in the local authority's standing orders within which the debate should take place to avoid decisions being unnecessarily delayed.

1   *New Council Constitutions: Guidance Pack*, Vol 1, chap 3, para 3.85.

The Extension to Cover Health Scrutiny

[5.10]
The Health and Social Care Act 2001 provides the legal basis for scrutiny of the health service by local authorities.

The National Health Service document *A New Voice for Patients* explains that:

> 'The proposals seek to address the democratic deficit in the NHS at local level by enabling democratically elected councillors to take on the important function of scrutinising local NHS services through local authority overview and scrutiny committees. Health bodies will have a duty to provide information about their activities and the operation of their services to the committees. Chief Executives of local NHS bodies will be required to attend their meetings twice a year to answer questions about their organisations. Overview and Scrutiny Committees will make reports and recommendations to the NHS bodies that they review. NHS bodies will have to provide clear justification for any recommendations that they do not accept. Health authorities will have a specific duty to consult overview and scrutiny committees on any major change to services in their area. If the overview and scrutiny committee finds that the proposed changes are not in the interest of the population it will be able to refer the matter to the new national Independent Reconfiguration Panel. It may also do so if it believes that the process of involving the public and patients in the development of the proposals was inadequate.
>
> The lead responsibility for scrutiny will lie with councils with responsibility for social services (Counties, London Boroughs and Unitary Authorities). In many places, overview and scrutiny committees from more than one local authority will need to work together to ensure an efficient scrutiny process. Subject to Parliament, regulations will be made setting out how overview and scrutiny committees can pool or share powers or co-operate together to do this'.

In order to facilitate the passage of the Health and Social Care Bill to enable it to receive the Royal Assent before the dissolution of Parliament the government had to make a number of concessions one of which was to retain Community Health Councils.

The result of these changes is that local authorities will still retain the power to scrutinise local health services and that the Community Health Councils will continue in their current form to provide patient representation in local areas.

Whilst there is some uncertainty about the arrangements for public and patient representation, local authorities will need to start discussion with all local relevant partners, including other local councils, Community Health Councils and health bodies about what arrangements will work best locally to ensure that there are effective and efficient mechanisms in place for scrutinising local health authorities and for improving the local health economy.

The government has not made any additional funds available in respect of the health scrutiny role, because 'as the powers are essentially permissive, the exact cost involved will depend on local decisions as to the level of NHS scrutiny each authority undertakes'. The Local Government Information Unit's Democratic Health Network has expressed concern that this could lead to insufficiently robust or even tokenistic scrutiny or to an inconsistent type of 'postcode scrutiny'.

It remains to be seen how local authorities will develop this new role with health authorities.

CHAPTER 6
Alternative Arrangements

Introduction

[6.1]
Political restructuring of local government, in accordance with the Local Government Act 2000 ('the Act'), presents all local authorities in England with three models which can be adopted – a directly elected mayor with cabinet, a leader with cabinet, or a mayor with council manager – with the choice of model to be based upon public consultation.

In addition to the above models, the Act provides specified authorities with a fourth model of 'alternative arrangements'. The fourth model is available as a primary option to district councils in two tier authorities with a population below 85,000 and as a fall-back option to all authorities holding a referendum[1].

The framework for the fourth model is set out in the Local Authorities (Alternative Arrangements) (England) Regulations 2001[2].

We begin by looking at the structure of alternative arrangements, before considering how they fit within the modernisation of local government provided for in the Act. Following this, we consider the issues likely to arise for local authorities who operate alternative arrangements, considering in particular those provisions which enable the fourth model to develop and change if need be.

While this fourth model is available to all Welsh local authorities, the particulars being considered by the Welsh Assembly (due to be published in July 2001) are slightly different, and is considered separately in brief at the end of this section.

1   LGA 2000, ss 27(2)(b) and 31(2).
2   SI 2001/1299.

Structure of Alternative Arrangements

What model arrangements can be adopted?

[6.2]
Under s 32 of the Act, the Secretary of State can specify arrangements for the discharge of functions which do **not** involve the creation and operation of an

executive for the authority. This is what distinguishes alternative arrangements from other models available to local authorities. This has the effect of
enabling authorities to retain a committee-style system, with the following
restrictions:

- the arrangements must appoint committees or sub-committees of the
  authority to review or scrutinise decisions made, or other action taken,
  in connection with the discharge of functions of the authority[1], and
- the Secretary of State considers the arrangements are *likely* to ensure
  that decisions of the authority are taken in an efficient, transparent and
  accountable way[2].

The Local Authorities (Alternative Arrangements) (England) Regulations
2001[3] ('the Regulations') and the DTLR Guidance, Chap 9 set out the form
alternative arrangements must take. Broadly, the arrangements will involve
the full council setting the policy framework and budget, up to five
committees to implement and make proposals on the policy framework,
regulatory committees/area committees/joint committees as required and
one or more overview and scrutiny committee(s) to hold the policy
committees to account. A standards committee is required to be appointed in
accordance with Pt III of the Act.

The Regulations provide that the local authority will continue to be able to
make arrangements for the discharge of its functions under ss 101 and 102 of
the Local Government Act 1972, in accordance with any other legislation
which governs the discharge of those functions. Political balance requirements in and under ss 15 to 17 of, and Sch 1 to, the Local Government and
Housing Act 1989 and the access to information requirements in Pt VA of the
Local Government Act 1972 continue to apply to arrangements made under
s 101 of the 1972 Act.

Regulation 5 provides that the number of members[4] on committees is to be
set by individual authorities. It specifies a maximum number[5] of members (15
for a committee and 10 for a sub-committee[6]) of policy committees and
sub-committees appointed by a policy committee.

The DTLR Guidance recommends that the number of policy committees
should be kept to a minimum and that in small shire districts this number
should be no more than five and that the use of sub-committees should be
restricted to time-limited projects[7].

A resolution of the local authority is required in order for the authority to
operate alternative arrangements[8]. As soon as practicable after passing such
a resolution, a local authority must comply with s 29(2) requirements
concerning publication of those arrangements[9].

1   LGA 2000, s 32(3) provides that Regulations under this section may make provision with
    respect to committees or sub-committees, including provision which applies or reproduces
    any provision of s 21 or paras 7 to 11 of Sch 1 which set up scrutiny committees.
2   LGA 2000, s 32(1).
3   SI 2001/1299.
4   It continues to be possible to have members of policy committees and sub-committees who
    are not members of the local authority, in line with the provisions of current legislation, in
    particular the Local Government (Committees and Political Groups) Regulations 1990, SI
    1990/1553.

5   The Guidance is clearly in favour of keeping the numbers of committees to a minimum, and recommends that the number of members should be substantially fewer than the prescribed maximum.
6   This does not apply to regulatory committees, area committees, joint committees, overview and scrutiny committees or standards committees.
7   DTLR Guidance, para 9.16.
8   LGA 2000, s 33(2).
9   LGA 2000, s 33(3).

What is the role of the council under alternative arrangements?

[6.3]
While acting together as the full council under alternative arrangements, councillors continue to have the role of agreeing the local authority's policy framework and budget, making appointments to committees, and making or confirming appointment of the chief executive. In addition, they also have a role in adopting the new constitution and new code of conduct.

Legislation, as supplemented by Regulations, provides that the full council under alternative arrangements may have a similar policy making role to the full council under executive arrangements. The Regulations require the following functions (and specified actions in connection with the discharge of functions) to be exercised by the full council[1]:

• the adoption or approval of specified plans and strategies of the local authority;
• the adoption or approval of the budget and any plan or strategy for the control of the local authority's borrowing or capital expenditure (the capital plan)[2];
• determining the scheme and amounts of member's allowances; and
• authorising applications to the Secretary of State for transfer of housing land.

Regulation 3 of, and Sch 1 to, the Regulations provide that the full council is responsible for approving or adopting specified plans and strategies[3]; while the Secretary of State *recommends* that local authorities consider including additional plans and strategies for approval or adoption by the full council[4].

1   Plans and strategies which are subject to full council approval or adoption are referred to collectively as the policy framework in the Guidance.
2   The full council's role in the budget setting process will continue to be as set out in the provisions of the Local Government Finance Act 1992.
3   Annual Library Plan; Best Value Performance Plan; Children's Services Plan; Community Care Plan; Community Strategy; Crime and Disorder Reduction Strategy plans and alterations which together comprise the Development Plan; Early Years Development Plan; Education Development Plan; Local Transport Plan; and Youth Justice Plan.
4   Food Law Enforcement Service Plan. The strategy and plan which comprise the Housing Investment Programme: Local Agenda 21 Strategy; Adult Learning Plan; Quality Protects Management Action Plan; The local authority's corporate plan or its equivalent.

What are councillors' roles under alternative arrangements?

[6.4]
Councillors under alternative arrangements are subject to the same ethical framework and code of conduct implemented under Pt III of the Act. They continue to have the roles of representing the views of their constituents, acting together as full council and membership of committees and sub-committees.

Under alternative arrangements, councillors may also act as members of overview and scrutiny committees.

Overview and Scrutiny

[6.5]
Great importance is attached to overview and scrutiny arrangements under the Act, and the DTLR Guidance indicates that this is particularly so in relation to authorities adopting alternative arrangements.

Regulation 6 requires a local authority to include provision for the appointment of one or more overview and scrutiny committee(s), and sets out their functions and powers.

Such committees, and any sub-committee, may include persons who are not members of the authority. Members of the overview and scrutiny committee(s) who are not members of the authority are not entitled to vote at any meeting (subject to regs 8 and 16, under which particular arrangements are made for education overview and scrutiny committees[1]). When drawing up proposals for alternative arrangements, the Secretary of State recommends that authorities ensure that at least a core group of five to ten councillors have overview and scrutiny as their principal responsibility. In practice, the Guidance recommends these members should not therefore be members of policy committees, except those committees which have sole responsibility for quasi-judicial functions.

The Secretary of State will keep the regulations under review and will consider introducing statutory provisions to achieve this if the experience of operating alternative arrangements shows this to be necessary.

---

1   In the case of a relevant local authority which maintain one or more Church of England or Roman Catholic Church schools, an education overview and scrutiny committee or sub-committee of an education overview and scrutiny committee must include at least one person nominated from each church, by either the Diocesan Board of Education for any Church of England diocese, or the bishop of any Roman Catholic diocese which falls wholly or partly in the authority concerned's area (reg 8). Such members are entitled to vote at a meeting on any question which relates to any education functions which are the responsibility of the authority concerned, and which fall to be decided at the meeting. The Secretary of State may by directions require the committee include persons appointed as representatives of the persons who appoint foundation governors for the foundation or voluntary schools maintained by the authority which are not Church of England or Roman Catholic Church schools. The authority shall also appoint at least two, but not more than five, parent governor representatives (reg 9), such representatives to be elected in accordance with regs 10 to 16.

Alternative arrangements as primary proposals (for authorities with a population of less than 85,000)

[6.6]
One type of authority to whom the model of alternative arrangements is available under the Local Authorities (Alternative Arrangements) (England) Regulations 2001[1] are those with a population below 85,000 (as estimated by the Registrar General on 30 June 1999). Section 31 of the LGA 2000 requires such small shire districts to either draw-up proposals for executive arrangements under s 25 of the Act *or* alternative arrangements as described at para **[6.2]** above. Section 31 of the Act sets out the requirements for authorities drawing-up proposals for executive arrangements including consultation with local electors.

1   SI 2001/1299.

Alternative arrangements as fall-back proposals (for ALL authorities)

[6.7]
Section 27(1)(*b*) provides that local authorities, where drawing-up proposals involving a form of executive for which a referendum is required[1], must also draw up and send to the Secretary of State an outline of the fall-back proposals they intend to implement in the event that their proposals are rejected by the electorate[2]. They may apply to the Secretary of State for the approval of outline fall-back proposals, involving arrangements not permitted by or under Pt II of the Act[3], but which are permitted by regulations made under ss 11(5) or 32[4].

Fall-back proposals are defined in s 27(2)(2) as proposals:
'(*a*)   for the operation of executive arrangements which do not involve a form of executive for which a referendum is required;
(*b*)   for the operation of alternative arrangements of a particular type permitted by Regulations made under section 32.'

Outline fall-back proposals must include a timetable with respect to the implementation of detailed fall-back proposals, in the event that the proposals are rejected in the referendum[5], and this must be done within the timetable set out[6].

Should the result of the referendum be a rejection of a local authority's proposals, the authority is required to draw up detailed fall-back proposals, based on their outline fall-back proposals, and again send a copy of these to the Secretary of State for approval[7].

Detailed fall-back proposals involving alternative arrangements are required[8] to:

- consider the extent to which the proposals, if implemented, are *likely* to assist in securing continuous improvement in the way in which the authority's functions are exercised, having regard to a combination of economy, efficiency and effectiveness; and

- contain details of any transitional arrangements which are necessary for the implementation of the proposals.

Before drawing-up such proposals, a local authority must take *reasonable* steps to consult the local government electors for, and other interested persons in, the authority's area.

Whilst the possibility of alternative arrangements as a fall-back proposal has always been on the face of the Act, the relevant Regulations under s 32 followed quietly after the Act's Royal Assent. It is not widely understood, or publicised, that *all* authorities can have alternative arrangements as a fall-back option when moving to a mayoral referendum and many have been confused into thinking that alternative arrangements are only available to small shire districts with a population of less than 85,000.

1   LGA 2000, s 25.
2   LGA 2000, s 27(1)(*b*).
3   LGA 2000, s 28.
4   The timetable referred to in s 27(13) shall be extended to the extent that there is any delay in making the necessary regulations under s 11(5) or 32 (as the case may be).
5   LGA 2000, s 27(4).
6   LGA 2000, s 27(13).
7   LGA 2000, s 27(8).
8   LGA 2000, ss 27(12) and 25.

What difference could alternative arrangements make in practice?

[6.8]
In the event that alternative arrangements are the preferred choice for small shire districts with a population of less than 85,000, or that alternative arrangements are implemented as fall-back proposals following a referendum, the effect of the model will largely depend upon the individual arrangements put forward by the local authority concerned.

If an authority adopts only the minimum amendment to their existing arrangements which are acceptable under the Act, then for an authority where the council meeting is already the forum at which all members of the local authority decide the local authority's policy framework and budget, this is not a dissimilar model to the one already in operation. What significant improvement would have been achieved by a transition to the alternative arrangements?

While criticism of the existing system had prompted the modernisation agenda[1], along the way there has been acknowledgement by those advocating change that the current legislative framework in some cases had been adapted by authorities to function effectively[2]. Retaining a system which does not separate executive and representational functions[3] (which the government had considered 'so easily confused in the committee system'[4]) still enables local authorities operating such arrangements to develop and demonstrate community leadership in view of the most significant change, the imposition of the review and scrutiny committee.

The expectation is that with overview and scrutiny committees in place, there will be greater clarity about who is responsible for decisions, who has taken and should be held to account.

Any proposals for alternative arrangements put forward are required also to consider ways in which, if implemented, they introduce change which assists in securing continuous improvement in the way the authority's functions are exercised, having regard to a combination of economy, efficiency and effectiveness.

With both those points in mind, turning then to the DETR Guidance. This document depicts modernisation as a process; not as a straightforward change in system, but rather a mechanism to develop the way in which local government operates. It is suggestive of ways in which the structural changes introduced can enhance the performance of decision-making which the initial changes are directed to improve.

Specific examples of recommendations in the Guidance, some of which may well operate for authorities under existing arrangements, include the following:

- effective and regular consultation and communication between the relevant policy committees, regulatory committees, area committees, joint committees, the relevant overview and scrutiny committees and other members of the local authority during the development of plans and strategies, in particular those which need the agreement of partner organisations;
- enabling the full council may receive policy proposals from regulatory committees, area committees, joint committees or overview and scrutiny committees.
- providing that prior to approval or adoption of a plan or strategy, that full council should receive proposals from any policy committees which have delegated authority to take decisions in the relevant policy areas.

Looked at in view of the overall objectives of the Local Government Act 2000, it is not surprising that the Guidance in particular recommends that authorities consider how policy determination can be enhanced under the new arrangements.

The Secretary of State makes further recommendations concerning the alternative arrangements model which echo the increased emphasis on accountability to the electorate under the new Act. Recommendations propose that where a local authority does not choose for a plan or strategy to be subject to full council approval, that the plan or strategy in question be subject to approval by *elected* members within the local authority, and goes on to suggest that where the full council can delegate to any policy committee freedom to make 'in year' modifications without having to seek full council approval for those modifications, that any such modification should be reported to the full council at the next available meeting.

In relation to the role of the council meeting, the DETR Guidance suggests that authorities consider whether decision-making could be enhanced by changing the frequency at which the full council meets, or by meeting more often at certain times of the year, and proposes that authorities examine how the structure and style of council meetings may need to change to allow for more debate, what arrangements will be necessary to enable open and informed debate, and how public participation can be encouraged.

1   The Green Paper *Moderninsing Local Government: Local Democracy and Community Leadership* (published by the DETR in February 1998, discussed in the House of Commons Library Research Paper *Cabinets, Committees and Elected Mayors* (Research Paper 98/38: 19/3/98) comments: 'The way local government currently operates, with its traditional committee structure, is inefficient and opaque. This committee system was designed over a century ago for a bygone age; it is no basis for modern local government'.
2   *Modernising Local Government: Local Democracy and Community Leadership*: 'But the story is not all bad. Many councils are already pushing at the boundaries of what is possible within the current legislative framework. They are trying innovative ways of involving the public in their decisions, adapting their committee structures to move away from the traditional functional structure and toward looking at strategic issues or devolving some matters to committees responsible for small parts of the overall council's area, for example'.
3   The Joint Committee established to consider the draft Local Government (Organisation and Standards) Bill published its report in August 1999, was not convinced that a separation of powers between executive and legislature was achievable. The Government's reply to this report, published in December 1999 (*Government Response to the Report of the Joint Committee on the Draft Local Government (Organisation and Standards) Bill* (Cm 4529)) was not persuaded that local authorities should be able to make new arrangements which did not entail a separation of powers.
4   *Modernising Local Government: Local Democracy and Community Leadership* (DETR, Feb 1998).

Further Development of Alternative Arrangements

Investment in the future of alternative arrangements

[6.9]
The Guidance acknowledges that in view of the developments concerning councillors role in local government, there is a need for members to have access to training and development opportunities to ensure that they can carry out their new roles effectively. Again, while much will depend upon the form of alternative arrangements adopted by individual authorities, clearly this is required in relation to the new scrutiny function. In view of its functions, overview and scrutiny committees need to be properly resourced and have effective support to function effectively.

Changing the local authority's member structures has consequential implications for the officer corps who will need to adapt in order support members more effectively and to deliver increasingly efficient and effective services.

Nowhere is this need more clear than in relation to the arrangements for overview and scrutiny committees. Local authorities require procedures to ensure that officers supporting decision-making bodies are not those supporting the overview and scrutiny committees, as there is a potential for conflict where overview and scrutiny committees will be questioning decision-makers' actions which will have been based on officers advice.

The Guidance recommends that local authorities develop appropriate conventions, setting out the roles, responsibilities and rights of officers and members and establishing the key principles governing officer/member relationships.

Developing and improving alternative arrangements

[6.10]
Once a local authority has passed a resolution under this section to operate alternative arrangements, they may not at any subsequent time cease to operate those arrangements unless the authority operates executive arrangements in place of those arrangements[1].

The Secretary of State may by Regulation make provision for or in connection with enabling a local authority which is operating alternative arrangements to operate alternative arrangements which differ from the existing alternative arrangements in any respect[2].

It is interesting to note that the Secretary of State may also by Regulation make provision for an authority to operate alternative arrangements in place of executive arrangements[3]. This enables the Secretary of State to make those 'alternative' models, presently available only to a limited number of smaller authorities, or alternatively available 'by default' to all local authorities should, over time, they prove in operation to be particularly effective.

1   LGA 2000, ss 33(4), (9), and 34 to 36.
2   LGA 2000, s 33(7).
3   LGA 2000, s 34(5), (6) and (9).

Alternative arrangements in Wales

[6.11]
In Wales, the fourth option now being considered by the Welsh Assembly is set out by the Local Authorities (Alternative Arrangements) (Wales) Regulations 2001[1] which came into force on 25 July 2001. This model envisages that the full committee[2] would be responsible for the policy framework as outlined above.

However, there are a number of significant differences with the English model, providing Welsh local authorities with greater flexibility in making decisions for themselves as to how they will operate:

- the committee of the council, called the Board, would be responsible for all council responsibilities bar judicial functions, such as licensing and planning;
- the Board would not be exempt from the political balance requirement and would have a maximum of 10 members – or 20% of the council[3];
- the Board could delegate to individual board members, sub-committees or area committees[4];
- in addition, there would be one principal scrutiny committee, where, again, there would be no membership crossover, and up to eight, but no less than three subject committees with the dual role of scrutiny and policy development.

1 SI 2001/2284.
2 For detail of limitations on which functions may be exercised by the full committee ('the Board') of a local authority, see regs 8 to 10 and Schs 1 to 4 of SI 2001/2284.
3 SI 2001/2284, reg 5(2).
4 SI 2001/2284, reg 13(*b*).

CHAPTER 7

Referendums, Mayoral Elections and Constitutions

Referendums

[7.1]
The conduct of referendums under the Local Government Act 2000 is regulated by the Local Authorities (Conduct of Referendums) (England) Regulations 2001[1] ('the referendum regulations'). These provisions relate both to the first mayoral referendums and subsequent referendums which occur when authorities propose to change their arrangements from one form of arrangement to another and either the original arrangements or the new proposals include an elected mayor.

Relevant provisions regarding publicity during the referendum are contained in Pt VII of the Political Parties Elections and Referendums Act 2000 and also the Code of Recommended Practice on Local Authority Publicity, Circular 20/88 (which was amended on 2 April 2001 to incorporate provisions in relation to referendums held under the Local Government Act 2000.)

The referendum regulations require a 'counting officer' to be responsible for exercising functions in relation to the conduct of the referendum. The counting officer must be the returning officer for elections in the local authority's area.

The DTLR has published (May 2001) a technical guide for counting officers and their staff on the conduct of referendums. The guide is endorsed by SOLACE and the Association of Electoral Administrators. It explains the referendum procedure, covering referendums taken alone, all-postal ballots and combined polls and includes some example forms and notices.

1   SI 2001/1298.

The referendum question

[7.2]
The wording of the referendum question is prescribed by the referendum regulations, and will read as follows[1]:

For a mayor and cabinet lead proposal

> 'Are you in favour of the proposal for [*insert name of local authority*] to be run in a new way, which includes a mayor who will be elected by

the voters of that [*borough, city, county, district*], to be in charge of the Council's services and to lead [*insert name of local authority*] and the community which it serves?'

For a mayor and council manager lead proposal

'Are you in favour of the proposal for [*insert name of local authority*] to be run in a new way, which includes a mayor who will be elected by the voters of that [*borough, city, county, district*], to lead [*insert name of local authority*] and the community which it serves?'

For Leader and Cabinet (for example, where proposing to move from a mayoral model to a leader and cabinet model)

'Are you in favour of the proposal for [*insert name of local authority*] to be run in a new way, which includes a councillor who will be elected by the councillors of [*insert name of local authority*], to lead the Council and the community which it serves?'

The persons entitled to vote in a local authority referendum are those:

- who would be entitled to vote as electors at an election of councillors within the authority's area; and
- are registered in the register of local government electors at an address within the local authority's area.

1   SI 2001/1298, regs 3, 9 and Sch 1.

Timetable

[7.3]
The referendum may not be held for two months after the proposals are sent to the Secretary of State[1]. The DTLR Guidance on *New Council Constitutions* further states that the referendum should be held within six months of sending the proposals to the Secretary of State.

The DTLR Guidance requires authorities to consult their returning officer about the date on which to hold a referendum, and to take into account any advice received from him or her.

1   LGA 2000, s 27(6).

Publicity for the referendum

[7.4]
Authorities must publish a public notice to contain specified information in at least one local newspaper as soon as reasonably practicable after the proposals have been sent in[1]. The public notice must contain:

- a statement that proposals have been sent to the Secretary of State;
- a description of the main features of the proposals and of the outline fall-back proposals;
- notice that a referendum will be held, the date on which it will be held, and the question to be asked in the referendum;
- where the authority have made a determination to hold an all-postal referendum, a statement that the votes in the referendum may be cast only by postal ballot, or, where no such determination has been made, that the referendum will be conducted in accordance with procedures similar to those used at local government elections;
- a statement of the referendum expenses limit that will apply in relation to the referendum, and the number of local government electors by reference to which that limit has been calculated;
- a statement of the address and times at which copy of the proposals, and of the local authority's outline fall-back proposals, may be inspected;
- a description of the procedures for obtaining a copy of the proposals and outline fall-back proposals;
- where appropriate, a statement that the referendum poll will be taken with another poll or polls (including details of that other poll or polls).

Authorities are permitted to include in the notice any other factual information relating to the proposals, the outline fall-back proposals, or the referendum itself. The information must be presented fairly, having regard to the Code of Recommended Practice on Local Authority Publicity.

Local authorities may, in practice, decide to combine the public notice with the notice of referendum required to be published under the Local Elections (Principal Areas) Rules 1986[2]. The Local Elections Rules require a notice of referendum to include additional information about applying for postal and proxy votes.

In order to comply with the referendum regulations, the public notice must be published between 55 and 28 days before the referendum (not including weekends or public holidays). A notice containing the information can be published earlier and in those circumstances the authority must publish a further notice, containing the same information, updated as necessary. The further notice must be published between 55 and 28 days before the referendum.

In publicising proposals, councils need to ensure that information about the poll is made widely available. Notwithstanding the consultation exercises undertaken, it is likely that the electorate will need much more information to adequately understand the options available. In addition to the newspaper notice described above, local authorities are required by the DTLR Guidance to consider other methods by which they might inform the public about the proposals (for example through displays, leaflets and on websites). Copies of the proposals must be available for inspection at the address and times specified in the notice and free of charge. Sufficient copies must be made available for those who wish to obtain them.

1   SI 2001/1298, reg 4.
2   SI 1986/2214.

Restriction on publicity during the referendum period

[7.5]
The Code of Recommended Practice on Local Authority Publicity states that:

> 'Local Authorities should ensure that any publicity about a referendum under Part II of the Local Government Act 2000 either prior to or during the referendum period is factually accurate and objective ... The publicity should not be capable of being perceived as seeking to influence public support for, or opposition to, the referendum proposals and should not associate support for, or opposition to, the proposals with any individual or group ...'

In the 28 days before the referendum (including weekends and public holidays), reg 5 of the referendum regulations places further restrictions on the ability of local authorities to produce material that relates to the referendum. In particular, the regulations do not permit any material that deals with any of the issues raised by the referendum, or that expresses support for, or opposition to, a particular answer to the referendum question, to be published by or on behalf of the local authority in the 28 day period, with the following exceptions:

- in response to specific requests for information;
- publication of press notices containing factual information, where the sole purpose of publication is to refute or correct any inaccuracy in material published by anyone other than the local authority;
- information relating to the arrangements for the poll at the referendum and encouraging participation.

During the final 28 day period, public debate on referendum issues should be conducted by individuals and groups in the political arena, without any further input from the local authority.

Maximising turnout

[7.6]
The DTLR Guidance indicates that local authorities should take all reasonable steps to maximise turnout at local referendums, and should ensure that, as far as possible, there are no barriers of conscience to voting in referendums, in particular in respect of the place, the day or in the period envisaged for the ballot.

With a view to researching ways to achieve a higher turnout in local polls, several pilot schemes were undertaken for an all-postal ballot when conducting local elections throughout 2000. All of the pilot schemes reported a significant increase in the electoral turnout. The high rates of increased turnout were only experienced in the pilot wards, indicating that this outcome was directly attributable to the method of voting.

Where further evaluation of the schemes was conducted, indications were that electors were generally highly satisfied with voting by post. Some of the reports give consideration to the impact of the increase in turnout to parties' respective share of the vote, the conclusion being that increasing turnout had remarkably little effect on vote share or outcome of the election.

The all-postal ballot pilots do indicate that there is a significant increase in cost for this method of voting. The increase in costs varied among the pilot authorities.

Further information on the evaluation of the pilot schemes is available for consideration at: www.homeoffice.gov.uk/ccpd/cnu/evalcont.htm

However, notwithstanding the results of the pilot research, at the time of writing three all postal ballot referendums have taken place in respect of proposals under the Local Government Act 2000 and the turnout has been very low[1]. The only other mayoral referendum that has been conducted was combined with the general election and achieved a much higher turnout of 64%[2].

1   In Watford, the turnout was 25%, in both Cheltenham and Gloucester it was 33%.
2   The outcome of the referendums at Cheltenham, Gloucester and Berwick-upon-Tweed was a 'No' vote in respect of proposals for a mayor and cabinet. In Watford, the vote was a 'Yes' vote.

Referendum expenses

[7.7]
Regulation 6 of the referendum regulations specifies a referendum expenses limit. This limit is a total of £2,000, plus 5p per elector. This limit applies to any expenses incurred by or on behalf of an individual or body for the purpose of promoting or securing a particular result in the referendum. When designing this formula, the government has chosen not to adopt the complex rules of the Political Parties, Elections and Referendums Act on what constitutes a campaign group. The formula is therefore a simpler one but leaves open the interpretation of when an individual is considered to be campaigning on behalf of another or for a body. Campaigners will therefore need to be mindful of whether they are campaigning on behalf of another individual or body and to apply the expenses limit accordingly. They will need to be mindful of the penalties (see below) and feel able to justify the approach taken if they are subsequently challenged.

Local authorities will wish to ensure that their members and those involved in campaigns are aware of the application of the expenses limit and to give guidance on when a campaign will be considered to be an individual one or as part of a body. To help the counting officer keep track of expenses, it may be sensible to invite campaigners to 'declare' their campaign to the counting officer and s/he will then be in a position to liaise with those individuals or bodies as to their expenses. One incentive for co-ordinating the campaign with the counting officer in this way could be the offer of tickets for the count. Those involved must also be clear that the limit begins to apply from the date that the proposals are sent to the Secretary of State (not the date that Notices are published as one might have expected from the normal electoral process). This is much earlier than some would imagine and invites authorities to get their guidance out as soon as possible after proposals are sent in.

A lists of items included as referendum expenses is set out in Sch 2 of the referendum regulations and includes the following (to the extent that they relate to the referendum):

- advertising of any nature;
- unsolicited material addressed to electors (by name or to households);
- any material which deals with any of the issues raised by the referendum, or argues for or against a particular answer to the referendum question;
- market research or canvassing conducted for the purpose of ascertaining voting intentions;
- the provision of any service or facilities in connection with press conferences or other dealings with the media.

Under reg 6(3) of the referendum regulations where any referendum expenses are incurred in excess of the limit, a person who knew or reasonably ought to have known that that limit would be exceeded, or who without reasonable excuse, authorises another person to exceed that limit, is guilty of an offence punishable by fine or imprisonment.

Result of the referendum

[7.8]
The result of the referendum is binding[1]. If the referendum approves the proposals they must be implemented in accordance with the timetable included in the proposals. If the proposals are rejected, they must not be implemented and the council will need to consult on, draw up and implement detailed fall-back proposals.

The referendum result can be challenged by a referendum petition on the grounds that the result was not in accordance with the votes cast or was void due to corruption.

1   LGA 2000, s 27(7) and (8).

Mayoral Elections

[7.9]
Following a referendum, if the vote supports a mayoral model, or at the end of the term of office of the elected mayor, a mayoral election will be held. The Local Government (Elected Mayors) (Elections, Terms of Office and Casual Vacancies) (England) Regulations 2001[1] set out the timing for the elections for the return of elected mayors.

The regulations require authorities to wait three months after the referendum before holding the mayoral election and then to hold the election on either the first Thursday in the next May or the third Thursday in the next October – whichever is sooner[2]. As the current regulations were not made in time for an October election in 2001, the first mayoral elections will take place on Thursday 2 May 2002.

The second mayoral election cannot take place within 23 months of the first. Subject to the 23 month minimum term, for metropolitan councils or councils who elect by thirds, the second election is to be held in the gap year, that is on the ordinary election day in the year when there is no election[3].

For other councils, the second election is to be held on the ordinary election day in any year not later than the fifth year after the first election (for councils who elect their first mayor in May) or the sixth year (for councils who elect their first mayor in October).

This means that the first term of office for the mayor could range from two to five-and-a-half years.

The normal term of office for an elected mayor will be four years[4] and subsequent elections will be held on the ordinary election day in every fourth year.

Where a referendum is held in respect of proposals to change the arrangements (see Chapter 4 above for details of changing arrangements), any subsequent mayoral election must take place either on the normal election day or the next third Thursday in October if the normal election day is within three months of the referendum.

The DTLR Guidance advises that the voting system for elected mayors will be the supplementary vote system:

> 'Under this system, voters cast first and second preference votes. After counting all of the first preference votes, all but the top two candidates are eliminated. Any of the eliminated candidates' second preference votes cast for the remaining candidates are added to those totals, and the one with the most votes is elected as elected mayor'[5].

The rules for mayoral elections have not yet been made but it is intended that they will cover nominations, election expenses and circumstances when polls should be taken together to maximise turnout.

1   SI 2001/2544.
2   SI 2001/2544, reg 2.
3   LGA 1972, s 7(2) and (8).
4   LGA 2000, s 39(6).
5   Paragraph 14.13 of the DTLR Guidance *New Council Constitutions*.

Constitutions

[7.10]
Authorities are required by the Local Government Act 2000 to prepare and update a 'constitution'[1]. This applies equally to councils who are operating executive and alternative arrangements. The constitution must include standing orders and the code of conduct for members. In addition, the Local Government Act 2000 (Constitutions) (England) Direction 2000 gives an A-to-Z list of what must be covered in the constitution. A copy of the Direction is set out at Division VI – Appendix 4 below for ease of reference as the starting-point for authorities when preparing and reviewing their constitutions.

The constitution must be made available on request (for a reasonable fee) and for inspection at the authority's principal office, and widely available to the public, for example, through libraries and websites[2]. The DTLR Guidance requires copies of the Guidance to be available in a range of formats and languages. There is no requirement to send the constitution to the Secretary of State as, or along with, the authority's proposals for new decision-making arrangements.

The aim of the constitution, as described in the DTLR Guidance, is to enable anyone who has dealings with the authority to work out who is responsible for the issue they are interested in and how they make representations. It must therefore be an accessible document which is clear, for example, about the delegations and where public representations can take place. Authorities will already have documented many of the matters that are required to be in the constitution under their old systems. The key change with the new arrangements will be for there to be an overriding document which collates all the relevant information in one place, with a clear explanation and summary of how the council is organised and makes its decisions.

In order to guide authorities in the direction of a 'single coherent document' the government has produced examples of new constitutions ('modular constitutions') for authorities to use as a template or for reference. The document *Modular Constitutions for English Local Authorities* sets out different options for each of the different form of decision-making structure available[3].

Several councils have completed their new constitutions, in particular, where authorities are adopting the Leader and Cabinet model and have been piloting those arrangements for some time. Examples of how these constitutions have been put together include that of Telford and Wrekin District Council, whose constitution is available on their website and is a good example of an accessible document which also appears to meet the statutory requirements[4].

1   LGA 2000, s 37(1).
2   LGA 2000, s 37(2) and (3); para 10.4 of the DTLR Guidance.
3   The document is available on the DTLR website: www.detr.gov.uk.
4   http://www.telford.gov.uk.

CHAPTER 8
Modernising Elections

Introduction

[8.1]
Electoral reform for local government is now on the agenda. The adoption of new voting systems for the election of the Scottish Parliament, the Welsh Assembly and members of the European Parliament has already established this principle in national elections. The use of alternative systems for the election of the Mayor and Assembly of London has introduced the principle into local elections. The probability of change in Scotland so that future elections are fought under Proportional Representation confronts England and Wales with the same possibility.

Local government has experienced a significant period of change represented by the Local Government White Paper in 1998, the Local Government Act 1999 and the Local Government Act 2000. Local authorities have been pressed to deliver Best Value in their services, to reform their political management structures and to represent their local communities, in particular, to increase turnout in local elections.

Process of Modernisation

[8.2]
Before the year 2000, the principal legislation was the Representation of the People Act 1983 ('the 1983 Act').

The 1983 Act was a consolidation of legislation dating back to the nineteenth century and its general thrust, and a good deal of the detail, dated from 1883. No one can doubt that things have changed since 1883 and the year 2000 saw the introduction of new legislation with aims to 'modernise' the electoral system to one that is appropriate for the twenty-first century.

The 1983 Act is still the main piece of legislation. However, it is now supported and in some part changed by the Local Government Act 2000, the Representation of the People Act 2000 and the Political Parties Elections and Referendums Act 2000.

In brief, these Acts have respectively introduced new provisions for directly elected mayors and new election cycles, new electoral procedures in relation to registration, absent voting and pilot election schemes and an electoral commission. This Commission will, in particular, assume the functions of the Local Government Boundary Commission. It will report on the conduct of elections and referendums and advise the Government on any necessary changes to the law. It will also take over a number of functions from the Home Office and act as a general reference point for advice, and on the conduct of elections and referendums.

Electoral Changes

Election schemes

[8.3]
Prior to the Local Government Act 2000, the pattern of elections to local authorities varied across England and Wales. Some Councils held 'all out' elections once every four years, others held 'annual elections' whereby a third of members were elected in each of three years out of four.

In the government's White Paper, *Modern Local Government: In Touch with the People 11*, it was proposed that elections by thirds should become the standard pattern for all Unitary Councils including London Boroughs, and for two-tier areas, it was proposed that both district and county councils would elect by halves in alternate years.

For Wales, the Welsh White Paper, *Modernising Local Government in Wales: Local Voices 12*, proposed giving the National Assembly of Wales a power to determine the frequency of elections for principal Councils and to rationalise the timing of electoral cycles for all local authorities in Wales.

The White Paper's recommendations were incorporated into Pt IV of the Local Government Act 2000. Part IV gives a power to the Secretary of State to alter, by order, the frequency of elections to local authorities and the year in which they are held.

Section 85 of the Local Government Act 2000 defines the three different schemes of elections that may be applied to principal councils.

The schemes are:

(1)   all-out elections with the whole council being elected once every four years;
(2)   elections by halves, with half the councillors being elected every other year;
(3)   elections by thirds, with one third of the councillors being elected each year for three years out of four.

In each case, councillors have a four year term of office.

Under s 86 of the Local Government Act 2000, the Secretary of State can specify by order:

(1)   that a particular scheme of elections should apply to a principal council;
(2)   the year or years in which elections should be held;
(3)   the wards electoral divisions and councillors that may be effected;

(4)   the method to be used for identifying the electoral divisions, wards and councillors; and

(5)   the principal councils to propose to the Secretary of State methods for identifying electoral divisions, wards and councillors.

Under s 87 of the LGA 2000, the Secretary of State can change, by order the years in which elections take place for any local authority but not the scheme or frequency of elections.

Further orders can be made under s 88 of the LGA 2000.

Mayoral Elections

[8.4]
The Local Government Act 2000 sets out the framework for electing mayors.

An elected Mayor

[8.5]
Section 39 of the LGA 2000 provides that an 'elected mayor' means an individual elected to that post by the local government electors in the authority's area.

The normal term of office for an elected mayor is four years unless as otherwise provided for in regulations made by the Secretary of State under s 41 of the LGA 2000.

An elected mayor is prohibited from being a councillor in the same authority (s 40) and sub-s (1) provides that if anyone stands for election to be and is elected as both the elected mayor and as councillor in the same authority in elections held at the same time, he or she cannot be appointed as councillor, and a vacancy will arise in the office of councillor. Likewise, sub-s (2) provides that where the election for the elected mayor is not held at the same time as elections for councillors and a sitting councillor is elected as mayor, a vacancy shall arise in the office of councillor.

The Secretary of State is given the power under s 41 to make regulations providing for the dates, years, and intervals at which elections for elected mayors can take place; for example, to provide for elections which are in accordance with the different electoral cycles of local authorities and can allow for an initial term of office to be more or less than four years to bring the mayoral electoral cycle in line with the named electoral cycle.

Methods for electing a Mayor

[8.6]
Section 42 and Sch 2 describe the method for electing a mayor.

There are two methods. If there are less than three candidates, each person entitled to vote has one vote to be given to the voter's first preference and the simple majority system is used. If there are three or more candidates, each person entitled to vote has two votes and the supplementary vote (SV) system is used.

The SV system

[8.7]
Under the SV system, the elector has two votes – for first and second preference.

Schedule 2 of the Act specifies the procedure. If any candidate receives more than half of the first preference votes cast, he or she is returned as elected mayor. If there is no candidate with an overall majority of first preference votes, the two candidates who received the greatest number of first preference votes remain in the contest. If, by reason, of an equality of first preference votes, three or more candidates are qualified to remain the contest by receiving the greatest number of first preference votes, all of them remain in the contest. All other candidates are eliminated from the contest. The number of second preference votes given for each of the candidates remaining in the contest by voters who did not given their first preference vote to any of those candidates is ascertained and then added to the number of first preference votes of each candidate to give the total number of preference votes. The candidate with the greatest total number of preference votes is returned as elected mayor.

Regulations

[8.8]
Under s 44, the Secretary of State can make regulations regarding the conduct of elections for elected mayors and the questioning of such elections and the consequences of irregularities. Such regulations may make provision about:

- the registration of electors,
- disregarding alterations in a register of electors,
- the limitation of election expenses (and the creation of criminal offences in connection with the limitation of such expenses),
- the combination of polls at elections for the return of elected mayors and other elections (including elections for the return of elected executive members),
- the combination of polls at elections for the return of elected executive members and other elections (including elections for the return of elected mayors),

and may apply, incorporate or modify any provisions under the Representation of the People Acts relating to the conduct of elections.

Rolling Registration and Absent Voting

[8.9]
The Representation of the People Act 2000 changed electoral procedures in relation to electoral registration and absent voting.

Background to the Representation of the People Act 2000

[8.10]
Before the Representation of the People Act 2000, the old method of compiling the register was that the register would be in force from 16 February for a year, the qualifying date was 10 October, an annual canvass took place each autumn, a draft register was available from 28 November, additions to the published register were made on a monthly basis, and no amendments or deletions were allowed.

The Working Party on Electoral Procedures (which contained representation from the main political parties, local government and electoral administrators) was set up in 1998 and its terms of reference required it to consider recommendations for changes to electoral practice. Its recommendations were published on 19 October 1999 in the House of Commons Official Report.

The recommendations it made included:

- that the annual register should be replaced with a system that would allow continuous or 'rolling registration' which would enable people to be added to (and deleted from) the electoral register at any time of the year rather than making registration contingent on residence on a single annual qualifying date;
- that registration under a rolling register should continue to include provision for an annual audit (including a canvass) but electors should be able to make a claim for their details to be transferred between registers on satisfactory proof of a change of address. Registration officers should be able to make deletions from the register where, for example, they are satisfied that an elector has made a claim to transfer registration out of the area or has died;
- that there should be changes to make it easier for the homeless, remand prisoners, people in mental institutions and service personnel to register. It recommended that remand prisoners should be entitled to register by way of a 'declaration of locality', the registration address being a previous address or the remand institution in which he or she was held;
- that those in mental institutions, but not those detained because of criminal acts, should also be entitled to register by way of a 'declaration of locality' this time in respect of the institution in which they were resident at or at the address they would otherwise be living. For members of the Armed Forces and their families it recommended that they should be able to register at their home address rather than solely by means of a service declaration;
- with regard to absent voting, that applications not on the standard form or made by fax should be acceptable, that an application for an absent

vote at a particular election should apply to all elections on the same day and that the grounds for late applications should be widened to include family bereavement, illness, or employment commitments;

- that postal votes should be able to be returned to a polling station and be treated as valid even if not returned in the official envelope, or if the ballot paper and the declaration of identity were returned separately; and
- that instead of limiting the availability of postal votes to certain requirements, all postal votes should be issued on demand.

1   (col WA 434).

The Representation of the People Act 2000 ('the Act')

[8.11]
Following the Working Party's recommendations, the Act introduced a new system of electoral registration or 'rolling registration' and new provisions for absent voting.

Rolling registration

[8.12]
In brief, the Act introduced a 'rolling register'.

Section 1 replaces the old ss 1, 2 and 4 of the Representation of the People Act 1983, ('the 1983 Act').

The old ss 1 and 2 of the 1983 Act set out who was entitled to vote but by reference to a single annual qualifying date and s 4 set that date to be 10 October. Section 1(1) of the Act (which inserts the replacement ss 1 and 2 of the 1983 Act) sets out the requirements for voting in parliamentary and local government elections which apart from re-enacting prohibitions against double voting, legal capacity, voting age and nationality allows a person who is registered in the register of parliamentary electors for that constituency or on the register of local government electors for that area on the date of the poll to vote.

Section 1(2) (which inserts the replacement s 4 of the 1983 Act) deals with entitlement to registration whereby a person is entitled to be registered if on the relevant date (the date on which an application for registration is made or the date on which a declaration of locality or a service declaration is made), he or she is resident in the constituency or local government area, is not subject to a legal incapacity, meets the nationality requirement and is of voting age or will shortly reach voting age (the entry on the register shall give the date voting age is attained).

The effect of s 1 is therefore that a person may be eligible to be registered as an elector at any time in the year rather than by reference to the single annual qualifying vote of old.

Section 2 inserts a new s 3A into the 1983 Act which disenfranchises offenders detained in mental hospitals as a result of committing a criminal offence.

[8.13]
Residence for the purposes of registration

Section 3 of the Act inserts a new s 5 into the 1983 Act and sets out the factors which registration officers must take into account when considering whether a person should be treated as resident. Sub-section (2) provides that a person who is staying somewhere other than on a permanent basis may be regarded as resident if he does not have a home elsewhere but not resident if he does have a home elsewhere. Residence is not taken as being interrupted by any absence due to employment or education commitments provided that absence is not more than six months or provided that the dwelling serves as a permanent place of residence and he or she would be in actual residence there but for his or her absence due to employment.

Section 4 of the Act replaces s 7 of the 1983 Act and enables those who are in mental institutions, other than those held as a result of a criminal activity, to register in respect of the institution if the period he or she is likely to spend there is sufficient for him to be regarded as resident and such registrations last for a maximum of 12 months.

Section 5 of the Act inserts a new s 7A into the 1983 Act and allows remand prisoners to register in respect of the remand establishment in which they are held if the period he is likely to spend there is sufficient for him to be regarded as resident up to a maximum of 12 months.

Section 6 of the Act inserts a new s 7B into the 1983 Act regarding declarations of local connection which can be made by those to whom s 7 (those in mental institutions) and s 7A (those remanded in custody) applies, and homeless persons. The address required in connection with a declaration of local connection is the address where he or she would be residing if he were not a patient in a mental institution or detained in custody or, if he or she cannot give such an address, an address in the United Kingdom at which he or she has resided. In the case of a homeless person, the address required is the address of, or which is nearest to, a place in the United Kingdom where he or she commonly spends a substantial part of his time (whether during the day or at night).

A declaration of locality is cancelled after 12 months and that person is removed from the electoral register unless the declaration is renewed.

Therefore people can be added to or deleted from the register at any time of the year.

[8.14]
The Representation of the People (England and Wales) Regulations 2001, SI 2001/341

The Act makes a large number of alterations to Sch 2 to the 1983 Act. This Schedule sets out the provisions which may be contained in Regulations as to registration etc. The new provisions, many of which are contained in the Representation of the People (England and Wales) Regulations 2001[1] include:

- a duty to maintain an electoral register, rather than producing one annually;

- an obligation on the registration officer to carry out an annual canvass;
- detailed provisions enabling the registration officer to deal with applications for registration, including the power to determine objections;
- the power for the registration officer to remove names from the register;
- a requirement for the registration officer to publish the revised versions of his registers by 1 December (or such later date as might be provided); and
- powers to alter the register.

Other provisions include:

- the register effective from 16 February 2001;
- additions/deletions/amendments made to the register at any time;
- monthly updates (the Notice of Alteration) produced on the first working day of each month;
- the reference date of 15 October replacing the previous qualifying date;
- two versions of the register – the complete register for electoral purposes of public inspection and credit referencing and the edited register for sale (these provisions are not due to be introduced until Autumn 2002);
- free supply of register and monthly updates to various specified bodies.

Schedule 1 to the 1983 Act is amended so that returning officers will be under an obligation to provide the partially sighted with large versions of the ballot paper and prescribed devices for enabling blind or partially sighted voters to vote without the need for assistance. The rules are also altered so as to allow those with disabilities other than blindness to be assisted by a companion in casting their vote.

1   SI 2001/341.

Absent voting

[8.15]
Under the old system, absent votes are available to people who are ill, have a physical disability, work away from home or are away on holiday when an election is held.

Relatively few people (on average under 2%) used this facility and evidence showed that the public found the system hard to understand. However, figures showed that when people did apply for a postal vote over 60% actually used it, nearly double the normal turnout rate for a local election.

Now, under s 12 of the Act, postal voting is available on demand. Sections 5 to 9 of the 1985 Act are replaced by Sch 4 to the 2000 Act. Much of those sections are the same, however, there is now no reason required for a postal vote. The main requirement will now be that the voter is registered in the register of electors. The forms will now only include provision for name, registered address, ballot paper address, signature, date and period for which postal vote is required. There is a tighter timescale. The deadline for new applications is now six working days before election and the deadline to cancel existing postal votes is 11 working days before election. Candidates and election agents are not now allowed to attend the issue of postal votes. Postal votes can now be sent out of the country.

Proxy voting

[8.16]
The Act has not changed the method for applying for a proxy vote, however, the dead-line for new applications is now six working days before the election instead of 11 days.

Alternative Forms of Voting

[8.17]
The electoral procedures that are used now remain largely unchanged over the last 100 years despite advances in technology and communications. The electoral system is appearing increasingly antiquated and not relevant to today's society. Turnout at elections is low and is on the decrease. This is recognised by both the government and councils up and down the country. Indeed, some councils are beginning to pioneer new ways of voting so as to make them more relevant and accessible to local people and therefore to increase turnout.

A two-way approach has been used. First, by using whatever flexibility there is within the existing rules to make voting literature more helpful and informative, and secondly by experimenting with new ways of voting, adapting the system and procedures to reflect modern lifestyles and trying to make voting processes more convenient and accessible to the electorate.

Section 10 of the Act enables local authorities to submit schemes for providing different electoral arrangements from those set down in the Act in terms of when, where, and how voting at elections is to take place, how the votes cast at the elections are to be counted, and the sending by candidates of elections communications free of charge. Local authorities were invited to apply for permission to pilot new schemes at the May 2000 local elections. The schemes had to be approved by order of the Secretary of State and once the election had taken place under the new arrangements, the pilot local authorities had to send to the Secretary of State a report assessing the scheme's success or otherwise including a statement as to:

(1)   whether the local authority is of the opinion that the turnout of voters was higher than usual;
(2)   whether voters found the procedures easy to use;
(3)   whether the procedures led to an increase in electoral offences and malpractice; and
(4)   whether the procedures led to any increase in expenditure.

A total of 44 authorities applied and 32 had their applications approved. Those 32 authorities ran a total of 38 pilot schemes.

Key findings

[8.18]
Postal voting

It is accepted that voters cannot always get to the polling station because of various factors such as work, holidays, emergencies etc.

One way to help such voters to allow them to cast their vote by post. In other countries where this is facilitated, greater numbers of voters participate than those required to attend polling stations.

Relatively few people (on average under 2%) use this facility and there is evidence indicating that the public finds this system difficult to understand.

[8.19]
All postal votes

This was confirmed in the May 2000 pilots, when seven councils ran all-postal ballots in their local elections and, for most, there was a 50% or greater turnout. Also, figures show that turnout more than doubled where no declaration of identity was required.

[8.20]
Postal votes on demand

Section 12 of the Act provides that all voters can now apply for a postal vote on demand without any explanation or criteria. In the May 2000 pilots, four authorities applied this. However, the results were inconclusive as in two cases, this increased turnout and in the other two, it did not. It was found that publicity for the scheme and dispensing with the statutory declaration of identity did increase turnout, however, overall, it was found that simply introducing postal voting on demand was unlikely to increase turnout.

However, some councils have written to their electorate inviting them to apply for a postal vote and some have launched campaigns to encourage the electorate to take up postal votes.

Most of those who voted by post said that they found the system easy to understand and use and would like to use it again.

[8.21]
Voting over more than one day

An alternative way of ensuring people vote is to extend the polling day. Fifteen councils ran early voting pilots at the May 2000 elections and extended voting over a few days.

Results show that between 0.4% and 3.7% of electors used the facility, with a majority of these saying that they were habitual local election voters. Most authorities said that they saw this as a convenience to electors rather than as a means of boosting turnout and there was evidence that electors were more inclined to use conveniently located polling stations.

[8.22]
Extending polling hours and changing the day of polling

Traditionally, Thursday has been the polling day. When 91% of working people work on weekdays this is probably not the most convenient day.

Weekend voting has been the norm in Europe for many years, and for the May 2000 elections, some authorities changed the polling day from Thursday to a day at the weekend.

Early and weekend voting was praised for convenience and novelty. In one authority, 25% of those who used the system said that they would not otherwise have voted. In another authority it was found that just over one-third of those voting during extended hours said that they would have been unlikely to do so in normal hours. However, the impact of the pilots on overall turnout appeared to be less than 1% overall.

[8.23]
Alternative venues

Whilst the traditional polling stations are located in schools or community halls, some councils have placed polling stations in supermarkets, shops, shopping centres and local libraries.

[8.24]
Taking the vote to the voters

Some voters find it difficult to vote in person. Some councils have taken the vote to the people. For example, Norwich supplied equipped vehicles with polling station teams to sheltered housing schemes, care homes, day centres and hospitals, and in Windsor and Maidenhead, a touring polling station was taken to various locations in two large rural wards. Electors using this system were found to be particularly appreciative and welcomed the sense of being able to be involved in the democratic process.

[8.25]
Electronic voting

Three of the May 2000 pilots involved electronic voting whereby touch screen facilities were provided at polling stations to record electors' votes and provide immediate results at the close of poll.

The majority of voters who used this system found it easy to use and claimed to prefer it to the traditional way.

[8.26]
Telephone voting (non-statutory elections)

Walsall, in collaboration with BT, allowed the electorate to vote for members of local community advisory committees by telephone, by issuing them with a polling card with a freephone number which invited simple yes/no answers.

[8.27]
Extending eligibility (non-statutory elections)

In Sheffield, people aged 15 and 16 were allowed, irrespective of nationality, to participate in a postal ballot to elect community representatives to a New Deal Partnership Board.

[8.28]
Alternative voting system

In the London Borough of Tower Hamlets, the single transferable vote was used in order to elect community representatives to the New Deal Partnership Board.

[8.29]
Electronic counting

In May 2000, two councils piloted electronic counting whereby votes are cast in the normal manner but are counted by machine. Some changes to the ballot paper are required to facilitate this, however results show that electronic counting is more accurate and quicker.

[8.30]
Electronic voting and counting

In three authorities votes were cast and counted electronically using a touch-screen voting machine. The verification of ballot papers appeared to be quicker and more accurate, voters reported few problems, however, a number of technical and logistical problems hampered the processing and counting of votes and the declaration of results and it would be very expensive for councils to introduce electronic voting and counting on a full cost basis.

Conclusions

[8.31]
MORI research conducted for the LGA (Encouraging People to vote: a MORI survey on people's attitudes to local elections – LGA 1998) revealed that of those who said they rarely vote in council elections:

* 56% would be more likely to vote if they could vote by telephone;
* 48% would be more likely to vote if they could vote by post;
* 47% would be more likely to vote if they could vote from home by digital TV/Internet; and
* 45% would be more likely to vote if there were polling stations at shopping centres.

More recent research shows that people would be more likely to vote electronically than doing many other things. The government is committed to the electronic delivery of services and its time for councils to now develop new voting procedures that reflect modern lifestyles.

The results of the May 2000 pilots show that turnout was noticeably higher than it might otherwise have been when votes were cast by post, that voters welcomed almost all the experiments and found them easy to understand and use, that there was no evidence of an increase in electoral fraud, and that all the new arrangements resulted in an increase in costs.

The Act allowed local authorities to try new ways of voting. The new Electoral Commission (to be established under the Political Parties, Elections and Referendums Act 2000) will have a role in encouraging awareness of electoral systems and advising the Home Office before any decisions are taken to roll-out successful pilots on a permanent basis. Under s 11 of the Act, the Secretary of State is entitled to make an order applying any scheme generally and on a permanent basis.

Best Value – Increasing Turnout at Local Government Elections

[8.32]

Elections are the prime way in which the political will of a community is expressed. Yet despite this, turnout at local government elections is on the decline and appears to be getting lower. In England and Wales, the turnout is one of the lowest in Europe. The average turnout in England from 1976 to 1996 was 41%. The 1999 election saw an average turnout of just 32% – with some areas achieving only 10% of eligible voters.

Although a higher turnout rate in most of the European countries can be explained by various factors such as proportional representation (which academics consider appears to add around 7% to turnout) and compulsory voting (as in Luxembourg, Italy and Belgium), it is clear that the low electoral turnout reflects an indifference to local democracy and the inability of local government to engage local people through the ballot box and effectively threatens the democratic legitimacy of local councils.

What causes low electoral turnout?

[8.33]
Political perception

Participation in local government elections is linked to voters' perceptions of whether or not it is worth voting – whether or not the local authority has the ability to make a difference. Local authorities' powers and abilities have been constrained over recent years by legislation, regulation, tight control over spending, and the transfer of functions to other bodies. In effect, local government's position and status in the community and its role in the governance of the country has been eroded. It needs to be restored by strengthening its position, role and capabilities within the local community.

Changing the electoral process

[8.34]
Proposals to do this, and to return greater freedom to raise and spend money locally, will, in the longer term, have a positive effect on participation and turnout at local government elections. However, these changes will take time to feed through and, in the meantime, voting systems and procedures will need to be made more accessible and user friendly to local people.

The Representation of the People Act 2000 ('the Act') contains certain provisions which address some of the problems that cause low electoral turnout.

Research shows that although many local authorities strive to improve the voting process, less than 50% of responding authorities have formally discussed improvements to their electoral registration process or improving electoral turnout over the last five years. Some authorities also appeared to be reluctant to pursue initiatives designed to encourage people to vote, believing that this was the role of the political parties. The Local Government Association considered that as part of a local authority's leadership role, it should increase its profile and should encourage the development of a healthy local democracy.

The Act

[8.35]
Many of the initiatives introduced by the Act reflect the recommendations of the Home Office Working Party on Electoral Procedures.

Good practice

[8.36]
All authorities should continue to review current procedures. The report published by DETR *Turnout at Local Government Elections – Influences on Levels of Voter Registration and Electoral Participation* contained some good practice initiatives designed to maximise registration such as designing a Form A which is pre-printed, bar coded and colour coded, using personal canvassers to produce the electoral register, training new canvassers, splitting the canvass areas into smaller units, using calling cards, setting up commission type objectives for canvassers, using telephones to contact non-responding households, using prize draws to encourage registration, using reminder/threatening letters, considering prosecuting non-responders, targeting students via advertising and Student Unions, working with other departments (eg council tax and housing), working in a consortia of authorities to try and increase registration and reviewing the policy of carrying names forward in the register.

Examples of good practice

[8.37]
Improving Public Response to Electoral Registration Canvass

For example, Newcastle City Council introduced a package of initiatives to improve the public response to the electoral registration canvass, including paying benefits to canvassers, extending the canvass, targeting areas with large ethnic minority communities, displaying posters and targeting students. Liverpool City Council ran a competition to reward the early return of Form A. Brighton & Hove City Council carried out a similar competition last year.

[8.38]
Absent votes

Most councils provide information about absent voting on Form A. There are other ways to increase awareness and the use of absent votes including:

(a)   inserting information about absent voting on Form A or on a leaflet delivered with Form A;

(b)   sending information about absent voting to residential homes, hospitals, hostels, universities and other such institutions;

(c)   inserting information about postal voting on poll cards and sending out poll cards earlier to allow more time to apply for an absent vote;

(d)   advertising the absent vote function by any other means.

West Berkshire Council issued poll cards in a larger format with an absent voting application form on the reverse and issued them earlier to allow for application. It also included information about absent voting on Form A. The same approach has been made by Basingstoke and Deane Borough Council who recorded an increase in postal voting. Epsom and Ewell Borough Council advertised the absent vote facility in all travel agents in the Borough to remind those going away on holiday to register as absent voters. Likewise the Borough of Charnwood placed an advertisement in the Loughborough University Students Union magazine

[8.39]
Poll cards and polling stations

At present, every eligible elector receives a personal poll card delivered to their registered address. This notifies registered electors about the date of the election and voting arrangements at their polling station.

Local authorities can review whether poll cards are hand delivered or posted, consider changing the text and appearance of the poll card, provide ramps and booths for the disabled at all polling stations and keep the location of polling places and stations under review.

Cambridge City Council reviewed the accessibility of all polling stations and installed several permanent large ramps as well as installing lower level polling booths for wheelchair users, providing magnifying glasses for each station to help voters who have impaired vision and updated the polling station checklist to ensure access issues are covered. Penwith District Council and Brighton & Hove City Council have cited polling stations in supermarkets.

[8.40]
Encouraging voting

As well as testing new voting procedures, all local authorities can take a number of steps to make the voting process more user-friendly and accessible and to encourage voting.

Advertising

Almost all local authorities advertise local elections in local newspapers, council newspapers and posters. Additionally, around 40% use local radio and around 25% leaflet every household.

New methods

Other initiatives authorities can undertake include exploring new ways to advertise an election (for example, the council website), leafleting every household providing information on the election and encouraging them to use their vote, asking local media to provide information on the election and encouraging them to use their vote, asking local media to provide information about the election, give presentations to schools about elections, have electoral services stalls at shows and exhibitions, work in a consortia of authorities to try to increase turnout and lastly, consult the public to discover the reasons for not voting in elections.

The City of Nottingham in May 2000 used its website for elections information such as information on the electoral register, first time voting, the council's citizen week, election results, lists of councillors and ward information.

Arun District Council leafleted homes in the district urging people to vote. This was part of the council's 'Make Your Mark Campaign' to raise awareness of local elections. Wycombe District Council ran an awareness campaign targeted at attainers, by sending a birthday card to each 18-year-old reminding them to vote. York City Council co-ordinated a consortium of over thirty local authorities to fund a TV campaign to promote voter turnout.

[8.41]
Issues of local importance

Brighton & Hove City Council held a referendum on the controversial siting of a new football stadium in the area in 1999 at the same time as local elections – turnout increased showing how local issues can be a factor in enhancing turnout.

Conclusion

[8.42]
Local authorities can take responsibility for increasing turnout by regularly reviewing the electoral registration processes in the light of good practice, considering what steps can be taken to encourage turnout in the light of good practice, setting realistic local targets for turnout at the next local elections, developing a strategy to increase turnout, and considering making an application to pilot new voting procedures at the next local elections.

The reasons for low turnout at elections in this country are varied and complex. Effective competition between the parties, a sense among the electorate that local authorities have the powers and freedoms to make a difference and media coverage of local issues and politics all play a part. However, new electoral arrangements brought about by the LGA 2000, and the RPA 2000 have a definite part to play.

The House of Commons Home Affairs Committee noted:

> 'it is clear that the present election procedures are not designed for the end of the twentieth and beginning of the twenty-first centuries. New technology has opened up possibilities which did not exist before'.

Councils are at the forefront of developing new systems and strategies with rolling registration, alternative forms of voting and Best Value in line with the programme for modernising elections set up by the new legislation and these systems can be developed and adapted to today's society and lifestyle so that today's voters and those of the future will be persuaded to take voting seriously and to take a part in forming local democracy.

DIVISION II
Ethical Standards

CHAPTER 9
What is meant by Ethics and Ethical Standards?

Background

[9.1]
The issue of ethics and standards in local government is not a new one, although the emphasis given to it by the Local Government Act 2000 has undoubtedly raised its profile within all Councils.

Although not by any means the first reference to ethics or ethical issues, the Widdicombe Committee on the Conduct of Local Authority Business[1] considered carefully the 1975 National Code of Local Government Conduct. This Code derived from the Redcliffe-Maud Committee on Local Government Rules of Conduct[2] and came to the view that it was in need of review. The report stated:

> 'The 1975 National Code . . . was issued in the wake of scandals where Councillors had been motivated by personal gain. As such it is concerned with conflicts between 'public duty' and 'private interest'. This dichotomy does not recognise the potential conflict between public duty and loyalties to sectional interests that are not motivated by private gain. There is nothing inherently improper in loyalties of this kind. They may of themselves by altruistic (eg loyalty to a voluntary body) and that may in practice coincide with the wider community interest. The problem arises where outside sectional loyalties are allowed to dictate Council policy as if they were co-terminus with the community interest'[3].

Widdicombe made a number of recommendations in respect of the conduct of local authority business, but in respect of the National Code of Local Government Conduct, suggested that it should be given statutory status, that new Councillors should declare upon accepting office that they would be guided by it, and that it should be amended to make it clear that:

- the Councillors hold office by virtue of the law and must act within the law; and
- sectional loyalties as well as private gain may create conflicts with Councillors' public duties[4].

Following Widdicombe, a review of the 1975 National Code was carried out by a joint working group representing the government departments concerned and the local authority associations. As a result, a Department of the Environment Circular[5] was issued which incorporates as its Annex the National Code of Local Government Conduct, this being a revised version of the 1975 Code. Until local authorities adopt the new Local Code of Conduct for Members, deriving from the Model Code approved by Parliament in accordance with the Local Government Act 2000, the 1990 National Code forms the backbone of any assessment of ethics and standards by Members in local government.

1   Cmnd 9797.
2   Cmnd 5636.
3   Paragraph 6.10.
4   Paragraphs 6.15, 6.16 and 6.23.
5   The National Code of Local Government Conduct (DoE 8/90); set out at Div VI – App 13 below.

The New Framework

[9.2]

The germination of the new Ethical Framework commenced with the Nolan Committee on Standards in Public Life, which was established in 1994 to consider the standards of conduct in public life (it later became the Neill Committee following the retirement of Lord Nolan). It was the Third Report, published in July 1997[1] which dealt with the Standards of Conduct in Local Government. Introducing the report, Lord Nolan said:

> 'What we have found elsewhere in our studies of public life holds good for local government. Despite instances of corruption and misbehaviour, the vast majority of councillors and officers observe high standards of conduct. The number of people who have used their position in local government for their own ends is small compared with the vast majority who genuinely wish to serve their community. We have been impressed by the positive attitude which local councillors and officers have taken to our inquiry and their awareness that high ethical standards are critical to maintain public confidence in local government'.

The government responded by issuing a consultation paper, *Modernising Local Government: A New Ethical Framework* in April 1998. The proposals were also summarised the White Paper *Modern Government – In Touch with the People*[2].

This set out a framework for modernisation for local government and covered many elements, one of which was the establishment of a new Ethical Framework. The White Paper tested this framework by explaining that high standards of conduct for Councillors and Officers was important, these would be based on strict codes of conduct with appropriate enforcement and disciplinary arrangements in place, an independent Standards Board, all Councils having Standards Committees and the end of surcharge. The White Paper spoke of the 'bond of trust between Councillors and their local people' as being essential. The Paper also recognised that a culture openness and accountability would contribute to a high standard of ethical probity in local government.

The government indicated its intention to introduce this new Ethical Framework based on the Nolan Committee report and on the proposals set out in the consultation paper published earlier in 1998.

In March 1999 the government published *Local Leadership, Local Choice*. In the forward, the Deputy Prime Minister, the Rt Hon John Prescott, MP, summarised the overall modernising agenda for local government in the following way:

> 'What Councils do and how they do it is crucial to the quality of life in Britain. That is why we have put our agenda to modernise local government at the heart of our plans to modernise Britain'.

Again, the paper looked at the modernising agenda in a broad sense and saw ethics and probity as being an integral part of decision-making, change management and improvements to democracy.

This paper acknowledged the existence of a new framework, a new Code of Conduct and a new national model for Councillors as well as a model code for employees. The role of the Standards Committee was fleshed out and, again, there is an acknowledgement that surcharge would be ended, although there would be powers to recover losses where a Councillor or Council employee had gained personally at the taxpayers expense. Again, it was stated that there would be an independent Standards Board to deal with complaints that Councillors have failed to observe the Code of Conduct with powers to suspend or disqualify.

The paper itself again recognised the bond of trust between the community and those that represent them. The paper spoke of 'restoring' the bond at a local level. This recognised the fact that prior to the Nolan Report there had been several instances of misconduct or alleged misconduct and government (both central and local) had been tainted by allegations and counter-allegations of sleaze and other forms of inappropriate conduct. Historians will no doubt look at this time in government and reflect upon it from afar, but it was perhaps one of the defining moments in terms of the relationship between the media and politicians – both at local and national level – when the media had the resources, technology and skill to be able to bring to bear the immense power that they wield, and politicians – those who were not fully aware by this stage anyway – came to be aware of how much their activities were always in the goldfish bowl of the public glare.

The government submitted the draft Bill to a joint parliamentary committee which reported their recommendations in July 1999. The government's response to the joint committee's recommendations (published in December 1999) were incorporated into the Local Government Bill, introduced in the November 1999 Parliamentary session, and by a series of government amendments.

From these papers came the Local Government Act 2000, Pt III of which deals with the conduct of local authority members and employees.

1   Cmnd 3702–1.
2   Cmnd 4014.

The Meaning of Ethics and Probity

[9.3]
Fundamental to understanding what this regime means and how it will work is an appreciation of what is meant by ethics and probity and ethical standards.

It is important to understand the history and some of the terminology used in taking local government from the position that it was in 1975 with the National Code of Local Government Conduct to the position it is in the new Millennium. The pressures identified in 1985 by Widdicombe, have come to fruition, and the role of the media and the intense scrutiny of those in positions of power has undoubtedly increased enormously. This in itself is no bad thing.

However, running a multi-million pound business with elected members who are derived from a pool frequently produced by political parties struggling to generate sufficient numbers of candidates, brings with it all the failings of human nature that we are all too familiar with and vulnerable to.

On the one hand, therefore, one can argue that ethics and probity reflects no more than bringing to bear the good qualities that one would expect to find in human beings, and promulgating to remove or at least control the poorer qualities.

A second, and far more unattractive interpretation, is that the regime was introduced to bring back to politics, particularly politics at a local level, a sense of civic responsibility, a sense of genuine accountability to the citizenship, and to try to remedy some of the worst excesses of the intervening decade. In other words, the purpose of the regime was to patch up the damaged reputation of local government and local politics. The difficulties with this view is that whilst undoubtedly there have been some severe and significant acts of misconduct in local government, they have, taken against the total number of Councillors, the total number of Council employees, the amount of business conducted in local government nation-ally, been very few and far between. The nature of the business conducted by local government means it is always subjected to the type of media scrutiny and exploitation that few other acts of misconduct in the private sector would ever receive. This analysis, whilst attractive to some, in reality does not stand up to scrutiny.

The third possible reason – and one that is far more sustainable – is that, and this comes from a careful reading of Widdicombe, both in respect of the 1975 National Code, but also in respect of local government politics and decision-making generally, that local government has moved on consider-ably, not only in the last 50 years, but in the 15 years or so since the Widdicombe report. Local government has always been a changing institu-tion, but the last decade has seen a fundamental shift and balance both in terms of the what local government is required to achieve, but also the pressures upon it in terms of delivery. The political organisation within local government has changed significantly from that identified by Widdicombe. Most, if not all, local authorities operate within some kind of political arrangement and in many authorities this is very strong. All operate in a situation where resources are an issue at all times, and Councillors are making decisions about the allocation of limited resources to priority issues, cases and matters, frequently in a political context.

Perhaps the most telling word in the consultation documents issued by the government is 'trust'. There is no doubt that in a few limited cases the bond of trust between citizens and politicians has been damaged. This has an impact on the citizens' perception of politics, politicians and political organisations. It is undoubtedly time for it to be restored. Citizens need to have reliance upon and confidence in those that they have elected. They need to know that they tell the truth, have value and are reliable. They need to have faith in them.

It is suggested that this definition – an approach to ethics and probity – is not only the most attractive, but is also, upon careful analysis, the correct approach. The aim must be to ensure that the citizens regard local government and those that they elect 'people worthy of being trusted, honest, reliable or dependable'.

That, perhaps, is the most useful definition that all Councillors should seek to achieve.

CHAPTER 10
The Monitoring Officer

Introduction

[10.1]
The roles of the three statutory officers – The Head of Paid Service, Chief Finance Officer and Monitoring Officer – are to be found in primary legislation, but the way in which those roles are performed are significant. All three will have roles to perform within the context of ethics and probity, but that of the Monitoring Officer is especially significant. It is a role that is frequently (though not exclusively) performed by a legally qualified individual and requires at times an almost impossible balance to be struck between meeting the obligations of the legislation and not interfering with the effective and smooth running of a political entity. It can, at times, be a remarkably lonely role, but one which, if managed effectively, can be of benefit to the local authority. This chapter examines the background to the role, the statutory provisions, particularly the amendments to s 5 of the 1989 Act by the Local Government Act 2000 and secondary legislation, and looks to practical ways in which the Monitoring Officer role can be performed to the best benefit of the authority, and in a way that places the individual with that responsibility in the least invidious position as possible.

Background

[10.2]
Every relevant authority[1] and now the Greater London Authority is required to have three designated posts:

- a Head of Paid Service;
- a Chief Finance Officer; and
- a Monitoring Officer.

The Monitoring Officer is not currently required by law to be a lawyer, but most are either Chief Executives or Heads of Legal Services/Chief Legal Officers.

It is a role that was introduced in Local Government and Housing Act 1989 and has been amended and significantly expanded by the Local Government Act 2000.

The role has been interpreted (and misinterpreted) in many ways – as a gate keeper, having a significant role, a burden that has to be put up with, a branch of the FBI or as an unnecessary statutory promulgation of a role that was generally being performed and performed well in local authorities by the legal officers.

Those who undertake the role have to wrestle with what is generally acknowledged as an unhelpful and unsatisfactory piece of legislation combined with the pressures, demands and expectations from Members, Officers and those outside the Council.

The Widdicombe report anticipated the role of the Monitoring Officer, and recommended that:

> 'The Chief Executive should additionally be given a formal statutory role in relation to the legality of Council decisions. Where Councillors propose to take any action that would be illegal, or alternatively risk breaking the law by failing to take an action, they should be advised by Officers before the illegality occurs'[2].

By the time the Local Government and Housing Act 1989 was promulgated, this had become a duty on every relevant authority to designate an Officer as Monitoring Officer, who, under the 1989 Act (this is no longer possible) could also be the Head of Paid Service, but could not be the Chief Finance Officer.

1   By virtue of s 5(1) of the Local Government and Housing Act 1989, it is the duty of every local authority to designate one of their officers as the Monitoring Officer. Section 21(1) of the same Act is set out at Division VI – App 5 below.
2   Paragraph 6.115.

Statutory Provision

[10.3]

Sections 5 and 5A of the Local Government and Housing Act 1989 (as amended) are set out at Division VI – Appendix 5 below.

The provisions as set out in the 1989 Act have been significantly amended over time, but perhaps the 2000 Act and subsidiary secondary legislation has had a bigger and more significant effect on it than any other provision. Specifically:

(1)   a Monitoring Officer may not also be the authority's Head of Paid Service (s 1A);

(2)   there is no duty under s 2 of the Act where the Local Government Ombudsman has not yet conducted an investigation (s 2A);

(3)   there is an express cross-reference to the provisions regarding conduct in Pt III of the Local Government Act 2000 (s 8A); and

(4)   there is a new s 5A inserted into the Act dealing with situations where the local authority is operating Executive Arrangements, and the proposal, decision or omission relates to illegality or maladministration by or on behalf of the Authority's Executive.

121

The Role of the Monitoring Officer

[10.4]

The cornerstone of the role are ss 5(2) and 5(2A) of the Local Government and Housing Act 1989, but the role cannot be seen to end there.

The essence of the role is that, quite simply, if it appears to the Monitoring Officer (this is an important qualification) that any proposal, decision or omission by the authority (this can be by the Executive, the Council, a Committee, Sub-Committee or employee) has given rise or is likely to give rise to illegality or maladministration (and note since the Local Government Act 2000, in respect of maladministration, there needs to be an investigation by the Local Government Commissioner in relation to this) that the Monitoring Officer has a duty to prepare a report.

Having prepared a report, the Monitoring Officer must consult, so far as practicable, the Head of Paid Service and Chief Finance Officer, and after such a report has been prepared, send a copy to each Member of the authority.

It is then a duty of the relevant authority or Executive in respect of any report that relates to an act or omission, etc by or on behalf of the Executive to consider the report. Meantime no steps should be taken to give effect to any proposal or decision to which any non-executive report relates until such time as the implementation of the proposal or decision is considered. In relation to Executive reports, the procedure is different. Implementation is suspended until the end of the first business day after which consideration of the report from the Monitoring Officer is concluded, and that report must be considered at a meeting held not more than 21 days after copies of the report are first sent to members of the Executive.

Following consideration of that, the Executive shall prepare a report which specifies:

- what action, if any, the Executive has taken in response to the report of the Monitoring Officer;
- what action, if any, the Executive proposes to take in response to that report and when it proposes to do that; and
- either the reasons for taking action or the reasons for taking no action.

As soon as practicable after the preparation of that report, the Executive must send copies of it to each Member of the Authority and the Monitoring Officer.

There are also provisions about appointment of a deputy in the event of illness.

Whilst that may seem simple, the reality is that for most Monitoring Officers facing an issue of illegality, unless they are in a 'worst case' situation, they have probably been involved with the issue prior to the need to write a statutory report, and they and/or their legal department (assuming they are the Chief Legal Officer) have given advice on the issue.

The purpose of the legislation is to provide a public audit trail for acts of illegality by a Council. However, is the role of the Monitoring Officer simply to enable third parties who wish to challenge local authorities for illegality to obtain evidence? It is suggested that the role of the Monitoring Officer is a pro-active one, and not a reactive one, whereas s 5 of the Local Government and Housing Act 1989 sets out the role as one that is purely a reactive response to actual or proposed illegality/maladministration.

It is suggested that the role of the Monitoring Officer should not be seen as solely confined by the legislation. It should in fact be interpreted fundamentally about enabling the authority to make decisions with confidence, whilst at the same time providing the appropriate, necessary and lawful backstop as required by the 1989 Act.

The Local Government Act 2000 and the Monitoring Officer

[10.5]
In Touch with the People provided:

> 'The enforcement and disciplinary arrangements . . . place important responsibilities on Monitoring Officers. They endorse the informal role that Monitoring Officers already play in keeping up standards of conduct by encouragement and persuasion, and they also establish a more formal role in the handling of allegations of Councillors breaches of their Council's code'[1].

This is how the White Paper referred to Monitoring Officers, having outlined the new Ethical Framework for Members and, indeed, the employees' Code of Conduct. There was an acknowledgement of the role carried out by Monitoring Officers under their statutory duty and an acknowledgement that these Officers had, for some years, grappled with issues of Member misconduct.

It was already understood that the National Code of Local Government Conduct could, where it was breached, lead to maladministration by Councils. This made breach of the National Code of Local Government Conduct a corporate issue and since maladministration was a specific criteria covered by s 5 of the 1989 Act, brought the issue within the purview of Monitoring Officers. However, the ability of the Monitoring Officer to investigate and/or take action or, indeed, of the Council to take action, had always been under dispute. Nevertheless, in those authorities which had been unfortunate enough to experience and have to deal with allegations of Member misconduct, the Monitoring Officer had been the fulcrum in the process, and this was recognised by the White Paper.

The White Paper also recognised the need to provide statutory protection against dismissal for both Monitoring Officers and Chief Finance Officers to protect their new role in the new regime, and this was endorsed in 'Local Leadership, Local Choice'.

This paper recognised the need for a close and good working relationship between the Standards Committee and the Monitoring Officer, given the

Monitoring Officer's enhanced role in providing advice and assistance on ethical standards issues to Members, Officers and also to the Standards Committee, and in maintaining the public Register of Interests.

As has already been stated, the 1989 Act as amended by the Local Government Act 2000 has an express cross-reference to Pt III of the 2000 Act. This is the part of that Act that deals with conduct issues.

The Monitoring Officer has a number of specific roles as laid out in Pt III. These are explained in the explanatory notes prepared by central government which accompanied the Act. The text of the legislation is set out at Division VI – Appendix 6; and a commentary on it (based on those explanatory notes) is set out below.

1   Paragraph 6.40.

[10.6]
LGA 2000, s 57(5)

Section 57(5) of the LGA 2000 is set out at Division VI – Appendix 6 below.

Section 57 provides for the creation of a Standards Board for England. Sub-section 5(c) enables the Board to issue guidance as to the qualifications and experience which monitoring officers should possess. This has been a lacuna in the law for some time. In respect of the statutory finance officer, s 113 of the Local Government Finance Act 1988 imposed professional qualification requirements for officers having responsibility under s 151 of the 1972 Act for the administration of an authority's financial affairs, except for those who were immediately before the commencement day already in such a post.

No such comparable provision exists in respect of Monitoring Officers, and it has for long been felt by many that a parallel provision in respect of those officers responsible for delivering s 5 duties should exist.

This provision will therefore enable this issue to be addressed.

[10.7]
LGA 2000, s 59(4)(c)

Section 59(4)(c) of the LGA 2000 is set out at Division VI – Appendix 6 below.

Section 59 specifies the functions of ethical standards officers. Their main function will be to investigate allegations that a member or former member has breached its code of conduct. Ethical standards officers may also investigate any associated cases that have come to their attention as a result of undertaking an investigation into a written allegation. Sub-section 4(c) provides that one of the findings that an Ethical Standards Officer may make is that the matter should be referred back to the monitoring officer of the relevant authority to deal with (in the case of a former member who is now a member of another relevant authority, the ethical standards officer must decide to which monitoring officer to refer the matter).

[10.8]
LGA 2000, s 60(2)(*b*)

Section 60(2)(*b*) of the LGA 2000 is set out at Division VI – Appendix 6 below.

This section deals with the conduct of investigations by ethical standards officers. Sub-section (2) provides that an ethical standards officer may cease an investigation at any stage before its completion and refer the matters which are the subject of the investigation to the monitoring officer of the relevant authority concerned. Attached to any such referral.

[10.9]
LGA 2000, s 60(3)

Section 60(3) of the LGA 2000 is set out at Division VI – Appendix 6 below.

Sub-section (3) clarifies references to the monitoring officer in cases where a former member is now a member of another relevant authority.

[10.10]
LGA 2000, s 64(1)

Section 64(1) of the LGA 2000 is set out at Division VI – Appendix 6 below.

This section provides that where an ethical standards officer concludes that there is no evidence of any failure to comply with the code of conduct of the relevant authority concerned or where no action needs to be taken in respect of the matters which are the subject of the investigation, he may produce a report and may provide a summary of the report to any newspapers circulating in the area of the relevant authority concerned. If a report is produced, a copy must be sent to the monitoring officer of the relevant authority. If the ethical standards officer does not produce a report, he must inform the monitoring officer of the relevant authority concerned of the outcome of the investigation.

Sub-section (4) makes provision for reports where a member may have committed a breach of a code of conduct at a relevant authority other that that at which he is presently a member.

[10.11]
LGA 2000, s 64(2)(*b*) and (*c*)

Section 64(2)(*b*) and (*c*) of the LGA 2000 are set out at Division VI – Appendix 6 below.

See further commentary at para **[10.12]** below.

[10.12]
LGA 2000, s 64(3)(*c*)

Section 64(3)(*c*) of the LGA 2000 is set out at Division VI – Appendix 6 below.

This sub-section places a duty on an ethical standards officer to produce a report when they conclude that the matters which are the subject of an investigation should be referred either to the monitoring officer of the relevant authority concerned or to the president of the Adjudication Panel. Copies of the reports must be sent to the monitoring officer of the relevant authority concerned, to the standards committee of the relevant authority concerned (where appropriate) or, as the case may be, to the president of the Adjudication Panel.

[10.13]
LGA 2000, s 64(4)

Section 64(4) of the LGA 2000 is set out at Division VI – Appendix 6 below.

Sub-section (4) makes provision for reports where a member may have committed a breach of a code of conduct at an authority other that that at which he is presently a Member and makes provision for the ethical standards officer to refer a report to the appropriate and relevant Monitoring Officer.

[10.14]
LGA 2000, s 65(5)(*b*)

Section 65(5)(*b*) of the LGA 2000 is set out at Division VI – Appendix 6 below.

Section 65 provides an ethical standards officer with the power to issue an interim report if, during an investigation, he considers that it would be in the public interest to do so. Such reports can recommend that the person being investigated should be immediately suspended or partially suspended from being a member of the relevant authority concerned or any of its committees or sub-committees for up to six months. The matter is then referred to the President of the Adjudication Panel for adjudication by an interim case tribunal. A copy of that report must be sent to the relevant Monitoring Officer.

[10.15]
LGA 2000, s 66

Section 66 of the LGA 2000 is set out at Division VI – Appendix 6 below.

This is a significant section for Monitoring Officers, as it relates, in its entirety to matters referred to monitoring officers. Section 66 gives the Secretary of State the power to make regulations to determine the way in which matters referred under ss 60(2) or 64(2) to a monitoring officer of a relevant authority should be dealt with. None have yet been made.

The regulations may:

- enable a monitoring officer to conduct an investigation in respect of matters referred to him and make a report or recommendations to the standards committee of the relevant authority in respect of those matters;
- enable the standards committee to consider any report or recommendations made by the monitoring officer, taking such action as may be prescribed by the regulations;

- make provisions for the publicity to be given to any such report, recommendations or action;
- confer powers of investigation on a monitoring officer and confer rights on any member who is the subject of an investigation;
- enable a standards committee to censure or suspend a member or former member. A right of appeal would be conferred on any member subject to such action;
- enable the ethical standards officer to direct the way in which matters referred should be dealt with by the monitoring officer.

[10.16]
LGA 2000, s 78(7)(*b*)

Section 78(7)(*b*) of the LGA 2000 is set out at Division VI – Appendix 6 below.

Section 78 makes provision for the decisions of interim Case Tribunals. It places a duty on the interim case tribunal to decide whether or not the member mentioned should be suspended on an interim basis (for a period not exceeding six months or, if shorter, the remainder of the person's term of office). The tribunal must give notice of its decision to the standards committee of the relevant authority concerned, including the details of the suspension or partial suspension and the date on which the suspension or partial suspension is to begin. The relevant authority is under a duty to comply with the notice. Section 78 also provides that the interim suspension or partial suspension shall cease to have effect on the day that a notice is given by a case tribunal under s 79. Copies of any notice to suspend or partially suspend on an interim basis must be given to the person who is the subject of the notice and to the relevant monitoring officer. The interim case tribunal must take reasonable steps to inform the person who made the allegation of its outcome.

[10.17]
LGA 2000, s 81(1)

Section 81(1) of the LGA 2000 is set out at Division VI – Appendix 6 below.

Section 81 makes provision with respect to the disclosure of interests by members, the maintenance of registers concerning those interests and the circumstances in which members are not entitled to take part in proceedings of those authorities. It also gives the monitoring officer of an authority a specific duty of establishing and maintaining the public register of interests. In particular, sub-ss (1) and (2) place the registration and declaration of interests within the model code of conduct.

[10.18]
LGA 2000, s 81(6)

Section 81(6) of the LGA 2000 is set out at Division VI – Appendix 6 below.

Sub-section (6) specifies that the register being maintained by the monitoring officer should be made available at an office where it can be inspected and viewed by members of the public.

[10.19]
LGA 2000, s 81(7)

Section 81(7) of the LGA 2000 is set out at Division VI – Appendix 6 below.

Sub-section (7) requires the authority to publish in one or more newspapers circulating in the area that the register is available, giving details of how the register can be obtained; the authority must also inform the Standards Board that the register is available. Whilst this task is not by law vested in the Monitoring Officer, given that the Monitoring Officer is required to maintain the register, it almost certain that this task will also pas to him/her.

[10.20]
LGA 2000, s 83(12) and (13)

Section 83(12) and (13) of the LGA 2000 is set out at Division VI – Appendix 6 below.

There has been much discussion over the effect and meaning of this provision, and its potential impact for Monitoring Officers for district or unitary authorities with parish councils. It is important to note that the cross-reference is to any function in this part, ie Pt III of the 2000 Act. Whilst this presents a significant raft of functions, it does not encompass the provisions of the 1989 Act. Nevertheless, it is to be hoped that the National Standards Board will look at this issue early in its life, and provide practical advice for the Monitoring Officers affected.

By implication, the Monitoring Officer will also have responsibility for certain matters under Pt III.

[10.21]
LGA 2000, s 51

Section 51 of the LGA 2000 is set out at Division VI – Appendix 6 below.

Section 51 places a duty upon relevant authorities to adopt a code of conduct within six months of the new model code coming into force. An authority's code of conduct must include any mandatory provisions of the model code that applies to the authority. However, the authority has discretion to incorporate in its code any optional or additional provisions it wishes to include, providing they are not inconsistent with any within the model code of conduct. Police authorities in Wales will be subject to the English model code of conduct as policing is a non-devolved matter.

This section also makes provision that if an authority fails to adopt a code of conduct within the specified period, the mandatory provisions of the model code relevant to the authority will apply to it by default until it adopts its own code. Once an authority has adopted or revised its code of conduct, it must publish the fact, make the code of conduct available for public inspection, state the address where it will be available for inspection, and send a copy to the Standards Board.

Clearly the Monitoring Officer will have a significant role in respect of this.

[10.22]
LGA 2000, s 60(1)

Section 60(1) of the LGA 2000 is set out at Division VI – Appendix 6 below.

Section 60(1) enables ethical standards officers to arrange for any person to assist them in the conduct of any investigation under s 59. As already stated, sub-s (2) provides that an ethical standards officer may cease an investigation at any stage before its completion and refer the matters which are the subject of the investigation to the monitoring officer of the relevant authority concerned. (Section 66 makes provision that directions may be attached to any such referral.)

This blanket provision may draw in the Monitoring Officer on a wider basis, or involve others who will require the assistance, support or direction of the Monitoring Officer.

[10.23]
LGA 2000, s 79

Section 79 of the LGA 2000 is set out Division VI – Appendix 6 below.

Section 79 provides for the decisions of Case Tribunals. It places a duty on the case tribunal to decide whether or not there has been a breach of the code of conduct in the case brought before it. Where the case tribunal decides that a person has not failed to comply with the code of conduct, it must notify the standards committee of the relevant authority concerned. The Monitoring Officer will almost certainly be involved in facilitating this.

Where the case tribunal decides that a person has failed to comply with the code of conduct, this section places the case tribunal under a duty to decide whether the person should be suspended or partially suspended from being a member of the relevant authority concerned or disqualified for being, or becoming (whether by election or otherwise), a member of that or any other relevant authority.

Section 79 also requires the case tribunal to decide on the period of suspension or partial suspension (up to one year, although this must not extend beyond the person's terms of office) or, where appropriate the period of disqualification (up to five years). The case tribunal must issue a notice to the standards committee of the relevant authority concerned, stating that the person has failed to comply with the code of conduct and specifying the details of the failure and stating, where appropriate, that the person must be suspended or partially suspended or is disqualified, with the period of suspension, partial suspension or disqualification. Again, the Monitoring Officer will almost certainly be involved in facilitating this.

Sub-section (9) provides that the relevant authority must comply with a notice stating that the person concerned must be suspended or partially suspended.

Section 79 also provides that a copy of the notice must be given to the Standards Board or the Commission for Local Administration in Wales (as appropriate) and to the person who is the subject of the notice. The notice must also be published in local newspapers in the relevant authority's area.

The case tribunal must also take reasonable steps to inform the person who made the initial allegation of the outcome of the tribunal's adjudication. Sub-section (15) introduces a right of appeal to the High Court for a person who a case tribunal decides has failed to comply with the code of conduct.

It is worthwhile noting – as many Monitoring Officers are also responsible for elections and the Returning Officer – that Sch 5 amends s 87 of the Local Government Act 1972 to provide that in a case where a case tribunal decides that a person is to be disqualified, the disqualification takes effect immediately; but a by-election only takes place once the person has either decided not to appeal or, in the event of an appeal, once the appeal process has been exhausted.

[10.24]
LGA 2000, s 80

Section 80 of the LGA 2000 is set out at Division VI – Appendix 6 below.

Section 80 makes provision that any case tribunal which has adjudicated on any matter may make recommendations about any matters relating to the exercise of the relevant authority's functions, code of conduct or standards committee. A copy of any recommendations must be sent to the Standards Board or the Local Commissioner in Wales.

The relevant authority to whom recommendations are made is under a duty to consider them within three months and it must prepare a report for the Standards Board or Local Commissioner outlining what action it has taken or proposes to take. Sub-section (4) states that the relevant authority's consideration of a report may be discharged only by the authority or by the standards committee of that authority. If the Standards Board or Local Commissioner is not satisfied with the action taken or proposed, sub-s (5) provides it with the power to require the relevant authority to publish a statement giving details of the recommendations made by the case tribunal and of the authority's reasons for not fully implementing them.

Again, the Monitoring Officer will almost certainly be involved in facilitating this.

In relation to the draft Model Code of Conduct for Members the Monitoring Officer will have a key role in respect of that.

Monitoring Officers will almost certainly be the officers in most if not all authorities who will lead the work of the Standards Committee, one of whose roles is the promotion/raising of awareness of the local code. On the basis that prevention is better than misconduct, the Monitoring Officer will therefore pick up much of this work.

Whist the draft Model Code of Conduct for Members is specifically addressed and analysed in full in Chapter 13 below, there are a number of specific references to the Monitoring Officer – paras 6, 7 and 14 to 17 – which are worthy of attention[1].

There are also duties (usually deriving from the existing law, but also fresh ones) relevant to the operation of the new executive arrangements, contained in the statutory guidance and Model Constitution.

---

1   The draft Model Code of Conduct for Members is set out at Div VI – App 16 below.

The Government Guidance on New Council Constitutions and the Monitoring Officer

[10.25]

The government issued comprehensive guidance – *Local Government Act 2000: Guidance to English Local Authorities*[1] to assist Council's in introducing the new executive and alternative arrangements. This Guidance was issued to English county councils, English district councils and London borough councils, and deals with:

- the content and operation of a new Constitution including executive arrangements or alternative arrangements; and
- the processes of changing to or revising a new Constitution including executive arrangements or alternative arrangements.

The Guidance includes a combination of description of the main statutory provisions of the 2000 Act and subordinate legislation, statutory guidance to which local authorities must have regard; and illustrative and good practice examples.

The statutory guidance underpins the provisions of Pt II of the Act and was issued primarily under s 38 of the 2000 Act.

The Guidance has been revised and updated, as the particularly the secondary legislation has been issued/revised.

The Guidance is both comprehensive and welcome, and its production should be warmly welcomed. It contains cross-references to the role of the Monitoring Officer that warrant consideration.

In the cited example of a conflict resolution process between the executive and council in setting the budget and policy framework, the example provides that the Monitoring Officer is the recipient of copies of the minutes of the meeting. While this should occur as a matter of course, where the Monitoring Officer is not responsible for the democratic processes – as is the case in a few authorities – it may be better if that officer is the recipient.

Paragraphs 2.50 to 2.52 analyse the need for advice from the Monitoring Officer and the Chief Finance Officer where there are doubts as to a proposed decision falling within (or outside) the budget and/or the policy framework.

> 'If the monitoring officer or other appropriate officers advise that a decision is likely to be considered contrary to the policy framework then the Secretary of State recommends that the decision should be treated as if it is indeed contrary to the policy framework and handled accordingly'[2].

The Guidance then goes beyond this and provides that if the advice is that it is likely to be contrary to etc, then decision should treated as if it were contrary etc to the policy framework and/or budget.

Paragraphs 4.44 and 4.45 contain recommendations from the Secretary of State that executives should put in place arrangements (referred to as mechanisms or protocols) to ensure that an individual executive member seeks advice from relevant officers before taking a decision within her or his delegated authority. Specific reference is made to consulting the monitoring officer where there is doubt about vires. In addition, in view of the legal and financial obligations that will arise from their decisions, members of the executive should always be aware of legal and financial liabilities (consulting the monitoring officer and chief finance officer as appropriate).

Section 13 of the 2000 Act specifically states that all functions of a local authority (including those conferred by future legislation) must be the responsibility of the executive unless they are specified in regulations under s 13(3) or there is express provisions to the contrary in any other legislation. The Guidance (para 5.2) provides that functions conferred by legislation (rather than by delegation from the local authority on (inter alia) named officers of a local authority (such as the monitoring officer, chief finance (s 151) officer etc are not affected by s 13 – they cannot be the responsibility of the executive and continue to be subject to the same legislative framework.

Accountable decision-making is a crucial aspect of the new arrangements the Guidance provides (at para 7.43) that authorities should ensure that (as with the council, its committees and sub-committees) all decisions made by members of the executive (either collectively or individually) are based on sound professional advice from officers, including advice from the monitoring officer and chief finance officer where appropriate.

In considering Officers' roles under executive arrangements, in recognition of their enhanced roles under executive arrangements and the ethical framework under Pt III of the Act the Secretary of State intends to amend the Local Government (Standing Orders) Regulations 1993[3] to provide that the statutory protections in those Regulations will also apply to the monitoring officer and the chief finance officer. This is addressed in Division V – Employment Implications.

The role of the chief executive is specifically referred to, and one aspect is that s/he should, together with the monitoring officer, be responsible for a system of record keeping for all the local authority's decisions (executive or otherwise).

In order to undertake their roles, the local authority needs to ensure (para 8.18) that the monitoring officer and chief finance officer have access as necessary to meetings and papers and that members consult with her or him regularly.

The Monitoring Officer is specifically referred to – in the context specifically of ethics and probity, the Guidance states:

> 'The monitoring officer will have a key role in promoting and maintaining high standards of conduct within a local authority, in particular through provision of support to the local authority's Standards Committee . . . Local authorities will need to recognise under executive arrangements the importance of the monitoring officer's key roles of providing advice on vires issues, maladministration, financial impropriety, probity and policy framework and budget issues to all members of the local authority. The monitoring officer should also be

the proper officer for the purposes of ensuring that executive decisions, together with the reasons for those decisions and relevant officer reports and background papers, are made publicly available'.

The Constitution (which is referred to in detail below) must, in respect of the Monitoring Officer, contain:

* the roles of officers of the local authority including–
    – the management structure of the local authority;
    – the functions of the head of paid service (chief executive), the monitoring officer and the chief finance officer.

1   Available at http://www.dltr.gov.uk/index/localgov.htm.
2   Paragraph 2.51.
3   SI 1993/202.

The Constitution and the Monitoring Officer

[10.26]
Authorities that are operating the new executive or alternative arrangements are required to have and maintain a Constitution. In essence, this explains how the Council will conduct its business. The document has to be publicly available (it is recommended that the Internet is made use of to facilitate this) and that it should contain, inter alia, the rules of procedure for the Council, executive, codes of conduct and all the detailed rules and procedures. In short, if an officer member or citizen wanted to know how a Council worked, they should find the answers in the Constitution.

This document – and its contents – therefore has a significant part to play in the ethical framework. Getting this right will ensure effective open and transparent decision-making, a local code and variations that are appropriate, a scheme of executive arrangements that balances effective decision-making with the effective checks and balances.

The Monitoring Officer, in looking at issues pro-actively of guidance, regulations and documentation has a fundamental role to play in the production, effective operation and monitoring of the Constitution. Clearly there is a balance to be drawn between 'over legalising' a document that should be reasonable digestible for all Members, Officers and, indeed, citizens. Nevertheless, given that the Constitution will form the very skeleton of every local authority operating new arrangements, its significance cannot be understated, and the importance of the having the Monitoring Officer involved in not only the production of the Constitution, but its review and monitoring, is absolutely crucial. Clearly, the Monitoring Officer does not need to draft every word, nor indeed does the Monitoring Officer have to be responsible for every issue referred to or contained in the Constitution. However, there are certain elements within the Constitution where, if the content of the documentation is effectively and appropriately drafted, will itself encourage high standards of behaviour, conduct, ethics and probity, and assist in preventing possible inadvertent (or, indeed, deliberate) acts of improper conduct. For example, the whole concept of individual Councillors making significant decisions involving large amounts of money, etc raised a spectre of potential misconduct. Therefore, the decision-making rules about who has to be involved in the decision-making process, systems whereby reports are cleared, the recording of decisions as well as the cultural aspects of decision-making, are very much at the heart of what the Monitoring Officer should be involved in looking at in the drafting and review of the Constitution.

The basis of the Constitution can be found in s 37 of the 2000 Act.

'(1)   A local authority which are operating executive arrangements or alternative arrangements must prepare and keep up to date a document (referred to in this section as their constitution) which contains –
(a)   such information as the Secretary of State may direct,
(b)   a copy of the authority's standing orders for the time being,
(c)   a copy of the authority's code of conduct for the time being under section 51, and
(d)   such other information (if any) as the authority consider appropriate.
(2)   A local authority must ensure that copies of their constitution are available at their principal office for inspection by members of the public at all reasonable hours.
(3)   A local authority must supply a copy of their constitution to any person who requests a copy and who pays to the authority such reasonable fee as the authority may determine.'

Guidance issued by the Government amplifies of the importance of this document:

'Local authorities should ensure that the constitution describes clearly and in a readily understandable form the way in which they conduct their business so that anyone who has dealings with the local authority on any matter can easily determine who is responsible for decisions in respect of those matters and so that they can also easily determine how best to make representations to the relevant person. The constitution should therefore, as far as possible, be written in plain language'[1].

In terms of its drafting, the Guidance states:

'The constitution should be drafted as a flexible document. For example, it should not be necessary to produce a revised constitution every time an ad-hoc committee or sub-committee is appointed to undertake a particular task. However, a constitution needs to be sufficiently detailed to allow anyone who has dealings with the local authority to use it, either by reference to it alone or by reference to it and other documents referred to in it (and for convenience available alongside it), to determine who is responsible for the matter with which they are concerned. It should also include the statutory derivation of all the provisions of the constitution (ie which powers and duties they are made under) to allow interested parties to check the constitution against those requirements'[2].

The Local Government Act 2000 (Constitutions) (England) Direction 2000 given under s 37(1)(a) of the Act sets out the broad themes to be included in a local authority's constitution.

The Direction is set out in full at Division VI – Appendix 4 below[3].

There are many styles and formats for approaching this, and it is submitted that there is not one 'correct' form of constitution. What matters is what works, and what suits an individual authority, its officers and members. However, the government have issued a model constitution, available as part of the Guidance and also to download (in HTML format) from the Internet[4].

The model – which has been adopted by many authorities with of course, alterations to reflect local circumstances – provides itself a wide range of possible options and variations.

1   Paragraph 10.3.
2   Paragraph 10.9.
3   Pay particular attention to para 3 of the Direction at Div VI – App 4 below.
4   http://www.local-regions.dtlr.gov.uk/conindex.htm.

Practical Issues and Considerations

[10.27]
The statutory role of the Monitoring Officer is as set out in s 5 of the 1989 Act (as amended). As already stated, that is a reactive role. It is suggested that in fact the role of the Monitoring Officer, if it is performed in its most effective form and to the benefit of the authority, is a proactive one.

It must never be forgotten that local government is a creature of statute and can only do that which it is statutorily empowered to perform. Despite the new powers in Pt I of the 2000 Act, there will still be many instances where the issue of vires is fundamental to an authority's actions.

The success or otherwise of its Legal Department and those who provide legal advice to the Council, whether in-house or external, will often be a barometer of the effectiveness of the Council in terms of its management and operation. To do all that Council's want to do in the new millennium, where Councils wish to be at the cutting edge and taking opportunities provided for by legislation and Government initiatives, the Legal Department must itself operate very much on that cutting edge. This means the role of the Monitoring Officer in making sure that the authority does not overstep the margin, is particularly important. It also requires an approach that acknowledges and makes use of opportunities.

How is this best to be undertaken? The answer is in a positive and pro-active manner by ensuring that the authority is aware of what it can do, as well as what it cannot.

The word 'enabling' is sometimes used to explain this, ie providing advice to enable the authority to achieve its key values, visions and objectives. Within this context, the Monitoring Officer has an important role, despite the fact that this is found nowhere in the legislation.

In order to ensure that the authority is, therefore, in a good position to be able to utilise the powers available to it, and not take actions that are unlawful or constitute maladministration, the Monitoring Officer should do a number of things:

[10.28]
The provision of legal advice and support to the authority

Where the Monitoring Officer is also the Head of Legal Services, clearly the individual will have a significant interest in ensuring that the pro-active, positive service/corporate advice given reflects high standards of probity and ethics and encourages all the things the Monitoring Officer is looking for. Where the Monitoring Officer is not the line manager of the legal function, the Head of Legal Services (or equivalent) will want to regularly discuss action taken by the Monitoring Officer to ensure that there is a consistency of approach. It is suggested that where the Monitoring Officer is not the line manager of the legal function, that is not always going to be easy, and is yet another argument as to why the senior legal officer in each authority should, in fact, be the Monitoring Officer, in the same way that the senior finance officer in every local authority will almost invariably be the Chief Finance Officer (by virtue of the requirement that Chief Finance Officers have to have a financial qualification).

Whether provided by an in-house team or externally or by a combination of the two, the Monitoring Officer has a responsibility to make sure that the advice that is provided is correct, cogent and appropriate to the authority even if s/he is not the line manager of the staff. However, with the decision that the Head of Paid Service cannot be the Monitoring Officer, it is likely that most, if not all, Monitoring Officers will, in time, be the heads of the legal profession in each Council.

In essence, legal support to Council can be divided into three blocks:

- Monitoring Officer, statutory role, probity and ethics;
- Corporate legal advice; and
- legal services.

The Monitoring Officer role and that provided under Pt III of the Local Government Act 2000 has already been discussed. Corporate legal advice consists of elements of both the statutory role, together with the highest level of enabling advice to be provided to an authority. The general legal services, which for the purposes of this definition includes issues such as conveyancing, legal advice to housing, child care support, etc. This bread and butter legal work is clearly fundamental to the authority, but there is a need to provide the corporate legal support at the highest level where the advice is perhaps less susceptible to be pigeon-holed into an understood formula, but where the advice is also given with a corporate perspective and destination in mind, the aim being to find a way for the authority to achieve something, rather than complete a transaction or Court case. This broader legal advice and support can be invaluable where it is provided effectively, and certainly contributes to the authority as a corporate whole achieving best or better value.

[10.29]
Appropriate consideration of decision/post decisions

Mention has already been made of the importance of the Constitution and the significance of the Monitoring Officer getting involved in the drafting of and operation of the Constitution.

In addition, there will need to be procedures and systems in place in local authorities for decision-making which will probably, rightly, not be replicated within the Constitution per se but will act to back up the Constitution and the principles contained within it. It is important that Monitoring Officer ensures that that systems address all the key issues – ie access to draft reports and proposals, proper access for the Monitoring Officer and also the Chief Finance Officer (the two Officers will be able to support each other in this approach), together with professional input from other areas which is so vital to the well-being of the authority, eg the Officer overall responsible for IS/IT, for Property, etc to reports.

Generally, any report proposing an action to be considered by the Council, Committee, Sub-Committee or by the Executive should be passed through a system ensuring that the appropriate Officers have the opportunity and time to consider the proposal and make an appropriate or timely contribution. Generally speaking, it is suggested that it is good practice for all reports to include a provision enabling legal implications to be added. Whilst on occasion, this paragraph may be drafted by other than the legal staff, it should ultimately be the legal staff who determine what the legal implications for any proposal are. In addition, it should not be for the authors or non-legally trained staff to decide that there are no legal implications, since frequently they may not appreciate that whilst the issue of vires may not be a matter for consideration, procedural issues may well bring significant legal implications for the Council.

As well as reports, it is important that the general system of decision-making within the Council is sufficiently robust, and that those involved in it have sufficient knowledge of the issues to be able to intervene. Those responsible for administrating the Committee system as well as the Internal Audit or Stewardship Department will have a significant role to play in this respect.

Furthermore, there are the bodies within the local authorities, such as management teams, whether Officer, Officer and Member, or Member where matters may be taken where appropriate advice should be sought from both the Chief Finance Officer and Monitoring Officer, together with other professions such as IS/IT, Property, Finance, etc. Whilst these bodies may be non-decision-making in the strict legal sense, their views and opinions can have a significant impact on proposals, and if those proposals are later shown to be flawed, it is sometimes extremely difficult to be able to reverse previously adopted positions. In addition, such Officers are then viewed as negative and unhelpful.

A well run authority does not put its statutory officers in this position, and affords them the opportunity to be able to input to proposals before such positions and prejudices are adopted or developed.

With the amendment to the 1989 Act and the requirement that the Monitoring Officer role should not be performed by the Head of Paid Service, many, if not most, Monitoring Officers are or will be the Chief Legal Officer for the Council. Whilst s 5 provides a statutory duty on authorities to provide Monitoring Officers with such resources as are necessary, in reality this provision is simply unattainable, given the current financial position of most Councils. Therefore, how Monitoring Officers perform their role, and the resources that they use to undertake that role, are crucial. Given the role of the Chief Legal Officer which surrounds providing and managing the legal support to the Council, a positive approach to the role will mean that much of the work needed to ensure statutory compliance directly intermeshes with the work appropriate and necessary to the provision of a quality legal service by any manager of a legal department.

The mystique surrounding the role of the Monitoring Officer can be off-set by a simple and well publicised guidance note distributed to Members and Officers explaining how the role will be performed and indicating how it will be kept within manageable bounds.

The Association of Council Secretaries and Solicitors has issued a Guidance paper on the new role of the Monitoring Officer which includes, as an Appendix, a draft Protocol, which authorities can consider incorporating within their arrangements which lays out the responsibilities of the Monitoring Officer in a clear and unequivocal manner. Clearly local arrangements may require some amendments to be made and local experience may suggest the need for additional paragraphs. However, this arrangement provides a clear basis for the Monitoring Officer in undertaking much of their statutory duties and such clear guidance can be of significant benefit. A copy of the Guidance produced by the Association of Council Secretaries and Solicitors is set out in full at Division VI – Appendix 7 below.

In addition, this Guidance can be supplemented by worked examples as to how the Monitoring Officer will keep the role within manageable bounds. For example:

- an indication that where the authority is involved in litigation, provided the authority's case is arguable, the Monitoring Officer does not consider that there is a duty to report, even though s/he may believe the authority will ultimately be unsuccessful will be sustainable. It would be different, however, if the authority were so plainly in breach of the law or putting forward arguments so tenuous that the Monitoring Officer felt that they could not possibly succeed.
- an indication that the Monitoring Officer does not consider that there is a general need to report on minor procedural irregularities or matters which have already been fully reported to Members by another Officer or where Members are fully aware of the illegality or maladministration involved may well appear to fly in the face of s 5 but it is suggested, is consistent with the purpose of the legislation which is to focus on major matters and provide an audit trail. This would mean, for example, there would be no need to make a statutory report where–
  - the Council is about to unavoidably fail to meet a statutory timescale;
  - matters are being resolved by other means, eg through the Council's insurers;
  - the Council has been convicted of a minor offence, for example, road traffic or health and safety, and a full report on the circumstances has already been submitted to Committee, Sub-Committee or the Full Council;
  - a matter is being dealt with through the Council's complaints procedure;
  - where the Ombudsman has made a finding of maladministration, where that has been reported to the Council / appropriate

Committee or Sub-Committee and where the Monitoring Officer has already made a comment in the context of that report.

Further, there are, as already indicated, effective systems to be put in place with regard to ensuring legality and good administration.

In each authority, these will vary, but by and large they will consist of the following:

- a Constitution that is regularly reviewed and updated. Whether the responsibility for the review and updating lies with the Monitoring Officer or with others, the Monitoring Officer will clearly be a significant trigger in this process, and should maintain the ability to be able to advise either the reviewing body (eg the Standards Committee or the Council) as to improvements that should be made;
- a system of corporate standards for legal and other services can be helpful. This goes beyond the Constitution and indicates, for example, in relation to Legal Services, circumstances where the taking of legal advice might be mandatory and/or discretionary;
- guidance on issues such as access to information, procedure rules, etc that supplement the Constitution and provide an easy route of access for Members and Officers to understand the rules is always valuable. Electronic media should be used whenever possible and where that is clearly going to be beneficial to the end user. Flow charts are always beneficial;
- reports on Ombudsman cases (annually) as well as the internal complaints procedure are beneficial. They provide an indication of areas of strength and weakness, and assist Members in understanding where, it there are problems, those problems may lie;
- lists of proper authorised officers, registers such as those of declaration of interest for Members and Officers are clearly crucial. These systems have to be clearly promulgated, in place and in existence; and
- elements of the Constitution, such as Contract Standing Orders, may not necessarily be the responsibility of the Monitoring Officer and may lie with other Officers. The Monitoring Officer should, nevertheless, seek to ensure him/herself such elements are regularly kept under review and maintained effectively.

CHAPTER 11
Standards Committee

Introduction

[11.1]
Whilst the Local Government Act 2000 will be the cornerstone of Standards Committees, a number of authorities have had them in existence for a number of years, reliant on provisions under the 1972 Act. This chapter looks at the background to Standards Committees, their operation prior to the 2000 Act, the impact of the 2000 Act and the wider governance role that it is suggested that Standards Committees should adopt, the roles, responsibilities and membership of the Standards Committee as well as some practical issues.

Background

[11.2]
Every local authority (in England and Wales) is now required, by virtue of s 53 of the Local Government Act 2000 to have a Standards Committee. Section 53 is set out at Division VI – Appendix 6 below.

This section places a duty upon all relevant authorities – except parish councils or community councils – to establish a standards committee. The section also specifies various details of the composition of an authority's standards committee. In summary, although the authority has discretion over the overall number of members of the standards committee, the committee must have at least three members – two who are elected members of the authority and one of whom is an independent person (ie not a member of that or any other authority). In an authority that operates under the executive arrangements set out in Pt II of the Act, a standards committee must not include a directly-elected mayor or executive leader, and may not be chaired by a member of the executive.

Section 54 of the 2000 Act addresses the function of a Standards Committee. Section 54 is set out at Division VI – Appendix 6 below.

This section sets out the functions of a standards committee. The general functions are to promote and maintain high standards of conduct within the authority and to assist members of that authority to observe the authority's code of conduct.

The section also outlines a range of specific functions. These are to:

- advise the authority on the adoption or revision of a code of conduct;

140

- monitor the operation of the authority's code; and
- advise members of the authority on matters relating to their code of conduct.

Clearly, these provisions should be cross-referenced to the Terms of reference of the Standards Committee in each authority.

However, many local authorities have been operating Standards Committees with some success for the past few years, and it is helpful to understand their background (and limitations) before looking at the powers that they will have under the 2000 Act.

Operation pre-Local Government Act 2000

[11.3]
Member misconduct is not a new issue and as has already been stated, prior to the 2000 Act, Members were governed by the National Code of Local Government Conduct in its various guises. What then was the action that an authority could take when a Member broke that Code of Conduct or in any other sense, committed misconduct.

Often the issue lay in the hands of the Monitoring Officer, and if the authority was to act, it would be a decision of Full Council that would be needed. Those Councils that found themselves having to deal with the situation realised early on realised that this was neither appropriate nor an effective way of dealing with, often, minor transgressions that required more than Officer intervention.

A number of authorities, therefore, adopted Standards Committees or equivalent several years prior to the 2000 Act. However, these bodies had a number of limitations:

(1) they were not expressly recognised with the Local Government Act 1972 or indeed any other legislation. Whilst local authorities had a power to establish Committees and Sub-Committees under the 1972 Act, the lack of an express authority to establish a body to dispense disciplinary measures was considered by some to be a fundamental issue of vires that went to the very root of their existence;

(2) their powers were limited. There is no provision within the Local Government Act 2000 to impose any sanction by Councils on Members for misconduct. There were frequently suggestions that, where sanctions were imposed, they were ultra vires.

The case of *R v Broadland District Council, ex p Lashley*[1] raised significant and important issues surrounding this that remain valid until authorities adopt the Model Code, affect Standards Committees in accordance with s 53 of the 2000 Act and are able to reply upon the activities of the National Standards Board et al.

This case revolved around an appeal by the applicant from a decision of Munby J (summarised below) dismissing her application for judicial review of a decision of the standards committee of Broadland District Council that her conduct fell short of the highest standards expected of Councillors. In September 1999 a report was submitted to the committee by the council's Chief Executive in which complaint was made as to her relations with a number of the council's officers. The report concluded that the allegations amounted to prima facie breach of the National Code of Local Government Conduct. The report was considered by the committee, which decided:

(i)   (by a majority, the two Labour members dissenting), that her conduct had fallen short of the highest standards expected of Councillors; and
(ii)   that no further action should be taken.

Munby J. dismissed the complaint that:

(a)   the committee was not discharging a statutory function of the council in hearing the complaint against her and, accordingly, the proceedings before it were ultra vires; and
(b)   there had been procedural unfairness. The decision was appealed.

It was held that the judge had correctly decided both issues for the right reasons. It was intra vires for a council, acting by a duly authorised standards committee, to investigate the propriety of a councillor's conduct and to report that her conduct had fallen below the expected standards. There had been no procedural unfairness in the investigation leading to that report.

Kennedy LJ stated:

> '. . . if a local government officer complains to his senior officer about the way in which he has been treated by a Councillor, the complaint has to be investigated. Ordinary principles of good management so require, and such an investigation is plainly a function which a local authority is entitled to carry out pursuant to its statutory powers as set out in the 1972 Act. In reality, it makes sense for the investigating officer to report to a Committee, such as the Standards Committee which can then consider what action to take. So far as the Councillor is concerned, the Committee's powers are restricted, but they are not non-existent. In extreme cases it can report matters to the Police or Auditors. In less extreme cases it may recommended to the Council removal of the Councillor from a Committee, or simply state its findings and perhaps offer advice. On the other side of the equation, the Committee can dismiss the complaint or, for example, suggest changes to working practices to prevent such problems arising in the future'.

1   [2000] LGR 708; affd sub nom *R v Broadland District Council, ex p Lashley* [2001] EWCA Civ 179 [2001] All ER (D) 71, Times, 20 March, CA.

Local Government Act 2000

[11.4]
As already mentioned, the Local Government Act 2000 establishes Standards Committees for local authorities (in England and Wales).

The powers of Standards Committees are laid out in the s 53 of the Act as already stated. The new regime, of course, establishes National Standards

Board, Adjudications Panels and Case Tribunals (see Chapter 15 below) and it is these bodies that now principally dispense justice when a Member has committed misconduct. However, the pro-active role of Standards Committees, as laid out in legislation, should not be under-estimated. The aim is not that there should be a regime which dispenses justice effectively, but that Councils should behave ethically, and Members should abide by the proper terms and conditions and Codes of Conduct.

The Standards Committee, therefore, has a significant role to play in ensuring, through its pro-active actions, that not only are the standards, ethics, rules and procedures for each local authority properly in place and understood, but training and development is properly managed and all the other associated activities to ensure that Members are aware of and abide the proper standards, codes and ethics for each local authority.

Wider Governance Role

[11.5]
In November 2000, the IDeA published a booklet 'Political Executives and the New Ethical Framework' by Dr Chris Skelcher and Dr Stephanie Snape (INLOGOV). This was an initiative that had the support of DETR, as well as the Local Government Modernisation Team. The study provides an excellent analysis of the New Ethical Framework and how it works within the context of the new Executive Arrangements.

There are, as the papers recognises, two interpretations of the way in which the New Ethical Framework can be construed in local government, a narrow and wide interpretation:

> '. . . The narrow interpretation sees it as being about the creation of Standards Committees, adoption of the Code and the behaviour of individual Members of the Council. The wide interpretation sees the New Ethical Framework as being about the overall approach to the Authority's governance, and the way this influences individual behaviour. It emphasises risk assessment and prevention, rather than cure. The wide interpretation sees a relationship between standards of conduct and transparency and openness in decision-making.
>
> Most local authorities currently operate within the narrow interpretation. Their Standards Committees are dormant or meet infrequently and with light agendas. In a few authorities, the Standards Committees have concentrated on hearing allegations of individual member misconduct. A small number of authorities are developing a wide interpretation. They are building links between standards of conduct and audit, and are undertaking self-assessments of ethical standing. Typically, the Standards Committee has wider terms of reference, including standards of conduct, audit, Ombudsman matters and – in some authorities – constitutional issues. The wider role has been termed the 'Governance Committee'. These authorities are also considering how Executive Arrangements can be designed to reflect ethical principles'.

The paper identifies several key issues for local authorities relating to the operation of the Executive, issues around declaration of interests, the role of Officers and specifically the role of the Monitoring Officer.

The paper recognises the importance of the principles that lie behind the new Executive Arrangements. Those principles include, inter alia, openness, accountability and transparency.

This is particularly significant when looking at the issue of individual decision-making which, as has been pointed out, not only represents a significant change in the way in which local government goes about discharging its business, but also raises a spectre, however unpalatable, of increased likelihood of allegations, at least, of misconduct by single Members.

Parallel to this, Officers will be dealing with a situation where, instead of advising a group of Members who will be making decisions, whether comprised as a Council, Committee or Standards Committee, they will be dealing with an entity – the Executive – where the power is far more concentrated and on many occasions will be dealing with individual Councillors in whom very significant powers are vested, whereas Officers may expect Committees to take a variety of view which, when taken as a whole, balance out, they will have to deal with individual Members who may not have that breadth of vision or, indeed, understanding of the issues and there may be conflicts, therefore, brought about by this. In addition, Officers will be working in a situation where they may, on occasion, be in a 1:1 situation with a decision-maker where it is their word against the decision-makers about what was done, what was considered, etc – this emphasises the point made previously about the need for an adequate and robust decision-making system with all of the right procedures, eg note taking, minute taking, record taking, presence of Officers, etc, reflect, however bureaucratic that might seem.

Officers will also be called to give evidence to Overview and Scrutiny when Executive decisions are investigated. There will be issues about what Officers can and cannot say, what advice may be tested by Overview and Scrutiny, where the dividing lines (if any) should be and so on. Often, Officers will be the fulcrum around which the Overview and Scrutiny Committee will want to operate to 'get at' the Executive. This is not to say that Overview and Scrutiny should, or indeed, will use their powers politically, but clearly they will want to bring the Executive to account and at the same time will want to be seen to and genuinely contribute to a better discharge of the local authority functions by the Executive by testing them and, perhaps, providing alternatives the Executive may not have thought of. To do that, they will need information, and much of that will come from Officers, whether it replicates that which is provided to the Executive or whether it is to test what the Executive have done.

All of this will bring additional pressures to the Officer core, and particularly the Heads of Service, Chief Officers and statutory officers who will be at the cutting edge of how this will function and operate.

Care will also need to be taken in respect of any transitional arrangements, ie moving from the traditional committee system to the New Executive

Arrangements. Many authorities have adopted some kind of transitional arrangements in the interregnum. That is good practice. As the New Ethical Framework is introduced, there will be a need to increase awareness, both amongst Officers, Members and, indeed, citizens of the ethical agenda, the role of the Standards Committee, if it has adopted the wider role (as is recommended) and how that will reflect within the Constitution, the way in which the independent bodies such as the National Standards Board, Adjudications Panel and Case Tribunals will work in the new arrangements, and how complaints will be addressed.

The paper identifies that:

'A number of authorities have undertaken investigations into allegations of misconduct. Research carried out by the Improvement and Development Agency (IDeA) and the Department of the Environment, Transport and the Regions (DETR) shows that nationally this has heightened Members' awareness of the Ethical agenda and ownership of the Code of Conduct. With the investigative role passing from Standards Committees to the National Standards Board, all Councils will need to ensure that the loss of local self-regulation does not result in a reduced level of awareness or ownership of the ethical agenda. This is unlikely in Southampton where the Standards Committee has visibly taken a pro-active role in determining the appropriate level, form and nature of standards for Members of the Council. This was a predominant aim of the transitional period and reflects well on all members of the Standards Committee.

Care will need to be taken in moving from the Transitional Arrangement Standards Committee to the statutory form of a Standards Committee with independent members present with a role which does not involve investigation and regulation. The formal dissolution of the current arrangement and the creation of a new committee with changed terms of reference will be a clean way of achieving that. It is likely that that is the approach which Officers will recommend to Members in due course. However, the Council may also want to consider whether they wish to develop a role for the Committee which relates to the wider interpretation of the Ethical agenda as discussed above'.

The paper also examines how the ethical agenda should be taken forward. The paper acknowledges that there are many agencies that will have a role in this – clearly, local authorities and their Standards Committees, but also the Standards Board for England, various national agencies and, of course, central Government have a role to play.

The focus of the local authority's Constitution and the importance of that has already been stressed and is reflected in the wider governance role supported by this paper.

The Standards Committee has a role to test the ethical content of the Constitution and advise the Authority. It is recommended that Standards Committees should endorse the wider role in the context of the new Executive Arrangements, one element of which would be to act as the Council's advisor on constitutional operation and revision. The draft DETR

Constitution recommends another option which is that the Monitoring Officer is the custodian of the Constitution. Whilst Officer advice is appropriate on the form, content and operation of the Constitution, that advice should be supplied to a body such as the Standards Committee who can take a broader governance role and recommend changes to the Constitution to Full Council (which will be the body which has the Authority to resolve to make changes to the Constitution). The Standards Committee could also determine to review the Constitution on its own volition, and also respond to issues raised by Members, the public, etc.

The Monitoring Officer will, of course, continue to have a role to play under these arrangements, and it is recommended that the Constitution could continue to reflect that by stressing the fact that the Monitoring Officer will, inter alia:

(1)   review the Constitution and make whatever recommendations are appropriate to him / her to the Standards Committee and its wider governance role;

(2)   in undertaking this, attend various meetings, make observations and seek the views of Officers, Members and citizens;

(3)   review papers, documents, commission examinations of decision-making, particularly in terms of testing the audit trail of the decision-making process;

(4)   seek to deliver and ensure the delivery of best practice by sharing operation methodologies with other Councils.

In devising the new Executive Arrangements, the way in which they are operated will contribute will contribute to high standards of ethics and probity. Taking the wider interpretation of the Standards Committee role, it may be helpful for the Standards Committee to issue some general guidance, where one is in place in the transitional arrangements, prior to the adoption of the new Executive Arrangements, to lay down some broad principles against which the Standards Committee will expect the new Arrangements to work.

Assuming that the Standards Committee and the transitional arrangements do take on the wider governance role, then the Standards Committee should review the detail of the Constitution, prior to it being promulgated and adopted by the Council on the commencement of the new Executive Arrangements.

The paper promotes three clear principles which are unlikely to be contentious as principles with any Council Member or Officer. However, the operation of these principles in practice can be more difficult. Nevertheless, as grass root principle, they provide an excellent basis for commencing consideration of any draft Constitution. They are:

- **Accountability** – where people can measure the actions taken against policies and plans on which those responsible were elected to office;
- **Transparency** – knowing who is responsible for making a particular decision, when and where, and having an explanation and justification for a decision;
- **Openness** – gaining access to meetings and documents.

For new structures to truly provide a system which nurture ethical well-being, some of the following conditions would appear to be necessary and should be included within any model:

(a)   Members and Officers need to be aware of the ethical dimensions of their behaviour;

(b)   the Authority's structures and processes need to integrate ethical considerations;

(c)   the Executive needs to work in a transparent and accountable manner;

(d)   decision-makers need to be identifiable and their powers set in the context of the Budget and Policy Framework, established by the Council who holds them accountable for their decisions;

(e)   a strong, influential and effective Overview and Scrutiny function needs to be in place, which itself is open, accountable and transparent in its methods of working;

(f)   there need to be fulfilling and meaningful roles for Members who are not on the Executive;

(g)   points (d) and (e) (decision-making / Overview and Scrutiny) need to be effectively integrated into the operation of the Executive Arrangements.

Roles and Responsibilities

[11.6]
In order to encompass the arrangements as set out in the Local Government Act 2000, and with the option of the wider governance role, suggested terms of reference for a Standards Committee operating currently under the 1972 Act, but with an eye to the wider governance role are set out at Division VI – Appendix 8 below.

Membership

[11.7]
In January 2001, the government issued a consultation paper – 'Standards Committees: Appointments and Procedures'. The paper addressed the issues surrounding the composition of standards committees, the appointment of independent members and the procedure of the committee.

The paper included, as an annex, a draft of the Relevant Authorities (Standards Committee) Regulations. These Regulations – the Relevant Authorities (Standards Committee) Regulations 2001 (SI 2001/2812) have now been issued and came into force on 28 August 2001.

As to size, reg 3 provides that:

'An authority must ensure that–

(a)   where its standards committee has more than three members, at least 25% are independent members; and

(b)   where it is operating executive arrangements under Part II of the Act, no more than one member of its standards committee is a member of the executive'.

147

For those authorities which are defined as 'responsible authorities' (which in this context means a district or unitary council which has functions in relation to the parish councils for which it is responsible under s 55(12) of the 2000 Act), they must include a parish member on their standards committees, even where they have adopted a sub-committee structure (reg 3(2)(*a*)). Despite reservations expressed by Counties and Districts (and unsurprisingly support from Parishes), the government's view is that a parish presence on both the main and sub-committees would help ensure there was a degree of continuity between their work. However, the government did accept that their draft proposals for validity of proceedings would be changed (see reg 6).

Reg 4 sets out the procedure for the appointment of independent members. This has been changed since the draft regulations. It is only necessary to have one local newspaper advertisement, the constitution of the appointment panel is left to local choice, and most importantly, the proposed requirement that any appointment would require the support of 75% of the Council has been dropped in favour of a simple majority.

Reg 6 requires meetings of standards committees to have a quorum. The draft proposals as to validity provided, inter alia, that, depending upon the size of the committee, at least two members and at least one independent would have to be present in a committee of two, three or four members (two independents if the committee was larger), and a parish representative would have to be present at any meeting of a district council standards committee for it to be quorate. This raised widespread (and understandable) concern.

The government has amended the regulations so that for a committee to be deemed quorate:

- a minimum of three members should be present;
- only one independent member need be present;
- the requirement that the parish representative has been dropped.

There is an additional (helpful) provision that provides that where the independent member is obliged to withdraw from the committee by virtue of the code of conduct (eg because of a conflict of interest), that shall not affect the validity of the proceedings.

Whilst these changes are of help, this still means that a disaffected (or simply unavailable) independent member may prevent the standards committee from discharging its responsibilities.

Practical Issues and Considerations

[11.8]
Given the changes that all local authorities are passing through in terms of their decision-making arrangements, the adoption of new Executive Arrangements and so forth, there is much room for flexibility and diversity. The ethos that appeared to be expressed at one time that all local authorities should, by and large, operate similar arrangements, will certainly not be the case.

This is equally applicable to Standards Committee.

Comment has already been made on the proposals regarding the appointment of independent Members, but the composition of Standards Committees generally requires some thought. Section 53(10) provides that a Standards Committee of a relevant authority in England or a Police Authority in Wales is not to be regarded as a body to which s 15 of the Local Government and Housing Act 1989 applies. This is the provision which deals with the duty to allocate seats to political groups.

Therefore, there is no mandatory obligation to ensure that Standards Committees are politically proportioned.

This, therefore, gives local authorities some room for options. Clearly one party Standards Committees, unless the authority is formed entirely from Members of one party, would be unacceptable. There will be at least one independent member present, and it is suggested that in a multi-party Council, the aim should be that the Standards Committee is apolitical. Give its role – as laid out above – there is perhaps an argument for having either unanimity across the parties in levels of representation, or at least ensuring that the normal 'politics' of debate, argument and disagreement is removed as much as possible from this arena.

One option is for the Chairman of the Council to chair the Standards Committee which has inherent attractiveness.

Clearly, it is a matter for local choice. However, careful consideration of this issue can bring benefits.

In addition, in considering how the Standards Committee will integrate with the remainder of the Authority, care needs to be given as to its reporting lines to Full Council. If it is to have the functions embodied in it by the legislation, then one argument is – why does it need to report to Full Council? There are a number of compelling reasons why some formal structured reporting system is of benefit to the Authority, to the Standards Committee and to the Monitoring Officer.

First of all, whilst the Standards Committee will clearly take responsibility for the functions allotted to it by the 2000 Act, they are matters of genuine interest (or ought to be of genuine interest) to all Members of every local authority. By putting a formal reporting line in, eg an item on every Council agenda for a reporting from the Standards Committee of the business transacted in the previous cycle – all Members will be advised of the Standards Committee's consideration of issues such as training, development, reviewing standards, IS/IT, etc. This will clearly have a dissemination benefit as well as an awareness raising benefit and for those who have to deal with problems that emanate from Members who say that they were 'not aware of' a particular matter, will provide a clear audit trail that all Members of the Council were officially informed that, for example, the Standards Committee adopted, promulgated and endorsed new IS/IT standards for Members.

In addition, it has a role of the heightening the significant and importance given by the Authority to the whole issue of ethics and probity. It is not a matter that is railroaded into a cul-de-sac of a Committee that meets perhaps only quarterly, the minutes of which are simply considered by the four or five Members who might attend that Committee.

Finally, it genuinely gives the Council an opportunity, were it minded to do so, to look at the decisions of the Standards Committee and say that it does or does not agree with them. That is not to say that the Council should be given a right of veto, etc, but it will allow the collective body of all elected members of that particular local authority to express views on the standards of conduct applicable to them, and how the Standards Committee is going about its role of proactively representing those interests and ensuring that the element of trust is maintained between the citizen and the Councillor. That role should not be underestimated.

1   [2000] 2 LGLR 933, QBD; [2001] JLEL D28, CA.

CHAPTER 12
Procedures and Documentation

Introduction

[12.1]
Whilst the importance of proper procedures and document cannot be over-emphasised, it is important to appreciate that the achievement of high levels of ethics and probity will not be achieved by the production of a high quantity of documentation. It is quality rather than quantity, quality in terms of thoroughness, coverage and understanding which is the key factor. It is important that the fundamental foundations for the effective operation of the Council are clearly documented and that documentation is properly and effectively communicated. This chapter looks at the importance of proper procedures and documentation and then analyses certain aspects of that documentation.

The Importance of Proper Procedures and Documentation

[12.2]
For the purposes of delivering ethical standards, whilst at times over-emphasis can be given to the existence of documentation which in itself will not deliver high standards of conduct, there is no doubt that having effective, simple and easy to understand standards and guidance properly and effectively documented and communicated will contribute to the achievement of high levels of conduct. Thus, any examination of procedures and documentation must be prefaced with a number of cautionary observations, namely:

(1)   The documentation will only be effective provided it is drafted and communication effectively. Plain English is a must. Over-use of jargon will mean that it will not be read by the target audience who, in most cases, will be Members of the Council. It must, therefore, be 'Member friendly'. This, therefore, also affects the length of the documentation. The propensity for lawyers is to clearly ensure that all levels of detail, all permutations and all options are covered. It is the natural approach to drafting, for example, a lease, to deal with all potential eventualities. However, drafting guidance for Members requires a different style and approach. Trying to promulgate for all eventualities will lead to a document that is so long and complex, Members will simply not read it.

(2)   How it is to be communicated is extremely important. A variety of methods is open to Officers, these range from simply sending the paper document to Members, circulating it during a training exercise (subject to attendance), or making it available via the internet or other electronic means.

It is suggested that all these and many other methods are equally valid and the appropriateness of each method will be determined by the relevance to the Members of the document in question, the preference of the Members and the way in which the authority operates.

However, it is suggested that simply supplying large amounts of paperwork to Members with an expectation that they will read, understand and abide, is unlikely to have the desired result. Therefore, Officers should be prepared to use a variety of approaches and wherever possible use as much electronic means of communication as possible.

In using an internet or intranet site to promulgate procedures, documentation and standards, one key benefit is that the master document can be updated with ease, and if all Members / Officer access from the same master document, the need to issue updates (and maintaining a list of those on the circulation or distribution list) becomes unnecessary.

In addition, in a world where much of the modern law, guidance, circulars, etc is available on the internet, the ability to cross-reference documents on the internet/intranet to other internet/intranet sites, links to central government guidance, the law etc, provides an opportunity to reduce the need to circulate documentation frequently – again making consumption easier for Members.

Some Key Documents and the Principles Behind Them

The constitution and decision-making framework

[12.3]
This has already been analysed in detail at paras **[10.26]** and **[10.27]** above. Its importance and inter-relationship between that and the Political Executive in the wider context of the Standards Committee has already been considered within this Division at Chapter 11 above.

Procedural standing orders / rules of procedure

[12.4]
These documents are embodied within the Constitution and, therefore, the comments set out above are applicable. But their significance is so great that they warrant specific mention. As always, one should adopt a purposive approach to applying the rules. Many authorities have significant bureaucratic rules in place, but the more bureaucratic, the tendency seems to be the less application.

Therefore, wherever possible, simplicity is of the essence. If the general intention, aim and purpose is clear, the way in which it is to be applied need not always be fully documented.

In addition, the general inherent common law powers should never be disregarded – for example, the Chair of any Council meeting has general powers to maintain good conduct, means that copious Standing Orders and procedural requirements as to the way in which the meeting is to be conducted, are not always strictly necessary, since it is unlikely that they will address every eventuality (even though they may attempt to do so).

Contract standing orders

[12.5]
Section 135 of the 1972 Act provides that a local authority may make standing orders with respect to the making of contracts, and must make such orders with respect to contracts for the supply of goods or materials or for the execution of works. In relation to those that they must make, they must include provisions for securing competition and for regulating the manner in which tenders are invited. They may exempt contracts for a price below that specified in the standing orders and may authorise the authority to exempt any contract from the relevant standing order when the authority is satisfied that the exemption is justified by special circumstances. An important provision to protect those contracting with local authorities is that they are not bound to inquire whether standing orders have been complied with, and non-compliance with such orders does not invalidate any contract entered into by or on behalf of the authority.

Regulation 8 of the Local Authorities (Executive Arrangements) (Modification of Enactments and Further Provisions) (England) Order 2001[1] is set out at Division VI – Appendix 9 below. This provision introduces a requirement for local authorities who are or will be operating executive arrangements under Pt II of the Local Government Act 2000 to make standing orders in respect of local authority contracts and specifies the provisions that are to be included in the standing orders, including the procedure to be followed in the making of such contracts.

Therefore, Councils cannot operate executive arrangements unless they have made Contract Standing Orders which include provisions about specifying that contracts should be in writing.

Secondly, Councils should be careful which contracts they specify ought to be in writing as para (4) of Art 8 then states that such contracts must be entered under seal.

One option may be to insert the following (and ensuring that there is no other requirement in Standing Orders for contracts to be written):

> 'Where it is the responsibility of the [Head of Legal Services] to accept a tender to create a contract, the Common Seal will be affixed to those documents (in writing or otherwise) which in the opinion of the [Head of Legal Services] should be sealed'.

---

1   SI 2001/1517.

Employees' Code of Conduct

[12.6]
Section 82 of the LGA 2000 is set out at Division VI – Appendix 6 below.

This section empowers the Secretary of State and the National Assembly for Wales to issue a code of conduct for all relevant authority employees. In drawing it up a code, they must consult representatives of relevant authorities and also of relevant authority employees. This code of conduct is to be incorporated into the terms and conditions of every relevant authority employee, unless excluded by regulations under sub-s (8).

Members' Code of Conduct (current and Model, plus local variations and guidance)

[12.7]
This is referred to in detail at para **[13.3]** below.

Confidential Reporting Procedure

[12.8]
On the basis that an authority will adopt principles of openness, transparency and accountability in terms of its decision-making, some robust guidance about when matters can and should be treated as confidential is helpful, so there is a clear dividing line (and understanding) as to what is and is not to be considered outside the public arena.

Executive Scheme of Delegation

[12.9]
By virtue of the 2000 Act, for those authorities that are operating executive arrangements, there is a range of delegations that may be applied to executive functions depending upon the nature of the executive in place (ss 14 to 17) as well as provisions dealing with area committees, joint arrangements etc.

The Local Government Act 2000 (Constitutions) (England) Direction 2000 requires, inter alia, that a Constitution should include:

'(h) a description of the functions of the local authority executive which, for the time being, are exercisable by individual members of the local authority executive stating as respects each function, the name of the member by whom it is exercisable;

(i) a description of the functions of the local authority executive which, for the time being, are exercisable by the executive collectively or a committee of the executive, stating as respects

154

each function, the membership of the body by who it is exercisable;

(j) a description of those powers of the executive which for the time being are exercisable by an officer of the local authority stating the title of the officer by whom each of the powers so specified is for the time being exercisable, other than any power exercisable by the officer for a specified period not exceeding six months'[1].

---

1 See para 3 of the Direction which is set out in full at Div VI – App 4 below.

Officer Scheme of Delegation

[12.10]

The Local Government Act 1972 grants wide-ranging powers for local authorities to delegate the discharge of their functions.

The 2000 Act also contains provisions on the delegation of Executive functions. The Act requires that those local authorities adopting Executive Arrangements must make arrangements for the discharge of their Executive functions. It makes provision (particularly in ss 14 to 16) for the delegation of the discharge of these functions.

In establishing a Scheme of Delegation for Officers – whether executive or non-executive functions, it is important to bear in mind that a number of principles exist in terms of delegations, none of which should be forgotten, failing which the authority will find itself in difficulty and, indeed, the Members granting the delegation could find themselves in difficulty.

As para 4.24 of the Guidance states:

'Where functions which are the responsibility of the Executive are delegated to Officers or other structures outside the Executive, the Executive should nevertheless remain accountable to the Council, through Overview and Scrutiny Committees, for the discharge of those functions. That is to say, the Executive should be held to account for both its decision to delegated a function and the way that the function is being carried out'.

Delegation means the conferring of authority on another, but does not imply that the delegator gives up the authority to act or decide him/herself. Generally, the delegatee may be considered as the operative mind – the delegatee is entitled to take the decision or act him/herself and bind the delegator by that decision or action, rather than simply making recommen-dations.

Therefore, the way in which a Scheme of Delegation is executed will be material and may reflect, whether in operation, political or in ethical/ probative terms upon, if it is an Executive function, the Executive and in some contexts, an individual Executive Member.

It is, therefore, helpful, if Schemes of Delegation do not simply reflect the powers that are expressly delegated, but also gives some guidance as to the operation of the Scheme, together with some indication of the way in which some authorisations may work. Whilst the maxim 'delegatus non potest delegare' is not a rule of law, it is a rule of construction or interpretation, and is a presumption that a discretion conferred by a statute should be exercised by an authority or person on whom the statute is conferred it and no other authority or person. Some model general notes are included as Appendix 10 of Division VI below.

In common with s 101 of the 1972 Act, ss 14 to 16 of the 2000 Act do not make express provision for an officer to whom the exercise of a function has been delegated to sub-delegate it to a subordinate officer.

However, in four cases in the 1980's, the courts considered the legality of the discharge of functions by officers of a local authority who were acting under the authority of and on behalf of their superiors (the superiors having themselves been formally delegated to discharge the relevant functions under the 1972 Act. In each case, the courts concluded that the performance by the other officer was lawful. Each case concerned different functions and the judgements raised some varied issues.

Therefore, as well as some general notes to assist in the interpretation and operation of a Scheme of Delegation, it is perhaps helpful to specify the safeguards that should be applied in terms of authorisations of subordinate officers to discharge particular functions (see further Division VI – Appendix 11 below). Care should be taken to ensure that the names of individual officers or their designated posts are approved by the council in relation to important decisions where the legal or financial strength of the council is brought to bear on third parties.

Register of Interests

[12.11]
Reference is made to the National Code of Local Government as well as the provisions in the Local Government Act 1972 at para **[13.3]** below. Detailed analysis is also undertaken of the draft Model Code with its provisions relating to the registration of interests of Members. It must be remembered that there is a need to register Officers' interests as well. Whatever arrangements are put in place, the system needs to be effective and robust as well as simple to understand for both Officers and Members. In respect of the Members' Code, it is ultimately an issue for Members to ensure compliance and, therefore, whatever regime is administratively to be operated, they need to find it supportive and helpful. Consideration should be given as to how frequently Members are reminded of this obligation, how frequently their memories are jogged that perhaps they should consider updating the Register, and what administrative steps are put in place so that Members have an opportunity to declare and have those interests recorded at meetings. Some authorities have a standing item of each agenda to remind Members of the possible need to do this, and that can be a useful *aide-memoir* whether the authority is operating Executive or alternative arrangements.

Members' Induction Process

[12.12]

The importance of an effective Members' induction process should not be underestimated. Both the Local Government Association and IDeA provide valuable assistance and guidance on Member training and development, and both organisations produce a range of useful publications on Member development. Frequently, when one compares the budget available for Member training and Member induction training, with say Officer training, or IS/IT upgrade costs, it is exceedingly low. Clearly, new Members will need to be made aware of the authority, how it works, the procedures, systems, etc. They will also need to be made aware of the big issues and for those who sit on specific Committees or Sub-Committees, or shadow or are to be Executive Member, there will be brief for them to get to grips with. There needs to be a balance between the policy issues and the probity and ethical issues. That is not always an easy balance to strike. Induction training needs to be planned well in advance of any election, and sufficient time, effort and resources needs to be devoted to it, not only in terms of individual training sessions, but also in ensuring that the Members have access and are guided to where they might find further detail and information, and how they might go about asking individual questions.

Frequently, Member induction is an area where there is insufficient thought or activity given to the topic in advance of the election, resulting in the training being hurried, inadequate and largely policy addressed as a balanced programme addressing a range of issues including ethics and probity.

Officers' Induction Process

[12.13]

Clearly, Officers need to be made aware of the processes and procedures that apply to them in terms of their contract of employment, terms and conditions, the authority's disciplinary rules and procedures and so on. In addition, the new Employee Code of Conduct will clearly be an issue that all employees will need to be made aware of.

They also need to be familiar with not only the Members' position, particularly for those Officers who work at the political interface, but surrounding the relationship between Officers and Members. Therefore, specific training for, for example, Committee and Democratic Services staff around the Officer/Member Protocol would be especially significant.

Members Continuing Development

[12.14]

It must never be forgotten that even in those authority's with annual elections, many Members may sit on the Council, being re-elected for many years, with little or no continuing development programme. Again, there is good support and guidance on this available from the various agencies that support local authorities, and there is clearly a drive towards an effective and planned continuing development programme for Members. That is unquestionably correct.

However, authorities do need to be particularly careful of the need to balance effective training and development with the amount of time that Members may have to devote to it, and there needs to be a sense of realism about whatever is being organised. It also needs to be borne in mind that training and development does not equate with courses, per se, and that 'on the job training' can be equally as effective.

Clearly, the training and development programme for Members in any authority is going to be tailored to meet the needs of those Members and that authority. Again, however, it is an area where traditionally the budget, time and effort allocated to this particular task has been minimal. That needs to be revisited by most authorities.

Officers' Continuing Development

[12.15]

Many authorities are pursuing or have achieved Investors in People (IiP). Those authorities that have not, are looking to put in place the sort of disciplines that IiP requires, including training plans and the like. Therefore, the issue of effective Officer Training and Development is, in most authorities, in hand or being addressed. That is to be warmly welcomed. It is important, however, that the programme does not simply address professional training, but reflects upon the business needs is to ensure that Officers are familiar with and up to date with the ethical and probity issues associated with the new Executive arrangements. That needs to be built into the training programme of certainly the senior managers, obviously the departments that have a direct interface with Members and, depending upon the nature, type and style of the authority, such other tiers of staff as is necessary. Clearly, not every officer is going to need to know every detail about, for example, Members' Code of Conduct, but it requires more than just the Monitoring Officer and the Head of Committee Services to have that information to hand.

Whistle-blowing / Duty to Act

[12.16]

Since July 1999, workers in the United Kingdom, including local authority employees, have enjoyed the protection of the Public Interest Disclosure Act 1998 – described as the most far-reaching whistle-blowing law in the world.

This Act protects employees from victimisation when they 'whistle-blow' inside and, if there is good reason, outside any organisation, including local authorities and covers varying issues and concerns. Whistle-blowing was not introduced per se by this legislation and was used in many well run and effective authorities and, indeed, other organisations, prior to this Act.

However, this Act gave statutory protection to workers who legitimately felt a need to advise others of a particular concern. Having an effective whistle-blowing or equivalent policy and procedure in place, is essential and, specific guidance was issued by Public Concern at Work, endorsed by CIPFA, including a series of checklists, displays and draft guidance which organisations could amend/adapt.

Most authorities now have a policy of this type in place in one form or another, but opportunity should always be taken to ensure that it is revised, updated and reflected upon.

An interesting quirk is, of course, the obligation contained within para 7 of the draft Model Code whereby a Member who believes another Member has failed to comply with the authority's code of conduct must report that other Member to both the Standards Board and to the Monitoring Officer, thus introducing an equivalent kind of whistle-blowing, but with a mandatory requirement upon Councillors. It remains to be seen how this will work, as compared to the Officer based whistle-blowing policy and approach, as endorsed and supported by Public Concern at Work, CIPFA and reflected on a national basis by the Government by the introduction of the Public Interest Act.

Other Council's specific additional Codes and Protocols

[12.17]
Clearly, authorities may introduce additional codes and protocols although a warning needs to be given about such activity. Whilst well intentioned, there needs to be a desire to avoid over legislating, production of excessive documentation can cause confusion, leads to doubt and uncertainty as to what the rules are and at times, provide such a volume of paper that all – Officers and Members – find it difficult to understand precisely what is required of them.

Nevertheless, it may be that given particular circumstances, additional codes, protocols or guidance may be of assistance.

For example, those authorities with a licensing function, may find it helpful to adopt and reflect a code or guidance that equates with the model Local Government Association Code on Planning. Licensing is a quasi-judicial function, issues can arise about the way in which a Licensing Committee discharges its responsibilities that are very much parallel with those that have arisen in the past in relation in which Planning Committee have discharged their responsibilities. Such guidance can, in certain circumstances, be exceedingly helpful. However, there should always be a good justification for producing and adopting such guidance, and it is suggested that the Standards Committee with its wider governance role should approach such additional guidance always with an eye to ensuring that there is a genuine need for further documentation and adopt such an approach on the basis of monitoring it carefully with a view, if it transpires that the additional guidance was unnecessary, being prepared to revoke it within a relatively short period of time.

CHAPTER 13
Setting the Standards – Legislation, Codes and Protocols

Introduction

[13.1]
This chapter analyses the actual standards themselves against which member conduct will be judged. The chapter looks first at the primary legislation. It then reflects upon the National Code and some key aspects of that, which although it will be replaced a Local Code in each authority, will remain more than a mere historical item of interest for some for some time. Then the chapter looks at the Local Code in detail, and finally the chapter looks at the use operation and content of the Officer/Member protocol as required within the Constitution.

Legislation

[13.2]
Sections 94 to 98 of the Local Government Act 1972 are to be repealed by the 2000 Act. In the meantime, they contain provisions that relate to restrictions on members as to when they may (may not) vote in circumstances where they have certain interests. These provisions therefore clearly lay down prescribed standards of conduct in respect of certain key matters, and are backed up by the criminal law for defaulters.

Section 94 of the LGA 1972 is set out at Division VI – Appendix 12 below. The purpose of this provision – which can trace its antecedents back to the nineteenth century is to prevent a conflict between private interest and public duty. The section places three duties on a member of a local authority who is present at a meeting at which any contract, proposed contract or other matter in which s/he has a direct or indirect pecuniary interest is considered. S/he must disclose his/her interest, s/he must not take part in the consideration or discussion and s/he must not vote on any question relating to it. If s/he fails to comply with the provisions he is liable on summary conviction to a fine not exceeding level 4 on the standard scale for each offence.

What is the situation that exists where a member insists on speaking *and* voting? This does not just arise under these sections, but also s 106 of the Local Government Finance Act 1992.

The question of members' interests was considered further by Redcliffe-Maud following which the 1975 Code was agreed between the government and the

160

local authority associations and circulated which, following consideration by Widdicombe led to the 1990 National Code. This is now to be superseded by the Local Code of Conduct for Members.

Section 95 of the LGA 1972 is set out at Division VI – Appendix 12 below. This section explains the meaning of a pecuniary interests for the purpose of s 94. The definition of an indirect pecuniary interest contained in this section is also applied to the indirect pecuniary interests of a member of a local authority contained in a general notice given in pursuance of the requirements of s 19 of the 1992 Act.

Sections 96 and 97 of the LGA 1972 are set out at Division VI – Appendix 12 below.

The Secretary of State may remove or modify a disability in relation to a member of a principal council or a joint authority, and the district council may remove or modify a disability in respect of a parish councillor and the principal council may do so in respect of a community council. A member desiring a dispensation is not precluded from voting on a motion to apply for a dispensation. Where a member's interest is so remote or insignificant that it is unlikely to affect his judgement, the member is not obliged to declare it. This is, of course, different to the arrangements laid out in the Model Code, which provide for the Standards Committee to have the power top provide dispensations in respect of interests arising under the Code.

These dispensations were revoked and replaced by the dispensations set out in DoE Circular 9/92, Circular 15/92, WO Circular 16/92. These are:

(1)   dispensation for Tenants of Unfurnished Accommodation;
(2)   dispensation for Children in Full-Time Education; and
(3)   dispensation for Members to discuss the Statutory Sick Pay Scheme under the Social Security and Housing Benefits Act 1982.

This Circular also revoked the dispensation for special responsibility allowances in DoE Circular 8/82. The dispensation for tenants of unfurnished accommodation was replaced by one in revised terms by DoE Circular 25/92 (WO Circular 50/92).

Section 98 provides some interpretative provisions for ss 95 and 97 and is set out at Division VI – Appendix 12 below.

Section 105 (set out at Division VI – Appendix 12 below) applies ss 94 to 98 relating to pecuniary interests in contracts, proposed contracts or other matters to members of committees including co-opted members, but restricts the right of co-opted members to inspect the record of disclosures to the book kept by the proper officer in respect of the particular committee or sub-committee on which they serve.

The Local Government Act 2000 (Sch 6) provides that ss 94 to 98 and 105 will be repealed. This is because the new Model Code comprehensively addresses the issue of interests.

These provisions repealing these parts of the 1972 Act are not yet in force, and will no doubt be brought into force when the Model Code is active in each local authority (which may mean for some Councils the provisions of the 1972 will remain in force for some time yet and hence, Officers and Members will need to refer to those particular provisions in at least the short-term).

Section 19 of the Local Government and Housing Act 1989 provides the Secretary of State with power to make regulations to require each member of a local authority to give a general notice setting out such information about his or her direct and indirect pecuniary interests as may be prescribed, or stating that he or she has no such interests, and to keep the declaration up to date. Failure to comply with the requirements of regulations made pursuant to s 19 of the Local Government and Housing Act 1989 is an offence but such an offence may only be prosecuted with the consent of the Director of Public Prosecutions. Regulations under s 19 of the 1989 Act may provide that a declaration pursuant to sub-s (1) thereof may constitute a sufficient disclosure under this section. A local authority is not entitled to impose any obligations on elected members to disclose any interests other than those they are required to disclose under this section or under any regulations made under s 19 of the Local Government and Housing Act 1989. The Local Authorities (Members' Interests) Regulations 1992[1], made under s 19, require each member to give the proper officer a notice about his direct and indirect pecuniary interests containing the information prescribed by the Regulations. However, there is no provision under s 19(4)(a) that the giving of a notice under the Regulations shall be deemed to be sufficient disclosure for the purposes of s 94[2].

The Local Authorities (Members' Interests) Regulations 1992 specify the records to be maintained by the proper officer prior to the Local Code coming into effect, and requires him to keep them open to inspection by members of the public without charge at all reasonable hours.

Section 106 of the LGA 1972 is set out at Division VI – Appendix 12 below. This section prevents certain members of the local authority from voting at meetings on any matters affecting the level of council tax or the arrangements for administering either the community charge or council tax. It does not, however, remove their right to speak at such meetings.

The position as to whether legally they can vote is open to interpretation, but it is suggested, the answer is that they can. This appears at first sight unsatisfactory – a member commits a criminal offence by voting, but their vote is to be counted. However, firstly, the offence is that they have failed to disclose and voted (there are in fact two possible offences in this section), not that they have attempted to vote. Clearly they will need to be advised (and it is suggested that the prudent Monitoring Officer will want to have an audit trail of that advice) but that is not advice that should provided in the public domain. To do so may result in a disclosure of information that is covered by the Data Protection Act 1998, and that in itself may be an offence. Secondly, there is no power for the person presiding in the meeting under the 1972 Act to deny them their vote, and indeed to do so on the basis of the possibility of criminal action may be highly dubious.

In most cases, where this arises, there will not be an issue. However, where the Council is hung (or balanced), it may well be an issue, and an issue for not only the member in question, but also one or more of the political groups – although the agendas may be different.

1   SI 1992/618.
2   Section 19 of the LGHA 1989 is set out at Div VI – App 5 below.

The National Code of Local Government Conduct

[13.3]
The background to the current and soon to be replaced Codes has already been mentioned. Given the possibility that some authorities may not adopt their local code for sometime, and residual matters of conduct falling under the National Code may require consideration, the National Code still warrants a degree of analysis.

The Code derives its authority from s 31 of the Local Government and Housing Act 1989 (which is set out at Division VI – Appendix 5 below).

The Code (reproduced at Division VI – Appendix 13 below) is embodied as an annex to DoE Circular 8/90. The general principles of conduct are also set out at Division VI – Appendix 14 below.

Paragraph 8 of the Circular states:

> 'Section 31 of the Act also provides that the form of declaration of acceptance of office under section 83 of the Local Government Act 1972 or section 33A of the Local Government (Scotland) Act 1973 may include an undertaking by the declarant to be guided by the National Code of Local Government Conduct in the performance of his functions. The Secretaries of State intend making orders to this effect to come into force on 3rd May 1990 for authorities other than parish and community councils, and 1st January 1991 for parish and community councils'.

The forms of declaration of acceptance of office prescribed by order of the Secretary of State, which must be made by all elected members of authorities within two months of their election, failing which they may not act, requires an undertaking to be guided by the Code. The form is laid out in regulations.

The interrelationship between the National Code and the Local Government Ombudsman has been a cause of some concern, and it will be interesting to see how the new Local Codes will inter-relate.

Paragraph 9 of the Circular states:

> 'In carrying out an investigation, the local ombudsman may find that a breach of the National Code of Local Government Conduct by any individual member of the authority, constitutes maladministration. Section 32 of the 1989 Act requires that in these circumstances the local ombudsman must name the member or members concerned in his report on the investigation and give particulars of the breach unless he is satisfied that it would be unjust to do so. The Secretaries of State also intend to bring this provision into force on 3rd May 1990'.

The introduction to the Code itself states:

163

> 'The Code represents the standard against which the conduct of members will be judged, both by the public, and by their fellow councillors. The local ombudsmen may also regard a breach of the Code as incompatible with good administration, and may make a finding of maladministration by the council in these circumstances'.

The Local Government Ombudsman may conclude, following an investigation, that a breach of the National Code by any individual member amounts to maladministration by the authority.

Section 26(1) provides the Ombudsman with the power to investigate:

> 'Subject to the provisions of this Part of this Act where a written complaint is made by or on behalf of a member of the public who claims to have sustained injustice in consequence of maladministration in connection with action taken by or on behalf of an authority to which this Part of this Act applies, being action taken in the exercise of administrative functions of that authority, a Local Commissioner may investigate that complaint'.

Section 30(3A) (inserted by s 32 of the 1989 Act) provides:

> 'Where the Local Commissioner is of the opinion–
> (a)   that action constituting maladministration was taken which involved a member of the authority concerned, and
> (b)   that the member's conduct constituted a breach of the National Code of Local Government Conduct,
> then, unless the Local Commissioner is satisfied that it would be unjust to do so, the report shall name the member and give particulars of the breach'.

This provision therefore provides that where a member's conduct is involved in action constituting maladministration and in breach of the National Code of Local Government Conduct, the member is to be named and the particulars of the breach given, unless the local commissioner is satisfied that it would be unjust to do so. This made such misconduct a corporate issue, and a matter that was of genuine concern to all local authorities, not just to the member or group concerned.

Therefore, since the Monitoring Officer has a statutory requirement to act in the event of actual or possible maladministration coming to his/her attention, this brought member misconduct with his/her direct purview.

Maladministration is of course widely defined though it is not defined in the 1974 Act. The expression does appear in the Parliamentary Commissioner Act 1967, and in the second reading debate on the Parliamentary Commissioner Bill, Mr Richard Crossman stated that the characteristics of maladministration include 'bias, neglect, inattention, delay, incompetence, ineptitude, perversity, turpitude, arbitrariness and so on'[1].

The courts have recognised the meaning as defined by 'the Crossman catalogue'[2].

Whilst the National Code's lifespan is clearly limited, there are certain paragraphs that are worthy of particular comment.

Paragraph 1 states:

> 'Councillors hold office by virtue of the law, and must at all times act within the law. You should make sure that you are familiar with the rules of personal conduct which the law and standing orders require, and the guidance contained in this Code. It is your responsibility to make sure that what you do complies with these requirements and this guidance. You should regularly review your personal circumstances with this in mind, particularly when your circumstances change. You should not at any time advocate or encourage anything to the contrary. If in any doubt, seek advice from your council's appropriate senior officer or from your own legal adviser. In the end however, the decision and the responsibility are yours'.

Members are tasked with making themselves aware of the rules of procedure, and for seeking advice from senior officers when issues arise. It is a matter for officers to draw attention to members that such advice is available, and from whom – and to make that advice as easily consumable as possible – but it is not the responsibility of officers to ensure that members comply with the code. As the last sentence says, compliance with the code is ultimately a matter for each member.

Paragraphs 2, 3, and 4 state:

> '2.   Your over-riding duty as a councillor is to the whole local community.
> 3.   You have a special duty to your constituents, including those who did not vote for you.
> 4.   Whilst you may be strongly influenced by the views of others, and of your party in particular, it is your responsibility alone to decide what view to take on any question which councillors have to decide'.

In exercising his right to vote, a councillor may be influenced by, but his discretion may not be fettered by, party loyalty and party policy. In *R v Waltham Forest London Borough Council, ex p Baxter*[3], members of the majority group on the council held a private, party meeting where they discussed what the policy of the group would be as to the setting of the rate at the forthcoming council meeting. After discussion, the group agreed to support significant rate increases for both domestic and non-domestic rates. The group's standing orders provided that members were required to refrain from voting in opposition to group decisions, the sanction being withdrawal of the party whip. A number of members who voted against this level of increase at the group meeting voted in favour at the council meeting, at which a resolution to increase the rate by the previously agreed amounts was passed by 31 votes to 26. A number of ratepayers sought judicial review on a variety of grounds. The Divisional Court rejected arguments to the effect:

(1)   that the councillors had fettered their discretion by regarding them-selves as bound by the terms of their election manifesto to undertake expenditure which rendered such a rate inevitable;

(2)   that the resolution was 'irrational' or 'Wednesbury unreasonable';

(3)   that there was no genuine or adequate consultation with representa-tives of commerce and industry; and

(4)   that six or seven councillors had voted contrary to their personal views. The Court of Appeal dismissed an appeal confined to issue.

The court held that had the councillors in question voted for the resolution not because they were in favour of it but because their discretion had been fettered by the vote at the group meeting, then the councillors would have been in breach of their duty to make up their own minds as to what rate was appropriate. However, that was not established on the facts. The councillors were entitled to take account of party loyalty and party policy as relevant considerations provided that they did not dominate so as to exclude other considerations. The court noted that the sanction was only withdrawal of the party whip: there was nothing to prevent a councillor who voted against the party line continuing as an independent member. Per Russell LJ:

> 'Party loyalty, party unanimity, party policy, were all relevant consid-erations for the individual councillor. The vote becomes unlawful only when the councillor allows those considerations or any outside influences so to dominate as to exclude other considerations which are required for balanced judgement. If, by blindly toeing the party line, the councillor deprives himself of any real choice or the exercise of any real discretion, then his vote can be impugned and any resolution supported by his vote potentially flawed'.

Furthermore, these procedures were widely adopted by political groups throughout the country and this had not been regarded by Widdicombe as a matter for concern.

In *R v Local Comr for Administration in North and North East England, ex p Liverpool City Council*[4], Court of Appeal held that para 4 of the National Code reflected the law as stated in the Waltham Forest case and that the Commissioner had been entitled to find maladministration (a breach of para 4) where voting on a planning application was 'heavily, and perhaps decisively, influenced by a sense of party political loyalty, whether or not councillors had a well-founded fear of disciplinary action which might follow a decision to vote against party preference'. The party pressure had made the subsequent debate in council meaningless. Three councillors had told the Commissioner that they would have voted differently if it had been a free vote; one that he would never vote against the view of his party group; and one that he voted against the application even though he felt that the proposal was acceptable.

Paragraphs 6 and 7 of the Code provide:

> '6.   You should never do anything as a councillor which you could not justify to the public. Your conduct, and what the public believes about your conduct, will affect the reputation of your council, and of your party if you belong to one.
> 7.   It is not enough to avoid actual impropriety. You should at all times avoid any occasion for suspicion and any appearance of improper conduct.'

These paragraphs are significant, but they can also cause problems in terms of interpretation. Whilst it is quite reasonable to include reputation and perception as concepts that members should be sensitive to, it provides an opportunity for those seeking to make mischief to allege that either a member has committed misconduct, or failing that, has acted in such a way as to raise suspicion of misconduct (perhaps raised itself by the complainant) and thus the Member is in breach of the Code.

Paragraphs 8 to 12 address pecuniary and other interests, and paras 13 to 19 dispensations (see Division VI – Appendix 13 below). This regime will be radically revised by the Local Code, but has caused many of the problems associated with the National Code during its life, and have been particularly difficult for officer to advice, and members to understand.

In essence, Councillors should disclose private or personal (non-pecuniary) interests, unless they are insignificant or are shared with other members of the public generally (eg as a council tax payer or inhabitant of the local area), and councillors should not create the impression that they are using their position to promote private or personal interests (defined to include the interests of friends and family). By para 11 of the Code, once an interest has been declared, the member must decide whether it is clear and substantial. If it is, he may take no further part in the proceedings, in the absence of special circumstances, and should withdraw from the meeting while the matter is being considered.

It is important to remember that the issue of interests is also addressed by primary legislation[5].

Paragraphs 23 to 25 state:

> '23.   Both councillors and officers are servants of the public, and they are indispensable to one another. But their responsibilities are distinct. Councillors are responsible to the electorate and serve only so long as their term of office lasts. Officers are responsible to the council. Their jog is to give advice to councillors and the council, and to carry out the council's work under the direction and control of the council, their committees and sub-committees.
> 24.   Mutual respect between councillors and officers is essential to good local government. close personal familiarity between individual councillors and officers can damage this relationship and prove embarrassing to other councillors and officers.
> 25.   The law and standing orders lay down rules for the appointment, discipline and dismissal of staff. You must ensure that you observe these scrupulously at all times. Special rules apply to the appointment of assistants to political groups. In all other circumstances, if you are called upon to take part in appointing an officer, the only question you should consider is which candidate would best serve the whole council. You should not let your political or personal preferences influence your judgement. You should not canvass the support of colleagues for any candidate and you should resist any attempt by others to canvass yours.'

These paragraphs attempted to set out the relationship between officers and members. With time, it became clear that these provisions alone were not acceptable, and the concept of some kind of protocol setting out the working relationship came into favour (see para **[13.5]** and Division VI – Appendix 15 below).

Paragraph 26 provides, in respect of the use of confidential and private information that:

> 'As a councillor or a committee or sub-committee member, you necessarily acquire much information that has not yet been made public and is still confidential. It is a betrayal of trust to breach such confidences. You should never disclose or use confidential information for the personal advantage of yourself or of anyone known to you, or to the disadvantage or the discredit of the council or anyone else'.

As the media have come closer and closer into politics, the world of spin and presentation became more critical, the desire to (and at times inability to) control information flows has become an issue for many Councils. This is of course counterbalanced by a desire by the Government for openness accountability and transparency. However, in the world of 'real politics', leading groups wish to maintain degrees of confidentiality about proposals which they will wish to announce to secure the best political advantage for their party. Therefore this provision can be used either to tackle leaks within Councils, or occasionally (and worse) there are attempts to use it to control leaks within party groups by warring factions.

Since the job of 'enforcement' usually falls to the Monitoring Officer, it is an issue of proof in this case as to who was the anonymous leaker – the media will rarely reveal sources, and proving the 'case' is therefore almost always impossible. It will be interesting to see whether the National Standards Board requires full proof of such matters, or the extent to which it will take into account circumstantial evidence.

Paragraph 32 states:

> 'You should always make sure that any facilities (such as transport, stationery, or secretarial services) provided by the council for your use in your duties as a councillor or a committee or sub-committee member are used strictly for those duties and for no other purpose'.

This has caused some difficulties for members and officers. Members sometimes find it difficult to appreciate the difference between party business, and Council business. Whether the new executive arrangements make this more acute is perhaps an issue of concern. Nevertheless, there is a need to ensure that both the members and the officers who support the members can distinguish between the two, so that members, deliberately or inadvertently, do not break the provision. Again, the Officer/Member protocol, may allow for an expansion and explanation to reflect local arrangements.

1   (H.C. Deb., Vol. 754, col. 51 (1966) *R v Local Comr for Administration for the North and East Area of England, ex p Bradford Metropolitan City Council.*
2   [1979] QB 287 at 311–312 per Lord Denning MR.
3   [1988] QB 419.
4   (2000) 2 LGLR 603.
5   See ss 94 to 97 of the LGA 1972 which are set out at Div VI – App 11 below.

The Local Code

[13.4]
The Nolan Report recommended, inter alia, that there should be a clear Code of Conduct for Councillors developed by each local council within a framework approved by Parliament.

In Touch with the People reflected this, acknowledging that there would be a new framework to govern the conduct of Councillors and Council employees, Councils being required to adopt a Code of Conduct based on a national model which Councillors would be under a duty to observe with a new Code of Conduct for Council Employees built into their conditions of employment.

By *Local Leadership: Local Choice*, it had been recognised that the starting-point for developing such a Code would be a general set of principles to be subject to Parliamentary approval.

These principles are clearly significant and have already been referred to. This paper also reflected the view that the concentration of decision-making powers would lead to an increased chance of unethical conduct. The government disagreed, stating that:

> 'The new ethical framework will minimise the likelihood of unethical conduct in all Councils, regardless of their management structure'.

The government has issued a draft Model Code of Conduct and a consultation paper with that raised a number of issues. It is likely that the draft Model Code will be laid before Parliament in an amended form shortly. Division VI – Appendix 16 below contains the draft Model Code, together with a commentary[1] on both the government's consultation paper and comments, views and suggestions from various Councils and their Monitoring Officers on the impact and likely effect of the draft Model Code, should it be adopted.

---

1   Note that the government's analysis and rationale for the form and content of the Model Code constitute a significant proportion of the commentary.

The Officer / Member Protocol

[13.5]
The Nolan Report, in examining the working relationship between Officers and Members, recognised the National Code's obligation that:

> 'Mutual respect between Councillors and Officers is essential to good local government'.

The Nolan Report approved those authorities who had drawn up statements defining how the relationship should work and appended to the report the Officer/Member Protocol from Birmingham City Council and recommended that all authorities should consider introducing such statements.

This has been reflected in the Constitutional requirements placed on authorities contained in the Local Government Act 2000 (Constitution)

(England) Direction 2000 which is referred to at para **[10.26]** above and set out in full at Division VI – Appendix 4 below.

Various authorities now already operate Officer/Member Protocols and a model is set out at Division VI – Appendix 15 below.

CHAPTER 14
Promoting and Monitoring Standards

Introduction

[14.1]
Having established the proper and effective role of the Monitoring Officer, set up a Standards Committee, drafted and made Officers and Members aware of the proper documentation, as well as having ensured that the effective and proper standards are set, whether by way of a local code with variations, or ancillary matters, eg the Officer/Member Protocol, it is important that those standards are promoted and monitored. This chapter examines who should own the standards, the roles of Officers and Members in promoting, maintaining and adhering to standards, as well as looking at a specific tool produced by the IDeA, LGA and a small group of local authorities called the Ethical Governance Audit, which may provide assistance to those Officers and Members who wish to promote the Ethical Framework as something of importance, at the same time as establishing where their authority lies, in terms of the quality of its ethics and probity.

Ownership

[14.2]
It is possible to see, particularly in those authorities which operate a Standards Committee which operates within the narrow interpretation of its role, that the ownership of standards, their promotion and monitoring, will fall almost exclusively on the shoulders of the Monitoring Officer. That has severe disadvantages for both the Council and the Monitoring Officer. From the authority's perspective, standards will really only be applied if they are understood, believed and owned by those who have to adhere to them, ie Members. If it is left to the Monitoring Officer to be the chief owner of the Council's standards for Members, s/he will be on a slippery slope from the moment they start. They will be trying to persuade Members to do things which Members will see as bureaucratic, unnecessary and imposed by a paid officer.

If, on the other hand, the standards are owned, particularly if they are seen to be owned, maintained, reviewed and endorsed by a group of Members through the Standards Committee, then those standards will be seen to be the standards of the Members and those Members who do not follow them, will have to answer to those Members who have endorsed them as being right, proper, appropriate and fair.

Therefore, the question of ownership, whilst in some senses a matter of principle rather than substance, is in fact very significant in this context.

In addition, as well as being owned by Members, the concept of an Ethical Framework should not be seen solely as an issue for the Monitoring Officer and/or the Standards Committee. In Officer terms, it is clearly an issue for all of the statutory officers, but it is also an issue for the Council's management team and the professional heads of all the various services, as well as specific units within local authorities – for example, Committee/Democratic Services, Internal Audit etc.

Role of Officers / Members

Role of Chief Executive

[14.3]
Given that the Head of Paid Service may no longer be the Monitoring Officer, the triumvirate of the statutory officers will generally be three individuals. However, given that the Head of Paid Service/Chief Executive will be senior to the Head of Legal Services, it is clearly important that the Chief Executive owns, responds, acknowledges and is supportive of the Ethical Framework and, indeed, the role of the Monitoring Officer. It should be stressed that this happens across local government already, but the importance of it should not be under-estimated.

Members faced with a situation which they find unattractive, promulgated, supported or communicated by an Officer of the authority, will seek to raise it at the highest level possibly with a view to trying to have it overturned or ameliorated.

It is important that the Chief Executive, Monitoring Officer and Chief Finance Officer for this reason speak as one and the Chief Executive needs to be seen to be supportive of the statutory role of his/her statutory Officers, and the significance and importance of a sound, solid ethical framework which will provide the underpinning for the effective delivery of quality services to the citizens.

This does not mean the three statutory officers have to be personally responsible for the nuts and bolts, but clearly they need to be aware of what is going on and communicate with each other on a regular basis so they are mutually informed of issues, concerns etc.

There is clearly nothing worse for a Chief Executive than having to face a Member with a complaint about a matter where the Member expects an immediate response when the Chief Executive is not briefed by the relevant officer as to what has been going on.

The contrary position is, of course, that for Chief Executives who are committed to the Ethical Framework, the appropriate approach of the Monitoring Officer and who are familiar with issues in their authority but imbue (and are seen to) trust in their statutory officers, they will manage (and be seen to manage) an authority with the confidence to address ethical issues in a way that is appropriate, robust and supportive of the Council.

Role of Executive Directors

[14.4]
Whether the Directors are Executive in style or not within a local authority, the Chief Officer tier is clearly predominantly policy/strategic focussed and has a role to play in ethics and probity. They need to understand the broad principles, in the same way the Chief Executive does, so that where issues arise, they are aware and familiar with them and, again, they should not either leave or be seen to leave the issue of the Ethical Framework to one or two individuals, ie the statutory officers. As the senior managers of any local authority, the Directors/Chief Officers and the senior management team need to own the principles that underpin the way in which the authority works, thereby bolstering the confidence that should be given to their views, opinions and advice to the elected Members.

The Monitoring Officer should be confident to have an expectation that the Chief Officers' management team (which s/he should obviously be a member of) in discharging their Executive/Director roles, will in promulgating the policies of the Councils, act in a lawful manner. The same clearly applies to the Chief Officer and his/her expectations of their staff.

Role of Heads of Services, Committee Services, Legal Services etc

[14.5]
The principles enunciated above are reflected in the officers who sit at Head of Service levels, although their level of knowledge and information, whilst it needs to have a breadth, will clearly in some circumstances be focussed around their particular service area. This is understandable, but the breadth of knowledge and understanding should not be omitted. In addition, particular services will have a particular focus. Reference has already been made to the Legal Services function within the Council, whether that is with or split from the Monitoring Officer. The Committee/Democratic Services function may not always be vested within the Legal Services function, although it is suggested that for good operational reasons it should be.

Where it is not, it is important that there is a close working relationship and understanding between the two, and that the Committee Services/ Democratic Services function should not be seen to be vested in the 'yes' culture to Members. They will have a significant role to play in decision-making, sometimes contrary to what Members wish to achieve. Of course, they should attempt to assist Members to achieve their objectives, but they also need to have the ability to say 'no'. This can be very unpalatable for junior Committee Services Members, and hence one of the reasons why a strong management culture where that division/function is headed by a statutory officer can be of assistance within an authority.

In addition, functions such as the Internal Audit function clearly have a role to play in terms of their investigative role and support to policies such as whistle-blowing/duty to act.

Role of statutory officers

[14.6]
In order to ensure that the three statutory officers – Head of Paid Services, Chief Finance Officer and Monitoring Officer – work effectively and well together, it is useful if there is a sharing of information between the three, and an understanding as to how the arrangements will be discharged. In some authorities, this takes the form of a regular meeting between the three statutory officers to discuss issues or areas of concern, commonality etc. In other authorities, it simply is an acknowledgement of the need to ensure that each of the statutory officers need to be briefed on any actual likely issues that are live, as soon as possible. This enables, for example and as indicated above, the Chief Executive to be fully aware, as Head of Paid Service, of an issues as soon as possible and ideally prior to a Member knocking on his/her door. The same goes for the inter-relationship of information between all three. In the days of electronic media, that should be very easy to achieve, but where there is perhaps not a developed working relationship or culture to use such devices or formalised arrangements may need to be put in place. However, that information flow – which can sometimes be information of an entirely rumour related basis, matters of innuendo etc, is crucial to the effective discharge of those three roles, and the support mechanism provided by the three sharing such information, should not be underestimated.

Role of Executive

[14.7]
Clearly, the Executive exists to provide the community leadership role within the Council, to lead on policy and strategy, subject to the Policy Framework as approved by the Council.

In ethical and probity terms, as already stated, there are those who have feared that the concentration of power in so few – the Executive – could lead to increased ethical issues. Therefore, it is for the Executive to robustly demonstrate that not only is that not going to be the case, but they would wish to show that their decision-making and their approach to conducting the business of the local authority is utterly and completely transparent, open and accountable, and that their actions, whilst there may be political differences about their judgements, are sound, honest, trustworthy and completely in line with the Codes of Conduct, ethical policy etc. To that extent, particularly as the new arrangements start, the new Executives will require significant guidance and assistance to ensure that they are probably going 10 to 25% beyond that which they might be required to do to demonstrate the soundness and robustness of their delivery of high ethical standards.

However, against that, there must be a caution not to require them to detach themselves from so many issues, due to potential conflicts of interests, and to go so overboard that their role as an Executive – the leadership role in particular – is seen to be watered down because they are unable to perform it due to a framework that is inhibiting the delivery of the Executive and its functioning. This is not an easy balance, but it is something that will need to be worked on.

Role of the Chairman of the Council

[14.8]
The Chairman of the Council will remain a significant figure because s/he will chair the Full Council meeting. In those authorities that have Executive arrangements involving a Leader and Cabinet, this post may, of course, be filled by a Mayor, but a Mayor who performs a ceremonial role as compared to an Executive one.

It must never be forgotten that the common law rules in terms of meetings apply to the person presiding at a Full Council meeting, and on the basis of the Local Government Act 1972, this person will, save in their absence, be the Chairman of the Council.

Given that the Full Council meetings will discharge significant aspects of business – approval of and variations to the Policy Framework, approval of and variation to the Constitution being but two, the role of the Chairman of the Council in this aspect is significant.

In addition, there are a number of authorities where that role is extended. For example, the Chairman of the Council, by virtue of their role, in a number of Councils automatically chairs the Standards Committee. This is seen as an impartial appointment and one that gives the important function and role to be discharged by the Standards Committee appropriate gravitas.

In addition, a number of Councils have taken the view that the Chairman of the Council should have a significant role in relation to the Overview and Scrutiny function, and that whilst perhaps that does not involve actually discharging any scrutiny functions per se given the time required to discharge the Chairman's functions, it may involve, for example, chairing the Management Committee, ie the body that has overall responsibility for formulating, time-tabling and organising the scrutiny function.

Regardless of the breadth and extent of the Chairman's role, it will change, and it will be significant within both the ambit of the authority and in terms of the ethical regime within the Council. Not least of these aspects will be the need for the Chairman of the Council or the person presiding at Full Council to be familiar with the revised Council Procedure Rules/Standing Orders, (or whatever they are called in the authority), which will undoubtedly have to change given the changing nature of business for Full Councils.

Role of back-bench Members

[14.9]
The role of back-bench Members in promoting and monitoring standards is an easy one to overlook. When one looks at all the structures, persons and entities involved in this regime, it can often be seen as the role of all of those bodies or persons to enforce standards against back-bench Members.

However, back-bench Members have a significant role in promoting their own standards, not just complying with them. For example, their behaviour will dictate the way in which the authority is viewed by the outside world.

There is no doubt that the Executive will have the binoculars placed on them for much of the time, as they will be discharging significant functions, often as individuals. However, the way in which back-benchers conduct themselves will have a significant impact upon the community and the way in which back-bench Members conduct themselves in Committees and Full Council is again an issue that will reflect broadly upon how the Council is viewed in terms of its ethical approach. All Members should be supplied with appropriate training and development in relation to ethics and standards, and back-bench Members are no exception. For example, the need to comply with the obligations regarding declarations of interest will be just as important to them as it is to Executive Members.

In addition, back-bench Members will carry the beacon of Overview and Scrutiny. The way in which that is conducted will in itself, be a significant barometer of the way in which the authority deals with and reacts to a variety of issues, questions and, perhaps at times, dilemmas.

If the back-bench Members view their role as being non-contributory, then the Executive will have an inappropriate level of freedom. If, however, the back-bench Members see their role as significant, both in terms of participation at Full Council and Policy Framework approval etc, and in terms of Overview and Scrutiny, not just in the negative sense but in the policy development arena as well, this will mean bringing the Executive to account, something that should be viewed as healthy, good practice and part of the important checks and balances that will help ensure not only effective decision-making, but also will deliver a system and regime that will be robust. A robust system is less likely to have ethical dilemmas.

Role of Standards Committees

[14.10]
The provisions of ss 53 and 54 of the 2000 Act have already been considered. Section 54, inter alia, provides that it is a function of the Standards Committee to promote and maintain high standards of conduct within that authority. How is the Standards Committee to go about promoting and monitoring standards. It is suggested that there are a number of routes available to it:

(1)   by endorsing and supporting the Ethical Framework and adopting a wider governance role, the Standards Committee will be seen to be proactively engaging across the authority with a view to ensuring that the rules, procedures as well as the standards to deliver high standards of ethics and probity but, at the same time, are owned and managed by the very Members who will have to operate those systems;

(2)   by endorsing such activities as the Ethical Governance Audit (referred to later);

(3)   by reviewing, monitoring and maintain the Members' and Officers' training and continuing development programme;

(4)   by advising and monitoring the Code of Conduct, Officer/Member Protocol, any local variations and any supplementary guidance;

(5)   by reviewing any other standards etc against which Members' conduct will have to be measured;

(6)   by proactively facilitating the discussion and raising of awareness of ethical issues and by being the 'champions' of ethics and probity within their Council.

Ethical Governance Audit

[14.11]
The Ethical Governance Audit is a device initiated by a combination of the Local Government Association, IDeA, DETR and a small group of local authorities who piloted an early version.

The purpose of the audit is to provide a self-help tool for local authorities to ascertain the level and standard of the Ethical Framework in place in their authority, to identify gaps and to assist them in remedying their gaps. It is being produced on the basis that it will provide a significant step for authorities in undertaking the proactive role so vital to the task of the Standards Committee, and so important to ensuring that the level of standards in each local authority is as high as possible.

The benefits of an Ethical Governance Audit should not be underestimated. Clearly, the way in which the tool is operated will deliver certain results and those results may not always been painless. Most authorities will probably have general feel for the likely outcome of any audit. However, the audit will bring those results into sharp focus and, therefore, the most important factor that comes out of an audit, is the action plan and the delivery against that action plan in terms of rolling forward any omissions, deficiencies or shortcomings within the Ethical Framework. Whilst a clear over-generalisation, most authorities have reasonably robust bureaucratic documentary arrangements in place, although they are always likely to benefit from revision, and will indeed have to have that with the production of the new Constitution. Those authorities that have conducted these audits have generally found that the principle outcomes are:

* a lack of knowledge and awareness of what the standards are and how to find them;
* a general lack of commitment to both the process of the audit, ie the number of returned questionnaires etc combined with a lack of inclination to necessarily see ethics and probity as a significant core issue for the Council.

The audit needs to start with an identification of a methodology and a suggested methodology is set out at Division VI – Appendix 17 below.

There is no prescribed way of doing the Ethical Governance Audit. Different authorities have in the pilot adopted different approaches. The methodology appended is that adopted by Southampton City Council. It worked for Southampton City Council, but for other authorities the methodology should reflect the needs of their audit process.

Clearly a key part of the methodology is the questionnaire and a copy of the questionnaire, which was used by the majority of the pilot authorities is set out at Division VI – Appendix 18 below.

Ethical Standards

The actual audit itself is contained within a document produced by the IDeA which has not yet been published but which is available on their website[1].

Those authorities starting out on consideration of ethics and probity will often wish to indicate to Members, either of the Standards Committee or generally, indicators of good and bad practice, and identify some objectives against either known deficiencies or general ethical issues against which the performance of their authority could or, indeed, should be measured. The audit contains, under a series of headings, both positive and contrary indicators of a high standard of ethics and probity, and those can be exceptionally useful in analysing and/or presenting either an analysis of one's own authority, or a prescription for what one might classify as an authority with a high standard of ethics and/or probity.

The core competencies (as the Ethical Governance Audit referred to them) are clearly at the fulcrum of this – these are:

- integrity;
- accountability; and
- standards management.

Within these core competencies are more specific characteristics, and it is these characteristics against these pro and contra indicator are set. The full set is as follows:

Integrity

- ethical vision;
- communication;
- commitment; and
- leadership.

Accountability

- organisational management;
- systems and process operation;
- objectivity; and
- scrutiny.

Standards Management

- standards integration;
- people and practice management;
- training and development; and
- planning and review.

The Ethical Governance Audit is strongly commended to all.

1   http://www.idea.gov.uk/member/ethicalgov.pdf.

CHAPTER 15
National Standards Board, the Adjudication Panel and Case Tribunals

Introduction

[15.1]
The Government, during the consultation on the Ethical Framework, moved away from the initial proposals of the Nolan Report to a regime whereby an independent body, with a split between the adjudicative and the investigatory function, would investigate written complaints for misconduct against Members of local authorities. This chapter examines how that arrangement will work, and the responsibilities of the various entities.

Background

[15.2]
The Nolan Report acknowledged that there was, at that time, no way in which a council collectively could act against an individual councillor for non-compliance with the Code of Conduct other than by exclusion from Committee with the consent of the councillor's party group. Nolan agreed that there should be a Standards Committee in every local authority, but recommended that in addition to this internal disciplinary procedure, there would need to be an external appeals mechanism. The recommendation was the introduction of a Local Government Tribunal to hear appeals from councillors who had been subject to disciplinary action by their own local authority for breaching its code of conduct. Therefore, Nolan recommended that the Standards Committee had genuine powers to discipline Members, but that this independent appellant body would be empowered to hear appeals, and whilst Standards Committees would be able to recommend the suspension of councillors for up to three months as well as the imposition of lesser penalties, the Tribunal would be empowered to disqualify councillors from office.

'In Touch with the People' identified the now familiar role of the Standards Committee, namely a proactive, non-enforcement body, and chose to remove the disciplinary element to the Standards Board, an independent body with a regional structure. The Standards Board would investigate complaints, quite possibly referring the matter back to the Monitoring Officer seeking further information or a report on the facts, and then in dealing with the matter would need to have proper separation between its investigative and judicative functions.

By 1999 and the publication of 'Local Leadership, Local Choice', the role of the Standards Committee had become firmly embodied, a new entity called an Ethical Standards Officer had been created who was to be responsible for receiving, investigating and reporting on allegations of breaches of an authority's code of conduct, these Ethical Standards Officers comprise a significant part of the Standards Board and it was proposed to establish Adjudication Panels independent of Ethical Standards Officers and their work, who would hear cases referred to them by the Standards Board decide whether a breach of the Code had taken place and, if so, impose an appropriate penalty. This brought about the effective separation of the investigative and adjudicative roles as referred to in 'In Touch with the People'.

Local Government Act 2000

[15.3]
Chapters II and III of Pt III of the Local Government Act 2000 deal with investigations in relation to conduct for England and Wales respectively.

In summary, a Standards Board for England will be established, comprising at least three members appointed by the Secretary of State which will employ Ethical Standards Officers to investigate and report on complaints of breach of a local code by a member of a local authority. In Wales, the functions of the Standards Board are to be taken by the Ombudsman, and the functions of the Ethical Standards Officer will be taken by the local commissioners.

When a written complaint is received by the Standards Board, or the Ombudsman in Wales, they shall take a preliminary view as to whether the matter should be investigated and then allocate it to an Ethical Standards Officer or local commissioner for investigation. The Ethical Standards Officer, or local commissioner, has extensive powers to require any person to respond to questions or produce documents for the purposes of the investigation, but will clearly require the assistance of the Monitoring Officer of the authority for the conduct of the investigation. This is clearly similar to the way in which the Local Government Ombudsman deals with complaints received and inter-reacts with link officers in every local authority (although not every link officer is the Monitoring Officer).

At the conclusion of the investigation, the Ethical Standards Officer or local commissioner will conclude either:

- that there is no evidence of a breach of the local code; or
- that there is such evidence but no action is required; or
- that the matter should be referred to the authority's Monitoring Officer; or
- that the matter should be referred to a case tribunal/adjudications panel for determination.

There are, as yet, no regulations which set out the powers/duties of the Monitoring Officer where a matter is referred to him/her by the Ethical Standards Officer or local commissioner. However, in the absence of such guidance and/or until such guidance is fully promulgated, it may be useful to adopt some local interim guidance (see Division VI – Appendix 19 below).

Section 60 of the 2000 Act provides for regulations which would allow an investigator to cease the investigation and refer the matter to the Monitoring Officer. This would enable, inter alia, the Monitoring Officer to carry out the investigation, report the results to the council's Standards Committee and prescribe the sanctions which the Standards Committee might impose.

Whilst the Act does not indicate the circumstances where these regulatory power making provisions might be implemented, the Government's stated intention is that the provision should only be implemented once the Acts have been operating for a period. There is a view – there are, however, conflicting views – that in the initial months of operation, there will be a significant number of cases which will swamp the resources available to the National Standards Board and, therefore, that these provisions should be triggered early to provide both a safety net to ensure that cases are investigated adequately, if necessary, in the first three months, by the Monitoring Officer and, secondly, that the consequences of not triggering these provisions at an early stage, either to deal with *de minimus* matters or to provide support, where directed and required of the National Standards Board, might result in the wait in a number of cases in the early months breaking the system down and thus causing discredit to the whole operation of the new Ethical Framework.

In all probability, however, it is likely that, subject to the sort of safety net provision as indicated above, the intention is that these provisions will be used for dispensations and relatively minor cases, perhaps relating to parish councils with the significant triggering of the provisions being related to utilisation and/or successful self-assessment perhaps (on an audited basis) of the Ethical Governance Audit.

Where an investigator concludes that the matter does have sufficient substance to be taken forward, their report is sent to the chair of the Adjudication Panel who sets up a case tribunal. There is, as yet, no procedure for how Case Tribunals will operate, but it is likely that the case to be presented will be, in essence, the report of the investigator, but there is clearly the possibility of witnesses being called which could include not only the Monitoring Officer, but also councillors, officers and, indeed, citizens. At the conclusion of the hearing, the tribunal decides whether there has been a breach of the code of conduct and where there has been, the tribunal has two sanctions available to it:

- suspension; or
- disqualification.

In the event that the tribunal decides that no breach has occurred, it must give notice to the Standards Committee.

If a case tribunal decides that there has been a breach of the code but the person concerned should not be suspended or disqualified, it will give notice to the Standards Committee, specifying the details of the breach.

Working with Local Government

[15.4]
It is clear from a rudimentary assessment of the new procedures that they are

complex, time-consuming and likely to be highly costly. In terms of needing to resolve these issues rapidly, it is clear that the amount of time and effort taken to deal with a substantive complaint, is going to be so considerable that authorities will look for ways for addressing those sorts of issues which might lend themselves to an 'internal' arrangement, and this inevitable system that the National Standards Board will need to look to and address and, it is suggested, support, is in its own interests.

Paragraph 7 of the draft Model Code requires that a Member must report to both the National Standards Board for England and the authority's Monitoring Officer any conduct of another Member which s/he believes a failure to comply with the authority's code of conduct.

There must, however, be certain more minor matters that can either be dealt with within the authority, or can be referred to the party groups to be dispensed with, thus avoiding the expense and complexities of the full procedure being brought into play.

In addition, councils retain the residual responsibilities acknowledged by the *Lashley* case (see para **[11.3]** above) and retain at least some sanctions available to them where they determine that there has been misconduct by a councillor.

For example, councils will be able to:

- give advice as to future conduct, which can be appropriate when the misconduct is not particularly serious, and the sanctions of suspension or disqualification are either inappropriate for a case tribunal, or the case tribunal has decided not to impose the sanctions but where the important aspect is to prevent a recurrence;

- going beyond merely giving advice, it is possible for a council to resolve to censure a Member for a particular item, aspect or pattern of conduct, thus recording publicly upon the record of the council the council's disapproval of the way in which a particular Member has conducted him/herself – this could even be seen as a form of caution, to be taken into account in any further misconduct;

- the council has, subject to some significant caveats, the ability to remove a Member from an office to which the councillor has been appointed by the council – it is important to note that there are particular provisions relating to Committees and Sub-Committees in terms of the allocation of Committee seats and regulations on political proportionality that means that councillors per se are not appointed to Committees, but this would be an issue for party groups but, if a councillor was found to have, for example, misconducted themselves in terms of the handling of a licensing application for, perhaps, a relative, it might be appropriate if that councillor was to no longer sit as a member of the Licensing Committee. There were also clearly appointments by the council to outside bodies, some of which are seen as genuinely a benefit and an indication of status, position and responsibility;

- the council may also consider withdrawing council facilities, although they will have to be mindful of the provisions in the National Code and, in the future, the Model Code, about the use of resources and the fact that such withdrawal of facilities should not be aimed at preventing the councillor from discharging his/her legitimate democratic and legal responsibilities;

- however, where the facilities have perhaps been abused, secretarial resources being used for party political purposes, then withdrawal of the provision of an office and/or secretarial or other support service, may be an appropriate response. Alternatively, where a Member has physically or verbally abused or assaulted staff, particularly where that takes place within Civic buildings, banning from council buildings, except for attendance at council meetings (as compared to political meetings) may well be an appropriate response, although it would no doubt be seen by many as draconian;

- it should never be forgotten that in many cases, serious misconduct will equate with misconduct in another place and/or under another set of rules and regulations. There are other agencies who may have a particular interest in the issue and the council may well wish to refer those matters to other agencies. It is suggested that as a matter of good practice, the three statutory officers should have automatic delegated authority to refer any matter where they believe there is criminality to the Police. It is further recommended as good practice that the three statutory officers should do so without delay whenever that situation arises, subject to whatever local protocols/procedures exist with the local Police. There should never be a situation where an Officer sits on a matter that is possibly reflecting criminal conduct for whatever reason. To do so, represents a risk for the council, the individual concerned and the Officer. If in doubt, the safest route is to refer the matter to the Police who may or may not decide to proceed with or without advice of the Crown Prosecution Service.

These arrangements give an indication (and there are others) of actions and sanctions that council may choose to take in relation to misconduct outside the responsibility of the National Standards Board, the Adjudication Panel and Case Tribunals.

These new bodies, as well as taking forward their important, significant and welcome independent role in terms of dealing with Member misconduct, need to work with local government to ensure that the Ethical Framework is delivered and the expectations of the citizens that 'trust' can be enhanced and preserved, are delivered.

The National Standards Board, by virtue of s 57(5) of the LGA 2000 (set out at Division VI – Appendix 6 below) has the power to issue, inter alia, guidance on the conduct of Members and co-opted Members.

Local government should welcome the opportunity that this presents, and encourage the National Standards Board not to codify, restrict or fetter the ability of authorities to deal with these matter, but to look to the National Standards Board to provide good practice guidance on how local government might work within the regime, and support the Ethical Framework by taking a relative view on the minor, low-level matters that do not warrant a full 2000 Act investigation and adjudication.

CHAPTER 16
Conducting An Investigation

Introduction

[16.1]
This chapter investigates the varying responsibilities of the parties, in terms of conducting an investigation, who will do what, what the process is and how each of the entities involved in the investigation, eg Monitoring Officer, Standards Committee, National Standards Board, will integrate.

Who Will Do What?

[16.2]
At the current time, the National Standards Board for England is still in its infancy, the legislation is not fully in force, secondary legislation is only partially in place and the guidance is not yet complete.

To understand how an investigation will be conducted and by whom will require considerably more work both by the National Standards Board and by Monitoring Officers working in partnership with the National Standards Board, Ethical Standards Officers and, indeed, the other agencies who are involved, eg the Local Government Ombudsman etc.

In due course, the picture will become clear about the way in which an investigation is to be processed, decisions are made about whether or not the Secretary of State intends to make regulations under s 66 of the 2000 Act and the processes and procedures are understood.

However, at the current time and prior to the implementation of the full legislative position, in the absence of a Local Code, and without any powers to take any action, the only way in which an investigation can be conducted and the only person who will conduct an investigation in most authorities is, of course, the Monitoring Officer, and Councils are, therefore, referred to Division VI – Appendix 20 below and the Model Special Procedure for dealing with such issues in the interim.

In due course, when the full position is known, this part of this text will be expanded, not only to provide a narrative as to the way in which investigations are to be conducted, but also appropriate guidance and precedents etc.

CHAPTER 17
Best Value, Overview and Scrutiny and Ethics and Probity

Introduction

[17.1]
This chapter looks at the inter-relationship between Best Value, Overview and Scrutiny and Ethics and Probity, looking at both Best Value and Overview and Scrutiny from the point of the Ethical Framework, the inter-relationship between the various aspects and the significance of ethics and probity to both concepts and their importance within the modernisation of local government.

Inter-Relationship Between Best Value and Ethics and Probity

[17.2]
In seeking to secure Best Value, the Executive will look to find new and better ways of delivering services to the citizens in order to improve their quality of life, bearing in mind the obligation to prepare a Community Strategy as set out in the 2000 Act and the new Pt I powers to promote economic, social and environmental well-being, also contained in the same legislation.

In meeting this statutory duty, the authority as a whole will, as well as looking to the Executive to lead the search for Best Value, need to comply with the statutory obligation to conduct a rolling programme of Best Value Reviews over a five year period. Thus, all functions, which in accordance with the primary and secondary legislation, will go through some kind of review process. Various aspects will be looked at during the course of that review process, including how effective the services are and, of course, the four C's:

- consult;
- challenge;
- compare; and
- compete.

Consideration may be given as part of the Best Value review, particularly for certain services, as to how well the ethical and probity regime operates. For example, an examination of how well the Committee Services function works in an authority will not only need to look at the efficiency with which

185

the decisions are recorded, promulgated, as well as the support systems to Members, but will also want in qualitative terms, to assess how problems have been resolved where there has been an issue about, for example, the recording of the rationale for a decision under the new Executive Arrangements.

The robustness of the operation, the training, development and awareness of the decision-making system and its application would clearly be a factor in assessing the efficiency of the service. Thus, whilst Best Value Reviews per se would not would necessarily address the issue of ethics and probity, it is an issue that should be built into Officer development training generally and for certain services there will be a direct inter-relationship which should be properly taken account of. Sometimes this will mean that, particularly from an outside perspective, the service may seem to be inefficient – because those who are evaluating or inspecting may not have the knowledge or experience to understand what is needed and required. This is why, at times, proper procedures and documentation can be useful so that at least there is a clearly documented rationale for the procedures. Again, sharing best practice across councils is an ideal way of achieving this in the most efficient and effective way possible.

Inter-Relationship Between Overview and Scrutiny and the Ethical Framework

[17.3]
There are clearly going to be circumstances where Members choose to undertake an Overview and Scrutiny exercise into a matter which has an ethical dimension. Obvious examples could be a situation where a particular issue of ethics or probity has arisen and the Overview and Scrutiny function is to be used to get at or behind that issue. There needs to be built into the Overview and Scrutiny arrangements a methodology whereby the Monitoring Officer (either of his/her own volition on behalf of the Standards Committee or possibly in due course on behalf of the National Standards Board/an Ethical Standards Officer) can either suspend, delay or remove from the terms of reference of Overview and Scrutiny a particular issue because to investigate it would fetter or in any other manner detract from an investigation into an ethical issue that should be addressed by others.

At first site, this seems a draconian and difficult provision, yet whilst the detail operation of this type of arrangement is new to local authorities, there has in many councils been an arrangement or understanding that where issues have arisen which have been rightly referred to other agencies, eg the police, councils do not get involved in looking at the issue whilst another agency is dealing with the matter.

It is simply, in essence, a rolling forward of that type of an arrangement.

In addition, it may be useful to differentiate between a matter relating to a service issue where, for example, there is a clear service issue wrapped up with an ethical issue, and it is frequently possible to delineate the terms of reference of an Overview and Scrutiny exercise so as not to tread on the toes of a matter being reviewed by either another body within the authority or a separate body. Therefore, the ability of the statutory officers to have both access to the reports of Overview and Scrutiny which could flag up salient issues which they would need to look at, as well as the ability to comment on and, if necessary, intervene in relation to terms of reference, is significant and important. If the rationale behind this is appreciated as being appropriate, necessary and frequently to the benefit of all concerned, then there should be no difficulty with this. Perhaps somewhat perversely, those authorities who have had problems with ethical issues in the past are more likely to be prepared to see those reviewed and addressed by an external body and, therefore, when approached by the Monitoring Officer on a matter that cuts across several functional boundaries, eg Best Value, Overview and Scrutiny, ethics and probity, are likely to be more prepared to acknowledge that the ethical issues should be addressed and addressed robustly and properly by that independent body without fetter or inappropriate intervention by the council through another one of its functions.

In order to achieve this, it is helpful within the arrangements that are established for Overview and Scrutiny to ensure that such intervention is acknowledged and understood.

Whilst it will still cause difficulty, if such possible intervention is indicated at the outset, it is easier then to use the facility provided rather than having to intervene without there having been any prior indication of that possibility.

Whilst there are Overview and Scrutiny procedure rules contained within the Constitution, there is clearly much guidance that the authority needs to consider about how Overview and Scrutiny will work, and this could be promulgated in a number of forms – for example, a Handbook approved by the parent Overview and Scrutiny Committee (if that is the model adopted).

If this is the case, then the Handbook can address these issues in some detail and pre-warn Members of the possibility that, in the event of the inter-relationship arising, there may be circumstances where their Overview and Scrutiny exercise has to take second place and fall down the list of priorities.

Ethical Standards in Best Value and Scrutiny

[17.4]
There is a clear need when looking at any part of the Modernising Agenda – whether it is ethics and probity, Best Value, the new Executive arrangements, local strategic partnerships, et al – to see the picture as a whole.

Underpinning all the new arrangements, structures, bodies, powers etc is a requirement to have a sound ethical framework.

It may not be the top of all the agendas in the Modernising Agenda, but it is contained within all the elements of the Modernising Agenda.

For without a robust ethical framework, Overview and Scrutiny will not operate – but an effective Overview and Scrutiny regime will contribute to a sound ethical authority.

The same, in essence, applies across all of the arrangements.

It is, of course, an issue that may in its own right be subject to a Best Value review, and may in its own right be subject to Overview and Scrutiny, although in having a Standards Committee in every authority, it may perhaps be considered to be wasteful to undertake this type of activity when indeed the Standards Committee should regularly be looking at and ensuring that the regime that is in place is appropriate for the council.

At an Officer level, assuming that a majority of the activity is to be carried out by the Monitoring Officer who, in most if not many authorities, will be located in the Legal Department, there would clearly be aspects of the work that will be brought within the Best Value Review process as set out in the Local Government Act 1999 and secondary legislation.

However, these are overlaps at the margins.

The key message about the way in which the Modernising Agenda inter-links is that no one aspect could or indeed should, succeed absolutely without the other aspect's contributing to it – and of all the aspects of the Modernising Agenda, the one element that underpins every other part is the sound ethical framework that the Government expects local authorities to adopt, put in place and maintain.

Division III
Community Focus

CHAPTER 18
Community Planning and Corporate Strategy

Introduction

[18.1]

'The only way by which any one divests himself of his natural liberty and puts on the bonds of civil society is by agreeing with other men to join and unite into a community'.
John Locke [1690]
'There is no such thing as Society. There are individual men and women, and there are families.'
Margaret Thatcher [1987]

In this Division we will look in some detail at the way the local authority interacts with the social fabric in which it lives, and which, after all, created it in the first place. We will look at the legal issues that arise from that interaction.

The first chapter in this Division (Chapter 18) is about planning – *planning ahead*, not town and country planning. It is a logical and topical place to start, logical because the plan should come before the activity, topical because the legislative framework for local authorities now is utterly plan based. This will introduce the new Community Strategy and the Local Strategic Partnership that should compose and deliver it, and their place in modernised structures and thinking.

The second chapter (Chapter 19) covers partnership. It takes us through the myriad relationships that this overworked word can describe, the drift away from legal personality in public law, the issues that can arise if a partnership goes wrong, and some of the intricacies of the partnership relationship for local authorities.

The third chapter (Chapter 20) is about consultation. What exactly is the duty to consult? And what does this mean in constitutional terms?

Then the fourth chapter (Chapter 21) deals with public access to information, a complex and developing topic, and one to which local government should pay more attention just now, else it will be caught unawares.

The Rise and Rise of the Statutory Plan

[18.2]
We will start with the statutory plan. The days when you got out the statute to look up the law have long gone. In the twenty-first century you need the Act,

the schedules, the regulations, the regulations that correct the mistakes in the first regulations, directions, guidance, statutory guidance, and several codes of practice.

The Local Government Act 2000 is bidding for the high water mark. Thanks to HMSO and an unexpected degree of liaison between the departments of state, material has accreted to the DETR Guidance Pack on Pt II of the Act like driftwood in a hurricane. There are no prizes at all for the first authority to be challenged for failing to take some of this into account, but how impressive it is to carry the Guidance Pack into a committee room.

Over-prescriptive government is an easy target, so it is only fair to redress the balance. The 1992 DETR publication *The Functions of Local Authorities in England* listed the different areas of local authority functions at the time. In about 7% of these areas, the local authority can choose whether or not to get involved at all. In about two-thirds the process is highly regulated, leaving little scope for local discretion. In the remaining third, the local authority can at least decide how to discharge the function.

But it is never as simple as that. Nowadays, you have to have a plan. In July 1948 the post-war labour government, having limbered up by inventing the welfare state and the nationalised industries, created town planning, as we know it today, and probably the first universal statutory duty on local government to prepare a plan. The development plan has had its ups and downs. It took a few years for anyone to take it seriously, and even in 1999 the local government minister was complaining that only 67% of authorities had adopted an area-wide plan. But the idea stuck. There are at least thirty statutory plans for local government, although this number excludes the plans the other people have to make which affect local government. Winnie-the-Pooh, counting his pots of Honey and never being quite sure of the number would recognise the problem. Under executive arrangements, 11 of these are so important that they have to be approved by a full council meeting. The statutory guidance lists another six that might be reserved to council. Government ministers have shown genuine interest in streamlining the planning requirements, it is to be hoped that the outcome will not be hedged around with conditions that are as complex as the plans themselves.

Here is a list of the main statutory plans. Of course, some, like the development plan, are in constant use to test decision-making. Others, one suspects, are rarely consulted except by the people whose job it is to update them. But it is better to have a plan than to potter on aimlessly. The various statutory Inspectorates do tend to take this part of the game rather seriously, so if you are interested in either securing good marks, or avoiding bad marks, it helps to get your plan in order.

The Community Strategy under s 4 of the Local Government Act 2000 is covered in some detail below.

The Best Value Performance Plan is compiled to meet a straightforward statutory duty under s 6(1) of the Local Government Act 1999, backed up by the Local Government (Best Value) Performance Plans and Reviews Order 1999[1] and the Local Government (Best Value) (Review and Performance Plans) (Wales) Order 2000[2]. It must set out the council's objectives for exercising its functions, any assessment it has made of how well it is discharging them, its performance in terms of the statutory performance indicators, its Best Value review timetable, and its progress and achievements in delivering the action plans and meeting the targets and standards set as a result of previous reviews.

The Children's Services Plan is required by para 1A of Sch 2 to the Children Act 1989. Originally Sch 2 just required local authorities to identify needs, do something about them, and publish information about what they did. In 1996 they were first required to review those services and publish a plan for them.

On the other hand, the Community Care Plan under s 46 of the National Health Service and Community Care Act 1990 is in the original version of the Act, in the form of a straightforward requirement to publish a plan for the provision of community care services in your area.

The Annual Library Plan is a requirement of the Secretary of State for Culture, Media and Sport under s 1(2) of the Public Libraries and Museums Act 1964, which gives him the right to require library authorities to 'furnish information' to enable him to superintend them. It dates from 1998.

The Crime and Disorder Reduction Strategy, under ss 5 and 6 of the Crime and Disorder Act 1998, derives from the simple but ambitious duty placed on the local authority and police to a prepare a strategy for the reduction of crime and disorder in the area.

Section 40 of the Crime and Disorder Act obliges local authorities to prepare a Youth Justice Plan setting out how youth justice services in their area are to be provided and funded, and how their multi-agency youth offending team is operating.

The Development Plan is a complex, many-headed being. It may be a county-level structure plan plus a district-level district plan. In London, metropolitan districts, and some unitary authority areas, it is a single unitary development plan. Where this is an issue, it will also include separate input on mineral planning and national park issues. It derives from ss 27 and 54 of the Town and Country Planning Act 1990 and contains the policies for land use and development that guide and to a large extent control planning decisions.

The Local Transport Plan is new. Under s 108 of the Transport Act 2000 each local transport authority must develop policies for the promotion and encouragement of safe, integrated, efficient and economic transport facilities and services to, from and within their area, and set these out in a plan.

The Early Years Development Plan comes from s 120 of the Schools Standards and Framework Act 1998. The local education authority has a duty to provide sufficient nursery education for pre-school children, must form a local partnership for this purpose, and prepare a plan in conjunction with the partnership which states how they intend to comply with the duty.

The Education Development Plan is prepared under s 6 of the same 1998 Act. It is a fundamental document setting out the proposals by the authority for developing their provision of education for children in their area, including by raising the standards of education improving the performance of schools.

There are many others, creatures of statute like the School Organisation Plan, creatures of policy like the Lifelong Learning Development Plan, creatures of bidding and funding regimes like the Housing Improvement Strategy. Listing them all is impossible, the list will be out-of-date before it is completed. Here are some quick cross references:

- **Food Law Enforcement Service Plan** – has statutory links with the Food Standards Act 1999 and the Food Safety Act 1990 but arises from a White Paper *The Food Standards Agency – A Force for Change* defining the relationship between the Agency and local authorities.
- **The Housing Investment Programme** – now called the Housing Strategy and (for authorities who manage their own housing) Housing Revenue Account Business Plan, has no direct statutory parentage but is a bidding document for government money.
- **Local Agenda 21 Strategy** – non-statutory, produced under DETR/LGA/ LGMB Guidance in January 1998.
- **Lifelong Learning Development Plan** – another bidding document, this time to access the Standards Fund, see The Education Standards Fund (England) Regulations 2000[3].
- **Quality Protects Management Action Plan** – required by Department of Health Local Authority Circular LAC (98)28 *The Quality Protects Programme : Transforming Children's Services.*
- **School Organisation Plan** – s 26 of the School Standards and Framework Act and the Education (School Organisation Plans) (England) Regulations 1999[4]; and the Education (School Organisation Plans) (Wales) Regulations 1999[5].

1   SI 1999/3251.
2   SI 2000/1271.
3   SI 2000/703.
4   SI 1999/701.
5   SI 1999/499.

The Duty to Prepare a Community Strategy

[18.3]
The White Paper *In Touch with the People* in July 1998 included a chapter on promoting the well-being of communities. It sought to place local authorities at the centre of public service within their area. It promised legislation, including a new power to promote well-being and a duty to develop a comprehensive strategy to bring this about.

The first Local Government Bill disappointingly contained none of this. Instead it concentrated on clearing away the undergrowth of CCT and crude and universal rate capping, replacing it with Best Value and sophisticated and targeted rate capping. It became the Local Government Act 1999. The next major publication was *Local Leadership Local Choice* which helpfully included a consultation Local Government (Organisation and Standards) Bill at the end. The Bill concentrated on structures and ethics, though, and once again the well-being power and the community strategy were missing. Part I, containing these elements, was introduced following strong representations from the LGA and the Joint Committee of both Houses of Parliament which scrutinised the draft Bill. The statutory community strategy was created.

Initially the Bill just included a power to prepare a Community Strategy. This became a duty right at the end of the parliamentary process, taking us back to the original intention.

It is interesting to speculate on the forces at work within government, and how far they impacted on this. Local government as such is of course within the remit of the Department of Transport, Local Government and the Regions. This is their consultation process, and their legislation. As a department promoting legislation – and there has been a great deal of local government legislation over the last two decades – they have a history of regulation and prescription, but a philosophy of partnership. On the other hand, many of the existing statutory plans belong to other Departments of State; those responsible for Education, Employment, Culture, or Health for example. They are the primary control mechanism for those departments, in so far as their own programmes need to be delivered by local government.

Meanwhile, though, Cabinet Office Policy Action teams were working on joined-up government, social inclusion and neighbourhood renewal, including the 'Joining it up locally ' report of PAT 17 in April 2000. This team was looking at strategies and the links between them. It recommended multi-agency working based on the principles of empowerment, leadership, prevention not cure, a new culture that looks for real outcomes, linking the different levels of intervention and government as a facilitator not a director. The local vehicle for this should be Local Strategic Partnerships (LSPs) driven by the emerging community planning requirement.

It was from the interplay between these streams of thought that the duty to prepare a Community Strategy was born.

The Community Strategy is in Pt I of the Local Government Act 2000, which s 1 applies to county councils, district councils, London boroughs, the Common Council of City of London (when acting as a local authority) and the Council of Isles of Scilly. In Wales it applies to a county or county borough council. So unlike Best Value, this is aimed full square at local government, not at the public sector generally.

Sections 2 and 3 contain the new statutory power to do anything considered likely to achieve the promotion or improvement of the economic, social or environmental well-being of a local authority's area, plus an indication of its scope. It includes a requirement to 'have regard' to the authority's Community Strategy when exercising the new power.

Section 4 says that every authority to which Pt I applies must prepare a Community Strategy for promoting or improving the economic, social and environmental well-being of their area, and for contributing to the achievement of sustainable development in the UK. The reference to sustainability has been located carefully. In earlier drafts, the exercise of the well-being power had to have regard to this principle as well as to the community strategy. Whether for tidiness or for fear of challenge, the final version jogged sustainability back into the Strategy itself.

This is now becoming something of a mantra for local and regional government. If regional government develops further, we may look back in

20 years time to the first time it appeared as a watershed in redefining the purpose of government below national level.

Look for example at the Greater London Authority. In essence, and within limits, it has power to do anything which it considers will further any one or more of its principal purposes. These are promoting economic development and wealth creation, social development and the improvement of the environment, all in Greater London, as you might expect. There is then a complicated formula designed to make the GLA at least try to do all of these things, not just one of them, and to improve Londoners' health and (impressively) the achievement of sustainable development in the United Kingdom.

Section 4 says that in preparing their, strategy, authorities must consult, and seek the participation, of such persons as they consider appropriate. This is covered in detail in Chapter 20 below.

Note also that the strategy must, unlike the exercise of well-being powers, address all the well-being purposes and sustainability. It is not sufficient to prepare a strategy that deals with economic development alone. When the duty to prepare an economic development plan under s 35 of the Local Government and Housing Act 1989 was repealed, word went out that one could be prepared nevertheless. True, but it will not wholly satisfy s 4.

Section 5 gives the Secretary of State power by order to amend, repeal, revoke or disapply any enactment that prevents or obstructs the exercise of the new well-being powers. This may be general, or limited to one or some local authorities. The change may be permanent or time-limited.

Sections 6 and 7 give similar power to disapply any statutory requirement to produce a plan or strategy if it is 'not appropriate', or so that the enactment in question 'operates more effectively'. These powers are also exercised by Order.

Before making an order under s 5 or 6 the Secretary of State must consult local government representatives, and for Wales the National Assembly. Then a draft of the order, with commentary on the proposals and the consultation, must be laid before Parliament for a minimum of 60 days. Any representations received must be considered and changes flagged up when the draft order itself is presented to Parliament. Orders under ss 5 and 6 require positive affirmation by Parliament.

Section 4 (3) says that, in producing the Strategy, local authorities must have regard to guidance issued by the Secretary of State (or in Wales the National Assembly) after consultation with representatives of local government and others if he or they so wish. The Guidance for England was issued in December 2000. For any strategy, it outlines a single aim, four objectives, four key components, and four underpinning principles. People who like this kind of thing will find it the kind of thing they like.

The aim of the Strategy should be to enhance the quality of life of local communities and contribute to the achievement of sustainable development in the UK through action to improve the economic, social and environmental well being of the area and its inhabitants.

There should be four objectives: to allow local communities to articulate their aspirations, needs and priorities; to co-ordinate the actions of the council and other local organisations; to focus and shape the actions of the latter to meet the aspirations of the former; to contribute to achieving sustainable development.

The four key components of a Community Strategy are as follows: first, a long term vision focussing on outcomes; secondly a shorter term action plan (designed to achieve the long-term outcomes); thirdly a shared commitment to the action plan; and fourthly arrangements to monitor, review and report progress to local communities.

The four underpinning principles are to engage and involve local communities, to secure the active participation of executive and non-executive councillors to create Local Strategic Partnerships, and to base planning on an assessment of local needs and resources.

Finally, and appropriately, authorities also need to consider the implications of the Race Relations (Amendment) Act 2000.

How Community Planning Should Work in Practice

[18.4]
So having established the principles, what are authorities actually expected to do? The Guidance tells us that community involvement and partnership working are crucial, and explains what that is likely to mean, but helpfully recognises that different authorities are working at different speeds, so there is no prescriptive timetable.

The process is to establish a vision, analyse resources and current activity, agree priorities and outcomes, then prepare an action plan.

Within each local authority the process should be executive led, but all members should contribute, either as members of Overview and Scrutiny Committees, or Area Committees, or because they have roles as members of outside bodies.

The Guidance suggests considering joint strategies for adjoining authorities, recognising that some headline issues may extend outside council boundaries. It also recommends a multi-tiered approach in shire counties.

Whose participation should be sought? The Guidance is tirelessly inclusive, and the list is recited in Chapter 20. Authorities need to work with them all, resolve differences in priorities, and explain the outcome, all without raising false expectations.

Finally, systems must be established to monitor and measure progress, and a review timetable (a full review after three to five years, with an interim review in between). The Strategy should include a power to make modifications. There should be progress reports back to the community.

This is all wonderful stuff, but back in the real world it will be hard enough to get all the people who want to take part into the same room more than once a year. Then there will be a huge challenge to synthesise an analysis of needs, resources and priorities, to collate the aspirations of the community, and produce a planning document, without falling back on the obvious platitudes that you could have come up with in the first place. But all in all, this is a positive and important exercise. If it is done well it will unify the public and voluntary sectors and the wider community behind a set of common goals and a robust high-level process to deliver them, with, as promised, the local authority in the thick of the battle.

Relationship with Other Plans under Executive Arrangements

[18.5]

The Community Strategy should be different from all the other plans. It should provide an overarching context to link other plans together. There should be a seamless flow of logic joining them all together. Everyone with local influence has got together and agreed the things that are most important to the area, and how they can be brought about. The statutory plans then set out how this is to be achieved in the specific area that they cover. If the Community Strategy contains a commitment to increasing literacy, the means to achieve it will be found in the Education Development Plan, the Libraries Plan and the Cultural Strategy. Increasingly, but not inevitably, the consultation requirement and guidance on these other plans will refer back to the Community Strategy, as will the plans themselves.

If the statutory plans had a pecking order (they do fight among themselves on the shelves when no one is looking) the traditional heavyweight must be the development plan. This plan sits within a pretty strict hierarchy. The Secretary of State issues regional planning guidance. The development plan must conform with the guidance. It is single-tier or two-tier. Where it is two-tier, as in shire Counties, the lower tier district plan must conform with the higher-tier structure plan. The Secretary of State has default powers to prevent mavericks. The plan is thoroughly tested, by consultation, by formal objection and by public inquiry or examination in public. It settles land use issues worth many millions of pounds. Planning applications should be determined in accordance with it unless material considerations indicate otherwise – a rebuttable presumption, but one that will usually prevail. Preparing a development plan takes years and costs a fortune. Many are out-of-date, so an entire doctrine has grown up about the status and weight of an old plan as against an emerging plan that has not yet completed the consultation and inquiry process.

The tough question is how this will stand if the development plan and the Community Strategy contradict each other. The statutory Guidance on *Preparing Community Strategies* says that the two should march together. It also acknowledges, though, that the contents of the Community Strategy can be a material planning consideration, and even suggests that part of it could be formally adopted as supplementary planning guidance if the requirements of DTLR's PPG 12 on content, consultation and adoption are met. So we can expect cases where there will be some conflict between an old out-of-date development plan and a new Community Strategy. A new regeneration scheme could have emerged, or the priorities between different land uses (industry and recreation, say) could be reversed. It will not be long before the presumption in favour of the development plan is overturned in favour of the contents of a new Community Strategy, and this leads to litigation.

The other contender for top council plan is the Best Value Performance Plan. After all, the Local Government Act 1999 hit the streets before the Local Government Act 2000. The statutory guidance suggests that the Community Strategy should provide the basis for the council to determine its own priorities and aspirations. Then the BVPP can both give practical expression to the council's activities to deliver these objectives and provide a system to monitor its delivery.

Under executive arrangements, the Executive side of the council (the Leader and Cabinet, Elected Mayor and Cabinet or Elected Mayor and Manager) prepare all plans and strategies. They are urged to consult and engage overview and scrutiny committees, and the model constitution which many authorities have followed contains a fairly rigid process. The constitution will also say which plans have to be reported to full council for adoption. Some plans are highly contentious; they provide a basis for closing schools, withdrawing facilities and unpopular projects in peoples' backyards. There is a great deal of process here and it will be easy to get this wrong.

There is another pitfall in the 2000 Act. The division of responsibility between the executive and the council is absolute. That which the council can do, the executive cannot, and vice versa. The statutory guidance makes clear the government's view that it would be illegal for the executive to take a decision that is reserved to full council. Assuming this is right, presumably the converse is also the case. And is this is illegal as in susceptible to judicial review, but with judicial discretion available, or as in void and of no effect? The issue gets especially pithy in that under Sch 4 to the Local Authorities (Functions and Responsibilities) (England) Regulations 2000[1] the executive must not take a decision (or as it puts it 'determine any matter in the discharge of a function'), which is a decision 'in relation to which a plan or strategy (whether statutory or non-statutory) has been adopted or approved by the authority ... in terms contrary to the plan or, as the case may be, the strategy adopted or approved by the authority'.

Two questions will illustrate how thin the ice could get. First, what happens if two plans contradict each other? These plans can be hundreds of pages thick and take years to complete. What if your Childrens Services Plan says 'more nursery schools' but your more recent Early Years Development Plan says 'fewer nursery schools, the numbers are dwindling'. Who can close a nursery school, the executive or full council?

Secondly what happens if your adopted plan is out-of-date, as is commonly the case for example with the development plan? If a ten-year-old development plan allocates a site for housing, how can the executive sell it to someone to build a factory?

Of course, you can get round the inconvenient plan by changing it. That is not always easy, in terms of the legislation under which the plan is made. There is an additional complication under executive arrangements. Regulation 4 of the same Regulations says that the executive may only alter a plan that has been approved by the council to the extent that it is giving effect to a ministerial requirement or authorised by a determination made by the council when approving or adopting it. This is fine from this point on, but many of these plans were made before it was known that this was going to be an issue. Sadly, reg 4 is retrospective. It says in so many words that it applies to these 'policy framework' plans made before the Regulations became law. But there may by a glimmer of hope here. The equivalent provision in Sch 4, banning executive decisions contrary to council plans, does not refer expressly to plans adopted before the regulations came into force. Perhaps one may assume that it only applies to new ones?

1   SI 2000/2853.

LSPs, PSAs and Deregulation

[18.6]
Returning to social exclusion and neighbourhood renewal, if the analysis is right, society is put at risk by the growth of a section of the community who are excluded in most ways from what everyone else does and values. This should be addressed through a new approach to regeneration and renewal in deprived neighbourhoods. The new approach must involve many different public, voluntary and private sector bodies, working together and thinking together. The definitive vehicle for this joined-up thinking at local authority level is the non-statutory Local Strategic Partnership, working to create and monitor the statutory Community Strategy.

It is an odd way round. Previously the legislation would have established the body and the body would have established the plan.

Guidance on LSPs was published in March 2001. According to the Guidance, a LSP is a body that brings together at a local level the different parts of the public sector as well as the private, business, community and voluntary sectors so that different initiatives and services support each other and work together. It is a non-statutory, non-executive organisation, which operates at a level which enables strategic decisions to be taken and is close enough to individual neighbourhoods to allow actions to be determined at community level. It should be aligned with local authority boundaries. Its agenda is developing the community strategy, launching local neighbourhood renewal strategies and piloting new forms of agreement between local and central government.

In the areas eligible for money from the Neighbourhood Renewal Fund, the distribution of government grant may be conditional on forming a LSP. There will also be a preliminary bag of start-up cash called the Community Empowerment Fund, which will go to the voluntary and community sector partners to bring them up to speed. In a June 2001 Circular they are urged to form a Community Network, broader and larger than the LSP, to work alongside it.

The new forms of agreement with central government are Public Service Agreements (PSAs). The authority (working with the LSP) agrees about a dozen improvement targets across a range of service areas. They should reflect local and national priorities. They should be built up from the Best Value Performance Plan, but commit the authority to even greater performance improvement. In return, there is direct pump-priming and 'reward' grant for meeting targets. The pilot examples include one authority improving attainment levels for 11-year-olds from Bangladeshi and Pakistani ethic origin by 10%, another increasing intensive home care for the elderly to help 9.3 people per thousand, from 6.6 per thousand, over three years, another reducing the numbers killed or seriously injured in road accidents by 25%. The 2001 roll out was announced in July 2001, and will involve 130 councils.

The second carrot is additional freedom. This may involve freeing up government controlled funding regimes, such as the schools standards fund. It may involve the exercise of order-making powers under ss 5 and 6 of the Local Government Act 2000, or s 16 of the Local Government Act 1999, defining a new public body under the Local Authorities (Goods and Services) Act 1970, permitting external discharge of a function under s 70 of the Deregulation and Contracting Out Act 1994 or perhaps even permitting charging under s 150 of the Local Government and Housing Act 1989. It is to be hoped, though, that the exercise of these powers will not be limited to PSAs. You can see the logic, but it would be a stifling approach.

So far, incidentally, no orders have been made under ss 5 and 6. There is consultation on an imaginative proposal to make a s 16 order providing parallel powers for Best Value purposes to those given under Pt I of the 2000 Act for well-being purposes. Many orders have been made under the 1970 Act, generic and specific. Charges have been allowed (subject to detailed conditions) for registering houses in multiple occupation, public path orders, local land charge enquiries, overseas assistance, and a number of highways, traffic management and transport fare concession functions. And the only deregulation orders are for local tax collection, investment services, housing and homelessness allocation, and some highways maintenance functions.

It is too early to tell whether PSAs are the icing, and conventional funding and performance measurement the cake, or the other way round. The beacon council scheme is still with us, so PSAs are different. We have moved from councils funded by local taxation topped up by government grant to funding by government grant topped up by local taxation. Local government has seen local taxes capped and uncapped, and the grants become conditional and their distribution arcane. It has found out the hard way that there are unexpected limits to what it can do itself through income-generation. It has jumped through hoops to bid for challenge funding, and found its own match funding from money that it had really intended to spend on something else. In the future will it all be about doing non-statutory deals with government about ten or twelve improvement targets?

CHAPTER 19
Partnership With Others

What Is Partnership All About?

[19.1]
Two quiet thoughts seem to underlie the well-being power, the community strategy, government thinking on social inclusion and neighbourhood renewal, and a clutch of recent statutes like the Crime and Disorder Act 1998 and the Health Act 1999. First, there is genuine acceptance that local government has something special to offer. It may be unruly and awkward, but there is more to it than a local mechanism for delivering statutory services and regulation.

Secondly, though, it cannot achieve anything interesting on its own. Collecting domestic refuse is not a complicated concept. There is scope for some local choice about how often it happens, and the choice of receptacles. It is a task that can be performed badly or well, expensively or cheaply, by employees or contractors. Beyond that, either it happens or it does not. The wattage of brain-power up and down the country that has been expended on testing this through elaborate notions like compulsory competitive tendering (CCT) and Best Value would illuminate a small city. But this is all just about service delivery by a single body. To make a real difference in an area that is truly difficult, like reducing criminal behaviour, or finding everyone a way out of poverty and ill-health, then a range of different agencies need to work together in a structured way.

'Partnership' is a word that has been put around all over the place over the last few years, accompanied by its curious sister 'partnering' (it means the same as partnership but sounds different). A bit of deconstruction will help.

The legal definition of a partnership is 'the relation which subsists between persons carrying on a business in common with a view of profit'[1]. The concept developed in the eighteenth and nineteenth centuries, essentially as a device for determining whether someone who had put money into a commercial enterprise was liable for its debts. Later on, it did not really fit well in the commercial world, because it is hard to buy and sell, but it was allowed to prosper for trustworthy professionals who sold their personal time and skills but needed to huddle together for mutual support. The idea of joint and several liability meant it did not get in anyone's way. It is a complex and plastic legal concept, and deeply misleading in this context. A law textbook on partnership will typically define partnership, describe those that are illegal, then comment at some length on the liability of partners both to each other and to third parties, and in the event of dissolution. It is all about what you can get away with.

202

Limited partnerships are a subspecies, perhaps a hybrid. Since 1907, a special kind of limited partnership has been allowed. Provided there are fewer than ten or twenty partners (depending on the type of business), and that one partner is 'general', the others may be 'limited' so long as they do not actively manage the concern. This means that their liability is limited to the funds that they have put in. These partnerships are registered with the Department of Trade.

The Limited Liability Partnerships Act 2000 created another hybrid, in its own words a 'new form of legal entity to be known as a limited liability partnership'. This is a registered corporate body, created by two or more persons carrying on a lawful business with a view to profit, whose membership is initially determined by the incorporation document, and thereafter by the existing members. Internal liability is determined by this document. To the outside world, all the partners are agents of the partnership.

Traditional thinking is that local authorities cannot enter into legal partnerships in this sense. They cannot carry on a business with others with a view of profit. It would be ultra vires to purport to do so.

How far will s 2 of the 2000 Act (and Regulations under s 16 of the Local Government Act 1999) change this, though?

Mainstream use of s 2 will see local authorities determining that it would improve the economic well being of their area to enter into a joint enterprise with a private sector partner which will generate profits. Despite the prohibition on activity under s 2 which amounts to 'raising money', government's statutory guidance tells us that it is permissible – and may even be mandatory – for a local authority to receive a return on its investment in a joint venture vehicle. Such a vast amount of regeneration activity up and down the country has depended on deals of this kind, under the economic development powers that preceded s 2, that the converse would be deeply alarming. But perhaps there is a true distinction, based on a test of purpose. The private sector partner will of course have a view of profit. This will be its predominant, possibly sole, purpose. The local authority's predominant purpose must be promoting well being: creating jobs, encouraging inward investment, enhancing the local tax base. This is not a view of profit, it is a view of economic development. The income that a view of profit must not only contemplate, but positively seek, is extremely likely to amount to 'raising money' and offend s 3. And for there to be a true partnership, each partner must have this intention.

So partnership in the local authority context really means anything but a partnership. This is always a good start. It is useful to take a tour around some of the different arrangements (a useful word, to be found in s 2, probably but not necessarily implying a contractual relationships) that can loosely be described as partnerships, and admire the architecture.

1   Partnership Act 1890, s1.

The Diminishing Importance of Legal Personality

[19.2]
The infinitely expanding universe of partnership bodies has one puzzling

outcome. A legal textbook on local government will start with the idea of the municipal corporation and the body corporate created by statute ('the corporation acting by the council'). Our appreciation of vires, the ability to hold land and enter into contracts, and to sue and be sued, derive from the certainty that a local authority is a body with clear legal personality. It can do things, and you know who has done them. This is the starting-point for most forms of legal analysis.

Partnership arrangements are not like that. There is a sliding scale of personality, often falling short of certainty.

Some partnerships have a statutory basis, others do not. A good example of the latter is the national network of Drug Action Teams. Launched by a White Paper in 1998, reporting direct to government on how well it is delivering a national strategy for tackling drug misuse, and bringing together the police, health authority and trusts, the probation service and the local authority, this is one of the most important areas of partnership activity and joined-up working you can imagine. Plainly the activities of the bodies that take part are within their legal powers, as separate entities, but the DAT itself it has no substantial statutory basis. It is mentioned in the Order wherein the Home Secretary sets out his objectives for the police in 1999/2000. It is prescribed as a body that must be invited to participate in developing a strategy under the Crime and Disorder Act 1998. It receives direct government funding. Otherwise, it does not exist at all in legal terms.

In real life, the importance of a public body depends on the resources it can deploy. Unless it can raise taxes, or precept or levy someone else who can do so, this usually depends on how much money others give it. So, therefore, the very substantial Home Office challenge funding for crime and disorder partnerships means that these statutory constructs have a significance that is greater than the bare statutory description of what they are there to do. The Crime and Disorder Act 1998 obliges local authorities and the police to lead a partnership and to work with a wide range of other bodies. They have to undertake an audit of crime and disorder, and prepare a strategy. This sounds high-level and arid, but it conceals the leverage that these bodies have from the money they can draw down from central government for crime reduction initiatives that meet government's priorities and requirements.

The DAT has government money but no statutory basis. The C&DA Partnership has government money, a statutory basis, but no legal personality. The local authority cannot get at the money except through the partnership, but at least has legal personality. This is an easy muddle, there are harder ones around. Let us look at some other types of partnership.

Different Kinds of Partnerships

Statutory and non-statutory bodies

[19.3]
Youth Offending Teams are also creatures of the 1998 Act. These are mandatory partnerships between top-tier councils, police, probation and

health authorities, to establish multi-disciplinary teams, ostensibly independent of any of the partners, bringing a joined-up and planned approach to dealing with young people who have, as they say, entered the criminal justice system.

Dotted round the country, in England at least, you will find Education Action Zones. They are established by order of the Secretary of State under the School Standards and Framework Act 1998. The order defines the zone by reference to the participating schools, each zone has its forum, and their statutory purpose is to improve educational standards in those schools. The forum is likely to include representatives of the schools, the education authority, employers and voluntary organisations. They are corporate bodies and charities, so that members are charitable trustees. They can act on behalf of schools, but the whole point of EAZs is to innovate and to create and deliver action plans through project directors. They are grant-aided by the Secretary of State but depend on broadly equivalent funding from local businesses.

Then there is the Learning and Skills Act 2000, and the new Learning and Skills Councils. These inherit the mantle of the TECs, and similarly cover the areas of several education authorities, with membership determined by the National Skills Council. Their purpose is to plan, fund and achieve the training of over 16s in their areas. Interestingly, and perhaps as a forerunner of legislation yet to come, they are under a statutory duty to consider the community strategy under the Local Government Act 2000. They should not be confused with the non-statutory advisory Lifelong Learning Partnerships, with which they work.

Within employment zones, established under the Welfare Reform and Pensions Act 1999 and the Jobseekers Act 2000, the contracts for managing active and innovative employment services are let to bidders. Government guidance expressed a preference for cross-sector partnership bids, and in practice successful bidders have been partnerships constructed by local Councils, TECs, LECs, private employment agencies and local employment service officers.

The Health Act 1999 has seven sections headed 'partnership'. It requires Health Authorities and Trusts and local authorities to co-operate with one another, and to help the Authority to prepare a strategy. It (and the NHS Bodies and Local Authorities Partnership Arrangements Regulations 2000[1]) make it possible for health bodies and local authorities to pay money to each other, discharge each other's functions, pool budgets and set up joint-arrangements and joint-committees, provided there are written agreements and clear lines of accountability

Then, with some trepidation, we need to peer into the alphabet soup of regeneration. The European Structural Funds include the European Social Fund (ESF) and the European Regional Development Fund (ERDF). Funds are targeted at areas of deprivation identified by their status, notably as 'objective one' (smallest number, biggest problems) or 'objective two'. To get at the money for your pet project you bid direct to a fund or to a sub-fund called an initiative. ERDF funds are administered by Monitoring Committees made up of government departments and RDAs, local authorities, higher and further education institutions, environmental bodies, the voluntary and private sectors and members of the business community.

RDAs are Regional Development Agencies established under the Regional Development Agencies Act 1998 for broad economic development purposes. Each has 13 members, of whom four come from local authorities. They work alongside broadly based voluntary Regional Chambers who scrutinise them. Their role is essentially strategic, but they have a big say in where the money goes, especially ERDF and SRB money.

You need to find match funding for your ERDF bid. One source has been SRB funding, and this has been the major source of national regeneration funding in its own right. The SRB is the Single Regeneration Budget. SRB bids have to be made by local partnerships to the RDA. The Partnership Boards will involve all the obvious local stakeholders and community representatives. It may link with smaller community bodies like Credit Unions (savings and loans schemes under the Credit Unions Act 1979), local development trusts, Local Exchange and Trading Systems (community barter) and Community Enterprise schemes. In Wales the system is looser knit, but again it is partnership based. Each board has an associated local authority through whom it acts – the board has the cash, the authority the legal competence. These structures are changing, and larger cluster partnerships are emerging.

There are other bidding regimes where you have to form a partnership: Lottery Funding bids; the New Deal for Communities which delivers targeted funding to combat social exclusion; People in the Communities Partnerships in Wales; Sure Start partnerships aimed at improving childrens' development within families and communities and described now as a kind of PSA; Children and Youth Partnerships in Wales.

The intention of Government is now to move from project-based SRB funding, to so the role of SRB partnerships and their relationship with LSPs is becoming less clear.

At the same time, a White Paper in 2000 gave rise to yet another non-statutory body, albeit one with legal personality. Urban Regeneration Companies (URCs) are new independent limited companies established by the local authority and RDA, as well as English Partnerships (unfortunately this is not a partnership, but the government agency that inherited the functions – and assets – of the Urban Regeneration Agency and the Commission for the New Towns under the Leasehold Reform, Housing and Urban Development Act 1993), the private sector and other key partners. These are new, only three were set up initially, and it will be interesting to see how far they act as facilitators and how far as property developers, holding and trading in assets.

1   SI 2000/617.

Companies

[19.4]
Companies exist in their own right. They can do anything that is within the

objects set out in their memorandum of association. The way they operate is regulated under the Companies Acts. They are run by directors, who have distinct personal legal accountability, and administered by a secretary. Almost all companies are limited, that is to say the liability of whoever set them up or owns them is limited. They can be limited by shares, so that the liability of the shareholder for the debts of the company is limited to the nominal value of the shares that they hold. This is the normal structure for companies that intend to make a profit, because the shareholding will determine the allocation of dividends, and assets if the company is wound up.

Companies can be limited by guarantee, in which case the participants' liability for the company's debts is limited to the guarantee they have given to pay a totally notional amount. Companies limited by guarantee are normally not-for-profit bodies – income is ploughed back into activity. They are often charitable. They offer an uncomplicated corporate vehicle for local authority partnership activity.

In either case, there is a wide range of structural options in terms of the powers of directors acting individually or as a board, the exercise of voting rights at board meetings or by shareholders (including the so-called 'golden share' that gives a shareholder with minority voting rights a special ability to veto big changes), and the distribution of assets on dissolution.

So it is simple. In order to create a partnership body that can actually own and buy and sell things on its own, you set up a company. If it is not designed to make a profit, or trade commercially, it should be limited by guarantee, otherwise by shares. Get out the precedents, fill in the forms, appoint directors and secretary, warn them about what they must and must not do, and arrange the first board meeting.

Well nearly. As usual there are some special issues for local government. First, is there legal power to set up the company in the first case? There are express powers in a few limited areas (to form housing associations, for further education establishments, waste disposal, bus undertakings and large airports, and until the 2000 Act for economic development). Generally, though, and despite some discouraging judicial asides to the contrary, it has in the past been necessary to rely on s 111 of the Local Government Act 1972 on the basis that the company assists in the discharge of a function. Now we have s 2 of the 2000 Act (plus in due course, perhaps, equivalent powers for Best Value purposes), so provided that there is a clear decision that the company will promote well-being, regard is had to the guidance and the community strategy, and you are not raising money or doing something that is prohibited elsewhere, life is a lot more comfortable.

The second issue is the quaint web of controls spun around local authority companies under Pt V of the Local Government and Housing Act 1989. Conceived alongside a host of probity controls on local government that now feel curiously dated, the idea was to stop local authorities setting up companies controlled by them which would then do things that they could not, or in a way that they could not. And in particular, of course, the worst thing that a local authority could do at the time was to increase the public sector borrowing requirement, so there were very close controls indeed over capital spending by local authority companies. There is a scale of council control and influence over the company. The rules are complicated, but in essence if you keep below 20% in terms of your holding or voting power or business influence, you only have to worry about some bureaucratic probity controls, whereas above that the company's spending tends to be your spending. And if you control or have a dominant influence over the company, a range of controls kick in that tend not to make the exercise worthwhile. But this is an oversimplification, and there is sadly no alternative to studying the Act and the Local Authorities (Companies) Order 1995[1] themselves.

1   SI 1995/849.

Industrial and Provident societies

[19.5]
Industrial and provident societies are associations registered with the Registrar of Friendly Societies under the Industrial and Provident Societies Acts. They are corporate bodies formed to carry out activities for the mutual benefit of their members. They are controlled by their members, who each have one vote – a workers co-operative would be an example. The value of the shares is capped. They can be useful vehicles for low level partnership activity where the concepts of involvement and mutuality are important, for example in housing management schemes. Housing associations tend to be industrial and provident societies. Friendly societies themselves are different. Members remain liable for their debts, and they have not been used as local authority partnership vehicles.

Trusts

[19.6]
Trusts look like corporate bodies with legal personality, but it is a disguise. Many local authorities administer trusts directly or with others, and have done so for years. Many unincorporated bodies have trustees to hold land, to take the lease of the premises that they use. And many local authorities have used trusts as a vehicle for transferring accountability for public services like leisure provision out of the council offices and into the community – and with tax advantages too. But trusts do not have legal personality. They only exist like contracts and leases exist, not like companies and people exist. The point is worth labouring because it is easy to get into an inescapable knot if you think of a trust as a thing rather than a relationship. Trustees become individually liable for trust contracts, debts and legal liabilities. Their duties under trust law are substantial but ill-defined. This is a useful non-corporate route to charitable status. It is a good way of nailing something down such that successors cannot undo it, which after all is what it was invented for. Beyond that though, a company limited by guarantee is probably better.

Charities

[19.7]
Charitable status may be a prize worth having. If the partnership body is content to plough income back into activity, and has charitable objects, it can avoid a variety of taxes. It will have some income tax exemption, its activities are likely to be zero rated or non-business for VAT, it will enjoy some relief from corporation tax, CGT, inheritance tax and stamp duty. Most significantly, it will receive at lease 80% relief from business rates (NNDR) most of the cost of which is absorbed nationally. Charitable purposes, which must be public purposes, are the relief of poverty, the advancement of education, the advancement of religion, and 'any other purpose beneficial to the community'. There is a lot of case law about the last one. Under the Recreational Charities Act 1958, certain facilities for recreation and leisure provided to the public in the interests of social welfare also qualify as charitable. Charities have been set up for festivals, auditoriums, libraries, historic buildings and wildlife sites and SSSIs. The bad news is, though, that charity law is very demanding and that charities (especially the larger ones) are subject to extremely careful supervision by the Charity Commissioners.

Everything else is a statutory body or an unincorporated association. Some statutory bodies are bodies corporate – local authorities for example. Others are not, but have such well defined powers and duties that it does not matter. Unincorporated associations do not exist as legal entities. They come about when a group of people or bodies that do have legal personality agree with each other to get together to do things. They typically set up a constitution, with a board, or a management committee, and rules and such. All this is fine, but all it amounts to is a criss-cross web of contractual agreements along the lines of 'if I as treasurer agree pay this bill, having followed the procedural rules appropriate to it, then you as a member agree to chip in one way or another to help me pay it'. The sports club model is infinitely transferable. A SRB partnership may be playing with millions of pounds of European money to tackle near impossible social and environmental conditions, but the legal relationships are not very different to those that prop up a village cricket club.

Other bodies

[19.8]
EAZs have already been mentioned, but not School Organisation Committees under the School Standards and Framework Act 1998, the Community Consortia for Education and Training in Wales, Connexions Partnerships for career guidance and mentoring for young people particularly those with special needs, or Excellence in Cities or LA 21 partnerships. Joint health bodies are evolving very rapidly at the moment, so as well as the Health Act 1999 infrastructure, consider what is happening in practice in areas like, for example, mental health commissioning. There are also Local Health Alliances and Local Health Groups in Wales, the partnership boards in Health Action Zones or Education and Health Partnerships. In the housing field there are Local Housing Companies, set up to take over management of council housing after stock transfer. These are usually companies limited by

guarantee registered as social landlords with the Housing Corporation. In employment, the New Deal is delivered by local partnerships based on Employment Service Districts. Under the Transport Act 2000 local transport authorities must engage with bus operators in Quality Partnership Schemes, whereas Rural Transport partnerships form to bid for funds from the RTP scheme run by the Countryside Agency. Not to be left out, the Lord Chancellor's Department has been pulling together CABs, other people who give legal advice, solicitors with (or wanting) Legal Services Commission contracts and local authorities into Community Legal Services Partnerships to work out local needs and local provision and illuminate the allocation of funding.

Back in the world of local government as we used to know it, there are innumerable and often mysterious joint-boards, statutory 'joint-authorities' and joint-committees and joint-advisory committees under s 102 of the Local Government Act 1972. In London in 1999, for example, the Association of London Government stopped being a unincorporated association (with a linked company holding property leases) to which member bodies paid subscriptions under s 143 of the 1972 Act, and became a nest of s 102 joint-committees.

Procurement

[19.9]
Then, finally, the term 'partnership' is often applied to some of the different ways of procuring services or service improvements.

The Private Finance Initiative (PFI) is a way of funding big projects such that assets and risk pass to a private sector partner who delivers a service back to the Council's customers. They are complex and expensive to set up, and opinions are divided as to whether this is a good way of obtaining funding, but they do give the maximum scope for private sector initiative, and there is grant aid from government to help support the cost of the payments. A broader concept is Public Private Partnerships, a government tag for long-term contractual and joint-venture relationships between the public sector and a private sector service provider, often like PFI involving a transfer of assets.

Partnership is also used to describe a procurement philosophy. A traditional contract for services, and especially a CCT contract, would try to specify in detail what the contractor was obliged to do. Then the contractor would tender the lowest price at which he thought he could make a profit. The lowest of these tenders would usually be accepted, that is to say the tender with the smallest profit margin, or sometimes the tender where the contractor had underpriced or decided to take risks. During the contract, the contractor's objective is to get away with not meeting the specification. The Council (which by this time has cut its annual budget down to the tender price, so has no room to manoeuvre) is struggling to get the contractor to do the job without making it insolvent. So the contract has driven down the quality of services, when that was not intended. The idea behind a partnership relationship is to reverse this process, to seek continual improvement, so that it is based on a mutual promise to work together in a non-adversarial way, to explore the scope for innovation and improvement, and to openness and joint-working.

Local authority consortia are another kind of partnership. They are to be found, for example, in the world of supplies and procurement. A consortium of this kind is an unincorporated association of local authorities acting (as must joint committees and some statutory bodies) through a 'lead authority' that acts as agents for the others on a contractual basis, or by an agency agreement under s 101 of the 1972 Act. There is a subtle difference between a contract for services and a s 101 agreement that delegates the discharge of functions.

This section has just listed about 55 different things that local authorities can, will and should get involved in, that can be called partnerships. Some have legal personality, some have money, some are statutory, but few have all of these. The list will change very quickly. The role of the local government lawyer is changing too. It is becoming increasing difficult to pin down who is doing what to whom, with what money, on what terms, on whose advice and with what accountability.

Unpicking Partnership Arrangements

[19.10]
Current thinking on partnership arrangements is based on a curious piece of magic. Effective partnership is built on trust. Partners must feel comfortable with what they are putting in and taking out, and with what the other partners are doing. Specifications, if they exist at all, must be flexible, and will change and develop as time goes by. The constitution, and the documentation around the relationship between the partners, must be invisible and unnecessary. All this is fine, and absolutely right, but not every partnership works. Sometimes things go wrong, so the task at the outset is to create and document a framework that allocates responsibility so effectively that no one will ever want to refer to it.

Assume a partnership involving the council, the Health Authority, a charitable voluntary organisation and a private sector sponsor, established to deliver a health improvement project under the well-being powers. The project is run by a steering group comprising a councillor, a health authority non-executive director, the chairman of the VO and the managing director of the sponsor. It has leased an office in the names of the steering group members, employed four people, entered into contracts with suppliers and to supply services to the partners and to other commercial organisations. The project is funded by a government grant and match funding from the partners. Then everything goes wrong. The project itself is discredited (research now shows it does more harm than good). One of the employees has absconded with the salaries of the other three, and with the chairman of the VO, having presented bogus accounts to the steering group. Another was pushed downstairs as she left, and is claiming wrongful dismissal, discrimination, victimisation assault and compensation for an industrial injury. Suppliers are suing for payment, customers are suing because the treatment does not work and everyone has come out in spots. The council has withdrawn the grant because of a budget crisis. The government has frozen its grant because the match funding has gone. The Health Authority has disowned the whole project claiming it never supported it in the first place and that the non-executive director was acting without authority. The sponsor has gone into liquidation without paying its contribution.

The partnership is an unincorporated organisation. The suppliers try to sue it in it's own name, discover it does not exist, so sue the members of the steering committee as individuals. So do the employees, the landlord and all the spotty customers. The potential liability is massive. The steering committee members claim indemnity from each other. The chairman of the VO has disappeared, and the sponsor's managing director seems to have no personal assets at all. The councillor and the non-executive director try to claim indemnity from the council and the Health Authority respectively. The council says it would like to, but cannot until regulations are made under s 101 of the Local Government Act 2000. The Health Authority refuses. The councillor judicially reviews the council for breach of legitimate expectation in relation to the grant. The council says that now it does not want to indemnify the councillor because he is not acting in the council's interests.

The councillor sues the council's lawyer for getting him into this mess. The council's lawyer claims indemnity from the council. The council's insurers refuse to indemnify him on the grounds that he ought not to have been acting for the councillor anyway. The council's auditor says that it is ultra vires the council to bail anyone out at all because the s 2 well-being purpose has evaporated. The sponsor's managing director takes the head of paid service and the chief finance officer out to dinner (his wife pays for the meal) and the council's lawyer writes a monitoring officer report. The council dismisses the lawyer, because the regulations under the Local Government Act 2000 requiring an independent investigation have not yet been made. The game is up. The councillor and the lawyer are led away in chains.

Delegation and Deregulation

[19.11]

Local authorities discharge functions, that is to say they perform duties and exercise powers given to them by statute. Any analysis of local authority law that cannot be traced back to this proposition is probably unsound. They are given explicit authority in the Local Government Act 1972 to discharge their functions by delegating them to committees, sub-committees, other authorities, joint committees with other authorities and officers. They are generally required by the Local Government Act 2000 to make executive arrangements for the discharge of executive functions by delegating them to, amongst others, an elected mayor, a leader, a cabinet, a cabinet committee, or a cabinet member. There are some odd additions, such as joint boards, but essentially that is the end of the list. Delegates may not delegate further, in the absence of statutory authority.

This matters because partnership is about doing things together. Two people can do the shopping together in three ways:

(1) they can both go into the shop and make the purchase, each paying a share;

(2) they can agree that one of them will go into the shop and make the purchase; or

(3) they can arrange for a third party to make the purchase for them.

In each case the shopping is done, but in the second and third case one or both of the partners is not actually making the purchase. In real life this does not matter. In local authority law it matters a great deal.

You have to draw a crude distinction between purpose (doing the shopping), function (making the purchase) and activity (looking at the shelves). Actually at this point the analogy breaks down because in most circumstances purchasing is activity rather than the discharge of a function. The distinction in terms of the 1972 Act is between 'arranging for the discharge of functions' under say s 101 and 'contracts for the supply of goods or materials or the execution of works' for which standing orders must be made under s 135(2).

A local authority involved in a partnership may – if it can find a statutory power to rely on – arrange for its partner, or a contractor engaged by them both, or a partnership vehicle like a joint venture company, to carry out activity for it as part of the partnership purpose. But (unless the partner is another local authority) it cannot delegate the discharge of functions to it. The distinction is not easy to draw, and there is little case law. In *R v Greater Manchester Police Authority, ex p Century Motors (Farnworth) Ltd*[1] the Court of Appeal had to decide if it was lawful for the authority to engage the Automobile Association as a main contractor who then sub-contracted the work of towing away vehicles. It decided that, although only a police officer could 'arrange for' vehicles to be removed, anyone could handle the actual removal. Many such fine distinctions had to be drawn for the purposes of so-called white collar compulsory competitive tendering under the Local Government Act 1992, as authorities reluctantly or enthusiastically sliced into their operations to decide what should and should not be contracted out: benefit administration but not determination, housing management but not housing allocation, highways repairs but not highways licensing.

As an attempt at assembling a test, can one say: 'I am doing this specific thing under section such and such?'. If a statutory decision has to be taken which materially affects someone's rights or well-being, then this is the discharge of a function. Otherwise it is activity. But if you fall into a pot-hole instead of bumping into a skip you will find the distinction hard to follow.

The concept is reasonable. A local authority is directly democratically accountable. If you voted for an administration because you liked the decisions that it took, you would be unimpressed if it handed the whole job over to someone else. But it gets in the way of partnership activity. It means that there is a range of things that the authority cannot vest in a partnership vehicle, whether a community partnership like a leisure trust or a commercial partnership like a joint venture company.

The government's answer is deregulation. Section 70 of the Deregulation and Contracting Out Act 1994 applies to any statutory function that can be delegated to an officer, apart from a few that are excluded under s 71. The exclusions are powers which impinge very directly on individual rights and liberties; judicial functions, those which interfere with liberty, or confer rights of entry, seizure or search (apart from the work of the Official Receiver, and some specified local tax collection powers, which can be delegated), power to make subordinate legislation such as by-laws. It gives the relevant minister power to make an order which would allow the functions described in the order to be discharged by someone other than the authority, if the authority authorises it. The minister must first consult local government representatives, and the order is just permissive – the authority can contract the work out, or it can keep it to itself, or both. And an authority that has delegated the work to another authority has to consent before the second authority contracts the work out. Authorisations must not be for more than ten years and may be revoked. Decisions taken by the contractor are taken to be those of the authority (but not in so far as there is a contractual dispute between the authority and the contractor, or the contractor or its staff commits a criminal offence).

The only Orders made so far are:

- the Contracting Out (Management Functions in Relation to Certain Community Homes) Order 1996, SI 1996/586 – managing childrens' homes, apart from those providing secure accommodation;
- the Local Authorities (Contracting Out of Tax Billing, Collection and Enforcement Functions) Order 1996, SI 1996/1880 – administration of certain functions relating to these local taxes, subject to provisions on the disclosure of information and unauthorised sub-contracting;
- the Local Authorities (Contracting Out of Investment Functions) Order 1996, SI 1996/1883 – investing money, but not pension or trust funds;
- the Local Authorities (Contracting Out of Allocation of Housing and Homelessness Functions) Order 1996, SI 1996/3205 – most functions relating to the allocation of housing and the determination of homelessness presentations, apart from certain 'back at the base' decisions about the allocation scheme and the some peripheral homelessness activities;
- the Contracting Out (Functions in Relation to the Provision of Guardian ad Litem and Reporting Officers Panels) Order 1997, SI 1997/1652 – providing panel of GALs and reporting officers; and
- the Local Authorities (Contracting Out of Highways Functions) Order 1999, SI 1996/2106 – a very miscellaneous list of highways functions.

It is an odd list. The flurry of orders in 1996 reflects the removal of impediments to externalisation of white collar work under the compulsory competitive tendering legislation. The highways order comes from the same stable, plus changes in trunk and special road maintenance regimes, but took longer to arrive. The two social services orders wandered in from left field. The most obvious omission is benefits administration, which is understood to be work in progress at the moment. In July 2001 the DFEE consulted on proposals to make an order for a long list of education functions – those not delegated to schools – in a way that those committed to the in-house provision of lea services will find a little ominous.

There are few other cracks in the plasterwork. The Health Act 1999 expressly allows health bodies and local authorities to carry out each others' functions.

Section 2 of the Local Government Act 2000 expressly gives a council exercising the new well-being powers authority to discharge the functions of others. This is in a list that is stated not to be exclusive, but it is probably the case that s 2 (notwithstanding that it is meant to be a power of first resort) does not operate the other way round, to allow councils to let others discharge their functions without an deregulation order.

In principle, the modernisation legislation is meant to take local authorities away from behaving like branch offices of government department, heads down, delivering services in accordance with rules and guidance. They should reinvent themselves as community leaders, working in partnership with others to find innovative solutions to cross-cutting social problems. Deregulation is a brake on the change that is needed to achieve this. If a partnership body wants to encompass any activity that amounts to discharging a council function, and it does not fall within a deregulation order, it will still have to get a council (or possibly health service body) employee of one sort or another into the room to do it.

1 (1996) Times, 31 May. The Court of Appeal judgment of 24 March 1998 is unreported.

Providing Services to Partners

[19.12]
Legal relationships with partners, or partnership bodies, are either statutory or contractual, or of course both. It is instructive to look at some of the implications of establishing a contractual relationship, calling the contracting body the 'partner', though it might be a body set up by a set of partners (a joint venture company, for example), or even an unincorporated organisation acting through some other body. In partnership arrangements it can be very difficult to work out who is doing what for whom, and why.

First, is there a contract? There is a wavy line, for example, between giving a conditional grant and placing a contract. The latter means, in this context, a full-blown contract for services, because there may well be a contractual relationship even in cases where the exchange is essentially giving a grant. There is no certain test, but the factors include the statutory basis for the arrangement, how easy it is to identify consideration, and whether or not the partner is doing things for the council. There is a difference between doing things that the council must, would or might otherwise do and doing things that the council approves of but cannot or would not usually do itself.

All this matters not only so that you know how to sue each other, but more importantly so that you know whether any procurement rules apply. Local authority contracts are most certainly caught by the European procurement regime, if they are of a high enough value and depending on the subject matter, and can be set aside if the procedures are not followed properly. Lower value contracts will still be caught by the rules about ignoring non-commercial considerations, publicity and giving reasons for decisions in Pt II of the Local Government Act 1998, and by the council's own contract standing orders.

What if the relationship is reversed? Can the council do things for its partners? This leads into an issue that used to be called municipal trading, but is now somewhat broader.

The question is this:

> Does a local authority have statutory power to provide goods or services to someone else?

There is fundamental tension between the wish for local authorities to innovate and engage with others, the principle that local authorities offer unfair competition to other suppliers because of the depth of their pockets and their ability to tax, and government reluctance to allow local authorities a free hand to extract money from the population or to carry out economic activity in the public sector that could be carried out in the private sector. This tension has worked itself out over the years in a series of battles about the ultra vires doctrine and the interpretation and alteration of a set of statutory provisions. This is a personal view of the current situation and more of a quick spin than an in-depth tour.

First, there are a few specific local authority powers. Obvious examples are s 38 of the Local Government (Miscellaneous Provisions) Act 1976 under which local authorities can sell-off spare computer capacity, or ss 141 and 142 of the Local Government Act 1972 relating to research and the provision of information.

Secondly, the issue may arise in an area where the authority clearly has powers, but has contracted out the activity to a partner agency or to a commercial contractor on a partnership basis. Arguably in these circumstances the support work associated with the activity can be supplied by the authority as a nominated sub-contractor. The argument is that if, say, the council could decide to provide (principally under s 111 of the Local Government Act 1972) legal services to support its in-house housing department, which discharges housing functions, then it could equally require that its legal service be a sub-contractor when the activity is contracted out (also under s 111). Of course it would have to be able to defend the decision in terms of its Best Value and fiduciary duties, but that applies to everything it decides to do.

Thirdly, there is the Local Authorities (Goods and Services) Act 1970. This says that a local authority and a specified public body may enter into an agreement for the supply by the authority to the body of goods or materials, the provision by the authority for the body of any administrative, professional or technical services, the use by the body of any vehicle, plant or apparatus belonging to the authority, the placing at the disposal of the body of the services of any person employed in connection with the vehicle or other property in question, and the carrying out by the authority of works of maintenance in connection with land or buildings for the maintenance of which the body is responsible. It also allows a local authority to purchase and store any goods or materials which they think they may require for the purposes of supply. Note that there are services that are not covered – construction as opposed to maintenance, for example. Note also that the other party must be a 'public body'. Some, such as other local authorities, are defined in the Act. Others, big and small, are prescribed in a series of statutory instruments, and if you ask nicely and do not mind waiting the Secretary of State will make an order adding to the list. There was along debate about the scope of the powers under the Act, resolved by an apparent change of view by Government and the case of *R v Yorkshire Purchasing Organisation, ex p British Educational Supplies Ltd*[1] so now it is safe to assume that this Act means just about what it says.

Once upon a time a great deal of trading activity by local authorities was justified in terms of s 111 of the Local Government Act 1972 as the sale of spare capacity. The argument, which applies now as it did then, was that if you employed staff and bought equipment and materials, or the discharge of your functions, and it just so happened that you did not need them all the time, or that you had some left over at the end, then you could hire them out or sell them commercially because it was ancillary or conducive to the purpose for which you engaged them in the first place. So you can sell left over plants from your nursery, if the parks are full. This got into deeper water when people tried to maintain that they could have a huge establishment for a small direct service because the income from the sale of spare capacity helped make the direct service cheaper. This is almost certainly outside s 111, either because it is not ancillary if the tail wags the dog, or because it is prohibited by other legislation, or because it fails a test of purpose.

Fifthly, there is s 2 of the Local Government Act 2000. This is the power to do anything which is considered likely to achieve the promotion or improvement of the economic, social or environmental well-being of the area. Sub-section 4 says this includes power to:

> 'enter into arrangements or agreements with any person ... co-operate with, or facilitate or co-ordinate the activities of, any person ... exercise on behalf of any person any functions of that person, and ... provide staff, goods, services or accommodation to any person.'

If the well-being test (and all other usual criteria for local authority decisions) is met, you can rely on this to provide services to partners. The fly in the ointment is s 3, which says the power 'does not enable a local authority to raise money (whether by precepts, borrowing or otherwise)'. Government appeared to insist as the Bill went through Parliament that this meant that councils could not charge for services provided to others, but the statutory guidance is more liberal and would allow income if it is incidental to the arrangement, or if partners make payments on a voluntary basis, or if a company or partnership vehicle is established which itself makes money. Some commentators have expressed the view that this interpretation is too liberal, but it has not yet been tested and may of course never be.

Finally, government is consulting on proposals to put orders in place under the Local Government Act 1999 which would confer powers that mirror the s 2 powers (and limitations) but substitute a Best Value purpose for the well-being purpose.

1   (1997) 95 LGR 727, CA.

CHAPTER 20
Consultation

Introduction

[20.1]
We started at the top, in the thin clear air of ambition, with the new community strategy and LSPs. We moved down the slopes into a jungle of tangled partnerships. Now the vegetation is thinning out, life is less complicated, we are in the world of consultation.

At first glance, the good thing about consultation is that either you have to do it or you do not, and either you have done it or you have not. It is more of an event than a relationship, a one-night stand of public participation. That probably accounts for all the trouble it causes. Because the not so good thing about consultation that it is easily misunderstood, and that it can feel unsatisfactory from both sides of the exchange. Nor is the law on the consultation as clear as it might be.

This chapter will look at the legal requirement for consultation, and contrast this with the participation regime for the Community Strategy.

Consultation – The Statutory Requirements

[20.2]

> 'No useful purpose would ... be served by formulating words of definition. Nor would it be appropriate to seek to lay down the manner in which consultation must take place . . . If a complaint is made of failure to consult, it will be for the court to examine the facts and circumstances of the particular case and to decide whether consultation was in fact held.'
>
> Morris J [1947]

The other problem with consultation is the way the rules keep changing.

Starting with statutory requirements, there are in fact fewer than one might think. Leaving aside environmental regulation, and concentrating on pure local government law, the statutory duties to consult the public are few and far between. The references to public consultation in the Local Government Act 2000 easily outnumber the references in the rest of the Local Government Acts, especially if one discounts the economic development chapter of the Local Government and Housing Act 1989, which the 2000 Act replaces.

218

There are countless requirements for one authority to consult another, but that is a different issue. Apportioning the balance of power between public bodies is different from asking the people affected by your actions and decisions what they think.

The language of statutory consultation has changed over the years. A few examples will illustrate this.

Section 13 of the Town and Country Planning Act 1990 is about preparing unitary development plans. It is headed 'public participation'. It says planning authorities must comply with Regulations. The Town and Country Planning (Development Plan) Regulations 1991[1] require 'pre deposit consultation' with a number of public bodies. Then the plan must be 'made available for inspection' and notice given in the paper and to pre-deposit consultees and any one else the planning authority chooses. During a six week period, people may make 'objections' under the Act or 'representations' under the Regulations. If objections are made, and are not withdrawn, s 16 requires a local inquiry or hearing to be held to consider them. If an inquiry is held, anyone with outstanding objections or representations may appear at it. The Inspector holding the inquiry will make a report, the council must prepare a detailed response, notify the other parties and publicise it generally. It can adopt the plan 28 days later. This process has not changed a great deal for 50 years, apart from the recognition that not every comment is an 'objection'. It is famous for taking forever and costing a great deal. It is also fundamentally adversarial.

Section 13 of the Rates Act 1984 introduced a new duty to consult industrial and commercial ratepayers before setting business rates. The logic is that business ratepayers do not vote, so this is the only way they can be given a chance to influence the spending that affects them and the rates that they pay. The idea survived the community charge, and the arrival of the national non-domestic rate, in terms of spending if not of local taxation, and is to be found in s 65 of the Local Government Finance Act 1992. This says that a billing or major precepting authority 'shall consult ... persons or bodies appearing to it to be representative of persons subject to non-domestic rates ...' and 'Consultations must be made as to each financial year, and must be about the authority's proposals for expenditure (including capital expenditure) in that financial year'. Regulations may prescribe matters which are to be treated as expenditure for this purpose. The duty must be performed before the annual budget-setting or precepting calculations are made. Authorities must have regard to government guidance as to whom, when and how to consult. The information that they are to be given in prescribed in regulations. Here, then, the language is of consultation. The ingredients, on which there is little scope for local discretion, are the timetable, the consultees, the information given and the method used

Section 3 of the Local Government Act 1999 contains the primary best value duty to make arrangements to secure continuous improvement in the way in which its functions are exercised, having regard to a combination of economy, efficiency and effectiveness. To decide how to do this, a best value authority must consult local taxpayer representatives, be they council tax or NNDR, representatives of persons who use or are likely to use services provided by the authority, and representatives of persons appearing to them to have an interest in the authority's area. Helpfully, the section says that 'representatives' in relation to a group of persons means persons who appear to the authority to be representative of that group. Regard must, as you might suspect, be had to statutory guidance, but DETR Circular 10/99 says that this is not likely to be issued, whilst at the same time making 'consultation' one of the 'four Cs' around which every best value review must be based, and giving what must be non-statutory guidance on how to do it. The language is still of consultation, but the obligatory thought process encompasses several open-ended decisions about whom to consult and how

Section 4 of the Local Government Act 2000 is about preparing the Community Strategy. It says that, in preparing or modifying their community strategy, a local authority must consult and seek the participation of such persons as they consider appropriate, and must have regard to any guidance issued by the Secretary of State. All being well, the inclusive, general and forward-looking character of the Community Strategy should reduce the chances of legal argument about the quality of this process. But just in case, the prudent authority will notice two features of this requirement.

First, consultation alone is not enough. There is a positive duty to seek the participation of others. The language has changed. Presumably the distinction relates to the nature and the quality of the process. Consultation equates to telling your consultee what you propose to do and listening to their comments before finally making up your mind. Participation must necessarily be different, otherwise why mention it separately, and supposes some joint working in drawing up the proposals in the first place and a degree of consensus in the outcome. The duty is to seek participation, not to ensure it, so a genuine and practicable invitation should be enough, even if it is turned down.

Secondly, there is a two-stage process. In the first stage, the authority decides whom it is appropriate to consult and whose participation to seek. In the second, it consults, seeks and participates.

Let us suppose that the Barchester Preservation Society is so deeply unhappy with the contents of the Barchester DC Community Strategy that it sought permission for judicial review. It would start by attacking the decision that it was not appropriate to seek its participation, move on to the decision not to consult it, then on to the adequacy of the seeking, and of the consultation, and the failure to have any or sufficient regard to the statutory guidance, before the final thrust at whether or not any reasonable authority could have determined that the strategy would promote or improve the economic, social and environmental well-being of their area, or contribute to the achievement of sustainable development in the UK.

1   SI 1991/2794.

Consultation – Case Law

The duty to consult

[20.3]
The case law has followed several strands. First, there is the duty to consult.

When does it arise, and how is it to be understood? Clearly enough, if there is a statutory duty then all that matters is the construction of the statute. For example in *R v Worcestershire Health Authority, ex p Kidderminster and District Community Health Council*[1] the CHC argued that the HA had wrongfully consulted on a single option for future care provision instead of the seven options that it had previously been contemplating. Regulation 18(1) of the Community Health Councils Regulations 1996[2] required consultation on 'proposals'. The case turned on whether all seven options had become proposals, or just the one that had been selected. The single-option consultation was held to be adequate. *R v Brent London Borough Council, ex p Morris*[3] established that the general duty of consultation under s 105 of the Housing Act did not impose a specific duty to consult individual tenants on housing management decisions.

In the absence of any statutory framework, though, the consultation requirement has tended to derive from the doctrine of legitimate expectation. This is a subset of the requirement for procedural fairness in public decision-making, but the two concepts intertwine. To start off with, a legitimate expectation will arise if you promise to consult someone. If you then fail to consult, the failure is a ground for judicial review where the subsequent decision may be quashed. For example in *R v Liverpool Corp, ex p Liverpool Taxi Fleet Operators' Association*[4], the Council had promised to consult the Association if it wanted to change its policy of limiting the number of hackney carriage licences it granted. The Court of Appeal quashed a decision changing the policy taken without consultation. As in *R v Governors of Small Heath School, ex p Birmingham City Council*[5] the court expressed the law in terms of general 'unfairness'. A legitimate expectation may arise if you express an intention to consult even though you do not tell the prospective consultee[6]. It may arise because you have a general practice of consultation on such issues[7]. It may arise because the interest is patent, and local authorities generally have a practice of consultation, see the leading case of *R v Brent London Borough Council, ex p Gunning*[8] on consulting parents before closing a school. It may arise because the would-be consultee has drawn special attention to himself. Thus, although there is no general legally enforceable duty in planning cases to notify in excess of the statutory requirement, notwithstanding a general informal practice of notification[9], failure to tell a prominent lead objector about a planning inquiry led to the decision being quashed[10].

Perhaps the logic is this. First, there may be a statutory duty. Secondly, there may have been a promise, express or implied. Thirdly, even in the absence of a promise, procedural fairness may give rise to a duty to consult. In *R v Powys County Council, ex p Hambridge*[11] the council had changed its policy for charging for adult social care without consulting the applicant. Government advice recommended consultation. There had been no promise. But procedural fairness did not require consultation with this applicant, because amongst other things the policy included a review procedure so she could represent that she should be made an exception.

1   (1989, unreported).
2   SI 1996/640.
3   (1996) 28 HLR 852.
4   [1972] 2 QB 299.

5   (1989) Times, 31 May.
6   *R v London Borough of Bexley, ex p Barnhurst* [1992] COD 382.
7   *R v Birmingham City Council, ex p Dredger* (1993) 91 LGR 532, [1993] COD 276.
8   (1985) 84 LGR 168.
9   *R v Secretary of State for the Environment, ex p Kent* (1988) 57 P&CR 431.
10   *Wilson v Secretary of State for the Environment* [1988] JPL 540.
11   [1998] 1 FLR 643, [1998] Fam Law 136.

Limits to the duty

[20.4]

There are other areas where the courts have occasionally held back. They do seem sometimes willing to be mindful of the practical implications. In addition to the planning cases, for example, *R v Falmouth and Truro Port Health Authority, ex p South West Water Ltd*[1] established both specifically that a port health authority was under no duty to consult a water undertaker before serving an abatement notice under the Environmental Protection Act 1990 concerning sewage discharge, and the principle that an enforcing authority was under no duty to consult a perpetrator before serving notices of this kind. This echoes *R v Birmingham City Council, ex p Ferrero Ltd*[2] where the court found no duty to consult before issue of a suspension notice under the Consumer Protection Act 1987 and *R v Hounslow London Borough, ex p Dooley and Bourke*[3] where there was held to be no duty to consult before service of a stop notice. Contrast, though, *R v Norfolk County Council Social Services Department, ex p M*[4] in which a decision to name a suspect as a child abuser, and place him on the child abuse register, was quashed for failure to notify or consult or offer a hearing. Likewise in *R v Wandsworth London Borough Council, ex p P*[5] a decision to remove the applicant from a list of approved foster mothers because of allegations of abuse was quashed for inadequate consultation with her.

Other cases confirm that there are limits to the doctrine. In *R v Gravesham Borough Council, ex p Gravesham Association of Licensed Hackney Carriage Owners*[6], in contrast to the *Liverpool* case, the court found there was no legitimate expectation to consult taxi drivers on a decision to lift the maximum number of licences to be granted. There had been no previous practice of consultation, no right of the taxi drivers was being infringed, and there had been no prior promise. And in *R v Secretary of State for the Home Department and the London Fire and Civil Defence Auhority, ex p London Borough of Greenwich*[7], an application for judicial review of a decision to close a fire station was unsuccessful. Apparently no legitimate expectation arose to consult again in changed circumstances, despite previous consultation and a government circular.

It is hard to draw out clear distinctions. Not only do the concepts of legitimate expectation and procedural unfairness interweave, but the more difficult cases take us from whether the legitimate expectation creates a duty to consult, and whether consultation has taken place, to whether it creates a duty to consult with a particular way group of people. So in the leading case on closing old peoples' homes, *R v Devon County Council, ex p Baker*[8], the Council was under a duty to consult residents in the home generally, but not each individual resident separately. But in *R v Wandsworth London Borough*

Council, ex p Beckwith[9] a decision to close a home was quashed because people living in other residential homes in the borough, who would be indirectly affected, had not been consulted even though the people in the home that was to be closed had been. The difficulty with these cases is that it is far easier to decide after the event whether or not the applicant ought to have been consulted, than it is to decide before the event whom to consult.

There is a difference between a duty to consult arising from a legitimate expectation and from statute. *R v Gwent County Council, ex p Bryant*[10] established that a breach of the former is curable at a later stage in the decision-making process, so it is sufficient if representations are properly considered by a Minister on appeal or review, whereas a breach of the latter will not be curable in this way.

1   [2001] QB 445.
2   [1993] 1 All ER 530.
3   (1999) P&CR 405.
4   [1989] QB 619.
5   (1988) 87 LGR 370.
6   (1987) Independent, 14 January.
7   (Unreported).
8   (1992) Times, 20 October.
9   (1995) 159 LG Rev 929.
10 [1988] COD 19.

Legitimate expectation

[20.5]
The doctrine of legitimate expectation has developed in its own right. In *R v North and East Devon Health Authority, ex p Coughlan*[1] the authority had promised extremely disabled patients that they could live at their special facility for as long as they chose, then decided to close it. The Court of Appeal said that if a promise or other conduct gave rise to a legitimate expectation that something would or would not happen, the court would examine the conduct and the circumstances to decide the legal consequences. The lowest level of intervention would simply apply the *Wednesbury* principles, so that the previous promise or conduct was a factor that had to be taken properly into account, but no more. Next, the promise or conduct may give rise to a legitimate expectation that consultation will take place before it is reversed. For a case falling somewhere between the first two, involving the closure of yet another residential home, see *R v Camden London Borough Council, ex p Bodimead*[2], where a handbook for residents contained a qualified statement aiming to provide residents with a home for life. This, and the consequential expectations of the residents, had not been taken into account, and the decision was quashed. Thirdly, though, if there is a very clear expectation that something substantial will happen or will not happen, such that doing something different would amount to an 'abuse of power', then the court is able to balance the competing interests and quash the decision on this ground alone. The judiciary are quietly introducing promissory estoppel into public law, and it will be fascinating to see what happens next. Ironically the Human Rights Act 1998 seems likely to inhibit this process, because there will be few if any cases where it is necessary to rely on abuse of power where there will not also be a breach of convention rights.

A recent train of thought derives from the increasing volume of government guidance. Some of it should be followed, especially if given under the National Assistance Act 1948[3]. Some statutory guidance must be taken into account and should be followed unless there is good reason to do otherwise, but need not be followed slavishly. Other non-statutory guidance probably ought to be taken into account, but you might get away with ignoring bits of it. The argument goes that if the guidance – depending on its status – tells you to consult, and you do not consult, you have failed to take a material factor into account, and are Wednesbury unreasonable. This will not succeed every time, for example in the *Powys* case (above), but it would be brave to ignore it.

1   (1998) 47 BLMR 27, affd [2001] QB 213, CA.
2   (Unreported)
3   See *R v London Borough of Islington, ex p Rixon* (1996) 32 BLMR 136.

Adequacy of consultation

[20.6]
The next strand is about the adequacy of consultation. This interrelates with the scope of the expectation that gave rise to the duty. It also raises a question as to whether there is a difference between 'consultation' in which you ask someone for their views on a proposal, and 'notification' in which you announce your intention publicly and give people the opportunity to make representations before you take a final decision. Probably there is not, it just adds a different flavour to the debate.

The ingredients of consultation have been listed in a number of cases, for example by the House of Lords in *R v Secretary of State for Social Services, ex p Association of Metropolitan Authorities*[1].

First, there must be a genuine invitation to give advice. This means, for example, that the consultation process must be genuine and not a sham, and that the decision-maker must not have a closed mind about the outcome. A false start is not necessarily fatal. In *R v London Borough of Barnet, ex p B*[2] a second consultation process, after a flawed process, was upheld as genuine and fair.

Secondly, the invitation must be made and expressed adequately. In *R v Lambeth London Borough, ex p N*[3] the court held consultation on proposals to close a special educational needs school to be inadequate, as there was no clear invitation to comment on the specific proposal to close the school, or the timetable for the closure, or the effect on the children using it. As a counterpoint, however, in *R v Shropshire Health Authority, ex p Duffus*[4] the court held that the Authority had not failed in its duty to consult the League of Friends of a hospital before deciding to close it. The League had been consulted on the authority's first proposals, but not on the second proposals which followed the comments on the first. The court held that the second proposals were not so different from the first as to constitute fresh proposals requiring fresh consultation.

Thirdly, the consultee must be given adequate information to be able to understand the proposition on which it is being consulted. In *R (on the application of Wainwright) v Richmond upon Thames London Borough*[5] there was a statutory duty to notify and consult residents before installing a toucan pedestrian crossing. The council's efforts were inadequate – the mailing process was deficient, the lamp-post notices gave a closing date that had already passed, and the newspaper adverts did not say exactly where the crossing was or that people could make representations. The court said the three ingredients for successful notification were:

(1)   a sufficient description of the proposal;
(2)   an invitation to comment; and
(3)   enough time to comment and respond.

Information must cover any issues as to the form and substance of the proposal, and its implications for the person being consulted, that they might not be aware of but that are known to the person carrying out the consultation.

Fourthly, the consultee must be given sufficient time to consider the issues and comment on them. The character of the consultee is important, for example it may have to consult its membership or arrange a meeting. So are the surrounding circumstances. For a case where a short period was acceptable, see *R v Leeds City Council, ex p N*[6]. The council proposed to close a school that was known to be failing or likely to fail. It published its consultation timetable in June. In line with this it consulted in early September with a deadline of 22 September. The formal procedure allowed a subsequent two-month objection period. The consultation period was adequate in the circumstances. Nor is it an excuse that the issue was so urgent that there was no time to consult. A health authority tried this argument in *R v North and East Devon Health Authority, ex p Pow*[7] and was told that it should have allowed enough time right from the start.

Finally, there must be a genuine receipt of that advice. This draws the obvious distinction between telling and asking. It also means that the comments made by consultees must be reported accurately to the decision-maker, who must have enough time to consider them. The decision must not be about something different from the subject-matter of the consultation.

1   [1986] 1 All ER 164.
2   [1994] 2 FCR 781.
3   [1996] ELR 299.
4   [1990] COD 131.
5   [2001] 18 EG 174 (CS).
6   [1999] Ed CR 735; affd [1999] ELR 324, CA.
7   (1997) 39 BMLR 77.

Checklist

[20.7]
In a sense the legal advice is easy. If in doubt, consult. If in doubt about how to consult, consult thoroughly and slowly. The following check list contains some dangerous generalisations, but may help:

- If the duty is statutory, check the statute. The court cannot waive omissions.
- Follow government guidance to consult unless you have excellent well-documented reasons to depart from it.
- If you have made a promise, or expressed an intention, or you or your peers have a settled practice of consultation, then you should consult. A promise to deliver a service may be enforceable in its own right.
- There is usually no need for prior consultation in regulatory enforcement cases (but it is good practice).
- But the impact of the proposals on a particular person may make it procedurally unfair not to consult him or her, depending on their other opportunities to make representations.
- Think about whom to consult, which groups or individuals are directly affected, and how you can be properly alert to their views.
- Ensure the consultation is genuine, not a sham.
- Invite comments properly. Ensure the invitation reaches the consultees, explains the proposition and tells them how to comment.
- Give consultees all the information you have about the proposal and its implications for them that you have, but they might not have. Be helpful.
- Allow the consultees sufficient time to respond.
- Make sure the proposal does not change too much during the process.
- Ensure comments are properly taken into account, and quality-assure the decision-making process generally. Think in particular about the matters that should and should not be taken into account and any government guidance.

Stakeholder Involvement in Community Strategies

[20.8]
It is very instructive to wind forward smartly from the nitty-gritty of inadequate consultation to the Community Strategy again. The language changes, the concept is different. Remember that s 4 of the 2000 Act requires authorities to consult and seek the participation of such persons as they consider appropriate, and to have regard to any guidance issued by the Secretary of State. Well, what does the guidance recommend?

The guidance stresses that the process is almost as important as the outcome. Giving people a voice is an aim in itself. It says that authorities should seek to involve all sectors of the community. They should actively reach out into the community to involve under-represented groups, especially to promote equality. They should seek to involve bodies covering LA 21 issues and regeneration, and residents groups.

They should work with the police, primary, secondary, further and higher education bodies, the Employment Service, the Benefits Agency, New Deal partnerships, the Small Business Service, Housing Associations and Trusts and other Registered Social Landlords, Health Authorities, Trusts and other bodies, Regional Development Agencies, Regional and local Chambers of Commerce, Learning and Skills Councils, Connexions, Department of the

Environment Transport and the Regions, Health Service and other regional Government Offices, in London the GLA and Mayor, Business in the Community, the private sector, voluntary groups, minority and hard to reach groups, Voluntary Service Councils, Rural Development Councils, community development agencies, and Community Legal Service Partnerships.

They should involve all the partnership bodies described in Chapter 19 (above) that they can find in their area. In multi-tier areas, they should consider 'nesting' (it does sound cosy) local strategies in county strategies, or some such arrangement. They might think about joining up with neighbours. And they must ensure that they drop down into local communities themselves, though community level partnership bodies or through targeted consultation.

They will need to use a variety of methods to engage with these different stakeholders. They need to think carefully about whether their consultation mechanisms accidentally exclude groups within the community such as disabled people and members of ethnic communities. Preferably, they should build on existing structures (around LA21, or New Deal or regeneration). Perhaps different groups will become involved in different ways at different times.

Then, of course, the task is to identify everyone's priorities, resolve differences and reach a common view on the highest priorities, but without raising false expectations. They should map out the gap between these ambitions and what everyone is currently delivering, and draw up an action plan to close it.

Public Participation in Modern Local Government

[20.9]
Perhaps the moral of this chapter should be that participation is better than consultation. In truth, it is too early to tell.

Consultation is certainly different from participation. If anything, it can create a stronger feeling of alienation than if you had not bothered in the first place. It is adversarial, there is a great deal of case law about it. If you do not ask people right at the start what they want to be built at the end of their road, then consult them later on the proposal for a nuclear powered pig farm with integral mobile telephone mast and home for the criminally insane, receive objections, then allow it to be built anyway, it is easy to understand if they are a little disenchanted. If one statutory body is obliged to consult another, either they will agree, in which case the exercise was futile, or they will disagree, in which case neither will be happy. Likewise, as consultation is about telling people what you have in mind to do, listening to what they have to say about it, then taking a final decision, if you do what you proposed, they say: *'They never intended to listen to us anyway'* and if you change your mind they say: *'It's a good job we persuaded them not to do it'*.

Neither consultation nor participation is about representative democracy, because they dilute the role of the elected decision-taker. It is now fairly common for local authorities to consult the whole electorate on their budget proposals, in addition to the obligatory consultation with non-domestic rate payers. What then if the budget coincides with local or national election pledges, but more people take part in the consultation than voted at the election, and reject a budget set by an administration voted in a few months earlier? Many of the community leaders who are consulted, or who participate in partnership bodies, are self-elected and represent very small numbers of people. And is it coincidence that the decline in interest in representational government has coincided with the growth of consultation and participation? Would more people turn out to vote if they thought the people they were voting for would take decisions without asking them about them first?

It remains to be seen how well the participative system of partnership working will perform. If it works well, it will lead to rounded and effective local government where everyone that matters feels they have played a full part and helps to deliver solutions to difficult problems. If it works badly, it will create uncertainty about who is actually responsible for what, aimless, unaccountable, introspective talking-shops, and failure to reach consensus on anything but the most banal platitudes.

CHAPTER 21
Openness and Freedom of Information

Access to Information – Where We Were Not Long Ago

[21.1]

> 'The concept of the official secret is bureaucracy's specific invention'.
> Max Weber [1921]

This Division started by looking at the new requirement under s 2 of the Local Government Act 2000 to prepare a community strategy. It examined the rules and the guidance, and thought about what the exercise would be like in practice. It looked at the community strategy alongside the other main statutory plans, at the Local Strategic Partnership that should compose and deliver it, and at the Public Service Agreement process that is muscling in on the government funding regimes that we are more familiar with. At this stage the local authority was truly leading a community that was anxious to agree priorities first locally, then with national government.

Then we looked at the concept of partnership, in all its odd guises. Now the council has moved off centre stage. It is part of the cast of characters, but it does not necessarily have a leading role. Old certainties and structures fade at the drop of a grant cheque, and curious new relationships and risks emerge.

Then we looked at consultation, the need to ask people what they think about things that you are going to do. Consultation evolved from objection to participation, and from a nice idea to an essential precondition.

Now we are moving even further away from the nirvana of joined-up consensus that would put all the lawyers out of a job. Never mind leading the community, never mind being partners with them, never mind asking what they think. This next bit is about keeping things secret from them.

The statutory guidance on new constitutions sets out the government's principles for local authority decision-making:

- proportionality;
- due consultation and professional advice;
- respect for human rights;
- a presumption in favour of openness; and
- clarity of aims and desired outcomes.

It is an interesting catechism. Where does it come from? The Human Rights Act 1998 issues are obvious, but why mention professional advice and not local democracy? And why should there be a presumption of openness in local authority decision-making when there is clearly none in central government. Anyway, transparency and openness are back on the modernisation agenda.

In 1908 the case of *Tenby Corpn v Mason*[1] established that there was no common law right to attend full council meetings, so the Local Authorities (Admission of the Press to Meetings) Act 1908 granted that right, subject to the ability to throw them out by resolution in special circumstances. Committee meetings were not subject to the Act, though, so a local authority could form a committee of the whole council and talk in private about the things that they did not want to talk about in public. You still occasionally hear the phrase 'going into committee' as a euphemism for excluding the press and public, although it has been overtaken in some parts by the no less impenetrable 'moving part two'.

This happy facility ended in 1960 with the Public Bodies (Admission to Meetings) Act 1960. Then in 1985 the Local Government (Access to Information) Act dug beneath the surface. It introduced ss 100A to K into the Local Government Act 1972, and the requirements for three clear working days notice of meetings, full public access to committee agendas and reports, public access to the background papers on which the reports are based, and public access to all council and committee meetings, unless there is a positive decision that the material in question is 'confidential' or 'exempt' from the right of public access. Material is only confidential in this narrow sense if the authority is prohibited from public disclosure by a government department or a court. To be 'exempt', the material must fall in one of the categories of exempt information in Sch 12A to the 1972 Act, and the council or committee must decide that it wishes to withhold it from the public (or the proper officer that it should not be published because of the likelihood of such a decision). Even then, the minutes must include a summary of the decision.

Local authorities then discovered in *R v Secretary of State for the Environment, ex p Hillingdon London Borough Council*[2] that only committees and officers could take decisions. Officers' decisions could be taken in total secrecy, committee decisions were subject to the access to information legislation. Procedures for chief officers to take decisions 'in consultation with' senior councillors soon emerged. The smoke filled room survived, or would have done but for the anti-smoking policy.

At the same time, an odd assortment of statutes has required local authorities to make information available to the public in obscure ways. The poor proper officer, for example, has to maintain things like the list of politically restricted posts under s 2 of the Local Government and Housing Act 1989, the register under s 100G of the Local Government Act 1972 which contains the name and address of every member of the Council and every co-opted committee member of each committee or the list under the same section which sets out officers' delegated powers. Section 100G also obliges him to keep a list of lists – a list of the enactments up to 1986 (but updated) which confer rights of access to meetings and papers. These are helpfully set out in the list of lists of lists, the little-known Local Government (Inspection of Documents) (Summary of Rights) Order 1986[3].

Add to this list Best Value inspection reports and the Best Value performance plan and the auditor's report on it, published under the Local Government Act 1999 and the Audit Commission Act 1998, the chief finance officer's report under the Local Government Finance Act 1998, reports from the head of paid service or the monitoring officer under the 1989 Act, ombudsman's reports under the Local Government Act 1974, and council tax information under the Local Government Finance Act 1974 including the information that must accompany the demand.

Think also about admission and exclusion arrangements under the School Standards and Framework Act 1998, school information, SEN information, information about the national curriculum and about complaints, pupil records that parents can access, reports from school governors and inspectors, and proposals to close or change the status of schools. Contemplate the Housing Act requirements for publishing information to Council tenants, and about big changes like stock transfer. Stand back in wonder at the raft of public information about planning and the environment, licensing and consumer protection.

Sadly the only certainty with a litany like this is that it is inevitably incomplete.

Finally, there are a lot of rules about what local authority accounts must be kept, and what information they must contain, and that is really a topic in its own right. But it is worth remembering that at one time the primary source of information for industrious journalists and assiduous ratepayers arose through the audit of the accounts. This is currently to be found in s 14 of the Audit Commission Act 1998, which gives electors a general if brief right of inspection of the accounts while they are being audited, and s 15 which allows an interested person, whether or not they are an elector, to look at 'all books, deeds, contracts, bills, vouchers and receipts' relating to the accounts, unless they contain personal information about a member of staff.

1   [1908] 1 Ch 457.
2   [1986] 1 All ER 810.
3   SI 1986/854.

Access to Information under Executive Arrangements

[21.2]
The Local Government Act 2000 was a real test. Heralded as an attempt to make decision-making more transparent, it gave decision-making power for most of the council's functions to no more than ten people. Welcome back the smoke filled room, if six of them decided to change the anti-smoking policy? After all, what is a cabinet for? Government rose effortlessly to the challenge of making a set of rules for others that are different from those that it follows itself. The Local Authorities (Executive Arrangements) (Access to Information) (England) Regulations 2000[1] apply to meetings of the executive, its committee, and to decisions on executive functions taken by executive members, officers and joint committees.

To understand them you first need to understand the concept of 'key decisions'. This was just meant to mean 'big decisions' and could have been left for local determination, but local government cannot be trusted with this sort of thing, so there had to be a definition. A decision is key if it crosses one or other of the following thresholds. The first is that it affects communities in more than one ward or electoral area. The second is that it involves expenditure or income that is significant in terms of the budget for the activity. This is getting a little complicated, and is still quite vague, but when in a hole keep digging, so the statutory guidance – which needed two attempts – says that authorities can decide that decisions are key even if they do not cross ward boundaries, and that they should have a look at what their neighbours are doing before deciding on a series of financial thresholds, likely to vary depending on the activity. This is what happens with lines on maps, of course. It is not very logical that you can get to go to the meeting about a small traffic management scheme which crosses ward boundaries but not the meeting about a larger one that does not. It is not very logical if you can go to a meeting to complain about spending £10,000 in one street, but not less than £100,000 in the next. Lines on maps are part of life in local government, though, and when they peeped over to see what their neighbours were doing, they saw them looking back to see what they were doing, so the government decided to consult before framing guidance on an indicative threshold, and that is the current position. Anyway, some big decisions are 'key' and the public stands more chance of getting to see them being taken.

Key decisions that the council knows about in advance must be flagged up in a published forward plan, covering the next four months and updated monthly. It must say:

- who is going to take the decisions;
- what reports are going to be considered;
- who will be consulted;
- when the decision is going to be taken; and
- how representations can be made.

This could come out like:

> 'In three months time the Cabinet Member for such things is going to decide whether or not to build something very unappealing next door to you, on the basis of some papers that have not been written yet, after consulting fewer people than you would like. Representations may be made in writing to the Town Hall in a shorter period than you would prefer.'

So we will have some fun about the adequacy of the consultation process for a start. If the council does not know about them far enough in advance, it should at least give three days public notice, subject to a careful urgency procedure involving the chair of the overview and scrutiny committee.

All executive decisions, including now all key decisions taken by officers, must be recorded. The record must give reasons and state alternatives rejected.

And the public can access all meetings of executive members at which key decisions are taken, or at which those that are going to be taken in the next 28 days are discussed in the presence of council officers. The background papers and reports are accessible to the public. The only exemptions (apart therefore from debates more than 28 days before the decision, and non-key decisions) are the familiar categories of confidential and exempt information, draft papers, reports by political assistants (who are subject to pay ceilings under the Local Government and Housing Act 1989) and meetings consisting principally of briefing by officers. Government is, incidentally consulting on amendments to the wording of the exempt information schedule, and on extending the three day prior publication requirement to five days.

1   SI 2000/3272.

The Data Protection Act 1998

[21.3]
The next piece of the jigsaw is a series of changes to data protection legislation under the Data Protection Act 1998, moving from access to information about the council, and about council decisions, to the right of an individual to see the information that the council holds about him or her, and to prevent its misuse.

This is a bigger change than is generally realised. Most local government officers, and quite likely most local government lawyers, think of the Data Protection Act as a rather woolly thing that applies to computer data, prevents you using data captured for one purpose for a different purpose, and has some sort of access rights attached that are rarely exercised. The most accurate part of this description is the wooliness. It is a paradox that access to information legislation is the least penetrable on the statute book. Two health warnings are necessary: first, please do refer to the Act itself because these notes are just an outline, second, doing this may seriously damage your health. The 1998 Act has moved matters on. It applies to non-computer records, there is a rolling programme of tougher compliance, and it is now the primary source of rights of access to personal information. The Act itself implemented an EU General Directive, which is always a good start.

People receiving personal social services, school children and their parents, and council tenants have all had a right of access to their personal files, backed up by a right of appeal to a council panel, for years. The source was the Access to Personal Files Act 1987 and regulations made under it. The Data Protection Act 1998 quietly repealed all this and substituted new provisions. Although these records (called 'accessible records' in the strange code in which the legislation is written) are not subject to the full swathe of the data protection principles until 2007, they are covered by a number of rights. These include the 'subject access rights', and from October 2001 rights to be informed of data processing activity, rights to rectify inaccurate records, rights to prevent processing and rights to compensation for breaches of the Act. They are also covered by rules requiring 'data controllers' (more code – the Council, or the school, probably in our case) to provide adequate security for these records. Note that this all generally applies to manual as well as computer records, if they are 'accessible records' that is to say personal records in the health, social services and education fields, or if the files are organised so you can get at information about individual people from them.

We will look at the subject access rights in more detail later, but at this stage a quick tour through the Act will be useful.

It applies to 'data', basically meaning any information processed automatically, or held in a filing system where the files are structured so you can find information about individuals, or in an accessible record, or (under the Freedom of Information Act 2000, when fully in force) held by a public authority. The chances are that if you have some information, it is data in terms of the Act. But the Act only applies to personal data, that is to say data about individual living people.

The bodies that control data must generally notify the Information Commissioner, who administers and enforces the legislation, of their details if they process automated data, and may do so for manual data. Advance permission is needed for some very sensitive processing. The Commissioner enforces primarily by serving an enforcement or information notice subject to a right of appeal to a Tribunal. The Act contains a series of offences concerning notification, failure to comply with notices, obtaining, disclosing, procuring and selling personal data and enforced subject access. Employees can be personally liable. There are powers of entry and inspection, and of forfeiture.

Subject to a number of exemptions, data must be processed in accordance with the data protection principles. 'Processing' means organising, altering, using, disclosing, analysing or destroying data and a whole lot more besides. The chances are that if you have done anything with your data, you have processed it.

This is a paraphase of the data protection principles:

The first principle

You must process personal data fairly and lawfully, and meet at least one of the Sch 2 conditions (and for sensitive personal data, one of the Sch 3 conditions). This means amongst other things that you must give people information when you process data about them. These conditions are set out below.

The second principle

You must obtain personal data only for specified and lawful purposes, and refrain from processing it in a way incompatible with those purposes.

The third principle

Personal data shall be adequate, relevant and not excessive for such purposes.

The fourth principle

Personal data shall be accurate and (reasonably) up-to-date.

The fifth principle

Personal data shall not be kept for longer than needed for such purposes.

The sixth principle

Personal data shall not be processed contrary to the rights of the person it is about, such as the subject access rights, and rights to give notice to inhibit processing.

The seventh principle

Technical steps shall be taken to prevent misuse or destruction of personal data.

The eighth principle

Personal data shall not be exported outside Europe without adequate safeguards (there is a whole body of law in the Act about the iniquity of non-Europeans and how to deal with them).

Also subject to exemptions, you cannot process personal data unless one of the Sch 2 conditions applies. They are as follows, again in outline only. It is hard to think of any local authority activity that would fall outside this list:

- the person concerned (the 'data subject', in data protection speak) has consented;
- the process is needed under or for a contract with the data subject;
- the process is needed for some other legal obligation of the data subject;
- the process is needed to protect the data subject's vital interests;
- the process is needed for the administration of justice, the exercise of statutory functions or the like;
- the process is needed for the legitimate interests of the data controller, or of a third party to whom data is disclosed, unless this is unwarranted and prejudicial to the data subject's rights, freedoms or legitimate interests.

If the data is 'sensitive' (about racial or ethnic origin, political views, faith, trades union membership, health, sex life or criminal activity) then one of the Sch 3 conditions must also be met:

- the data subject has given explicit consent;
- the process is needed under employment law;
- the process is needed to protect someone's vital interests, and there are certain specified problems getting consent;
- this is a limited process for members and so on of not-for profit political, religious, or trades union organisations;
- the data subject has publicised the data already;
- the process is needed for legal proceedings, legal advice and the like;

235

- the process is needed for the administration of justice, the exercise of statutory functions and the like;
- the process is needed for medical purposes and covered by a professional duty of confidence;
- the data is about ethic and racial origins and the process is needed to promote equal opportunity;
- (by a separate order) the process is needed in the substantial public interest to prevent or detect law breaking, incompetence and such things; involves giving family details for insurance and pension purposes, confidential counselling, some activities of registered political parties; archives, or the actions of a police constable.

And, subject to exemptions as ever, data subjects have some very specific rights.

The right to information

Schedule 1 imposes a duty to provide information to the data subject, so far as practicable, about the processing, or at least to make the information readily available. This should happen before the data is obtained, and before it is processed or disclosed to (or withheld from) a third party, unless this would involve disproportionate effort, or concerns a record needed to discharge a legal obligation. The information is the identity of the data controller, the purpose of the processing, and further information needed for example to ensure the processing is fair.

Subject access rights

Data subjects are entitled to be told, if they ask, if any data about them is being processed by the data controller, its nature, the purpose of the process and any recipients. They are also entitled to access the information itself (and be given a copy in permanent form if no disproportionate effort is required) and to be told its source. They can also ask about any automated process that is likely to be the sole basis of a decision affecting them. A small fee may be charged, and there is a timetable for responding which allows a little time to verify the request.

If compliance would release information about a third party (for example that they were the source), the data controller must either get that person's consent, or decide that it is reasonable to disclose without it. One option is to alter the information to make it anonymous.

There are special rights about credit agencies derived from consumer credit legislation, and a ban on making people consent to accessing their data (as in 'you have to supply me with this personal information before you get the job').

If this is not a case where the first four of the Sch 2 conditions apply, there is a right to require the data controller to stop the process on the ground that it is unwarranted, and that it is causing or likely to cause substantial damage or substantial distress. There is a right to give notice to prevent direct marketing

– cold-calling and junk-mail. And there are rights to interrupt and prevent certain types of automated decision-making.

Under s 13, the data subject has a right to compensation for damage and in some cases distress. Finally there is the right to rectify, block or seek the destruction of personal data, if it is inaccurate or if there has been a contravention of the Act.

The exemptions need careful study. Different exemptions apply to different aspects of the legislation and many are just exempt from the subject access and subject information rights. The list is as follows:

- national security;
- crime and taxation;
- regulation (if it would prejudice proper discharge of specified functions);
- the 'special purposes' of journalism, art, and literature (where more licence is allowed);
- research;
- history;
- statistics;
- disclosures required by law;
- domestic purposes;
- confidential references;
- the armed forces;
- judicial appointments;
- honours;
- crown employment and the like;
- management forecasts;
- corporate finance;
- negotiations with the data subject;
- some examinations;
- legal professional privilege; and
- self-incrimination.

There are detailed exemptions from the information and subject access rights in relation to health, education and social services. These are to be found in three Subject Access Modification Orders of 2000[1]. The information exemption is mainly around court reports. The subject access rights exemption is available if disclosure is likely to cause serious harm to anyone's physical or mental health or condition. To rely on this for health data, a data controller that is not a health professional must get an opinion from one, and there is a process that this should follow.

There is an exemption for education and social services records if it is against a child's interests to reveal information about abuse to a person with a parental role. And there is a limitation to the general exemption for third party rights (you will remember that their consent must be obtained, or the data controller must decide it is unreasonable to require it). If the third party is a teacher or education professional, the exemption only applies if disclosure carries a likelihood of serious harm.

Because the Directive allowed derogation, the Act is coming into force piecemeal, which is lulling us all into a false state of security. To follow this, divide the data into that which was being processed before October 1998 (called 'eligible data') and data which started being processed after that date. Then divide it another way, into automated (computers) and manual (paper). Then slice it again into an 'accessible record ' (a health, education, social services or housing record that used to be covered by the Access to Personal Files Act) and all the rest.

The First Transitional Period comes to an end in October 2001. Archaeological though it sounds, this has been a period in which the old consumer credit legislation, and the subject access rights over accessible records, has been in force albeit in their new forms. Eligible automated data – old computer systems effectively – were covered by a modified version of the Act that goes back somewhat to 1984 Act. Eligible manual data was generally exempt. New automated and manual systems were fully covered.

From the 25 October we are in the Second Transitional Period, which lasts until 2007. During this period eligible manual data, and all accessible records, still enjoy limited exemption from data protection principles 1 (apart from the duty to inform), 2, 3, 4 and 5 and from the rights of rectification, destruction and the like. They are still subject, though, to subject access rights, processing rights and the right to compensation. There is a special derogation for historical research. Anything else has to comply fully.

Before leaving the Data Protection Act, why not ask yourself a few questions about your organisation? For example, which of your manual filing systems are covered by the Act, and which of those are 'eligible'? How many requests for information under the subject access rights do you get a month, and how many of those are dealt with as requests under this legislation? And, perhaps the most curious of all, what difference did the 24 October 1998 and the 24 October 2001 make to your organisation, and, especially if the answer is 'none', why?

1   SI 2000/413; SI 2000/414; and SI 2000/415.

The Freedom of Information Act 2000

[21.4]
It helps to reverse the usual order of events and set out the timetable before explaining what the Act says. In a nutshell, the Act obliges public authorities to produce a 'publication scheme' telling the public what they can and cannot get to see, and gives them a general right to access all information held by the public authority, subject to a series of exemptions. The Act is to be brought into force between now and the end of 2005. The timetable is unofficial, and may of course change, but envisages central government coming on stream in the summer of 2002, followed by local government in the winter of 2002/2003, then at roughly six-monthly intervals the health service, police, schools (in 2004), Non-Departmental Public Bodies and finally private sector organisations such as local authority contractors in 2005.

This means that local government probably has less than 18 months to prepare. Apathy is raging in most authorities. After all, most already have an open government policy, and everyone knows that the Act is a lot less tough than open government lobbyists would have liked. On the other hand, the Home Office and other commentators are telling everyone to wake up and do things.

The Act gives anyone, for any reason, a right to find out if a public authority has any information about whatever topic they choose. If it does, they have a right to have that information communicated, and they can choose the means of communication back to them within reason (inspection, letter, copying, disc, video or email for example). If it came from someone else and is defamatory, publishing it in this way has qualified privilege and is only actionable if malice is proved.

The phrase 'public authority' refers to a long list of bodies set out in the Act, and to be supplemented by order, plus any company wholly owned by a public authority.

While we are defining things, let us, purely for our immediate purposes, call the member of the public 'Mr Smith' and the public authority 'the Council'.

Mr Smith may first look at the Council's Publications Scheme. This must say what information the Council publishes, how it is published, and whether or not it is free. It should follow a model produced by the Information Commissioner (the same one as under the Data Protection Act), and the Council's scheme has to be approved by her. It must be prepared and reviewed periodically 'having regard to the public interest ... in allowing public access to information ... and in the publication of reasons for decisions made ...'.

But Mr Smith does not have to look at the scheme. His request just has to be in writing (including email or via the website) stating his name and address and what information he wants. He can drop it in at the nearest Depot, or Area Office, or wherever he likes. Mr Smith is in fact fanatically interested in beetles. He wants to know what kind of beetles are to be found on Council premises. He can address this question to the nearest social worker, and, provided he has written it down, he has made it and the Council has received it. Whether the social worker will understand that this is what has happened is another matter. The Council can, incidentally, stop the duty running by asking for further information to identify and locate the information. It can serve a 'fees notice' or invoice requiring a modest fee to be paid. There will be regulations to limit the fee levels. But time starts running when the request is made, stops to clarify the request and while the Council asks for the fees, then runs again. And the amount of time allowed is 20 days.

Unfortunately for Mr Smith, the Council has a loophole if the cost of finding the information exceeds a prescribed limit (starting at £550) so he may have to rephrase the beetles question (*'Do you have death watch beetle in the Town Hall?'*). It can refuse to answer repeated requests if a reasonable time has not elapsed (*'We told you yesterday'*) and it can refuse to answer a request that is 'vexatious'. Devotees of the frivolous will be delighted to discover that they are not ruled out of order at this stage, but exactly what 'vexatious' means in this context is tricky to penetrate. Most awkward questions vex someone. There is also a general duty to provide advice and assistance by reference to a national code of practice (*'The library is over there, they have books on beetles'*).

Then either the Council answers the beetle question or it refuses to do so. In some cases the refusal can be because the request is premature, in which case a time scale must be given. Otherwise the refusal notice must give proper reasons depending on the exemption claimed.

There are two types of exemption. Some cover all information falling into the statutory description. Others only cover information so described if, in addition, disclosure would be likely to cause 'prejudice'. This is all set out in each of the sections covering the exemption. The exemptions make it clear how far the authority is also exempt from the duty to confirm or deny the existence of the information. In addition, most exemptions are subject to an overriding 'public interest' test. Not only must the information fall within the terms of the exemption, but also the public interest in maintaining the exemption must outweigh the public interest in disclosure. If it does not, the information cannot be withheld.

These, then, are the exemptions, paraphrased and cut short somewhat. In particular have repeatedly truncating 'would, or would be likely to' which is an ugly phrase and comes very close to tautology. Those of real significance to local government – unless there is a defence establishment in the area, which is not uncommon – appear later on.

- The information is available elsewhere, for example in books available in the library, or in shops (*'Beetles, and Where to Find Them Locally'*), or is communicated to the public through some other statutory process.
- The information was and is intended for future publication, and it is reasonable to expect Mr Smith to wait.
- The information relates to a range of bodies that deal with government security (in the espionage sense), or to national security generally, or disclosure would prejudice defence, or the armed forces, or international relations.
- The information was provided by a State, or an international organisation or court, confidentially.
- Disclosure would be likely to prejudice relations between the UK Government and the Scottish Administration, the Northern Ireland Executive or the National Assembly for Wales.
- Disclosure would be likely to prejudice the economic interests of the UK, or any part of it, or the financial interests of the administration of any of the bodies mentioned in the last exemption.
- The information is held for the purposes of criminal investigation or proceedings. There is some rather convoluted drafting here, so care is needed.
- Disclosure would be likely to prejudice the prevention or detection of crime, the apprehension or prosecution of offenders, the administration of justice, tax assessment or collection, operating immigration controls, running prisons, or the exercise of functions for a list of purposes. These are ascertaining if anyone has broken the law or acted improperly, or if regulatory action might be taken, or the fitness of an individual to run a

company or undertake a profession, or the cause of an accident, plus protecting charities and the like, and securing the health and safety and welfare of people at work and so on. Civil or Fatal Accidents Acts proceedings brought for these purposes are included.

- Court papers, including those of tribunals, inquiries and arbitration are exempt.
- Disclosure would be likely to prejudice audit functions, either the audit of accounts or the examination of the economic, efficient and effective use of resources.
- The information is covered by parliamentary privilege.
- The information is held by a government department or the National Assembly for Wales and relates to the formulation or development of government policy, Ministerial communications, Law Officers' advice or a Ministerial Private Office. Statistical background information is not exempt.
- (This is an important one.) 'In the reasonable opinion of a qualified person', disclosure would be likely to do one of three things. The first is that it would prejudice the maintenance of the convention of collective cabinet responsibility (in government and the Northern Irish and Welsh Assemblies only, though). The second is that it would be likely to inhibit either 'the free and frank provision of advice' or 'the free and frank exchange of views for the purposes of deliberation'. The third is that it would be 'likely otherwise to prejudice the effective conduct of public affairs'. The debate with the Leader about the municipal beetle cull was recorded, including the Chief Environmental Health Officer's advice that it was senseless cruelty. But telling Mr Smith about it would stop the CEHO ever offering honest advice again, or the Leader ever asking him for it, or cause every cabinet meeting to dissolve in chaos at the embarrassment. Pity the poor 'qualified person', who must certify his or her reasonable opinion of this. There is a list. In a Government Department it is the Minister. In the House of Commons it is the Speaker. In the Greater London Assembly, it is the Mayor. In a local authority, it is a blessing conferred by Ministerial designation either on the Council itself or on an 'officer or employee', but not a member.
- The information is about Crown honours, or communication with the Royal Family.
- Disclosure would be likely to endanger the safety or physical or mental health of any individual.
- This is environmental information that is accessible under different regulations and a different treaty obligation.
- This is personal information that is covered by the Data Protection Act, or where disclosure contravenes that Act. This avoids duplication, but remember that the Freedom of Information Act extends all the DPA controls to all manual records containing personal data, even those not in a structured filing system.
- The information was provided by another person in confidence, where a breach of the duty of confidence would be actionable in law.
- The information is covered by legal professional privilege.
- These are trade secrets, or information that would be likely to 'prejudice the commercial interests of any person (including the public authority holding it)'. This is another important exemption.

• Disclosure is prohibited by statute, or EC obligation or would be contempt of court.

Happily there will be Codes of Practice to guide everyone all through this, and the Information Commissioner has a duty to promote good practice. A consultation draft code was issued in May 2001. It emphasises the need to be helpful and timely, and the need to consider how to handle requests that need to be transferred to third parties, or on which third parties should be consulted. It advises against entering into unnecessary contractual confidentiality agreements, and the need for an internal complaints procedure as a first port of call. The Commissioner will also handle Mr Smith's appeal for failure to comply, or against refusal, unless she believes that he has not exhausted the Council's complaints procedure, or there has been undue delay, or the application is frivolous or vexatious or has been dropped. It appears that although the Council is under a duty to respond to frivolous requests, there is no right of appeal if it fails to do so. There is a further right of appeal to an Information Tribunal. The Commissioner can serve information and enforcement notices, and there is a goal-line clearance provision enabling a Minister to defeat one of these by issuing a certificate, which is unlikely to be much used. Failure to comply is referred to the court, and is treated as contempt. It is an offence to alter or destroy a record to prevent disclosure and a whole Schedule of rights of entry and inspection.

We need to think about two things. First, there is potentially a huge logistical problem. Systems and training will be needed, computer systems must be changed, contracts checked. Secondly, there needs to be a complete change of culture. In practice, outside the work of the regulators, enforcers, lawyers and those involved in commercial deals, just about every bit of information held on any file or computer record anywhere is potentially accessible. The qualified person can play the 'free and frank provision of advice' or 'the free and frank exchange of views for the purposes of deliberation' or 'likely otherwise to prejudice the effective conduct of public affairs' card occasionally, subject to appeal and guidance, but this is really about high level stuff, not the everyday contents of everyday files used by millions of public sector staff up and down the country. We have to get used to the idea that the man sitting next to us on the bus going home has a perfect legal right to look at what we were doing all day. This may take a little time.

The Exchange of Information Between Community Partners

[21.5]
Imagine a local authority committed to planning ahead. It has prepared its community strategy, involved everyone in sight, set up a LSP and entered into a PSA. It has ended up with more partners than you can shake a stick at, statutory and advisory, cash rich and cash poor, local and regional, commercial and social, good companies and bad company, trusts and mistrust. It has delegated and deregulated, and it and its partners are taking in each other's washing. It consults assiduously, and there are online real-time webcams in all the offices. Only one problem remains. The authority and its

partners do not know what to say to each other. It is not, of course, that they have nothing to say. The problem is that they are not sure what they are allowed to say. There is tension between the craving for joined-up government, with full community participation, and the fear that a joined-up state will oppress the individual. What legal principles should they apply?

Remember how wide the range of partner bodies can be, and that they are usually answerable legally or in practice to others. It is no use saying: *'we think you cannot do that'* if the answer is: *'but we are advised that we have no choice'*. A company's primary duty is to its shareholders, a trust's to its objects, a statutory body to its statutory duties, a community partnership to its members. Pity the police officer who does not know whether to conceal the information he has been given about the potentially dangerous criminal because of Art 8 of the Human Rights Act 1998, or to pass it on to the people at risk because of Art 2[1]. So, if you pass information on, you lose control.

The first question is 'do we have legal power to provide the information?'. For local authorities at least, s 2 of the Local Government Act 2000 has significantly augmented existing powers. Hitherto great reliance had been placed on s 111 of the Local Government Act 1972, as a basis, for example, for information sharing between housing authorities and the police to enable the council to pass on information about its tenants. Another curiosity is s 115 of the Crime and Disorder Act 1998, which allows disclosure which is 'necessary or expedient for the purposes of any provision of this Act'. Outside the specific orders covered by the Act, this can be interpreted either narrowly as authorising the exchange of information to prepare a crime and disorder strategy, or generously to authorise the exchange of information to help combat crime in accordance with the strategy.

There is a slight variant, taking us into Data Protection Act territory, along the lines of 'Is the use you propose to make of the information you have obtained consistent with the purposes of the statute under which you obtained it?'. This train of thought lay behind a famous opinion obtained by the Information Commissioner that said that local authorities could not (at that time – the legislation has changed) use council tax records to cross-check benefit claims to detect fraud.

On the other hand, does the person receiving the information have the legal power to accept it? Once again, this is really just a problem for statutory bodies, and most now have a fairly wide remit, but when databases start flying around as currency this will become more important. Did the regeneration body really have power to store information about residents' health problems?

This does take us back into the Data Protection Act, if the information is about a living person. Passing information to others is processing, so all the principles and rights come into play. In particular, do you have the consent of the data subject to the processing? If not, which of the other paragraphs of Sch 2, and Sch 3 if the data is sensitive, are you relying on? And the data is being processed in a manner compatible with the purpose for which it was obtained, and is it accurate and up-to-date? And is there an obligation to notify the data subject?

But there is more. The information may have been obtained in confidence. How can that happen? Well, the easiest ways are by statute or by contract. A number of statutes impose a direct duty of confidentiality on a local authority or an officer holding information, section 28 of the Health and Safety at Work etc Act 1974 for example. And a duty of confidentiality can arise in a contractual relationship under the express terms of the contract, or by implication ('Is that meant to be a secret?' says the officious bystander 'Of course', say the parties) or under an implied collateral contract such as may arise during tendering notwithstanding that the main contractual relationship has been expressly kept at bay. A contract of employment may very well contain express or implied terms on individual privacy. But even in the absence of legislation or a contract the courts have long been willing to recognise an equitable duty of confidentiality if the circumstances are right. Such circumstances may include the relationship between a professional social worker or health professional or probation officer an their client, so if they are likely to come under a duty to pass information on they will need to be careful about how they set the situation up.

The Human Rights Act 1998 is usually about saying the same thing in a different way, so let us pass swiftly by Art 8 and the right to respect for private and family life, home and correspondence, and of course Art 10 and the right to freedom of expression, noting them and that they are both qualified, and balancing them proportionately as one must.

What is the person receiving the information going to do with it? Are they, for example, going to misuse it, or give it to someone else? If they do, what can be done about it? You need an agreement with them that they will not do this, and you have to be thoughtful about how you frame it because once information has been released it cannot be recovered, and the courts are reluctant to grant injunctions to bring about the impossible. So a bare agreement will not do, an indemnity is essential, but above all you need effective mechanisms for sharing information about what each partner is doing about information.

There is work for the lawyers here. There are some good protocols in operation on child protection, crime and disorder, fraud detection and the like, but there are many that exist on paper but not in reality, because they were signed but no-one read them, and there are many gaps. The issue has, for example, set particular ethical conundrums for health authorities. It would be helpful to see the development of national models, but the task has so far fallen down one of the many partnership cracks.

1   See for example *Venables v News Group Newspapers Ltd* [2001] 1 All ER 908; or *R v Chief Constable of North Wales Police, ex p AB* [1997] 4 All ER 691; affd sub nom *R v Chief Constable of North Wales Police, ex p Thorpe* [1999] QB 396, CA.

Division IV

Financial Propriety

CHAPTER 22
Introduction

What Do We Mean By 'Financial Propriety'?

[22.1]

Propriety is defined in dictionaries variously as 'moral correctness of behaviour or of actions' or 'the quality or state of being proper' or 'conformity to what is socially acceptable in conduct or speech'. These definitions are useful in that they relate 'Proper' and 'Correctness' to social acceptability.

In relation to accounting and finance, the 'Government Accounting' definition places a strong emphasis on Parliamentary control stating: 'Propriety is the further requirement that expenditure and receipts should be dealt with in accordance with Parliament's intentions and the principles of Parliamentary control, including the conventions agreed with Parliament (and in particular the Public Accounts Committee)'. Whilst Parliamentary control is somewhat remote it terms of local government expenditure it is useful to consider propriety in these terms as this adds the sense of accountability (ultimately to Parliament) to the sense of correctness and social acceptability given in dictionary definitions.

However as in many areas the Nolan Committee in its first report *Standards in Public Life* manages to distil the essence of meaning in its definition, 'we take propriety to encompass not only financial rectitude, but a sense of the values and behaviour appropriate to the public sector'. The Nolan Committee also defined the principles governing the values and behaviour of those involved in the pubic sector as:

* selflessness;
* objectivity;
* integrity;
* accountability;
* openness;
* honesty; and
* leadership.

Taking the above definitions together we can say that Financial Propriety includes:

* 'Correct Accounting' – Compliance with the CIPFA Code, appropriate SSAPs and generally accepted accounting principles;

- financial and performance information which can be understood by members and the public;
- sound, objective, financial management and advice for members;
- financial processes and controls that promote accountability, openness and honesty as well as the effective use of public funds; and
- a financial strategy designed to maximise the effective use of resources for the benefit of the public.

However as propriety is a quality that is recognised only in the perception of others it is not sufficient that the criteria above are met. It must be obvious to all stakeholders and interested third parties that the criteria are met.

The Role of the 'Section 151 Officer' or Chief Financial Officer – The Statutory Provisions

[22.2]
Within local government finance there are numerous references to 'the 151 Officer'. It can seem that all power, in financial term anyway, is derived from this almost legendary entity and that every financial action was to be overseen by the 'Section 151 Officer', or called to question on the grounds of '151 officer approval'. Many quite junior finance officers use the term to justify their appropriate, or in some cases quite inappropriate actions. The truth whilst somewhat different to the legend, does place a considerable **personal** responsibility on the '151 Officer', far more than is the case for the finance director of a PLC. It is therefore not surprising that '151 Officers' have a powerful role in local authorities, or that they are protective of the powers they need to discharge what is a personal responsibility which is not diluted by delegation.

The Local Government Act 1972 (the 1972 Act) requires local authorities 'to appoint such officers as they deem necessary for the proper discharge of their functions'. Furthermore in s 112(2) of the 1972 Act 'officers hold office on such reasonable terms and conditions as the appointing authority thinks fit'.

The Term 'Section 151 Officer' derives from s 151 of the 1972 Act. This Act requires that every local authority in England and Wales should:

> '... make arrangements for the proper administration of their financial affairs and shall secure that one of their officers has responsibility for the administration of those affairs'.

There is a considerable body of Case Law and Counsel Opinion both prior to and since the 1972 Act which defines and clarifies the nature of the role and responsibilities of the CFO, which can be summarised as follows:

- **Fiduciary Duty** – CFO's hold an office of Public Trust. The responsibilities of the CFO as financial administrator encompass the general fiduciary duty owed to local taxpayers. This is to say that council funds are considered held in trust for the benefit of all local taxpayers and there is a duty to deploy the resources available to the best advantage of all the local community, maintaining a balance between conflicting interests;

- **The responsibility is a personal responsibility** – the 1972 Act clearly refers to 'one of their officers', and it is the view of the Chartered Institute of Public Finance and Accountancy (CIPFA) that responsibilities under section 151 cannot be shared with any other member or officer of a local authority. This does not mean that the CFO cannot employ staff to assist in the financial administration. However, it does have implications in relation to responsibility for the actions of finance staff working on the direct instruction of the CFO, and to responsibility for specific advice given to members of the Local Authority.

- As a minimum the standard of financial administration needs to demonstrate to the external auditor that:
  - expenditure is not contrary to the law (s 161);
  - the accounts are prepared in accordance with the regulations made under section 166, and comply with the requirements of all other enactments and instruments applicable to the accounts (s 157(a));
  - proper accounting practices have been observed in the compilation of the accounts (s 157(b));

- The CFO also needs to have regard for the duty of the external auditor 'to consider whether, in the public interest he should make a report on any matters arising out of or in connection with the accounts in order that those matters may be considered by the body concerned or brought to the attention of the public'.

There may be occasions where the CFO needs to decide between making a payment which they, after taking legal advice, consider to be contrary to law, or deliberately disobeying a specific council instruction. The considered view in such circumstances is that the general responsibility under s 151 takes precedence because it is derived from an overriding statutory obligation placed on local authorities by Parliament.

Fortunately in such circumstances the course of action for a CFO is prescribed in the Local Government Finance Act 1988 (the 1988 Act).

Section 114 of the Local Government Finance Act 1988

[22.3]
Section 114 of the Local Government Finance Act 1988 sets out the circumstances where a CFO must make a report to the authority's external auditor and all the members of the authority. These are where the authority has or is likely to incur expenditure which is unlawful or will result in a deficit. The full text of s 114 is set out at Division VI – Appendix 20 below.

The Act also goes on to specify that the Authority must meet to consider the report and decide what action to take, making provision that unlawful or excessive expenditure is ceased or prohibited during the intervening period.

The effect of this part of the Act is to place responsibility with members of the authority to decide if the expenditure should go ahead against specific advice to the contrary from the Chief Financial Officer. Section 114 reports are rare occurrences. In my experience the threat of issuing such a report is sufficient for members to consider the circumstances and approve appropriate measures prior to the actual issue of a formal report under s 114.

This Act is helpful in a number of further respects. In s 114(1) (see above) the Act introduces the term 'Chief Finance Officer', which is a significant improvement for ease of understanding of the role. However the term '151 Officer' whilst somewhat inane seems to have become embedded into local government culture, and it is difficult to see any decline in its use in the near future.

The 1988 Act also sets standards of qualification for Chief Finance Officers. Prior to the implementation of the Act there was no requirement for the CFO to be a qualified accountant, although there was an implied duty that the post holder was suitably educated and experienced. The 1988 Act requires that the CFO is a member of one of the six main accountancy bodies, although it also allows for CFOs in post prior to commencement date of the Act to continue in office. This is set out in s 113 of the Act[1].

1   Section 113 of the LGFA 1988 is set out at Div VI – App 20 below.

Section 113 of the Local Government Finance Act 1988

[22.4]
Section 113 of the Local Government Finance Act 1988 is set out at Division VI – Appendix 20 below.

The last area of note relevant to the role of Chief Finance Officer is that the 1988 Act specifies that the authority must provide adequate resources to undertake the duties.

In s 114(7) it states:

> 'A relevant authority shall provide its chief finance officer with such staff, accommodation and other resources as are in his opinion sufficient to allow his duties under this section to be performed'.

This statement appears only to relate to the specific duties of reporting specified in s 114, however there is a view that it must be applied more widely to allow the CFO to determine if the section is applicable at any point in time. Although to my knowledge this view has not been tested in the courts.

If one considers the statutory provisions for the role and responsibilities of the Chief Financial Officer (or Section 151 Officer) in comparison to what is required for Financial Propriety, the requirement can be mapped to the statutory provision. It can be seen that the statutory provisions provide some basis for the delivery of Financial Propriety, and at the very least there is no conflict between the two requirements:

Requirement for Financial Propreity	Statutory provision
Correct Accounting – Compliance with the CIPFA Code, appropriate SSAPs and generally accepted accounting principles	CFO as a qualified accountant is bound by Professional standards, codes of practice, and disciplinary provision from their professional body
Financial and performance information which can be understood by members and the public	External audit and Professional standards of accounting bodies go some way to encourage this but understanding is more difficult to measure than compliance with standards and codes of practice
Sound, objective, financial management and advice for members	Independence of CFO in extreme circumstances of s 114, provides some level of protection for objective advice
Financial processes and controls that promote accountability, openness and honesty as well as the effective use of public funds	External Audit to 'police' satisfactory framework of control, with powers to 'go public' about concerns
A financial strategy designed to maximise the effective use of resources for the benefit of the public	Fiduciary relationship with Taxpayers and the trustee status of CFO, places substantial personal responsibility on CFO to secure this

Quality Standards

[22.5]
Quality Standards in accounting and financial management can be difficult and time consuming to determine. However any finance function that wishes to ensure Financial Propriety must have quality standards and must measure its performance against those standards. Without quality standards and measurement the finance function cannot know if it is operating in a manner which will deliver financial propriety for the organisation.

There are many ways of categorising quality standards but is firstly useful to separate standards and measures that are concerned with the performance of the organisation from those that measure the performance of the finance function. For example an appropriate standard for organisational financial performance may be to maintain total expenditure within +1% and –5% of budget. This is not a quality standard for the finance function. Quality standards for the finance function are generally concerned with provision of information or advice and may be standards of accuracy, timeliness or usefulness. A local authority should have a range of quality standards of both types to measure performance against.

Financial Propriety is also an organisational quality that is judged by the public and external organisations. The external perception of propriety is unlikely to be based entirely, if at all, on fact. It is therefore important that quality standards include measures of perception by the general public, third party organisations, and service partners.

Disclosure and Open Accounting

[22.6]
Local government with the requirement to open accounts for inspection, and to publication of reports and decisions probably has the most open framework of management and financial decision-making of any type of organisation in the United Kingdom. Certainly far greater than plcs, central government and the NHS. This degree of openness should be regarded as a strength of local government, however in many local authorities the opening of accounts for inspection seems to be regarded as an irksome task and the effort expended to publicise the process is the minimum to meet the statutory requirements.

The opening of accounts for inspection is an opportunity to publicise the work of the authority, to get over the full picture of how money has been spent on behalf of the local taxpayers and residents, and to ensure that the full context of the council's financial position is made available to the public and the press. Local authorities should consider, after taking appropriate public relations advice, opening the accounts with a presentation of the accounts and the financial position to the press and public. This has the advantage of providing a platform for the authority to present the whole picture from a balanced viewpoint, before those who may wish to provide a suitably sensational headline, or to further a sectional interest have the opportunity to ask questions.

The Annual Financial Report

[22.7]
The annual financial report is a major opportunity for local authorities to demonstrate financial propriety. However if it is restricted to the statutory format it may show that the authority can produce a good set of accounts, and sound finances but only to those who have the time and the technical knowledge to read and understand it, a fairly limited audience.

To gain the maximum effect from any publication there are a few key questions to ask before consideration of the format and content. First, who are the people we want to communicate with, secondly what are the messages we need to pass on, and thirdly what we want these people to think about the organisation and the message. In answering these questions you may find that you need to get slightly different messages to different groups of people, and that you want to have a different effect on each group. This will require a range of additional information, and alternative presentations. The table below gives some examples:

Inward Investors and Financial Partners	Current and Potential Service Partners	Residents and Taxpayers
Message	*Message*	*Message*
Information about the financial size of the authority, Gross expenditure, Capital Programme expenditure, Loan & Investment portfolios. Sources of Capital. Information about investment in the Borough, and the activities of other investment partners	Information about the financial size of the authority, the range of services provided, and the diversity of service providers. An indication of the authority's expectations on value for money and increasing efficiency	An understanding of what resources the authority has, where the money comes from, and what it is spent on. An indication of the pressure on resources from competing demand for services, and information about how the authority has become more efficient
Impression	*Impression*	*Impression*
Secure, financially prudent, and well managed. Innovative in project financing. Efficient in project management and delivery	Effective and efficient financial processes. Flexibility in dealings with partners. Financially secure but forward thinking and innovative	Financially sound and well managed. Becoming more efficient to enable the provision of additional services

Given the different target groups and intended messages it will be sensible to consider if one single report can deliver all the right messages and impressions, particularly as the physical attributes of the document (the shape, binding and the quality of finish) will inevitably influence the impression given. In addition the most appropriate methods of distribution for each target group are likely to differ. For example for residents and taxpayers it may be best to use a local newspaper insert, or a direct mailing, but for financial partners the document may accompany an individual letter of introduction or be handed out following a presentation. This will require a different document format to suit the method of distribution. Whatever is decided professional design and production is best left to experts. I have not found many accountants with graphic design, corporate image or copy-writing skills.

There are two important final considerations for the content of any financial report. Firstly does the information and presentation represent the authority and its financial position fairly. There is no requirement for additional financial information to be audited, but the authority's reputation for financial propriety will not be enhanced if the report presents an optimistic view of the financial position, which the authority cannot live up to. Secondly the annual financial report is the opportunity to publicise the authority's financial position, financial performance, and financial management. The messages will be diluted if the document is also used for promoting policy or service performance.

CHAPTER 23
Risk Management of Strategic and Operational Risks

Introduction

[23.1]
Risk management is an essential element in the framework of good corporate governance, and must be the basis of all activity to achieve financial propriety. It is important to have a wide definition of risk to ensure that all risks are considered. One frequently used definition is:

> 'the threat or possibility that an action, a lack of action, or an event will adversely affect an organisation's ability to achieve its objectives'.

All organisations have objectives, express or implied. Risk management supports the achievement of those objectives by identifying the circumstances that threaten their achievement and the likelihood of those circumstances occurring. With this knowledge it is possible to plan a course of action which, either minimises the likelihood of occurrence, or takes an alternative approach given the changed circumstances to achieve the original objective. Risk Management is not a process for avoiding all risk. Even if this were possible it is unlikely to be desirable. When used well it can allow an organisation to take on activities that have a higher level of risk to achieve a greater return, or wider benefits. The residual risk to an organisation is lower if all risks have been identified, are understood and are being well managed. Risk management should not be considered as a simply negative approach that seeks to ensure that bad things are less likely to happen, but also a positive force that increases the likelihood that good things will happen. It may be that if we described this side of Risk Management as Opportunity Management, a more positive approach to the concept could be engendered.

Understanding Risk

[23.2]
In order to understand risk it is useful to examine the concept at its fundamental levels. At a basic level risk can be defined as the probability that something bad happens. Whereas 'chance' is often thought of as the probability that something good happens. These are useful descriptions in that they allay the two factors that are most useful in measuring risk the first is

254

probability, which describes how frequently a particular event will occur, and the second, impact, the effect the event will have to the organisation or environment. Once you have separated these two fundamentals its is possible to assess and rank organisational risks and opportunities. Very simply, *Risk* equals *Probability* multiplied by *Impact*:

$$R = P \times I$$

In some ways if the matter was as simple as the above formula implies, risk management would not be needed at all because all decisions and alternatives could be compared on a like for like basis. So for example there is a risk of cost and time overrun on major capital projects and in Upper Riskington District Council eight out of 10 projects in the last few years have overspent by 10% of the originally approved capital allocation excluding contingencies. The borough have done some research and found that their experience is similar to other boroughs on similar sized projects. They are looking at their risks as part of their annual planning process to make they have two capital projects amounting to a total estimated cost of £1.5 million. The risk inherent in the projects is the probability 0.8 multiplied by the Impact (£1.5M x 0.1) or £120,000. This does not mean that they should automatically provide a further £120,000 as a budget contingency, the council may wish to introduce tighter controls over capital expenditure, or to delay one of the projects into the following year. It may be that this risk is insignificant compared to other risks. The action taken will depend on the organisation's attitude to risk and the overall risk profile across the Council as a whole. The use of risk information is dealt with later in this section.

The difficulty lies in that for most decisions or courses of action the probability can only be guessed and if the impact can be measured, it is likely that the unit of measurement will differ from the units that can be measured for an alternative course or outcome. However in most cases it is sufficient to calculate risk using a scale of one to three for both the probability and the impact factors. This has advantages in that it enables comparison of risk where the impact effects are of a different nature. The disadvantage being that this introduces a range of value judgements into the risk assessment. As an indication of how this process works the table below has some examples, which are taken from a Year 2000 project's initial risk analysis.

Description of Risk	Probability	Impact	Risk Score
Payroll software will not cope with Year 2000 dates	High	High	9
General Ledger will not cope with year 2000 dates	Medium	Medium	4
PC Network Cards will fail on 01/01/00 as result of embedded timer chip problems	Low	Low	1
School heating systems fail on 01/01/00 as result of embedded timer chip problems	High	Low	3

Fire alarm and control systems fail on 01/01/00 as result of embedded timer chip problems	Low	High	3
Lift Control systems fail on 01/01/00 as result of embedded timer chip problems	Medium	High	6

As can be seen from the table even with a quite unsophisticated scoring system it is possible to get a meaningful ranking of risk, certainly enough to prioritise the workload for the project. As a result of the initial risk analysis one of the decisions taken was that apart from securing a small supply of new PC network cards, no further action was taken or time expended on the issue of network card compliance. This removed a substantial potential workload from the project plan.

Types of Risk

[23.3]
It is self evident that every organisation is different, and will have its own unique risk profile. In addition both the probability of an event and its impact change over time. The identification of risk in an organisation will therefore be specific to the organisation at any particular point in time. However there are categories of risk which are common to all organisations and more specifically to all Local Authorities. The table below is a useful checklist that can be used to identify areas of risk in a local authority. The top level risk categories follow the widely used PESTLE analysis categories. I have attempted to cover all the major areas of risk, but this list can only be used as an aid to risk identification and cannot be a substitute for a specific rigorous risk review.

Risk Category	Risk Area
Political	Local Policy Changes National Policy Changes Changes in political leadership Impact of policy changes in other councils
Environmental	Building & property risks Office and Industrial Space constraints Open space risks Weather effects Transport system failures Traffic changes and growth

Social	Demographic Change Community Group and Pressure Group actions Human Resource Management Risk Effects of change (eg. reorganisation, outsourcing) on individual and group performance Public Liability Service Liability
Technological	Key Systems failures Computer & Email viruses System Implementation Risk Communications system failures Obsolescence Network overload or failure
Legal	Legislation Changes Contract Disputes Employee Relations disputes
Economic	Income reduction or restriction Expenditure Control Grant Regime changes Treasury management Risks Balance sheet control

Assessing Risk

[23.4]

Where the probability and the impact can be measured risk assessment is relatively easy. However as stated above for most risks this is not the case, as the probably and the impact can only be estimated. At the micro level business or service units should assess the main service risks and produce a business or service continuity plan as part of the business planning process. At the macro level for directorate or corporate risks using a risk assessment workshop. Risk assessment workshops use a combination of brainstorming, consensual definition, and scoring techniques to identify, specify and evaluate relative risks for an organisation. They need to involve all the senior managers within the area concerned to ensure that the widest range of potential risks are considered and examined. They are likely to be more productive when facilitated by a risk management specialist as an experienced risk manager will be able to promote discussion of a wide range of generic risks and to assist the participants to assess probability and impact in relation to external benchmarks from experience. The outcome of the workshop should be a ranked list of potential risks that can be further examined in detail by small groups of participants to firstly validate the probability and impact by further research, and secondly develop action plans to reduce the probability and lessen or avoid the impact. The value of the exercise is contained in the action plans. It is therefore advisable to follow up the workshop with a further meeting of the participants to review and agree the action plans developed.

Developing Risk Reducing Strategies

[23.5]
There are only two ways to reduce risk. Either reduce the probability that the event will occur, or reduce the impact of the event. There are two primary strategies to reduce the probability that an event will occur. These are to increase the level of compliance through control, and to increase performance through training. Impact reduction strategies are primarily associated with either planning a response to the event occurrence that lessens the consequences through additional actions, or insuring or hedging against the event to reduce or eliminate the financial consequences.

Controls

[23.6]
Increasing the controls that prevent the event can reduce the probability of an event occurring. Controls can be physical, systematic or process related, or supervisory.

Physical Controls

[23.7]
These are controls where a barrier is introduced to prevent the event, this could be an additional guard on a machine to prevent trapping of clothing, a fence to prevent access to a dangerous area, or use of a safe to control access to valuables. This type of control is often ignored when looking at large or strategic risks. However physical controls do have a role and should be considered. Computer viruses are a major risk to all networked systems. Even with the growth of email and Internet access, floppy disks remain a major source of the introduction of viruses to networked systems. Removal of floppy disks from networked personal computers is a powerful physical barrier to the risk of introduction of viruses and will reduce the probability of virus introduction.

System or Process Related Controls

[23.8]
These are controls that involve modification of a system or process to prevent or deter an event. This could be an additional verification stage in a computer programme. For example a user password verification check for authorisation of a payment, or a simple 'do you really want to do this now' check box before initiating a none reversible system or data change. In manual systems this could involve keeping a log of documents received with control totals to ensure that it is possible to check that all items have been processed. In automated systems this may involve checking system status before allowing a user initiated event to occur. For example a check that a guard is in place before allowing a machine to be switched on or checking if a backup has been taken before a major system update in commenced.

The design of system or process controls needs to be undertaken with care and an understanding of their effect on system users. If the control is too onerous on the user or the value of the control is not understood, the user can often find most ingenious ways of avoiding the controls altogether sometimes removing other basic controls at the same time resulting in the complete opposite of the intended effect. In one case a fraud occurred where a manager gave his authorisation password to a junior temp. When questioned he said that a system change that required him to re-enter his password individually for each payment had caused a backlog of authorisations so he employed a temp to process the authorisations on his behalf. The temporary staff member colluded with another member of staff to process dummy invoices for payment.

Supervisory Controls

[23.9]
These are controls that involve greater supervision of individual or process events. This could be a manager checking the decisions or work of a junior member of staff, the random sampling of cases for senior review, increased frequency of audit checks or automated IT system control checks. Typical examples are:

- the review of letters before mailing;
- Benefit or Social Services case file reviews;
- random cash balance or stock checks; or
- the production of database control reports to ensure that control totals balance with detailed amounts.

There is no doubt that supervisory controls correctly implemented can be immensely valuable in the reduction of risk. However, they always involve duplication of work to some extent and as such tend to be more costly to implement than other forms of control. In addition they tend to be a manager's first reaction to a problem, following the adage if you want something doing right do it yourself. For these reasons it is sensible to look into alternative forms of control or the alternative to control, which is training, before taking what always seems the obvious step of greater supervision.

Training

[23.10]
Where reasonable basic controls are in place, the alternative to increased controls is training. In many organisations training is seen as either altruistic or penal. A staff benefit only given to those who deserve development, or conversely a prelude to disciplinary action or dismissal, following a mistake or misfeasance. It should however be seen as tool to increase performance and reduce risk. It is never a soft option and should be seen as a hard-edged reaction to under performance, as it is the most cost-effective way of

achieving more effective output from staff resources. Generally at least 60% of local authority costs are for staff resources it follows therefore that a relatively small increase in staff performance can have a significant effect on total cost.

The conversely altruistic or penal view of training in organisations leads to a lack of focus on the organisational and performance benefits from training. This results in a reduction in the value obtained from training activity. If training is seen as an investment to achieve performance improvement it should be managed in the same way that a capital investment or a systems improvement project is managed with:

- clear objectives and outcome targets;
- a control system that ensures that the outcomes are evaluated, and if deficient that the training is modified;
- a reporting system to monitor progress and achievement of the training plan.

The recognised standard for good practice is Investors in People and organisations wishing to ensure that they make maximum use of their staff resources should assess their practice against this standard.

Impact Reduction

[23.11]
Strategies to reduce risk will generally include both probability reduction measures and impact reduction measures. However where the event is outside the control of the organisation the only option is to reduce the impact of the event. When considering if an event is outside the control of the organisation care needs to be taken. Often the organisation will have some influence over an event even if it cannot fully control the circumstances that lead the occurrence of the event. It may be thought that, for example changes to grant regimes or legislation are outside the control of local authorities. However, use of lobbying and publicity, particularly where a number of similarly affected authorities agree a joint approach and campaign, can be effective tools in reducing the likelihood and the impact of this type of threat.

Scenario planning is the key tool to reduce the impact of events. Most local authorities make use of scenario planning in their emergency-planning role. Emergency planning is almost entirely concerned with impact reduction, and it is surprising that local authorities do not make more use of the skills they possess in this area to reduce the impact of risks other than physical and environmental catastrophes. Scenario planning reduces the impact of events by pre-planning the response to a range of possible events. It allows managers to consider the consequences of alternative courses of action outside of the time constraints and pressure that will be present in real life. This allows considered rational responses that minimise the consequential effect of the impact, and in many cases will produce credible immediate alternative long-term strategies that reduce the impact of the event in advance.

For example one local authority, wishing to examine and reduce the impact of a decision to join the Euro, used scenario planning to model the effect of exchange and interest rate movements on its loan and investment portfolio, in the run up to Euro membership. It found that in practically all circumstances a change in its balance between fixed and variable loan rates was advantageous. This led to an immediate change in treasury policy and resulted in considerable gains to the authority when interest rates reduced (partially at least for other economic reasons). The real point is not that they were able to predict exactly what would happen as a result of joining the Euro, this is still unknown, but that they were able to develop a strategy that was better in all the foreseeable circumstances.

Scenario planning is also useful as part of the initial follow up to a risk assessment workshop. As previously indicated estimates of probability and impact are often inexact. Scenario planning can assist the process of risk assessment. By using scenario planning to examine how the probability of an event can be reduced, considering what sort of controls or training would reduce risk and how much this would cost to implement, one can begin to put a value scale to the control of probability. In addition detailed scenario planning will enable calculations of the cost of impact, allowing at least a financial scale for impact to be developed. Whilst financial scales are difficult to compare to loss of reputation or the impact of loss or impairment of life This will allow some objectivity it the decisions of which risks are and are not acceptable.

CHAPTER 24
Monitoring and Reviewing Performance

Performance Review – Why?

[24.1]
Regular and frequent performance review must be an intrinsic part of a local authority's routine if it is to achieve propriety. To achieve goals or targets, an organisation must measure its position and compare to its target or plan, and allocate resources accordingly. The more frequently an organisation measures performance and adjusts resources the more likely it will be to achieve its plans. In addition frequent measurement and adjustment is likely to result in an overall reduction in resource use. It is easier to understand this concept by use of the analogy of an aircraft flying between two points using auto-pilot.

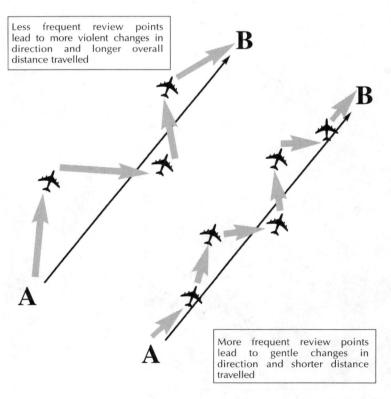

Less frequent review points lead to more violent changes in direction and longer overall distance travelled

More frequent review points lead to gentle changes in direction and shorter distance travelled

Without frequent performance review an organisation is likely to find that its progress is so far from target that when measured it is impossible to get back to target within the time available, or that to achieve target the change in activity or behaviour required is too drastic to be achievable.

It is useful to identify the expected time lag for action as part of introducing performance review. This enables a sensible consideration of the review frequency and also aids the future monitoring of future performance, as the expectation of improvement will be at the appropriate point. This avoids the disappointment and anxiety of over ambitious expectations. For a monthly review cycle the earliest indication that action to correct a performance issue from month one is in the report for month three, which will be received during month four. If the action taken is not fully effective immediately then the full effect will not be seen in the results until the report for month four is received, during month five.

[24.2]
Monthly Reporting Timeline

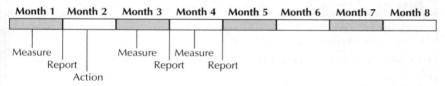

For a quarterly review cycle the time lag to confirm effective action is even greater. As can be seen from the diagram below the first indication that action has been effective or otherwise is not given until the second quarterly report which will not be received until month seven.

[24.3]
Quarterly Reporting Timeline

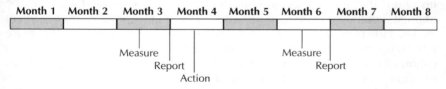

Clearly there is a significant advantage in monthly performance review, in fact it is difficult to understand how any organisation would be prepared to wait over six months to know if corrective action to deal with under-performance was successful.

The Corrective Action Cycle

[24.4]
Quality management experts recommend a number of extra steps for

performance management when looking at the performance of processes. This approach known as 'The Corrective Action Cycle' is easily applicable to financial and operational performance in local authorities. Typically the stages in the cycle are described as:

- define the problem;
- assemble the required expertise (Team);
- establish and Implement a containment plan;
- analyse the problem using data;
- establish root cause(s);
- identify permanent corrective action(s);
- implement the permanent corrective action(s);
- verify the effectiveness of the action(s).

These stages can be mapped to the typical performance management approach as indicated in the table below:

Corrective Action Cycle	Performance Management
Define the Problem Assemble the required expertise (Team)	*Identify areas of under-performance*
Establish and implement containment plan Analyse the problem using data Establish root cause(s) Identify permanent corrective action(s) Implement the permanent corrective action(s)	*Manager takes action to get back on track*
Verify the effectiveness of the action(s)	*Check performance at next review cycle*

Clearly the additional stages required in undertaking the full corrective action cycle approach would involve considerable extra resources. There is no doubt that many may question the need for the extra stages and the implicit additional workload on inevitably highly pressed management teams. However the benefit of a lasting solution to some of the more intractable performance issues can outweigh the short-term resource implications. This must be particularly true where similar performance problems re-occur month after month and year after year.

A local authority wishing to introduce the corrective action cycle into its management arrangements should undertake formal training for the group of managers and staff who will be involved. A number of stages involve the use of specific quality improvement techniques, the effectiveness of which will not be fully realised without adequate training and some practical experience. However to give an indication of what is involved and how the technique differs from the basic performance review process, the key features of each stage are set out below.

Problem Definition

[24.5]
This stage is key to the outcome of the process as it defines the scope of the project and will inevitably shape the final outcome. It is important that the definition is wide enough to allow the team to get to grips with all the key issues, but not so wide that the project becomes too large to complete in a reasonable time scale. It is sensible to involve the proposed team leader in the problem definition stage, and also to allow some flexibility for the team to revisit the definition once they have begun to examine and understand the relevant issues.

Team Building

[24.6]
It is important that a team is put together to work on the problem. The use of a team is to bring different viewpoints experiences and skills to the issues involved. It is important that the team have the individual skills and experience to deal with the type of issues involved. Teams would normally include people with operational experience in the area concerned, people with finance skills, and people with operational experience from different areas. Obviously it is useful to include people who already have team problem experience, or those who have been trained in the use of problem solving techniques. The size of the team will be dependent on the nature and complexity of the problem but as a general rule, not less than four (leads to too much individual work) or more than seven (too wide a span of control for the team leader) seems to work best. It is valuable if team members can be chosen with regard to their Belbin[1] team roles. There is considerable evidence to show that balanced teams are more likely to succeed.

1   Dr Meredith Belbin, *Management Teams Why They Succeed or Fail* (1981).

Problem Containment

[24.7]
The first task of the team is to look at containing the problem and what can be done to reduce or eliminate the current symptoms. This stage is sometimes known as the 'quick fix'. The objective is to find a way to bring performance back into line in the quickest most cost-effective way for the short-term.

Problem Analysis

[24.8]
This stage and the following stage (root cause identification) are critical to the process, and form the main difference to the method of coping with under performance which is usually employed. During this stage the team will gather as much data about the problem as possible. They will use

problem-solving tools such as force field analysis, Pareto Analysis, Cause and
Effect Diagrams, and Concept mapping. The objectives of this stage are that
the team understands as much about the problem as possible, and that they
arrive at a list of possible root causes.

Root Cause Identification

[24.9]
The objectives of this stage are to narrow down the possible root causes to
those which are most likely to be the true causes of the problem. During this
stage, the team, using the knowledge they have gained in the previous stages,
evaluates the possible root causes to arrive at the agreed root causes for the
problem. The tools used at this stage can include:

- Affinity Diagrams;
- Weighted Matrices;
- Decision Trees;
- Solution Circles; and
- Process Simulation.

Identify Permanent Corrective Action

[24.10]
Once the root causes have been identified the team concentrate on finding
permanent solutions. This should be a process to achieve consensus and the
team are likely to use number of the tools from the previous stages but in
particular Weighted Matrices, Decision Trees, Solution Circles and Process
Simulation, will be useful.

Implement the Permanent Corrective Action

[24.11]
It is important that the same team are kept together to undertake the planning
and implementation of the corrective action. The team will have built up a
close working relationship and have a considerable interest in the outcome
of the project. They will be very committed to delivering a successful
outcome.

Verify the Effectiveness of the Action

[24.12]
There are three key factors to consider for this stage. The first is that for the
same reasons that the team need to be kept together for the previous stage,
verification should also include people that are outside the team to ensure
that there is some independence. The second is that verification should

include close monitoring (in terms of depth and frequency) of the process and the changes introduced. The third factor is that if the solutions do not have the required effect (which will inevitably happen on some occasions) the team need to go back to the problem analysis stage to work through the problem and solutions again.

Performance Review as Part of Internal Control

[24.13]
Financial and operational performance review is a key part of internal control. It is unlikely that internal controls will be effective without frequent and regular performance review. If budgets are reasonably constructed fraud is most likely to result in either expenditure in excess of budget or performance below target. This is simply because resources will have been expended which will not have contributed to performance of the service. It is equally likely that financial performance review will point to operational performance difficulties, in my experience poor operational management is always associated with poor financial management, and in the vast majority of cases poor financial management occurs with or leads to poor operational management. Internal control at the micro level (separation of duties, dual authorisation etc) relies on reasonably good management to ensure its implementation. Performance review operates at the macro level and will provide a good indicator of the effectiveness of the micro level controls.

Accrual Accounting, Cash Accounting, Resource Accounting, Commitment Accounting – What Does It All Mean?

[24.14]
These four technical terms are often used when describing a local authority's accounting and financial reporting systems. It is useful to understand these terms and how they relate to the information included in reports used for performance review.

Cash Accounting

[24.15]
This term describes the form of accounting where cost or expenditure is not included in the accounts until payment for the goods or services is actually made. It is fairly obvious that this form of accounting can cause substantial distortion of the true financial position, as unless payment for goods and services is actually made in the same reporting time period as the use of the good or service the accounts will not reflect the real position. Most goods or services are provided on credit terms or, in the case of utilities, charged for in arrears. Property rentals, however, are normally paid quarterly in advance. Accounts prepared on this basis will contain a mix of inaccuracies dependent on the type of expenditure and the credit terms or payment

arrangements. As an accounting methodology it has major drawbacks, and does not comply with the fundamental accounting principle of accruals. This principle which is also known as the matching concept requires that income and expenditure must be reported in the period in which they are generated or incurred. So that the financial statements 'match' the activity of the organisation.

Accrual Accounting

[24.16]
A basis of accounting in which revenues are recognised in the period earned, and expenses are recognised in the period when the resource purchased is used or disposed. The principle of accruals accounting is universal in the commercial world. This methodology overcomes the deficiencies of cash accounting as goods bought on credit or services paid for in advance are charged into the correct accounting period, recognising their use or consumption in achieving the objectives of the organisation. Local authorities have been required to produce their annual Statutory Accounts using Accrual Accounting since the 1980's. However, despite the known deficiencies of the cash accounting methodology many local authorities still use cash accounting for their internal periodic reporting.

Resource Accounting

[24.17]
This is the UK Government's term for Accrual Accounting. Resource accounting was introduced in April 2001. All government departments are now required to account and control on the basis of expenditure incurred. This means that for income and expenditure (revenue) accounts, expenditure will be charged when the goods have been received or when services performed and items held in stores will be charged to expenditure when issued. For capital expenditure the changes will mean that capital projects and equipment are charged to expenditure over their lifetime (depreciation) and there will be a charge to expenditure for the economic cost of capital assets (similar to interest or cost of borrowing). These changes bring Central Government in line with the internationally accepted standards for accounting and financial reporting, commonly referred to as Generally Accepted Accounting Principles or GAAP.

Commitment Accounting

[24.18]
Commitment Accounting is a methodology that measures expenditure where a commitment has been made to spend at some point in the future, and provides a total of actual expenditure and committed expenditure to compare against the annual budget. For financial management and control purposes this has advantages over accrual accounting. In circumstances

where expenditure is limited to an annual budget amount but spending does not occur evenly through the year. It is not possible to tell from accounts showing total current expenditure how much of the annual budget remains available to spend. This is because at any one time there will be an amount of the budget which whilst not spent, (ie the goods or services have not been received or used), is nonetheless already irreversibly committed. This may be simply that an order has been placed, but more significantly and increasingly commonly with the growth in outsourced services that there is a contract for delivery of services for a period in the future. Commitment accounting enables managers to see how much of the annual budget is available for use in the remainder of the financial year.

Commitment Accounting is not a substitute for Accrual or Resource Accounting, as managers still need to know the total cost of the services actually delivered so that they can judge or calculate the cost efficiency of the service delivered. It is however a useful additional tool for managers to use to help control expenditure.

Revenue Account Reporting and Review

[24.19]
For effective performance review revenue account reporting should consist of a hierarchy of reports that summarise the financial position at each level of management control through the organisation. Typically this will be from cost centre, through business (or service) unit, and directorate to the total for the local authority. The reports must be accrual based, although it will be an advantage if committed expenditure can also be shown.

The reports should show an analysis of income and expenditure in a common format across the organisation. Typically reports will show the actual expenditure for the period monitored together with expenditure for the year to date. Reports need to also include the budgeted expenditure for the same time periods and the variance between actual and budgeted expenditure. The report showing the actual financial position is a valuable control tool in itself, however of equal if not greater value is a written report from the responsible manager that explains the reasons for any variances and includes an up to date forecast of the out-turn for the year. The finance function in the local authority should review the reports to identify any inconsistency, ask further questions of the responsible managers where explanations are unclear and prepare a summary written report for the Chief Executive and Corporate Management Team.

It is generally possible to tell how seriously the Management Team regard the importance of financial performance review by looking at how much time is devoted to review of the reports at Management Team meetings.

Capital Expenditure – Reporting and Review

[24.20]
Effective capital expenditure control relies on accurate accrual based capital

project accounting. Given the nature of capital projects commitment accounts and remaining expenditure forecasts are particularly valuable, as at any time in the project the key question to be answered is will the project be completed within budget. Analysis of expenditure within a project total should be specific to the project and designed to highlight different project phases or sub projects where there is some flexibility in the design or the total cost to be incurred. For example a building refurbishment project may include options for different standards of final finish, whilst the building cost estimates may be dependent on actual site conditions which cannot be determined in advance. In such a case the project cost analysis should separate the building and finishing phases so that if the building phase incurs an unavoidable overspend, this can be identified before final decisions are taken on the standard of finish.

Where final project selection and timing are devolved within annual capital budget totals, hierarchical reports summarising project totals at the levels of devolved budgets are needed so that managers can be held responsible for their decisions.

Frequency of expenditure reporting can be an issue. Senior managers will most likely wish to see performance measured on the same frequency as the revenue accounts. Project managers will often require more frequent reports that tie in (or can be matched to) to the specific project time-scales. If this flexibility cannot be achieved within the accounting or reporting system, a sensible compromise is often weekly reporting, with senior managers using the weekly report most appropriate to the revenue account period ends.

Operational Performance Reporting and Review

[24.21]
Operational review is the monitoring of the operational performance of a business or service unit and is as critical to financial propriety as Revenue reporting and review. Local authorities deliver a multiplicity of services, and therefore have a complex mix of service and organisational objectives. This increases the need for effective operational performance. In the private sector sales or profit can be used as a proxy for operational performance, and in some ways this reduces the importance of operational performance measurement. However, most large private sector organisations will measure a range of operational outcomes, and particularly those that are seen as precursor to or component of sales or profit. The value of financial reporting is significantly reduced if operational reporting is absent or ineffective. Judgement of financial performance is limited if there is no measure of the output delivered for the resources consumed.

Progress against operational targets must be monitored alongside the financial performance of the unit. Operational performance reports should show the performance of the business or service unit against operational performance indicators determined as part of the business or service planning process. Clearly most operational targets will be service specific, but should also include targets for the unit's contribution to corporate targets. Because of the varied nature of services delivered hierarchical summaries of performance are limited. However where summation or averaging is possible totals should be produced to match the management and responsibility hierarchy within the organisation. This will be particularly valuable for corporate targets as it will allow an understanding of the variability of performance and allow targeted management action in those areas where improved performance will have the greatest effect on the corporate position.

Balance Sheet Reporting and Review

[24.22]

The nature of balance sheet reporting in a local authority will depend on the organisation of balance sheet accounting. Practically all accounting systems allow revenue expenditure to be analysed by cost centre and/or business unit. However, unless specific internal structures are set up at the development stage, accounting systems are generally designed to have a single cost centre or business unit structure for balance sheet accounting. It can therefore be difficult to analyse balance sheet components at the same level of detail as the revenue accounts.

The three balance components for which it is critical to have cost centre or business unit analysis are external creditors, external debtors and stock. These are the components which will affected by the performance within business or service units. The level and movement of business unit or cost centre balances for these components of the balance sheet are critical financial control issues. In many cases the analysis required can be obtained from subsidiary systems. For example, rent debtors are normally managed and reported using a specific rent and housing management system.

However, where subsidiary systems are not used or do not provide the analysis required specific reports must be developed to maintain control of the balance sheet. Reports should provide as a minimum, the period end balance, the movements within the period, and the movements from the start of the year. This should be accompanied by an analysis of the balance that relates the absolute size of the balance to the movement within the time period. The simplest analysis to understand is where the balance is expressed as a number of days, ie debtor days, creditor days or days stockholding, however for debtors it can be useful to show the percentage collection rate. This has the advantage of being easily understood, relatively easy to calculate, and free from the distortion that is experienced with the debtor days calculation where the level of debt created on a daily basis is subject to wide variation.

Most local authorities have relatively sophisticated reporting of major corporate debts such as Council Tax and National Non-Domestic Rates. Typically the percentage collection rate, the absolute value outstanding, and the level of arrears collection reported on at least a monthly basis, along with operational statistics such as the number of reminders, and summonses for non-payment issued. Housing benefit overpayment debt, whilst significant in many local authorities is often poorly reported and reviewed. The best practice is to report the level of debt created, the percentage collection rate and the level of debt written off as not collectable. Ideally these should be reported in terms of value and the number of benefit cases.

Treasury Operations

[24.23]
The value of treasury operations in any given period, particularly where a local authority has large housing debt, can be significant in relation to the size of the revenue account. Well-managed treasury functions can make a significant financial contribution to revenue. Income can be generated from short-term investment of surplus cash, and from the active management of borrowing. Local authority's are required to operate within stringent controls over both the level of borrowing and the level of cash invested. The controls are intended to preclude money market speculation whilst encouraging the maximisation of income for the authority. Financial propriety requires that the letter and the spirit of the regulations are followed, and that where opportunities exist to generate income these should be taken with regard to individual and overall portfolio risks. At the level of an individual decision, the failure to take opportunities where risk is low is just as serious as a decision to take too great a risk. Both decisions will result in overall increased risk for the organisation.

The frequency of treasury reporting will depend on the stability of financial markets. However, it should never be less frequent than monthly. When markets are unstable the frequency may need to be increased to fortnightly or weekly. In addition as treasury review is often associated with proposals for tactical changes in investment or loan portfolios, where decisions need to be made, ad-hoc reports in advance of or immediately following interest rate announcements or other key market announcements are frequently required. The ideal set of information is as follows:

- up-to-date cash flow forecast;
- details of current loan portfolio with debt due for renewal in the next 12 months highlighted;
- details of current cash investment portfolio with investments due for renewal in next month highlighted;
- graph of debt pool rate over time;
- calculation of effective credit ceiling; and
- details of Public Works Loan Board remaining capacity.

Chapter 25
Internal and External Audit – Reporting and Controls

The Managed Audit Approach

[25.1]
This is the term used by the Audit Commission to describe their preferred approach to audit. The approach was introduced in 1995, and has been progressively implemented since then. Whilst the approach introduces no new principles, and does not change the District Auditors responsibilities or duties, it does promote a more productive way of working and encourages District Auditors and local authorities to develop a better working relationship.

The Audit Commission envisages that where a local authority meets the following conditions:

* sound financial systems;
* effective controls;
* good internal audit; and
* reliable accounts production processes.

The District Auditor should make maximum use of the local authorities own work in meeting its stewardship and governance responsibilities. This would allow a greater emphasis on high level controls and less on more detailed controls, and would involve close co-ordination with internal audit.

The Audit Commission recognises that the above conditions will not be met in full in all local authorities, and encourages the District Auditor and the local authority to work together to improve compliance with the conditions. More specifically it stated that it was the auditors role to:

'promote the concept of the Managed Audit with officers and other interested parties ... This proactive approach required the auditor to–
* Work with management and internal audit to help achieve improved conditions;
* Undertake a more formal and comprehensive review of the control environment;
* Make greater use of the work of internal audit;
* Adopt an approach with a presumption towards system and controls testing and a move away from transaction testing;
* Make greater use of the audited body's working papers; and
* Improve project management of the audit process'[1].

The Audit Commission also has legitimate expectations of local authorities to play their part in enabling the Managed Audit approach. It is realistic enough to realise that achieving the right conditions for the full implementation of Managed Audit will take time. However, it does expect local authorities to demonstrate both commitment and real progress to achieving the conditions. The key areas that a local authority needs to address to achieve this are:

- **Corporately**
    - corporate governance arrangements that recognise the impor-tance of financial reporting and the audit function;
    - a risk management approach to planning and effective risk management strategies;
    - clearly defined roles and responsibilities for officers;
    - an environment of management control, and good internal control systems;
    - an Internal Audit function that is adequately resourced and effective.
- And more specifically for the **finance** function:
    - procedures and processes that are documented with a high level of compliance;
    - capable and knowledgeable staff who are adequately trained to meet their responsibilities;
    - the appointment of specific finance officers to co-ordinate the authorities work in relation to the audit and to liase with the audit team on progress of work;
    - a good track record of delivery for accounts, performance indicators, and grant claims enabling the audit team to rely on the timing in planning the audit.

Whilst technically the Managed Audit approach only applies to the part of the audit that supports the opinion on the accounts, many local authorities have reported other benefits that appear to arise from the closer working relationship with the audit team and the District Auditor. In particular they have valued the opportunity afforded by closer contact to discuss accounting treatment or legality issues on an informal basis, before making final decisions. Some of the features of managed audit have also transferred to other audit areas. For example, one London authority has reported an improvement in preparation and audit of grant claims (technically outside of managed audit arrangements) resulting from the willingness of the audit manager to run seminars for staff, explaining the format and standards required for claim files to achieve audit approval promptly.

1   The Managed Audit Review Report (The Audit Commission, May 2001).

Relationships with the District Auditor

[25.2]
Clearly the relationship with the District Auditor is important and a local authority has much to gain in achieving financial propriety from a relationship that delivers mutual trust and co-operation. The relationship is

also fairly complex as within what can be described as the local authority's relationship are four separate relationships (ie with The Chief Executive, The Chief Finance Officer, The Monitoring Officer, and Members). Whilst, as one may expect, in most cases the primary relationship is with the Chief Financial Officer, the other relationships cannot be ignored. The basic objectives of the District Auditor and the local authority in achieving financial propriety should be the same. It is, in some ways, difficult to comprehend why there are so many reports from both District Auditors and Chief Financial Officers of difficult and challenging relationships. However there must be at least a suspicion that the conflict arises from the nature of the individual personalities rather than the specific qualities of the auditor/audited relationship.

It is fairly easy to describe the attributes of a good relationship, but much more difficult to achieve, particularly if there has been a difficult and challenging history. The table below sets out the attributes of a good relationship with the District Auditor and proposes some practical steps that will go some way towards this end. However, the practical steps cannot substitute for the right attitude toward the individual, and where a bad relationship exists it must be up to the individuals involved to question their own attitude and willingness to change.

Attributes	Constructive Behaviours for the Local Authority
Open	Hold regular meetings and keep the DA informed about long term plans, current issues and difficulties, as well as progress with the accounts, PIs and audit queries Give the DA and their team unrestricted access to staff and members. Attempting to control access wastes your time and theirs Give the DA copies of relevant reports without being asked
Honest	Be realistic about what can be achieved Do not hide issues that you are attempting to resolve, but explain the issue and the steps you are taking Make sure that you keep the DA informed if you are unhappy with any aspects of the audit or the performance of his staff, but be constructive with criticism, always suggesting an alternative approach that is reasonable
Trusting	Use the DA as a sounding board if there are complex accounting or legality issues
Understanding	Make sure you understand any areas of concern the DA has Make sure you understand the audit code of practice, and get the DA to discuss how the code is applied in your audit
Shared Goals	Develop joint goals for improving the final accounts, and PI processes and the relevant audits
Co-operative	Treat the DA as an equal. If you are able to co-operate with requests for changes to plans or timetables, do so. You may need the DA's co-operation on occasion too

Friendly	Make the DA welcome when they visit Don't play power games, like keeping them waiting or cancelling meetings at short notice Provide reasonable accommodation (to the same standard as for your own employees) for the DA's staff If the DA attends formal meetings, make sure they understand the protocols, have copies of the papers, and know if and when they may be called upon to speak

Relationships with the Chief Executive and the Monitoring Officer

[25.3]
It is clear from the paragraph above that the council's relationship with the District Auditor will also depend upon the relationships between the Chief Executive, the Monitoring Officer and the District Auditor. It is important that the council presents a unified view to the District Auditor, to ensure that it does not present mixed messages. The three statutory officers need to discuss and agree the approach to the relationship with the District Auditor. Equally important is that they ensure open communication between themselves concerning any issues raised with or by the District Auditor. The council's relationship with the District Auditor will in many ways be dependent on good working relationships between the three statutory officers, and they may also wish to consider if their relationships on an individual basis meet the attributes set out above for the relationship with the District Auditor.

Audit Planning – The Risk Based Approach

[25.4]
The risk based approach to audit planning uses an assessment of relative risk by service area and system to determine the type frequency and scope of audit needed. There are a number of different risk scoring systems in use, but the principles followed for the development of plans are the same. The theory behind the approach is that if audit resources are targeted proportionately to higher risk areas, a higher level of reliance can be obtained for the same level of audit resources.

In principle this appears sound and relatively simple. However, in practice it is a little more complex. Different types of audit require a different mix of skills and experience to achieve a reliable result. Whilst the number of audit days for an effective transaction audit will be considerably greater than the number of days needed to undertake an internal controls review for the same system or service. The level of skills and experience (and therefore the audit day cost) for most of the work in a transaction audit is much lower than will be required for a control review. In addition there is the issue of audit coverage. All systems and areas require some level of audit, depending on the overall level of risk and compliance within an organisation and, realistically, the level of resources available, the overall plan need to ensure full coverage within a three to five year period.

That said, once a risk assessment has been undertaken, it becomes fairly obvious that applying a single audit methodology in all circumstances is an injudicious waste of resources.

As mentioned previously there are a number of risk scoring systems. All the systems (known to me) use gross expenditure as the impact measure and it is in the estimate of probability that systems make use of different factors or criteria. Typically, high risks are associated with three particular circumstances:

- direct payments to individuals;
- opportunity for external collusion;
- access to cash or cash equivalents.

Other factors that can be used are:

- previously identified audit issues;
- significant changes to systems or processes.

Anecdotally one county council includes a factor for 'subjective evidence of risk' which turns out to be the 'gut feeling' of the chief internal auditor based on his personal experience over a considerable number of years.

This last factor is an interesting one as it brings out the fact that the risk approach the audit planning has, in reality, been in use for many years. Auditors and Chief Financial Officers have always allocated greater resources to areas of high risk. Indeed most planning systems previously used gross expenditure or level of materiality to allocate audit days, which is, after all, a measure of the impact part of risk. They may not have specifically identified the risks or even considered that their approach was other than personal experience or judgement. In the current methodology all that has really changed is that we have become more sophisticated and perhaps somewhat more objective is assessing the probability part of the risk equation.

Internal Audit – What Reporting Line?

[25.5]
The traditional approach has been that Internal Audit is part of the Finance Service and reports to the Chief Financial Officer. This issue has had some considerable debate over the last few years and various arguments have been proposed for Internal Audit to report to the Chief Executive. This view primarily proposed by the Institute of Internal Auditors, follows the views expressed in Cadbury Report, (now part of what is known as the 'combined code'). In summary this view is that to maintain the independence of Internal Audit it should report directly to the chairman of the board of directors, or to an Audit Committee that is chaired by a non-executive director. The IIA considered that an equivalent reporting line in a local authority was to the Chief Executive and that this would give the required independence from the finance function and the Chief Financial Officer. In many ways this is a

compelling argument, having worked in the private sector for a considerable number of years before joining local government it has seemed odd that Internal Audit was considered very much the domain of the Chief Financial Officer.

However the structure of responsibility for finance in local government is very different from the structure in the private sector, and CIPFA[1] restated their strongly held view that Internal Audit was a critical part of the organisation structure needed for the CFO to discharge their duties and responsibilities. It is perhaps not surprising to some that CIPFA would take a view which supported the role of the CFO, who are mostly CIPFA members, however their undoubted pre-eminence in knowledge of local government finance ensure that their arguments will be somewhat more than just soundly based.

To understand their views we need to go back to statutory provisions and case law discussed above. The CFO (perhaps '151' officer, is the more appropriate term here), has a personal responsibility and fiduciary duty to taxpayers, that cannot be delegated. Internal Audit plays a key role in ensuring financial probity and in providing assurance concerning the effective operation of internal control. As such it is a critical part of the mechanism used by the CFO to discharge their duties, and perhaps more importantly the primary source of information they need to ensure that they are delivering on their personal responsibility. Many CFOs take the view that if internal audit were to report to the Chief Executive, they would need to re-create it in another guise within their own organisation to ensure their personal responsibilities and duties were met.

Not being a member of CIPFA, and having held the position of CFO in both the private sector and in a local authority, I find myself in an unusually independent position of being able to give a truly personal view. The personal responsibilities and the clear fiduciary duty lead me in the end to the conclusion that internal audit should be part of the responsibilities of the CFO. If internal audit were managed elsewhere it would be considerably more difficult to gain the assurance that personal control allows. In addition it could lead to circumstances where the CFO and the officer responsible for internal audit disagreed over issues of risk, audit coverage or the level of assurance required. This would put the CFO in a difficult perhaps untenable position. However I think that there do need to be some safeguards to protect the independence of the Chief Internal Auditor (CIA), and would recommend that all or some of the following are put in place:

- standing orders provide for the right of the CIA to put independent reports to the appropriate committee;
- appointment, discipline or dismissal of CIA to be undertaken only with approval of the Chief Executive and the Monitoring Officer;
- audit reports on any area under control of the CFO to be routinely copied to the Monitoring Officer for comment;
- the establishment of an audit committee to oversee audit arrangements.

1   Chartered Institute of Public Finance and Accountancy (CIPFA).

Audit Committees

[25.6]

The Audit Commission in its paper *Called to Account – The Role of Audit Committees in Local Government* encourages councillors and officers to review their procedures for establishing effective corporate governance in those aspects relating to audit issues. In particular the Commission suggests that they consider the establishment of an audit committee to oversee the authorities audit arrangements.

Audit Committees in public companies have been in existence in the USA and the UK since about 1870, In the UK, the pressures from the Cadbury Committee recommendations led to a rapid increase in formation of audit committees within PLCs. However the extent of the take up of Audit Committees in local government has been fairly limited. It is fairly certain that the low take up is at least in part the result of the nature of the CFO's responsibilities, where the issues are similar to the issues about control of the internal audit service. In addition I have no doubt that there is some confusion in local authorities regarding the relationship of an audit committee to the formal committee structure.

In summary the key issues seem to be:

- if the audit committee is a formal committee of the council what is the position of the CFO in relation to that committee;
- if the CFO has delegated responsibility for internal audit what is the role of the audit committee and is it purely advisory;
- in the new structures proposed by the Local Government Act 2000 where should and audit committee be located, as part of the executive role, reporting to the cabinet, or as part of the scrutiny role and does it fit well in either.

This is not to say that Audit Committees have not been seen to work well where they have been established. There are a number of examples of Audit Committees as both full committees of council and as informal committees or 'working parties' with a purely advisory role. In some cases however the full committee approach has led to a role which has become more akin to the role of the Public Accounts Committee in Parliament.

The treasury has published a set of policy principles for audit committees in central government and its explanation of the purpose of audit committees is helpful in considering appropriate arrangements in local government. 'The purpose of an Audit Committee is to give advice to the Accounting Officer on the adequacy of audit arrangements (internal and external) and on the implications of the assurance provided in respect of risk and control in the organisation'

Whilst the role of 'Accounting Officer' usually combines the functions of Chief Executive and CFO, the definition of purpose, substituting the CFO for the Accounting Officer appears to be appropriate for local government. If this were taken as the purpose it would point to an informal committee approach. This would then point to any role similar to the role of the Public Accounts

Committee as part of a local authority's scrutiny arrangements, which also appears to be the intention of the Local Government Act 2000.

Whichever approach is taken there are a number of considerations for the constitution of audit committees that can be drawn from the private sector, central government and other areas of the public sector. The following principles for an audit committee should be considered:

- the Audit Committee is appointed to give advice to the Accounting Officer. Although the Accounting Officer may chair the Audit Committee, the objectivity of the advice given can be enhanced if another member (particularly a non-executive) is the Chair of the Committee;
- the terms of reference for the Audit Committees should be drafted by the CFO and agreed with the Chief Executive and The Monitoring Officer and should include a remit to consider the adequacy of risk management and internal control through review of–
  - the mechanisms for the assessment and management of risk;
  - the internal audit plan ;
  - issues arising from internal audit reports;
  - the external audit plan and in particular the choice of value for money studies;
  - the annual management letter from the District Auditor, and any issues arising from external audit studies;
  - the adequacy of management response to issues identified by audit activity; and
  - the authorities corporate governance arrangements and any matters raised by the District Auditor in relation to corporate governance.
- it is normal for Audit Committees to be constituted with significant proportion of members that are no non-executive or independent, appropriate individuals should be sought for appointment as external members of the Audit Committee. Ideally two or three independent members should be sought;
- in large authorities (eg Counties and Unitary Authorities) the Audit Committee should ideally have no fewer than five and no more than ten members. For smaller authorities (eg Districts) a minimum membership of three may be more practicable;
- Audit Committee members who are also Senior Officers should be rotated on an appropriate cycle (perhaps three years) to provide for objectivity in the long term and to avoid over or under representation of particular aspects of the body's business and administrative interests;
- the Chief Internal Auditor and the District Auditor should have the right of access to the Audit Committee and should normally be present at meetings (as attendees rather than members). It may be appropriate for the CIA to be formally the committee secretary;
- the Audit Committee should meet regularly and at least three times a year.

Monitoring Audit Performance

[25.7]
As with any other service performance monitoring and management is

critical to service quality efficiency and value for money. Typically audit performance measures include:

- number of audit days delivered compared to plan;
- actual days used compared to planned days for audits delivered;
- percentage completion of annual audit plan; and
- some form of quality measures from post audit questionnaires (eg how valuable was the audit, did you agree with the recommendations, did the auditor turn-up on time).

All of the above are valuable measures and will help keep track of empirical performance and the perception of audit staff and teams across the organisation, although it is always good to be fairly sceptical of the questionnaire responses. Many managers will privately admit to some level of fear of audit which, is not a bad thing in itself, but does tend to skew questionnaire responses considerably to the positive side. One measure that is often used, somewhat unwisely, is the number of recommendations or audit points raised. This always seems to lead to a high level of petty and superficial recommendations, which do nothing for the standing of the Audit Service.

However the one of the main purposes of audit, alongside the purpose of reassurance, is to instigate change. If this is one of the main purposes then to measure performance you need to measure how successful it is at instigating change. The best way to measure this is by looking at how many audit recommendations are implemented and how quickly they are implemented. It is true that the level of implementation is not entirely within the control of the audit service but they do have a substantial input to this. The factors that govern the implementation of an audit recommendation are:

- the level to which the manager responsible agrees with the recommendation;
- the risk that the manager associates with the area of the recommendation;
- the practicality of implementation;
- the resources available to the manager;
- the availability and practicality of alternative action to address the same problem; and
- the commitment of the manager to perform well.

The auditor in developing and framing the recommendation and explaining it to the manager has some level of control over the first three, should be taking the next two into account, and whilst individually has no control over the last, as part of the audit service, has an influence over how acceptable to the organisation it is to ignore audit recommendations.

The only danger in using this as measure of audit performance (apart from upsetting the Chief Internal Auditor) is that it could possibly lead to auditors watering down recommendations in order that more are implemented. I think we can rely on the professionalism of auditors as a body to know that this is unlikely.

Implementation Audit

[25.8]

Internal and external auditors are capable of producing lists of well framed, sensible, recommendations. However apart from giving us a warm feeling that we know what to do to put things right, what value do the recommendations have to the organisation. Their only true value is when they are implemented. Most individual audits include a review of the implementation of previous recommendations, but in most cases this is at least a year and possibly two or three years later. Surely if we thought it was important enough to issue an audit recommendation we want to know much more quickly if the recommendation is being implemented. The stock answer to this type of questioning is that once the recommendation has been accepted by the responsible manager, it should be part of the performance management regime within the department concerned to follow through implementation. One has to question if this is really good enough or if it is really possible to know the level of implementation without some formal method of checking.

In addition where there is an issue of manager commitment or motivation are they more likely or less likely to implement if they know that their actions will be checked after six months. Implementation audit is powerful tool to drive up the level of compliance with audit recommendations.

Implementation audit can be introduced at fairly low cost, if it is added into the work of audit teams and the teams are given sufficient flexibility to undertake the audit interviews when it is geographically convenient. A target of 90% implementation audits undertaken between five and seven months following the issue of the final report is relatively easy to achieve without any significant disruption of the planned audit programme. The alternative is to employ a specialist resource but depending on the volume of work, this may be less cost effective. A suggested audit methodology is set out below.

Audit Brief	To ascertain if high and medium priority audit recommendations have been implemented but specifically not to examine the adequacy of the implementation.
Frequency/ Timing	Audit to be undertaken between five and seven months following issue of final audit report in question.
Methodology	Initial telephone interview with the responsible manager asking simply what action had been taken to implement the recommendations. In cases where the manager reports that no action has been taken on the high and medium priority recommendations, the report is completed and no further action is taken. Where the manager reports that action had been taken a face-to-face interview at an appropriate time is arranged. Structured interview using appropriate interview template to ascertain if the recommendations have been fully or partially implemented, taking copies of appropriate supporting documentation as evidence. Further interview with the staff involved and inspection of supporting system documentation, if appropriate.

Report format	List of recommendations with each listed as implemented, not implemented, or partially implemented. Monthly summary by Directorate and audit team showing percentage Not Implemented, Partially Implemented, and Fully Implemented.

Planned and Investigative Audit – Getting the Right Balance

[25.9]
This is similar to the 'chicken and egg' question, which comes first? Where planned audit is insufficient, the level of investigative audit, as problems are discovered, is higher. When the level of investigative audit is too high, resources are taken away from planned audit and this leads to a downward spiral. More and more resources are sucked into investigations, so that eventually no planned audit is undertaken and there are not enough resources to deal with all the requests for investigations. Whilst circumstances have to be extreme for lead to total breakdown many audit teams will have experienced the symptoms to a greater or lesser extent, and a total breakdown has happened in at least one London borough.

There is no one easy solution once the downward spiral has started, and the real trick is to prevent it starting in the first place, but some tips gained from personal experience are set out below:

- get extra resources. This may be difficult and embarrassing for the audit service, but realistically without extra resources, in the short-term at least, breaking the cycle will be impossible;
- devise a minimum audit plan, using a risk based approach, with the lowest coverage you can accept. Separate out the resources to deliver the plan, and stick to it (whatever happens!);
- be ruthless in sifting the requests for investigative work. Only take on those where there is either a significant indication of fraud, or where the impact of control failure is high. (Small petty cash imbalances are definitely out!);
- complete investigations as soon as possible, reporting the findings and recommendations as rapidly as possible. Do not get involved in collating evidence for disciplinary matters, leave this to the department or to HR staff;
- put in place management arrangements to allow directorates to fund investigations themselves if they so desire, using additional temporary staff;
- have faith that the level of investigative work will reduce, it may take some time but it will eventually.

Relationship Between Audit and Fraud Investigation

[25.10]
Where Internal Audit and Fraud Investigation are managed separately, it is

essential that the two services maintain close links, as in many cases they will need to rely on each other's work. In addition whilst much of the work of fraud investigation is unplanned, some work will be part of an annual programme and as such should be co-ordinated with the internal and external audit plans. To facilitate the working relationship it is useful to put in place a number of measures that formalise the relationship. The following suggestions will ensure that certain matters are discussed on a regular basis and that there is a rationale to determine the boundaries of their respective work areas:

- agreed criteria to determine if cases will be handled by Internal Audit or by the Fraud Investigation team;
- an agreed protocol for hand over of cases where the work identified crosses the boundaries. (eg suspicion of fraud during an internal audit, or where a fraud enquiry identifies issues of internal control failings but no fraudulent activity);
- formal monthly liaison meetings to keep the units informed about current work and issues, and to agree the hand over of cases; and
- joint annual risk assessment and planning.

CHAPTER 26
Involvement of Staff and Partners

Who Knows What Happens Round Here Anyway?

[26.1]
Financial propriety is not achieved through great strategy documents, detailed financial regulations or the perfect risk based audit plan, it has to be delivered by the staff working in the authority. It is in their attitude, vigilance, and behaviour that propriety is to be found. Without their commitment and involvement, the strategies and plans are only as useful as the doorstops they will become. Staff will only become committed to the strategies an plans if they are involved in their creation, and staff involvement is more about listening that telling.

Any experienced auditor knows that to find out what happens in an organisation you have to talk to and more importantly listen to the junior staff. The manager will tell you what should happen, or what they would like to think happens, but only from the junior staff will discover what actually happens. They know what works, and what does not, which bit of the process are skipped, the system shortcuts, and if you ask them, they often know a much better way to get the job done. The only thing they often do not know is why, because nobody has ever really explained. Internal control and process compliance is achieved in the long-term through a real dialog with the staff operating the processes and the process designer. Furthermore unless there is a real commitment to training and coaching, process compliance will deteriorate as soon as there is a change in staff.

Financial Regulations – Does Anyone Read Them?

[26.2]
It always seems surprising when reading an audit report about a control failure, that the people involved, could possibly do that! Haven't they read the financial regulations? Don't they know anything about internal control?

Its even more surprising that there will probably be no correlation between the answers to the two questions, and there will be no correlation between control failures and the manager reading the financial regulations. So, why are these wonderful documents produced if people do not read them, and even if they do, they do not understand them or take notice of them?

Well, the sample used is just a little skewed! It is all the cases where controls failed, not a random sample of all staff across the organisation. However this does tell us something. A control failure is either a failure to properly communicate the financial regulations or it must be a deliberate act of omission. If it is the latter then the person must be intent on organisational sabotage, and discipline or dismissal is the only answer. Fortunately most organisations do not employ many people like this. So in most cases it is the failure to communicate that is cause.

Reading even the most well written set of financial regulations is about as exciting as doing your tax return, so what is really the most surprising is that financial regulations that are published without some form of training or support programme are read at all. Given that the subject matter is hardly captivating, developing a training or support programme for financial regulations is an interesting challenge, and there is a danger that the training sessions end up as turgid as the subject matter. However with a little creative thought and a participative approach there is much that can be done to make the sessions productive. The best approach that I have seen, was brief introduction to the subject followed by a specially designed board game that took the participants through their working month showing how the financial regulations affected their working lives. Participants gained points for recognising the issues where the regulations applied and for correctly identifying what action was needed to comply.

Controls Awareness Workshops

[26.3]
Controls awareness workshops are another good tool to increase understanding and compliance with financial regulations. The objectives are to make the participants understand the purpose and operation of financial controls in their working environment, and to help them develop and action plan to improve the operation of controls in their own team or business/service unit. A typical programme might be:

- explanation of the need for internal control and how it protects both staff individually and the organisation as a whole;
- role play of a potential fraud situation with and without the correct operation of a key control;
- structured group discussion of types of internal control;
- syndicate examination of financial regulations, relating them to the types of control they represent;
- learning points feedback;
- individual action planning.

Internal Audit – A Support for Managers?

[26.4]
Why is it that managers often regard auditors as the enemy, and internal auditors as the enemy within? It is clearly not just specific to the profession, as it seems that there is a general resentment in society to any form of

inspection. Anecdotes about auditors, Tax and VAT inspectors abound and seem to follow the pattern that if you keep them in the dark, treat them badly, and never volunteer any information, you manage to get away with some misfeasance or profit from the system in some way. I have no doubt that there is an evolutionary psychologist somewhere that will be able to show that this behaviour relates to some distant behavioural trait that gave early humans an evolutionary advantage over another species of ape. However this will not tell us why we have this urge to treat auditors or inspectors badly. I have met quite a few socially, and they seem to be quite nice people.

What is clear is that if the attitude to audit or inspection is overcome, and managers came to regard the audit as an opportunity to improve their processes, and reduce the risk of failure. The whole audit or inspection process would become much more productive and much less stressful for all concerned. So what can be done to help this occur.

Audit Issues for Out-sourced Contracts

[26.5]
As a result of introduction of Compulsory Competitive Tendering, Public Private Partnerships and subsequent governments' encouragement for out-sourcing, almost all local authorities have one or more services that are delivered through third party contracts. The varied nature of services delivered through contract arrangements raise a number of issues for audit arrangements.

Where the service delivered is self-contained (ie all the risk in delivery has passed to the contractor and they have no update access to council systems) the contract can be treated for audit purposes as an ordinary supply contract with no special audit needs. A significant number of CCT type contacts, eg building maintenance, refuse collection, street lighting fall into this category.

At the opposite extreme are contracts where the service process is only partially delivered by the contractor, or where the contractor operates the service on behalf of the authority but does not take on the risk in the service, eg Housing Benefit, Trade Waste Collection. In this type of contract the level of audit need is high, indeed probably higher that if the service were to remain with the authority. The audit issues for this type of contract fall into three main areas; Contractual, Systems, and Personnel Management.

Contractual

[26.6]
The contract must provide for unfettered access to processes and data for audit purposes, In addition as the contractors staff will need to co-operate for any audit to be successful. The contract must provide for the full co-operation of the contractors staff during any audit process. The contract must have firm arrangements for responding to the audit, including the maximum time allowed for response to audit points and the report, and maximum time allowed for implementation of audit recommendations. Finally although not

287

specifically an audit issue all such contracts must be clear that all data and information used in performing the service remain the property of the authority, to be handed back on termination in the original format or such format as agreed by the authority. This last point in crucial where document management systems are employed as the authority may not wish to take on such systems on termination.

Systems

[26.7]
If the authority continues to own and manage the systems concerned this is less of an issue, as the audit of the system will be much as if it were operated internally. However the authority will still need access to the contractors premises to inspect any prime records or supporting documentation. Where the systems are entirely under the control of the contractor, internal audit will require full access to the contractors systems, and this will include access to system management arrangements, emergency and disaster cover arrangements. The authority will need to undertake full systems audit and to audit the IT management arrangements and operating controls. This can be very complex particularly if the contractor has a number of similar contracts with other authorities, as it will probably manage and operate the IT jointly for all contracts. With the growing complexity and specialist nature of systems auditing, many authorities find that subcontracting these audits to a large audit practice the most convenient and cost-effective approach.

Human Resource Management

[26.8]
The primary HR issue for auditors involved in auditing the operation of third party contractors is that the staff are not employees of the authority. This is the potential cause of a number of problems. The staff will most likely be subject to different disciplinary arrangements. To avoid compromising any disciplinary arrangements, it is wise to discuss and agree with the contractor's management how poor performance, negligence, or any suspicious activity should be reported. It may be more appropriate to pass over any further investigation to the contractor's management team as soon as any such behaviour is identified. This protects the audit team from being drawn in to further investigatory or disciplinary work that is likely to be time-consuming.

CHAPTER 27
Regulation of Investigatory Powers Act 2000

General Synopsis

[27.1]
The Act, which received Royal Assent on 28 July 2000, is intended to ensure that investigatory powers respect the human rights of the individual. The powers covered by the Act include:

- the interception of communications;
- the acquisition of communications data (eg billing data and system use data);
- intrusive surveillance (on residential premises/in private vehicles);
- covert surveillance in the course of specific operations;
- the use of covert human intelligence sources (agents, informants, undercover officers); and
- access to encrypted data.

In each of these areas the Act means to ensure that the law clearly determines:

- the purposes for which these powers may be used;
- which authorities can use the powers;
- who should authorise each use of the power; and
- the use that can be made of the material gained.

In addition the Act makes provision for independent judicial oversight of the use of the powers and a means of redress for the individual.

Areas Covered by the Act

[27.2]
The five main areas of the Act are as follows:

(1) Interception of Communications and the Acquisition and Disclosure of Communications Data

[27.3]
This part of the Act provides for a new regime for the interception of

communications incorporating a number of changes form the provisions within the Interception of Communications Act 1985, which it repeals. It establishes a basic principle that communications may not be recorded or monitored without the consent of the senders and recipients. However it is important to note that new regulations[1] under the Act, which set out the circumstances in which businesses can record and monitor e-mails and phone calls came into force on 24 October 2000.

1   Telecommunications (Lawful Business Practice) (Interception of Communications) Regulations 2000, SI 2000/2699.

(2)   Surveillance and Covert Human Intelligence Sources

[27.4]
The Act provides a statutory basis for the authorisation and use by the security and intelligence agencies, law enforcement and other public authorities of covert surveillance, agents, informants and undercover officers. It regulates the use of these techniques and is intended to safeguard the public from unnecessary invasions of their privacy. Under this part of the Act local authorities (within the meaning of s 1 of the Local Government Act 1999) are given powers to authorise and undertake, directed (but specifically not intrusive) surveillance, and to authorise the use of covert intelligence sources.

(3)   Investigation of Electronic Data Protected by Encryption etc

[27.5]
The Act contains provisions to maintain the effectiveness of existing law enforcement powers in the face of increasing criminal use of encryption. Specifically, it introduces a power to require disclosure of protected (encrypted) data.

(4)   Scrutiny of Investigatory Powers and Codes of Practice

[27.6]
The Act establishes an independent judicial Tribunal as a means of redress for those who wish to complain about the use of the powers. The Act provides for the appointment of Commissioners to provide oversight of powers where necessary, and it also provides for the Secretary of State to issue Codes of Practice covering the use of the powers covered by the Act.

(5)   Miscellaneous and Supplemental

[27.7]
This makes minor amendments to Wireless Telegraphy Act 1949, Pt III of the

Police Act 1997 in the light of operational experience and extends those provisions to the Ministry of Defence Police, the British Transport Police and the Service Police.

Issues for Local Authorities

[27.8]

The Act (and the Bill before it became law) has been the subject of a good deal of debate, primarily because of the powers it gives to the government in two areas, the access to encrypted material and encryption keys, and the access to communications data. However these issues are not particularly significant for local authorities and are not dealt with in detail here. The areas of most significance for local authorities and their implications are set out below.

Where local authorities intend or are likely to make use of such powers they are advised to take specific legal advice on the definitions and provisions within the Act. In any event given that the Act now provides specific powers local authorities are advised to ensure that they do not undertake any of the activities which are subject to the provisions within the Act without appropriate approval process to ensure regulatory compliance with the Act. In addition local authorities should consider taking appropriate measures on a periodic basis to ensure that compliance is maintained.

Interception of Communications

[27.9]

The Regulations[1] brought in under the Act, provide for a number of circumstances in which it will be lawful for an authority to intercept, monitor and record communications without the consent of sender, recipient or caller. In short, these include the following purposes:

- to establish the existence of facts relevant to the business;
- to ascertain compliance with regulatory or self regulatory rules or guidance;
- to ascertain or demonstrate standards which are or ought to be achieved by persons using the telecommunications system in the course of their duties;
- to prevent or detect crime;
- to investigate or detect the unauthorised use of their systems – for example, to ensure that employees do not breach company rules on the use of the system; and
- to ensure the effective operation of the system – for example monitoring for viruses.

In addition monitoring, but not recording, without consent is available for the purposes of determining whether or not the communications are relevant to the business and in relation to confidential anonymous counselling or support help-lines.

There are three caveats in relation to the use of the powers:

- the interception is solely for the purpose of monitoring or (where appropriate) keeping a record of communications relevant to the business;
- the telecommunication system in question is provided for use wholly or partly in connection with that business; and
- if an authority wishes to use the powers contained in the Regulations to monitor or record without an individual's consent, then the authority must make all reasonable efforts to inform every person who may use the system that communications may be intercepted.

1 Telecommunications (Lawful Business Practice) (Interception of Communications) Regulations 2000, SI 2000/2699.

Authorisation of Surveillance or Covert Operations

[27.10]
As indicated above the Act provides for local authorities the power to authorise the use of directed surveillance and to use covert intelligence sources. Local authorities do not have powers to authorise intrusive surveillance. These terms are defined in detail in s 26 of the Act, but in brief:

- directed surveillance is any operation, conducted covertly, that is likely to result in the obtaining of information about a person's family life or private life;
- covert intelligence sources are persons who establish a relationship with another to covertly obtain or provide access to private information, and use of a source includes inducing, asking or assisting;
- intrusive surveillance is directed surveillance that relates to anything taking place on any residential premises or in any private vehicle and involves the presence of an individual on the premises or in the vehicle or is carried out by means of a surveillance device, in or on the vehicle or premises.

The circumstances in which the powers may be used are specifically regulated by the Act, with the further caveat that they are used proportionately in relation to what is sought to be achieved. The circumstances that permit use are:

- in the interests of national security;
- for the purpose of preventing or detecting crime or of preventing disorder;
- in the interests of the economic well-being of the United Kingdom;
- in the interests of public safety;
- for the purpose of protecting public health;
- for the purpose of assessing or collecting any tax, duty, levy or other imposition, contribution or charge payable to a government department;

- for any purpose (not specifically mentioned above) which is specified for the purposes of this sub-section by an order made by the Secretary of State.

The power to authorise use is given to the local authority and the local authority will need to ensure that its scheme of delegation provides appropriate arrangements for decisions to be taken at an appropriate level within the organisation. Whilst this is a matter for individual authorities to consider it is suggested that such decisions are restricted to Chief Officers.

The Home Office has prepared draft forms for use in an approval process, use of these forms will go some considerable way to ensure that appropriate consideration is given to approval. The forms are available on the Home Office web site at http://www.homeoffice.gov.uk/ripa/p2forms.htm.

CHAPTER 28
Countering Fraud and Corruption

Anti-Fraud Culture

[28.1]
It is unfortunate, but a fact of life that minor theft and fraud are endemic in society today. In particular the attitude to minor theft and fraud against government and major business tends towards the view of fair game, with comments such as:

- 'Well they take enough tax from me'; and
- 'They're big enough, they can afford it'.

Local government is not immune to this culture, as much as we would like to think that our employees work in local government because they are committed to the public service ethic. We all know that in reality most staff have the same strengths and weaknesses as staff anywhere else. However most 'honest' people have a fairly low threshold of what they consider acceptable, and will identify with actions to reduce and eliminate fraud and theft, if they believe that the action is universal and proportionate. So, providing people believe that enough action is being taken to prevent serious fraud, and that any measures taken are effective across the whole organisation, they will not reject measures to eliminate petty fraud and theft.

It is however important that these matters are dealt with sensitively and that there is no explicit or implicit accusation of individuals or groups where the issue is potentially organisation wide. That is not to say that an organisation should back away from dealing with specific provable cases of petty fraud or theft, in fact the opposite, as staff are probably more likely to be aware or at least suspicious of individual fraud or theft, than are their managers. Simply that any measures taken are implemented fairly with no one section of the organisation more frequently targeted or harshly treated. Accusations of fraud or theft go to an individual's sense of their own integrity and will be taken much more personally than issues of performance or ability.

Conscious of the above caveats there is no special trick or treatment to changing attitudes and behaviours to fraud, in comparison to say changing attitudes and behaviours towards customer service. As for any change in organisation culture, it is difficult to achieve, easy to start and fail, and more difficult to implement once people get the feeling that it is just 'flavour of the month'. The key factors that lead to successful changes in organisational culture are set out in the table below together with some suggestions for practical actions. The suggestions are intended to stimulate debate and

294

discussion rather than be implemented blind. What will work best in any particular organisation may well be considerably different. The important factor is that whatever action is taken it is discussed and agreed by the whole management team. In culture change there is no room for dissent or mild acceptance. The whole team needs to be, and be seen to be, fully supportive of the change.

Culture Change Success Factors	Suggestions Specific to Anti-Fraud
Senior managers understand the need for change, the benefits of change, the time scale (years rather than months) and the need for demonstration of their commitment	Presentation from Fraud Investigation Team that highlights the problem, its scale and how a change in culture will deter internal and external fraud. Examples of best practice elsewhere, and of failings within should be highlighted. Managers encouraged to share experiences in syndicate work. Change Management specialist follows with presentation of the how change in culture can be effected. Highlighting pitfalls and successes elsewhere.
All staff are consulted about the need to change and are asked for their views and suggestions about how change can be effected	Consultation should be undertaken at workplace team meetings. A short, centrally developed presentation about the problem, followed by group work which asks what the council should do and what can be done in each team. Team action plan developed.
Change starts and is seen to start at the top	Launch register of members and senior managers interests. Top team take up one or more suggestions from the consultation exercise.
Activities and events associated with the change are small scale, infrequent, but regular at the start so that the momentum for change is seen to build rather than be launched with a fanfare followed by an anti-climax	Programme of Fraud Awareness Seminars, for all teams, not compulsory but expected (and followed up by senior managers). Strongly branded completion certificate or badge for all attendees. Possibly allow use of logo on stationery. Anti-Fraud training introduced to corporate training programme for follow up and specialist training. Specific events for staff working in areas where there is a high risk of external fraud; for example benefits, purchasing, invoice processing, trade waste etc.

Information about the change, about how staff can get involved, about progress and successes is widely published using a range of channels. This should be primarily drip feed approach with the occasional special feature of a good idea or well supported event. Staff driven events should be particularly featured	Features regularly in team brief, Staff news and external publications. PR team also concentrates on getting some external press coverage but not too high profile at first. It is important that publicity does not anticipate the momentum for change.
The top management team demonstrates their continuing interest and commitment to the change by asking junior staff about their experiences and sharing the ideas that they hear about	The value of this can not be stressed too much.
Once momentum has been seen to build (probably at least a year or so into the process) the change is converted to a mainstream or routine activity, and built into planning processes	Business or service plans include an anti-fraud strategy. Fraud awareness training and the council's attitude to fraud incorporated into induction process. Questions about council and individual attitudes to fraud included in annual staff survey.

Fraud Awareness Workshops

[28.2]
Fraud awareness workshops are extremely useful tools to spread the fight against fraud across your organisation. They will be most effective if facilitated by a trained facilitator with experience in Fraud Detection. The objectives of the workshop are to:

- raise general awareness of fraud in the workplace;
- stimulate discussion of fraud risks in participant's individual working areas; and
- empower participants to take responsibility for fraud avoidance and detection.

They can generally be delivered in a half-day session (feedback from full day sessions was that they were too long). Typically the programme would cover the following:

- introduction to fraud in the workplace: types of fraud, and the effects of fraud: specific fraud risks affecting local authorities;
- discussion and syndicate work to identify fraud risks in participants' own workplaces;
- an explanation of internal control as a tool to prevent and detect fraud;
- syndicate work for participants to review fraud controls in their individual working areas;

- an explanation of what action to take where fraud is suspected, including the arrangements for reporting suspected fraud; and
- individual action planning for participants.

Internal Audit and Fraud Investigation – Separate or Joint Functions?

[28.3]
As you may expect there is no single correct answer to this question. My preference is for separate units, but only because in my experience, audit work, particularly routine audit work, gets put to one side when what is perceived as much more interesting, investigative work, is on offer. The other advantages of separate units come from the organisational focus that can be achieved in a single function unit.

However there are some disadvantages to splitting the functions into separate units separate units. The most obvious of which is the loss of economy of scale, at the very least you need to have two managers and it may well be that some administrative functions are duplicated also. However since the Regulation of Investigatory Powers Act 2000 was passed the opportunity for sharing resources are more limited as formal training requirements have increased. Furthermore, having separate units can make liaison more difficult and lead to at least some element of 'turf war'. Surprisingly, however, in my experience, the 'turf war' effect is more about wanting to pass borderline cases on rather than retaining cases more appropriately dealt with by the other unit.

In conclusion there are advantages and disadvantages to each approach. It is important to consider both options, and to choose what is most appropriate for the organisation at the time.

Fraud Reporting – A Strategy for the Media

[28.4]
Media reporting of fraud in the context of local authorities tends to concentrate on the issue of lack of control that allowed the fraud to be perpetrated rather than the fact the fraud has been discovered and dealt with. Whilst the media will never be seen to condone fraud, their focus on the authorities failings rather than the crime of the fraudster, inevitably leads to some public impression that the authority is partially to blame, and by implication that the fraudster is only partially to blame. Obviously this is not the image that the authority wishes to portray. Not only does this reflect badly for the image of the authority, but also as a result of the impression of shared blame it does not augment the social disapproval required to enhance the deterrent effect of the detection. Furthermore, this treatment in the media has a negative effect on staff morale, particularly those who were involved in the investigation and detection.

This presents something of a dilemma for the local authorities media strategy. There is potentially a positive message to publicise but the likely media reaction will be at best neutral and at worst fairly detrimental to the authority's image. There are a number of strategy options:

- it can choose to give no publicity to the detection of fraud in the hope that the story will not leak in such a way to draw any significant attention, and prepare press releases and statements should the story break. The risk being that if the story breaks it will always be on the back foot responding to events rather than attempting the shape the news. In addition it may be accused of covering the matter up which will result in entirely the wrong image portrayed;

- it can chose to publicise the issue in a matter of fact way, with prepared backup statements and details about its anti-fraud strategy available for release as soon as there is any press interest. It may take the line that the detection of fraud is simply a routine part of what a well-managed local authority does. Perhaps highlighting the effective relationship it has with the police and the co-operation it has received in the particular case (obviously only if that is true);

- the further option, which will be particularly appropriate if the authority suffers a high level of attempted fraud is that it publishes its anti-fraud strategy aggressively. Showing the latest detection as proof of its success in dealing with crimes of this nature. If this approach is taken it may be advantageous to invite relevant media representatives to visit the fraud unit at an early stage to see some of the strategies and techniques used to combat fraud; or

- whichever strategy is chosen it is important that any of the staff involved who are likely to be questioned or interviewed by the media have been briefed on the strategy and have been given appropriate media skills training.

DIVISION V
Employment Implications

CHAPTER 29
Cultural Issues

Introduction

[29.1]
Although the Local Government Act 2000 is primarily about the democratic and community aspects of local governance, these inevitably have a major impact on the role of the local authority as an employer.

Despite a greatly increased focus over the last two decades on the outsourcing of local government services, local authorities still employ over two million people, about one in thirteen of the national workforce. Typically, between 60 to 70% of a local authority's budget is spent on employees. Any change in the way an authority is democratically organised and the interface with the community is bound therefore to affect the workforce.

The employees and their representatives are major stakeholders and should be consulted on all aspects of local government governance. This issue is discussed in more detail in respect of Best Value in this chapter.

This chapter examines the cultural issues that arise from the Local Government Act 2000 which impact on the workforce and covers:

- The local authority as one employer;
- Employee/member relationships;
- Serving cabinet, scrutiny and the council;
- Best value and employment.

The Local Authority as One Employer

[29.2]
Each local authority in England, and Wales (and Scotland) is a single employer in law. For the purposes of individual rights under the Employment Rights Act 1996, s 230(4) of that Act defines 'employer' as the person by whom the employee or worker is (where the employment has ceased, was) employed. Section 230(5) defines 'employment' as:

(a)   in relation to an employee, employed under a contract of employment; and

(b)   in relation to a worker, employed under the worker's contract (eg self-employment).

The contracts of all employees are with the local authority and this continues under the Local Government Act 2000.

Section 231 of the Employment Relations Act 1996 says that for the purposes of the Act (and for Equal Pay legislation) any two employers shall be treated as **associated employers** if:

(a) one is a company of which the other (directly or indirectly) has control; or

(b) both are companies of which a third person (directly or indirectly) has control.

The definition of 'associated employer' is exhaustive. The fact that the legislation refers to 'companies' is crucial. It means that local authorities, who are not 'companies' in law, cannot be associated employers as it is impossible for two local authorities – not being companies - to meet the definition of associated employer. It is however possible for a local authority-owned company, and the local authority which owns it, to be associated employers under (a) above – the local authority is an employer (it does not have to be a 'company' to meet the first element of the definition) and controls a company.

Where two employers are associated employers, this gives their employees additional employment protection rights. In particular, it means that service with one employer counts as service with the other. For example, for the purposes of determining whether or not an employee has sufficient continuous service with his/her employer under s 108(1) of the Employment Rights Act 1996 to make a complaint of unfair dismissal to an employment tribunal, continuous service with the employer and associated employer(s) will count. (Section 108(1) currently requires one year's continuous service before an employee can make a complaint of unfair dismissal.)

Where an employee employed by one local authority resigns and is appointed by another local authority, the calculation of continuous service for the purposes of employment legislation will start with the date the employee joins the second authority. This is despite the fact that there may be a contractual entitlement to count previous local government service for pay and conditions purposes including pensions, annual leave and sick pay. Such entitlement may be provided by the relevant national agreement, eg the National Joint-Council for Local Government Services – the Green Book, or through other legislation, eg the Local Government Pension Scheme Regulations 1997[1].

Where an employee is transferred by law from one local authority to another, eg under the Transfer of Undertakings (Protection of Employment) Regulations 1981[2] ('TUPE') (as amended), or by a statutory transfer order, eg those that were made during local government re-organisation between 1995 and 1998, statutory employment rights also transfer and continuous service is preserved for those purposes.

There is case-law to support the view that local authorities are not associated employers in law[3].

There is one exception to this. The Local Government Redundancy (Continuity of Employment in Local Government etc) (Modification) Order

1999[4] ('the Modification Order') makes local authorities and other specified bodies associated employers for the sole purposes of entitlement to and calculation of statutory redundancy payments. The provisions mirror those of s 146 of the Employment Rights Act in relation to the offer of re-employment on redundancy by an employer or associated employer. The effect of the Modification Order is as follows:

- all continuous service with local authorities and other bodies specified by the Order counts towards the entitlement to and calculation of a redundancy payment;
- if a redundant employee employed by a local authority or other body covered by the Order is offered and accepts alternative employment by another local authority or body covered by the Order *before* the date of redundancy, and the new job starts within four weeks of the date of redundancy, continuity of employment is preserved. There is no dismissal and therefore no entitlement to a redundancy payment. If the offer is made any time *after* the date of redundancy, there will have been a dismissal in law, continuity will have been broken and there will be an entitlement where appropriate to a redundancy payment.

There have been some recent significant developments in respect of the area of 'same employment' for the purposes of **equal pay legislation**. Currently, employees working for one employer are unable to name as equal pay comparators those working for another employer unless they are 'associated employers' (which local authorities are not – see above) – they are not in the 'same employment' for the purposes of s 1(3) of the Equal Pay Act 1970 (as amended). But the local government trade unions have for some time now been campaigning for cross-local authority equal pay claims to be permitted. Their argument has been that Art 141 of the Treaty of Rome (formerly Art 119) permits applicants and comparators to be employed by different employers where there is a community of interest between the employers for them to be regarded as being in the same 'service' for the purposes of same employment under Art 141.

This argument seems to have been given some credence by the decision of the Scottish Employment Appeal Tribunal (EAT) in *South Ayrshire Council v Morton*[5], but this decision needs to be treated with some caution as it affects teachers whose pay levels are determined in general by the Scottish National Joint-Council which had been set up by the Education (Scotland) Act. Under the general control of the Secretary of State. The EAT upheld the employment tribunal's decision that Ms Morton was entitled to compare herself with a man employed by a different LEA because while education authorities are not associated employers, 'they do (at least in the area of education) have a sufficient community of interest for the whole structure of education to be regarded as a service'. But the *Morton* case concerns teachers salaries determined by a body set up by an Act of Parliament, which strengthens the 'community of interest' argument. In the context of employees covered by the NJC for Local Government Services (the Green Book) and some other pay bodies, it is worth noting that the arrangements are non-statutory and voluntary in nature with authorities having wide discretion to determine pay and conditions. It may therefore be much harder to argue successfully that there is 'community of interest' between applicants and comparators of different employers of Green Book employees.

The Court of Appeal have referred the question of comparison for equal pay purposes to the European Court of Justice in the case of *Lawrence v Regent Office Care*[3] and a decision is awaited. The union's argument is that employees of a local authority and a contractor to whom some of the council's employees have been transferred are in the 'same employment' because they share a community of interest. One question asked of the ECJ in *Lawrence* is whether an applicant can only rely on Art 141 if the employer of the applicant is able to explain why the employer of the comparator pays him/her as they do.

With the growing emphasis in the local government modernisation agenda of partnerships and outsourcing, the issue of the local authority as one employer gains importance. As explained, where employees are transferred by law, eg under TUPE, from a local authority to a service provider they will take their continuous service with them for the purposes of statutory employment rights. Trade union recognition rights will also transfer. Depending on the decision of the ECJ in *Lawrence*, 'same employment' might include both the local authority and the service provider to whom employees are transferred. Where a local authority establishes a company to undertake services, that company and the local authority may be 'associated employers'.

The fact that a local authority is 'one employer' in law impacts not only on the employment rights of individual employees but also the duties of those employees towards the authority.

As referred to in para **[29.2]** above, para 8.4 of the DETR *Guidance on New Council Constitutions* says that contracts for all 'officers' (or employees) continue to be with the local authority. Local authority employees will continue to be under a duty to advise the council as a whole. This is considered in more detail below.

1   SI 1997/1612 (as amended).
2   SI 1981/1794.
3   See *London Borough of Merton v Gardiner* [1981] QB 269.
4   SI 1999/2277.
5   [2001] IRLR 28.
6   [2000] IRLR 608.

Employee / Member Relationships

[29.3]
The DETR *Guidance on New Council Constitutions* (para 8.25) says that it is a matter for local choice as to how local authorities choose to organise officer support for the different roles, eg cabinet, scrutiny, within the local authority. But para 8.26 adds that authorities should do so within the following broad **key principles**:

- all officers (Note – the term covers all paid employees) are employed by, and accountable to, the local authority as a whole;

- support from officers is needed for all the local authority's functions and the roles of the full council, overview and scrutiny, committees, the executive, individual members representing their committees etc;
- overview and scrutiny in particular will need to be properly resourced and effectively supported by officers;
- day-to-day managerial and operational decisions should remain the responsibility of the chief executive and other officers;
- local authorities should seek to avoid potential conflicts of interest for officers arising from the separation of the executive and the overview and scrutiny role; and
- all officers will need access to training and development (see Chapter 35 below) to help them support the various member roles effectively and to understand the new structures.

Local authority officers, whilst free to join a political party, and vote in elections, and (if not politically restricted – see Chapter 31 below) allowed to stand as an elected member for a local authority other than the one by whom they are employed, must be politically neutral and not show any political bias in the way they undertake their official duties. The Conditions of Service of the Joint-Negotiating Committee (JNC) for Chief Executives of Local Authorities (para 9) and the JNC for Chief Officers of Local Authorities (para 57) both provide that an officer shall not be required to advise any political group of the council, either as to the work of the group or as to the work of the council. Neither can they be required to attend any meetings of any political group. But this is without prejudice to any arrangements to the contrary which may be made in agreement with the officer and which includes safeguards to preserve the political neutrality of the officer in relation to the affairs of the council. This remains unchanged by the Local Government Act 2000. But in councils with a strong and determined executive the role of chief officers in relation to the giving of advice to political groups will need careful defining.

The codes of conduct for local authority members and officers cover the relationships between them and this is discussed in Chapter 30 below.

Serving Cabinet, Scrutiny and the Council

[29.4]
Chapter 8 of the DETR (DTLR) *Guidance on New Council Constitutions* provides advice on the arrangement of officer support under the provisions introduced under Pt II of the Local Government Act 2000. In particular it gives advice on support for the council, cabinet and overview and scrutiny committees. Figure 8.1 of the Guidance gives some examples of effective officer support for various member roles.

The Guidance sets out the following principles:

Paragraph 8.27 – says that 'in organising support for the executive, local authorities will need to *take into account the potential for tension between chief officers and cabinet members with portfolios*. It may be helpful to arrange the officer and member responsibilities so that they are not exactly coincident'. Many local authorities have reviewed their officer structures along with the introduction of new democratic arrangements. Practice inevitably varies, but it is not uncommon for the top management team to be small in number with the members of the team either having a range of service responsibilities, which may change from time to time, or indeed no fixed service responsibilities at all. The emphasis in all cases is on creating a corporate approach to the management of the authority, and the dangers of the service responsibilities of individual cabinet members and chief officers coinciding exactly have been greatly reduced or removed altogether by such arrangements.

Paragraph 8.28 – says that 'changing the local authority's member structures should, in many local authorities, provide an opportunity to *restructure the officer corps* to support members more effectively and, more importantly, to deliver more efficient and effective services'. As referred to in the above paragraph, such restructuring is taking place on a wide-scale, with the emphasis normally being placed on a corporate approach at the top of the officer structure with service heads reporting either to the top team as a whole or to individual members of that team. The day-to-day relationship in such a structure is more likely to be between the cabinet member with an individual portfolio for a service and the service head rather than between the member and a member of the top officer team. Relationships within the top officer team (and with the executive) may present particular problems for statutory officers such as the monitoring officer who owe a personal duty in law to the council as a whole.

Paragraph 8.29 – says that 'local authorities should develop *appropriate conventions* setting out the roles, responsibilities and rights of officers and establishing the key principles governing officer/member relationships'. This could be done as part of a locally developed code of conduct for officers (and members) based on the statutory codes (see Chapter 30 below). The conventions should cover inter alia:

- how and when members can ask officers for information;
- the arrangements for officers attending executive and cabinet meetings;
- how overview and scrutiny committees can require the attendance of officers; and
- if and how officers could be asked to advise political groups.

As regards support to the executive, the DETR (DTLR) Guidance gives the example of the chief executive attending every meeting of the cabinet and arranging for chief officer attendance as necessary for items on the agenda. Officers in general may attend any meeting in order to have an understanding of political priorities and the debate around them. Councils may wish to ensure that statutory officers such as the monitoring officer have access to all such meetings.

Paragraph 8.30 – says that 'overview and scrutiny committees need properly resourced and effective support. Where the same officers are supporting both the executive and overview and scrutiny committees there is potential for conflict – overview and scrutiny committees will be questioning the executive's decisions which will have been based on officer advice. This might discourage officers from pointing an overview and scrutiny committee to fruitful lines of enquiry. Local authorities will need to draw up procedures for resolving such conflicts of interest'. Procedures should cover inter alia:

- the arrangements for providing administrative support to executive/ cabinet and overview/scrutiny meetings – eg the roles of cabinet secretaries and scrutiny secretaries and their staff;
- the arrangements for scrutiny committees to know the professional advice that was given to the cabinet;
- the arrangements for scrutiny committees to have access to documents considered by executive/cabinet; and
- assurances to officers that their professional integrity in advising both executive/cabinet and scrutiny committees will be respected.

The DETR (DTLR) Guidance gives the example of an authority appointing a chief officer or senior manager to support overview and scrutiny. Some local authorities have identifiable teams supporting overview and scrutiny. Roles vary from traditional secretariat functions to strong advice and leadership in selecting what the DETR (DTLR) describes as 'fruitful issues' for review and scrutiny and in establishing review processes. One local authority has used an independent facilitator to assist overview and scrutiny committees. Another large metropolitan authority has a combined officer team supporting both Best Value and Overview and Scrutiny.

Paragraph 8.31 – makes the point that 'the Secretary of State does not believe that a formal separation of officer support between the executive and overview and scrutiny is necessary. The Secretary of State recognises that, particularly in smaller authorities, it may not be possible to separate support in this way. Local authorities should, however, consider whether some separation of officer support is appropriate when considering how to support overview and scrutiny committees effectively'. The developing practice amongst authorities seems to point to a number not separating the roles in this way. One reason for this is the professional tension that may arise between officers in the same service area who could have separate responsibilities for advising the executive and scrutiny committee.

Paragraph 8.32 – says that where an authority does decide to separate officer support, 'it should ensure that there is appropriate exchange of staff between those supporting overview and scrutiny and others and that all staff have rewarding career development opportunities'.

Paragraph 8.33 – says that 'similar conflict may occur for officers supporting both the full council and the executive, particularly in the budget and policy setting process'. Practice so far points to most authorities not choosing to make such a separation of roles, although the DETR (DTLR) Guidance says that in some cases it might be appropriate for there to be dedicated support for the full council, although it does not give examples where this could be necessary.

There will still be a continuing need for support for elected members' local roles, and as the DETR (DTLR) Guidance points out, many have teams to support members' representational roles. These can vary from basic administrative support to personal assistants for small groups of members.

Best Value and Employment

[29.5]

Under s 3 of the Local Government Act 1999, Best Value local authorities are required, with effect from 1 April 2000, to make arrangements to secure continuous improvement in the way in which their functions are exercised, having regard to a combination of economy, efficiency and effectiveness. The implications for local government employment of Best Value is a subject in its own and cannot be dealt with in full in this publication. What will be attempted here is a study of those aspects of the modernisation agenda and the Local Government Act 2000 which impact most on Best Value from the point of view of the workforce.

The government has defined Best Value as a duty to deliver services to clear standards – covering both cost and quality – by the most economic, efficient and effective means available. This represents a challenging new performance framework for local authorities. Best Value local authorities will be required to:

- publish annual *Best Value performance plans* that report on past and current performance and identify forward plans, priorities and targets for improvement; and
- review all of their functions over a five year cycle.

Best Value will require local authorities to ask themselves fundamental questions about the underlying objectives and priorities of their work and about their performance in relation to other organisations in the public, private and voluntary sectors. In addition, Best Value will require authorities to consult with local residents and the users of local services about their views and priorities.

The government will require local authorities, including parish councils with budgeted incomes over £500,000, to publish an annual Best Value performance plan (BVPP) by 31 March every year, covering the entire range of the authority's functions. The BVPP will be a key public document that identifies each authority's assessment of its past and current performance against nationally and locally defined standards and targets, and its vision of future priorities and targets for improvement. It will also set out a programme of Best Value reviews scrutinising all of the authority's functions over a period of five years. The BVPP will be the main instrument by which authorities will be held accountable by the local community for delivering Best Value.

Circular 10/99, published in December 1999, sets out statutory guidance on Best Value. Whilst the guidance stresses that one aim of Best Value is to ensure that public services are responsive to the needs of citizens, not the convenience of service providers (para 5), it also makes the point (at para 84) that the government recognises the importance of fair employment and that a well-motivated and well-trained workforce is vital to the provision of public services, whether the workforce is employed in the public, private or voluntary sectors. Sustained improvement under Best Value depends on employees being committed to providing the public with high quality and cost-effective services.

The review process must use the so-called 4Cs – challenge, compare, consult and compete – as a framework.

Under the third C, the authority has to **consult** with a range of relevant 'persons', including, under s 3(2)(*d*), 'representatives of persons appearing to the authority to have an interest in any area within which the authority carries out functions'. The duty to consult should therefore be assumed to include the workforce and their representatives, including the recognised trade unions.

Perhaps the most important aspect is the wish of government for local authorities to enter into partnership with providers from the public, private and voluntary sectors and what this might mean for the workforce. But whatever model for Best Value is chosen, it is essential that the workforce and its representatives are fully consulted throughout the process. The law requires consultation on certain issues, eg potential redundancies and transfers under TUPE, whilst good practice demands consultation on other areas such as organisation of work, performance management etc.

This part of the Chapter will concentrate on the areas of partnership, outsourcing and the role of the workforce in Best Value. Amongst other sources, acknowledgement is given in particular to the publication by the East Midlands Provincial Council on Employee Involvement in Best Value (2001).

Role of the workforce

[29.6]
In its Guidance on Best Value (Circular 10/99), the DETR stresses the important role to be played by employees in the Best Value process. As already stated, para 84 of the Guidance says that sustained improvement under Best Value depends on employees being committed to providing the public with high quality and cost-effective services, and that a well-motivated and well-trained workforce is vital to the provision of public services.

Council employees have a number of important roles to play in the Best Value process, including as:

* managers;
* service providers;
* trade unionists;
* employee representatives; and
* users of council services.

Managers have an obvious role including participating in service reviews, meeting Best Value performance indicators, motivating, encouraging and supporting employees, and considering and implementing service delivery changes.

Paragraph 17 of the DETR (DTLR) Guidance on Best Value stresses the need for reviews to involve those currently delivering services, the **service**

providers. This applies to all employees, but particularly to frontline staff whose experience of face-to-face contact with the public and service users can bring an important perspective as to how a service is perceived and valued, and how it can be improved. The DETR (DTLR) acknowledges that the support of employees is critical to successful implementation of Best Value reviews.

Trade union representatives will have a legitimate role in seeking to safeguard the position of their members during times of review and change, especially in respect of staffing levels, the quality of employment, including terms and conditions, equalities and training needs. UNISON points out in its *Best Value Toolkit* that Best Value can have either a positive or negative impact on jobs and the quality of employment for employees. It could mean one or a combination of the following:

- new organisation and management culture;
- integration of services;
- increased focus on performance;
- increased inspection and auditing;
- changes to working practices and procedures;
- changes in responsibility;
- more rapid use of information and communications technology (ICT);
- generic working; and
- transfer, externalisation and privatisation.

Employee representatives will have a vital role to play in review teams in assessing the impact of proposed changes to the organisation and operation of services and functions and to represent the views of service providers.

The local authority is often the largest employer in the area and its employees are major **users of its services**. Their experience can be fed back into the review process and it is helpful if authorities make arrangements for this to happen.

As relationships between the council and its employees and trade unions are vital for the success of Best Value, formal arrangements, or 'protocols', for consultation, information and communications generally may be helpful.

The NJC for Local Government Services (document available from the Employers Organisation or UNISON web-sites and attached as an Appendix to the UNISON Toolkit) and the JNC for Local Authority Craft and Associated Employees (as set out in Circular CR 5/00) have both adopted *Framework Agreements* for dealing with employee relations issues surrounding Best Value. The NJC and JNC encourage local authorities to enter into local negotiations on Best Value in the spirit of the Framework Agreements and the agreements could form the basis of any locally agreed protocols.

Any protocol should recognise the following key elements of the national Framework Agreements and that to succeed Best Value needs the active support of the workforce. To gain this it is essential:

- that employers and trade unions work together in co-operation, based on a clear commitment to high quality services to the community;

- that employees and their unions are involved at the start and throughout the process of review, eg as members of review teams;
- that employees and their unions are provided with appropriate training to enable them to be effective in their new role;
- that employees and their trade unions are involved in the process of consulting the community;
- that employees and their unions are involved in the implementation of the outcome of Best Value reviews;
- to ensure that employees are treated fairly and that Best Value is not used as a mechanism to drive down terms and conditions of service;
- the approach should be seen as a partnership to achieve quality services provided by a quality workforce.

Any protocol should also detail the arrangements for:

- *consulting* with the workforce through existing joint-machinery and/or specially established consultation forums, including the provision of appropriate financial information;
- keeping the workforce *informed* through bulletins, newsletters, videos, meetings etc, with special regard to keeping the 'hard to reach' employees, eg part-time peripatetic workers, up to date with developments. It is also important that managers review their usual consultation and communication channels to ensure that they are not excluding any particular group that may be under-represented in the normal processes;
- seeking the *views of employees* through attitude and employee satisfaction surveys, suggestion schemes, focus groups etc. Employees and their representatives could be involved in the design and analysis of such surveys;
- detailing the arrangements for identifying training and learning needs of employees, in particular the acquisition of additional skills to enhance the flexibility of the workforce.

Locally agreed protocols, whether or not based on the national Framework Agreement, should be kept under review to ensure that they are working effectively and meeting the needs of the council and its employees.

Partnerships and out-sourcing

[29.7]
In its Guidance on Best Value, the government makes the following points:

- the government recognises the importance of fair employment and that a well-motivated and well-trained workforce is vital to the provision of public services whether employed in the public, private or voluntary sectors. Sustained improvement under Best Value depends on employees being committed to providing the public with high quality and cost-effective services;

- getting the best from employees and maximising the potential of the labour market generally involves more than compliance with minimum standards. It also depends on a positive and effective approach to equal opportunities;
- new forms of partnership with the private and voluntary sectors and other public bodies will co-exist with, and often supersede, the way in which authorities have tendered previously. In either case, if it is to be effective, competition must be fair and conducted in a spirit where employees' rights are fully respected.

Guiding principles

[29.8]
These points are underlined in the Cabinet Office *Statement of Practice on Staff Transfers in the Public Sector*, published in January 2000, which sets out the following three guiding principles relating to employment and partnerships:

- the government is committed to ensuring that the public sector is a good employer and a model contractor and client. The people employed in the public sector, directly and indirectly, are its biggest asset and critical in developing modern, high quality, efficient, responsive, customer focused and environmentally friendly public services;
- the government's approach to public services is a pragmatic one, based on finding the best supplier who can deliver quality services and value for money for the taxpayer. This involves some services or functions being provided by, or in partnership with, the private or voluntary sector, or restructured and organised in a new way within the public sector. The involvement, commitment and motivation of employees are vital for achieving smooth and seamless transition during such organisational change.
- Public/Private Partnerships and the process of modernisation through organisational change in the public sector will best be achieved by clarity and certainty about the treatment of the employees involved. The government is committed to ensuring that employees involved in all such transfers are treated fairly and consistently and their rights respected. In the government's view this will encourage a co-operative, partnership approach to the modernisation of the public sector with consequential benefits for all citizens.

It is clear therefore that the government expects local authorities to enter into partnerships and outsource services where appropriate, and although local government has had a long history of using outside suppliers to provide services, the expectation is that this will grow as the Best Value regime develops. Partnerships and outsourcing clearly have a major impact on the employees concerned who may transfer to the new provider, and the government is anxious to take 'the fear out of transfer'. It is seeking to do this through a number of ways:

- strengthening TUPE;
- guidance on public sector transfers;
- safeguarding the pension provision of those transferred;
- ensuring that the new provider employs workers on fair terms and conditions.

TUPE

[29.9]

The Transfer of Undertakings (Protection of Employment) Regulations 1981, SI 1981/1794 ('TUPE') (as amended) arose from the need for the UK to implement the European Acquired Rights Directive (ARD). Originally TUPE applied only to transfers that were in the nature of a commercial venture, but the regulations were changed some years ago to allow for public sector transfers to be covered, at least in principle.

In 1998 the EC adopted a revised Acquired Rights Directive (Council Directive No 98/50/EC) which made a number of changes to the previous provisions, including clarifying when a relevant transfer takes place for the purposes of the Directive and allowing Member States to include occupational pensions within the contractual terms that transfer. The UK Government has to implement the revised ARD by July 2001, but so far formal proposals have not yet been put forward. The following summary is therefore correct at the time of writing.

TUPE requires that where there is a relevant transfer of an undertaking, the employees employed in that undertaking must transfer from their current employer (the transferor) to the new employer (the transferee) on their existing terms and conditions of service (at present with the exception of occupational pensions). Any dismissal of employees for a reason connected with the transfer is automatically unfair unless it is for an economic, technical or organisational (ETO) reason. The transferee cannot lawfully change the terms and conditions of the transferred employees, even with their consent, if the reason for the change is connected with the transfer, unless it is for an ETO reason.

Before the transfer takes place, both the transferee and the transferor must consult with the accredited representatives of the employees (usually trade union representatives) on the impact of the transfer and the effect it will have on the workforce.

The case-law at both UK and European level on TUPE and the ARD is some of the most complex in employment legislation, and it is not possible here to go into detail. But it is now generally agreed that a transfer involving public sector employees will be covered by TUPE so long as the entity is in the nature of an economic activity (which does not necessarily have to make a profit). In practice, the activities of a local authority which are capable of forming the basis of a partnership or outsourcing contract will meet the definition of economic activity.

But in order to avoid uncertainty, the Cabinet Office has issued guidance on the transfers of staff in the public sector.

Cabinet Office Statement

[29.10]
The Cabinet Office *Statement of Practice on Staff Transfers in the Public Sector* was published on 7 January 2000, and is available on the Internet at http://www.cabinet-office.gov.uk/civilservice/2000/tupe.

The statement sets out a framework on TUPE that the government expects all public sector organisations to work within. The statement says that, with the support of the public, private and voluntary sectors, and employee representatives, TUPE should, with some genuine exceptional circumstances, apply to all general situations where a service is:

- contracted out;
- re-tendered and brought back into the public sector;
- transferred within the public sector; or
- restructured and organised in a new way in a different part of the public sector.

Where TUPE may not strictly apply in law (eg to certain types of transfer between different parts of the public sector), the principles of TUPE should still be followed.

Although at the time of writing **pensions** have yet to be brought within the remit of TUPE itself, the Cabinet Office statement says that there should be appropriate arrangements to protect occupational schemes, redundancy and severance terms where transfers take place. Attached as an Annex to the statement is the Treasury Statement of Practice on transfers and pensions *A Fair Deal for Staff Pensions*, published on 14 June 1999. There is now statutory provision for the admission of private contractors to the Local Government Pension Scheme (LGPS) through the LGPS (Amendment etc) Regulations 1999 (see below).

The government intends the statement to be followed by local government, subject to the duty of Best Value being complied with. The statement stresses the support of the Personnel and Human Resources Panel of the Local Government Association for the principles contained in the statement, and its encouragement of their adoption by individual local authorities.

As far as **public private partnerships** are concerned, the statement makes the point that the strict legal application of the TUPE regulations will be a matter of law based on the facts, but that the parties should through the contracting exercise make it clear that TUPE should apply and potential bidders should be advised accordingly. This does not prevent potential bidders from making a non-TUPE bid, but if they do so they will need to make it clear that it falls within one of the 'exceptional circumstances' summarised below. If TUPE does not apply, then the statement makes it clear that redundancy and redeployment costs will need to be taken into account in assessing such a bid. Where there is a contractual requirement that TUPE should apply (presumably once the contract has been awarded), then the requirements of TUPE must be 'scrupulously' followed.

In essence, the same principles apply to second and subsequent transfers and transfers back into the public sector as with private public partnerships. The application of TUPE will be the norm, unless there are exceptional circumstances.

The statement lists the **exceptions** to the application of TUPE in 'a small number of cases' that may arise. There must be 'genuinely exceptionally reasons' why this should be the case. The circumstances that may qualify for such exceptions are broadly as follows:

- where a contract is for the provision of both goods and services, but the provision of services is ancillary to the purpose to the provision of the goods; or
- where the activity for which the public sector organisation is contracting is essentially a new or a one off project; or
- where services are essentially a commodity bought 'off the shelf' and no grouping of staff are specifically and permanently assigned a common task; or
- where the features of the service or function subject to the contracting exercise are significantly different from the features of the function previously performed within the public sector, or by an existing contractor, eg a function to be delivered electronically and in such a way that it requires radically different skills, experience and equipment.

Where TUPE does not apply because of one of the above exceptions, then in the case of so-called 'first generation' contracts, the public sector organisation should seek to identify with the contractor any staff that the contractor will take on voluntarily, and seek where possible to redeploy the remainder within the public sector organisation.

Whilst TUPE as currently drafted does not include **occupational pensions**, the Cabinet Office Guidance makes it clear that in transfers involving local government employees their pension position should be protected. To this effect, the government have passed the Local Government Pension Scheme (Amendment etc) Regulations 1999[1] which came into force on 13 January 2000 and which were amended by the Local Government Pension Scheme (Amendment) Regulations 2000[2].

The regulations as amended contain provisions relating to admitted bodies. In particular, subject to certain conditions being met, they allow for employees transferred from a local authority to a private contractor under a Best Value arrangement to remain in the LGPS if the private contractor seeks and obtains admitted body status.

The main points of the regulations are as follows:

- a private contractor is defined as a body which provides services or assets referred to in a Best Value arrangement or part of such services or assets;
- a 'Best Value arrangement' means a contract or other arrangement made with a local authority for the provision of, or making available of, services or assets, for the purposes of, or in connection with, the exercise of a function of that authority. In practice, this would seem to cover most if not all outsourcing arrangements;

- a contractor may choose to apply for admitted body status. The authority cannot make the application of admitted body status a condition of the contract as such. But under Best Value guidance, if a contractor chooses not to apply for admitted body status, the contractor must provide a broadly comparable pension scheme;
- where the local authority entering into the admission agreement with the contractor is not an Administering Authority, the authority must be a party to the admission agreement along with the relevant Administering Authority;
- a private contractor seeking admitted body status will be required to provide an indemnity or bond in an approved form and with an authorised insurer or a relevant institution;
- under the admission agreement the transferred employees will remain in the LGPS on transfer, although they are of course free to make other appropriate pension arrangements if they so wish;
- the admission agreement can apply only in respect of employees who transfer from the local authority to the contractor (it cannot apply to existing members of the contractor's workforce) and will continue to apply all the while the transferred employee is employed in connection with the provision of services or assets referred to in the Best Value arrangement.

The above is a summary of the effect of the regulations. The Local Government Pensions Committee have issued detailed guidance on the issue which is available from the Employers Organisation.

Non-commercial matters

[29.11]
Under the CCT regime, local authorities were not allowed under the Local Government Act 1988 to take into account **non-commercial matters** when awarding contracts, and the personnel policies and practices of the contractor were regarded as a non-commercial matter. Through an Order made under the Local Government Act 2000, the 1988 Act has been changed and allows so-called workforce matters to be taken into account by local authorities when entering into partnerships or outsourcing services as part of Best Value.

DETR Circular 02/2001 dated 15 March 2001 contains guidance on the handling of workforce matters and contracting. It follows the Local Government Best Value (Exclusion of Non-commercial Considerations Order) 2001[3] which came into force on 13 March 2001. The regulations permit local authorities to take workforce matters into account when awarding contracts under Best Value (in its broadest sense).

The regulations provide for certain matters to cease to be non-commercial matters for the purposes of s 17 of the Local Government Act 1988. The matters concerned relate to the terms and conditions of employment etc. of a contractor's workforce, and the conduct of contractors or their workers in internal disputes. However, those matters cease to be non-commercial matters only so far as necessary or expedient to permit compliance with Best Value or where there is a transfer of staff under TUPE.

The Order applies to all Best Value authorities in England and police and fire authorities in Wales. (At the time of writing, similar regulations are expected to come into force in respect of Best Value authorities in Wales.)

The Circular's section on principles of procurement (Pt 2) identifies some of the matters which authorities will need to examine in tendering procedures under Best Value including:

- the connection between service quality and appropriately skilled and motivated workforces;
- the need to keep a proper balance between quality and cost, which recognises that driving down workforce costs too far will have an adverse effect on service to customers;
- the need for transparent tendering procedures which make clear how a judgment will be made of what constitutes the optimum combination of cost and quality;
- the scope for continuous improvement in the way in which the contract is structured;
- the relevance of equal opportunities to the delivery of contracts;
- the need to ensure that TUPE and associated workforce communication and consultation issues are properly handled.

Taking account of these matters (along with other non-workforce matters) will mean that the council is likely to select the 'most economically advantageous' tender rather than necessarily the lowest priced one.

If an authority is going to look at workforce matters, it follows that tenderers should:

- be asked to provide sufficient information about the competence of their workforce, without such a requirement being too onerous;
- be told about how competence and other issues will be assessed, and about what information they will be expected to provide and what service standards will be expected;
- be given some scope to propose different ways about how the service could be provided;
- be fully aware of the basis on which bids will be judged, and the stages in the bidding process;
- have access to the council's written policy on tender evaluation, which should be a public document.

Any in house bid must be judged on exactly the same basis as bids from outside contractors.

The core 'guidance' section of the Circular (Pt 3) looks at how workforce matters can be take into account at each of the following stages:

- pre-qualification to tender;
- service specification and conditions of contract;

- invitation to tender;
- tender evaluation;
- contract management.

In compiling a short-list of contractors capable of performing the contract at the **pre-qualification stage**, a council should be looking only at the contractor's personal standing, economic and financial standing, technical capacity, and, for service contracts, ability. Thus workforce questions at this stage should focus on:

- the contractor's experience and track record in providing similar services over the last three years (or five years for works contracts);
- the contractor's procedures (including accreditation and documentation) relating to health and safety (including policies on detailed issues relating to the work concerned), equal opportunity practices (provided these are relevant to the delivery of the services in the contract), HR procedures (staff management and employment practices) relevant to the contract - this would include details of the staff involved in the provision of the service in question, their qualifications and training, and the contractors TUPE track record;
- any convictions relating to the conduct of the contractor's business, including findings by a Tribunal of breaches of employment protection, discrimination or health and safety requirements.

On racial equality matters, councils are still free to ask the '6 questions' set out in DoE Circular 8/88, but they are no longer restricted to these questions and may be able to ask about other matters on racial equality which are relevant to the contracted services.

A local authority's aim at the **service specifications and conditions of contract stage** should relate to quality levels for the work. As such it may incorporate staff management practices which help create a suitably skilled and motivated workforce. These should be specified in terms of output or performance. Requirements to meet national standards will be useful in this context, but care must be taken not to infringe EU procurement rules by seeking compliance with UK standards: contractors should be given an opportunity to indicate that they meet equivalent, non-UK, standards. Again the standards being sought must be relevant and proportionate to the services in question. Any specific requirements for attributes relating to fair treatment and equal opportunities must be set out clearly at this stage – they must relate to outputs (so that inputs, such as the ethnic composition of a contractors workforce could not be specified), but they could include a requirement to meet any existing equalities policies or procedures affecting the service in question.

At the **invitation to tender stage**, councils should give very clear instructions about information to be included with their bid. This may well include a plan for how transfer/TUPE matters will be handled; and staff training and development plans (linked to improving the service over the life of the contract).

The tender evaluation stage should not be a re-run of the pre-qualification stage, but should focus on examining and clarifying the bidders' response to the requirements on workforce matters set out in the invitation to tender, including any relating to equal opportunities. As such, they must relate to the bidders ability to deliver the service in question.

Monitoring of workforce matters at the contract management stage should focus on those matters identified as relevant to the performance of the contract, compliance with statutory and regulatory requirements. They should be monitored in the same way and at the same time as other aspects of the contractor's performance. On equalities, there may be scope for the authority to work with the contractor to consider how good practice can be promoted during the life of the contract.

SOCPO and SOLACE have published a joint-guide entitled *Public/Private Partnerships – the HR Dimension* which as well as summarising the background to the government's current policy on partnership, includes a model questionnaire on workforce matters for completion by prospective external providers.

1   SI 1999/3438.
2   SI 2000/1005.
3   SI 2001/909.

CHAPTER 30
Codes of Conduct

Existing Provisions for Employees

[30.1]
The highest standards of behaviour are expected from those who are employed in local government, and these have long been reflected in both national conditions of service and the law in general. Before the Local Government Act 2000, they have also been contained in a Code of Conduct for Local Government Employees, which applies to England and Wales, was issued in 1994 by the Local Government Management Board (LGMB) (now the Employers Organisation (EO)), and the then Association of County Councils (ACC), the Association of District Councils (ADC) and the Association of Metropolitan Authorities (AMA) (now the Local Government Association (LGA)).

The code outlines existing laws, regulations and conditions of service and provides further guidance to assist local authorities and their employees in their day-to-day work. The code was voluntary in status, and some authorities adopted separate provisions relating to official conduct. The Code is reproduced at Division VI – Appendix 21 below.

Apart from codes of conduct, there are other provisions which relate to official conduct of local government employees. Under s 117 of the Local Government Act 1972, an officer who knows about a contract in which he or she has a pecuniary interest must give notice of that interest to the authority. Section 117(2) forbids an officer 'under colour of his office or employment' from accepting 'any fee or reward' whatsoever other than proper remuneration.

Under the Prevention of Corruption Acts 1906 and 1916 it is an offence for employees in public service, including local government, corruptly to receive any gifts or consideration as an inducement or reward from doing, or refraining from doing, anything in their official capacity or showing favour or disfavour to any person in their official capacity. In addition, under the 1916 Act, any money, gift or consideration received by an employee in public service from a person or organisation holding or seeking to obtain a contract will be deemed by the courts to have been received corruptly, unless the employee proves to the contrary.

The former Scheme of Conditions of Service of the National Joint-Council for Local Authorities' Administrative, Professional, Technical and Clerical Services (the 'Purple Book') contained detailed provisions on official conduct. These were replaced in 1997 by those set out in Section 2 of Pt 2 of the

National Agreement on Pay and Conditions of Service of the National Joint-Council for Local Government Services (the 'Green Book') by the statement that 'employees will maintain the highest standard such that public confidence in their integrity is sustained. Local codes of practice will be developed to cover the official conduct and the obligations of employees and employers'.

Code of Conduct for Members – Dealings with Employees

[30.2]
Section 49 of the Local Government Act 2000 provides for the Secretary of State to specify by order principles which are to govern the conduct of elected members and co-opted members or local authorities. The government has consulted on a set of principles and the Local Government Association has given advice to the government on the content of a Model Code for members. Once the Model Code is issued, s 51 of the Local Government Act requires all relevant authorities to adopt a local code of conduct, incorporating any mandatory elements of the Model Code, within six months from the date of the order issuing the Model Code.

The Code has been issued under the Relevant Authorities (Model Code of Conduct) Order 2001, and came into force in July 2001. Most of the provisions of the code relate to the activities of elected members in their representational capacity, and are not directly relevant to this part of this Division, but a number do impact on their relationship with local authority employees.

A key obligation is set out in the seventh general principle relating to members' conduct. This says that a member must promote equality by **not discriminating unlawfully against any person and by treating people with respect**, regardless of their race, age, religion, gender, sexual orientation or disability. Members should respect the impartiality and integrity of the authority's statutory officers and its other employees.

This obligation is reflected in para 2(*a*) of the Code which repeats the principles that a member must promote equality by not discriminating unlawfully against any person and by treating people with respect, regardless of their race, age, religion, gender, sexual orientation or disability. 'Any person' includes any employee of the council and so an important provision of the code is that elected members treat employees with respect and do not discriminate unlawfully against them. In any claim by an employee against their authority, a breach of this provision by an elected member could lead to a claim of constructive dismissal, and/or be used in evidence against the authority in, say, a claim for unfair dismissal. This will be especially relevant in the relationships between elected members and senior officers.

Paragraph 2(*b*) goes on to say that a member must not do anything **which compromises or which is likely to compromise the impartiality of an employee** of the authority. This reinforces the requirement on employees to serve the council as a whole and act without political bias.

Paragraph 3 provides that a member must **not disclose information given in confidence** by anyone without the consent of that person, or unless the member is required by law to do so. 'That person' will include any local authority employee who provides a member with confidential information and it would be advisable for authorities to draw up a procedure for the supply of information, including confidential information, by employees to members. In particular, local authorities should make clear the status of information contained in reports to members.

Paragraph 5(*a*) says that a member must not in his/her official capacity use his/her position improperly to confer or secure for any person an advantage or disadvantage. This would include the improper influencing of decision in relation to employees including their appointment, training, pay and conditions, any grievance they might bring, any disciplinary action taken against them, including dismissal, and the terms on which the employee leaves the council's service.

Paragraph 6 of the code covers **advice from statutory officers**. It provides that a member must have regard to any relevant advice provided to him/her by the authority's chief finance officer acting in pursuance of s 114 of the Local Government Finance Act 1988[1], and the authority's monitoring officer in pursuance of his/her duties under s 5 of the Local Government and Housing Act 1989[2].

Paragraph 7 says that a member must report to the Standards Board for England and the council's monitoring officer any conduct by another member which he/she believes involves a failure to comply with the authority's code of conduct. Authorities may wish to draw up a procedure for members to report such matters to the monitoring officer. This might usefully include protocols for dealing with complaints or expressions of concern about possible misconduct which falls short of a 'belief' that misconduct has taken place.

Part 3 of the Code covers the register of members' interests which must be notified to the monitoring officer. Again, authorities may wish to draw up a procedure for members to notify the monitoring officer of any such interests.

1   See para 6(*b*)(i) of the Code.
2   See para 6(*b*)(ii) of the Code.

Code of Conduct for Employees

[30.3]
Until the passing of the Local Government Act 2000, there had been no statutory code of conduct for local government employees. As referred to above, the various national conditions of service had contained provisions relating to official conduct and the local authority associations adopted a model code in 1994, although this does not have the force of law. Many local authorities developed codes of conduct, often based on the national model code, and a breach of the provisions of the code might constitute misconduct (or even gross misconduct) for the purposes of the disciplinary procedure.

However, under s 82 (1) of the Local Government Act 2000, the Secretary of State may by order issue a code as regards the conduct which is expected of qualifying employees of relevant authorities in England and police authorities in Wales. Under s 82(2), a similar order has been issued by the National Assembly for Wales in respect of employees of local authorities in Wales.

Under s 82(8) 'qualifying employees' includes all employees with the possible exception of council managers, for whom a separate code may be issued under s 82(3)(*a*).

'Relevant authority' is defined in s 49(6) of the Act. It means:

- a county council;
- a county borough council;
- a district council;
- a London borough council;
- a parish council;
- a community council;
- the Greater London Authority;
- the Metropolitan Police Authority;
- the London Fire and Emergency Planning Authority;
- the Common Council of the City of London in its capacity as a local authority or police authority;
- the Council of the Isles of Scilly;
- a fire authority constituted by a combination scheme under the Fire Services Act 1947;
- a police authority;
- a joint-authority established by Pt IV of the Local Government Act 1985;
- the Broads Authority; or
- a National Park authority established under s 63 of the Environment Act 1995.

Section 82(7) of the Act provides that the terms or conditions of employment of every qualifying employee of a relevant authority – whether appointed or employed before or after the commencement of s 82 – are to be deemed to incorporate any code issued by order under the Act. Teachers and firefighters are excluded from the definition of 'qualifying employee' and are therefore not covered by the code. The incorporation of the code into the terms and conditions of employees is discussed in more detail at para **[30.6]** below.

Draft Code

[30.4]
At the time of writing (June 2001), the issuing and approval of a code of conduct for employees has been delayed, partly by the General Election held on 7 June 2001. A draft has however been discussed by the partners' working party established by the Local Government Association, the Employers' Organisation and the local government trade unions (UNISON, TGWU, GMB, ALACE and MPO).

The partners' working party took the view that although the voluntary code published by the Associations and the LGMB in 1994 had been adopted in some form by around 90% of local authorities in England and Wales, it was not an ideal model for a statutory code. This was because the voluntary code was a mixture of statutory requirements, good practice and exhortation. The working party took the view that a statutory code needed to be a more focussed document, concentrating on the essential elements of conduct.

Nevertheless, the working party thought that the voluntary code did provide a valuable starting point by highlighting several of the basic elements of a statutory code. In addition, the working party was conscious of the need to take account of the parallel work on the model code of conduct for members (see above), and in certain areas, eg relations between members and employees, there was a need for a consistent approach between the two codes. The experience of the voluntary code, and the work on the elected members' code, shaped the core provisions of the draft employees' code. These are:

- **General principles** – a short overall statement on the qualities expected of local authority employees in undertaking their duties; followed by further short statements on specific aspects of conduct.
- **Accountability** – an important statement on the duty owed by the employee to the whole of the authority, particularly in the context of the move to new political management arrangements in many authorities.
- **Political Neutrality** – a re-statement of an essential principle of public sector employment.
- **Relations with Councillors, the public and other employees** – a recognition that good relationships are essential for an effective public service.
- **Stewardship** – reflects the importance to be given to the appropriate use of public funds and resources.
- **Personal Interests** – emphasises the need in public services to make a clear and transparent separation between an employee's public duties and private interests.
- **Whistle-blowing** (see Chapter 33 below) – recognises that every employee has a responsibility to play a part in bringing to the attention of the employing authority illegalities or unethical conduct. (It should be noted that the working party is of the view that whilst code of conduct for elected members provides that a member must report to the Standards Board for England and to the authority's monitoring officer any conduct by another member which he/she believes involves a failure to comply with the authority's code of conduct, it does not consider that there should be a similar contractual duty through an employee's terms and conditions to report breaches of the employee code. This recognises the practical difficulties of legally enforcing such a provision.)
- **Treatment of Information** – a recognition of the requirement to be as open as possible, whilst recognising the need to maintain confidentiality in certain circumstances.
- **Appointment of Staff** – a specific requirement on a sometimes sensitive issue, serving to reinforce the basic requirement on employees to act impartially and to avoid furthering the interests of family or friends.

The draft has sought to identify the irreducible components of a statutory code covering expected standards of conduct. The working party has said that it is not intended to be comprehensive in specifying all the duties applying to employees in local government. Issues such as isolated incidents of neglect of duty, failure to follow reasonable instructions or other forms of misconduct will be covered by the council's disciplinary procedure. The working party expects that authorities might wish to supplement the statutory code to take account of local circumstances or extend it to employees not covered by the regulations (eg teachers, firefighters).

The code as drafted applies to all employees (excluding teachers and firefighters) of all local authorities, including parish and town councils, national park authorities, and civilian employees of police and fire authorities. But the working party has said that it would also like to see authorities extending the code to other externalised workers performing local government services (eg contractors, agency workers etc) under the Local Government Best Value (Exclusion of Non-commercial Considerations Order) 2001[1] and DETR (now DTLR) Circular 02/2001 in relation to the non-commercial workforce matters aspects of the Best Value procurement process.

The working party intends to produce guidance to supplement the statutory code to point the way to good practice on matters of conduct. The Employers' Organisation is also expected to produce a model code, building upon the statutory code, for adoption or modification by authorities.

The working party considers that the code addresses the essential elements of conduct which should be expected of a local government employee. The working party says that the elements of the code are not new, but draw upon the accepted conventions and best traditions of public service in local government.

1   SI 2001/909.

Welsh Code

[30.5]
Although the code for England is awaited, the code for employees in local authorities in Wales has been approved by Parliament. It is thought the English version will not differ significantly from this. The Welsh code is set out at Division VI – Appendix 22 below.

Incorporating the Code into Employment Contracts

[30.6]
As explained at para **[30.3]** above, s 82(7) of the Act provides that the terms or conditions of employment of every qualifying employee of a relevant authority are deemed to incorporate any code issued by order under the Act. This means that the provisions of the **statutory** code once approved by Parliament and brought into effect have automatic contractual force and the terms and conditions of all relevant employees amended accordingly.

However, it would be good practice for all affected employees to be notified of the change and provided with a copy of the code. This could be done through an advisory note contained with pay slips etc, although obviously an individual letter would be preferable.

But it is only the provisions of the statutory code that are automatically incorporated in this way. If the local authority wishes to adopt additional provisions to the statutory code – the statutory code is a mandatory minimum and must apply to all relevant employees – and give them contractual force, then the contracts of individual employees will need to be varied in the usual way. It should be made clear in any local code that it supplements/ incorporates, and does not replace, the statutory code.

It will also be necessary to agree changes to contracts with the employees, and/or their trade unions, if the statutory provisions are to be applied locally to excluded groups, such as teachers and fire-fighters.

An attempt to introduce changes to the contract without the consent of the other party will amount to a breach of contract which an employee can accept, for example by resigning and claiming constructive dismissal or by suing for damages arising from the breach. To succeed in a claim of constructive dismissal, the employee must show that there was a fundamental breach which went to the root of the employment relationship. As an alternative to claiming constructive dismissal, the employee may claim damages for breach of contract which will enable the individual to remain in employment. The damages payable will be calculated on the basis of the period during which the employer was in breach. If the employer purports to change the contract by issuing notice that the change will be implemented from a future date, this will merely be giving notice to the employee of the intention to breach the contract if the change is unilateral and outside any flexibility provided within the contract.

The employee may agree to the change sought by the employer, either expressly or by working on without protest and thereby agreeing impliedly, by conduct. If the employee continues to work without resistance he or she will be taken to have acquiesced to the change, and even though the employer is strictly speaking in breach, the employee will be taken to have waived the breach and will not be able to rely on it later, for example, to found a claim for damages.

Agreements reached with recognised trade unions are binding and enforceable against the individual, provided that there is an embodiment term in the contract whereby collective agreements are incorporated into the individual's contract of employment. By agreeing a change in terms and conditions in the collective bargaining forum, the employer effects the change for all employees within scope of the agreement. There is no need to agree the change with each employee individually, but the employer will be obliged to inform all employees of the change to their terms and conditions within one month under s 1 of the Employment Rights Act 1996 (ERA).

Where changes to contracts are made through collective agreement, which is the norm in local government, it would be advisable for any locally amended code of conduct to be collectively agreed with the recognised trade unions. The code will then have automatic contractual effect, although it will be necessary to let individuals know, perhaps through a note with the pay slip, of the change.

If the locally-amended code is not collectively agreed, it will be necessary to reach agreement with individual employees for the code to have contractual force, if the authority is to avoid being challenged in law (see above).

In any event, it would be good employee relations practice to gain the commitment of the recognised trade unions to any locally amended code (the trade unions are a party at national level to the statutory code). It would also facilitate the making of any breach of the code a disciplinary offence (see below).

Handling Breaches of the Code

[30.6]
As explained above, there have long been provisions in both national and local conditions of service relating to the official conduct of local government employees, although the statutory code issued under s 82 is the first time that the issue has been given the force of law as such. It is not suggested that special arrangements should be adopted for breaches of the statutory code. Such breaches will in effect be a breach of contract by the employee, should be regarded in the same way as any other such breach, and therefore dealt with under the council's disciplinary procedure.

It would be advisable however for the local disciplinary procedure to be amended to make it clear that breaches of the statutory code, and any local supplement, will be regarded as misconduct and dealt with under the disciplinary procedure. It should also be explained that serious breaches of the code(s) might constitute gross misconduct and could lead to the employee's dismissal without notice. Most local authority disciplinary procedures are collectively agreed with the recognised trade unions, and so the changes reflecting the statutory code should be agreed with the trade union side in the usual way. This in turn will mean that the contracts of individuals will have been changed automatically to reflect the revised disciplinary procedure.

CHAPTER 31
Changing Roles of Statutory Officers

Introduction

[31.1]
The Local Government Act 2000 makes changes to provisions relating to a number of the statutory officers of local authorities – the Head of the Paid Service (HAPS), the Monitoring Officer and the Finance Officer responsible for financial matters under s 151 of the Local Government Act 1972.

Head of Paid Service

[31.2]
Section 4(1) of the Local Government and Housing Act 1989 provides that every relevant local authority (as defined by s 21(1)) must designate on of their officers as head of their paid service (HAPS). 'Relevant authority' includes:

- a county council;
- a district council;
- a London borough council;
- the Common Council of the City of London in its capacity as a local authority, police authority or port health authority;
- the Council of the Isles of Scilly;
- a fire authority;
- a police authority;
- a joint-authority;
- a waste disposal authority; and
- the Broads authority.

There is no requirement on a parish or town council to designate an officer as head of paid service.

Section 4 the HAPS is to advise the council on:

(a) the manner in which the discharge by the authority of its different functions is co-ordinated;
(b) the number and grades of staff required by the authority for the discharge of its functions;
(c) the organisation of the authority's staff; and

(*d*)　the appointment and proper management of the authority's staff.

The authority must provide the HAPS with such staff, accommodation and other resources which are, in the opinion of the HAPS, sufficient to allow these duties to be carried out.

Whilst a relevant authority must designate an officer as the HAPS, there is no statutory requirement on a local authority to appoint a chief executive as such.

The Local Government Act 2000 makes one significant change to the designation of the HAPS. Paragraph 24 of Sch 5 of the Act provides that the officer designated as the council's Monitoring Officer under s 5(1) of the Local Government and Housing Act 1989 (see below) cannot also be the HAPS. So where currently the HAPS also acts as the Monitoring Officer, another officer will need to be designated as Monitoring Officer if the HAPS is to continue as head of the paid service.

In addition, where the council has adopted an executive arrangement involving a mayor and council manager, the council manager can be the HAPS (and chief executive) but cannot by virtue of para 13 of Sch 1 to the Local Government Act 2000 also be the monitoring officer or finance (s 151) officer.

But where the council has adopted the leader and cabinet model, the HAPS can be the s 151 Finance Officer (but not the monitoring officer).

Although there is still no statutory requirement for a local authority to appoint a chief executive, Chapter 8 of the DTLR (DETR) Guidance on New Council Constitutions says in para 8.1 that:

> 'a local authority operating executive arrangements should have a professional chief executive (who should be the statutory head of paid service, responsible for securing and managing the professional body of staff needed to deliver modern, effective, well focussed services'.

Paragraph 8.14 of the Guidance says that the core roles of the chief executive (who as stated should be the statutory head of paid service) should be:

- overall corporate management and operational responsibility (including overall management responsibility for all staff);
- the provision of professional advice to all parties in the decision-making process (the executive, overview and scrutiny, full council and other committees);
- together with the monitoring officer, responsibility for a system of record keeping for all the local authority's decisions (executive or otherwise); and
- representing the local authority on partnership and external bodies (as required by statute or the local authority).

These roles are underpinned by the fundamental principles of political neutrality and service to the whole council (see Chapter 29 above).

Monitoring Officer

[31.3]
Under s 5 of the Local Government and Housing Act 1989, every authority in England and Wales (excluding parish and community councils, but including joint-police and fire authorities) must designate an officer as monitoring officer. As with the HAPS, the authority must provide the monitoring officer with such staff, accommodation and other resources to allow the officer's statutory duties under s 5 to be performed. Local authorities have normally designated their legal officer or HAPS as monitoring officer. The Act prevents them, however from designating the chief financial officer as monitoring officer, and as referred to above, the Local Government Act 2000 now prevents the HAPS from also being designated as monitoring officer.

The monitoring officer's role is to report to the authority on any proposal, decision or omission by the authority or any of its committees, sub-committees or officers which has given rise to, is likely to or would give rise to, a breach of law or statutory code of practice or lead to a possible finding of maladministration by the ombudsman. In preparing his or her report, the monitoring officer must consult as far as practicable with the HAPS and the chief finance officer. The authority or relevant committee must consider the monitoring officer's report within 21 days of first receiving it, and must not take action in respect of the matter covered by the report whilst it is under consideration. To ignore a monitoring officer's report could lead to a finding of wilful misconduct against the members and/or officers involved.

As para 8.20 of the DTLR (DETR) Guidance points out, with the introduction of the ethical framework under Pt III of the Local Government Act 2000, there are significant changes to the role of the monitoring officer. The monitoring officer will have a key role in promoting and maintaining high standards of conduct within a local authority, in particular through provision of support to the local authority's Standards Committee. It is for this reason that the monitoring officer cannot be the HAPS (and therefore chief executive) or the council manager, where this model is adopted.

The DTLR Guidance (para 8.21) says that local authorities will need to recognise under executive arrangements the importance of the monitoring officer's key roles of providing advice on vires issues, maladministration, financial impropriety, probity and policy framework and budget issues to all members of the authority. The DTLR also says that the monitoring officer should be the proper officer for the purposes of ensuring that executive decisions, together with the reasons for those decisions and relevant officer reports and background papers, are made publicly available.

Section 5 of the Local Government and Housing Act 1989 is to be modified to provide that a monitoring officer's report about lawfulness or maladmin-istration should be to the executive where it relates to functions which are the responsibility of the executive, but that all members of the local authority should receive a copy of such a report. As is the current position with a monitoring officer's report under s 5, all action in respect of the matter in the report would be suspended until after the executive had considered the report. After considering the report the executive will have to make a report to the local authority on its consideration of the report and any action taken in consequence of it.

The Secretary of State recommends that where such a report is made, the relevant overview and scrutiny committee should consider whether it would be appropriate to hold a short enquiry into the matter which is the subject of the report, prior to the executive's consideration of it.

Chief Finance Officer

[31.4]
Section 151 of the Local Government Act 1972 requires every relevant local authority to 'make arrangements for the proper administration of their financial affairs and shall secure that one of their officers has responsibility for the administration of those affairs'. As with the monitoring officer, 'relevant authority' includes:

- a county council;
- a district council;
- a London borough council;
- the Common Council of the City of London in its capacity as a local authority, police authority or port health authority;
- the Council of the Isles of Scilly;
- a fire authority;
- a police authority;
- a joint-authority;
- a waste disposal authority; and
- the Broads authority.

The DTLR Guidance (para 8.24) says that local authorities will need to recognise under executive arrangements the importance of the chief finance officer's key roles of providing advice on vires issues, maladministration, financial impropriety, probity and policy framework and budget issues to all members of the local authority. The chief finance officer will also have an important role in the management of the local authority, in particular by:

- contributing to corporate management, in particular through the provision of sound professional financial advice;
- maintaining financial administration and stewardship;
- supporting and advising members and officers in their respective roles;
- providing financial information to the media, members of the public and the community.

Implications for Organisational Structures

[31.5]
Chapter One discusses the DTLR advice on the arrangement of officer support under the new arrangements. There are also a number of organisational issues which relate to the new roles of HAPS, monitoring officer and chief finance officer under the new arrangements.

Although the DTLR Guidance is firm in saying that a local authority should appoint a chief executive, a number of authorities have considered not having a chief executive as such on the grounds that it does not fit easily with the increased responsibilities the executive may have. Instead, they have nominated a lead chief officer as, 'primus inter pares', HAPS. This may either be an arrangement that goes with one particular post (eg Chief Finance Officer, although this would not be possible with the council manager model – which however by definition is a 'chief executive') or one that rotates between members of the corporate management team. It cannot however be given to the monitoring officer. It has to be acknowledged that authorities who in the past have decided against having a post of chief executive have tended to go back to the concept at a later date. It will be interesting to see how this issue develops I councils with a strong executive, especially a 'mayor with cabinet' model.

The increased responsibilities (and powers) of chief finance officers and particularly monitoring officers may have implications for their position within the officer management hierarchy. Before the coming into force of the Local Government Act 2000, there was a tendency for some local authorities to place the head of legal services (often the monitoring officer) and the chief finance officer at a head of service level, reporting to a corporate director. Whilst there is nothing specific in the new executive arrangements to prevent this from continuing, it may be difficult in practice for an officer at third tier (or below) to exercise their statutory powers with confidence. At the very least, it would seem sensible to ensure that the monitoring officer and chief finance officer are either members of, or in attendance at meetings of, the top corporate management team.

Disciplinary Provisions for Statutory Officers

[31.6]
There are special provisions in the national conditions of service for chief executives and chief officers relating to disciplinary matters, as negotiated by the relevant Joint-Negotiating Committees. These procedures are contractual where the terms and conditions of the JNCs have been incorporated into the contracts of employment of the officers concerned, and failure to abide by them may result in a finding of unfair or wrongful dismissal. In addition, if the procedures have not been complied with, the officer concerned and his or her trade union or other representative may seek a judicial review of the case.

In cases of disciplinary action against chief executives, it is necessary for an **Independent Person** to be appointed, in accordance with reg 3(1) of the Local Authorities (Standing Orders) Regulations 1993[1] once it has been decided that a full investigation should be carried out into the matter in question, after a preliminary investigation has been undertaken by a politically balanced group of not fewer than three elected members. If the parties cannot agree on an independent person, he or she is appointed by the Secretary of State. An independent person is not required to be appointed in cases of redundancy or permanent ill health. The statutory provisions have been incorporated into s 16 – Procedures for Redundancy, Capability and Discipline of the Handbook of the Joint-Negotiating Committee for Chief Executives of Local Authorities.

A local authority may suspend the chief executive on full pay pending an investigation into a disciplinary matter for two months, but the independent person has to agree to any suspension beyond that initial two-month period.

The independent person's role is to prepare a report on the matter. The authority is required to pay the independent person remuneration and any costs incurred by him or her in connection with the discharge of his or her functions under the regulations. The independent person shall, at his or her discretion, have power at any stage in the proceedings to act as follows, as he or she considers appropriate:

(1) to direct that no further steps (whether by the authority or any committee, sub-committee or officer of theirs) should be taken in respect of the disciplinary action proposed or contemplated;

(2) to direct that any suspension shall end, and the chief executive shall be reinstated;

(3) to direct that before the independent person has prepared his or her report no steps towards disciplinary action or further disciplinary action are to be taken against the chief executive, other than in the presence of, or with the agreement of, the independent person;

(4) to inspect any documents in the possession, or under the control, of the authority, and any other documents which any person is prepared to show to him or her;

(5) to require any employee of the authority to answer questions concerning the conduct of the chief executive providing that if any such employee has not been called to give evidence the person presenting the complaint on behalf of the authority and the chief executive (or his or her representative) may question the employee (in an appropriate forum) on the answers given to the independent person.

The independent person's report shall:

(a) state his or her opinion as to whether (and if so the extent to which) the evidence he or she has obtained supports any allegations of misconduct against the chief executive;

(b) recommend the disciplinary action or range of actions which appear to him or her to be appropriate for the authority to take against the chief executive.

The independent person is required to send a copy of his or her report to the chief executive. Before the council or appropriate committee as the case may be considers the report or the recommendations of the independent person, the chief executive or his/her representative has the right to address the council or committee, but, unless the council or committee consents, has no right to call witnesses. The council or committee cannot apply a disciplinary sanction in respect of the chief executive greater than that recommended by the independent person.

The regulations are to be amended however so that the statutory provisions will **not** apply to the HAPS who is also council manager in a 'mayor and council manager' form of executive.

1   SI 1993/202.

Extended Independent Person Provisions

[31.7]
In recognition of their enhanced roles under executive arrangements and the ethical framework under Pt III of the Local Government Act 2000 the Local Government Act 2000, the Local Authorities (Standing Orders) Regulations 1993[1] are to be amended to provide that the statutory protections summarised above applicable to the HAPS will also apply to the monitoring officer and chief finance officer. This will mean that the monitoring officer and the chief finance officer may not be suspended on full pay for more than two months for the purposes of investigating misconduct unless it is in accordance with a recommendation in a report made by an independent person whose appointment has been agreed between the officer in question and the authority. It will also mean that no disciplinary action can be taken against either the monitoring officer or the chief finance officer unless it is in accordance with a recommendation made by an independent person.

Most monitoring officers and chief finance officers are subject to the conditions of service of the JNC for Chief Officers of local authorities, and steps are expected to be taken by the JNC to amend Part 4 – Discipline, Capability and Redundancy – to reflect the new statutory protections for monitoring officers and chief finance officers. Once the JNC conditions have been changed they will be incorporated automatically into the contracts of employment of the officers concerned. In the meantime it is suggested that a similar procedure is followed for them as is set out in s 16 – Procedures for Redundancy, Capability and Discipline of the Handbook of the Joint-Negotiating Committee for Chief Executives of Local Authorities.

Where the monitoring officer and chief finance officer are not subject to JNC conditions, the authority should take steps to ensure that the local disciplinary procedure which does apply to them is amended to reflect the new statutory provisions, again using the JNC for Chief Executives' provisions as a model. It is suggested that any such changes are agreed with the individuals in order for them to be given contractual effect.

1   SI 1993/202.

CHAPTER 32
Employee Relations Implications

Introduction

[32.1]
The Local Government Act 2000 makes significant changes to the role of elected members in the appointing and disciplining of employees. Successive governments have long had concerns that elected members could show bias or favouritism to employees and those wishing to become employees who may have family, business or political connections and the provisions of the Act significantly reduce councillors' involvement in day to day personnel matters.

Appointment Procedures

[32.2]
In the past, elected members have often played a major part in the appointment of staff, sitting on appointments panels for employees at all levels. Member involvement has varied widely depending on the type of authority (councillor involvement is more usual in smaller district councils) and sometimes the political party(ies) in control.

Schedule 1 of the Local Authorities (Functions and Responsibilities) (England) Regulations 2000[1] now provide that, under the 'leader and cabinet' model the power to appoint staff in accordance with s 112 of the Local Government Act 1972 cannot be the responsibility of the executive. Furthermore, under regulations (yet to be issued) made under s 8 of the Local Government and Housing Act 1989 local authorities will be required to incorporate provisions in their standing orders that the appointment of all staff below deputy chief officer level is the responsibility of the head of paid service or his/her nominee. 'Deputy chief officer' is defined by s 2(8) of the Local Government and Housing Act 1989 as a person who, as respects most or all of the duties of his/her post, is required to report directly or is directly accountable to one or more of the statutory or non-statutory chief officers.

Section 2(6) of the Local Government and Housing Act 1989 defines a 'statutory chief officer' as:

- the chief education officer or director of education;
- the chief officer of a fire brigade;
- the director of social services;
- the s 151 chief finance officer.

Section 2(7) defines 'non-statutory chief officer' as:

- a person for whom the head of paid service is directly responsible;
- a person who, as respects all or most of the duties of his/her post is required to report directly to or is directly accountable to the head of paid service;
- any person who, as respects all or most of the duties of his/her post is required to report directly to or is directly accountable to the local authority (or any committee or sub-committee of the authority) – this definition covers the monitoring officer.

(A person whose duties are solely secretarial or clerical or are otherwise in the nature of support services is not regarded as a chief officer, regardless of whether they would otherwise meet the definition under the Act.)

The Employers Organisation in Advisory Bulletin 433 on 'Councillors' Involvement in the Appointment of Senior Officers' (May 2001) asks the question as to whether the changes mean that members are excluded from the appointments process as a whole for staff below deputy chief officer level, or that they simply must not be the chairperson on interview panels. The intention of the legislation would appear to be however that elected members have no involvement at all in the appointments process below deputy chief officer level, and it would be advisable for authorities to exclude members at all stages in respect of those posts. This would include not only the selection process itself but also the drawing up of person specifications, job descriptions, advertisements and consideration of the detailed arrangements for making the appointment.

Under regulations (yet to be made at the time of writing), under executive arrangements which involve the 'mayor and council manager' form of executive, the council manager or her/his nominee must be responsible for the appointment and dismissal of all other staff.

The DTLR Guidance (para 8.11) says that under the 'leader and council manager' type arrangements the chief executive (and therefore head of paid service) or his/her nominee should be responsible for the appointment (and dismissal) of all staff.

These restrictions do not apply to assistants to political groups appointed under s 9 of the Local Government and Housing Act 1989, where the appointment can be made in accordance with the wishes of that political group.

Where there is a mayoral form of constitution, an assistant to the mayor can be appointed only by the mayor.

It should be noted that these restrictions do not apply to parish and town councils.

In the light of these changes, local authorities need to review their appointments procedures to ensure they comply with the new provisions set out above.

1   SI 2000/2853.

Senior officers

[32.3]
The Local Government Act 2000 has also heralded changes to the appointments processes for senior officers (ie those at deputy chief officer level and above).

[32.4]
Head of Paid Service

Regulations (yet to be made at the time of writing) will require that under executive arrangements which involve either the mayor and cabinet or leader and cabinet form of executive, the head of paid service must be appointed (and dismissed – see below) by the full council. Any committee or sub-committee which undertakes the selection process and makes recommendations to the full council must contain at least one member of the executive.

The Employers Organisation in Advisory Bulletin 433 identifies two variations for the appointment process for the head of paid service.

Variation 1 – has the full council approving the appointment of the head of paid service following the recommendation of the appointment by a committee or sub-committee, where no well-founded objection has been made by any member of the executive.

Variation 2 – has the full council appointing the head of paid service, again where no well-founded objection has been made by any member of the executive.

Up to now, it has been the usual practice for chief executive (head of paid service) appointments to be made by a committee or sub-committee, often advised by external consultants. Such committees/sub-committees normally have delegated powers to make the appointment, although the appointment could be reported for information to the full council at its next meeting. It has also been the (less-common) practice in some authorities for the whole council to make the appointment of chief executive, or for the whole council to approve a recommendation of the appointments committee/sub-committee.

Under the new provisions, it would appear that it will no longer be possible for an appointments committee/sub-committee to be given delegated powers as such to make the appointment, but that their decision will need to be ratified by the full council. It is also unclear as to how 'well-founded objection' will be defined in practice, and the position could well be reached where such an objection is made by a member of the executive who has not been involved in any stage of the appointment up until ratification by the full council. The full council must consider any objections to the intended appointment from any member of the executive and satisfy itself that the objection is not well-founded or that it has taken action in respect of the objection.

Whilst the power to appoint staff is explicitly excluded from the duties of the executive under Sch 1 of the Local Authorities (Functions and Responsibilities) (England) Regulations 2000[1] (see above), one way forward might be to ensure that all the members of the executive are appointed to the committee/sub-committee making the appointment so that 'well-founded objections' can be discussed at that stage rather than after an appointment has been offered. (It cannot be assumed that appointments panels will be dominated by executive members otherwise.)

As the new process means that it will not be possible for an appointment of head of paid service to be confirmed until after the full council has approved it, consideration may need to be given to arranging for a meeting of the full council to be held on the last day the appointments process itself in order to avoid delays and uncertainties.

1　SI 2000/2853.

[32.5]
Chief Officers and Deputy Chief Officers

Regulations (yet to be made at the time of writing) under s 8 of the Local Government and Housing Act 1989 will govern the appointment of chief officers under executive arrangements which involve either the mayor and cabinet or leader and cabinet form of executive. In such cases, where the appointment is made by the local authority, or a committee or sub-committee of the local authority (which must contain at least one member of the executive) or full council, the regulations will provide that the appointment cannot be made until:

* the local authority, committee or sub-committee has considered any objections to the intended appointment from any member of the executive; and
* the local authority, committee or sub-committee has satisfied itself that the objection is not well-founded or has taken action in respect of the objection.

As explained above, elected members may only be involved in appointments at deputy chief officer level or above. The Employers Organisation in Advisory Bulletin 433 identifies three variations for the appointment process for the head of paid service.

Variation 1 – has a committee or sub-committee of the council (with at least one member of the executive) appointing chief officers and deputy chief officers, with an offer of appointment being made only where there has been no objection to the appointment from any member of the executive, or where any such objection is considered by the body making the appointment not to be well-founded. (Again, one way forward might be to ensure that all the members of the executive are appointed to the committee/sub-committee making the appointment so that 'well-founded objections' can be discussed and resolved before an appointment is offered.)

Variation 2 – has the full council appointing chief and deputy chief officers, with the offer of appointment only being made where no well-founded objection from any member of the executive has been received.

Variation 3 – envisages the appointment of chief and deputy chief officers being the responsibility of the head of paid service or his/her nominee (which would appear to avoid the 'well-founded objection' issue.).

It is unlikely in practical terms that authorities would wish to go down the route of variation 2, or variation 3 (except perhaps for the appointment of some deputy chief officer posts). So the probability is that the model of variation 1 will be the one authorities will seek to adopt for the appointment of chief and deputy chief officers.

Disciplinary Action

[32.6]
As explained in Chapter 31 above there have long been special provisions in the national conditions of service for chief executives and chief officers relating to disciplinary matters, as negotiated by the relevant Joint-Negotiating Committees. These procedures are contractual if the terms and conditions of the JNCs have been incorporated into the contracts of employment of the officers concerned, and failure to abide by them may result in a finding of unfair or wrongful dismissal. In addition, if the procedures have not been complied with, the officer concerned and his or her trade union or other representative may seek a judicial review of the case.

As also explained in Chapter 31, in cases of disciplinary action against the head of paid service (the chief executive) and now the monitoring officer and the chief finance officer, it is necessary for an Independent Person to be appointed, in accordance with reg 3(1) of the Local Authorities (Standing Orders) Regulations 1993[1], once it has been decided that a full investigation should be carried out into the matter in question. If the parties cannot agree on an independent person, he or she is appointed by the Secretary of State for the Environment. An independent person is not required to be appointed in cases of redundancy or permanent ill-health.

But as well as extending the 'independent person' provisions to the monitoring officer anf chief finance officer, the Local Government Act 2000 also makes some changes to the general provisions relating to disciplinary action against employees.

1   SI 1993/202.

Head of paid service

[32.7]
By regulations (yet to be made at the time of writing) under s 8 of the Local Government and Housing Act 1989, under executive arrangements which involve either the 'mayor and cabinet' or 'leader and cabinet' form of executive, the head of service can only be dismissed by the full council. This can only take place once an independent person has reported and that report says that the dismissal of the head of paid service is justified. This new provision will require an amendment to the disciplinary procedure set out in

s 16 – Procedures for Redundancy, Capability and Discipline – of the conditions of service of the JNC for Chief Executives. As presently drafted, the model procedure set out there allows for a committee to act with delegated powers to take disciplinary action, including dismissal, against the chief executive. Presumably this will need to be amended so that the final decision, perhaps on the recommendation of a committee, and taking into account the report of the independent person, is taken by the full council.

Chief and deputy Chief Officers

[32.8]

Elected members will still be able to take part in disciplinary proceedings against chief and deputy chief officers as defined by the Local Government and Housing Act 1989, and apart from the need to extend the independent person provisions to the monitoring officer and the chief finance officer (see above), there should be no need for any substantial change to the disciplinary provisions set out in Part Four of the conditions of service of the JNC for Chief Officers of Local Authorities.

It should be noted however that the JNC procedures will not apply to chief and deputy chief officers in authorities with the 'leader and council manager' arrangement, where the chief executive (head of paid service) has responsibility for the dismissal of all staff. In these cases the same disciplinary procedure can apply to all staff below head of paid service. Such changes should be notified to employees currently subject to JNC chief officer conditions, whose contracts will have been changed by the operation of statute.

Employees below deputy Chief Officer

[32.9]

As with appointments, regulations (yet to be made at the time of writing) will provide that elected members cannot be involved at any stage in disciplinary proceedings against staff below deputy chef officer level. In practice this is probably the case now in most local authorities.

The regulations will however allow elected members to be involved in appeals against dismissal or other disciplinary action where this is provided for in the disciplinary, capability or related procedures of the local authority. There is however no requirement for elected members to be involved in this way. Where elected members are currently involved in appeals, and an authority wishes to review such involvement, it must be remembered that disciplinary procedures may be contractual and that where they are the contracts will need to be changed lawfully (eg by collectively agreed amendments to the disciplinary procedure) for the amendments to take effect.

Grading and Grievance Appeals Committees

[32.10]
Some authorities' procedures provide for the final stage of certain grading and grievance appeals to be to elected members.

There would appear to be nothing in the Local Government Act 2000, and the regulations to be made as a result of the Act, which would necessarily prevent this, although it must be remembered that elected members may not be involved in appointment or discipline matters in respect of employees below deputy chief officer level. Grading, and especially grievance, issues may concern issues arising from appointments processes, and in order to avoid any inconsistency or breaches of regulation, authorities may consider the time is now right for all appeals procedures in relation to employees below deputy chief officer level to stop with officers, and not provide an appeal to elected members.

Such changes may of course need to be renegotiated with the recognised trade unions where they form collective agreements and where those collective agreements in turn form part of the employees' contracts of employment.

Joint Negotiation and Collective Bargaining

[32.11]
The revised executive and scrutiny arrangements arising from the Local Government Act 2000 may have implications for joint-negotiating and collective bargaining arrangements at local level.

Again there would appear to be nothing in principle in the Act and regulations to prevent elected members from continuing to serve on joint-negotiating/consultation committees (JNCs) (unless they are considering individual appointment and disciplinary issues), but the decision-making processes will need to be reviewed.

Until the Local Government Act 2000, it was not uncommon for a local JNC either to have delegated power to determine certain personnel and employment issues or to make recommendations to a personnel committee. Unless the committee system continues (as may be the case with district councils with a population of less than 85,000), such decisions, if they are not delegated to officers, may need to be made by the executive member with responsibility for personnel matters. The executive as a whole does not have the power to make appointments under s 112 of the Local Government Act 1972 by virtue of Sch 1 of the Local Authorities (Functions and Responsibilities) (England) Regulations 2000[1] and it is assumed this extends to the setting of reasonable terms and conditions, including remuneration, under s 112(2) of the Local Government Act 2000.

The setting of terms and conditions for posts at deputy chief officer level and above (where elected members can be involved in the appointments process) can presumably be the responsibility of committees set up for that purpose.

1   SI 2000/2853.

Chapter 33
Whistle-blowing

[33.1]

The new political arrangements, and particularly the requirements of the codes of conduct for members and employees, place a greater emphasis on the need for cases of malpractice to be brought to the attention of the council and for those doing so to be protected from victimisation. Central to this for employees is the Public Interest Disclosure Act 1998 (PIDA), which came into force on 2 July 1999.

This chapter concentrates on the protection of employees under the PIDA, which is the legislation's central purpose.

The Act started out as a Private Members Bill introduced in the House of Commons in June 1997 by Richard Shepherd MP, sponsored by the 'Public Concern at Work' action group. The PIDA works by making substantial amendments and additions to the Employment Rights Act 1996 (ERA). The core provision inserts eleven new sections, ss 43A to 43L, into the ERA as a new Pt IVA generically entitled 'Protected disclosures'[1]. These new ERA sections define what disclosures will qualify for protection and by whom and to whom protected disclosures can be made. Complaints brought under the Act are made to an employment tribunal.

1   Public Interest Disclosure Act 1998, s 1.

What Is Whistle-Blowing?

[33.2]

The dictionary definition of 'whistle-blowing' is 'giving information (usually to the authorities) about illegal and underhand practices'. The Act was passed in response to events including the controversy surrounding the Bristol Royal Infirmary heart operations, the child abuse scandal in North Wales, the Maxwell pensions affair and the Clapham Rail and Zebrugge disasters. After each of these, official enquiries revealed that workers had been aware of dangers but were afraid of making their fears public.

The PIDA gives legal protection to any worker against dismissal or other penalty as a result of his/her disclosing information (a qualifying disclosure – see para [33.4] below) relating to crimes, breaches of a legal obligation, miscarriages of justice, dangers to health and safety or the environment and to the concealing of evidence relating to any of these. The Act applies whether or not the information is confidential and whether the malpractice is occurring in the UK or overseas.

A 'worker'

[33.3]
There is an extended definition of 'worker' under the Act to whom its provisions apply. As well as covering employees in the normal sense of the word for the purposes of employment protection under the ERA, the definition also covers contractors and sub-contractors, agency staff, home-workers and those providing general medical, dental ophthalmic or pharma-ceutical services and those undertaking work experience, either by means of a contract of employment or as part of an educational course run by for example a college or university. It does not cover the genuinely self-employed, volunteers, the intelligence services, the army or the police.

To qualify for protection, the worker must act in good faith and have reasonable grounds for believing that the information disclosed indicates the existence of one of the above problems.

Qualifying Disclosures

[33.4]
A 'qualifying disclosure' is the term used in the PIDA to identify the categories of information which a worker will be able to disclose to a suitable person without fear of reprisal (or more accurately which will give the worker rights if reprisals are taken against him/her for making the disclosure) provided the disclosure is made in good faith.

A 'qualifying disclosure' for the purpose is defined as one which tends to show one or more of the following:

*   that a criminal offence has been committed, is being committed or is likely to be committed;
*   that a person has failed, is failing or is likely to fail to comply with any legal obligation to which he is subject;
*   that a miscarriage of justice has occurred, is occurring or is likely to occur;
*   that the health or safety of any individual has been, is being or is likely to be endangered;
*   that the environment has been, is being or is likely to be damaged, or
*   that information tending to show any matter falling within any one of the preceding paragraphs has been, is being or is likely to be deliberately concealed.

A disclosure of information is not a qualifying disclosure if the person making the disclosure commits an offence by making it. A disclosure of information in respect of which a claim to legal professional privilege (or, in Scotland, to confidentiality as between client and professional legal adviser) could be maintained in legal proceedings is not a qualifying disclosure if it is made by a person to whom the information had been disclosed in the course of obtaining legal advice.

There are three types of disclosure under the Act:

(1) **Internal disclosures** – a disclosure to a manager or the employer will be protected if the whistle-blower has an honest and reasonable suspicion that a malpractice has occurred, is occurring or is likely to occur. Where a third party is responsible for the malpractice, this same provision will apply. There will also be protection if a 'proper' disclosure is made to the sponsoring department by someone in the public sector – in local government's case presumably the DTLR or other relevant department.

(2) **Regulatory disclosures** – the Act makes a special provision for disclosure to prescribed bodies. These will include bodies such as the Health and Safety Executive and the Financial Services Authority. Again, such disclosures will be protected where the whistle-blower has an honest and reasonable suspicion that a malpractice has occurred, is occurring or is likely to occur.

(3) **Wider disclosures** – wider disclosures (eg to the police, the media, and non-prescribed regulators) are also protected if, in addition to the tests for regulatory disclosures, they are reasonable in all the circumstances and are not made for personal gain. There are two parts to the test of reasonableness for wider disclosures. First, unless the whistle-blower reasonably believes he/she would be victimised, the concern must have been raised with the employer or the prescribed regulator, as applicable. This requirement does not apply if the matter is exception-ally serious. Nor does it apply where there is no prescribed regulator and the whistle-blower reasonably believes there would be a cover-up. If these provisions are met and an employment tribunal is satisfied that the disclosure was reasonable the whistle-blower will be protected. In deciding reasonableness, the tribunal will:

– consider the identity of the person to whom the disclosure was made;
– the seriousness of the concern;
– whether the risk or danger remains;
– whether it breached a duty of confidence the employer owed a third party;
– where the concern was raised with the employer or prescribed regulator, the reasonableness of their response.

A Worker's Rights Under the PIDA

[33.5]
It will be automatically unfair dismissal to dismiss a worker, or select him/her for redundancy, for making a qualifying disclosure in good faith to someone to whom he/she is entitled to make it, or to penalise him/her (subject him to a detriment) for doing so. The protection is available regardless of how long the worker has been employed and without age limit.

The Public Interest Disclosure (Compensation) Order 1999[1] provides that there is no maximum limit on the compensation that a tribunal can award where an employee has been dismissed for making a protected disclosure under the Act.

Section 9 of the PIDA extends the ERA provisions for interim relief to employees making protected disclosures. If the employee seeks interim relief within seven days and the tribunal considers it likely that it will find that he/she was dismissed for making a protected disclosure, it may order the employer to reinstate him/her. If the employer fails to comply with such an order, the employee is deemed to remain in employment until the hearing, and entitled to continue to be paid as such.

1   SI 1999/1548.

'Gagging' Clauses

[33.6]
'Gagging' clauses in employment contracts (and compromise agreements) are void insofar as they conflict with the protection given by the Act.

Implications for Local Authorities

[33.7]
The PIDA follows similar legislation in the USA, but is stronger in three respects – it applies across all sectors, covers malpractice overseas and controls gagging clauses in contracts. Although not obligatory under the PIDA, a number of local authorities have brought in procedures to reflect the Act's provisions, in particular those enabling employees to raise internal issues with the employer.

An important task is to inform the workforce about the provisions of the PIDA and to reassure them that if they have genuine concerns it is safe for them to raise them. Employees should be encouraged to raise concerns with the employer, as they are often the first to see malpractice and an effective, early disclosure may prevent a greater problem arising for the local authority at a later stage. If there is no safe and clear way for employees to raise concerns internally, they may for example leak them to the media instead.

By discussing, and perhaps agreeing, a whistle-blowing procedure with the trade unions, and by informing the employees about the procedure, the workforce may have an ownership of the policy. In the context of Best Value, as well as the modernisation agenda, the employees' interest in the reputation and success of the organisation is vital. The advantages of a formal whistle-blowing policy are that it may:

*   deter and detect malpractice;
*   demonstrate accountability;
*   reduce the likelihood of disclosures to outside bodies;
*   reduce the risk of claims under the PIDA.

The procedure will also need to address issues such as:

*   when, where, how and with whom can an employee raise a concern;
*   what if the employee participated in the malpractice;
*   what if the employee is malicious;

- respecting confidentiality;
- what if the whistle-blower is dissatisfied with the employer's response, eg should there be access to elected members.

Whistle-Blowing and the Code of Conduct

[33.8]
Authorities may wish to adopt a whistle-blowing procedure, or revise an existing one, at the same time as implementing the statutory employee code of conduct, or introducing a local code which builds on the statutory provisions. In particular, it should be stressed to employees that under the statutory code an employee who becomes aware of activities which he or she believes are illegal, improper, unethical or otherwise inconsistent with the code, should report the matter in accordance with the authority's confidential reporting procedure or any other procedure designed for that purpose. Employees should also be reminded of their rights under the PIDA at the same time.

Further Advice

[33.9]
Further advice on the implementation of the PIDA is available from Public Concern at Work, (http://www.pcaw.co.uk) the organisation which originally sponsored the Private Member's Bill which led to the PIDA becoming law.

CHAPTER 34
Human Rights

Introduction

[34.1]
The provisions of the Human Rights Act 1998, and the European Convention on Human Rights, to which the Act gives force in UK legislation, apply to local government employees in the same way as other workers. The Local Government Act 2000 does not change this position as such, but there are a number of specific provisions from local government law which limit the human rights of local government employees in some respects.

Politically Restricted Postholders (PRPs)

[34.2]
The most significant of these restrictions are the provisions contained in the Local Government and Housing Act 1989 in relation to politically restricted postholders (PRPs).

Section 1 of the Local Government and Housing Act 1989 introduced the principle of 'politically restricted posts' (PRPs) and of restricting political activities of local authority employees. Before the Act, local authority employees were already prevented from being an elected member of the authority for which they worked, although they were able to be members of another authority – the so-called 'twin-tracking' practice, which had attracted government criticism before the 1989 Act was passed. The Act now prevents PRPs from becoming an elected member of another authority as well as their own. The disqualification also applies to election as an MP and an MEP.

PRPs fall into three broad categories, as follows:

(1) Certain 'specified' posts, namely–
    (a) the Head of Paid Service (HAPS);
    (b) the statutory chief officers, ie education, social services;
    (c) non-statutory chief officers;
    (d) deputy chief officers;
    (e) the monitoring officer;
    (f) the chief finance officer;
    (g) assistants to political groups appointed under s 9 of the Act;
    (h) officers to whom certain powers are delegated;
    (i) other officers reporting direct to the HAPS or directly to the authority and/or its committees and sub-committees.

(2)   A post for which the remuneration level is or exceeds 'spinal column point' (SCP) 44 (excluding London or regional weighting) on the national local government scales or equivalent, and where the post-holder is not successful in seeking exemption;

(3)   A 'sensitive' post, which meets the following duties-related criteria–

(a)   giving advice on a regular basis to the authority, its committees and sub-committees and any joint-authority on which it is represented; and/or

(b)   speaking on behalf of the authority on a regular basis to journalists or broadcasters.

(Secretarial and support staff who might otherwise meet the above definitions are excluded, as are teachers, including head teachers, and lecturers. Support staff in educational establishments are, however, subject to the provisions of the Act.)

Each local authority has to draw up, and keep up to date, a list of those employees who are PRPs.

The government appoints an Independent Adjudicator for the operation of the PRP criteria. The adjudicator's role is to:

- issue guidance and advice on the application of the criteria for designation of a PRP, which local authorities will have to take into account;
- consider applications from employees designated on remuneration grounds for exemption from political restriction;
- consider appeals from employees that an authority has misapplied the 'sensitive post' criteria;
- direct that a particular post should be included on a authority's list of PRPs.

The Local Government Officers (Political Restrictions) Regulations 1990[1] were made under s 1 of the 1989 Act. They restrict PRPs from announcing their candidature for election to a local authority, the House of Commons or the European Parliament. They may stand for election to a parish or community council, but they are not able to canvass on behalf of a political party in that respect. The regulations also prohibit PRPs from being an officer of a political party or any of its branches or a member of any of its committees or sub-committees where the duties would be likely to require:

- participation in the general management of the party or branch; or
- acting on behalf of the party or branch in dealing with non-party members.

PRPs are also prevented from canvassing on behalf of a candidate standing for election to a local authority or as an MP or MEP, including acting as an agent or sub-agent. PRPs are not allowed to speak in public if there is an apparent intention to affect public support for a political party. ('Political party' is not defined by the regulations.) Neither can they publish any work they may have written or edited nor authorise or permit someone else to publish or edit such a work if the work appears to be intended to affect support for a political party. PRPs are, however, allowed to display political notices at his or her home or on his or her car.

Political assistants appointed under s 9 are prevented from speaking in public if this gives the impression that they are an authorised representative of a political party, nor may they publish or edit any 'political' work. For the activity to be covered by the Act, however, it must be the intention of the PRP or political assistant to affect public support for a political party – this does not mean that such a person cannot refer to a political party in any speech or published work.

UNISON argued that the political restrictions on senior local government officers and/or those in politically restricted posts introduced by the Local Government and Housing Act 1989 were an infringement of human rights. But this argument was rejected by the European Court of Human Rights in *Ahmed and Others v the United Kingdom*[2] which said that the UK Government was within its rights to introduce such restrictions.

1   SI 1990/851.
2   Application 22954/93 (1998) 29 EHRR 1.

Employees – Freedom of Thought and Outside Interests

[34.3]
Article 10 of the European Convention of Human Rights on Freedom of Expression is incorporated into Sch 1 to the Human Rights Act 1998, as follows:

(1)   Everyone has the right to freedom of expression. This right shall include freedom to hold opinions and to receive and impart information and ideas without interference by public authority and regardless of frontiers. This Article shall not prevent States from requiring the licensing of broadcasting, television or cinema enterprises.

(2)   The exercise of these freedoms, since it carries with it duties and responsibilities, may be subject to such formalities, conditions, restrictions or penalties as are prescribed by law and are necessary in a democratic society, in the interests of national security, territorial integrity or public safety, for the prevention of disorder or crime, for the protection of health or morals, for the protection of the reputation or rights of others, for preventing the disclosure of information received in confidence, or for maintaining the authority and impartiality of the judiciary.

The European Court of Human Rights have held in the *Ahmed* case[1] that the politically restricted post provisions of the Local Government and Housing Act 1989 do not breach this article.

Local government terms and conditions have long recognised that local government employees off-duty hours are their own personal concern, but that they should not subordinate their duty to their private interests or put themselves in a position where their duty and private interests conflict. A local government officer who is not politically restricted is free to express political and personal opinion publicly and to stand for election as a councillor in another local authority or as an MP or MEP.

The code of conduct for local government employees (see Chapter 30 above) makes it clear however that local authority employees, whether or not politically restricted, must follow every lawfully expressed policy of the authority and must not allow their own personal or political opinions to interfere with their work. Where they are politically restricted, they must comply with any statutory restrictions on their political activities.

With the coming into force of the PIDA (see Chapter 33 above), local government officers, like other employees, are protected if they make a lawful 'whistle-blowing' complaint against their employing authority.

1   See para [34.2] above.

Right to a Fair Hearing

[34.4]
Article 6(1) of the European Convention on Human Rights, again incorporated into Sch 1 to the Human Rights Act 1998, says that:

> 'in the determination of his/her civil rights and obligations or of any criminal charge against him/her, everyone is entitled to a fair and public hearing within a reasonable time by an independent and impartial tribunal established by law.'

Ever since the Human Rights Act came into force, there has been some speculation by lawyers that internal disciplinary appeals and indeed employment tribunals do not meet the requirement under Art 6 of the European Convention on Human Rights for an individual to have a fair and public hearing within a reasonable time by an *independent and impartial* tribunal established by law. The position of appeals bodies under the Act has now been examined by the Scottish Court of Session in *Tehrani v United Kingdom Central Council for Nursing, Midwifery and Health Visiting*[1].

The case has established that Art 6 will apply to a professional disciplinary hearing which determines an individual's right to practice. But the Court of Session have said that it is not necessary for a professional disciplinary tribunal to met all the requirements of an independent and impartial tribunal if the disciplinary procedure provides a statutory right to a court of law. In his commentary on the case, Michael Rubenstein, Editor of *Industrial Relations Law Reports* (IRLR), doubts whether Art 6 applies to purely internal disciplinary procedures. But if it did, then on the face of it the fact that an individual will have a right to go to an employment tribunal presumably gives the statutory right of appeal which may put right any 'deficiency' there may be in the internal appeals process as far as independence is concerned.

But Michael Rubenstein goes on to say that:

> 'it remains to be seen whether Article 6 would be satisfied merely by the availability of unfair dismissal proceedings in an employment

tribunal. The weakness of the remedy of reinstatement and the resurrection of the range of reasonable responses test (the Court of Appeal in *HSBC Bank plc (formerly Midland Bank plc) v Madden*[2]) might suggest that the employment tribunal does not exercise sufficient control of the disciplinary tribunal so as to guarantee the right to a fair hearing'.

Only time will tell, but at this stage it would not appear that local authorities will need to make changes to their current internal appeals procedures in the light of the human rights legislation. If the process is challenged as not being truly independent, one response could be that it is doubtful whether the human rights provision applies to internal hearings, but nevertheless there remains a right of appeal to an employment tribunal, which until proved otherwise, provides the statutory right of appeal to an independent body required by the Convention on Human Rights.

And following the decision of the Scottish Court of Session in *Tehrani* (see above) the EAT have held in *Scanfuture UK Ltd v Secretary of State for Trade and Industry; Link v Same*[3] that under the new procedures for appointing lay members of employment tribunals, those tribunals are now compliant with the European Convention of Human Rights, even where the Secretary of State was a party to the proceedings.

The EAT held that although in 1999, when the cases under appeal were heard, Art 6 of the Convention had been breached, changes in the power and practices of the Secretary of State in relation to lay members of employment tribunals were such that panels composed of members appointed under the current system were compliant with Art 6 and that the appeals could now be remitted to an employment tribunal for rehearing. The EAT allowed an appeal by Scanfuture UK Ltd and Mrs J Link from a decision of a Hull employment tribunal sitting in April 1999 with a decision promulgated in June, dismissing claims against the Secretary of State for payment from the national insurance fund.

Article 6 requires a test of impartiality and independence to be applied to the employment tribunal. The EAT said that ' independence' plainly included independence from the parties but where one of the parties was the Secretary of State, a member of the executive, and where the executive was properly to be regarded as indivisible, it must also include independence from the executive branch of government as a whole. It was the appellants' case that the employment tribunal was not truly independent within the meaning of Art 6 by reason of an aggregate of factors, namely that the two lay members were appointed by the secretary of state, a party to the proceedings, because:

(i)   their remuneration was fixed by him;
(ii)   their short term of office was fixed by him; and
(iii)   their potential for further appointment depended on him.

The EAT said that the:

> 'fair-minded and independent observer ... would have harboured (in 1999) an objectively justifiable fear that the employment tribunal

lacked both impartiality and independence within the meaning of that expression in article 6'.

The obvious course upon Art 6 being found to have been breached was to set aside the decision of the employment tribunal. The appeal was allowed and the decision set aside.

But The EAT said that the changes made in the tribunal appointment rules since 1999 now made the employment tribunal system compliant with Art 6. Lay members were now appointed under a system which included an element of open competition and were made for a renewable period of three years. There was no reason for any lay members to think that they could curry favour and that it would help them acquire a renewal of office by their leaning in favour of the Secretary of State in any hearing. There were now in place sufficient guarantees to exclude any legitimate doubt. Neither the appellants nor any reasonable person could have any objectively justifiable view as to a lack of impartiality or of independence in an employment tribunal appointed and operating under the current system.

The EAT remitted the case for a fresh hearing by a panel composed of members appointed under the current system.

1   [2001] IRLR 208.
2   [2000] IRLR 827.
3   [2001] IRLR 416.

Trade Union Rights

[34.5]
Article 11(1) of the European Convention on Human Rights, again incorporated into Sch 1 to the Human Rights Act 1998, says that:

'everyone has the right to freedom of peaceful assembly and to freedom of association with others, including the right to form and to join trade unions for the protection of his/her interests'.

Local government has a long tradition of encouraging membership of appropriate trade unions and has recognised a range of trade unions at national regional and local level. Paragraph 3 of Part 1 of the conditions of service of the NJC for Local Government Services (the Green Book) continues this tradition by stating that the 'NJC has a strong commitment to joint-negotiation and consultation at all levels, and to this end encourages employees to join and remain in recognised trade unions'.

Paragraph 18.1 of Part 2 of the Green Book states that:

'authorities shall provide the recognised trade unions with facilities necessary to carry out their functions, including paid leave of absence to attend meetings of the NJC and Provincial Councils and the operation of a check off system whereby, with the consent of the individual, trade union dues are deducted from pay'.

Trade union rights are of course also recognised in UK employment legislation and it is not appropriate in this Division to go into these in detail.

But the rights of an individual trade union member can be summarised as follows.

Dismissal on trade union grounds is automatically unfair[1]. A dismissal on trade union grounds will be deemed to have occurred when the reason for it is that the employee:

- was or proposed to become a member of an independent trade union;
- took part or proposed to take part in trade union activities; or
- refuses to become a member of a trade union.

In such circumstances, it is not necessary for the employee to have met the qualifying period normally required for the right to make a complaint of unfair dismissal before an employment tribunal (one year as from 1 June 1999). Neither are employees over normal retirement age or over the age of 65 necessarily barred from pursuing a claim[2].

The protection against dismissal contained in the s 152(1)(a) of the Trade Union and Labour Relations (Consolidation) Act 1992 protects an employee against dismissal on grounds of past, present or proposed membership of an independent trade union (or a branch or section of one). Membership of a union, includes for the purposes of the legal protection, taking advantage of union membership (eg using the services of a trade union).

The Trade Union and Labour Relations (Consolidation) Act 1992 protects union members against dismissal for having 'taken part, or proposed to take part, in the activities of an independent trade union at an appropriate time'[3]. 'Appropriate time', according to s 152(2) of the Trade Union and Labour Relations (Consolidation) Act 1992, means either:

- a time outside the employee's working hours;
- a time within the employee's working hours at which, in accordance with arrangements agreed with, or consent given by, the employer, it is permissible for him or her to take part in the activities of a trade union.

The protection of individuals against dismissal extends only to members of an independent trade union. A distinction needs to be drawn between the activities of an ordinary member and those of an accredited representative of the union. There is no legal definition of 'activities of an independent trade union', but they are likely to include:

- discussions/consultations with union officials;
- attending union meetings and conferences;
- voting in union elections;
- distributing union literature;
- recruitment activities.

As long as the activities are either carried out outside working hours (eg during lunch or tea breaks), or undertaken with permission during working hours, they will be protected.

Under s 152 of the Trade Union and Labour Relations (Consolidation) Act 1992, it is also automatically unfair to dismiss an employee for not being a member of a trade union (or a member of a particular trade union), for refusing to become a member, or for refusing to remain a member. This provision effectively renders the operation of any form of closed-shop arrangement unlawful.

1   Trade Union and Labour Relations (Consolidation) Act 1992, s 152.
2   Trade Union and Labour Relations (Consolidation) Act 1992, s 154.
3   Trade Union and Labour Relations (Consolidation) Act 1992, s 152(1)(*b*).

Right to a Safe Working Environment

[34.6]
The Health and Safety at Work etc Act 1974 (HSWA) and numerous European Directives impose general duties on employers, including local authorities, and the self-employed to secure the health, safety and welfare of people at work. It is not appropriate for this Division to give detailed advice on such a complex subject but the main principles of the law on health and safety can be summarised as follows:

- to secure the health, safety and welfare of people at work;
- to protect others from risks arising from the activities of people at work;
- to control the use and storage of dangerous substances;
- to control the emission into the atmosphere of noxious or offensive substances.

The HSWA applies to virtually all persons at work, this includes:

- employers;
- self-employed;
- employees;
- trainees (including work experience);
- manufacturers, suppliers, designers and importers; and
- people in control of premises.

It also affords protection to the general public, but it does not apply to people working in domestic positions in private residences.

The HSWA is superimposed upon previously enacted legislation, such as the Factories Act 1961 and the Offices, Shops and Railway Premises Act 1963. Some of the provisions of this earlier legislation are still in force, but much has been repealed.

Under the legislation the employer owes a number of duties to the employee. These are defined in general terms in s 2 of the Health and Safety at Work etc Act 1974 as follows:

'an employer must ensure, so far as is reasonably practicable, the health, safety and welfare of all his employees while they are at work'.

The main areas covered are:

- provision and maintenance of a safe workplace, and safe means of access and egress;

- safe arrangements for storage, transport, handling and use of articles and substances;
- provision of adequate instruction, training, supervision and information;
- provision of a safe working environment and adequate welfare facilities;
- provision and maintenance of a safe plant and equipment and of a safe system of work;
- appointment of safety representatives and committees; and
- provision of a written safety policy where five or more people are employed.

What constitutes 'safe' or 'adequate' is not defined. Previous and extensive case law has established how the courts expect employers to fulfil their duties. 'Health' is taken to include mental well-being as well as physical.

Because the Health and Safety at Work etc Act 1974 is designed to protect individuals at work, it is necessary to take into account the particular circumstances of any individual, especially where that person may have an additional need of protection. Under the act the duty of care is not an absolute standard and it may be that the duty of care is greater, for example, to a pregnant woman, than to other employees in more standard circumstances. This has to be reflected in the risk assessment carried out after she has informed her employer of her pregnancy.

The Health and Safety at Work etc Act 1974 is a criminal statute. A breach of statutory duty is a criminal act; penalties for a breach of statutory duty may be a fine, imprisonment or both. Statutory duties lay down specific obligations which must be complied with, and a criminal act will occur if the duty is breached. In criminal law the question is: '*has the duty been performed or not?*' Criminal prosecutions arise through failure to comply with the requirements of the relevant acts or regulations.

Common law also requires that an employer takes reasonable care to provide a safe workplace, safe equipment, safe systems of work and competent fellow employees. The standard of care is that which 'an ordinary prudent employer would take in all the circumstances'. Prudence includes what could be held in particular circumstances as identifying and guarding against a reasonably foreseeable risk. If a risk is reasonably foreseeable, the common law duty of care is likely to apply. The common law duties are invoked where employers' liability for negligence is an issue.

In a claim for compensation arising from the tort of negligence, the burden of proof is on the person making the claim. He/she must prove, on the balance of probabilities, that his/her injuries were a reasonably foreseeable consequence of the negligent act by the defendant. To succeed in his/her claim he/she must argue that the employer owed him/her a duty of care in respect of the activity which has caused injury, that the employer failed in this duty, and that he/she suffered injury as a consequence.

There are also duties imposed in law on employees to take reasonable care of themselves and of other persons who may be affected by their work activities.

Both acts and omissions are included. This part of the Health and Safety at Work etc Act 1974 is generally taken to cover instances of 'horseplay' or 'skylarking' and in particular the refusal of workers to comply with procedures issued by the employer. Employees must also co-operate with their employers, or any other person, so far as is necessary to enable that person to comply with their duties under any relevant statutory provision.

A duty is imposed generally on all people, including employees, not to interfere or misuse anything provided in the interests of health, safety or welfare. This would include fire precautions, fencing, warning notices, protective clothing and equipment, etc.

As it is the general duty of all employers to ensure the health, safety and welfare of employees and people affected by the work, s 2(3) of the Health and Safety at Work etc Act 1974 requires employers with five or more employees to prepare a written health and safety policy and to bring this to the attention of their employees. The policy is a written document which contains the statement of the employer's commitment and aims regarding safety, the organisational structure that supports this general statement and the arrangements (procedures, rules and instructions) that ensure that the principles in the statement can be carried out. As things change with time – both within the organisation and as technology changes - it is necessary for employers to review the policy on a regular basis and revise it as necessary.

There is also a duty on employers to consult employees under the Health and Safety at Work etc Act 1974, which now extends to the whole of the workforce, unionised or not.

CHAPTER 35
Training and Information

Introduction

[35.1]
The significant changes brought about by the governance and modernisation agenda through the Local Government Act 2000, associated regulations, and other relevant legislation require local authorities to adopt a communications and training strategy to ensure that all elected members and employees are aware of the implications of the relevant issues and able to operate effectively within the new regime.

Elected Member Training

[35.2]
As well as keeping elected members informed of the issues, some authorities are developing training strategies for councillors which concentrates on looking at their management styles and at the climate within the council, with the aim of improving both. A leading example is the programme devised by Tameside Metropolitan Borough Council, in partnership with Hay Management Consultants[1].

Unlike training for employees, it is not possible to insist on councillors attending training, and therefore the training programme has to be seen as relevant and adding value. By devising a programme which was seen as beneficial, the Tameside experience saw attendance reaching 60% of all councillors, across the political groups, for the workshops. One way used by Tameside of gaining support for the training from elected members was to involve them in designing the programme. Members were invited to attend focus groups and one-to-one sessions beforehand to discuss what they saw as the key qualities of an effective councillor within the new member structure adopted by the council. From these discussions the programme leaders were able to identify 14 core competencies – which included trustworthiness, service orientation and teamwork – that councillors needed in order to perform their new roles. That in turn gave them an insight into what new behaviours they needed to adopt.

The Tameside development programme consists of one-day workshops spread over eight months. Members use what they learn in these sessions to develop their own performance improvement plans. Further training and support is available for those who feel they need it as a result of issues raised in the workshops. But according to Tameside perhaps the most valuable

357

Employment Implications

aspect of the programme has been the opportunities it has created for councillors to learn from each other.

One key issue to emerge from the workshops which is essential if the new political structures are to function effectively is how members co-operate with officers.

A programme of workshops for elected members could also cover the following key areas:

- the new legislation;
- members involvement (and non-involvement) in personnel management issues;
- Best Value;
- budgetary control;
- IT;
- conduct of meetings;
- council standing orders; and
- partnership working.

The Improvement and Development Agency (IDeA) have produced a member development programme. 'Modern Members' is a systematic attempt to provide a national framework for member development. The programme is delivered by experienced trainers and facilitators from the IDeA to individual councils, or on a regional basis by regional employers organisations and Syniad (the Employers Organisation for Wales).

An added value of this programme is the opportunity to involve elected members of all parties in the delivery of the programme. Based on the principles of adult learning, the programme will build on member's existing knowledge and skills.

The 2001/2002 'Modern Members' modules are as follows:

Overview and scrutiny

The introductory level programme is aimed at authorities where members are about to start the overview and scrutiny process. The advanced level is for members who have some experience of carrying out overview and scrutiny and want to improve their skills in particular areas.

Better Council Services – performance monitoring and continuous improvement

How the Best Value process can be used by members to generate performance improvement and major change to meet the needs of communities.

Partnerships and Community Leadership

Gives participants an opportunity to think more deeply about partnerships and community engagement and suggests ways in which engaging more effectively could raise the political credibility of councillors.

358

Finance for Councillors

Emphasises the role and importance of performance monitoring and describes the accountability framework of councils including roles and responsibilities. For members who have already received a general introduction to local government finance from their own authority.

Effective Member/Officer Relationships

Allows participants to reflect on the formal and informal relationships between members and officers, explores the various roles they can take within the new political framework and the skills and knowledge needed to work effectively with each other.

Ethics and Probity

Gives the opportunity to consider roles and responsibilities within the new ethical framework and an understanding of the standards committee and Standards Board. Will incorporate the national codes of conduct for members and officers.

Raising Standards in Education – the role of members

Looks at the councillor's role in securing improvements in the quality of education in the local area, taking account of national and local policies. Highlights partnership working with other agencies and stakeholders.

Effective Casework and Advice Surgeries for Councillors

Advice on how to meet the community's interests and problems through effective casework and publicity.

E-Governance – implications for members

Designed to keep members informed about the changes in technology and the way they effect the way services are delivered. The content includes understanding the internet and developing an e-government strategy.

Each programme is designed to run as a one-day event either on a regional/sub regional basis or in house within one authority. Alternative delivery methods may be available, particularly for in house programmes, for some of the modules. Details are available from IDeA on 020-7296-6600.

There may also be a need for specialist training for certain members, especially in respect of their involvement (albeit more limited now) in personnel management issues. Any elected member who is likely to be involved in recruiting officers at deputy chief officer level and above must have undergone recruitment and equalities training. Any elected member who serves on a disciplinary appeals panel should receive training in their role and employment legislation.

A continuing programme of refresher training is also important.

1   See *People Management* (31 May 2001).

Employee Training

Induction training

[35.3]
Many local authorities have well-developed induction training programmes for new employees which cover general areas such as the Council's functions, the political make-up as well as detailed advice and guidance. It is important that the relevant modernisation issues covered by the Local Government Act 2000 are now included, whilst recognising that they may not always seem relevant to all employees at all levels.

But areas arising from the new agenda which it would be important to cover in induction training include:

- general background to the government's modernisation agenda;
- the political structure – which model has been adopted and why – eg leader/cabinet;
- political balance;
- the role of the executive and scrutiny;
- general powers of the local authority;
- financial management;
- Best Value;
- e-government;
- code of conduct for employees (and members);
- role of elected members in personnel matters; and
- officer/member relationships.

Management training

[35.4]
It is essential that all aspects of the modernisation programme are covered in management training. The areas appropriate for induction training outlined above are also relevant for management training but special emphasis should be given to the following:

- the operation of the political model in the authority;
- the role of executive and scrutiny;
- officers' roles at meetings involving elected members;
- officer/member relationships;
- officer code of conduct; and
- the implications of partnership working.

A continuing programme of workshops to update officers on developments is essential.

The IDeA is available to assist with the design and running of such programmes, including their own 'Modern Managers' programme.

Communicating with the Workforce

[35.5]

Communicating the modernisation issues to the workforce on a regular and continuing basis is essential. This can be done in a number of ways including:

- making it a regular part of team briefing;
- special employee focussed leaflets;
- staff magazines and newspapers;
- regular workshops and seminars;
- internet and intranet; and
- e-mail updates.

Authorities may also want to give consideration to the production of an employee handbook, perhaps in loose-leaf form to enable updating. This could cover the following areas:

- general background to the government's modernisation agenda;
- the political structure – which model has been adopted and why – eg leader/cabinet;
- political balance;
- the role of the executive and scrutiny;
- general powers of the local authority;
- council procedures;
- role of the statutory officers, eg monitoring officer;
- audit procedures and processes;
- financial management;
- Best Value;
- e-government;
- code of conduct for employees;
- role of elected members in personnel matters;
- officer/member relationships; and
- whistle-blowing procedures.

DIVISION VI
Appendices

APPENDIX 1

Examples of Local Strategic Partnerships in Development and Contact Details

(Chapter 3)

Arun: 'Our Kind of Place'
Jacqui Ball (Head of Strategy)
Arun District Council
Arun Civic Centre, Maltravers Road,
Littlehampton, West Sussex BN17 5LF
Tel: 01903–737602
Fax: 01903–733585
Email: jacqui.ball@arun.gov.uk

Kieran Stigant (Asst Chief Executive)
West Sussex County Council
County Hall, Chichester
West Sussex P019 1RQ
Tel: 01243–777940
Fax: 01243–777697
Email: kieran.stigant@westsussex.gov.uk

Bournemouth Partnership
Lee Green (Principal Officer)
Corporate Development Team
Chief Executive's Office
Bournemouth Borough Council
Town Hall, Bourne Avenue
Bournemouth BH2 6DY
Tel: 01202–454608
Fax: 01202–451000
Email: lee.green@bournemouth.gov.uk

Cherwell Community Planning Partnership
Mrs Alison Davies (Corporate Strategy Manager)
Cherwell District Council
Bodicote House
Bodicote, Banbury
Oxfordshire OX15 4AA
Tel: 01295–252535
Fax: 01295–250652
Email: alison.davies@cherwell-dc.gov.uk

Appendix 1

Croydon Partnership
Moira Skinner (Strategic Partnership Manager)
Economic and Strategic Development Unit
LB Croydon
Taberner House, Park Lane
Croydon CR9 3JS
Tel: 020–8760–5692
Email: moira_skinner@croydon.gov.uk

Devon Strategic Partnership
Ian Hobbs (County Community Strategy Officer)
Devon County Council
County Hall
Topsham Road
Exeter EX2 4QD
Tel: 01392-382-000
Email: ihobbs@devon.gov.uk

Leeds Initiative
Martin Dean (Programme Manager)
Leeds Initiative
Cathedral Chambers, Great George Street
Leeds LS2 8DD
Tel: 0113-247-8989
Fax: 0113-247-8988
Email: martin.dean@leeds.gov.uk
Internet: www.leedsinitiative.org.uk

Lewisham's Local Strategic Partnership
Ashley Pottier (Head of Policy and Partnerships)
London Borough of Lewisham
Room 408, Town Hall
Catford
London SE6 4RU
Tel: 020–8314–6707
Fax: 020–8314–3077
Email: ashley.pottier@lewisham.gov.uk

Liverpool Partnership Group
Penny Wakefield (Director – Liverpool Partnership Group)
5th Floor, Hamilton House
24 Pall Mall
Liverpool L3 6AL
Tel: 0151–285–2310
Fax: 0151–285–2004
Email: penny.wakefield@liverpool.gov.uk

Middlesbrough Partnership
Steve Stewart (Head of Corporate Strategy)
Middlesbrough Council
PO Box 99A
Town Hall
Middlesbrough TS1 2QQ
Tel: 01642–263-564
Fax: 01642–263-517
Email: steve_stewart@middlesbrough.gov.uk

Newham 2010 Local Strategic Partnership
Louise Jacklin (Senior Corporate Projects Manager)
Newham Council
Town Hall, East Ham
London E6 2RP
Tel: 020–8430–3096
Fax: 020–8430–6891
Email: louise.jacklin@newham.gov.uk

Martin Lews (Corporate Strategy Manager)
(*details as opposite*)

Email: martin.lewis@newham.gov.uk

Salford Partnership
Sheila Murtagh (Salford Partnership Manager)
City of Salford
Civic Centre, Chorley Road
Swinton
Salford M27 5FJ
Tel: 0161–793–3406

South Wiltshire Strategic Partnership
Debbie Dixon (Policy Director)
Salisbury District Council
The Council House, Bourne Hill
Salisbury SP1 3UZ
Tel: 01722–434-260
Fax: 01722–434-437
Email: ddixon@salisbury.gov.uk

Telford and Wrekin Partnership
John Pay (Partnership Manager)
Partnership Development Unit
Telford & Wrekin Partnership
University of Wolverhampton
Telford Campus, Priorslee Hall
Telford TF2 9NT
Tel: 01902–323-950 / 01952–202-463
Email: sh1011@wbs.wlv.ac.uk or
john.pay@wrekin.gov.uk

APPENDIX 2

Regulations and Directions under the Local Government Act 2000

(Chapter 4)

Regulations under the Local Government Act 2000

- Local Authorities (Proposals for Alternative Arrangements) (England) Regulations 2000, SI 2000/2850;
- Local Authorities (Arrangements for the Discharge of Functions) (England) Regulations 2000, SI 2000/2851;
- Local Authorities (Referendums) (Petitions and Directions) (England) Regulations 2000, SI 2000/2852 (and two amending SIs: SI 2001/760 and SI 2001/1310);
- Local Authorities (Functions and Responsibilities) (England) Regulations 2000, SI 2000/2853;
- Local Authorities (Executive Arrangements) (Access to Information) (England) Regulations 2000, SI 2000/3272;
- Parent Governor Representatives (England) Regulations 2001, SI 2001/478;
- Local Authorities (Changing Executive Arrangements and Alternative Arrangements) (England) Regulations 2001, SI 2001/1003;
- Local Authorities (Alternative Arrangements) (England) Regulations 2001, SI 2001/1299;
- Local Authorities (Conduct of Referendums) (England) Regulations 2001, SI 2001/1298 (and one amending SI: SI 2001/1494);
- Local Authorities (Executive Arrangements) (Modification of Enactments and Further Provisions) (England) Order 2001, SI 2001/1517.

Directions under the LGA 2000

- The Local Government Act 2000 (Proposals for Executive Arrangements) (England) Direction 2000;
- The Local Government Act 2000 (Proposals for Alternative Arrangements) (England) Direction 2000;
- The Local Government Act 2000 (Constitutions) (England) Direction 2000*;
- The Local Government Act 2000 (Fall-back proposals) (England) Direction 2000;
- The Local Government Act 2000 (Changing Executive Arrangements and Alternative Arrangements) (England) Direction 2001.

* Set out at App 4 below.

Regulations and Directions under the Local Government Act 2000

(Chapter 4)

Regulations under the Local Government Act 2000

APPENDIX 3

Main Similarities and Differences Between the Mayor and Cabinet, Leader and Cabinet and Mayor and Council Manager Models

(Chapter 4)

Defining Features	Mayor and Cabinet Model	Leader and Cabinet Model	Mayor and Council Manager Model
Summary of Model	A directly elected Mayor (four year term) following a referendum, who appoints an executive cabinet	A Council Leader, elected by the full Council, who then either appoints an executive drawn from the Council or heads an executive appointed by and drawn from the Council	A directly elected Mayor (four year term) following a referendum with an Officer of the Authority appointed by the Council as a Council Manager
Make-up of Executive	A Cabinet chosen freely by the Mayor from elected Councillors. Minimum of three and maximum of 10 Councillors in the Cabinet (including the Mayor)	If 'strong leader' model – size and composition of Cabinet chosen by the Leader. If 'weak leader' model – size and composition chosen by full Council. Both will have a minimum of three and maximum of 10 Councillors in the Cabinet	Executive consists of the directly elected Mayor and the Council Manager. The Council Manager is an Officer appointed to the Executive by the Council as a whole, who will also be the Head of Paid Service and Chief Executive

Schemes of Delegation (to be publicly available)	Decided by the Mayor – possible delegations to: • Individual executive members • Committees (area/joint) • Sub-Committees of executive Members • Other authorities • Officers	If 'strong leader' model, delegations could be decided by Leader in same way with same possibilities as directly elected Mayor. However, the Leader is likely to have restrictions placed on his/her power to delegate as the Leader is not directly elected. If 'weak leader' model, full Council could set out the scheme of delegations either broadly or specifically	Decided by the Council Manager – possible delegations to: • Other Officers • Area Committees • Joint Committees • Other authorities • Advisory Committees of Councillors provided for to give advice to the Council Manager
The Role of Full Council	Full Council responsible for adoption of overall policy framework and budget	Full Council responsible for adoption of overall policy framework and budget. Council appoints leader and can appoint cabinet	Full Council responsible for adoption of overall policy framework and budget. Council appoints the Council Manager
Accountability (see also 'Implications for Overview and Scrutiny Role' below)	The Mayor is accountable to the electorate	The Leader is accountable to the Council and not the Electorate in the way that an elected Mayor is and the Council has the power to remove a Leader and/or the whole cabinet	The Council Manager has day-to-day decision-making responsibility with political steer from the Mayor in line with the Mayor's manifesto commitments and the policy framework agreed by Council. The Council Manager has the right to attend and speak but not vote at all meetings (other than overview and scrutiny meetings)

Deputy	A member of the Executive appointed by the Mayor	A member of the Cabinet	Appointed by Mayor but not Chair or Vice-Chair of the Authority, nor a member of Overview and Scrutiny Committee
Ceremonial Function	Carried out by the Deputy Mayor or Chair of the Council or another nominated person	Continue to be carried out by Ceremonial Mayor	Deputy Mayor, Chair or some other nominated person (as in mayor and cabinet model)
Implications for Overview and Scrutiny Role	All Members outside the Executive can be engaged in the Overview and Scrutiny function	All Members outside the Executive can be engaged in the Overview and Scrutiny function	Advisory Councillors to the Council Manager with delegated powers would not be involved in the Overview and Scrutiny function

APPENDIX 4

Local Government Act 2000 (Constitutions) (England) Direction 2000

(Chapters 7 and 10)

The Secretary of State for the Environment, Transport and the Regions, in the exercise of his powers under sections 37(1)(a) and 48(7) of the Local Government Act 2000 (c 22) (the Act) and all other powers enabling him in that behalf, hereby directs all local authorities in England to which Part II of the Act applies as follows:

1
Miscellaneous and interpretation

In the direction:

'constitution' has the meaning given by section 37(1) of the Act,

'overview and scrutiny committee':

(a) in the case of a local authority which is operating executive arrangements has the meaning given by section 21(1) of the Act; or

(b) in the case of a local authority which is operating alternative arrangements means any committee or sub-committee appointed by the authority in accordance with regulations made under section 32(1)(b) of the Act to review or scrutinise decisions made, or other action taken, in connection with the discharge of functions of the authority.

2

In complying with this direction a local authority must have regard to any guidance issued for the time being by the Secretary of State under section 38 of the Act.

3
The constitution

The constitution prepared and kept up to date in accordance with section 37(1) of the Act by a local authority which is operating executive arrangements or, as the case may be, alternative arrangements must include:

(a) a summary and explanation of the purpose and content of the constitution;

(b) a description of the composition of the council, the scheme of ordinary elections for members of the council and their terms of office;

(c) a description of the principal roles and functions of the members of the council under executive arrangements or, as the case may be, alternative arrangements including the rights and duties of those members;

(d) the scheme of allowances for members of the authority drawn up in accordance with regulations made under section 18 of the Local Government and Housing Act 1989 (c 42);

(*e*)   a description of the rights and responsibilities of inhabitants of the authority's area including:

   (i)   their rights to vote in elections for the return of members of the authority;

   (ii)   their rights to access to information about the authority's activities;

   (iii)   their rights of access to meetings of the council, its committees and sub-committees and any joint committees established with any other authority; and

   (iv)   their rights of access to meetings of the executive and committees of the executive;

(*f*)   a description of the roles of the authority itself under executive arrangements or, as the case may be, alternative arrangements including:

   (i)   the functions which may be exercised only by the authority itself or which may to some extent be exercised only by the authority itself (including, in the case of a local authority operating executive arrangements any plans and strategies which are subject to approval or adoption by the authority itself by virtue of regulation 5 of, and paragraph 1 of Schedule 4 to, the Local Authorities (Functions and Responsibilities) (England) Regulations 2000 (SI 2000/2853)); and

   (ii)   any rules governing the conduct and proceedings of meetings of the authority itself whether specified in the authority's standing orders or otherwise;

(*g*)   a description of the roles and functions of the chairman of the council (including a chairman entitled to the style of mayor);

(*h*)   a description of the functions of the local authority executive which, for the time being, are exercisable by individual members of the local authority executive stating as respects each function, the name of the member by whom it is exercisable;

(*i*)   a description of the functions of the local authority executive which, for the time being, are exercisable by the executive collectively or a committee of the executive, stating as respects each function, the membership of the body by who it is exercisable;

(*j*)   a description of those powers of the executive which for the time being are exercisable by an officer of the local authority stating the title of the officer by whom each of the powers so specified is for the time being exercisable, other than any power exercisable by the officer for a specified period not exceeding six months;

(*k*)   a description of the arrangements for the operation of overview and scrutiny committees including:

   (i)   the terms of reference and membership of those committees and any rules governing the exercise of their functions; and

   (ii)   any rules governing the conduct and proceedings of meetings of those committees whether specified in the authority's standing orders or otherwise;

(*l*)   in the case of a local authority which is operating executive arrangements, a description of the roles of the executive, committees of the executive and members of the executive including:

   (i)   the roles, functions, rights, responsibilities and duties of members of the executive;

   (ii)   in the case of a local authority which is operating executive arrangements which include a leader and cabinet form of executive, any rules governing the election of the executive leader;

   (iii)   any rules governing the appointment of members of the executive;

   (iv)   any provisions in the local authority's executive arrangements with respect to the quorum, proceedings and location of meetings of the executive;

    (v)   any provisions in the local authority's executive arrangements with respect to the quorum, proceedings and location of meetings of any committees of the executive;

    (vi)   any provisions in the local authority's executive arrangements with respect to the appointment of committees of the executive; and

    (vii)   in the case of a local authority which is operating executive arrangements which include a mayor and council manager form of executive, any roles of committees appointed by the elected mayor to advise the executive in accordance with paragraphs 3(14) and (15) of Schedule 1 to the Act;

(*m*)   in the case of a local authority which is operating executive arrangements which include a mayor and council manager form of executive, a description of the roles, functions, rights, responsibilities and duties of the deputy mayor appointed in accordance with paragraph 3(3) of Schedule 1 to the Act;

(*n*)   a description of the roles of any committees or sub-committees appointed by the authority in accordance with section 101 of the Local Government Act 1972 (c 70) including:

    (i)   the membership, terms of reference and functions of such committees or sub-committees; and

    (ii)   any rules governing the conduct and proceedings of meetings of those committees or sub-committees whether specified in the authority's standing orders or otherwise;

(*o*)   a description of those powers of the council which for the time being are exercisable by an officer of the local authority stating the title of the officer by whom each of the powers so specified is for the time being exercisable, other than any power exercisable by the officer for a specified period not exceeding six months;

(*p*)   a description of the roles of the local authority's Standards Committee and any parish council sub-committee of the Standards Committee appointed in accordance with sections 53 or 55 of the Act including:

    (i)   the membership, terms of reference and functions of that committee or sub-committee; and

    (ii)   any rules governing the conduct and proceedings of meetings of that committee or sub-committee whether specified in the authority's standing orders or otherwise;

(*q*)   a description of the roles of any area committees appointed by the authority to exercise functions in accordance with regulations 16A of the Local Government (Committees and Political Groups) Regulations 1990 (SI 1990/1553) or, as the case may be, section 18 of the Act and the Local Authorities (Arrangements for the Discharge of Functions) (England) Regulations 2000 (SI 2000/2851) including:

    (i)   the membership, terms of reference and functions of such committees; and

    (ii)   any rules governing the conduct and proceedings of meetings of those committees whether specified in the authority's standing orders or otherwise;

(*r*)   a description of any joint arrangements made with any other local authorities under section 101(5) of the Local Government Act 1972 including:

    (i)   the terms of those arrangements;

    (ii)   the membership, terms of reference and functions of any joint committees established under those arrangements; and

    (iii)   any rules governing the conduct and proceedings of meetings of those joint committees whether specified in the authority's standing orders or otherwise;

(*i*) a description of any arrangements made with another local authority for the discharge of functions by that other local authority or the executive of that other local authority in accordance with section 101(1)(*b*) of the Local Government Act 1972 or, as the case may be, Local Authorities (Arrangements for the Discharge of Functions) (England) Regulations 2000;

(*t*) a description of the roles of officers of the local authority including:

(i) the management structure for officers of the authority;

(ii) any arrangements made under section 101 of the Local Government Act 1972 or, as the case may be, section 14, 15 or 16 of the Act for the discharge of functions by officers of the authority;

(iii) the roles and functions of the head of paid service, monitoring officer and chief finance officer;

(iv) the code of conduct for local government employees issued by the Secretary of State in accordance with section 82 of the Act;

(v) any rules governing the recruitment, appointment, dismissal and disciplinary action for officers of the authority;

(vi) any protocol established by the authority in respect of relationships between members of the authority and officers of the authority;

(*u*) a description of the arrangements the authority has in place for access of the public, members of the authority and officers of the authority to meetings of the authority, committees and sub-committees of the authority, joint committees established with any other local authority, the executive and committees of the executive;

(*v*) a description of the arrangements the authority has in place for access of the public, members of the authority and officers of the authority to information about the decisions made or to be made by in respect of local authority's functions and activities;

(*w*) a register stating:

(i) the name and address of every member of the local authority executive for the time being and the ward or division (if any) which he represents; and

(ii) the name of every member of each committee of the local authority's executive for the time being;

(*x*) a description of the rules and procedures for the management of its financial, contractual and legal affairs including:

(i) procedures for auditing of the local authority;

(ii) the local authority's financial rules or regulations or such equivalent provisions as the local authority may have in place whether specified in the authority's standing orders or otherwise;

(iii) rules, regulations and procedures in respect of contracts and procurement including authentication of documents whether specified in the authority's standing orders or otherwise; and

(iv) rules and procedures in respect of legal proceedings brought by and against the local authority; and

(*y*) a description of the register of interests of members and co-opted members of the authority required under section 81 of the Act, together with the procedures for publicising, maintaining and updating that register;

(*z*) a description of the rules and procedures for review and revision of the authority's constitution and executive arrangements or, as the case may be, alternative arrangements.

4

This direction shall have effect from 19th December 2000.

APPENDIX 5

Local Government and Housing Act 1989
ss 5, 5A, 19, 21, 31

(Chapter 10)

5
Designation and reports of monitoring officer
(1) It shall be the duty of every relevant authority —
   (a) to designate one of their officers (to be known as 'the monitoring officer')
      as the officer responsible for performing the duties imposed by this section
      and, where relevant, section 5A below; and
   (b) to provide that officer with such staff, accommodation and other resources
      as are, in his opinion, sufficient to allow those duties and, where relevant,
      the duties under section 5A below to be performed;
      and subject to subsection (1A) below the officer so designated may be the
      head of the authority's paid service (or, in the case of a police authority
      established under section 3 of the Police Act 1996 or the Metropolitan
      Police Authority, the clerk to the authority) but shall not be their chief
      finance officer.
(1A) The officer designated under subsection (1) above by a relevant authority to
which this subsection applies may not be the head of that authority's paid service.
(1B) Subsection (1A) above applies to the following relevant authorities in
England and Wales —
   (a) a county council,
   (b) a county borough council,
   (c) a district council,
   (d) a London borough council,
   (e) the Greater London Authority, and
   (f) the Common Council of the City of London in its capacity as a local
      authority, police authority or port health authority.
(2) Subject to subsection (2B), it shall be the duty of a relevant authority's
monitoring officer, if it at any time appears to him that any proposal, decision or
omission by the authority, by any committee, or sub-committee of the authority, by
any person holding any office or employment under the authority or by any joint
committee on which the authority are represented constitutes, has given rise to or is
likely to or would give rise to —
   (a) a contravention by the authority, by any committee, [or sub-committee of
      the authority, by any person holding any office or employment under the
      authority] or by any such joint committee of any enactment or rule of law
      or of any code of practice made or approved by or under any enactment;
      or
   (b) any such maladministration or injustice as is mentioned in Part III of the
      Local Government Act 1974 (Local Commissioners) or Part II of the Local

Government (Scotland) Act 1975 (which makes corresponding provision for Scotland),

to prepare a report to the authority with respect to that proposal, decision or omission.

[(2A) No duty shall arise by virtue of subsection (2)(*b*) above unless a Local Commissioner (within the meaning of the Local Government Act 1974) has conducted an investigation under Part III of that Act in relation to the proposal, decision or omission concerned.]

[(2B) Where a relevant authority are operating executive arrangements, the monitoring officer of the relevant authority shall not make a report under subsection (2) in respect of any proposal, decision or omission unless it is a proposal, decision or omission made otherwise than by or on behalf of the relevant authority's executive.]

(3) It shall be the duty of a relevant authority's monitoring officer—

    (*a*) in preparing a report under this section to consult so far as practicable with the [person who is for the time being designated as the head of the authority's paid service under section 4 above] and with their chief finance officer; and

    (*b*) as soon as practicable after such a report has been prepared by him or his deputy, to arrange for a copy of it to be sent to each member of the authority [and, in a case where the relevant authority have a mayor and council manager executive, to the council manager of the authority].

(4) The references in subsection (2) above, in relation to a relevant authority in England and Wales, to a committee or sub-committee of the authority and to a joint committee on which they are represented shall be taken to include references to any of the following, that is to say—

    (*a*) ...

    (*b*) any local fisheries committee the members of which include persons so appointed;

    (*c*) ... and

    (*d*) any sub-committee appointed by a committee falling within paragraphs (*a*) to (*c*) above;

but in relation to any such committee or sub-committee the reference in subsection (3)(*b*) above to each member of the authority shall have effect as a reference to each member of the committee or, as the case may be, of the committee which appointed the sub-committee.

(5) It shall be the duty of a relevant authority and of any such committee as is mentioned in subsection (4) above—

    (*a*) to consider any report under this section by a monitoring officer or his deputy at a meeting held not more than twenty-one days after copies of the report are first sent to members of the authority or committee; and

    (*b*) without prejudice to any duty imposed by virtue of section 115 of the Local Government Finance Act 1988 (duties in respect of conduct involving contraventions of financial obligations) or otherwise, to ensure that no step is taken for giving effect to any proposal or decision to which such a report relates at any time while the implementation of the proposal or decision is suspended in consequence of the report;

and nothing in section 101 of the Local Government Act 1972 or in section 56 of ... the Local Government (Scotland) Act 1973 (delegation) shall apply to the duty imposed by virtue of paragraph (*a*) above.

(6) For the purposes of paragraph (*b*) of subsection (5) above the implementation of a proposal or decision to which a report under this section relates shall be suspended in consequence of the report until the end of the first business day after the day on which consideration of that report under paragraph (*a*) of that subsection is concluded.

(7) The duties of a relevant authority's monitoring officer under this section shall be performed by him personally or, where he is unable to act owing to absence or

illness, personally by such member of his staff as he has for the time being nominated as his deputy for the purposes of this section.

(8)　In this section [and in section 5A]—

'business day', in relation to a relevant authority, means any day which is not a Saturday or Sunday, Christmas Day, Good Friday or any day which is a bank holiday under the Banking and Financial Dealings Act 1971 in the part of Great Britain where the area of the authority is situated;

'chief finance officer', in relation to a relevant authority, means the officer having responsibility, for the purposes of section 151 of the Local Government Act 1972, section 73 of the Local Government Act 1985, section 112 of the Local Government Finance Act 1988[, section 127(2) of the Greater London Authority Act 1999] or section 6 below or for the purposes of section 95 of the Local Government (Scotland) Act 1973, for the administration of the authority's financial affairs; and

'relevant authority'—

    (a)　in relation to England and Wales, means a local authority of any of the descriptions specified in paragraphs (a) to [(k)] of section 21(1) below; and

    (b)　in relation to Scotland, means a local authority.

[(8A)　Any reference in this section to the duties of a monitoring officer imposed by this section, or to the duties of a monitoring officer under this section, shall include a reference to the functions which are conferred on a monitoring officer by virtue of Part III of the Local Government Act 2000.]

(9)　This section shall come into force at the expiry of the period of two months beginning on the day this Act is passed.

Amendment

Amended by the Police and Magistrates' Courts Act 1994, s 43, Sch 4; the Local Government etc (Scotland) Act 1994, s 180, Schs 13, 14; the Environment Act 1995, s 120, Sch 24; the Police Act 1996, s 103, Sch 7; the Greater London Authority Act 1999, ss 132, 325, Sch 27; Local Government Act 2000, ss 107, 108, Sch 5; SI 2001/2237, arts 1, 2, 23;

5A
Reports of monitoring officer—local authorities operating executive arrangements

[(1)　Where a relevant authority are operating executive arrangements, the monitoring officer of that authority shall be responsible for performing the duties imposed by this section.

(2)　It shall be the duty of the monitoring officer of a relevant authority that is referred to in subsection (1) above, if at any time it appears to him that any proposal, decision or omission, in the course of the discharge of functions of the relevant authority, by or on behalf of the relevant authority's executive, constitutes, has given rise to or is likely to or would give rise to any of the events referred to in subsection (3), to prepare a report to the executive of the authority with respect to that proposal, decision or omission.

(3)　The events referred to for the purposes of subsection (2) are—

    (a)　a contravention, by the relevant authority's executive or any person on behalf of the executive, of any enactment or rule of law; or

    (b)　any such maladministration or injustice as is mentioned in Part III of the Local Government Act 1974 (Local Commissioners).

(4)　No duty shall arise by virtue of subsection (3)(b) above unless a Local Commissioner (within the meaning of the Local Government Act 1974) has conducted an investigation under Part III of that Act in relation to the proposal, decision or omission concerned.

(5)　It shall be the duty of an authority's monitoring officer—

(a) in preparing a report under subsection (2) to consult so far as practicable with the person who is for the time being designated as the head of the authority's paid service under section 4 above and with their chief finance officer; and

(b) as soon as practicable after such a report has been prepared by him or his deputy, to arrange for a copy of it to be sent to each member of the authority and, where the authority has a mayor and council manager executive, the council manager.

(6)   It shall be the duty of the authority's executive—

(a) to consider any report under this section by a monitoring officer or his deputy at a meeting held not more than twenty-one days after copies of the report are first sent to members of the executive; and

(b) without prejudice to any duty imposed by virtue of section 115B of the Local Government Finance Act 1988 (duties of executive as regards reports) or otherwise, to ensure that no step is taken for giving effect to any proposal or decision to which such a report relates at any time while the implementation of the proposal or decision is suspended in consequence of the report.

(7)   For the purposes of paragraph (b) of subsection (6) above the implementation of a proposal or decision to which a report under this section, by a monitoring officer or his deputy, relates shall be suspended in consequence of the report until the end of the first business day after the day on which consideration of that report under paragraph (a) of that subsection is concluded.

(8)   As soon as practicable after the executive has concluded its consideration of the report of the monitoring officer or his deputy, the executive shall prepare a report which specifies—

(a) what action (if any) the executive has taken in response to the report of the monitoring officer or his deputy;

(b) what action (if any) the executive proposes to take in response to that report and when it proposes to take that action; and

(c) the reasons for taking the action specified in the executive's report or, as the case may be, for taking no action.

(9)   As soon as practicable after the executive has prepared a report under subsection (8), the executive shall arrange for a copy of it to be sent to each member of the authority and the authority's monitoring officer.

(10)   The duties of an authority's monitoring officer under this section shall be performed by him personally or, where he is unable to act owing to absence or illness, personally by such member of his staff as he has for the time being nominated as his deputy for the purposes of this section.]

Amendment
Inserted, in relation to England, by SI 2001/2237, arts 1, 2, 23.

19
Members' interests

(1)   The Secretary of State may by regulations require each member of a local authority—

(a) to give a general notice to the proper officer of the authority setting out such information about the member's direct and indirect pecuniary interests as may be prescribed by the regulations, or stating that he has no such interests; and

(b) from time to time to give to that officer such further notices as may be so prescribed for the purpose of enabling that officer to keep the information provided under the regulations up to date.

(2)   Any member of a local authority who—

(a) without reasonable excuse fails to comply with the requirements of any regulations under this section; or (*b*)   in giving a notice in compliance with any such requirement, provides information which he knows to be false or misleading in a material particular or recklessly provides information which is false or misleading in a material particular,

shall be guilty of an offence and liable, on summary conviction, to a fine not exceeding level 4 on the standard scale.

(3)   Proceedings for an offence under subsection (2) above shall not be instituted in England and Wales except by or with the consent of the Director of Public Prosecutions.

(4)   Neither section 96 of the Local Government Act 1972 (general notice of pecuniary interests) nor section 40 of the Local Government (Scotland) Act 1973 (corresponding provision for Scotland) shall apply in relation to any notice given in pursuance of any regulations under this section; but such regulations may provide—

(*a*)   that the giving of a notice in pursuance of any such regulations shall be deemed to be sufficient disclosure for the purposes of section 94 of the said Act of 1972 (disability of members of authorities for voting on account of interest in contracts etc) or for the purposes of section 38 of the said Act of 1973; and

(*b*)   that the proper officer of a local authority is to maintain such records of the information contained in notices given to him as may be prescribed by the regulations and is to keep those records open to inspection by members of the public.

(5)   A local authority shall not be entitled (whether by means of making it a condition of any appointment or by any other means whatever) to impose any obligations on their members to disclose any interests other than those that they are required to disclose by virtue of section 94 of the Local Government Act 1972, section 38 of the Local Government (Scotland) Act 1973 or any regulations under this section.

(6)   Regulations under this section may contain such incidental provision and such supplemental, consequential and transitional provision in connection with their other provisions as the Secretary of State considers appropriate.

(7)   References in this section to the indirect pecuniary interests of a member of a local authority shall include references to any such interests as, by virtue of any connection between that member or his spouse and any other person, would fall to be disclosed—

(*a*)   in the case of a local authority in England and Wales, under section 94 of the Local Government Act 1972; or

(*b*)   in the case of a local authority in Scotland, under section 38 of the Local Government (Scotland) Act 1973,

if the authority were proposing to enter into a contract with that other person.

21
Interpretation of Part I

(1)   Any reference in this Part to a local authority is, in relation to England and Wales, a reference to a body of one of the following descriptions —

(*a*)   a county council;

(*aa*)   a county borough council;

(*b*)   a district council;

(*c*)   a London borough council;

(*d*)   the Common Council of the City of London in its capacity as a local authority, police authority or port health authority;

(*e*)   the Council of the Isles of Scilly;

(*f*)   a fire authority constituted by a combination scheme under the Fire Services Act 1947;

(*g*)   a police authority established under section 3 of the Police Act 1996, the Metropolitan Police Authority or the Service Authority for the National Crime Squad;

(*h*)   an authority established under section 10 of the Local Government Act 1985 (waste disposal authorities);

(*i*)   a joint authority established by Part IV of that Act (... fire services, civil defence and transport) or the London Fire and Emergency Planning Authority;

(*j*)   any body established pursuant to an order under section 67 of that Act (successors to residuary bodies);

(*k*)   the Broads Authority;

(*l*)   any joint board the constituent members of which consist of any of the bodies specified above; ...

(*m*)   ... and

(*n*)   a joint planning board constituted for an area in Wales outside a National Park by an order under section 2(1B) of the Town and Country Planning Act 1990.

Amendment

Para (*aa*): inserted by SI 1996/3071. Para (*g*): substituted by the Police and Magistrates' Courts Act 1994, ss 43, Sch 4. Para (*g*): amended by the Police Act 1996, s 103, Sch 7; the Greater London Authority Act 1999, s 325, Sch 27; Police Act 1997, s 88, Sch 6. Para (*i*): amended by the Police and Magistrates' Courts Act 1994, ss 43, 93, Schs 4, 9; Greater London Authority Act 1999, s 328, Sch 29. Para (*l*): amended by the Environment Act 1995, s 78, Sch 10. Para (*m*): repealed by the Environment Act 1995, s 120, Sch 24. Para (*n*): inserted by the Environment Act 1995, s 78, Sch 10.

31
National Code of Local Government Conduct

(1)   The Secretary of State, for the guidance of members of local authorities, may issue a code of recommended practice as regards the conduct of members of such authorities to be known as the National Code of Local Government Conduct.

(2)   The Secretary of State may revise or withdraw a code issued under this section.

(3)   The Secretary of State, before issuing, revising or withdrawing a code, shall consult—

(a)   as respects England and Wales, such representatives of local government, and

(b)   as respects Scotland, such associations of local authorities,

as appear to him to be appropriate.

(4)   A code shall not be issued unless a draft of it has been laid before and approved by a resolution of each House of Parliament.

(5)   Where the Secretary of State proposes to revise a code, he shall lay a draft of the proposed alterations before each House of Parliament and—

(a)   he shall not make the revision until after the expiration of the period of 40 days beginning with the day on which the draft is laid (or, if copies are laid before each House of Parliament on different days, with the later of those days); and

(b)   if within that period either House resolves that the alterations be withdrawn, he shall not proceed with the proposed alterations (but without prejudice to the laying of a further draft).

(6)   In reckoning any period of 40 days for the purposes of subsection (5) above no account shall be taken of any time during which Parliament is dissolved or prorogued or during which both Houses are adjourned for more than four days.

[(6A)   Subsections (4) to (6) above do not apply to a code which applies only to Scotland and such a code shall not be issued unless a draft of it has been laid before and approved by a resolution of the Scottish Parliament.

(6B)   Where the Scottish Ministers propose to revise such a code as is mentioned in subsection (6A), they shall lay a draft of the proposed alterations before the Scottish Parliament and—

(*a*) they shall not make the revision until after the expiration of the period of 40 days beginning with the day on which the draft is laid; and

(*b*) if within that period the Parliament resolves that the alterations be withdrawn, they shall not proceed with the proposed alterations (but without prejudice to the laying of a further draft).

(6C) In reckoning any period of 40 days for the purposes of subsection (6B) above no account shall be taken of any time during which the Parliament is dissolved or is in recess for more than 4 days.]

(7) The form of declaration of acceptance of office under section 83 of the Local Government Act 1972 or section 33A of the Local Government (Scotland) Act 1973 may include an undertaking by the declarant to be guided by the National Code of Local Government Conduct in the performance of his functions.

(8) In this section—

'local authority' means—

(*a*) as respects England and Wales, a county council, [a county borough council,] a district council, a London borough council, a parish council, a community council, the Common Council of the City of London or the Council of the Isles of Scilly;

(*b*) as respects Scotland, a [council constituted under section 2 of the Local Government etc (Scotland) Act 1994] or a joint board or joint committee within the meaning of section 235(1) of the Local Government (Scotland) Act 1973; and

'member', in relation to a local authority, includes any person who, whether or not a member of the authority, is a member of a committee or sub-committee of the authority or of any joint committee of theirs.

Amendment
Amended by the Local Government etc (Scotland) Act 1994, s 180(1), Sch 13; SI 1996/3071, art 2, Sch; SI 1999/1820, art 4, Sch 2.

APPENDIX 6

Local Government Act 2000
ss 51, 53, 54, 57, 59, 60, 64, 65, 66, 78, 79, 80, 81, 82, 83

(Chapters 10, 11 and 12)

Part III
Conduct of Local Government Members and Employees

51
Duty of relevant authorities to adopt codes of conduct

(1)   It is the duty of a relevant authority, before the end of the period of six months beginning with the day on which the first order under section 50 which applies to them is made, to pass a resolution adopting a code as regards the conduct which is expected of members and co-opted members of the authority (referred to in this Part as a code of conduct).

(2)   It is the duty of a relevant authority, before the end of the period of six months beginning with the day on which any subsequent order under section 50 which applies to them is made, to pass a resolution—

(a)   adopting a code of conduct in place of their existing code of conduct under this section, or

(b)   revising their existing code of conduct under this section.

(3)   A relevant authority may by resolution—

(a)   adopt a code of conduct in place of their existing code of conduct under this section, or

(b)   revise their existing code of conduct under this section.

(4)   A code of conduct or revised code of conduct—

(a)   must incorporate any mandatory provisions of the model code of conduct which for the time being applies to that authority,

(b)   may incorporate any optional provisions of that model code, and

(c)   may include other provisions which are consistent with that model code.

(5)   Where a relevant authority fail to comply with the duty under subsection (1) or (2) before the end of the period mentioned in that subsection—

(a)   they must comply with that duty as soon as reasonably practicable after the end of that period, and

(b)   any mandatory provisions of the model code of conduct which for the time being applies to the authority are to apply in relation to the members and co-opted members of the authority for so long as the authority fail to comply with that duty.

(6)   As soon as reasonably practicable after adopting or revising a code of conduct under this section, a relevant authority must—

387

(a) ensure that copies of the code or revised code are available at an office of the authority for inspection by members of the public at all reasonable hours,

(b) publish in one or more newspapers circulating in their area a notice which—

  (i) states that they have adopted or revised a code of conduct,

  (ii) states that copies of the code or revised code are available at an office of the authority for inspection by members of the public at such times as may be specified in the notice, and

  (iii) specifies the address of that office, and

(c) send a copy of the code or revised code—

  (i) in the case of a relevant authority in England or a police authority in Wales, to the Standards Board for England,

  (ii) in the case of a relevant authority in Wales, to the Commission for Local Administration in Wales.

(7) Where a relevant authority themselves publish a newspaper, the duty to publish a notice under subsection (6)(b) is to be construed as a duty to publish that notice in their newspaper and at least one other newspaper circulating in their area.

(8) A relevant authority may publicise their adoption or revision of a code of conduct under this section in any other manner that they consider appropriate.

(9) A relevant authority's function with respect to the passing of a resolution under this section may be discharged only by the authority (and accordingly, in the case of a relevant authority to which section 101 of the Local Government Act 1972 applies, is not to be a function to which that section applies).

53
Standards committees

(1) Subject to subsection (2), every relevant authority must establish a committee (referred to in this Part as a standards committee) which is to have the functions conferred on it by or under this Part.

(2) Subsection (1) does not apply to a parish council or community council.

(3) The number of members of a standards committee of a relevant authority in England or a police authority in Wales and their term of office are to be fixed by the authority (subject to any provision made by virtue of subsection (6)(a)).

(4) A standards committee of a relevant authority in England or a police authority in Wales must include—

(a) at least two members of the authority, and

(b) at least one person who is not a member, or an officer, of that or any other relevant authority.

(5) A standards committee of a relevant authority in England which are operating executive arrangements—

(a) may not include the elected mayor or executive leader, and

(b) may not be chaired by a member of the executive.

(6) The Secretary of State may by regulations make provision—

(a) as to the size and composition of standards committees of relevant authorities in England and police authorities in Wales,

(b) as to the appointment to such committees of persons falling within subsection (4)(b),

(c) with respect to the access of the public to meetings of such committees,

(d) with respect to the publicity to be given to meetings of such committees,

(e) with respect to the production of agendas for, or records of, meetings of such committees,

(f) with respect to the availability to the public or members of relevant authorities of agendas for, records of or information connected with meetings of such committees,

(g) as to the proceedings and validity of proceedings of such committees.

(7) The Standards Board for England—

    (*a*)   may issue guidance with respect to the size and composition of standards committees of relevant authorities in England and police authorities in Wales, and

    (*b*)   must send a copy of any such guidance to the Secretary of State.

(8)   A member of a standards committee of a relevant authority in England or a police authority in Wales who is not a member of the authority is entitled to vote at meetings of the committee.

(9)   A relevant authority in England and a police authority in Wales must send a statement which sets out the terms of reference, or any revised terms of reference, of their standards committee to the Standards Board for England.

(10)   A standards committee of a relevant authority in England or a police authority in Wales is not to be regarded as a body to which section 15 of the Local Government and Housing Act 1989 (duty to allocate seats to political groups) applies.

(11)   The National Assembly for Wales may by regulations make provision—

    (*a*)   as to the size and composition of standards committees of relevant authorities in Wales other than police authorities (including provision with respect to the appointment to any such committee of persons who are not members of the relevant authority concerned),

    (*b*)   as to the term of office of members of any such committees,

    (*c*)   as to the persons who may, may not or must chair any such committees,

    (*d*)   as to the entitlement to vote of members of any such committee who are not members of the relevant authority concerned,

    (*e*)   for or in connection with treating any such committees as bodies to which section 15 of the Local Government and Housing Act 1989 does not apply,

    (*f*)   with respect to the access of the public to meetings of such committees,

    (*g*)   with respect to the publicity to be given to meetings of such committees,

    (*h*)   with respect to the production of agendas for, or records of, meetings of such committees,

    (*i*)   with respect to the availability to the public or members of relevant authorities of agendas for, records of or information connected with meetings of any such committees,

    (*j*)   as to the proceedings and validity of proceedings of any such committees,

    (*k*)   for or in connection with requiring relevant authorities in Wales (other than police authorities) to send to the Commission for Local Administration in Wales statements which set out the terms of reference of their standards committees.

(12)   The provision which may be made by virtue of subsection (6)(*c*) to (*f*) or (11)(*f*) to (*i*) includes provision which applies or reproduces (with or without modifications) any provisions of Part VA of the Local Government Act 1972.

54
Functions of standards committees

(1)   The general functions of a standards committee of a relevant authority are—

    (*a*)   promoting and maintaining high standards of conduct by the members and co-opted members of the authority, and

    (*b*)   assisting members and co-opted members of the authority to observe the authority's code of conduct.

(2)   Without prejudice to its general functions, a standards committee of a relevant authority has the following specific functions—

    (*a*)   advising the authority on the adoption or revision of a code of conduct,

    (*b*)   monitoring the operation of the authority's code of conduct, and

    (*c*)   advising, training or arranging to train members and co-opted members of the authority on matters relating to the authority's code of conduct.

(3)   A relevant authority may arrange for their standards committee to exercise such other functions as the authority consider appropriate.

(4) The Secretary of State may by regulations make provision with respect to the exercise of functions by standards committees of relevant authorities in England and police authorities in Wales.

(5) The National Assembly for Wales may by regulations make provision with respect to the exercise of functions by standards committees of relevant authorities in Wales (other than police authorities).

(6) The Standards Board for England may issue guidance with respect to the exercise of functions by standards committees of relevant authorities in England and police authorities in Wales.

(7) The National Assembly for Wales may issue guidance with respect to the exercise of functions by standards committees of relevant authorities in Wales (other than police authorities).

57
Standards Board for England

(1) There is to be a body corporate known as the Standards Board for England.

(2) The Standards Board for England is to consist of not less than three members appointed by the Secretary of State.

(3) The Standards Board for England is to have the functions conferred on it by this Part and such other functions as may be conferred on it by order made by the Secretary of State under this subsection.

(4) In exercising its functions the Standards Board for England must have regard to the need to promote and maintain high standards of conduct by members and co-opted members of relevant authorities in England.

(5) The Standards Board for England—
- (a) must appoint employees known as ethical standards officers who are to have the functions conferred on them by this Part,
- (b) may issue guidance to relevant authorities in England and police authorities in Wales on matters relating to the conduct of members and co-opted members of such authorities,
- (c) may issue guidance to relevant authorities in England and police authorities in Wales in relation to the qualifications or experience which monitoring officers should possess, and
- (d) may arrange for any such guidance to be made public.

(6) Schedule 4 makes further provision in relation to the Standards Board for England.

59
Functions of ethical standards officers

(1) The functions of ethical standards officers are to investigate—
- (a) cases referred to them by the Standards Board for England under section 58(2), and
- (b) other cases in which any such officer considers that a member or co-opted member (or former member or co-opted member) of a relevant authority in England has failed, or may have failed, to comply with the authority's code of conduct and which have come to the attention of any such officer as a result of an investigation under paragraph (a).

(2) The Standards Board for England may make arrangements in relation to the assignment of investigations under this section to particular ethical standards officers.

(3) The purpose of an investigation under this section is to determine which of the findings mentioned in subsection (4) is appropriate.

(4) Those findings are—
- (a) that there is no evidence of any failure to comply with the code of conduct of the relevant authority concerned,
- (b) that no action needs to be taken in respect of the matters which are the subject of the investigation,

(c) that the matters which are the subject of the investigation should be referred to the monitoring officer of the relevant authority concerned, or

(d) that the matters which are the subject of the investigation should be referred to the president of the Adjudication Panel for England for adjudication by a tribunal falling within section 76(1).

(5) Where a person is no longer a member or co-opted member of the relevant authority concerned but is a member or co-opted member of another relevant authority in England, the reference in subsection (4)(c) to the monitoring officer of the relevant authority concerned is to be treated as a reference either to the monitoring officer of the relevant authority concerned or to the monitoring officer of that other relevant authority (and accordingly an ethical standards officer who reaches a finding under subsection (4)(c) must decide to which of those monitoring officers to refer the matters concerned).

60
Conduct of investigations

(1) An ethical standards officer may arrange for any person to assist him in the conduct of any investigation under section 59.

(2) An ethical standards officer to whom an investigation under section 59 is assigned may—

(a) cease the investigation at any stage before its completion, and

(b) refer the matters which are the subject of the investigation to the monitoring officer of the relevant authority concerned.

(3) Where a person is no longer a member or co-opted member of the relevant authority concerned but is a member or co-opted member of another relevant authority in England, an ethical standards officer may, if he thinks it more appropriate than making such a reference as is mentioned in subsection (2)(b), refer the matters which are the subject of the investigation to the monitoring officer of that other relevant authority.

(4) An ethical standards officer may not at any time conduct an investigation under section 59 in relation to a member or co-opted member (or former or co-opted member) of a relevant authority if, within the period of five years ending with that time, the ethical standards officer has been a member or an officer of the authority or a member of any committee, sub-committee, joint committee or joint sub-committee of the authority.

(5) An ethical standards officer who is directly or indirectly interested in any matter which is, or is likely to be, the subject of an investigation under section 59—

(a) must disclose the nature of his interest to the Standards Board for England, and

(b) may not take part in any investigation under that section which relates to that matter.

(6) The validity of any acts of an ethical standards officer are not to be affected by any contravention of subsection (4) or (5) or paragraph 3(2) of Schedule 4 or any breach falling within paragraph 3(3) of that Schedule.

64
Reports etc

(1) Where an ethical standards officer determines in relation to any case that a finding under section 59(4)(a) or (b) is appropriate—

(a) he may produce a report on the outcome of his investigation,

(b) he may provide a summary of any such report to any newspapers circulating in the area of the relevant authority concerned,

(c) he must send to the monitoring officer of the relevant authority concerned a copy of any such report, and

(d) where he does not produce any such report, he must inform the monitoring officer of the relevant authority concerned of the outcome of the investigation.

(2)   Where an ethical standards officer determines in relation to any case that a finding under section 59(4)(*c*) is appropriate he must—

    (*a*)   produce a report on the outcome of his investigation,

    (*b*)   subject to subsection (4)(*b*), refer the matters which are the subject of the investigation to the monitoring officer of the relevant authority concerned, and

    (*c*)   send a copy of the report to the monitoring officer, and the standards committee, of the relevant authority concerned.

(3)   Where an ethical standards officer determines in relation to any case that a finding under section 59(4)(*d*) is appropriate he must—

    (*a*)   produce a report on the outcome of his investigation,

    (*b*)   refer the matters which are the subject of the investigation to the president of the Adjudication Panel for England for adjudication by a tribunal falling within section 76(1), and

    (*c*)   send a copy of the report to the monitoring officer of the relevant authority concerned and to the president of the Adjudication Panel for England.

(4)   Where a person is no longer a member or co-opted member of the relevant authority concerned but is a member or co-opted member of another relevant authority in England—

    (*a*)   the references in subsections (1)(*b*), (*c*) and (*d*), (2)(*c*) and (3)(*c*) to the relevant authority concerned are to be treated as including references to that other relevant authority, and

    (*b*)   an ethical standards officer who reaches a finding under section 59(4)(*c*) must refer the matters concerned either to the monitoring officer of the relevant authority concerned or to the monitoring officer of that other relevant authority.

(5)   A report under this section may cover more than one investigation under section 59 in relation to any members or co-opted members (or former members or co-opted members) of the same relevant authority.

(6)   An ethical standards officer must—

    (*a*)   inform any person who is the subject of an investigation under section 59, and

    (*b*)   take reasonable steps to inform any person who made any allegation which gave rise to the investigation,

    of the outcome of the investigation.

65
Interim reports

(1)   Where he considers it necessary in the public interest, an ethical standards officer may, before the completion of an investigation under section 59, produce an interim report on that investigation.

(2)   An interim report under this section may cover more than one investigation under section 59 in relation to any members or co-opted members (or former members or co-opted members) of the same relevant authority.

(3)   Where the prima facie evidence is such that it appears to the ethical standards officer producing the interim report—

    (*a*)   that the person who is the subject of the report has failed to comply with the code of conduct of the relevant authority concerned,

    (*b*)   that the nature of that failure is such as to be likely to lead to disqualification under section 79(4)(*b*), and

    (*c*)   that it is in the public interest to suspend or partially suspend that person immediately,

    the interim report may include a recommendation that that person should be suspended or partially suspended from being a member or co-opted member of the relevant authority concerned for a period which does not exceed six months or (if shorter) the remainder of the person's term of office.

(4) Where an ethical standards officer produces an interim report under this section which contains such a recommendation as is mentioned in subsection (3), he must refer the matters which are the subject of the report to the president of the Adjudication Panel for England for adjudication by a tribunal falling within section 76(2).

(5) A copy of any report under this section must be given—

    (a)   to any person who is the subject of the report,

    (b)   to the monitoring officer of the relevant authority concerned, and

    (c)   to the president of the Adjudication Panel for England.

(6) Where a person is no longer a member or co-opted member of the relevant authority concerned but is a member or co-opted member of another relevant authority in England—

    (a)   the second reference in subsection (3) to the relevant authority concerned is to be treated as a reference to that other relevant authority, and

    (b)   the reference in subsection (5)(b) to the relevant authority concerned is to be treated as including a reference to that other relevant authority.

(7) In this Part 'partially suspended' and cognate expressions are to be construed in accordance with section 83(7) and (8).

66
Matters referred to monitoring officers

(1) The Secretary of State may by regulations make provision in relation to the way in which any matters referred to the monitoring officer of a relevant authority under section 60(2) or 64(2) are to be dealt with.

(2) The provision which may be made by regulations under subsection (1) includes provision for or in connection with—

    (a)   enabling a monitoring officer of a relevant authority to conduct an investigation in respect of any matters referred to him,

    (b)   enabling a monitoring officer of a relevant authority to make a report, or recommendations, to the standards committee of the authority in respect of any matters referred to him,

    (c)   enabling a standards committee of a relevant authority to consider any report or recommendations made to it by a monitoring officer of the authority (including provision with respect to the procedure to be followed by the standards committee),

    (d)   enabling a standards committee of a relevant authority, following its consideration of any such report or recommendations, to take any action prescribed by the regulations (including action against any member or co-opted member (or former member or co-opted member) of the authority who is the subject of any such report or recommendation),

    (e)   the publicity to be given to any such reports, recommendations or action.

(3) The provision which may be made by virtue of subsection (2)(a) includes provision for or in connection with—

    (a)   conferring powers on a monitoring officer of a relevant authority to enable him to conduct an investigation in respect of any matters referred to him,

    (b)   conferring rights (including the right to make representations) on any member or co-opted member (or former member or co-opted member) of a relevant authority who is the subject of any such investigation.

(4) The provision which may be made by virtue of subsection (2)(d) includes provision for or in connection with—

    (a)   enabling a standards committee of a relevant authority to censure a member or co-opted member (or former member or co-opted member) of the authority,

    (b)   enabling a standards committee of a relevant authority to suspend or partially suspend a person from being a member or co-opted member of the authority for a limited period,

(c) conferring a right of appeal on a member or co-opted member (or former member or co-opted member) of a relevant authority in respect of any action taken against him.

(5)   Nothing in subsection (2), (3) or (4) affects the generality of the power under subsection (1).

(6)   An ethical standards officer who refers any matters to the monitoring officer of a relevant authority under section 60(2) or 64(2) may give directions to the monitoring officer as to the way in which those matters are to be dealt with.

78
Decisions of interim case tribunals

(1)   An interim case tribunal which adjudicates on any matters which are the subject of an interim report must reach one of the following decisions—

(a) that the person to whom the recommendation mentioned in section 65(3) or 72(3) relates should not be suspended or partially suspended from being a member or co-opted member of the relevant authority concerned,

(b) that that person should be suspended or partially suspended from being a member or co-opted member of the authority concerned for a period which does not exceed six months or (if shorter) the remainder of the person's term of office.

(2)   An interim case tribunal must give notice of its decision to the standards committee of the relevant authority concerned.

(3)   If the decision of an interim case tribunal is that a person should be suspended or partially suspended from being a member or co-opted member of the relevant authority concerned—

(a) the notice must give details of the suspension or partial suspension and specify the date on which the suspension or partial suspension is to begin, and

(b) the relevant authority must suspend or partially suspend the person in accordance with the notice.

(4)   A decision of an interim case tribunal under this section shall not prevent an ethical standards officer from continuing with the investigation under section 59 which gave rise to the interim report concerned and producing a report under section 64, or a further interim report under section 65, in respect of any matters which are the subject of the investigation.

(5)   A decision of an interim case tribunal under this section shall not prevent a Local Commissioner in Wales from continuing with the investigation under section 69 which gave rise to the interim report concerned and producing a report under section 71, or a further interim report under section 72, in respect of any matters which are the subject of the investigation.

(6)   The suspension or partial suspension of any person under this section shall not extend beyond the day on which a notice under section 79 is given to the standards committee of the relevant authority concerned with respect to that person.

(7)   A copy of any notice under this section must be given—

(a) to any person who is the subject of the notice, and

(b) to the monitoring officer of the relevant authority concerned.

(8)   In a case where section 65(6) or 72(6) applies, the references in subsections (2) and (7)(b) to the relevant authority concerned are to be treated as including a reference to the relevant authority of which the person concerned was formerly a member or co-opted member.

(9)   An interim case tribunal must take reasonable steps to inform any person who made any allegation which gave rise to the investigation under section 59 or 69 of its decision under this section.

(10)   A person who is suspended or partially suspended under this section may appeal to the High Court—

(a) against the suspension or partial suspension, or

(b) against the length of the suspension or partial suspension.

79
Decisions of case tribunals

(1)   A case tribunal which adjudicates on any matter must decide whether or not any person to which that matter relates has failed to comply with the code of conduct of the relevant authority concerned.

(2)   Where a case tribunal decides that a person has not failed to comply with the code of conduct of the relevant authority concerned, it must give notice to that effect to the standards committee of the relevant authority concerned.

(3)   Where a case tribunal decides that a person has failed to comply with the code of conduct of the relevant authority concerned, it must decide whether the nature of the failure is such that the person should be suspended or disqualified in accordance with subsection (4).

(4)   A person may be—

  (a)   suspended or partially suspended from being a member or co-opted member of the relevant authority concerned, or

  (b)   disqualified for being, or becoming (whether by election or otherwise), a member of that or any other relevant authority.

(5)   Where a case tribunal makes such a decision as is mentioned in subsection (4)(a), it must decide the period for which the person should be suspended or partially suspended (which must not exceed one year or, if shorter, the remainder of the person's term of office).

(6)   Where a case tribunal makes such a decision as is mentioned in subsection (4)(b), it must decide the period for which the person should be disqualified (which must not exceed five years).

(7)   Where a case tribunal decides that a person has failed to comply with the code of conduct of the relevant authority concerned but should not be suspended or disqualified as mentioned in subsection (4), it must give notice to the standards committee of the relevant authority concerned—

  (a)   stating that the person has failed to comply with that code of conduct, and

  (b)   specifying the details of that failure.

(8)   Where a case tribunal decides that a person has failed to comply with the code of conduct of the relevant authority concerned and should be suspended or partially suspended as mentioned in subsection (4)(a), it must give notice to the standards committee of the relevant authority concerned—

  (a)   stating that the person has failed to comply with that code of conduct,

  (b)   specifying the details of that failure, and

  (c)   stating that the person must be suspended or partially suspended by the relevant authority concerned for the period, and in the way, which the tribunal has decided.

(9)   A relevant authority must comply with any notice given to its standards committee under subsection (8).

(10)   Where a case tribunal decides that a person has failed to comply with the code of conduct of the relevant authority concerned and should be disqualified as mentioned in subsection (4)(b), it must give notice to the standards committee of the relevant authority concerned—

  (a)   stating that the person has failed to comply with that code of conduct,

  (b)   specifying the details of that failure, and

  (c)   stating that the person is disqualified for being, or becoming (whether by election or otherwise), a member of that or any other relevant authority for the period which the tribunal has decided.

(11)   The effect of a notice given to the standards committee of a relevant authority under subsection (10) is to disqualify the person concerned as mentioned in subsection (10)(c).

(12)   A copy of any notice under this section—

  (a)   must be given—

    (i)   to the Standards Board for England, where the relevant authority concerned is in England,

(ii) to the Commission for Local Administration in Wales, where the relevant authority concerned is in Wales,

(b) must be given to any person who is the subject of the decision to which the notice relates, and

(c) must be published in one or more newspapers circulating in the area of the relevant authority concerned.

(13) Where the person concerned is no longer a member or co-opted member of the relevant authority concerned but is a member or co-opted member of another relevant authority in the same country (that is to say, England or Wales)—

(a) a copy of any notice under subsection (2), (7) or (10) must also be given to the standards committee of that other relevant authority,

(b) the references in subsections (4)(a) and (8)(c) to the relevant authority concerned are to be treated as references to that other relevant authority,

(c) the duty to give notice to the standards committee of the relevant authority concerned under subsection (8) is to be treated as a duty—

(i) to give that notice to the standards committee of that other relevant authority, and

(ii) to give a copy of that notice to the standards committee of the relevant authority concerned,

(d) the reference in subsection (12)(c) to the relevant authority concerned is to be treated as including a reference to that other relevant authority.

(14) A case tribunal must take reasonable steps to inform any person who made any allegation which gave rise to the adjudication of the decision of the case tribunal under this section.

(15) Where a case tribunal decides under this section that a person has failed to comply with the code of conduct of the relevant authority concerned, that person may appeal to the High Court against that decision, or any other decision under this section which relates to him.

80
Recommendations by case tribunals

(1) A case tribunal which has adjudicated on any matter may make recommendations to a relevant authority about any matters relating to—

(a) the exercise of the authority's functions,

(b) the authority's code of conduct, or

(c) the authority's standards committee.

(2) A case tribunal must send a copy of any recommendations it makes under subsection (1) to the relevant person.

(3) A relevant authority to whom recommendations are made under subsection (1) must consider the recommendations and, within a period of three months beginning with the day on which the recommendations are received, prepare a report for the relevant person giving details of what action the authority have taken or are proposing to take as a result of the recommendations.

(4) A relevant authority's function of considering a report under subsection (3) may be discharged only by the authority or by the standards committee of that authority (and accordingly, in the case of a relevant authority to which section 101 of the Local Government Act 1972 applies, is not to be a function to which that section applies).

(5) If the relevant person is not satisfied with the action the relevant authority have taken or propose to take in relation to the recommendations, the relevant person may require the authority to publish a statement giving details of the recommendations made by the tribunal and of the authority's reasons for not fully implementing the recommendations.

(6) In this section 'the relevant person' means—

(a) the Standards Board for England where the relevant authority concerned is in England,

(b) a Local Commissioner in Wales where the relevant authority concerned is in Wales.

81

Disclosure and registration of members' interests etc

(1)   The monitoring officer of each relevant authority must establish and maintain a register of interests of the members and co-opted members of the authority.

(2)   The mandatory provisions of the model code applicable to each relevant authority ('the mandatory provisions') must require the members and co-opted members of each authority to register in that authority's register maintained under subsection (1) such financial and other interests as are specified in the mandatory provisions.

(3)   The mandatory provisions must also—

(a)   require any member or co-opted member of a relevant authority who has an interest specified in the mandatory provisions under subsection (2) to disclose that interest before taking part in any business of the authority relating to that interest,

(b)   make provision for preventing or restricting the participation of a member or co-opted member of a relevant authority in any business of the authority to which an interest disclosed under paragraph (a) relates.

(4)   Any participation by a member or co-opted member of a relevant authority in any business which is prohibited by the mandatory provisions is not a failure to comply with the authority's code of conduct if the member or co-opted member has acted in accordance with a dispensation from the prohibition granted by the authority's standards committee in accordance with regulations made under subsection (5).

(5)   The Secretary of State may prescribe in regulations the circumstances in which standards committees may grant dispensations under subsection (4).

(6)   A relevant authority must ensure that copies of the register for the time being maintained by their monitoring officer under this section are available at an office of the authority for inspection by members of the public at all reasonable hours.

(7)   As soon as practicable after the establishment by their monitoring officer of a register under this section, a relevant authority must—

(a)   publish in one or more newspapers circulating in their area a notice which—

(i)   states that copies of the register are available at an office of the authority for inspection by members of the public at all reasonable hours, and

(ii)   specifies the address of that office, and

(b)   inform the Standards Board for England that copies of the register are so available.

(8)   In its application to standards committees of relevant authorities in Wales (other than police authorities), subsection (5) has effect as if for the reference to the Secretary of State there were substituted a reference to the National Assembly for Wales.

82

Code of conduct for local government employees

(1)   The Secretary of State may by order issue a code as regards the conduct which is expected of qualifying employees of relevant authorities in England and police authorities in Wales.

(2)   The National Assembly for Wales may by order issue a code as regards the conduct which is expected of qualifying employees of relevant authorities in Wales (other than police authorities).

(3)   The power under subsection (1) or (2) to issue a code includes power—

(a)   to issue a separate code for council managers (within the meaning of Part II of this Act), and

(b)   to revise any code which has been issued.

(4)   Before making an order under this section, the Secretary of State must consult—

    (*a*)   such representatives of relevant authorities in England, and of employees of such authorities, as he considers appropriate,

    (*b*)   the Audit Commission, and

    (*c*)   the Commission for Local Administration in England.

(5)   Before making an order under this section so far as it relates to police authorities in Wales, the Secretary of State must consult—

    (*a*)   such representatives of police authorities in Wales, and of employees of such authorities, as he considers appropriate,

    (*b*)   the Commission for Local Administration in Wales, and

    (*c*)   the National Assembly for Wales.

(6)   Before making an order under this section, the National Assembly for Wales must consult—

    (*a*)   such representatives of relevant authorities in Wales, and of employees of such authorities, as it considers appropriate,

    (*b*)   the Audit Commission, and

    (*c*)   the Commission for Local Administration in Wales.

(7)   The terms of appointment or conditions of employment of every qualifying employee of a relevant authority (whether appointed or employed before or after the commencement of this section) are to be deemed to incorporate any code for the time being under this section which is applicable.

(8)   In this section 'qualifying employee', in relation to a relevant authority, means an employee of the authority other than an employee falling within any description of employee specified in regulations under this subsection.

(9)   The power to make regulations under subsection (8) is to be exercised—

    (*a*)   in relation to England, by the Secretary of State, and

    (*b*)   in relation to Wales, by the National Assembly for Wales.

83
Interpretation of Part III

(1)   In this Part—

'the Audit Commission' means the Audit Commission for Local Authorities and the National Health Service in England and Wales,

'case tribunal' has the meaning given by section 76(1),

'code of conduct' means a code of conduct under section 51,

'co-opted member' has the meaning given by section 49(7),

'elected mayor' and 'elected executive member' have the meaning given by section 39(1) and (4),

'ethical standards officer' means a person appointed under section 57(5)(*a*),

'executive' is to be construed in accordance with section 11,

'executive arrangements' has the meaning given by section 10,

'executive leader' has the meaning given by section 11(3)(*a*),

'interim case tribunal' has the meaning given by section 76(2),

'Local Commissioner in Wales' has the meaning given by section 68(5),

'model code of conduct' is to be construed in accordance with section 50(1) and (2),

'police authority' means a police authority established under section 3 of the Police Act 1996,

'the relevant Adjudication Panel' means—

    (*a*)   in relation to matters referred or to be referred by an ethical standards officer, the Adjudication Panel for England,

    (*b*)   in relation to matters referred or to be referred by a Local Commissioner in Wales, the Adjudication Panel for Wales,

'relevant authority' has the meaning given by section 49(6).

(2)   Any reference in this Part to a committee of a relevant authority, in the case of a relevant authority to which Part II of this Act applies, includes a reference to a committee of an executive of the authority.

(3)   Any reference in this Part to a member of a relevant authority, in the case of a relevant authority to which Part II of this Act applies, includes a reference to an elected mayor or elected executive member of the authority.

(4)   Any reference in this Part to a member of a relevant authority, in the case of the Greater London Authority, is a reference to the Mayor of London or a London Assembly member.

(5)   Any reference in this Part to a joint committee or joint sub-committee of a relevant authority is a reference to a joint committee on which the authority is represented or a sub-committee of such a committee.

(6)   Any reference in this Part to a failure to comply with a relevant authority's code of conduct includes a reference to a failure to comply with the mandatory provisions which apply to the members or co-opted members of the authority by virtue of section 51(5)(*b*).

(7)   Any reference in this Part to a person being partially suspended from being a member or co-opted member of a relevant authority includes a reference to a person being prevented from exercising particular functions or having particular responsibilities as such a member or co-opted member.

(8)   The reference in subsection (7) to particular functions or particular responsibilities as a member of a relevant authority, in the case of a relevant authority to which Part II of this Act applies, includes a reference to particular functions or particular responsibilities as a member of an executive of the authority.

(9)   A person who is suspended under this Part from being a member of a relevant authority shall also be suspended from being a member of any committee, sub-committee, joint committee or joint sub-committee of the authority, but this subsection does not apply to a person who is partially suspended under this Part.

(10)   A person who is suspended under this Part from being a member of a relevant authority to which Part II of this Act applies shall also be suspended, if he is a member of an executive of the authority, from being such a member; but this subsection does not apply to a person who is partially suspended under this Part.

(11)   A person who is disqualified under this Part for being or becoming a member of a relevant authority shall also be disqualified—

(*a*)   for being or becoming a member of any committee, sub-committee, joint committee or joint sub-committee of the authority, and

(*b*)   if the authority is one to which Part II of this Act applies, for being or becoming a member of an executive of the authority.

(12)   Any function which by virtue of this Part is exercisable by or in relation to the monitoring officer of a relevant authority which is a parish council is to be exercisable by or in relation to the monitoring officer of the district council or unitary county council which are the responsible authority in relation to the parish council; and any reference in this Part to the monitoring officer of a relevant authority which is a parish council is to be construed accordingly.

(13)   Any function which by virtue of this Part is exercisable by or in relation to the monitoring officer of a relevant authority which is a community council is to be exercisable by or in relation to the monitoring officer of the county council or county borough council in whose area the community council is situated; and any reference in this Part to the monitoring officer of a relevant authority which is a community council is to be construed accordingly.

(14)   Any functions which are conferred by virtue of this Part on a relevant authority to which Part II of this Act applies are not to be the responsibility of an executive of the authority under executive arrangements.

(15)   Any functions which are conferred on the Greater London Authority by virtue of this Part are to be exercisable by the Mayor of London and the London Assembly acting jointly on behalf of the Authority.

(16)   Subsections (12) and (13) of section 55 are to apply for the purposes of subsection (12) as they apply for the purposes of that section.

APPENDIX 7

The New Role of the Monitoring Officer

(Chapter 10)

2 July 2001
Reproduced with the permission of:
Association of Council Secretaries and Solicitors
150 Mountbatten Close
Ashton-on-Ribble
Preston PR2 2XE
Telephone/Fax: (01772) 739073
Email: acsesny@cybase.co.uk
Website: www.acses.org.uk

1
Introduction

This paper has been prepared by the Association of Council Secretaries and Solicitors in response to a widespread call for a clear statement of the new role of the Monitoring Officer as a result of the Local Government Act 2000. That role has substantially changed not only in relation to the new ethical framework in Part III of the Act but also as a result of the implementation of executive arrangements under Part II.

The Association's membership includes the most senior lawyers and administrators in local government in England and Wales and its members comprise the great majority of Monitoring Officers. This paper is published not only for the benefit of Monitoring Officers but also in the expectation that it will be of interest to senior councillors and Chief Executives concerned to ensure the fluent implementation of the new political structures.

In preparing this paper the Association recognises that in the great majority of Councils Monitoring Officers enjoy excellent working relationships with colleagues especially Heads of Paid Service and this paper is intended not only to explain the Monitoring Officer's role but to support and further develop those relationships.

2
Background

The Local Government and Housing Act 1989 (LGHA 1989) introduced the statutory office of Monitoring Officer but left Councils' free to decide whether or not the appointment should be held also by the Head of Paid Service. Unlike the provisions relating to the appointment of Chief Financial Officer no professional qualifications were specified.

The Government has now established a strong external regime for dealing with serious misconduct and has substantially enhanced the role of Monitoring Officers giving them a key role in supporting the Standards Committee and by keeping up standards by encouragement and persuasion. Regulations are likely to provide a more

401

formal role in the handling of allegations of misconduct. The White Paper 'A new ethical framework' published in 1998 proposed that it should be a requirement for Monitoring Officer posts to be established at Chief Officer level reflecting the duty to report directly to the Council. So far at least, this seems to have been overlooked although undoubtedly appointments at that level represent current best practice.

3
Qualifications for Appointment

There are no statutory requirements as to who may be appointed Monitoring Officer save that it cannot be the Head of Paid Service under Local Government Act 2000 (LGA 2000) (para 24(3), Schedule 5) nor can it be the Chief Finance Officer appointed under s 151 of the Local Government Act 1972 (LGA 1972). It is interesting to note that the Standards Board for England (s 57(5)(c) of the LGA 2000), and the Commission for Local Administration in Wales (s 68(2)) may issue guidance in relation to the qualifications or experience which Monitoring Officers should possess. It would be surprising if early guidance did not emphasise the desirability of a legal qualification and substantial experience in constitutional issues affecting local government. The Association hopes that such guidance will also advise on such matters as the need for resources, access to meetings and the organisational location of the Monitoring Officer and has recommended the Standards Board to do so.

4
Selection Appointment and Dismissal

Save for Heads of Paid Service Monitoring Officers currently designated under s 5 of the LGHA 1989 will continue in office subject to any review by Councils as a result of Standards Board guidance. The appointment of staff generally, including Monitoring Officers, is not a function of the Executive under new constitutions (Local Government (Functions and Responsibilities) (England) Regulations 2000). There are two important points to make here. Firstly, the role of Monitoring Officer should be considered with care by those making the designation. The personal duty to the Council, the need for impartial and independent judgement often in the face of political pressure require many attributes including analysis, resolution, consistency and steadfastness. Secondly where Monitoring Officers are chief officers (or deputy chief officers) the Secretary of State intends to make regulations in relation to executive arrangements which involve a mayor with cabinet or leader with cabinet, requiring the Council to consider any objections from a member of the Executive and not to make the appointment unless they conclude that the objection is not well founded. A member of the Executive will also be required to be included on any appointments committee or sub-committee. The Association recommends that the full Council should approve the designation. The Monitoring Officer will often be required to give advice on the vires of executive decisions or the interpretation of the constitution which affects the executive and for this reason the executive influence on the appointment should not be dominant. These duties also strongly suggest that the Monitoring Officer should be Chief Officer, on the senior management board of the authority, to have sufficient weight and independence from senior colleagues, as well as involvement in the decision making and formulation processes at the highest level. Where Councils are operating a Mayor with Council Manager model it would seem wrong that the person responsible for the majority of decision-making, the Council Manager, should also be the person appointing the Monitoring Officer.

The Secretary of State as advised by Nolan, and the Joint Committee of both Houses intends to extend the protection from dismissal provision in the Local Government (Standing Orders) Regulations 1993 (which currently apply to the head of paid service) to the Monitoring Officer (see para 8.12 of the DETR Statutory Guidance). The Joint Committee in their report in July 1999 said:

> 'There appears to be a risk that these officers may have become more vulnerable to abuses of power as a result of their investigative responsibilities and as the primary advisor to the Standards Committee.'

The effect of extending the regulations will be that the Monitoring Officer will not be the subject of disciplinary action (except suspension for a limited time with full pay to allow alleged misconduct to be investigated) other than in accordance with a recommendation in a report made by a designated independent person. This personal protection from dismissal extends not only to the exercise of Monitoring Officer duties but also to any other duties that person discharges under his or her contract of employment. It will be important for the Monitoring Officers to build a strong working relationship with the Standards Committee and especially the chairman to whom they should be able to look for support in difficult times.

5
Personal Duty and appointment of Deputy
The Monitoring Officer owes a personal duty to the Council as a whole in carrying out his or her statutory functions which cannot be discharged through an intervening officer or committee. As with all functions of the Council the exercise of the Monitoring Officer's functions are susceptible to judicial review. Monitoring Officers need to check that their council operates adequate insurance and indemnity arrangements should their decisions be challenged. This may be particularly important for Monitoring Officers in district and unitary authorities who also exercise their ethical framework functions on behalf of Parish Councils.
Section 5(7) of the LGHA 1989 requires Monitoring Officers to appoint a deputy to act when they is unable to do so through absence or illness. It is suggested that good practice would be to appoint a deputy at an early stage and to advise colleagues and the Council of his identity even though the deputy can only act in the Monitoring Officer's absence. Where Monitoring Officers have a conflict of interest in an issue which requires their advice it would be best if he were to find a good reason to be absent so that the deputy could act.

6
Primary Statutory Responsibilities
The basic responsibilities of the Monitoring Officer are contained in s 5 of the LGHA 1989. These provisions will be substantially amended with effect from 28 July 2001 by paragraph 24 of Schedule 5 to the LGA 2000. The duties prior to the 28 July 2001 were to report to the Council on any proposal, decision or omission by the Council or any committee or officer which has given or is likely to give or would give rise to any contravention of any enactment or rule of law or statutory code of practice. From that date the duty to report on contraventions of statutory codes (ie primarily the National Code of Local Government Conduct) is removed. At the same time the duty to report on maladministration or injustice (which was widely regarded as a legislative drafting error and largely unworkable) is amended to apply where the Ombudsman has carried out an investigation. Why it should be necessary for the Monitoring Officer to prepare a report where the Ombudsman has found no maladministration, or maladministration but no injustice, is difficult to imagine save that it would provide the Monitoring Officer with the opportunity to take a wider view on process within the organisation and make recommendations.

7
Consultation
In the course of preparing a report under s 5 of the LGHA 1989 the Monitoring Officer must consult so far as it is practicable with the Head of Paid Service (normally the Chief Executive) and the Chief Finance Officer. This requirement reflects the key role of the three Statutory Officers in the corporate governance of the council and the importance of early warning to enable them to consider whether they also should issue reports. It also gives a chance to reflect on the views of colleagues before the green button is pressed.

8
Report to the Council

Having prepared a report under s 5 the Monitoring Officer must send a copy to each member of the Council. The Council must meet to consider the report not more than 21 days after copies of the report are first sent to members. The decision or proposal the subject of the Monitoring Officer's report remains suspended until the end of the first business day after the day on which the consideration of the report is concluded. Presumably this is designed to give some time, although precious little, for any person aggrieved to challenge the decision by taking legal proceedings.

It should be noted that the Secretary of State intends to modify s 5 of the LGHA 1989 to provide that where a Monitoring Officer's report relates to executive functions the report should be made to the Executive although all members of the Council would receive a copy of the report (Statutory Guidance paragraph 8.22).

9
Some Monitoring Officer Issues in relation to Section 5

Section 5 of the LGHA 1989 does not assist the Monitoring Officer on a number of matters. There is no guidance as to when a report is to be made although it might reasonably be assumed that it should be made as soon as is practicable after the Monitoring Officer is satisfied that a contravention of law has taken or is about to take place. Difficulties can arise where another investigative body is carrying out enquiries, eg the District Auditor, the Police, the Ombudsman and within a few months time possibly also the Standards Board. There would certainly be a fair case at least for deferring a report if say the police were to take the view that it would hinder their enquiries.

Monitoring Officers under Section 5 have no duty to search or find contraventions of law but they must act when circumstances come to their attention and are satisfied as to the legal position. We all recognise of course that at best the role of the Monitoring Officer is proactive and not judgmental after the event and this issue is developed later in this paper.

10
Resources

Each Council has a duty under s 5 of the LGHA 1989 to provide the Monitoring Officer:

> '. . . with such staff, accommodation and other resources as are, in his opinion, sufficient to allow these duties to be performed; ...'

Monitoring Officers will wish to note that paragraph 24(8) of Schedule 5 to the LGA 2000 adds all the duties of the Monitoring Officer under Part III of the LGA 2000 (the ethical framework) to s 5 of the LGHA 1989. Monitoring Officers will wish to reflect on the need to report to their Councils on resources where in his or her opinion they are insufficient to properly discharge the scope of their new duties. In addition, in the event that the Secretary of State makes regulations under s 66 of the LGA 2000 enabling Monitoring Officers to formally conduct investigations, Monitoring Officers may need to keep the issue of resources under review. This could well include an adequate budget for counsel's advice. Most importantly he will need clear protocols which will ensure access to all meetings and early reports from colleagues where there is uncertainty about vires or proper process within the constitution. Such protocols should include a positive duty on colleagues to advise the Monitoring Officer where they believe the Council may have acted or be about to act unlawfully. Appendix 1 contains a draft protocol which local authorities may wish to consider and adapt to local circumstances.

Councils must provide Monitoring Officers with the resources they consider are needed. It is recommended that if staff and resources are inadequate and a report is required it should be made this year and not delayed until after the LGA 2000 is fully in operation.

11
The draft Model Code

There are a number of points worth reference at this stage which add to the responsibilities of the Monitoring Officer. It is clear that the Secretary of State will expect Monitoring Officers to be available to give advice generally to members on the application of Local Codes of Conduct and particularly to assist members to evaluate whether their personal interest is so significant that it would be regarded as likely to prejudice judgement.

The Monitoring Officer is also to be the recipient of whistle blowing notifications from members. This was the advice of the Local Government Association to DETR although the draft Model Code also requires the notification to be made to the Standards Board. It is regrettably unclear at this stage as to what the Monitoring Officer is expected to do in this instance. Hopefully the Standards Board will look to the Monitoring Officer to investigate and report in all but the more serious cases.

It is also worthwhile noting at this point that the draft in paragraph 6 requires members when reaching decisions to 'have regard' to any relevant advice provided by the Monitoring Officer in any formal report under Section 5. This arguably adds weight to such Monitoring Officer's reports making them akin to statutory guidance ie members should either accept the guidance or only reject it on clear and reasonable grounds. It is interesting that the LGA's advice to DETR on the draft Model Code was also that Monitoring Officers with party group leaders should play a role in helping to resolve complaints by members alleging breaches of conduct. It is hoped at least in practice that such a role will be performed.

12
Registers

The responsibility of the Monitoring Officer under s 81 of the Act to establish and maintain a register of interests of members and co-opted members of the Council should be noted. It will be important for Monitoring Officers to ensure sound advice to all members on these potentially difficult questions and to ensure regular updates are sought.

The Monitoring Officer will also be obliged to maintain a register of gifts and hospitality if the draft Model Code provisions are made in that form by the Secretary of State by Order.

13
The New Ethical Framework

The statutory guidance at paragraph 8.20 states that the Monitoring Officer will have a key role in promoting and maintaining high standards of conduct within a local authority in particular through the provision of support to the Standards Committee. In effect the Monitoring Officer in partnership with the Standards Committee will be the source of advice and training for members and officers on conduct and the adoption of a local code of conduct.

Monitoring Officers may well find that they are consulted at an early stage by the Standards Board who are considering whether or not to investigate and by the Ethical Standards Officer (ESO) at various stages in deciding how to carry out his investigation or, for instance, under what terms the complaint should be passed to the Monitoring Officer. This could well prove to be an important additional task.

The functions of the Monitoring Officer in District and Unitary Councils under the ethical framework are to be discharged also for parishes in that area. This will be a particular burden when Councils are managing the introduction of executive arrangements and the new ethical framework. One District Council has over a hundred parishes! The issue of resources (paragraph 10 above) will be particularly important for them. It is interesting to note that these arrangements suggest an acceptance that Monitoring Officers do not need to be exclusively concerned with the business of their Council and may exercise judgement across a number of Councils without regular contact with them. The duties in relation to parishes do not extend to the responsibility to report on contraventions of the law or maladministration investigations under s 5 of the LGHA 1989.

Especially in two-tier areas where members are elected quite often to both County and District, Monitoring Officers may judge it beneficial to meet from time to time with colleagues in their County to share issues and to reach consensus, if possible, on advice. This may prove particularly important in advance of a range of advice published by the Standards Board.

Regulations under s 66 of the LGA 2000 may be made by the Secretary of State which govern the way Monitoring Officers are to deal with references to them by ethical standards officers under ss 60(2) or 64(2). The Regulations are expected to cover the power to conduct an investigation, reports to the Standards Committee, its procedures, powers (including censure, partial suspension, suspension, and appeal) and publicity. The Association firmly believe that less serious complaints would prove to be best dealt with speedily and effectively locally through the Monitoring Officer and the Standards Committee.

14
Allegations of misconduct in the absence of a written complaint to the Standards Board

Complaints or concerns may be received by the Monitoring Officer from members of the public, or other persons who do not wish, at least at that stage, to make a formal written complaint to the Standards Board. A councillor may raise issues of potential concern with the Monitoring Officer which have not yet reached the point where the member has a duty to report to the Standards Board. Allegations of misconduct may relate also to other matters of concern to the Council, eg as a result of a failure to declare a personal interest the validity of decision is challenged. The Association is of the view that the Council should look to the Monitoring Officer to make enquiries into the position and following consideration report if appropriate to the Standards Committee. He or she would liaise with the Standards Board should it subsequently receive a written complaint.

15
Maladministration

Section 92 of the LGA 2000 enables Councils to make a payment or provide some other benefit to a person who has been or may have been adversely affected by action which amounts to or may amount to maladministration. Bearing in mind the Monitoring Officers duties under s 5 of the LGHA 1989 Monitoring Officers should advise on any such circumstances. Decisions under s 92, which cannot be an executive function, would best be delegated to the Standards Committee on the advice of the Monitoring Officer.

16
New Constitutions and Executive Arrangements

The role of the Monitoring Officer under new constitutions will be just as demanding as the new ethical framework and in some Councils even more so. DETR guidance states:

> 'Local authorities will need to recognise under executive arrangements the importance of the Monitoring Officer's key roles of providing advice on vires issues, maladministration, financial impropriety, probity and policy framework and budget issues to all members of the local authority'.

The Secretary of State clearly envisages the Monitoring Officer playing a vital role in advising both the Overview and Scrutiny committees and the Executive. The guidance at paragraph 3.48 advises that Scrutiny Committees should seek the advice of the Monitoring Officer where they consider there is doubt about the vires for a decision or an executive decision is contrary to the policy framework and should have been referred to the full Council. Paragraph 4.44 also advises the executive to consult the Monitoring Officer where there is doubt about vires. Advice of this kind in highly charged political situations will prove very difficult especially where for instance the balance of opinion in the executive is different to the full Council. DETR guidance in paragraphs 2.51 and 2.52 is that advice from the Monitoring Officer that a decision is contrary to the policy framework, budget, standing orders or financial regulations should be treated and handled accordingly.

The implementation of new constitutions however, quite separately from vires issues, will prove demanding for the Monitoring Officer especially where for example questions are raised as to whether or not a decision should have been treated as a 'key decision' and included in the forward plan, and whether or not a matter before the executive can be called in by Scrutiny. These questions in an atmosphere of political tension will test Monitoring Officers as much as any aspect of their new ethical framework functions.

These issues will put the Monitoring Officer in a very difficult position when reporting to another more senior tier of management within the authority, who may not necessarily agree with the Monitoring Officer's views.

DETR guidance (paragraph 8.21) advises that the Monitoring Officer should also be the proper officer for the purpose of ensuring that executive decisions, together with the reasons for those decisions and relevant officer reports and background papers, are made publicly available. With the Chief Executive he is responsible for a system of record keeping for all the local authority's decisions (executive or otherwise).

17
Further Issues for the Monitoring Officer

Monitoring Officers more than most senior officers will face potential difficulties in advising both the executive and scrutiny. Paragraph 8.30 of DETR guidance points to the potential conflict where scrutiny committees are questioning executive decisions. Monitoring Officers who are also Chief Legal Officers may find themselves being examined in public by scrutiny in connection with politically sensitive advice given in private to the executive by one of their Senior Legal staff, eg the Monitoring Officer may not personally wholly agree with the advice given, or possibly the executive will be concerned that advice received in private which they did not accept will be exposed.

Another issue concerns confidentiality and the strict duty a solicitor owes to his client. Section 62(2) of the LGA 2000 requires any person to give such information or explanation as the Ethical Standards Officer (ESO) considers necessary in his investigation. The Monitoring Officer may have confidential information about a member which could be of assistance but is not strictly requested by the ESO. Disclosure could risk a complaint to the Law Society. Many Councils may be willing formally to give the Monitoring Officer authority to disclose any information held by the Council to the ESO whether confidential or otherwise whether requested or not which he considers would be of assistance. Such an authority might be appropriately included in the protocol between the Monitoring Officer and his Council referred to in the following paragraph.

18
Position of the Monitoring Officer within the Organisation

The role of the Monitoring Officer as described in this paper is significantly increased. The Statutory Guidance emphasises his key role in terms of standards and vires and ensuring proper process within the constitution. The Association firmly believes that

Monitoring Officers will be in a position to discharge their responsibilities if they have or are:
(i)   Chief Officers with a place on the Chief Officers' Management Board, or receive copies of all agenda and minutes and has a right to attend and speak on matters of concern;
(ii) A right of access to all meetings of the Council without reservation including member briefings;
(iii) Recognised as the principal advisor to the Standards Committee and is the point of reference for advice on vires and interpretation of the constitution;
(iv) Have a protocol approved by the full Council setting out how they are expected to discharge their functions and the support and reporting arrangements required, including positive duties on fellow officers to report situations where they believe the Council has acted unlawfully or may be about to do so;
(v)   A team with sufficient expertise to keep under regular review the Council's constitutional documents.

19
It is a matter of regret that the present version of the statutory guidance does not reflect Monitoring Officers' new responsibilities in terms of their position within the organisation. The role of the Chief Financial Officer in the corporate affairs of the Council is acknowledged; the Association will continue to press for a future edition of the statutory guidance to make a similar recommendation in respect of the Monitoring Officer whose duties imply a similar corporate contribution.

20
Conclusion
The role of Monitoring Officers has substantially increased not only as a result of their key role in the ethical framework but also because they will be the focal point of advice for compliance with complex procedural rules under new constitutions. It is essential that Monitoring Officers ensure that they have the reporting mechanisms and colleague support which will enable them to discharge their new functions effectively. A place in the organisation is required which is either engaged in or well informed about the development of new initiatives and the approach to difficult decisions. This is not about personal profile. It is about making sure you have the access and support you need to do your job well.
RICHARD LESTER
Member of ACSeS and formerly County Secretary and Monitoring Officer at Cornwall County Council. He is a consultant with Eversheds.
26 June 2001

Appendix 1
DRAFT PROTOCOL
(Local authorities may wish to consider incorporating some or all of the following statement in a local protocol).

1
The Monitoring Officer undertakes to discharge his or her responsibilities outlined in this paper with determination and a manner which will enhance the reputation of the Council. In general terms his or her ability to discharge these duties depends on excellent working relations with colleagues and members but also the flow of information and access to debate particularly at early stages.

2
The following arrangements and understandings between Monitoring Officers and colleagues and members are designed to help ensure the effective discharge of their functions:

(a) If not a member of the Chief Officer's Management Team Monitoring Officers will have advance notice of those meetings and agenda and reports and the right to attend and speak;

(b) Advance notice of meetings whether formal or informal between Chief Officers and members of the Executive or Committee Chairmen will be given to Monitoring Officers where any procedural, vires or other constitutional issues are likely to arise;

(c) Chief Officers will alert Monitoring Officers to all emerging issues of concern including legality, probity, vires and constitutional issues;

(d) Monitoring Officers or their staff will have copies of all reports to members;

(e) Monitoring Officers are expected to develop good liaison and working relations with the Standards Board, the District Auditor and the Ombudsman including the giving and receiving of relevant information whether confidential or otherwise;

(f) Monitoring Officers will have a special relationship with the Chairman of the Council, Chairman of the Standards and Overview and Scrutiny Committees and will ensure the Head of Paid Service and Chief Financial Officer have up-to-date information regarding emerging issues;

(g) Monitoring Officers will be expected to make enquiries into allegations of misconduct in the absence of a written complaint being received by the Standards Board and if appropriate will make a written report to the Standards Committee unless the Monitoring Officer and Chair of Standards Committee agree a report is not warranted;

(h) The Head of Paid Service, Chief Financial Officer and Monitoring Officer will meet regularly to consider and recommend action in connection with current governance issues and other matters of concern regarding probity;

(i) In carrying out any investigation (whether under Regulations or otherwise) Monitoring Officers will have unqualified access to any information held by the Council and any employee who can assist in the discharge of their functions;

(j) Monitoring Officers will have control of a budget sufficient to enable him to seek Counsel's opinion on any matter concerning their functions;

(k) Monitoring Officers will be responsible for preparing a training programme for members on the ethical framework subject to the approval of the Standards Committee;

(l) Monitoring Officers will report to the Council from time to time on the Constitution and any necessary or desirable changes following consultation in particular with the Head of Paid Service and Chief Financial Officer;

(m) In consultation with the Chairman of the Council and Standards Board Monitoring Officers may defer the making of a formal report under s 5 of the LGHA 1989 where another investigative body is involved;

(n) Monitoring Officers will make a report to the Council from time to time as necessary on the staff, accommodation and resources they requires to discharge his/her functions;

(o) The Monitoring Officer will appoint a deputy and keep him or her briefed on emerging issues;

(p) Monitoring Officers will make arrangements to ensure good communication between their office and Clerks to Parish Councils.

Appendix 2
SUMMARY OF MONITORING OFFICER FUNCTIONS

	Description	Source
1	Report on contraventions or likely contraventions of any enactment or rule of law.	Section 5 of the Local Government and Housing Act 1989
2	Report on any maladministration or injustice where Ombudsman has carried out an investigation.	Section 5 of the Local Government and Housing Act 1989
3	Appointment of Deputy.	Section 5 of the Local Government and Housing Act 1989
4	Report on resources.	Section 5 of the Local Government and Housing Act 1989
5	Receive copies of whistle-blowing allegations of misconduct.	Draft Model Code
6	Investigate misconduct in compliance with Regulations (when made) and directions of Ethical Standards Officers.	Regulations when made. Directions when made in individual cases. Section 66(1) and (6) of the Local Government Act 2000
7	Establish and maintain registers of members interests and gifts and gifts and hospitality.	Section 81 of the Local Government Act 2000 and Draft Model Code
8	Advice to members on interpretation of Code.	Draft Model Code and Consultation Paper
9	Key role in promoting and maintaining high standards of conduct through support to the Standards Committee.	Statutory Guidance, paragraph 8.20
10	Liaison with Standards Board and Ethical Standards Officers.	New ethical framework, practical implications
11	New ethical framework functions in relation to Parish Councils.	Section 83(12) of the Local Government Act 2000
12	Compensation for maladministration.	Section 92 of the Local Government Act 2000
13	Advice on vires issues, maladministration, financial impropriety, probity and policy framework and budget issues to all members.	DETR guidance

APPENDIX 8

Terms of Reference of Standards and Governance Committee

(a) The Committee is a committee appointed by the Council under s 102(1) of the Local Government Act 1972.

(b) The Council has arranged under s 101(1) of that Act for the Standards Committee to exercise and discharge all the functions of the Council as are within its terms of reference (set out below), such functions not being:
- otherwise reserved by Corporate Committee to be exercised by another committee or sub-committee, or
- reserved by law to a meeting of full Council.

(c) The Committee shall have the power to establish Sub-Committees of itself, appoint members to those Sub-Committees (under s 102(1) or 102(4) of the 1972 Act), delegate matters to them and manage those Sub-Committees.

(d) Where a function or matter within the Standards Committee's competence has been delegated to an officer, the Committee may exercise that function/matter concurrently with the officer to whom it has been delegated.

(e) The exercise of any function or matter within the Committee's competence is always subject to any relevant requirement of Contract Standing Orders, Financial Regulations and Council Standing Orders (as amended from time to time).

(f) The Council may amend the Committee's terms of reference at any time.

Terms of Reference

1. To design, implement, monitor, approve and review the ethical framework of the Council, both for Councillors and employees. The Committee's powers shall include responding to consultation documents and the promulgation of Codes of Conduct but the adoption and revisions to the local Code of Conduct for Councillors shall be reserved to the Council.

2. To promote a culture of openness, accountability, transparency and probity in order to ensure the highest standards of conduct of Councillors and employees.

3. To recommend, monitor and review the operation of the Constitution.

4. To promote the values of putting people first, valuing public service and creating a norm of the highest standards of personal conduct.

5. To oversee and manage programmes of guidance, advice and training on ethics, standards and probity for Councillors and employees and on the local Code of Conduct for Councillors.

6. To receive reports from the Monitoring Officer on the operation of the Register of Members' Interests from time-to-time.

7. To be responsible for written guidance and advice on the operation of the system of declarations of Members' Interests and to receive reports form the Monitoring Officer on the operation of the system of declarations from time-to-time.

8. * To establish, monitor, approve and issue advice and guidance to Councillors on a system of dispensations to speak on, or participate in, matters in which they have interests and give dispensation in appropriate cases.
9. * To exercise the functions of the Council in relation to the ethical framework and standards of conduct of Joint Committees and other bodies.
10. * To determine appropriate action on matters referred to the Council by the National Standards Board for England.
11. To support the Monitoring Officer in his/her statutory role and the issuing of guidance on his/her role from time-to-time.
12. To support the Head of Financial Services in his/her statutory role in connection with financial probity and the issuing of guidance on his/her role from time-to-time.
13. * To establish and maintain a process to reprimand Councillors for breaches of the local Code of Conduct, Protocols and other rules and regulations subject to any guidance or requirements issued by the National Standards Board for England.
14. In the interim, to determine complaints on matters of conduct relating to Members and to pass such sanction as legally available to the Council in such form as the Committee thinks appropriate.

Notes

1 Functions marked with an asterix may only be exercised, or fully exercised, when appropriate powers have been introduced by legislation.
2 When the Local Government Act 2000 and appropriate secondary legislation and guidance is in force, and the Council adopts the local Code of Conduct for Members, these terms of reference will be revised and amended.

Appendix 9

Local Authorities (Executive Arrangements) (Modification of Enactments and Further Provisions) (England) Order 2001, SI 2001/1517 reg 8

(Chapter 12)

8
Standing orders with respect to local authority contracts

(1)   Before a local authority operate executive arrangements under Part II of the 2000 Act they shall make standing orders under section 135 of the 1972 Act (contracts of local authorities) with respect to the making of contracts on their behalf in the course of the discharge of functions which are the responsibility of the executive of that authority.

(2)   The standing orders shall include provision for securing that any contract which—

    (a)   is of or above a value specified in the standing orders by the authority; or

    (b)   is of a description specified in the standing orders by the authority,

    must be in writing.

(3)   The function of specifying a value or a description of contracts for the purposes of the provisions required by paragraph (2) shall be discharged by the authority themselves and section 101 of the 1972 Act (arrangements for the discharge of functions by local authorities) shall not apply to that function.

(4)   The standing orders shall include provision for securing that any contract to which the provisions required by paragraph (2) apply must—

    (a)   be made under the authority's seal and be attested by at least one officer of the authority who, in the case of an authority having a mayor and council manager executive, is not the council manager, whether or not the seal is also attested—

        (i)   by any member of the authority; or

        (ii)   in the case of an authority having a mayor and council manager executive, by the council manager; or

    (b)   be signed by at least two officers of the authority, whether or not the contract is also signed by any member of the authority.

(5)   In relation to an authority which are operating executive arrangements on the date on which this Order comes into force, the requirement of paragraph (1) to make the standing orders before they operate executive arrangements shall be treated as a requirement to make the standing orders as soon as reasonably practicable after that date.

Local Authorities (Executive Arrangements) (Modification of Enactments and Further Provisions) (England) Order 2001, SI 2001/1517, reg 8

APPENDIX 10

Notes to Scheme of Delegation

(Chapter 12)

These notes form part of the Register of Delegated Powers:

1
The powers in this document are subject to the provisions of Standing Orders Financial Regulations and Contract Standing Orders and the delegations contained therein.

2
All delegated functions shall be deemed to be exercised on behalf of and in the name of the Council.

3
The exercise of a delegated power, duty or function shall:
(a)   be subject to the City Council's policies and criteria;
(b)   not amount to a new policy or extension of or amendment to an existing policy;
(c)   be subject to any Special Procedure and/or Protocol; and
(d)   be subject to the requirements of Standing Orders, Financial Regulations and Corporate Standards.

4
An officer to whom a power, duty or function is delegated may nominate or authorise another officer to exercise that power, duty or function, provided that officer reports to or is responsible to the delegator.

5
References to any enactment, regulation, order or byelaw shall be construed as including any re-enactment or re-making of the same, whether or not with amendments.

6
Any reference to any Act of Parliament includes reference to regulations, subordinate and EU legislation upon which either UK legislation is based, or from which powers, duties and functions of the Council are derived.

7
Where the exercise of powers is subject to prior consultation with another officer, that officer may give his or her views in general terms in advance to apply to any particular circumstances, to remove the need for consultation for each proposal.

8

Subject to any express instructions to the contrary from the Council, Committee or Sub-Committee, any power to approve also includes the power to refuse, and the power to impose appropriate conditions.

9

Delegations to officers is subject to:
(a) the right of the Council, Committee or Sub-Committee to decide any matter in a particular case;
(b) the Head of Service or other officer may in any case in lieu of exercising his/her delegated power refer to a Committee or Sub-Committee for a decision; and
(c) any restrictions, conditions or directions of the delegating committee or Sub-Committee.

10

In exercising delegated powers, the Head of Service or other officer shall:
(a) take account of the requirements of the Corporate Standards and Special Procedures and shall address all legal, financial and other professional safe-guards as if the matter were not delegated;
(b) shall exercise the delegation so as to promote the efficient, effective and economic running of that Division, Directorate and the Council, and in furtherance of the Council's visions and values; and
(c) shall, where and when appropriate, report back to the appropriate Committee as to the exercise of those delegated powers.

11

Except where otherwise expressly provided either within this Scheme of Delegation or by resolution of the Council, a Committee or Sub-Committee, the exercise of any delegated power, duty or function is subject to having the appropriate and necessary budgetary provision in place to take the action in the name of and/or on behalf of the Council.

12

Save in respect of any statutory roles that are not capable of delegation, any power conferred on a subordinate officer shall be exercisable by the Head of Service, Executive Director or the Chief Executive.

13

The compilation of a Register of Delegated Powers is a statutory requirement. The Register is maintained by the Head of Democratic Services, and delegations are added to it as they are made by Committees and Sub-Committees. This is a 'snap-shot' of the Register as at 17th May 2000 (amended to reflect an internal reorganisation in May 2001). Officers should take care to inform themselves of any subsequent changes to the Register before solely relying on this document.

14

Following consultation with the Head of Legal Services, the Head of Democratic Services shall have the power to amend this Register to reflect re-organisations, changes in Job Titles and vacancies, where said changes result in re-distributing existing delegations and not the creation of new ones.

15

Any post specifically referred to below shall be deemed to include any successor post, or a post which includes within the job description, elements relevant to any particular delegation, which were also present in the earlier post and shall include anyone acting up or seconded.

16

Any reference to a Committee or Sub-Committee shall be deemed to include reference to a successor Committee or Sub-Committee provided that the subject matter of a particular delegation can be found within the terms of reference of both the earlier and the successor Committee or Sub-Committee.

17

Where a power or duty is delegated to an officer, and the exercise of that power or duty is contingent upon the opinion of the Council that particular conditions or factual circumstances exist, then the officer in question has the power to determine whether or not those circumstances exist or those conditions have been fulfilled in the name of and with the authority of the Council.

18

With respect to any reference to a delegation being exercised following consultation with the appropriate Executive Member, the decision is vested with the delegatee who shall be responsible and accountable for the decision, the delegatee is required to bring independent judgement to bear on the decision, and the decision must not consist of the officer adding an imprimatur of approval to what a Councillor has decided.

19

strike="on"All enquiries about this register should be made to the Committee and Members Services Manager.

20

All matters of interpretation of this document will be determined by the Head of Legal Services.

21

If a matter is delegated to an officer, but that delegation cannot be implemented, that should be reported to the delegating Committee or sub-Committee.

22

Functions, matters, powers, authorisations, delegations, duties and responsibilities etc within this Scheme shall be construed in a broad and inclusive fashion and shall include the doing of anything which is calculated to facilitate or is conducive or incidental to the discharge of anything specified.

23

This Register of Delegated Powers was approved under delegated powers on 1st May 2001. Additional delegated powers when added to the Register will refer to the appropriate Committee minute.

APPENDIX 11

Safeguards for Authorisation of Subordinate Officer to Discharge Particular Function in Scheme of Delegation

---

(Chapter 12)

1

The nature and statutory context of the function which is to be discharged by a subordinate officer is relevant. The greater the extent to which the discharge of the function affects individual rights or requires the exercise of discretion or professional judgement, the less likely it would be lawful to authorise the subordinate to act. It would be rare to authorise a subordinate to institute criminal proceedings.

2

Administrative inconvenience is a very important rationale for the power to authorise subordinates to act. Therefore, authorisation should only be given where the administrative burden of personally discharging functions would be significant.

3

The degree of control maintained by the senior officer over the authorised subordinate may be a material factor in determining the validity of the authorisation. In cases where significant discretion or judgement must be exercised, a high degree of control should be retained.

4

An authorisation may simply involve authorising the making of recommendations, which the senior officer himself considers whether or not to implement. In such a situation, the senior officer may retain a substantial degree of control over the discharge of the function that he may be said to direct his own mind to it. In nearly all cases, this approach would include a finding that there was an unlawful authorisation to the subordinate.

5

The subordinate may be authorised to make decisions in the name of the senior officer, if necessary be using a facsimile signature or requiring the senior officer simply to sign decisions without personally considering them. This system takes advantage of s 234(2) of the 1972 Act.

6

In the case of the simplest administrative tasks, involving a minimal exercise of discretion or judgement, there would be less need for formality.

7

A subordinate officer who is authorised to discharge a particular function should not subsequently authorise another officer or third party to discharge that function. The responsibility of the Head of Department or other senior officer has formed a basis for the decisions which allowed authorisations. Any kind of 'sub-authorisation' will undermine and lessen this responsibility and would, therefore, greatly increase the likelihood that it will be found to be unlawful.

8

The ability and experience of the authorised officer should be taken into account, so that an officer with appropriate experience and skills is authorised to act.

9

The nature and extent of the authorisation should be set down in writing.

Appendix 12

Local Government Act 1972
ss 94, 95, 96, 97, 98, 105, 106

(Chapter 13)

94
Disability of members of authorities for voting on account of interest in contracts, etc

(1)   Subject to the provisions of section 97 below, if a member of a local authority has any pecuniary interest, direct or indirect, in any contract, proposed contract or other matter, and is present at a meeting of the local authority at which the contract or other matter is the subject of consideration, he shall at the meeting and as soon as practicable after its commencement disclose the fact and shall not take part in the consideration or discussion of the contract or other matter or vote on any question with respect to it.

(2)   If any person fails to comply with the provisions of subsection (1) above he shall for each offence be liable on summary conviction to a fine not exceeding [level 4 on the standard scale] unless he proves that he did not know that the contract, proposed contract or other matter in which he had a pecuniary interest was the subject of consideration at that meeting.

(3)   A prosecution for an offence under this section shall not be instituted except by or on behalf of the Director of Public Prosecutions.

(4)   A local authority may by standing orders provide for the exclusion of a member of the authority from a meeting of the authority while any contract, proposed contract or other matter in which he has a pecuniary interest, direct or indirect, is under consideration.

(5)   The following, that is to say—

    (a)   the receipt by the chairman, vice-chairman or deputy chairman of a principal council of an allowance to meet the expenses of his office or his right to receive, or the possibility of his receiving, such an allowance;

    (b)   the receipt by a member of a local authority of an allowance or other payment under any provision of sections 173 to 176 below [or paragraph 25 of Schedule 2 to the Police Act 1996] [or paragraph 17 of Schedule 2 to the Police Act 1997] [or under any scheme made by virtue of section 18 of the Local Government and Housing Act 1989] or his right to receive, or the possibility of his receiving, any such payment;

shall not be treated as a pecuniary interest for the purposes of this section.

Amendment
Amended by the Local Government and Housing Act 1989, Sch 11; the Police Act 1996, s 103, Sch 7; and the Police Act 1997, s 88, Sch 6.

95
Pecuniary interests for purposes of section 94

(1)   For the purposes of section 94 above a person shall be treated, subject to the following provisions of this section and to section 97 below, as having indirectly a pecuniary interest in a contract, proposed contract or other matter, if—

(a)   he or any nominee of his is a member of a company or other body with which the contract was made or is proposed to be made or which has a direct pecuniary interest in the other matter under consideration; or

(b)   he is a partner, or is in the employment, of a person with whom the contract was made or is proposed to be made or who has a direct pecuniary interest in the other matter under consideration.

(2)   Subsection (1) above does not apply to membership of or employment under any public body, and a member of a company or other body shall not by reason only of his membership be treated as having an interest in any contract, proposed contract or other matter if he has no beneficial interest in any securities of that company or other body.

(3)   In the case of married persons living together the interest of one spouse shall, if known to the other, be deemed for the purpose of section 94 above to be also an interest of the other.

96
General notices and recording of disclosures for purposes of section 94

(1)   A general notice given in writing to the proper officer of the authority by a member thereof to the effect that he or his spouse is a member or in the employment of a specified company or other body, or that he or his spouse is a partner or in the employment of a specified person, or that he or his spouse is the tenant of any premises owned by the authority, shall, unless and until the notice is withdrawn, be deemed to be a sufficient disclosure of his interest in any contract, proposed contract or other matter relating to that company or other body or to that person or to those premises which may be the subject of consideration after the date of the notice.

(2)   The proper officer of the authority shall record in a book to be kept for the purpose particulars of any disclosure made under section 94 above and of any notice given under this section, and the book shall be open at all reasonable hours to the inspection of any member of the local authority.

97
Removal or exclusion of disability, etc

(1)   The district council, as respects a member of a parish [council, the principal council, as respects a member of a] community council, and the Secretary of State, as respects a member of any other local authority, may, subject to such conditions as the ... council or the Secretary of State may think fit to impose, remove any disability imposed by section 94 above in any case in which the number of members of the local authority disabled by that section at any one time would be so great a proportion of the whole as to impede the transaction of business, or in any other case in which it appears to the ... council or the Secretary of State in the interests of the inhabitants of the area that the disability should be removed.

(2)   The power of a ... council and of the Secretary of State under subsection (1) above includes power to remove, either indefinitely or for any period, any such disability which would otherwise attach to any member (or, in the case of the power of the Secretary of State, any member or any class or description of member) by reason of such interests, and in respect of such matters, as may be specified by the council or the Secretary of State.

(3)   Nothing in section 94 above precludes any person from taking part in the consideration or discussion of, or voting on, any question whether an application should be made to a ... council or the Secretary of State for the exercise of the powers conferred by subsections (1) and (2) above.

(4)   Section 94 above does not apply to an interest in a contract, proposed contract or other matter which a member of a local authority has as [a person who is liable [to pay an amount in respect of any community charge or in respect of council tax] or who would be so liable but for any enactment or anything provided or done under any enactment or as] a ratepayer or inhabitant of the area or as an ordinary consumer of water, or to an interest in any matter relating to the terms on which the right to participate in any service, including the supply of goods, is offered to the public.

(5)   For the purposes of section 94 above a member shall not be treated as having a pecuniary interest in any contract, proposed contract or other matter by reason only of an interest of his or of any company, body or person with which he is connected as mentioned in section 95(1) above which is so remote or insignificant that it cannot reasonably be regarded as likely to influence a member in the consideration or discussion of, or in voting on, any question with respect to that contract or matter.

(6)   Where a member of a local authority has an indirect pecuniary interest in a contract, proposed contract or other matter by reason only of a beneficial interest in securities of a company or other body, and the total nominal value of those securities does not exceed [£5,000] or one-hundredth of the total nominal value of the issued share capital of the company or body, whichever is the less, and if the share capital is of more than one class, the total nominal value of shares of any one class in which he has a beneficial interest does not exceed one-hundredth of the total issued share capital of that class, section 94 above shall not prohibit him from taking part in the consideration or discussion of the contract or other matter or from voting on any question with respect to it, without prejudice, however, to his duty to disclose his interest.

[(7)   Section 94 above shall not prohibit a director of a public transport company, or a subsidiary of such a company, who is neither—

(a)   paid for acting as such; nor

(b)   an employee of the public transport company or subsidiary,

from taking part in the consideration or discussion of, or from voting on any question with respect to, a local transport plan or bus strategy; and in this subsection 'public transport company' and 'subsidiary' have the same meanings as in Part IV of the Transport Act 1985.]

Amendment
Amended by SI 1990/10, art 2; the Local Government and Housing Act 1989, s 194, Sch 11; the Local Government Finance Act 1992, s 117, Sch 13; the Local Government (Wales) Act 1994, s 66, Schs 15, 18; and the Transport Act 2000, s 161, Sch 11.

98
Interpretation of sections 95 and 97

(1)   In sections 95 and 97 above 'securities' [means—

(a)   investments falling within any of paragraphs 1 to 6 of Schedule 1 to the Financial Services Act 1986 or, so far as relevant to any of those paragraphs, paragraph 11 of that Schedule; or

(b)   rights (whether actual or contingent) in respect of money lent to, or deposited with, any society registered under the Industrial and Provident Societies Act 1965 or any building society within the meaning of the Building Societies Act 1986.]

[(1A)   In sections 94 and 97 above 'local authority' includes a joint authority [, the London Fire and Emergency Planning Authority] [and a police authority established under [section 3 of the Police Act 1996]] [and the Metropolitan Police Authority] [and the Service Authority for the National Crime Squad] ... and in section 94(5)(a) above 'principal council' includes any such authority.]

[(1B)   In the application of section 97 above to a member of the Service Authority for the National Crime Squad, subsection (1) of that section shall apply as if the words from 'or in any other case' to the end were omitted.]

(2)   In section 95 above 'public body' includes any body established for the purpose of carrying on under national ownership any industry or part of an industry or undertaking, the governing body of any university, university college or college, school or hall of a university and the National Trust for Places of Historic Interest or Natural Beauty incorporated by the National Trust Act 1907.

Amendment
Amended by the Local Government Act 1985, s 84, Sch 14; Financial Services Act 1986, s 212(2), Sch 16; the Education Reform Act 1988, s 237, Sch 13; the Police and Magistrates' Courts Act 1994, s 43, Sch 4; the Police Act 1996, s 103, Sch 7; the Police Act 1997, s 88, Sch 6; and the Greater London Authority Act 1999, ss 325, 328, Schs 27, 29.

105
Disability for voting on account of interest in contracts, etc

Sections 94 to 98 above shall apply as respects members of a committee of a local authority or of a joint committee of two or more local authorities (including in either case a sub-committee), whether the committee or joint committee are appointed or established under this Part of this Act or under any other enactment, as they apply in respect of members of local authorities, subject to the following modifications—

    (a)   references to meetings of any such committee shall be substituted for references to meetings of the local authority; and

    (b)   in the case of members of a committee of a local authority or any sub-committee the right of persons who are members of the committee or sub-committee but not members of the local authority to inspect the book kept under section 96(2) above shall be limited to an inspection of the entries in the book relating to the members of the committee or sub-committee.

106
Standing orders

Standing orders may be made as respects any committee of a local authority by that authority or as respects a joint committee of two or more local authorities, whether appointed or established under this Part of this Act or any other enactment, by those authorities with respect to the quorum, proceedings and place of meeting of the committee or joint committee (including any sub-committee) but, subject to any such standing orders, the quorum, proceedings and place of meeting shall be such as the committee, joint committee or sub-committee may determine.

APPENDIX 13

National Code of Local Government Conduct (DoE Circular 8/90)

This code was issued to local authorities in April 1990 under cover of DoE circular 8/90. It applies to all councillors and all members of committees, joint committees and sub-committees, whether or not they are councillors and whether or not they are voting members. The code represents the standard against which the conduct of members will be judged, both by the public and by their fellow councillors. The local ombudsmen may also regard a breach of the code as incompatible with good administration, and may make a finding of maladministration by the council in these circumstances.

The Code

The law and standing orders
1.
Councillors hold office by virtue of the law, and must at all times act within the law. You should make sure that you are familiar with the rules of personal conduct which the law and standing orders require and the guidance contained within this code. It is your responsibility to make sure that what you do complies with these requirements and this guidance. You should regularly review your personal circumstances with this in mind, particularly when your circumstances change. You should not at any time advocate or encourage anything to the contrary. If in any doubt, seek advice from your council's appropriate senior officer or from your own legal advisor. In the end, however, the decision and the responsibility are yours.

Public duty and private interest
2.
Your over-riding duty as a councillor is to the whole local community.

3.
You have a special duty to your constituents, including those who did not vote for you.

4.
Whilst you may be strongly influenced by the views of others, and of your party in particular, it is your responsibility alone to decide what view to take on any question which councillors have to decide.

5.
If you have a private or personal interest in a question which councillors have to decide, you must not take any part in the decision, except in the special circumstances described below. Where such circumstances do permit you to participate, you must not let your interest influence the decision.

6.
You should never do anything as a councillor which you could not justify to the public. Your conduct, and what the public believes about your conduct, will affect the reputation of your council, and of your party if you belong to one.

7.
It is not enough to avoid actual impropriety. You should at all times avoid any occasion for suspicion and any appearance of improper conduct.

Disclosure of pecuniary and other interests
8.
The law makes specific provision requiring you to disclose both direct and indirect pecuniary interests (including those of a spouse with whom you are living) which you may have in any matter coming before the council, a committee or a sub-committee. It prohibits you from speaking or voting on that matter. Your council's standing orders may also require you to withdraw from the meeting while the matter is discussed. You must also by law declare certain pecuniary interests in the statutory register kept for this purpose. These requirements must be scrupulously observed at all times.

9.
Interests which are not pecuniary can be just as important. You should not allow the impression to be created that you are, or may be, using your position to promote a private or personal interest, rather than forwarding the general public interest. Private and personal interests include those of your family and friends, as well as those arising through membership of, or association with, clubs, societies and other organisations such as the Freemasons, trade unions and voluntary bodies.

10.
If you have a private or personal non-pecuniary interest in a matter arising at a local authority meeting, you should always disclose it, unless it is insignificant, or one which you share with other members of the public generally as a ratepayer, a community charge payer or an inhabitant of the area.

11.
Where you have declared such a private or personal interest, you should decide whether it is clear and substantial. If it is not, then you may con-tinue to take part in the discussion of the matter and may vote on it. If, however, it is a clear and substantial interest, then (except in the special circumstances described below) you should never take any further part in the proceedings, and should always withdraw from the meeting whilst the matter is being considered. In deciding whether such an interest is clear and substantial, you should ask yourself whether members of the public, knowing the facts of the situation, would reasonably think that you might be influenced by it. If you think so, you should regard the interest as clear and substantial.

12.
In the following circumstances, but only in these circumstances, it can still be appropriate to speak, and in some cases to vote, in spite of the fact that you have declared such a clear and substantial private or personal interest:

(*a*) if your interest arises in your capacity as a member of a public body, you may speak and vote on matters concerning that body; for this purpose a public body is one where, under the law governing declaration of pecuniary interests, membership of the body would not constitute an indirect pecuniary interest;

(*b*) if your interest arises from being appointed by your local authority as their representative on the managing committee, or other governing body, of a charity, voluntary body or other organisation formed for a public purpose (and not for the personal benefit of the members), you may speak and vote on matters concerning that organisation;

(*c*) if your interest arises from being a member of the managing committee, or other governing body of such an organisation, but you were not appointed by your local authority as their representative, then you may speak on matters in which that organisation has an interest; you should not vote on any matter directly affecting the finances or property of that organisation, but you may vote on other matters in which the organisation has an interest;

(*d*) if your interest arises from being an ordinary member or supporter of such an organisation (and you are not a member of its managing committee or other governing body), then you may speak and vote on any matter in which the organisation has an interest.

Dispensations
13.
Circumstances may arise where the work of your authority is affected because a number of councillors have personal interests (pecuniary or non-pecuniary) in some question.

14.
In certain circumstances, you may be able to get a dispensation to speak, and also to vote, in spite of a pecuniary interest. Such dispensations are given under statute by the Secretary of State in the case of county, regional, islands, district and London borough councils, and (in England and Wales) by the district council in the case of town, parish and com-munity councils.

15.
In the case of non-pecuniary interests, there may be similar exceptions to the guidance contained in paragraphs 9 to 12 of this code. In the circumstances below it may be open to you to decide that work of the council requires you to continue to take part in a meeting discussing a matter in which you have a clear and substantial private or personal interest.

16.
Before doing so, you should:
(*a*) take advice from the chairman of your local authority (if this is practicable) and from the appropriate senior officer of the authority as to whether the situation justifies such a step;

(*b*) consider whether the public would regard your interest as so closely connected with the matter in question that you could not be expected to put your interest out of your mind (for example, the matter might concern a decision by the council affecting a close relative); if you think that you would, you should never decide to take part in a discussion of, or a vote on, the matter in question; and

(*c*) consider any guidance which your council has issued on this matter.

17.
The circumstances in which (after such consultation and consideration) you may decide to speak and vote on a matter in which you have a clear and substantial private or personal non-pecuniary interest are if, but only if:

(a) at least half the council or committee would otherwise be required to withdraw from consideration of the business because they have a personal interest; or

(b) your withdrawal, together with that of any other members of the council or committee who may also be required to withdraw from consideration of the business because of a personal interest, would upset the elected party balance of the council or committee to such an extent that the decision is likely to be affected.

18.

If you decide that you should speak or vote, notwithstanding a clear and substantial personal or private non-pecuniary interest, you should say at the meeting, before the matter is considered, that you have taken such a decision, and why.

19.
The guidance set out in paragraphs 15 to 18 above also applies to sub-committees. However, if the sub-committee is very small, or if a large proportion of members declare a personal interest, it will usually be more appropriate for the matter to be referred to the parent committee.

Disclosure in other dealings
20.
You should always apply the principles about the disclosure of interests to your dealings with council officers, and to your unofficial relations with other councillors (at party group meetings, or other informal occasions) no less scrupulously than at formal meetings of the council, committees and sub-committees.

Membership of committees and sub-committees
21.
You, or some firm or body with which you are personally connected, may have professional, business or other personal interests within the area for which the council are responsible. Such interests may be substantial and closely related to the work of one or more of the council's committees or sub-committees. For example, the firm or body may be concerned with planning, developing land, council housing, personnel matters or the letting of contracts for supplies, services or works. You should not seek, or accept, membership of any such committee or subcommittee if that would involve you in disclosing an interest so often that you could be of little value to the committee or sub-committee, or if it would be likely to weaken public confidence in the duty of the committee or sub-committee to work solely in the general public interest.

Leadership and chairmanship
22.
You should not seek, or accept, the leadership of the council if you, or any body with which you are associated, has a substantial financial interest in, or is closely related to, the business or affairs of the council. Likewise, you should not accept the chairmanship of a committee or sub-committee if they have a similar interest in the business of the committee or sub-committee.

Councillors and officers
23.
Both councillors and officers are servants of the public, and they are indispensable to one another. But their responsibilities are distinct. Councillors are responsible to the

electorate and serve only so long as their term of office lasts. Officers are responsible to the council. Their job is to give advice to councillors and the council, and to carry out the council's work under the direction and control of the council, their committees and sub-committees.

24.

Mutual respect between councillors and officers is essential to good local government. Close personal familiarity between individual councillors and officers can damage this relationship and prove embarrassing to other councillors and officers.

25.

The law and standing orders lay down rules for the appointment, discipline and dismissal of staff. You must ensure that you observe these scrupulously at all times. Special rules apply to the appointment of assistants to political groups. In all other circumstances, if you are called upon to take part in appointing an officer, the only question you should consider is which candidate would best serve the whole council. You should not let your political or personal preferences influence your judgement. You should not canvass the support of colleagues for any candidate and you should resist any attempt by others to canvass yours.

Use of confidential and private information
26.

As a councillor or a committee or sub-committee member, you necessarily acquire much information that has not yet been made public and is still confidential. It is a betrayal of trust to breach such confidences. You should never disclose or use confidential information for the personal advantage of yourself or of anyone known to you, or to the disadvantage or the discredit of the council or anyone else.

Gifts and hospitality
27.

You should treat with extreme caution any offer or gift, favour or hospitality that is made to you personally. The person or organisation making the offer may be doing, or seeking to do, business with the council, or may be applying to the council for planning permission or some other kind of decision.

28.

There are no hard or fast rules about the acceptance or refusal of hospitality or tokens of goodwill. For example, working lunches may be a proper way of doing business, provided that they are approved by the local authority and that no extravagance is involved. Likewise, it may be reasonable for a member to represent the council at a social function or event organised by outside persons or bodies.

29.

You are personally responsible for all decisions connected with the acceptance or offer of gifts or hospitality and for avoiding the risk of damage to public confidence in local government. The offer or receipt of gifts or invitations should always be reported to the appropriate senior officer of the council.

Expenses and allowances
30.

There are rules enabling you to claim expenses and allowances in connection with your duties as a councillor or a committee or sub-committee member. These rules must be scrupulously observed.

Dealings with the council
31.
You may have dealings with the council on a personal level, for instance as a ratepayer or community charge payer, as a tenant, or as an applicant for a grant or a planning permission. You should never seek or accept preferential treatment in those dealings because of your position as a councillor or a committee or sub-committee member. You should also avoid placing yourself in a position that could lead the public to think that you are receiving preferential treatment: for instance, by being in substantial arrears to the council, or by using your position to discuss a planning application personally with officers when the other members of the public would not have the opportunity to do so. Likewise, you should never use your position as a councillor or a committee or sub-committee member to seek preferential treatment for friends or relatives, or any firm or body with which you are personally connected.

Use of council facilities
32.
You should always make sure that any facilities (such as transport, stationery, or secretarial services) provided by the council for your use in your duties as a councillor or a committee or sub-committee member are used strictly for those duties and for no other purposes.

Appointments to other bodies
You may be appointed or nominated by your council to another body or organisation – for instance, to a joint authority or a voluntary organisation. You should always observe this Code in carrying out your duties on that body in the same way that you would with your own authority.

APPENDIX 14

The General Principles of Conduct

(Chapter 13)

1
Selflessness
Members should serve only the public interest and should never improperly confer an advantage or disadvantage on any person.

2
Honesty and Integrity
Members should not place themselves in situations where their honesty and integrity may be questioned, should not behave improperly and should on all occasions avoid the appearance of such behaviour.

3
Objectivity
Members should make decisions on merit, including when making appointments, awarding contracts, or recommending individuals for rewards or benefits.

4
Accountability
Members should be accountable to the public for their actions and the manner in which they carry out their responsibilities, and should co-operate fully and honestly with any scrutiny appropriate to their particular office.

5
Openness
Members should be as open as possible about their actions and those of their authority, and should be prepared to give reasons for those actions.

6
Personal Judgement
Members may take account of the views of others, including their political groups, but should reach their own conclusions on the issues before them and act in accordance with those conclusions.

7
Respect for Others
Members should promote equality by not discriminating unlawfully against any person, and by treating people with respect, regardless of their race, age, religion, gender, sexual orientation or disability. They should respect the impartiality and integrity of the authority's statutory officers, and its other employees.

8
Duty to Uphold the Law
Members should uphold the law and, on all occasions, act in accordance with the trust that the public is entitled to place in them.

9
Stewardship
Members should do whatever they are able to do to ensure that their authorities use their resources prudently and in accordance with the law.

10
Leadership
Members should promote and support these principles by leadership, and by example, and should act in a way that secures or preserves public confidence.

APPENDIX 15

Officer/Member Protocol

(Chapter 13)

Introduction and Principles
1.1
The purpose of this Protocol is to guide Members and Officers of the Council in their relations with one another in such a way as to ensure the smooth running of the Council.

1.2
Given the variety and complexity of such relations, this Protocol does not seek to be either prescriptive or comprehensive. It simply offers guidance on some of the issues which most commonly arise. It is hoped, however, that the approach which it adopts to these issues will serve as a guide to dealing with other circumstances.

1.3
This Protocol is to a large extent a written statement of current practice and convention. It seeks to promote greater clarity and certainty. If the Protocol is followed it should ensure that Members receive objective and impartial advice and that Officers are protected from accusations of bias and any undue influence from Members.

1.4
It also seeks to reflect the principles underlying the respective Codes of Conduct which apply to Members and Officers. The shared object of these codes is to enhance and maintain the integrity (real and perceived) of local government and the Codes, therefore, demand very high standards of personal conduct.

1.5
This Protocol is a local extension of the Members' and Employees' Codes of Conduct. Consequently, a breach of the provisions of this Protocol may also constitute a breach of those Codes.

1.6
This Protocol should be read in conjunction with the Members' and Employees' Codes of Local Government Conduct, the Council's Constitution and any guidance issued by the Standards and Governance Committee and/or Monitoring Officer.

The Relationship: General Points
2.1
Both Councillors and Officers are servants of the public and they are indispensable to one another. But their responsibilities are distinct. Councillors are responsible to the electorate and serve only so long as their term of office lasts. Officers are responsible to the Council. Their job is to give advice to Councillors and the Council, and to carry out the Council's work under the direction and control of the Council, the Executive,

their committees and subcommittees.

2.2
At the heart of the Code, and this Protocol, is the importance of mutual respect. Member/Officer relationships are to be conducted in a positive and constructive way. Therefore, it is important that any dealings between Members and Officers should observe standards of courtesy and that neither party should seek to take unfair advantage of their position or seek to exert undue influence on the other party.

2.3
Inappropriate relationships can be inferred from language/style. To protect both Members and Officers, Officers should address Members as 'Councillor XX/Mr or Madam Mayor/Sheriff' save where circumstances clearly indicate that a level of informality is appropriate, eg a one to one between a Head of Service and their respective Cabinet Member.

2.4
A Member should not raise matters relating to the conduct or capability of an Officer in a manner that is incompatible with the objectives of this Protocol. This is a long-standing tradition in public service. An Officer has no means of responding to such criticisms in public. If a Member feels s/he has not been treated with proper respect, courtesy or has any concern about the conduct or capability of an Officer, and fails to resolve it through direct discussion with the Officer, s/he should raise the matter with the respective Head of Service of the Division. The Head of Service will then look into the facts and report back to the Member. If the Member continues to feel concern, then s/he should report the facts to the Executive Director who heads the Directorate concerned, or if, after doing so, is still dissatisfied, should raise the issue with the Chief Executive who will look into the matter afresh. Any action taken against an Officer in respect of a complaint, will be in accordance with the provisions of the Council's Disciplinary Rules and Procedures.

2.5
An Officer should not raise with a Member matters relating to the conduct or capability of another Officer or to the internal management of a Section/Division/Directorate at or in a manner that is incompatible with the overall objectives of this Protocol.

2.6
Where an Officer feels that s/he has not been properly treated with respect and courtesy by a Member, s/he should raise the matter with his/her Head of Service, Executive Director or the Chief Executive as appropriate, especially if they do not feel able to discuss it directly with the Member concerned. In these circumstances the Head of Service, Executive Director or Chief Executive will take appropriate action either by approaching the individual Member and/or group leader or by referring the matter to the Head of Legal Services in the context of the Standards Committee considering the complaint.

The Relationship: Officer Support to Members: General Points
3.1
Officers are responsible for day-to-day managerial and operational decisions within the authority and will provide support to both the Executive and all Councillors in their several areas.

3.2
Certain statutory officers – the Chief Executive, the Monitoring Officer and the Chief Finance Officer – have specific roles. These are addressed in the Constitution. Their roles need to be understood and respected by all Members.

3.3
The following key principles reflect the way in which the officer core generally relates
to Members:
- all officers are employed by, and accountable to the authority as a whole;
- support from officers is needed for all the authority's functions including Full
  Council, Overview and Scrutiny, the Executive, individual Members representing their communities etc;
- day-to-day managerial and operational decisions should remain the responsibility of the Chief Executive and other officers;
- the authority will seek to avoid potential conflicts of interest for officers arising
  from the separation of the Executive and Overview and Scrutiny role; and
- all officers will be provided with training and development to help them support
  the various Member roles effectively and to understand the new structures.

3.4
On occasion, a decision may be reached which authorises named Officers to take
action between meetings following consultation with a Member or Members. It must
be recognised that it is the Officer, rather than the Member or Members, who takes the
action and it is the Officer who is accountable for it.

3.5
Finally, it must be remembered that Officers within a Division or Directorate are
accountable to their Head of Service and Executive Director and that whilst Officers
should always seek to assist a Member, they must not, in so doing, go beyond the
bounds of whatever authority they have been given by their Head of Service or
Executive Director.

The Relationship: Officer Support: Members and Party Groups
4.1
It must be recognised by all Officers and Members that in discharging their duties and
responsibilities, Officers serve the Council as a whole and not any political group,
combination of groups or any individual Member of the Council.

4.2
There is now statutory recognition for party groups and it is common practice for such
groups to give preliminary consideration to matters of Council business in advance of
such matters being considered by the relevant Council decision making body.
Officers may properly be called upon to support and contribute to such deliberations
by party groups but must at all times maintain political neutrality. All Officers must, in
their dealings with political groups and individual Members, treat them in a fair and
even-handed manner.

4.3
The support provided by Officers can take many forms. Whilst in practice such
Officer support is likely to be in most demand from whichever party group is for the
time being in control of the Council, such support is available to all party groups

4.4
Certain points must, however, be clearly understood by all those participating in this
type of process, Members and Officers alike. In particular:
4.4.1 Officer support must not extend beyond providing information and advice in
      relation to matters of Council business. Officers must not be involved in
      advising on matters of party business. The observance of this distinction will be
      assisted if Officers are not present at meetings or parts of meetings, when
      matters of party business are to be discussed;
4.4.2 party group meetings, whilst they form part of the preliminaries to Council
      decision making, are not empowered to make decisions on behalf of the
      Council. Conclusions reached at such meetings do not therefore rank as

Council decisions and it is essential that they are not interpreted or acted upon as such; and

4.4.3 similarly, where Officers provide information and advice to a party group meeting in relation to a matter of Council business, this cannot act as a substitute for providing all necessary information and advice to the relevant Committee or Sub-Committee when the matter in question is considered.

4.5

Special care needs to be exercised whenever Officers are involved in providing information and advice to a party group meeting which includes persons who are not Members of the Council. Such persons are not bound by the National Code of Local Government Conduct (in particular, the provisions concerning the declaration of interests and confidentiality) and for this and other reasons, Officers may not attend and/or give advice to such meetings.

4.6

Officers must respect the confidentiality of any party group discussions at which they are present in the sense that they should not relay the content of any such discussion to another party group.

4.7

Whilst any Member may ask a relevant Head of Service, Programme Manager, Executive Director or the Chief Executive for written factual information about a Directorate or service, such requests must be reasonable and not seek information relating, for instance, to case work of a similar nature, eg Social Services, employment etc. Requests will be met subject to any overriding legal considerations (which will be determined by the Head of Legal Services), or if the recipient of any request considers the cost of providing the information requested or the nature of the request to be unreasonable. If a Member requesting such information is dissatisfied by such a response, s/he should raise the matter in the first place with the relevant Executive Director, and if still dissatisfied should raise the matter with the Chief Executive who will discuss the issue with the relevant Group Leader(s).

4.8

In relation to budget proposals:

(a) the Administration shall be entitled to confidential discussions with Officers regarding options and proposals. These will remain confidential until determined by the Administration or until published in advance of Committee/Council meetings, whichever is the earlier; and

(b) the opposition groups shall also be entitled to confidential discussions with Officers to enable them to formulate alternative budget proposals. These will remain confidential until determined by the respective opposition groups or until published in advance of Committee/Council meetings, whichever is the earlier.

4.9

It must not be assumed by any party group or Member that any Officer is supportive of any policy or strategy developed because of that Officer's assistance in the formulation of that policy or strategy.

4.10

Any particular cases of difficulty or uncertainty in this area of Officer advice to party groups should be raised with the Chief Executive who will discuss them with the relevant group leader(s).

The Relationship: Officer Support: The Executive
5.1

It is clearly important that there should be a close working relationship between Executive Members and the Officers who support and/or interact with them.

However, such relationships should never be allowed to become so close, or appear to be so close, as to bring into question the Officer's ability to deal impartially with other Members and other party groups.

5.2

Whilst Executive Members will routinely be consulted as part of the process of drawing up proposals for consideration or the agenda for a forthcoming meeting, it must be recognised that in some situations an Officer will be under a professional duty to submit a report. Similarly, a Head of Service or other senior Officer will always be fully responsible for the contents of any report submitted in his/her name. This means that any such report will be amended only where the amendment reflects the professional judgement of the author of the report. This is to be distinguished from a situation where there is a value judgement to be made. Any issues arising between an Executive Member and a Head of Service in this area should be referred to the Chief Executive for resolution in conjunction with the Leader of the Council.

5.3

The Executive and its members have wide ranging leadership roles. They will:

- lead the community planning process and the search for Best Value, with input and advice from Overview and Scrutiny Committees, area committees and any other persons as appropriate;
- lead the preparation of the local authority's policies and budget;
- take in-year decisions on resources and priorities, together with other stakeholders and partners in the local community, to deliver and implement the budget and policies decided by the Full Council; and
- be the focus for forming partnerships with other local public, private, voluntary and community sector organisations to address local needs.

5.4

Where functions which are the responsibility of the Executive are delegated to Officers or other structures outside the Executive, the Executive will nevertheless remain accountable to the Council, through Overview and Scrutiny Committees, for the discharge of those functions. That is to say, the Executive will be held to account for both its decision to delegate a function and the way that the function is being carried out.

5.5

Under Executive Arrangements, individual Members of the Executive will, for the first time, be allowed to formally take decisions. The Executive and Cabinet members must satisfy themselves that they are clear what exactly they can and cannot do.

5.6

The Council has put in place mechanisms/protocols which ensure that (as with the Council, its Committees and Sub-Committees, and the Executive and its Committees) an individual Executive Member seeks advice from relevant Officers before taking a decision within her or his delegated authority. This includes taking legal advice, financial advice and professional officer advice (particularly about contractual matters) as well as consulting the Monitoring Officer where there is doubt about vires.

5.7

Decisions taking by individual Members of the Executive give rise to legal and financial obligations in the same way as decisions taken collectively. Therefore, Members of the Executive should always be aware of legal and financial liabilities (consulting the Monitoring Officer and Chief Finance Officer as appropriate) which will arise from their decisions,. To ensure effective leadership for the local authority and the communities it serves, there are arrangements to ensure co-ordination of and haring responsibility for Executive decisions including those made by individuals.

5.8
Officers will continue to work for and serve the local authority as a whole., Nevertheless, as the majority of functions will be the responsibility of the Executive, it is likely that in practice many Officers will be working to the Executive for most of their time. The Executive must respect the political neutrality of the Officers. Officers must ensure that, even when they are predominantly supporting the Executive, that their political neutrality is not compromised.

5.9
In organising support for the Executive, there is a potential for tension between Chief Officers and Cabinet Members with portfolios. All Members and Officers need to be constantly aware of the possibility of such tensions arising and both Officers and Members need to work together to avoid such tensions an conflicts existing or being perceived.

The Relationship: Officer Support: Overview and Scrutiny
6.1
It is not Overview and Scrutiny's role to act as a disciplinary tribunal in relation to the actions of Members or Officers. Neither is it the role of Officers to become involved in what would amount to disciplinary investigations on a Panel's behalf. This is the Chief Executive's function alone in relation to staff, the Monitoring Officer's and the Standards and Governance Committee as regards the conduct of Members. This means:
- Overview and Scrutiny's questioning should *not* be directed to the conduct of individuals, not in the sense of establishing the facts about what occurred in the making of decisions or implementing of Council policies, but with the *implication* of allocating criticism or blame;
- in these circumstances, it is for the Chief Executive to institute a formal enquiry, and Overview and Scrutiny may ask (but not require) him to do so.

6.2
Overview and Scrutiny should not act as a 'court of appeal' against decisions or to pursue complaints by individuals (Councillors, Officers or members of the public) as other procedures exist for this. These are internal, eg the Corporate Complaints Procedure, and external/statutory, eg Local Government Ombudsman or appeal to the Courts. That said,
- Overview and Scrutiny may investigate the manner in which decisions are made but should not pass judgements on the merits of a decision in individual cases;
- they can comment, however, on the merits of a particular policy affecting individuals.

6.3
It would be unfair to invite someone to appear before a Panel without telling them in general terms what they will be asked, or not giving them adequate time to prepare. Overview and Scrutiny ought to provide written questions ('Indicative Topics') beforehand, so that the answers can form the basis of the questioning and discussion. In addition, speakers ought to be told the general line that further questioning is likely to take. Questioning should not stray outside the subject area that the Panel had previously indicated.

6.4
The Overview and Scrutiny Handbook contains guidelines as to the procedure at Evidence Meetings, and guidance for Members and Officers.

Support services to Members and Party Groups
7.1
The only basis on which the Council can lawfully provide support services (eg, stationery, typing, printing, photo-copying, transport etc) to Members is to assist them in discharging their role as Members of the Council. Such support services must therefore only be used on Council business. They should never be used in connection with party political or campaigning activity or for private purposes.

Members' Access to Information and to Council Documents
8.1
Members are have the ability to ask for information pursuant to their legal rights to information. This right extends to such information, explanation and advice as they may reasonably need in order to assist them in discharging their role as a Member of the Council. This can range from a request for general information about some aspect of the Council's activities to a request for specific information on behalf of a constituent. Such approaches should normally be directed to the Head of Service or another senior Officer of the Division concerned. In cases of doubt, Members should approach the Head of Democratic Services for assistance.

8.2
As regards the legal rights of Members to inspect Council documents, these are covered partly by statute and partly by the common law.

8.3
Members have a statutory right to inspect any Council document *which contains material relating to any business which is to be transacted by the Council.* This right applies irrespective of whether the Member is a Member of the Committee or Sub-Committee concerned and extends not only to reports which are to be submitted to the meeting, but also to any relevant background papers. This right does not, however, apply to documents relating to certain items which may appear as a confidential (Pink) item on the agenda for a meeting. The items in question are those which contain exempt information relating to employees, occupiers of Council property, applicants for grants and other services, the care of children, contract and industrial relations negotiations, advice from Counsel and criminal investigations.

8.4
In relation to business of the Executive, by virtue of Regulation 17 of the Local Authorities (Executive Arrangements) (Access to Information) (England) Regulations 2000:
(i)   where there is a meeting (eg Cabinet) and there is a document which is in the possession/under the control of the Executive relating to the business to be conducted at that meeting, that document shall be available for inspection;
(ii) where the decision is made at a private meeting by a Cabinet Member or is a Key Decision delegated to an Officer, the document shall be available either after the meeting closes or when the decision is made;
(iii) there are savings for exempt and confidential material and any document that contains advice provided by a political advisor or assistant.

8.5
The common law rights of Members remains intact, are much broader and are based on the principle that any Members has a prima facie right to inspect Council documents *so far as his/her access to the document is reasonably necessary to enable the Members properly to perform his/her duties as a Member of the Council.* This principle is commonly referred to as the 'need to know' principle.

8.6
The exercise of this common law right depends therefore, upon an individual Member being able to demonstrate that s/he has the necessary 'need to know'. In this

respect a Member has no right to 'a roving commission' to go and examine documents of the Council. Mere curiosity is not sufficient. The crucial question is the determination of the 'need to know'. This question must initially be determined by the particular Head of Service whose Division holds the document in question (with advice from the Head of Legal Services). In the event of dispute, the question falls to be determined by the relevant Committee – ie the Committee in connection with whose functions the document is held.

8.7
In some circumstances (eg, a Committee Member wishing to inspect documents relating to the business of that Committee) a Member's 'need to know' will normally be presumed. In other circumstances (eg, a Member wishing to inspect documents which contain personal information about third parties) the Member will normally be expected to justify the request in specific terms. Furthermore, there will be a range of documents which, because of their nature are either not accessible to Members or are accessible only by the political group forming the administration and not by other political groups. An example of this latter category would be draft documents compiled in the context of emerging Council policies and draft committee reports, the disclosure of which prematurely might be against the Council's and the public interest.

8.8
Whilst the term 'Council document' is very broad and includes for example, any document produced with Council resources, it is accepted by convention that a Member of one party group will not have a 'need to know' and therefore, a right to inspect, a document which forms part of the internal workings of another party group.

8.9
Further and more detailed advice regarding Members rights to inspect Council documents may be obtained from the Head of Legal Services.

8.10
Finally, any Council information provided to a Member must only be used by the Member for the purpose for which it was provided, ie in connection with the proper performance of the Member's duties as a Member of the Council. Therefore, for example, early drafts of Committee reports/briefing papers are not suitable for public disclosure and should not be used other than for the purpose for which they were supplied. This point is emphasised in paragraph 3 of the Code of Local Government Conduct:

> 'A Member:
> (a)   must not disclose information given to him in confidence by anyone without the consent of a person authorised to give it, or unless he is required by law to do so; and
> (b)   must not prevent another person from gaining access to information to which that person is entitled by law'.

Correspondence
9.1
Correspondence between an individual Member and an Officer should not normally be copied (by the Officer) to any other Member. Where exceptionally it is necessary to copy the correspondence to another Member, this should be made clear to the original Member. In other words, a system of 'silent copies' should not be employed.

9.2
Official letters on behalf of the Council should normally be sent in the name of the appropriate Officer, rather than in the name of a Member. It may be appropriate in certain limited circumstances (eg, representations to a Government Minister) for a

letter to appear in the name of a Cabinet Member or the Leader, but this should be the exception rather than the norm. Letters which, for example, create legal obligations or give instructions on behalf of the Council should never be sent out in the name of a Member, Executive or otherwise.

Publicity and Press Releases
10.1
Local authorities are accountable to their electorate. Accountability requires local understanding. This will be promoted by the Authority, explaining its objectives and policies to the electors and rate-payers. In recent years, all local authorities have increasingly used publicity to keep the public informed and to encourage public participation. Every Council needs to tell the public about the services it provides. Increasingly, local authorities see this task as an essential part of providing services. Good, effective publicity aimed to improve public awareness of a Council's activities is, in the words of the Government, to be welcomed.

10.2
Publicity is, however, a sensitive matter in any political environment because of the impact it can have. Expenditure on publicity can be significant. It is essential, therefore, to ensure that local authority decisions on publicity are properly made in accordance with clear principles of good practice. The Government has issued a Code of Recommended Practice on Local Authority Publicity. The purpose of the Code is to set out such principles. The Code affects the conventions that should apply to all publicity at public expense and which traditionally have applied in both central and local government. The Code is issued under the provisions of the Local Government Act 1986 as amended by the Local Government Act 1988 which provides for the Secretary of State to issue Codes of Recommended Practice as regards the content, style, distribution and cost of local authority publicity, and such other matters as s/he thinks appropriate. That section requires that all local authorities shall have regard to the provisions of any such Code in coming to any decision on publicity.

10.3
Officers and Members of the Council will, therefore, in making decisions on publicity, take account of the provisions of this Code. If in doubt, Officers and/or Members should initially seek advice from the Head of Marking and Information who will refer the matter to the Head of Legal Services, if necessary/appropriate. Particular care should be paid to any publicity used by the Council around the time of an election. Particular advice will be given on this by the Head of Legal Services as appropriate.

Involvement of Ward Councillors
11.1
Whenever a public meeting is organised by the Council to consider a local issue, all the Members representing the Ward or Wards affected should as a matter of course, be invited to attend the meeting. Similarly, whenever the Council undertakes any form of consultative exercise on a local issue, the Ward Members should be notified at the outset of the exercise. More generally, Officers should consider whether other policy or briefing papers, or other topics being discussed with an Executive Member, should be discussed with relevant Ward Members. Officers should seek the views of the appropriate Executive Member(s) as to with whom and when this might be done.

Conclusion
12.1
Mutual understanding, openness on these sort of sensitive issues and basic respect are the greatest safeguard of the integrity of the Council, its Members and Officers.

Officer/Member Protocol
13.1
This Protocol was drafted by [.......................], and adopted by the Council as part of the Constitution on [...........................].

13.2
Copies of the Protocol will be issued to all Members as part of the Constitution upon election.

13.3
Questions of interpretation of this Protocol will be determined by the [*Head of Legal Services*].

Appendix 16

Draft Model Code of Conduct for Members

(Chapter 13)

Note

Note that the government's analysis and rationale for the form and content of the Model Code constitute a significant proportion of the commentary set out below.

Part 1
General Provisions

1
Scope

(1)   A member must observe the authority's code of conduct wherever he—
 (a)   conducts the business of the authority;
 (b)   conducts the business of the office to which he has been elected or appointed, or
 (c)   acts as a representative of the authority.

(2)   A relevant authority's code of conduct shall not have effect in relation to the activities of a member undertaken other than in an official capacity, except and insofar, as otherwise indicated.

(3)   Where a member acts as a representative of that authority on another body, he must, when acting in that capacity, comply with the authority's code of conduct, except and insofar as it conflicts with any other legal obligations to which he may be subject.

Commentary

Paragraph 1(1) provides that the model code applies to a member whenever s/he conducts the business of the authority, or of the office to which they have been elected or appointed, or acts as a representative of their authority. So the code will apply whenever a member is carrying out official duties, such as meetings of the authority or any of its committees, meetings of any executive, meetings with other members and officers, meetings of any political groups on the authority, surgeries for constituents, public meetings and area committees and forums. The code does not apply to members' activities outside their official duties, except and insofar as otherwise indicated.

There are some provisions in the code which apply outside a member's official duties:

- paragraph 4, under which a member must not commit a criminal offence or act in a way that might reasonably be regarded as bringing his or her office or their authority into serious disrepute;

443

- paragraph 5(*a*), which prohibits a member from using his or her position improperly to confer on or secure for any person, (including the member), an advantage or disadvantage.

Paragraph 1(3) provides clear advice that when a member is acting as a representative of the authority on another body, he or she must comply with the authority's code of conduct, except and insofar as it conflicts with any other legal obligations to which he or she may be subject. So when the member, having been appointed to a body, is taking part in the business of that body, the legal obligations of the outside body take precedence over the code in the event of any conflict between the two.

2
General Obligations
A member—

    (a) must promote equality by not discriminating unlawfully against any person and by treating people with respect, regardless of their race, age, religion, gender, sexual orientation or disability, and

    (b) must not do anything which compromises or which is likely to compromise the impartiality of an employee of the authority.

Commentary
This provision deal with non-discrimination and the impartiality of employees. The first promotes equality by prohibiting members from unlawfully discriminating against anyone and requiring them to treat people with respect, regardless of their race, age, religion, gender, sexual orientation or disability. The second enshrines the impartiality of the authority's employees, and prohibits a member from doing anything that compromises it.

3
A member—

    (a) must not disclose information given to him in confidence by anyone, without the consent of a person authorised to give it, or unless he is required by law to do so, and.

    (b) must not prevent another person from gaining access to information to which that person is entitled by law.

Commentary
This provision deals with the treatment of information. A member is required to respect information that has been given to him or her in confidence by not divulging it without the consent of a person authorised to give such consent, or unless there is a legal requirement to do so. This latter provision would mean, among other things, that the confidentiality requirement would be over-ridden if a member needed to report a suspected breach of the code under the provisions in para 7.

4
A member must not in his official capacity or otherwise commit a criminal offence, or conduct himself in a manner which could reasonably be regarded as bringing his office or authority into serious disrepute.

Commentary
This paragraph, which applies to a member's outside activities as well as to their official duties, makes committing a criminal offence a breach of the code. The range of such offences is of course very wide. Some are serious, others less so; some might bear particularly on a person's suitability to hold public office, others will not. Serious

offences - those resulting in a sentence of imprisonment (whether suspended or not) of not less than three months - will, as now, result in a member's automatic removal from office under the provisions in s 80(1)(d) of the Local Government Act 1972. For other offences, the Adjudication Panel / Case Tribunals will decide what, if any, sanction should be imposed. Any sanction will need to reflect the nature and seriousness of the offence and its proximity to the member's public duties and the functions of the authority.

This paragraph also prohibits misconduct which could reasonably be regarded as bringing the office of the member, or the authority, into serious disrepute. This provision acknowledges that there are actions which, while not resulting in a criminal conviction, may nevertheless have a damaging effect on the public's confidence in the member or their authority. There is clearly an element of subjectivity in the provision – what constitutes serious disrepute is open to a variety of interpretations. The Guidance states that Members must reach their own judgement on the sorts of activities that might fall foul of this provision. This is **not** helpful. In assessing an allegation that such an activity has taken place, the Standards Board for England, the Adjudication Panel and Case Tribunals will need to consider how a reasonable person might view the activity, and whether it really could be regarded as bringing the member, or their authority, into serious disrepute.

5

A member—

    (a)   *must not, in his official capacity or otherwise, use his position improperly to confer on or secure for any person, an advantage or disadvantage.*

    (b)   *must, when using or authorising the use by others of the resources of the authority, act in accordance with the authority's requirements and ensure that such resources are not used for the activities of a registered political party.*

Commentary

This provision concerns the principle that in performing their public duties members must behave selflessly. Members are prohibited from improperly benefiting from their membership of the authority, or from securing benefits improperly for third parties. The provision also prohibits members from using their position to disadvantage other people (for instance to settle a score or give practical effect to a personal dislike of someone).

Members have a duty to comply with their authority's requirements when using or authorising the use of its resources. Such resources would typically relate to the use of equipment or facilities belonging to the authority, or decisions as to levels of hospitality, accommodation on visits and so on. Authorities should have rules or policies in place relating to such issues, and members will be required to comply with them. For example, it is helpful to have IS/IT Standards in lace, to address issues as to their use (and misuse) for non-council purposes, but also to address the plethora of other legal requirements – data protection for one – that members need to have highlighted. The Code means that such ancillary codes/protocols/standards must be complied with, and breach of such requirements would constitute breach of the Code. This provision also contains a specific prohibition on using the resources of the authority for party political activities.

6

A member must when reaching decisions—

    (a)   *not act unreasonably;*

    (b)   *have regard to any relevant advice provided to him by-*

        (i)   *the authority's chief finance officer acting in pursuance of his duties under section 114 of the Local Government Finance Act 1988(b), and*

        (ii)   *the authority's monitoring officer acting in pursuance of his duties under section 5 of the Local Government and Housing Act 1989(c), and*

(c) give the reasons for those decisions in accordance with the authority's
requirements.

Commentary

This provision deals with the decisions taken by members and their accountability for
them. The Consultation paper refers to the Oxford English Dictionary's definition of
unreasonableness as 'not guided by, or based on good sense or beyond the limits of
acceptability'. The term has, of course, been the subject of much judicial comment –
the *Wednesbury* case and others), and has taken on a meaning in the context of public
decision-making of not taking irrelevant factors into account in reaching a decision.
The government says that in the code, 'unreasonable' is used in both legal and
common senses, and the Monitoring Officer who will tend to be lawyer must take
care that their interpretation is that broad.

Paragraph 6(*b*) requires members to have regard to the advice provided by the
monitoring officer or the chief finance officer.

The code requirement makes each member responsible individually for his part in a
council's failure to give proper consideration to a statutory officer's advice. This does
not mean that members have to agree with the advice given to them by officers.
However, they must be satisfied – and be able to demonstrate – that they took it into
account and had good reason to disregard it, particularly if, subsequently, the action
is found by the courts or auditor to have been unlawful.

Paragraph 6(*c*) requires members to give the reasons for their decisions. This is a key
measure to ensure that members can be held accountable for their decisions by fellow
members and by the public.

7

A member must report to the Standards Board for England and to the authority's
monitoring officer any conduct by another member which he believes involves a
failure to comply with the authority's code of conduct.

Commentary

This is the least attractive provision in the Model Code. Despite the fact that the Local
Government Association agreed that members should be placed under a duty to bring
suspected breaches of the code by other members to the attention of the monitoring
officer, this has been described and may become a 'grassers charter'.

Members must report in writing both to the Standards Board for England and to their
authority's monitoring officer, (where one exists), any conduct by another member
that he or she believes involves a failure to comply with the code.

It is to be hoped that the National Standards Board may provide some guidance to
make these provisions workable, and avoid a politically based culture of 'tit-for-tat'
type allegations and counter-allegations from permeating all local authorities.

Part 2
Interest

8
Personal Interests

(1) A member must in all matters consider whether he has a personal interest,
and whether the authority's code of conduct obliges him to disclose that interest.

(2) A member must regard himself as having a personal interest in a matter if he
anticipates that a decision upon it might reasonably be regarded as affecting the
well-being or financial position of–

(a) himself, a member of his family or a friend, or
(b) a body which employs those persons, or for which those persons have any
degree of ownership, control or management to a greater extent than other
council tax payers, ratepayers, or inhabitants of the authority's area.

(3)   A member may regard himself as not having a personal interest in a matter if it relates to–
- (a)   another relevant authority of which he is a member;
- (b)   another public authority where he holds a position of general control or management;
- (c)   a body to which he has been appointed or nominated by the authority as a representative;
- (d)   the housing functions of the authority where the member may hold a tenancy or lease with a relevant authority, provided that he does not have arrears of rent of more than two months;
- (e)   the functions of the authority in respect of school meals, transport and travelling expenses, where the member is a parent of a child in full time education, unless it relates particularly to the school which the child attends;
- (f)   the functions of the authority in respect of statutory sick pay under Part XI of the Social Security Contributions and Benefits Act 1992, where the member is in receipt of, or is entitled to the receipt of such pay from a relevant authority, and
- (g)   the functions of the authority in respect of an allowance or payment made under sections 173 to 176 of the Local Government Act 1972, section 18 of the Local Government and Housing Act 1989, paragraph 25 of Schedule 2 to the Police Act 1996, and paragraph 17 of Schedule 2 to the Police Act 1997.

9
Disclosure of Interests

(1)   A member with a personal interest in a matter who attends a meeting of the authority at which the matter is discussed must disclose the existence and nature of the interest at the commencement of that discussion, or when it becomes apparent.

(2)   A member with a personal interest in any matter who has made an executive decision in relation to that matter must record in the written statement of that decision, the existence and nature of the interest.

10
Prejudicial Interests

(1)   A member with a personal interest in a matter must consider whether it is a 'prejudicial interest'.

(2)   A member must regard himself as having a prejudicial interest if it is a personal interest which a member of the public with knowledge of the relevant facts would regard as so significant and particular that it could prejudice the member's judgement of the public interest.

11
Overview and Scrutiny Committees

For the purposes of paragraphs 9 and 10, a member must regard himself as having a personal and a prejudicial interest in a matter if he is present at a meeting of the authority's overview and scrutiny committee or sub-committee which considers any matter that was the subject of, or which relates to a decision of another committee, sub-committee, joint committee or joint sub-committee of which he may also be a member.

12
Participation in Relation to Disclosed Interests

(1)   A member with a prejudicial interest in any matter must—
- (a)   withdraw from a meeting wherever it becomes apparent that the matter is being considered, unless he has obtained a dispensation from the authority's standards committee, and

(b) not exercise executive functions in relation to that matter.

(2)   Notwithstanding paragraph (1) (a), a member with a prejudicial interest may, unless that interest is of a financial nature and unless it is an interest of the type described in paragraph 11, participate in a meeting of the authority's—

(a)   overview and scrutiny committees, and

(b)   joint or area committees to the extent that such committees are not exercising functions of the authority or its executive.

13

For the purposes of this code, 'meeting' means any meeting—

(a)   of the relevant authority;

(b)   of any executive of the authority;

(c)   of any of its committees, sub-committees, joint-committees, joint sub-committees, or area committees, or

(d)   where members or officers of the authority are present.

Commentary

Part 2 of the draft model code relates to interests, and provides a consolidated regime. That is to be welcomed.

This currently is one of the most complex areas for officers to advise on and members to comprehend the requirements of. It remains to be seen whether the proposed new arrangements will improve on that.

The government identified to in designing these provisions, there was a need to balance three desirable goals:

'•   Retention of public trust in the member and the working of the authority;

•   Maximising opportunities for members to contribute to the work of their authority;

•   Simplicity and clarity in the operation of the model code.'

Paragraph 4.3 of the consultation paper made a crucial point that few could or would disagree with:

'The retention of public confidence is not so much a desirable goal, as a fundamental necessity. Without the public's trust, an authority would quickly become discredited. So Ministers see the requirements of public probity as paramount. The system we design must, first and foremost, meet those requirements.'

The draft code is clear that the declaration and participation rules do not apply to interests that are shared with council taxpayers, ratepayers, or inhabitants in the area of the authority. This is entirely correct.

In addition, the draft model code provides, unless the member is prevented from doing so by any other interest, that:

• a member who is also a member of any other relevant authority may participate in any discussion or decision-making on any matter relating to that authority;

• a member sitting on the management board of any public body may participate in any discussion or decision-making on any matter relating to that body;

• a member formally appointed or nominated to represent their authority on an external body may participate in any discussion or decision-making on any matter relating to that body.

There are also a range of narrower (but nonetheless vital in operational terms) which allow:

- members who are council tenants to participate and vote in debates on housing matters – the government propose (rightly) that this should be extended to cover council leaseholders, too;
- members who are parents of children in full-time education to participate and vote in debates on school meals, school transport and the reimbursement of school travelling expenses, except if the matter under discussion relates particularly to the school which the child attends;
- members to participate and vote in debates on the payment of statutory sick pay and in decisions on members' allowances.

All of these seem entirely sensible and reasonable.

In respect of members interest that arise in respect of participation in a [personal capacity, as compared to being appointed by the Council, after consideration (and the various issues are weighed and considered in the consultation paper), their proposed approach is to exclude from the new model code the provision in the current code permitting members either to speak and vote on matters relating to outside bodies on which they sit in a private capacity, or to speak, but not vote if the matter under discussion concerns the body's finances or property.

This will have a consequence for members, Councils and communities. Members frequently sit on and/or participate in organisations/bodies as community representatives/leaders at the request of the community. This enhances their community role.

Any interest arising from their personal involvement in such bodies in the future will be treated in the same way as any other interest. This may restrict the contribution that they can make to debates and decisions in matters concerning some outside organisations. Members and their authorities will need to recognize this and take steps to ensure that this is understood – and the rationale – or else members may be perceived as withdrawing from activities carried out in the past – and Council's may need to revisit their consultation arrangements to ensure that the links that may be lost through member participation are retained in other forms.

The first task of a member under the draft model code is to consider whether s/he has a personal interest in the outcome of any issue before them. This is addressed in paras 8(1) and 8(2). The word 'anticipate' will no doubt raise some issues – what is the test here – is it the reasonable member, a prudent member or what? To what extent are members expected to anticipate? And at what time – now or in the future, and if the latter, how far into the future?

If a Member has a personal interest, then s/he must declare it before the issue is considered or (if the interest is not apparent until the issue is under consideration) then as soon as the interest becomes apparent. This is the purpose of para 9 which requires the disclosure of both the existence and nature of any personal interest.

The code in this respect is of concern. Clearly, the member who intends to remain and participate should declare not only that they have an interest, but what that interest is. But for the member who does not intend to remain and/or participate, but in essence says that they will leave the room while the issue is discussed, this provision requires them to also specify the nature of that interest.

The government considers that the interests of openness outweigh any disadvantage to loss of member's privacy.

This is not a convincing argument. Once a member has said 'I will not participate in this as I have an interest then the reason for that information needing to be known is entirely unclear. However, where members have (for example) pecuniary interests, then they may wish not to actually disclose details of them, but would wish to abide by any requirements regarding non-participation.

The effect of this will be two-fold – people will be put off from remaining/becoming members if they have to disclose information for so little reason. Members will also seek to find ways around the issue. Neither of these options bode well for the Code or those trying to police it.

The definition of a meeting – referred to in para 9 – can be found in para 13. This is unsatisfactory, since the term can, based on para 13, be construed as including any meeting where members or officers are present. Does that include a party group meeting? Or a social dinner party? This needs clarification.

Having declared an interest, there are going to be some circumstances where a personal interest will be so significant that in order to 'ensure public confidence in the probity of the authority' (para 4.24 of the consultation paper), the member should play no part in the consideration of the issue that has given rise to that interest. Paragraphs 10 to 12 of the draft code address this issue.

The government's proposal is that Members, when they have identified a personal interest, should consider:

> 'whether a member of the public with knowledge of the relevant facts of the situation would reasonably think that the interest was so significant and particular that it could prejudice the member's judgement of the public interest.' (para 10.2 of the draft model code)

If that is the case, then the interest should be regarded as a 'prejudicial interest', and the member should abstain from participation in the consideration of the issue that has given rise to that interest (para 12 of the draft model code).

Notwithstanding the general requirement, the model draft code provides that a member participating in a meeting of:

(a) an overview and scrutiny committee

(b) a joint or area committee on occasions when it is not exercising the functions of the authority or the executive

should be required to withdraw only if they have a prejudicial interest of a financial nature (see para 12(2) of the draft code).

This is because the government is of the view that for authorities operating new constitutional arrangements under the 2000 Act, that where decisions are not being taken, the code could take a less restrictive approach to handling conflicts of interest. The functions of overview and scrutiny committees are constrained by statute to prevent them exercising any traditional decision-making function. Area committees and joint committees may carry out decision-making functions formally delegated to them by the authority, or the executive, but they may well also conduct discussions in order to review or inform policy decisions, rather than actually to make those decisions.

Paragraph 11 contains a further ground for withdrawal. This relates to scrutiny, a fundamental principle of which is to allow members who have not been involved in a decision to scrutinise that decision if it is felt that the issue needs a 'second look'. Whilst Members of the Executive cannot sit on overview and scrutiny committees, some decisions may be made by committees etc. Therefore, para 11 provides that members of that decision-making body who also sit on the Overview and Scrutiny Committee would have to withdraw from the scrutiny of that decision so as not to prejudice the independent nature of scrutiny.

Parallel transitional arrangements for those authorities who commence Part II arrangements prior to their Local Code being adopted can be found in reg 45 of the Local Authorities (Executive and Alternative Arrangements) (Modification of Enactments and Other Provisions) (England) Order 2001, SI 2001/2237.

Part 3
The Register of Members' Interests

14
Registration of Financial and Other Interests
A member must notify the authority's monitoring officer of—
- (a) any employment, office, trade or profession carried on by him for profit or gain;
- (b) the name of the person who employs or has appointed him, the name of any firm in which he is a partner, and the name of any company for which he is a remunerated director;
- (c) the name of any person, other than a relevant authority, who has made a payment to him in respect of his election or any expenses incurred by him in carrying out his duties;
- (d) the name of any corporate body which has a place of business or land in the authority's area, where the member has a beneficial interest in a class of securities of that body which exceeds the value of £25,000 or one hundredth of the total issued share capital of that body;
- (e) a description of any contract for goods, services or works made between the authority and himself, a firm in which he is a partner, a company of which he is a director, or a body of the description in paragraph (d);
- (f) the address of any land in which he has a beneficial interest and which is in the area of the authority;
- (g) the address of any land where the landlord is the authority and the tenant is a firm in which he is a partner, a company of which he is a director, or a body of the description in paragraph (d);
- (h) the address of any land in the authority's area in which he has a licence (alone or jointly with others) to occupy for a month or longer, and
- (i) the cost of any visit outside the United Kingdom for which the authority has paid or will pay.

15
A member must notify the authority's monitoring officer of his membership of or position of general control or management in any—
- (a) body to which he has been appointed or nominated by the authority as a representative;
- (b) public authority or body exercising functions of a public nature;
- (c) company, industrial and provident society, charity, or body directed to charitable purposes;
- (d) private club;
- (e) body whose principal purposes include the influence of public opinion or policy, and
- (f) trade union or professional association.

16
A member must notify the authority's monitoring officer of any—
- (a) other matter that he believes a member of the public might reasonably regard as likely to influence him, and
- (b) change to the interests specified under paragraphs 14 and 15.

17
Registration of Gifts and Hospitality
A member must notify the authority's monitoring officer of the existence and nature of any gifts or hospitality he has received over the value of £ [ ].

Commentary

Part 3 is reasonably self explanatory and in essence requires members to notify the Monitoring Officer of interests, and the Monitoring Officer to establish and maintain a register of the interests of their authority's members.

For those Monitoring Officers who are not personally to undertake this task (perhaps where committee and members services are managed elsewhere in the Council), they must ensure that a robust system is in place, and that the staff who do operate are aware that they must not, regardless of management instructions, depart from the prescribed regime.

The register of members' interests is described by the government as ' ... an important instrument of openness and good governance' (para 5.3 of the consultation paper).

The draft model code contains specific requirements as to what must be registered (although the list in para 15 is a generic one).

However, there is also a catch all in para 16 whereby in addition to the requirements with regard to financial and non-financial interests, a member should also register any interest that s/he believes might be regarded by the public as likely to influence the member's work on the authority.

In relation to para 17, the government considers that it is appropriate within the context of an ethical framework, to require members to register hospitality or gifts. The draft model code requires members to register gifts and hospitality received in the course of their official duties above an (as yet unspecified) value. The consultation paper sought views upon whether gifts and hospitality offered but not accepted should be registered and whether the code should specify that gifts above a specified value should become the property of the authority. No doubt these issues will be addressed in the final draft.

APPENDIX 17

Ethical Governance Audit – Methodology

(Chapter 14)

1. Desk Top Review of Policies (eg what policies and processes do we think we have in place?)

Standing Orders		❏
Scheme of Delegation	Officers	❏
	Members	❏
Terms of Reference		❏
Contracts Standing Orders		❏
Financial Standing Orders		❏
Standards Document:		❏
⇒ National Code of Local Government Conduct – Members		❏
⇒ Code of Conduct – Employees		❏
⇒ Officer/Member Protocol		❏
⇒ Code of Practice – Whistle-blowing		
⇒ Guidance – for Members on Outside Bodies		❏
⇒ Standards Committee		❏
◆ Terms of Reference		❏
⇒ Monitoring Officer Guidance		❏
⇒ Conflicts of Interest		❏
⇒ Guidance on Support for Councillors		
⇒ Guidance on Members' Correspondence		❏
⇒ Dissemination of Local Government Ombudsman decisions		
⇒ Decision making and Legal and Financial advice		❏
⇒ Audit Reports - dissemination		❏
⇒ Audit Code of Conduct		❏
Declarations		❏
Gifts and Hospitality		❏
Proper Officer Arrangements		
Recording of decisions		❏
Induction	Officers	❏
	Members	❏

453

Training	Officers	❑
	Members	❑
Risk Management Protocol		❑
Health and Safety Policy		❑
IT Security Policy		❑
Management Letter		❑
Statutory Plans (various)		❑
Best Value Performance Plan		❑
Members Allowance Scheme		❑
Officer Expense Scheme		❑
Arrangements for Head of Paid Service		❑
Arrangements for Monitoring Officer		❑
Arrangements for Section 151 Officer		❑
Employment Policies (including local agreements)		❑

2. Desk Top Review of Communication of Policies (eg how we think we do this)

To Officers
To Members
To the public
To others   Government
               Local Government Associations
               The Press and Media
               District Audit
               Others

3. Desk Top Review of Processes (eg How do we think we apply policies and processes?) (Cross Reference to 1 and 2 above)

4. Reality Check (eg What is the true picture?)

Surveys/Questionnaires   – Officers
                          – Members
                          – Partners
                          – Public
                          – District Audit
                          – Others
Interviews
Site Visits
Other Methods as appropriate

5.   External Validation (eg by someone outside the organisation)

Review 1 – 4 above
Inspection Visit
Agree – programme
Programme – process
Interviews of   – Officers
                           – Members
                           – Partners
                           – Public?
                           – Others?

6.   Report Findings

To Standards Committee
To Executive Board
To Leader's Advisory Board
To all Members
To public
To Partners
To Others

7.   Action Plan

Draft and implement Action Plan

8.   Review

Annually?
Every 2 years?
Every 5 years?

Appendix 18

Ethical Governance Audit – Questionnaire

(Chapter 14)

INTRODUCTION

In the context of local government, an ethical framework is a set of principles which govern our behaviour. Values like accountability, openness and observance of the law should determine the way we conduct ourselves in the carrying out of our duties in the public interest.

The Local Government Act 2000 provides for a new ethical framework for Members requiring them to observe a Code of Conduct which will be largely set nationally and a disciplinary procedure for dealing with complaints alleging misbehaviour. The Act also provides for a new Code of Conduct for employees which will automatically be incorporated into contracts of employment.

QUESTIONNAIRE

This audit has been approved by the Council's Standards Committee. Responses from a sample of Members and Officers will assist in assessing any ethical vulnerabilities facing the Council. The responses will be collated and are non-attributable. The results will help the Committee in particular in deciding how best to devote resources to training on conduct matters. Members or Officers who would like to participate in further confidential discussions on the issues raised are asked to complete the statement at the end of the questionnaire.

Please tick the answers you feel best reflect your view.

NO	QUESTIONS	ANSWER				COMMENTS (IF ANY)
		Yes	To a large extent	Not really	Not at all	
1	Is it important for local government to establish and operate by a set of strong ethical values?					
2	Do you think the public perceive ethical standards within the Council to be good?					
3	Do you believe standards of ethical conduct in this authority are high?					
4	Is there good access to information for: (a) Members (b) the public?					
5	Are you aware of and have a broad understanding of the following documents? ● Standing Orders ● Scheme of Delegation ● National Code of Local Government Conduct for Members ● Officer/Member Protocol ● Financial Regulations ● Contract Standing Orders ● Special Procedures and Protocols Do you know where you can put your hands on the above documents?					

6	Do you have a reasonable understanding of the role of the following statutory officers? • Head of Paid Service • Monitoring Officer • Chief Finance Officer							
7	Do you have a good understanding of the processes for the conduct of local authority business?							
8	Do you receive clear information about the work of the Council which is relevant to you?							
9	Do you think there is any complacency about standards of conduct? (a) within Members (b) within Officers							
10	Do you think Members see themselves as having a role in ensuring good conduct and high standards on the part of others?							
11	Do you think Officers see themselves as having a role in ensuring good conduct and high standards on the part of others?							
12	Is there an understanding throughout the authority of the new ethical framework proposed in the Local Government Act 2000?							
13	Are Officers clear as to their role and accountabilities?							

14	Are Members clear as to their role and accountabilities?								
15	Are Members and Officers clear as to who is responsible for what under the new transitional arrangements?								
16	Do non-executive Members identify strongly with the overview and scrutiny role?								
17	In respect of ethical governance are the Council's practices and procedures relevant, up-to-date and clear?								
18	Does the Council consistently follow such proper procedures?								
19	Does the Council deal effectively with misconduct? • of Members • of Officers								
20	Do Members have a common understanding on how to deal with conflict of interests?								
	Do Officers have a common understanding on how to deal with conflict of interest?								
21	Do you believe the role of the Standards Committee is widely understood?								
22	Are Standards issues perceived as owned by Members and Officers generally?								

23	Do you know where (or from whom) you can obtain advice and support to help you on Standards issues?				
24	Have you had relevant training on issues relating to standards of conduct?				
25	Are there any questions you would want the Ethical Governance Audit to answer for you?				

WHAT PART DO YOU PLAY IN THE BUSINESS OF THE COUNCIL?

As a Member   Chair of a Committee/Panel ❑
Vice Chair of a Committee/Panel ❑
Member of the Executive ❑
Other ❑

As an employee   Executive Director ❑
Level One/head of Service ❑
Other ❑

Please add your name and signature **only** if you would like a specific response to any issue that you have raised – or if you would like to!

Name (in block capitals) _____ Member/Officer

Signed   _____

Date   _____

THANK YOU FOR COMPLETING THIS QUESTIONNAIRE. THE STANDARDS COMMITTEE AND I ARE VERY GRATEFUL FOR YOUR CO-OPERATION.

Please use the attached addressed envelope to return the questionnaire to:

Special Procedure and Protocol Standards Committee

(Chapter 15)

THE STANDARDS COMMITTEE IS A 'SPECIALIST COMMITTEE' WITHIN THE TERMS OF THE STANDING ORDERS OF THE COUNCIL AND COMMITTEES

This Special Procedure requires the Committee, in dealing with matters within its Terms of Reference–

1. to apply best practice based on the law including the provisions of the Human Rights Act 1998, and on the principles of natural justice, in particular providing that:
   - each party has the right to be heard;
   - no member serving on the Committee will hear any matter in which s/he has an interest or in which any reasonable member of the public could take the view that there was bias on the part of the Committee member;
   - all relevant matters will be taken into account;
   - all irrelevant matters will be ignored; and
   - Members serving on the Committee will come to reasonable decisions based upon the evidence in front of them, and the law.
2. to comply with the requirements of the Council's Standing Orders, with particular reference to Standing Orders 34(3) and (5).
3. to have regard to the following:
   - the maintenance of standards;
   - the protection of the public interest; and
   - the rights of all interested parties;
4. to conduct its business in a non-political manner in relation to decisions of a quasi-judicial nature.

Definitions

'Misconduct' means any conduct by a Councillor which is in breach of:
- the National Code of Local Government Conduct (as issued by the Secretary of State for the Environment in April 1990);
- the Council's Officer/Member Protocol; or
- any other Codes, Protocols, Procedures, Rules or Guidance that the Council may from time to time adopt.

'Sanctions' means (subject to the lawfulness of the Council or another body imposing such a sanction) any of the following either singularly or in conjunction with each other:
- the removal of a Councillor from membership of some or all Committees;
- the removal of a Councillor as representative of the Council on any outside body;
- the barring of a Councillor from representing the Council at conferences, seminars and other similar events;

- the recommendation to an appointing Committee that the Councillor be removed from the Office of Chairman or any other office;
- public censure; or
- a request that a political party consider instituting its own disciplinary measures against the Councillor

'Complainant' means any Councillor, Officer or member of the public who has made a formal written complaint in accordance with this procedure.

'Representative' means any representative including a professional or legal representative, save in so far as legal representative shall not include a Solicitor employed by Southampton City Council.

1. General

1.1   This procedure applies to complaints against Members of [....................] Council only. Complaints against Officers will be considered in accordance with the Councils Disciplinary Rules and Procedures as laid down from time to time. Complaints from Citizens about services shall be considered under the Council's Customer Complaints Procedure.

1.2   The Special Procedure set out below may be ended at any time by the Standards Committee where they conclude that continuing will serve no useful purpose eg;

- the Councillor concerned acknowledges the complaint is justified, apologies and accepts any sanction the Committee may feel necessary; or
- the Councillor concerned has resigned or died.

1.3   The Special Procedure set out below may take place in the absence of any party if they fail to co-operate with any reasonable request of the Committee or the Head of Legal Services or fail to attend a hearing without good cause.

1.4   Nothing in this Special Procedure detracts from the authority of the Chief Executive, Chief Finance Officer or Monitoring Officer to decide that any matter, whether involving a Member or not, should be reported to the Police **at any time**.

2. Receipt of Complaint

2.1   Any complaint of misconduct should be made in writing to the Head of Legal Services setting out the conduct complained of and giving particulars of any alleged breaches of any relevant legislation or codes of conduct. Any complaint not containing the above information may still go forward to the Preliminary Investigation Stage if, in the opinion of the Head of Legal Services, the matter complained of merits further investigation. The Head of Legal Services will acknowledge receipt of any complaint within five working days. The Head of Legal Services may also determine of his own volition that a matter should be investigated without a receipt of a complaint.

3. Preliminary Investigation Stage

3.1   The Head of Legal Services will send a copy of any complaint received to the Leader of that Councillor's Political Group for information purposes, to the Councillor concerned, the Chief Executive and the Chair of the Standards Committee within five working days of receipt. The Councillor will be invited to respond to the complaint in writing and/or to discuss the issue with the Head of Legal Services within such reasonable time as the Head of Legal Services may allow. The Head of Legal Services may take such steps as are necessary at this point to gather information in order to assist him in determining whether a prima facie case exists.

3.2   On receipt of the Councillors' written or verbal comments the Head of Legal Services will consider whether or not a prima facie case is made out, which process shall not be time limited. Where a Councillor has failed to respond to a complaint within the reasonable time allowed as above, the Head of Legal Services will not be estopped from determining whether or not a prima facie case is made out as above.

4. Minor Infractions

4.1   At this point the Head of Legal Services will determine whether or not the case should be referred to the Standards Committee, it should be investigated by some other agency eg the Police or whether it should be dealt with other than by the Standards Committee. Where a Police or other external investigation is already underway in relation to the matter complained of it shall not be referred to the Standards Committee until such time as it has been properly disposed of by that body.

4.2   In certain circumstances, it may be appropriate to 'caution' a Councillor rather than refer them to the Standards Committee. This is likely to take the form of a reminder of the Procedure or Protocol that has been breached and advice that should a further occurrence occur, then the matter will be reported to the Standards Committee. Such a further occurrence would also bring forward the initial issue for consideration by the Standards Committee. If the Head of Legal Services reaches such a view, that will be shared with the Chief Executive and Chair of the Standards Committee on the basis that should either or both the Chief Executive and Chair of the Standards Committee have a different view, the Head of Legal Services has an opportunity to revisit the matter and if appropriate bring the case before the Standards Committee for consideration. The determination of the matter in these circumstances shall be shared with the Chair of the Standards Committee, Group Leaders and the Chief Executive.

5. Substantive Cases: Preparatory Matters

5.1   If a prima facie case is established in a matter that has been determined should be considered by the Standards Committee, a management meeting of the relevant Officers and the Chair of the Committee will be called as soon as reasonably practical to determine the timeframe for the further investigation of the matter and to give directions as to:

- any additional witnesses be interviewed by the Head of Legal Services;
- any additional documents to be produced during the investigation;
- the appointment of specialist advisors to supply information not readily available to the Committee or to clarify complex matters.

where it is felt necessary or expedient to do so.

5.2   The Chair of the Standards Committee may, at his/her absolute discretion, involve other Members of the Standards Committee to participate in any management meeting referred to in para 5.1 above.

5.3   As soon as reasonably practicable after the management meeting the Head of Legal Services will write to all parties advising them of the proposed date on which the matter will be heard by the Standards Committee. The Head of Legal Services will at all times retain the right to alter the proposed date of the Committee in the event of any delay in the investigation procedure, provided always that all parties be advised in writing as soon as possible of such delay and of any new date set for the hearing of the matter.

6. Substantive Complaint: Investigation

6.1   In the event of a full investigation the Head of Legal Services will, as soon as reasonably practical after the Committee management meeting, invite the complainant for a formal interview. The complainant will be afforded the opportunity to submit further material in support of the allegations made.

6.2   The Head of Legal Services will provide the Councillor with a copy of the complaint any further supporting material. S/he will be invited to comment on the material and may submit material of their own which they consider relevant.

6.3   Following the above the Head of Legal Services will prepare a report for the Standards Committee. The report will be copied to the Complainant and Councillor a minimum of 10 working dates in advance of the Committee meeting to consider the complaint. The complainant and Councillor may at this stage submit further written comments for submission with the report if required. Such comments must be made available within any timeframe laid down by the Head of Legal Services.

6.4   The Head of Legal Services may exclude documents s/he considers confidential from the information sent to the complainant or Councillor.

7.   Standards Committee Hearing

7.1   The procedure at the full hearing of the complaint will be as follows:

- the Head of Legal Services will present the report;
- the Complainant or his/her representative will be invited to speak to their complaint if they wish to do so;
- the Head of Legal Services and the Committee may ask questions of the complainant if present;
- the Councillor or his/her representative may present their case;
- the Head of Legal Services and the Committee may ask questions of the Councillor;
- witnesses may be called at the discretion of the Committee. Witnesses will be called in any order and may be questioned by:
  - the complainant/Councillor;
  - the Head of Legal Services and the Committee;
- the Councillor may sum up his/her case;
- the Head of Legal Services will sum up.

7.2   Any witnesses will be entitled to be accompanied by a representative of their choice.

7.3   The Complainant and Councillor will normally be entitled to be present at the meeting throughout the Committee's consideration of the complaint.

7.4   Any procedural questions or issues which may arise during the course of the hearing will be determined by Committee ensuring at all times that the parties to the complaint are treated fairly.

7.5   At any time before or during the hearing the Committee may send for persons, papers and or records not currently before it and may adjourn so that this can take place.

7.6   The Committee will determine how much of the information available at the hearing should not be made available for public inspection after the announcement of the decision (having regard to the Access to Information provisions of the Local Government Act 1972 and the need to ensure fairness to the persons involved).

7.7   The Committee will be supported at all times by a suitably qualified Lawyer who will advise them as to practice and procedure, together with any relevant points of Law in relation to their decision making process.

8.   Sanctions/Costs

8.1   The Committee, after considering all the evidence before it, may determine whether or not a complaint is upheld or not. Where a complaint is upheld the Committee may impose such sanctions as it thinks fit, are within the law and within its powers to impose. In making its decision the Committee will have regard to the severity of the misconduct found and will determine the type, length and duration of such sanctions accordingly.

8.2   Alternatively or in addition to the imposition of sanctions the Committee may offer advice or comments to the Councillor about his or her future conduct.

8.3   The costs of attendance at the meetings must be borne by the individuals concerned and the Committee has no power to award costs or expenses to any party and or their representatives.

9. Notification of Committee decision

9.1 The Committee will deliver its decision, together with reasons, in public session. The Head of Legal Services will send written confirmation of that decision to all parties within five working days of the hearing.

9.2 All members of the Council will be notified of the Committee's decision for information.

9.3 The attached chart, which forms part of this Special Procedure, sets out the process referred to above including such parts of the process as should be closed to the public in the interests of fairness and to preserve the confidentiality of such material as is not in the public domain.

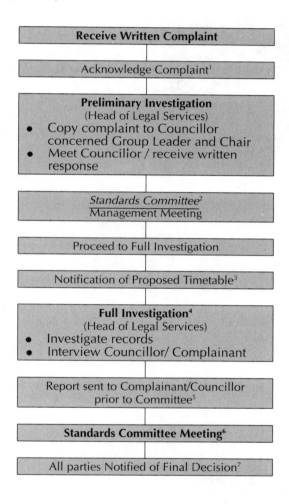

Receive Written Complaint

Acknowledge Complaint[1]

Preliminary Investigation
(Head of Legal Services)
- Copy complaint to Councillor concerned Group Leader and Chair
- Meet Councillor / receive written response

*Standards Committee[2]
Management Meeting*

Proceed to Full Investigation

Notification of Proposed Timetable[3]

Full Investigation[4]
(Head of Legal Services)
- Investigate records
- Interview Councillor/ Complainant

Report sent to Complainant/Councillor prior to Committee[5]

Standards Committee Meeting[6]

All parties Notified of Final Decision[7]

Notes

1   Within five working days.
2   Closed to General Public; Restricted access; Determines nature of investigation.
3   Within five working days.
4   Not time-limited.
5   10 days prior to Meeting.
6   Open to General Public.
7   Within five working days.

APPENDIX 20

Local Government Finance Act 1988
ss 113 and 114

(Chapter 22)

113
Qualifications of responsible officer
(1)   On and after the commencement day the person having responsibility for the administration of the financial affairs of a relevant authority under section 151 of the 1972 Act, section 73 of the 1985 Act[, section 127 of the 1999 Act] or section 112 above shall fulfil the requirement in one (or the requirements in each) of the paragraphs of subsection (2) below.

(2)   The requirements are that—
    (a)   he is a member of one or more of the bodies mentioned in subsection (3) below;
    (b)   immediately before the commencement day he had responsibility for the administration of the financial affairs of any of the authorities mentioned in section 111(2)(a) to (k) above under section 151 of the 1972 Act or section 73 of the 1985 Act.

(3)   The bodies are—
    (a)   the Institute of Chartered Accountants in England and Wales,
    (b)   the Institute of Chartered Accountants of Scotland,
    (c)   the Chartered Association of Certified Accountants,
    (d)   the Chartered Institute of Public Finance and Accountancy,
    (e)   the Institute of Chartered Accountants in Ireland,
    (f)   the Chartered Institute of Management Accountants, and
    (g)   any other body of accountants established in the United Kingdom and for the time being approved by the Secretary of State for the purposes of this section.

(4)   The authority mentioned in subsection (2)(b) above need not be the same as that under consideration for the purpose of applying subsection (1) above.

Amendment
Amended by the Greater London Authority Act 1999, s 129.

114
Functions of responsible officer as regards reports
(1)   On and after the commencement day the person having responsibility for the administration of the financial affairs of a relevant authority under section 151 of the 1972 Act, section 73 of the 1985 Act[, section 127 of the 1999 Act] or section 112 above shall have the duties mentioned in this section, without prejudice to any other functions; and in this section he is referred to as the chief finance officer of the authority.

(2) [Subject to subsection (2A),] the chief finance officer of a relevant authority shall make a report under this section if it appears to him that the authority, a committee [of the authority, a person holding any office or employment under the authority, a member of a police force maintained by the authority,] or a joint committee on which the authority is represented—

    (a) has made or is about to make a decision which involves or would involve the authority incurring expenditure which is unlawful,

    (b) has taken or is about to take a course of action which, if pursued to its conclusion, would be unlawful and likely to cause a loss or deficiency on the part of the authority, or

    (c) is about to enter an item of account the entry of which is unlawful.

[(2A) Where a relevant authority is operating executive arrangements, the chief finance officer of the relevant authority shall not make a report under subsection (2) in respect of any action referred to in paragraph (a), (b) or (c) of that subsection unless it is action taken otherwise than by or on behalf of the relevant authority's executive.]

(3) The chief finance officer of a relevant authority shall make a report under this section if it appears to him that the expenditure of the authority incurred (including expenditure it proposes to incur) in a financial year is likely to exceed the resources (including sums borrowed) available to it to meet that expenditure.

[(3A) It shall be the duty of the chief finance officer of a relevant authority, in preparing a report in pursuance of subsection (2) above, to consult so far as practicable—

    (a) with the person who is for the time being designated as the head of the authority's paid service under section 4 of the Local Government and Housing Act 1989; and

    (b) with the person who is for the time being responsible for performing the duties of the authority's monitoring officer under section 5 of that Act.]

[(3B) Subsection (3A) above shall have effect in relation to the London Development Agency with the substitution for paragraphs (a) and (b) of the words 'with the person who is for the time being appointed under paragraph 4(2) of Schedule 2 to the Regional Development Agencies Act 1998 as the chief executive of the London Development Agency'.

(3C) Subsection (3A) above shall have effect in relation to Transport for London with the substitution for paragraphs (a) and (b) of the words 'with the person who is for the time being designated for the purpose under subsection (3D) below'.

(3D) Transport for London shall designate a member of Transport for London, or a member of the staff of Transport for London, as the person who is to be consulted under subsection (3A) above.]

(4) Where a chief finance officer of a relevant authority has made a report under this section he shall send a copy of it to—

    (a) the person who at the time the report is made has the duty to audit the authority's accounts, and

    (b) each person who at that time is a member of the authority[; and

    (c) in a case where the relevant authority has a mayor and council manager executive, the person who at the time the report is made is the council manager of that authority].

[(4A) The duty under subsection (4)(b) above—

    (a) in a case where the relevant authority is the Greater London Authority, is to send a copy of the report to the Mayor of London and to each member of the London Assembly; and

    (b) in a case where the relevant authority is a functional body, within the meaning of the 1999 Act, includes a duty to send a copy of the report to the Mayor of London and to the Chair of the Assembly, within the meaning of that Act.]

(5) Subject to subsection (6) below, the duties of a chief finance officer of a relevant authority under subsections (2) and (3) above shall be performed by him personally.

(6)   If the chief finance officer is unable to act owing to absence or illness his duties under subsections (2) and (3) above shall be performed—

(a)   by such member of his staff as is a member of one or more of the bodies mentioned in section 113(3) above and is for the time being nominated by the chief finance officer for the purposes of this section, or

(b)   if no member of his staff is a member of one or more of those bodies, by such member of his staff as is for the time being nominated by the chief finance officer for the purposes of this section.

(7)   A relevant authority shall provide its chief finance officer with such staff, accommodation and other resources as are in his opinion sufficient to allow his duties under this section to be performed.

(8)   In this section—

(a)   references to a joint committee are to a committee on which two or more relevant authorities are represented, and

(b)   references to a committee (joint or otherwise) include references to a sub-committee.

[(9)   The National Crime Squad shall be treated as a police force for the purposes of subsection (2) above.]

Amendment
Amended by the Local Government and Housing Act 1989, s 139, Sch 5; the Police and Magistrates' Courts Act 1994, s 43, Sch 4; the Police Act 1997, s 88, Sch 6; the Greater London Authority Act 1999, s 130; and SI 2001/2237, arts 1, 2, 20.

APPENDIX 21

LGMB Code of Conduct for Local Government Employees (1994)

(Chapter 30)

Standards

Local government employees are expected to give the highest possible standard of service to the public, and where it is part of their duties, to provide appropriate advice to councillors and fellow employees with impartiality. Employees will be expected, through agreed procedures and without fear of recrimination, to bring to the attention of the appropriate level of management any deficiency in the provision of service. Employees must report to the appropriate manager any impropriety or breach of procedure.

Disclosure of Information

It is generally accepted that open government is best. The law requires that certain types of information must be available to members, auditors, government departments, service users and the public. The authority itself may decide to be open about other types of information. Employees must be aware of which information their authority is and is not open about, and act accordingly.

Employees should not use any information obtained in the course of their employment for personal gain or benefit, nor should they pass it on to others who might use it in such a way. Any particular information received by an employee from a councillor which is personal to that councillor and does not belong to the authority should not be divulged by the employee without the prior approval of that councillor, except where such disclosure is required or sanctioned by the law.

Political Neutrality

Employees serve the authority as a whole. It follows they must serve all councillors and not just those of the controlling group, and must ensure that the individual rights of all councillors are respected.

Subject to the authority's conventions, employees may also be required to advise political groups. They must do so in ways which do not compromise their political neutrality. Employees, whether or not politically restricted, must follow every lawful expressed policy of the authority and must not allow their own personal or political opinions to interfere with their work.

Political assistants appointed on fixed-term contracts in accordance with the Local Government and Housing Act 1989 are exempt from the standards set above.

Relationships

Councillors

Employees are responsible to the authority through its senior managers. For some, their role is to give advice to councillors and senior managers and all are there to carry out the authority's work. Mutual respect between employees and councillors is essential to good local government. Close familiarity between employees and individual councillors can damage the relationship and prove embarrassing to other employees and councillors, and should therefore be avoided.

The Local Community and Service Users

Employees should always remember their responsibilities to the community they serve and ensure courteous, efficient and impartial service delivery to all groups and individuals within that community, as defined by the policies of the authority.

Contractors

All relationships of a business or private nature with external contractors, or potential contractors, should be made known to the appropriate manager. Orders and contracts must be awarded on merit, by fair competition against other tenders, and no special favours should be shown in the tendering process to businesses run by, eg friends, partners or relatives. No part of the local community should be discriminated against. Employees who engage or supervise contractors, or who have any other official relationship with contractors and have previously had or currently have a relationship in a private or domestic capacity with contractors, should declare that relationship to the appropriate manager.

Appointment and Other Employment Matters

Employees involved in appointments should ensure that these are made on the basis of merit. It would be unlawful for an employee to make an appointment which was based on anything other than the ability of the candidate to undertake the duties of the post. In order to avoid any possible accusation of bias, employees should not be involved in an appointment where they are related to an applicant or have a close personal relationship outside work with him or her.

Similarly, employees should not be involved in decisions relating to discipline, promotion or pay adjustments for any other employee who is a relative, partner, etc.

Outside Commitments

Some employees have conditions of service which require them to obtain written consent to take any outside employment. All employees should be clear about their contractual obligations and should not take outside work which conflicts with the authority's interests. Employees should follow their authority's rules on the ownership of intellectual property or copyright created during their employment.

Personal Interests

Employees must declare to an appropriate manager any non-financial interests that they consider could bring about conflict with the authority. Employees must declare to an appropriate manager any financial interests which could conflict with the authority's interests.

Employees should declare to an appropriate manager membership of any organisation not open to the public without formal rules of membership and commitment of allegiance and which has secrecy about rules of membership or conduct.

Equality Issues
All local government employees should ensure that policies relating to equality issues as agreed by the authority are complied with in addition to the requirements of the law. All members of the local community, customers and other employees have a right to be treated with fairness and equity.

Separation of Roles During Tendering
Employees involved in the tendering process and dealing with contractors should be clear on the separation of client and contractor roles within the authority. Senior employees who have both a client and contractor responsibility must be aware of the need for accountability and openness. Employees in contractor or client units must exercise fairness and impartiality when dealing with all customers, suppliers, other contractors and sub-contractors.

Employees who are privy to confidential information on tenders or costs for either internal or external contractors should not disclose that information to any unauthorised party or organisation.

Employees contemplating a management buyout should, as soon as they have formed a definite intent, inform the appropriate manager and withdraw from the contract awarding processes.

Employees should ensure that no special favour is shown to current or recent former employees or their partners, close relatives or associates in awarding contracts to businesses run by them or employing them in a senior or relevant managerial capacity.

Corruption
Employees must be aware that it is a serious criminal offence for them corruptly to receive or give any gift, loan, fee, reward or advantage for doing, or not doing, anything or showing favour, or disfavour, to any person in their official capacity. If an allegation is made it is for the employee to demonstrate that any such rewards have not been corruptly obtained.

Use of Financial Resources
Employees must ensure that they use public funds entrusted to them in a responsible and lawful manner. They should strive to ensure value for money to the local community and to avoid legal challenge to the authority.

Hospitality
Employees should only accept offers of hospitality if there is a genuine need to impart information or represent the local authority in the community. Offers to attend purely social or sporting functions should be accepted only when these are part of the life of the community or where the authority should be seen to be represented. They should be properly authorised and recorded.

When hospitality has to be declined, those making the offer should be courteously but firmly informed of the procedures and standards operating within the authority.

Employees should not accept significant personal gifts from contractors and outside suppliers, although the authority may wish to allow employees to keep insignificant items of token value such as pens, diaries, etc.

When receiving authorised hospitality employees should be particularly sensitive as to its timing in relation to decisions which the authority may be taking affecting those providing the hospitality.

Acceptance by employees of hospitality through attendance at relevant conferences and courses is acceptable where it is clear the hospitality is corporate rather than personal, where the authority gives consent in advance and where the authority is satisfied that any purchasing decisions are not compromised. Where visits to inspect equipment, etc are required, employers should ensure that authorities meet the cost of such visits to avoid jeopardising the integrity of subsequent purchasing decisions.

Sponsorship – Giving and Receiving

Where an outside organisation wishes to sponsor or is seeking to sponsor a local government activity, whether by invitation, tender, negotiation or voluntarily, the basic conventions concerning acceptance of gifts or hospitality apply. Particular care must be taken when dealing with contractors or potential contractors.

Where the authority wishes to sponsor an event or service neither an employee nor any partner, spouse or relative must benefit from such sponsorship in a direct way without there being full disclosure to an appropriate manager of any such interest. Similarly, where the authority through sponsorship, grant aid, financial or other means, gives support in the community, employees should ensure that impartial advice is given and that there is no conflict of interest involved.

APPENDIX 22

Code of Conduct (Qualifying Local Government Employees) (Wales) Order 2001, SI 2001/2280 Schedule

(Chapter 30)

Code of Conduct for Qualifying Employees of Relevant Authorities in Wales

General Principles
1. The public is entitled to expect the highest standards of conduct from all qualifying employees or relevant authorities. The role of such employees is to serve their employing authority in providing advice, implementing its policies, and delivering services to the local community. In performing their duties, they must act with integrity, honesty, impartiality and objectivity.

Accountability
2. Qualifying employees of relevant authorities work for their employing authority and serve the whole of that authority. They are accountable to, and owe a duty to that authority. They must act in accordance with the principles set out in this Code, recognising the duty of all public sector employees to discharge public functions reasonably and according to the law.

Political Neutrality
3. Qualifying employees of relevant authorities, whether or not politically restricted, must follow every lawfully expressed policy of the authority and must not allow their own personal or political opinions to interfere with their work. Where qualifying employees are politically restricted (by reason of the post they hold, the nature of the work they do, or the salary they are paid), they must comply with any statutory restrictions on their political activities.

Relations with members, the public and other employees
4. Mutual respect between qualifying employees and members is essential to good local government, and working relationships should be kept on a professional basis.
5. Qualifying employees of relevant authorities should deal with the public, members and other employees sympathetically, efficiently, and without bias.

Equality
6.   Qualifying employees of relevant authorities must comply with policies relating to equality issues, as agreed by the authority, in addition to the requirements of the law.

Stewardship
7.   Qualifying employees of relevant authorities must ensure that they use public funds entrusted to them in a reasonable and lawful manner, and must not utilise property, vehicles or other facilities of the authority for personal use unless authorised to do so.

Personal Interests
8.   Whilst qualifying employees' private lives are their own concern, they must not allow their private interests to conflict with their public duty. They must not misuse their official position or information acquired in the course of their employment to further their private interests, or the interests of others. In particular, they must comply with:
(1)   any rules of their relevant authority on the registration and declaration by employees of financial and non-financial interests;
(2)   any rules of their relevant authority on the declaration by employees of hospitality or gifts offered to or received by them, from any person or organisation doing or seeking to do business, or otherwise benefiting or seeking to benefit from a relationship with the authority. Qualifying employees must not accept benefits from a third party unless authorised to do so by their relevant authority.

Whistle-blowing
9.   In the event that a qualifying employee becomes aware of activities which that employee believes to be illegal, improper, unethical or otherwise inconsistent with this Code, the employee should report the matter, acting in accordance with the employee's rights under the Public Interest Disclosure Act 1998, and with the relevant authority's confidential reporting procedure, or any other procedure designed for this purpose.

Treatment of Information
10.   Openness in the dissemination of information and decision-making should be the norm in relevant authorities. However, certain information may be confidential or sensitive and therefore not appropriate for a wide audience. Where confidentiality is necessary to protect the privacy or other rights of individuals or bodies, information should not be released to anyone other than a member, relevant authority employee or other person who is entitled to receive it, or needs to have access to it for the proper discharge of their functions. Nothing in this Code can be taken as overriding existing statutory or common law obligations to keep certain information confidential, or to divulge certain information.

Appointment of Staff
11.   Qualifying employees of relevant authorities involved in the recruitment and appointment of staff must ensure that appointments are made on the basis of merit. In order to avoid any possible accusation of bias, such employees must not be involved in any appointment, or any other decisions relating to discipline, promotion or pay and conditions for any other employee, or prospective employee, to whom they are related, or with whom they have a close personal relationship outside work.

Investigations by Monitoring Officers

12. Where a monitoring officer is undertaking an investigation in accordance with regulations made under section 73(1) of the Local Government Act 2000 a qualifying employee must comply with any requirement made by that monitoring officer in connection with such an investigation.

INDEX

A

Absent voting
background, **8**.10—**8**.11
generally, **8**.15
introduction, **8**.9
turnout, and, **8**.38
Access to information
background, **21**.1
executive arrangements, **21**.2
Accommodation, provision of
well-being powers, and, **2**.18
Accountability of cabinet government
access to information, **4**.21
forward plan, **4**.20
generally, **4**.16
individual executive decisions, **4**.19
key decisions, **4**.18
recording decisions, **4**.17
Accounting
accrual, **24**.16
cash, **24**.15
commitment, **24**.18
introduction, **24**.14
resource, **24**.17
Accrual accounting
generally, **24**.16
Acquisition of communications data
investigatory powers, and, **27**.3
Adjudication Panels
ethics, and, **15**.2
Admission to meetings
openness, and, **21**.1
Alternative arrangements
council's role, **6**.3
councillors' role, **6**.4
effect, **6**.8
fall-back proposals, as, **6**.7
further development, **6**.9—**6**.10
introduction, **6**.1
overview and scrutiny, **6**.5
primary proposals, as, **6**.6
structure, **6**.2
Wales, in, **6**.11
Amendment of enactments
generally, **2**.33
procedure, **2**.38
s.137 LGA 1972, **2**.36
ss.33—35 LGHA 1989, **2**.37
Annual financial report
generally, **22**.7

Annual library plan
community planning, and, **18**.2
Anti-social behaviour, action against
well-being powers, and, **2**.41
Appointment of employees
Chief Officers, **32**.5
Head of Paid Service, **32**.4
introduction, **32**.1
procedures, **32**.2—**32**.5
Associated employers
generally, **29**.2
Audit of accounts
Audit Committee, **25**.6
Chief Executive's role, **25**.3
District Auditor's role, **25**.2
fraud, and, **25**.10
implementation audit, **25**.8
internal arrangements, **25**.5
investigative audit, **25**.9
managed approach, **25**.1
Monitoring Officer's role, **25**.3
performance monitoring, **25**.7
planned audit, **25**.9
planning, **25**.4
Awareness workshops
financial controls, **26**.3
fraud, **28**.2

B

Backbench members
ethics, and, **14**.9
Balance sheet reporting
generally, **24**.22
Beacon Council Scheme
generally, **3**.7
Phase One, **3**.8
Phase Two, **3**.9
Best value
consultation, and, **20**.2
employment issues, and
employees, role of, **29**.6
guiding principles, **29**.8
introduction, **29**.5
non-commercial matters, **29**.11
outsourcing, **29**.7
partnerships, **29**.7
transfer of undertakings, **29**.9—**29**.10
ethics, and
inter-relationship with ethics, **17**.2
introduction, **17**.1
local strategic partnerships, and, **3**.3
non-commercial matters, **29**.11

Best value—*contd*
transfer of undertakings
best value, **29**.9
Cabinet Office statement, **29**.10
generally, **29**.2
well-being powers, and, **2**.43
Best value inspection reports
openness, and, **21**.1
Best value performance plan
community planning, and, **18**.2
openness, and, **21**.1
Business rates
consultation, and, **20**.2

C

Cabinet government
access to information, and, **21**.2
accountability
access to information, **4**.21
forward plan, **4**.20
generally, **4**.16
individual executive decisions, **4**.19
key decisions, **4**.18
recording decisions, **4**.17
conclusion, **4**.25
conflict resolution, **4**.14
councillors' role, **4**.15
executive's role, **4**.10—**4**.12
Full Council's role, **4**.13
functions
cannot be responsibility of executive, **4**.11
generally, **4**.10
may be responsibility of executive, **4**.12
introduction, **4**.1
local choice functions, **4**.12
Mayoral elections, **7**.9
monitoring, **4**.24
officers, **4**.23
options
introduction, **4**.3
Leader and Cabinet, **4**.6
Leader and Council Manager, **4**.8
Mayor and Cabinet, **4**.5
Mayor and Council Manager, **4**.7
other, **4**.9
overview and scrutiny function
comparison with Parliamentary system, **5**.3
conflict resolution, **5**.9
health service, of, **5**.10
introduction, **5**.1—**5**.2
models, **5**.4—**5**.5
types, **5**.6—**5**.8
referendums
eligible voters, **7**.2
expenses, **7**.7
introduction, **7**.1
maximisation of turnout, **7**.6
publicity, **7**.4—**7**.5
results, **7**.8
timetable, **7**.3

Cabinet government—*contd*
referendums—*contd*
wording of question, **7**.2
review, **4**.24
Standards Committee, **4**.22
statutory basis
generally, **4**.2
key features, **4**.4
options, **4**.3
Cabinet Office statement
best value, and, **29**.10
Call-in
overview and scrutiny function, and, **5**.9
Capacity building
Community Empowerment Fund, **3**.25
generally, **3**.24
Capital expenditure reporting
generally, **24**.20
Case Tribunals
ethics, and, **15**.3
Cash accounting
generally, **24**.15
CCTV
well-being powers, and, **2**.42
Chairman of the Council
ethics, and, **14**.8
Chairs of Committees
local strategic partnerships, and, **3**.33
Charging
generally, **2**.29
incidental, **2**.28
Charities
partnerships, and, **19**.7
Chief Executive
audit of accounts, and, **25**.3
ethics, and, **14**.3
Chief Finance Officer
appointment, **32**.5
change of role, **31**.4
discipline
generally, **32**.8
independent person provisions, **31**.6—**31**.7
generally, **10**.2
organisational structures, **31**.5
political restrictions, **34**.2
reporting, **22**.3
resources, **22**.4
role, **22**.2
Children's services plan
community planning, and, **18**.2
Codes of Conduct
employees, for
current status, **30**.4
generally, **30**.3
handling breaches, **30**.7
incorporation into contracts, **30**.6
introduction, **30**.1
Wales, for, **30**.5
whistle-blowing, **33**.8
members, for, **30**.2

Collaborative working
joint commissioning, **2**.21
lead commissioning, **2**.20
Collective bargaining
employment, and, **32**.11
Communications
employment, and, **35**.5
Commitment accounting
generally, **24**.18
Community care plan
community planning, and, **18**.2
Community Empowerment Fund
local strategic partnerships, and, **3**.25
Community Enterprise schemes
partnerships, and, **19**.3
Community leadership
meaning, **3**.1
partnership, and
and see **Local Strategic Partnership**
context, **3**.3
development proposals, **3**.10—**3**.11
elected members, role of, **3**.30—**3**.34
funding sources, **3**.4—**3**.9
generally, **3**.12—**3**.29
introduction, **3**.2
well-being powers, and, **2**.10
Community planning
Community Strategy
generally, **18**.3
practical issues, **18**.4
relationship with other plans, **18**.5
consultation, and, **20**.2
introduction, **18**.1
Local Strategic Partnerships, **18**.6
Public Service Agreements, **18**.6
statutory plans, **18**.2
Community Strategy, preparation of
consultation, and
generally, **20**.8
introduction, **20**.2
generally, **18**.3—**18**.6
introduction, **2**.32
nature of power, and, **2**.14
practical issues, **18**.4
relationship with other plans, **18**.5
Companies
partnerships, and, **19**.4
Company formation
well-being powers, and, **2**.24
Confidential reporting procedure
ethics, and, 12.8
Conflict resolution
executive arrangements, and, **4**.14
overview and scrutiny function, and, **5**.9
Connexions
partnerships, and, **19**.8
Constitution of council
ethics, and, 12.3
generally, **7**.10
Consultation
case law
adequacy of consultation, **20**.6
duty to consult, **20**.3

Consultation—*contd*
case law—*contd*
legitimate expectation, **20**.5
limits to duty, **20**.4
checklist, **20**.7
Community Strategy, and, **20**.8
conclusion, **20**.9
introduction, **20**.1
statutory basis, **20**.2
Continuing development
members', **12**.14
officers', **12**.14
Contract standing orders
ethics, and, 12.5
Controls awareness workshops
financial propriety, and, **26**.3
Co-operation with activities of person
well-being powers, and, **2**.17
Corrective action cycle
analysis of problem, **24**.8
containment of problem, **24**.7
definition of problem, **24**.5
identification of permanent solution, **24**.10
implementation of permanent solution,
24.11
introduction, **24**.4
root cause identification, **24**.9
team building, **24**.6
verification of effectiveness, **24**.12
Council tax information
openness, and, **21**.1
Council tenant information
openness, and, **21**.1
Covert operations7
generally, **27**.4
local authority issues, **27**.10
Credit unions
partnerships, and, **19**.3
Crime and disorder reduction strategy
community planning, and, **18**.2

D

Data protection
openness. and, **21**.3
Delegation
ethics, and
executive scheme, **12**.9
officers' scheme, **12**.10
partnership, and, **19**.11
register of officers' powers, and, **21**.1
Development plan
community planning, and, **18**.2
Disciplining of employees
Chief officers, **32**.8
generally, **32**.6
Head of Paid Service, **32**.7
independent person provisions, **31**.6—**31**.7
introduction, **32**.1
other employees, **32**.9
Disclosure
financial propriety, and, **22**.6

Disclosure of communications data
  investigatory powers, and, **27**.3
District Auditor
  role, **25**.2

E

Early years development plan
  community planning, and, **18**.2
Economic development
  consultation, and, **20**.2
Economic well-being, promotion of
  accommodation, provision of, **2**.18
  amendment of enactments
    generally, **2**.33
    procedure, **2**.38
    s.137 LGA 1972, **2**.36
    ss.33—35 LGHA 1989, **2**.37
  background
    generally, **2**.1—**2**.2
    s.111 LGA 1972, **2**.3
    s.137 LGA 1972, **2**.4—**2**.5
    ss.33—35 LGHA 1989, **2**.6—**2**.7
  best value, and, **2**.43
  charging
    generally, **2**.29
    incidental, **2**.28
  collaborative working
    joint commissioning, **2**.21
    lead commissioning, **2**.20
  community leadership, **2**.10
  Community strategy, preparation of
    generally, **18**.1—**18**.6
    introduction, **2**.32
    nature of power, and, **2**.14
  company formation, **2**.24
  conclusion, **2**.44
  co-operation with activities of person, **2**.17
  enter into arrangements, **2**.17
  exercise functions on behalf of any person, **2**.18
  financial assistance, **2**.16
  generally, **2**.9
  goods, provision of, **2**.18
  incur expenditure, **2**.16
  introduction, **2**.8
  joint commissioning, **2**.21
  lead commissioning, **2**.20
  limitations on power
    charging, **2**.29
    incidental charging, **2**.28
    introduction, **2**.25
    observe express restrictions, **2**.26
    other, **2**.31
    raising money, **2**.27
    trading, **2**.30
  London, **2**.23
  modification of plan-related enactments
    England, **2**.34
    procedure, **2**.38
    Wales, **2**.35

Economic well-being, promotion of—*contd*
  nature of power
    beneficiaries, **2**.13
    introduction, **2**.12
    regard to Community Strategy, **2**.14
  non-collaborative working, **2**.22
  possible uses
    activities outside authority's area, **2**.19—**2**.24
    co-operation with activities, **2**.17
    enter into arrangements, **2**.17
    exercise functions on behalf of any person, **2**.18
    financial assistance, **2**.16
    incur expenditure, **2**.16
    introduction, **2**.15
    provision of staff, etc., **2**.18
  proposed uses
    CCTV, **2**.42
    combating anti-social behaviour, **2**.41
    introduction, **2**.39
    pooling of budgets, **2**.40
  relevant local authorities, **2**.11
  repeal of enactments
    generally, **2**.33
    procedure, **2**.38
    s.137 LGA 1972, **2**.36
    ss.33—35 LGHA 1989, **2**.37
  restrictions on power
    charging, **2**.29
    incidental charging, **2**.28
    introduction, **2**.25
    observe express restrictions, **2**.26
    other, **2**.31
    raising money, **2**.27
    trading, **2**.30
  services, provision of, **2**.18
  staff, provision of, **2**.18
  trading, **2**.30
Education Action Zones
  partnerships, and, **19**.3
Education development plan
  community planning, and, **18**.2
Election of mayors
  conduct, **8**.8
  generally, **8**.4—**8**.5
  introduction, **7**.9
  methods of election
    generally, **8**.6
    SV system, **8**.7
Electoral reform
  absent voting
    background, **8**.10—**8**.11
    generally, **8**.15
    introduction, **8**.9
    turnout, and, **8**.38
  background, **8**.2
  introduction, **8**.1
  local authority elections, **8**.3
  mayoral elections
    conduct of election, **8**.8
    generally, **8**.4—**8**.5
    introduction, **7**.9
    methods of election, **8**.6—**8**.7

Electoral reform—*contd*
  postal voting
    all-postal ballots, **8**.19
    generally, **8**.18
    on demand ballots, **8**.20
  proxy voting, **8**.16
  rolling registration
    background, **8**.10—**8**.11
    generally, **8**.12
    introduction, **8**.9
    Regulations, **8**.14
    residence requirement, **8**.13
  turnout
    absent voting, **8**.38
    advertising, **8**.40
    causes of low turnout, **8**.33
    changes in electoral process, **8**.34—**8**.35
    conclusion, **8**.42
    incentives, **8**.37
    introduction, **8**.32
    local importance issues, **8**.41
    polling cards, **8**.39
    polling stations, **8**.40
    review of procedures, **8**.36
  voting
    alternative systems, **8**.28
    alternative venues, **8**.23
    conclusions, **8**.31
    electronic, **8**.25
    eligibility extension, **8**.26
    extended hours, **8**.22
    introduction, **8**.17
    mobile stations, **8**.24
    over more than one day, **8**.21
    postal, **8**.18—**8**.20
    telephone, **8**.26
    weekend, **8**.23
Electronic counting
  generally, 8.26
Electronic voting
  generally, 8.25
Electronic voting and counting
  generally, 8.27
Employee/member relationships
  Codes of Conduct, **30**.2
  cultural issues, **29**.3
Employees' Code of Conduct
  ethics, and, 12.6
Employment
  appointment of employees
    Chief Officers, **32**.5
    Head of Paid Service, **32**.4
    introduction, **32**.1
    procedures, **32**.2—**32**.5
  associated employers, **29**.2
  best value
    employees, role of, **29**.6
    guiding principles, **29**.8
    introduction, **29**.5
    non-commercial matters, **29**.11
    outsourcing, **29**.7
    partnerships, **29**.7
    transfer of undertakings, **29**.9—**29**.10

Employment—*contd*
  Chief Finance Officer
    appointment, **32**.5
    change of role, **31**.4
    disciplinary provisions, **31**.6—**31**.7, **32**.8
    organisational structures, **31**.5
    political restrictions, **34**.2
  Code of Conduct
    current status, **30**.4
    employee/members relationships, **30**.2
    generally, **30**.3
    handling breaches, **30**.7
    incorporation into contracts, **30**.6
    introduction, **30**.1
    Wales, for, **30**.5
    whistle-blowing, **33**.8
  collective bargaining, **32**.11
  communications, **35**.5
  cultural issues
    authority as employer, **29**.2
    best value, **29**.5—**29**.11
    employee/member relationships, **29**.3
    executive arrangement support, **29**.4
    introduction, **29**.1
  disciplining of employees
    Chief officers, **32**.8
    generally, **32**.6
    Head of Paid Service, **32**.7
    independent person provisions, **31**.6—**31**.7
    introduction, **32**.1
    other employees, **32**.9
  employee/member relationships
    Codes of Conduct, **30**.2
    cultural issues, **29**.3
  equal pay, **29**.2
  executive arrangements, **29**.4
  grading, **32**.10
  grievance, **32**.10
  Head of Paid Service
    appointment, **32**.4
    change of role, **31**.2
    disciplinary provisions, **31**.6—**31**.7, **32**.7
    organisational structures, **31**.5
    political restrictions, **34**.2
  human rights
    fair hearing, right to, **34**.4
    freedom of thought, **34**.3
    introduction, **34**.1
    politically restricted positions, **34**.2
    safe working environment, **34**.6
    trade union rights, **34**.5
  joint negotiating and collective bargaining, **32**.11
  Monitoring Officer
    appointment, **32**.5
    change of role, **31**.3
    disciplinary provisions, **31**.6—**31**.7
    organisational structures, **31**.5
    political restrictions, **34**.2
  negotiating with employees, **32**.11

Employment—*contd*
  statutory officers, role of
    Chief Finance Officer, **31**.4
    Head of Paid Service, **31**.2
    introduction, **31**.1
    Monitoring Officer, **31**.3
  training
    employees, **35**.3—**35**.4
    introduction, **35**.1
    members, **35**.2
  transfer of undertakings
    best value, **29**.9
    Cabinet Office statement, **29**.10
    generally, **29**.2
  whistle-blowing
    Code of Conduct, **33**.8
    further advice, **33**.9
    'gagging' clauses, **33**.6
    introduction, **33**.1
    local authority issues, **33**.7
    meaning, **33**.2
    qualifying disclosures, **33**.4
    relevant workers, **33**.3
    worker's rights, **33**.5
Employment Service Districts
  partnerships, and, **19**.8
Employment zones
  partnerships, and, **19**.3
Encrypted electronic data
  investigatory powers, and, **27**.5
Entering into arrangements
  well-being powers, and, **2**.17
Environmental regulation
  consultation, and, **20**.2
Environmental well-being, promotion of
  accommodation, provision of, **2**.18
  amendment of enactments
    generally, **2**.33
    procedure, **2**.38
    s.137 LGA 1972, **2**.36
    ss.33—35 LGHA 1989, **2**.37
  background
    generally, **2**.1—**2**.2
    s.111 LGA 1972, **2**.3
    s.137 LGA 1972, **2**.4—**2**.5
    ss.33—35 LGHA 1989, **2**.6—**2**.7
  best value, and, **2**.43
  charging
    generally, **2**.29
    incidental, **2**.28
  collaborative working
    joint commissioning, **2**.21
    lead commissioning, **2**.20
  community leadership, **2**.10
  Community strategy, preparation of
    generally, **18**.1—**18**.6
    introduction, **2**.32
    nature of power, and, **2**.14
  company formation, **2**.24
  conclusion, **2**.44
  co-operation with activities of person, **2**.17
  enter into arrangements, **2**.17

Environmental well-being, promotion of—*contd*
  exercise functions on behalf of any person, **2**.18
  financial assistance, **2**.16
  generally, **2**.9
  goods, provision of, **2**.18
  incur expenditure, **2**.16
  introduction, **2**.8
  joint commissioning, **2**.21
  lead commissioning, **2**.20
  limitations on power
    charging, **2**.29
    incidental charging, **2**.28
    introduction, **2**.25
    observe express restrictions, **2**.26
    other, **2**.31
    raising money, **2**.27
    trading, **2**.30
  London, **2**.23
  modification of plan-related enactments
    England, **2**.34
    procedure, **2**.38
    Wales, **2**.35
  nature of power
    beneficiaries, **2**.13
    introduction, **2**.12
    regard to Community Strategy, **2**.14
  non-collaborative working, **2**.22
  possible uses
    activities outside authority's area, **2**.19—**2**.24
    co-operation with activities, **2**.17
    enter into arrangements, **2**.17
    exercise functions on behalf of any person, **2**.18
    financial assistance, **2**.16
    incur expenditure, **2**.16
    introduction, **2**.15
    provision of staff, etc., **2**.18
  proposed uses
    CCTV, **2**.42
    combating anti-social behaviour, **2**.41
    introduction, **2**.39
    pooling of budgets, **2**.40
  relevant local authorities, **2**.11
  repeal of enactments
    generally, **2**.33
    procedure, **2**.38
    s.137 LGA 1972, **2**.36
    ss.33—35 LGHA 1989, **2**.37
  restrictions on power
    charging, **2**.29
    incidental charging, **2**.28
    introduction, **2**.25
    observe express restrictions, **2**.26
    other, **2**.31
    raising money, **2**.27
    trading, **2**.30
  services, provision of, **2**.18
  staff, provision of, **2**.18
  trading, **2**.30

Equal pay
employment, and, **29**.2
Ethical Governance Audit
generally, **14**.11
Ethical standards
Adjudication Panels, **15**.2
background, **9**.1
best value, and
inter-relationship with ethics, **17**.2
introduction, **17**.1
Case Tribunals, **15**.3
documentation
importance, **12**.2
introduction, **12**.1
key documents, **12**.3—**12**.17
Ethical Governance Audit, **14**.11
Ethical Standards Officers, **15**.3
framework, **9**.2
key documents
confidential reporting procedure, **12**.8
constitution of council, **12**.3
contract standing orders, **12**.5
employees' Code of Conduct, **12**.6
executive delegation scheme, **12**.9
members' Code of Conduct, **12**.7
members' continuing development, **12**.14
members' induction process, **12**.12
officers' continuing development, **12**.14
officers' delegation scheme, **12**.10
officers' induction process, **12**.13
other Codes and Protocols, **12**.17
procedural standing orders, **12**.4
register of interests, **12**.11
whistle-blowing law, **12**.16
legislation, **13**.1
Local Code of Conduct, **13**.4
meaning, **9**.3
Monitoring Officer
background, **10**.2
constitution, and, **10**.26
introduction, **10**.1
new councils, and, **10**.25
practical issues, **10**.27—**10**.29
role, **10**.4—**10**.24
statutory basis, **10**.3
National Code of Local Government
Conduct, **13**.3
National Standards Board
background, **15**.2
conduct of investigation, **16**.1—**16**.2
introduction, **15**.1
statutory basis, **15**.3
working with members, **15**.4
Officer/Member Protocol, **13**.5
officers and members, role of
backbench members, **14**.9
Chairman of the Council, **14**.8
Chief Executive, **14**.3
executive, **14**.7
executive directors, **14**.4
heads of service, **14**.5
statutory officers, **14**.6

Ethical standards—*contd*
overview and scrutiny, and
inter-relationship with ethics, **17**.3
introduction, **17**.1
ownership, **14**.2
procedures and documentation
importance, **12**.2
introduction, **12**.1
key documents, **12**.3—**12**.17
promotion and monitoring
Ethical Governance Audit, **14**.11
introduction, **14**.1
members/officers' role, **14**.3—**14**.9
Standards Committee' role, **14**.10
Standards Committee
background, **11**.2
establishment, **11**.4
introduction, **11**.1
membership, **11**.7
practical issues, **11**.8
pre-LGA 2000 operation, **11**.3
role, **11**.5—**11**.6
Ethical Standards Officers
generally, **15**.3
European Regional Development Fund
partnerships, and, **19**.3
European Social Fund
partnerships, and, **19**.3
Excellence in Cities
partnerships, and, **19**.8
Executive
ethics, and, **14**.7
local strategic partnerships, and, **3**.33
Executive arrangements
access to information, and, **21**.2
accountability
access to information, **4**.21
forward plan, **4**.20
generally, **4**.16
individual executive decisions, **4**.19
key decisions, **4**.18
recording decisions, **4**.17
alternatives
and see **Alternative arrangements**
further development, **6**.9—**6**.11
introduction, **6**.1
structure, **6**.2—**6**.8
conclusion, **4**.25
conflict resolution, **4**.14
constitution, **7**.10
councillors' role, **4**.15
employment, and, **29**.4
executive's role, **4**.10—**4**.12
Full Council's role, **4**.13
functions
cannot be responsibility of executive,
4.11
generally, **4**.10
may be responsibility of executive, **4**.12
introduction, **4**.1
local choice functions, **4**.12
Mayoral elections, **7**.9
monitoring, **4**.24

Executive arrangements—*contd*
officers, **4**.23
options
  introduction, **4**.3
  Leader and Cabinet, **4**.6
  Leader and Council Manager, **4**.8
  Mayor and Cabinet, **4**.5
  Mayor and Council Manager, **4**.7
  other, **4**.9
overview and scrutiny function
  comparison with Parliamentary system, **5**.3
  conflict resolution, **5**.9
  health service, of, **5**.10
  introduction, **5**.1—**5**.2
  models, **5**.4—**5**.5
  types, **5**.6—**5**.8
referendums
  eligible voters, **7**.2
  expenses, **7**.7
  introduction, **7**.1
  maximisation of turnout, **7**.6
  publicity, **7**.4—**7**.5
  results, **7**.8
  timetable, **7**.3
  wording of question, **7**.2
review, **4**.24
Standards Committee, **4**.22
statutory basis
  generally, **4**.2
  key features, **4**.4
  options, **4**.3
Executive delegation scheme
ethics, and, **12**.9
Executive directors
ethics, and, **14**.4
Exercising functions on behalf of any person
well-being powers, and, **2**.18
Extended hours voting
generally, **8**.22

F

Financial assistance
well-being powers, and, **2**.16
Financial propriety
accounting
  accrual, **24**.16
  cash, **24**.15
  commitment, **24**.18
  introduction, **24**.14
  resource, **24**.17
annual report, **22**.7
audit of accounts
  Audit Committee, **25**.6
  Chief Executive's role, **25**.3
  District Auditor's role, **25**.2
  fraud, and, **25**.10
  implementation audit, **25**.8
  internal arrangements, **25**.5
  investigative audit, **25**.9
  managed approach, **25**.1
  Monitoring Officer's role, **25**.3

Financial propriety—*contd*
audit of accounts—*contd*
  performance monitoring, **25**.7
  planned audit, **25**.9
  planning, **25**.4
Chief Financial Officer
  reporting, **22**.3
  resources, **22**.4
  role, **22**.2
disclosure, **22**.6
fraud
  awareness workshops, **28**.2
  internal audits, and, **28**.3
  introduction, **28**.1
  reporting, **28**.4
human resource management, **26**.8
investigatory powers
  coverage, **27**.2—**27**.7
  introduction, **27**.1
  local authority issues, **27**.8—**27**.10
meaning, **22**.1
openness, **22**.6
outsourced contracts
  contractual issues, **26**.6
  introduction, **26**.5
  systems issues, **26**.7
performance review
  corrective action cycle, **24**.4—**24**.12
  internal control, as, **24**.13
  purpose, **24**.1
  reporting timelines, **24**.2—**24**.3
quality standards, **22**.5
reporting and review
  balance sheet, **24**.22
  capital expenditure, **24**.20
  operational performance, **24**.21
  revenue account, **24**.19
risk management
  assessment of risk, **23**.4
  controls, **23**.6—**23**.9
  impact reduction, **23**.11
  introduction, **23**.1
  nature of risk, **23**.2
  reduction strategies, **23**.5
  training, **23**.10
  types of risk, **23**.3
staff involvement
  controls awareness, **26**.3
  financial regulations, **26**.2
  introduction, **26**.1
  management support, **26**.4
treasury operations, **24**.23
Food law enforcement service plan
community planning, and, **18**.2
Fraud
audit of accounts, and, **25**.10
awareness workshops, **28**.2
internal audits, and, **28**.3
introduction, **28**.1
reporting, **28**.4
Freedom of information
openness, and, **21**.4

Full Council
  executive arrangements, and, **4**.13
  local strategic partnerships, and, **3**.31

G

'Gagging' clause
  whistle-blowing, **33**.6
Golden share
  companies, and, **19**.4
Goods, provision of
  well-being powers, and, **2**.18
Grading
  employment, and, **32**.10
'Green' book
  employee conduct, **30**.1
Grievance
  employment, and, **32**.10

H

Head of Paid Service
  appointment, **32**.4
  change of role, **31**.2
  disciplinary provisions
    generally, **32**.7
    independent person provisions, **31**.6—
      31.7
  generally, **10**.2
  openness of reports, and, **21**.1
  organisational structures, **31**.5
  political restrictions, **34**.2
Heads of service
  ethics, and, **14**.5
Health Action Zones
  partnerships, and, **19**.8
Health authorities' and trusts
  partnerships, and, **19**.3
Housing investment programme
  community planning, and, **18**.2
Human resource management
  financial propriety, and, **26**.8
Human rights
  fair hearing, right to, **34**.4
  freedom of thought, **34**.3
  introduction, **34**.1
  openness, and, **21**.1
  politically restricted positions, **34**.2
  safe working environment, **34**.6
  trade union rights, **34**.5

I

Implementation audit
  generally, **25**.8
Incurring expenditure
  well-being powers, and, **2**.16
Induction process
  members', **12**.12
  officers', **12**.13
Industrial and Provident societies
  partnerships, and, **19**.5

Interception of communications
  generally, **27**.3
  local authority issues, **27**.9
Internal control
  performance review, and, **24**.13
**'Introduction to Local Democracy and
  community leadership' (Green Paper,
  1998)**
  modernisation agenda, **1**.1
Investigative audit
  generally, **25**.9
Investigatory powers
  coverage
    acquisition of communications data, **27**.3
    covert operations, **27**.4
    disclosure of communications data, **27**.3
    encrypted electronic data, **27**.5
    interception of communications, **27**.3
    introduction, **27**.2
    surveillance operations, **27**.4
  introduction, **27**.1
  local authority issues
    covert operations, **27**.10
    interception of communications, **27**.9
    introduction, **27**.8
    surveillance operations, **27**.10
  modification of enactments, **27**.7
  scrutiny, **27**.6

J

Joint commissioning
  well-being powers, and, **2**.21

L

LA 21
  partnerships, and, **19**.8
Lead commissioning
  well-being powers, and, **2**.20
Leader and Cabinet
  executive arrangements, and, **4**.6
Leader and Council Manager
  executive arrangements, and, **4**.8
Learning and Skills Councils
  partnerships, and, **19**.3
Legal personality
  partnerships, and, **19**.2
Lifelong learning development plan
  community planning, and, **18**.2
Lifelong Learning
  partnerships, and, **19**.3
Limited liability partnerships
  generally, **19**.1
Limited partnerships
  generally, **19**.1
Local Agenda 21 plan
  community planning, and, **18**.2
Local authorities, powers of
  background
    generally, **2**.1—**2**.2
    s.111 LGA 1972, **2**.3
    s.137 LGA 1972, **2**.4—**2**.5
    ss.33—35 LGHA 1989, **2**.6—**2**.7

Local authorities, powers of—*contd*
economic, environmental and social well-
being
amending enactments, **2.33—2.38**
community strategy, **2.32**
generally, **2.9—2.10**
introduction, **2.8**
limits on power, **2.25—2.31**
modifying enactments, **2.34—2.36**
promotion of well-being, **2.12—2.24**
proposed uses, **2.39—2.42**
relevant local authorities, **2.11**
repealing enactments, **2.33—2.38**
s.111 LGA 1972, **2.3**
s.137 LGA 1972
generally, **2.4**
modification, **2.5**
ss.33—35 LGHA 1989
generally, **2.6**
repeal, **2.7**
Local choice functions
executive arrangements, and, **4.12**
Local Code of Conduct
ethics, and, **13.4**
Local development trusts
partnerships, and, **19.3**
Local Exchange and Trading Systems
partnerships, and, **19.3**
Local Housing Companies
partnerships, and, **19.8**
'Local Leadership, Local Choice' (consultation
paper, 1998)
ethical standards, **9.2**
modernisation agenda, **1.1**
political management structures, **4.1**
Standards Committee, **15.2**
Local public service agreements
generally, **3.5**
Local Strategic Partnership (LSP)
background, **3.10**
best value, and, **3.3**
capacity building
Community Empowerment Fund, **3.25**
generally, **3.24**
Chairmanship, **3.23**
community involvement, **3.16**
context, **3.3**
core functions, **3.13**
elected members, role of
Chairs of Committees, **3.33**
Executive, **3.33**
Full Council, **3.31**
introduction, **3.30**
non-executive councillors, **3.34**
Overview and Scrutiny Committee, **3.32**
establishment, **3.17—3.18**
funding sources
Beacon Council Scheme, **3.7—3.9**
introduction, **3.4**
local public service agreements, **3.5**
Neighbourhood Renewal Fund, **3.6**
generally, **3.12—3.29**
introduction, **3.2**

Local Strategic Partnership (LSP)—*contd*
leadership, **3.23**
meaning, **3.10**
membership
generally, **3.19**
key partners, **3.20**
multi-tier authority partners, **3.22**
principles governing relationship, **3.26—
3.29**
relationship between members
accountability, **3.28**
equality, **3.27**
introduction, **3.26**
transparency, **3.29**
resources, **3.11**
structure, **3.14**
training, **3.24**
'Local Strategic Partnerships' (Guidance,
2001)
local strategic partnerships, **3.2**
Local transport plan
community planning, and, **18.2**
London
well-being powers, and, **2.23**
Lottery Funding bids
partnerships, and, **19.3**

M

Management of risk
assessment of risk, **23.4**
controls
introduction, **23.6**
physical, **23.7**
process, **23.8**
supervisory, **23.9**
system, **23.8**
impact reduction, **23.11**
introduction, **23.1**
nature of risk, **23.2**
reduction strategies, **23.5**
training, **23.10**
types of risk, **23.3**
Mayor and Cabinet
executive arrangements, and, **4.5**
Mayor and Council Manager
executive arrangements, and, **4.7**
Mayoral elections
conduct, **8.8**
generally, **8.4—8.5**
introduction, **7.9**
methods of election
generally, **8.6**
SV system, **8.7**
Members'
Code of Conduct, **12.7**
continuing development, **12.14**
ethics, and
backbench members, **14.9**
Chairman of the Council, **14.8**
induction process, **12.12**
name and address register, **21.1**

Mobile polling stations
generally, **8**.24
'Modern Local Government: In Touch with the People' (White Paper, 1998)
election schemes, **8**.3
ethical standards, **9**.2
modernisation agenda, **1**.1
Monitoring Officer, **10**.5
overview and scrutiny, **5**.1
political management structures, **4**.1
Standards Committee, **15**.2
Modernisation agenda
introduction, **1**.1
Local Government Act 2000, **1**.2
Modification of enactments
investigatory powers, and, **27**.7
plan-related, and
England, **2**.34
procedure, **2**.38
Wales, **2**.35
Monitoring
executive arrangements, and, **4**.24
Monitoring Officer
appointment, **32**.5
audit of accounts, and, **25**.3
background, **10**.2
change of role, **31**.3
constitution, and, **10**.26
disciplinary provisions, **31**.6—**31**.7
introduction, **10**.1
new councils, and, **10**.25
openness of reports, and, **21**.1
organisational structures, **31**.5
political restrictions, **34**.2
practical issues, **10**.27—**10**.29
role, **10**.4—**10**.24
statutory basis, **10**.3

N

National Code of Local Government Conduct
ethics, and, **13**.3
National Standards Board
background, **15**.2
conduct of investigation, **16**.1—**16**.2
introduction, **15**.1
statutory basis, **15**.3
working with members, **15**.4
Negotiations
employees, with, **32**.11
Neighbourhood Renewal Fund
generally, **3**.6
New Deal
partnerships, and, **19**.8
Nolan Committee report
ethical standards, **9**.2
financial propriety, **22**.1
Non-collaborative working
well-being powers, and, **2**.22
Non-commercial matters
best value, and, **29**.11

Non-executive councillors
local strategic partnerships, and, **3**.34
Non-statutory bodies
partnerships, and, **19**.3

O

Officer/Member Protocol
ethics, and, **13**.5
Officers
continuing development, and, **12**.14
delegation scheme, and, **12**.10
ethics, and
Chief Executive, **14**.3
executive, **14**.7
executive directors, **14**.4
heads of service, **14**.5
statutory officers, **14**.6
executive arrangements, and, **4**.23
induction process, and, **12**.13
Ombudsman's reports
openness, and, **21**.1
'151 Officer'
generally, **10**.2
reporting, **22**.3
resources, **22**.4
role, **22**.2
Openness
access to information
background, **21**.1
executive arrangements, **21**.2
data protection, **21**.3
financial propriety, and, **22**.6
freedom of information, **21**.4
intra-partner information exchange, **21**.5
Operational performance reporting
generally, **24**.21
'Organisation and Standards' (draft Bill, 1999)
modernisation agenda, **1**.1
Outsourced contracts
contractual issues, **26**.6
introduction, **26**.5
systems issues, **26**.7
Outsourcing
best value, and, **29**.7
Overview and Scrutiny Committee
comparison with Parliamentary system, **5**.3
conflict resolution, **5**.9
ethics, and
inter-relationship with ethics, **17**.3
introduction, **17**.1
health service, of, **5**.10
legal basis, **5**.1—**5**.2
local strategic partnerships, and, **3**.32
models, **5**.4—**5**.5
types of scrutiny
developing and reviewing policy, **5**.7
holding executive to account, **5**.8
introduction, **5**.6

P

Partnership
best value, and, **29**.7
categories
charities, **19**.7
companies, **19**.4
Industrial and Provident societies, **19**.5
non-statutory bodies, **19**.3
other bodies, **19**.8
statutory bodies, **19**.3
trusts, **19**.6
delegation, **19**.11
introduction, **19**.1
legal personality, and, **19**.2
openness, and, **21**.5
procurement, and, **19**.9
provision of services, **19**.12
termination, **19**.10
Performance monitoring
audit of accounts, and, **25**.7
Performance review
corrective action cycle
analysis of problem, **24**.8
containment of problem, **24**.7
definition of problem, **24**.5
identification of permanent solution,
24.10
implementation of permanent solution,
24.11
introduction, **24**.4
root cause identification, **24**.9
team building, **24**.6
verification of effectiveness, **24**.12
internal control, as, **24**.13
purpose, **24**.1
reporting timelines
monthly, **24**.2
quarterly, **24**.3
team building, **24**.6
PESTLE analysis
risk management, **23**.3
Planned audit
generally, **25**.9
Planning, community
Community Strategy
generally, **18**.3
practical issues, **18**.4
relationship with other plans, **18**.5
introduction, **18**.1
Local Strategic Partnerships, **18**.6
Public Service Agreements, **18**.6
statutory plans, **18**.2
Politically restricted posts
openness, and, **21**.1
Polling cards
turnout, and, **8**.39
Polling stations
mobility, **8**.24
turnout, **8**.40
Pooling of budgets
well-being powers, and, **2**.40
Postal voting

Postal voting—*contd*
all-postal ballots, **8**.19
generally, **8**.18
on demand ballots, **8**.20
'*Powerpack*' (LGA, 2000)
well-being powers, **2**.39—**2**.42
'*Preparing Community Strategies*' (Guidance, 2000)
local strategic partnerships, **3**.2
local authority elections, **8**.3
Private Finance Initiative (PFI)
procurement, and, **19**.9
Probity
meaning, **9**.3
Procedural standing orders
ethics, and, **12**.4
Procurement
partnership, and, **19**.9
Proportionality
openness, and, **21**.1
Proxy voting
generally, **8**.16
Public consultation
case law
adequacy of consultation, **20**.6
duty to consult, **20**.3
legitimate expectation, **20**.5
limits to duty, **20**.4
checklist, **20**.7
Community Strategy, and, **20**.8
conclusion, **20**.9
introduction, **20**.1
statutory basis, **20**.2
Public Service Agreements
community planning, and, **18**.6
'Purple' book
employee conduct, **30**.1

Q

Quality partnership schemes
partnerships, and, **19**.8
Quality projects management action plan
community planning, and, **18**.2
Quality standards
financial propriety, and, **22**.5

R

Rates for business
consultation, and, **20**.2
Redcliffe-Maud report
ethical standards, **9**.1
Referendums
eligible voters, **7**.2
expenses, **7**.7
introduction, **7**.1
maximisation of turnout, **7**.6
publicity
generally, **7**.4
restrictions, **7**.5
results, **7**.8
timetable, **7**.3
wording of question, **7**.2

Regional development agencies
partnerships, and, **19**.3
Register of interests
ethics, and, **12**.11
Repeal of enactments
generally, **2**.33
procedure, **2**.38
s.137 LGA 1972, **2**.36
ss.33—35 LGHA 1989, **2**.37
Reporting and review
balance sheet, **24**.22
capital expenditure, **24**.20
fraud, **28**.4
operational performance, **24**.21
revenue account, **24**.19
Residence
rolling registration, and, **8**.7
Revenue account reporting
generally, **24**.19
Risk management
assessment of risk, **23**.4
controls
introduction, **23**.6
physical, **23**.7
process, **23**.8
supervisory, **23**.9
system, **23**.8
impact reduction, **23**.11
introduction, **23**.1
nature of risk, **23**.2
reduction strategies, **23**.5
training, **23**.10
types of risk, **23**.3
Resource accounting
generally, **24**.17
Rolling registration
background, **8**.10—**8**.11
generally, **8**.12
introduction, **8**.9
Regulations, **8**.14
residence requirement, **8**.13
SV system, **8**.7

S

School Organisation Committees
partnerships, and, **19**.8
School organisation plan
community planning, and, **18**.2
School-related information
openness, and, **21**.1
Services, provision of
partnerships, and, **19**.12
well-being powers, and, **2**.18
Single Regeneration Budget
partnerships, and, **19**.3
Social well-being, promotion of
accommodation, provision of, **2**.18
amendment of enactments
generally, **2**.33
procedure, **2**.38
s.137 LGA 1972, **2**.36
ss.33—35 LGHA 1989, **2**.37

Social well-being, promotion of—*contd*
background
generally, **2**.1—**2**.2
s.111 LGA 1972, **2**.3
s.137 LGA 1972, **2**.4—**2**.5
ss.33—35 LGHA 1989, **2**.6—**2**.7
best value, and, **2**.43
charging
generally, **2**.29
incidental, **2**.28
collaborative working
joint commissioning, **2**.21
lead commissioning, **2**.20
community leadership, **2**.10
Community strategy, preparation of
generally, **18**.1—**18**.6
introduction, **2**.32
nature of power, and, **2**.14
company formation, **2**.24
conclusion, **2**.44
co-operation with activities of person, **2**.17
enter into arrangements, **2**.17
exercise functions on behalf of any person,
2.18
financial assistance, **2**.16
generally, **2**.9
goods, provision of, **2**.18
incur expenditure, **2**.16
introduction, **2**.8
joint commissioning, **2**.21
lead commissioning, **2**.20
limitations on power
charging, **2**.29
incidental charging, **2**.28
introduction, **2**.25
observe express restrictions, **2**.26
other, **2**.31
raising money, **2**.27
trading, **2**.30
London, **2**.23
modification of plan-related enactments
England, **2**.34
procedure, **2**.38
Wales, **2**.35
nature of power
beneficiaries, **2**.13
introduction, **2**.12
regard to Community Strategy, **2**.14
non-collaborative working, **2**.22
possible uses
activities outside authority's area, **2**.19—
2.24
co-operation with activities, **2**.17
enter into arrangements, **2**.17
exercise functions on behalf of any
person, **2**.18
financial assistance, **2**.16
incur expenditure, **2**.16
introduction, **2**.15
provision of staff, etc., **2**.18
proposed uses
CCTV, **2**.42
combating anti-social behaviour, **2**.41

Social well-being, promotion of—*contd*
proposed uses—*contd*
introduction, **2**.39
pooling of budgets, **2**.40
relevant local authorities, **2**.11
repeal of enactments
generally, **2**.33
procedure, **2**.38
s.137 LGA 1972, **2**.36
ss.33—35 LGHA 1989, **2**.37
restrictions on power
charging, **2**.29
incidental charging, **2**.28
introduction, **2**.25
observe express restrictions, **2**.26
other, **2**.31
raising money, **2**.27
trading, **2**.30
services, provision of, **2**.18
staff, provision of, **2**.18
trading, **2**.30
Staff, provision of
well-being powers, and, **2**.18
Standards Committee
background, **11**.2
establishment, **11**.4
executive arrangements, and, **4**.22
introduction, **11**.1
membership, **11**.7
practical issues, **11**.8
pre-LGA 2000 operation, **11**.3
role, **11**.5—**11**.6
Statutory bodies
partnerships, and, **19**.3
Statutory officers
ethics, and, **14**.6
Statutory plans
community planning, and, **18**.2
Supplementary vote (SV)
mayoral elections, **8**.7
Sure Start
partnerships, and, **19**.3
Surveillance operations
generally, **27**.4
local authority issues, **27**.10

T

Team building
performance review, and, **24**.6
Telephone voting
generally, **8**.26
Trading
well-being powers, and, **2**.30
Training
employees, **35**.3—**35**.4
introduction, **35**.1
members, **35**.2
risk management, and, **23**.10
Transfer of undertakings
best value, **29**.9
Cabinet Office statement, **29**.10
generally, **29**.2

Treasury operations
generally, **24**.23
Trusts
partnerships, and, **19**.6
Turnout
absent voting, **8**.38
advertising, **8**.40
causes of low turnout, **8**.33
changes in electoral process, **8**.34—**8**.35
conclusion, **8**.42
incentives, **8**.37
introduction, **8**.32
local importance issues, **8**.41
polling cards, **8**.39
polling stations, **8**.40
review of procedures, **8**.36

U

Unitary development plans
consultation, and, **20**.2
Urban Regeneration Companies
partnerships, and, **19**.3

V

Voting
alternative systems, **8**.28
alternative venues, **8**.23
conclusions, **8**.31
electronic, **8**.25
eligibility extension, **8**.26
extended hours, **8**.22
introduction, **8**.17
mobile stations, **8**.24
over more than one day, **8**.21
postal
all-postal ballots, **8**.19
generally, **8**.18
on demand ballots, **8**.20
proxy, **8**.16
telephone, **8**.26
weekend, **8**.23

W

Weekend voting
generally, **8**.23
Whistle-blowing
Code of Conduct, **33**.8
ethics, and, **12**.16
further advice, **33**.9
'gagging' clauses, **33**.6
introduction, **33**.1
local authority issues, **33**.7
meaning, **33**.2
qualifying disclosures, **33**.4
relevant workers, **33**.3

Whistle-blowing—*contd*
    worker's rights, **33**.5
Widdicombe report
    ethical standards, **9**.1

Y

Youth offending teams
    partnerships, and, **19**.3